The Investment Banking Handbook

Edited by

J. PETER WILLIAMSON
Professor of Business Administration
The Amos Tuck School of Business Administration
Dartmouth College
Hanover, New Hampshire

John Wiley & Sons
New York · Chichester · Brisbane · Toronto · Singapore

ISBN 0-471-81562-4

10 9

Contributors

Edward I. Altman is professor of finance and chairman of the MBA program at NYU. He has been visiting professor at the Hautes Études Commerciales and Université de Paris–Dauphine in France, at the Pontifica Catolica Universidade in Rio de Janeiro, Brazil, and the Australian Graduate School of Management. Altman has an international reputation as an expert on corporate bankruptcy and credit analysis. Editor of the international *Journal of Banking and Finance* and two publishers' series, Wiley Professional Banking and Finance Series (Wiley) and Contemporary Studies in Economics and Finance (JAI Press), Altman has also published several books and over 60 articles in scholarly finance, accounting, and economics journals. He is the current editor of the *Finance Handbook* and the author of two recently published books, *Corporate Financial Distress* and *Recent Trends in Corporate Finance*. A consultant to several government agencies, major financial and accounting institutions, and industrial companies, he has lectured to executives in North America, South America, Europe, and Asia, has testified before the U.S. Congress on several occasions, and is on the Scientific and Technical Committee of Italy's Centrale dei Bilanci.

Tanya Styblo Arnold was a swap specialist at the First Boston Corporation when she prepared her chapter. She has also written on the subject of interest rate swaps in *Harvard Business Review*.

Van Burger, Jr. is a managing director of Donaldson Lufkin & Jenrette and chairman of the firm's Pershing Division. He is also chairman of Pershing, Keen Ltd., the firm's London-based international clearing subsidiary. Burger joined Pershing in 1968 when it was a private partnership. He received a BA from Yale University in 1962 and an MBA from Harvard Business School in 1967. He has served as a director of the Chicago Board Options Exchange.

David E. Dougherty is managing director and head of the Mergers and Acquisitions Group at Bankers Trust Company, New York. He joined Bankers Trust in 1980 as vice president and manager of the Bank's Public Finance Group. Under his leadership, the Bank became the largest originator of floating rate tax-exempt securities. He was named senior vice president in 1983 and was appointed to his current position in February 1985. Prior to joining Bankers Trust, Mr. Dougherty was vice president and manager of municipal finance in the Philadelphia office of Kidder, Peabody & Company, Inc. A graduate of Georgetown University, Mr. Dougherty studied public administration at the University of Pittsburgh and earned a JD degree from Temple University.

Charles D. Ellis is managing partner of Greenwich Associates. He is the author of four books, including *The Second Crash*, *Institutional Investing*, and *The Repurchase of Common Stock*. He has written articles for a number of business and professional magazines, including *Harvard Business Review*, *Fortune*, *Institutional Investor*, and *The Financial Analysts' Journal*. He has taught at the Harvard Business School and currently teaches at the Yale School of Management. A member of the Advisory Council of the Salomon Brothers Center at New York University and of the Visiting Committee for the Harvard Business School, he is also an Overseer of New York University Graduate School of Business and a director of the Gartner Group and of Analysis and Technology. Before founding Greenwich Associates in 1972, he was a vice-president of Donaldson Lufkin & Jenrette. He holds a BA from Yale, an MBA from the Harvard Business School, and a PhD from New York University.

Frederick G. Fisher III is managing director of Arab Banking Corporation's merchant banking arm, based in London. In that capacity, he oversees a variety of Euromarket-related activities, including new issues, mergers and acquisitions, corporate financial counseling, and other services to a variety of clients in the Middle East and other parts of the world. He joined the First Boston Corporation in 1974 and, after an initial assignment in New York, was transferred to the firm's London office in 1976. He has been based in London ever since. Subsequent to leaving First Boston, he headed the Corporate Finance Department of Blyth Eastman Dillon International, was executive director of Orion Royal Bank, and since 1982 has led the corporate finance activities of Arab Banking Corporation. He is the author of *The Euro Dollar Bond Market* (1979) and *International Bonds* (1981), and has co-authored *International Mergers and Acquisitions* (1986). He graduated from Harvard College in 1969, received a senior honors degree from Oxford University in 1972, and received an MBA from the Harvard Business School in 1974.

Ronald W. Forbes is department chairman and associate professor of finance in the School of Business, State University of New York at Albany. He has published extensively on the tax-exempt securities market and has served as a consultant to a number of investment banking firms, including First Boston Corporation, Donaldson Lufkin & Jenrette, and Shearson Lehman Brothers. He has undertaken studies for the Twentieth Century Fund, the Advisory Commission on Intergovernmental Relations, the National Council on Public Works Improvement, and the Public Securities Association. He received an AB in economics from Dartmouth College and a PhD in finance from the State University of New York at Buffalo.

Peter E. Frank is partner-in-charge, Investment Services Consulting Practice, Peat Marwick, Mitchell and Company, New York. He is a member of the Securities Industry Association and of the board of directors of the Greater New York Council of the Boy Scouts of America. He holds a BS in economics from Rensselaer Polytechnic Institute and an MA from the City University of New York.

James L. Freeman is a managing director of the First Boston Corporation. He presently is the firm's manager of sales and research activities for all fixed-income and equity products, a member of the Management Committee and of the Capital Commitment Committee, chairman of the Investment Policy Committee, a director of Credit Suisse First Boston Investment Management, president and director of First Boston Income Fund, Inc. (a NYSE company), Global Growth and Income Fund, Inc. (a NYSE company), a director of the International Convertible Growth Fund, a member of the Investment Committee—The Japan Society, a member of the SIA Institutional Committee, and an official of the NYSE Disciplinary Committee. Additionally, he is an adjunct professor at the Columbia University School of Business where he teaches a course on sales, trading, and research within the Investment Bank. He began his First Boston career in 1975 as the Philadelphia branch office manager, and subsequently became co-manager of the Equity Division, director of research and manager of the European branch offices at The First Boston Corporation. He had previously worked as an institutional salesman and later in New York as the equity sales manager at White, Weld & Co. He began his Wall Street career as a security analyst at Goldman, Sachs & Co. He holds an AB in English with honors from the University of Pennsylvania (1967) and an MBA in finance from the University of Pennsylvania's Wharton School (1969).

Laurie S. Goodman is a vice president in the Capital Markets Analysis Unit of Citicorp Investment Bank. She specializes in research in fixed-income financial markets, with an emphasis on mortgage-backed securities, futures, and options. Prior to joining Citibank, Goodman was a senior economist at the Federal Reserve Bank of New York. She holds a BA from the University of Pennsylvania and an MA and PhD in economics from Stanford University. Goodman has published extensively in professional and popular journals.

Peter D. Goodson is a senior vice president of Kidder, Peabody & Company, Incorporated. He is director of the firm's merchant banking and acquisition advisory group, and co-director of the high-yield finance group. He joined Kidder, Peabody in 1966, after selling a plastics manufacturing company of which he was the founder and chief executive officer. As founder of Kidder's mergers and acquisition practice and current director of merchant banking, he has personally participated in over five hundred corporate assignments. Under his leadership, the M&A group has completed transactions exceeding $62 billion over the past three years. He is a recognized authority on corporate finance, and is frequently quoted in the *Wall Street Journal*, the *Financial Times of London*, the *New York Times*, and *Business Week*.

Jeanne Gustafson is a senior vice president with Evaluation Associates, Inc., which she joined in 1986. She consults with pension plans, endowments, and foundation on asset allocation, manager selection, performance monitoring, and all other investment-related issues. She worked previously for Peat Marwick where she was senior manager in charge of investment supervision. Prior to that she was at Bankers Trust Company, Hewitt Associates, The Hartford Insurance Group, and

TIAA–CREF. She is a chartered financial analyst, a chartered life underwriter, and a fellow of Life Management Institute. She holds a BA degree from the University of Nebraska.

Samuel L. Hayes holds the Jacob H. Schiff Chair in Investment Banking at the Harvard Business School. He has taught at the School since 1971, prior to which he was a tenured member of the faculty of the Columbia University Graduate School of Business. His research has focused on capital markets and the corporate interface with the securities markets. He has written numerous working papers and articles on related topics for publication in the *Harvard Business Review*, *The Accounting Review*, *The Financial Analysts' Journal*, the *Economic Review*, and *Financial Management*, and has contributed chapters to a number of books. He is the co-author of *Competition in the Investment Banking Industry*, published by Harvard University Press in 1983. He received a BA in political science from Swarthmore College in 1957 and an MBA (with distinction) and DBA from the Harvard Business School in 1961 and 1966, respectively.

C. Edward Hazen is active in corporate finance and venture capital with Robertson, Colman & Stephens. He was previously a vice president of DLJ Capital, the venture capital subsidiary of Donaldson Lufkin & Jenrette. Previously he was an associate in the firm's investment banking group. He received a BA from Brown University in 1973 and an MBA from the Harvard Business School in 1979.

Peter C. Jachym is a vice president of the First Boston Corporation, where his work is primarily with financial corporations. He joined First Boston in 1981. He holds a BA from Yale University and an MBA from the Amos Tuck School at Dartmouth College.

Edward C. Johnson III is director and chairman of Fidelity Investments, as well as chairman and chief executive officer of FMR Corp. He has been associated with Fidelity since 1957, first as a research analyst, and subsequently as portfolio manager of Fidelity Trend Fund. He has held the positions of chairman of Fidelity Management and Research Company, chairman of Fidelity International, Ltd. (United Kingdom), chairman of Fidelity International, Ltd. (Japan), and chairman of the Fidelity Group of International Funds. He is a member of the Corporation of the Boston Biomedical Research Institute, the Eye Research Institute of Retina Foundation, the Massachusetts General Hospital, and New England Deaconess Hospital. He is also a member of the American Antiquarian Society, the Boston Society of Security Analysts, and a trustee and Investment Committee member of the Boston Museum of Fine Arts. He is a graduate of Harvard University.

Toshiaki Kamijo is president of Nomura Investment Management Co., Ltd. After joining the Nomura Securities Company in 1954, he moved to the Nomura Research Institute in 1965, the year the Institute was established, to become manager of the Economic Research Department, then director and finally executive vice president, the position he held when he prepared the chapter on investment banking in Japan.

In 1986 he assumed his present position. He is the author of several articles on the Japanese economy and is a graduate of the Economics Department of Hitotsubashi University. The Nomura Research Institute serves as the heart of the information network of the Nomura group.

Paul Kazilionis is a vice president with Morgan Stanley Realty, Inc. He is a graduate of Colby College and received an MBA from the Amos Tuck School at Dartmouth College.

Stephen C. Kirmse is a senior vice president of Morgan Guaranty Trust Company of New York, the principal subsidiary of J.P. Morgan & Co. Inc. He joined Morgan after graduating from Princeton and has held a number of positions within the J.P. Morgan group of companies. Currently he heads Morgan Guaranty's Corporate Finance Services Department. Between 1983 and mid-1987 he headed the Commercial Paper Advisory Group, which developed and implemented Morgan Guaranty's entry into the commercial paper market.

Warren Law is the Edmund Coggswell Converse Professor of Banking and Finance at the Graduate School of Business Administration, Harvard University, where he has been a faculty member since 1958. Previously he taught at Southern Methodist University and was associate economist for the First National Bank of Dallas. At Harvard he has been chairman of the International Business Area and of the Program for Management Development. He received a BBA degree from Southern Methodist and MBA and PhD degrees from Harvard.

Dennis E. Logue is the Nathaniel Leverone Professor of Management at the Amos Tuck School of Business Administration at Dartmouth College. Before joining the Tuck School faculty he taught at Indiana University and worked as a senior international economist at the U.S. Treasury. He has authored, co-authored, or edited seven books, including *Legislative Influences on Corporate Pension Plans*, *Managing Corporate Pension Plans: The Impact of Inflation*, *The Investment Performance of Corporate Pension Plans*, and *The Handbook of Modern Finance*. He is a director of the Dartmouth National Bank, EXOGEN Corporation, and ANDROX, Inc. He holds a AB degree from Fordham University, an MBA from Rutgers University, and a PhD from Cornell University.

David Van Praag Marks is a Harvard-trained economist and lawyer. One of his research interests is the organization and regulation of the financial services sector. He formerly headed a consulting firm specializing in strategic planning for firms in regulated industries, including those within the financial services sector.

John E. Petersen is senior director, Government Finance Research Center in Washington, D.C. He has served as financial advisor to many federal agencies, state governments, and municipalities, including the U.S. Treasury, the U.S. Environmental Protection Agency, the Department of Transportation, and the states of Oregon, Alaska, Tennessee, and New York. In addition, he has undertaken studies for a number of nonprofit and private organizations, including the Twentieth

Century Fund, the National Science Foundation, and the Time–Life Corporation. He is recognized as an expert in the evaluation of financing alternatives, as well as in the structuring, rating, and marketing of municipal debt. He received a BA in economics from Northwestern University, an MBA from the Wharton School, and a PhD from the University of Pennsylvania.

Howard Platzman is a vice president for Public Policy and Corporate Issues at Chase Manhattan Bank, and was formerly an adjunct lecturer in philosophy at Baruch College and Brooklyn College of the City University of New York. He received a BA degree from Brooklyn College in 1971 and a PhD from the City University of New York Graduate School in 1981.

Calvin Potter is, since 1968, a professor of finance at Concordia University. Before that he was professor of commerce at McMaster University. He has been a visiting professor in the faculty of business at the University of British Columbia, at Monash University in Australia, and at the University of Aix-en-Province/Marseille in France. For one year he was a Simon Research Fellow at Manchester University in England. He is a Fellow of the Ontario Institute of Chartered Accountants and a member of the Quebec Order of Chartered Accountants. For six years he was a member of the Standards Setting Committee of the Canadian Institute of Chartered Accountants, and later was a member of the Special Committee on Standards Setting of that Institute. He has been a consultant to securities commissions and governments on financial issues, and is the author of many articles and monographs, and a text, *Finance and Business Administration in Canada*.

Tadeusz M. Rybczynski is economic advisor to Lazard Brothers & Company, Ltd. and director of Lazard Securities, Ltd. He is also a visiting professor at the City University in London, England. He is a Fellow of the Institute of Bankers of the United Kingdom, and is a governor and member of the Council of Management and Executive Committee of the National Institute of Economic and Social Research. He is also a council member and treasurer of the Royal Economic Society, a vice president of the British Association for the Advancement of Science, a member of the editorial board of *World Economy*, and received the Harms Medal for Outstanding Contribution to the Economic Profession from the Institute of Economic Research at the University of Kiel. He received Bachelor of Commerce and Master of Science degrees from the University of London.

Anthony Saunders is professor of finance at the Graduate School of Business Administration, New York University, and research advisor at the Federal Reserve Bank of Philadelphia. He is editor of Salomon Brothers Center *Monograph Series in Finance and Economics* and associate editor of the *Journal of Banking and Finance* and the *Journal of Financial Services Research*.

David Shaw is a professor of business administration at the University of Western Ontario. He has published extensively in academic and management journals on the topic of capital markets, and has testified before commissions on the structure of securities markets in Canada. Currently he is undertaking research into the role of domestic markets within global capital markets. His teaching interests span the area of corporate financial management and capital markets. He received a PhD in business and applied economics and an MBA from the Wharton School of Finance at the University of Pennsylvania.

Clifford W. Smith, Jr. is a professor of finance and economics at the William E. Simon Graduate School of Business Administration at the University of Rochester. He is the author of more than thirty published papers in the areas of corporate financial policy, financial institutions, and option pricing, and is editor of *The Modern Theory of Corporate Finance*, with Michael C. Jensen. He is an editor of the *Journal of Financial Economics*, an associate editor of the *Journal of Accounting and Economics*, the *Journal of Financial and Quantitative Analysis*, and the *Journal of Real Estate Finance and Economics*. He is also a member of the editorial review board of the *American Real Estate and Urban Economics Association Journal*, and *Current Issues in Finance*, and he is on the Advisory Board of the *Midland Corporate Finance Journal*. He received a BA from Emory University and a PhD from the University of North Carolina, Chapel Hill.

A. Michael Spence, dean of the Faculty of Arts and Sciences at Harvard since 1984, oversees the finances, organization, and educational policies of Harvard and Radcliffe Colleges, the Graduate School of Arts and Sciences, and the Office of Continuing Education. After teaching at Stanford, he returned to Harvard in 1977 as a professor of economics and in 1979 was named professor of business administration at the Business School. In 1983 he was named chairman of the Economics Department and George Gund Professor of Economics and Business Administration. He was awarded the John Kenneth Galbraith Prize for excellence in teaching and the John Bates Clark medal for his contribution to economic thought. He earned an undergraduate degree in philosophy at Princeton *summa cum laude* and was selected for a Rhodes Scholarship. He was awarded a BA–MA from Oxford and earned a PhD in economics at Harvard.

Joel M. Stern is managing partner of Stern Stewart & Co. Before founding Stern Stewart, he was President of Chase Financial Policy, the financial consulting arm of The Chase Manhattan Bank. Stern has served on the faculty of the University of Cape Town Graduate School of Business and now is visiting professor at the University of Witwatersrand in Johannesburg, and adjunct professor at Columbia University Graduate School of Business. He has participated since 1973 as rotating panelist on the national television program *Wall Street Week*. He serves on the Faculty Committee at the Lincoln Institute of Land Policy. Stern is the author of four books: *Analytical Methods in Financial Planning, Measuring Corporate Performance, The Revolution in Corporate Finance*, and *Six Roundtable Discussions of Corporate Finance with Joel Stern*.

A. Robert Towbin is a managing director at Shearson Lehman Brothers, Inc. He joined Shearson after leaving L.F. Rothschild, Unterberg, Towbin, of which he had been vice chairman. He joined one of that firm's predecessors, C.E. Unterberg, Towbin Company in 1959, and became a partner in 1961. He has been a director of a number of public corporations, including Convergent Technologies, Inc. and Lafayette Radio Electronics. He has also been a director of the National Black Network, and he has been vice chairman of the New York State Council on the Arts and vice chairman and treasurer of the Film Society of Lincoln Center. He received a BA degree from Dartmouth College in 1957.

Ingo Walter is the Dean Abraham L. Gitlow Professor of Economics and Finance at the Graduate School of Business Administration, New York University, and currently holds a joint appointment as the John H. Loudon Professor of International Management, INSEAD, Fontainebleau, France. He has been on the faculty of New York University since 1970. From 1971 to 1979 he was Associate Dean for Academic Affairs, serving as chairman of International Business from 1980 to 1983, and as chairman of Finance from 1983 to 1985. He is the author of a number of published papers and the author or editor of sixteen books, the most recent of which is *Global Competition in Financial Services*, published in 1987. He has served as a consultant to various U.S. and foreign government agencies, international institutions, banks, and other corporations. He received his AB and MA degrees from Lehigh University and a PhD degree from New York University.

J. Peter Williamson is professor of business administration at the Amos Tuck School of Business Administration at Dartmouth College. He has been at the Tuck School since 1961 and has taught at the Harvard Business School, the Darden School at the University of Virginia, and the University of Toronto Law School. He is the author of numerous articles and over a dozen books, on investments, taxation, and corporate finance. He teaches courses in investments, corporate finance, and financial institutions. He serves as a consultant to a number of business corporations and public organizations, is an active professional witness in utility cases, and is a trustee of the Common Fund, which manages investment portfolios for over 800 educational institutions. He received a BA from the University of Toronto, an LLB from the Harvard Law School, and MBA and DBA degrees from the Harvard Business School.

Charles Wolf is a professor of business at the Graduate School of Business, Columbia University. He is currently on leave working in the Equity Research Department of First Boston Corporation where he follows personal computer companies. Wolf is coauthor (with Professor Eli Shapiro) of *The Role of Private Placements in Corporate Finance* (Harvard University Press). He has also written numerous articles in the area of fixed-income investments. Wolf received BA, MBA, and DBA degrees from Harvard University.

Series Preface

The worlds of banking and finance have changed dramatically during the past few years, and no doubt this turbulence will continue through the 1980s. We have established the Wiley Professional Banking and Finance Series to aid in characterizing this dynamic environment and to further the understanding of the emerging structures, issues, and content for the professional financial community.

We envision three types of book in this series. First, we are commissioning distinguished experts in a broad range of fields to assemble a number of authorities to write specific primers on related topics. For example, some of the early handbook-type volumes in the series concentrate on the Stock Market, Investment Banking, and Financial Depository Institutions. A second type of book attempts to combine text material with appropriate empirical and case studies written by practitioners in relevant fields. An early example is a forthcoming volume on The Management of Cash and Other Short-Term Assets. Finally, we are encouraging definitive, authoritative works on specialized subjects for practitioners and theorists.

It is a distinct pleasure and honor for me to assist John Wiley & Sons, Inc. in this important endeavor. In addition; to banking and financial practitioners, we think business students and faculty will benefit from this series. Most of all, though, we hope this series will become a primary source in the 1980s for the members of the professional financial community to refer to theories and data and to integrate important aspects of the central changes in our financial world.

EDWARD I. ALTMAN

Professor of Finance
New York University,
School of Business

Series Preface

When John Wiley and I launched the Wiley Professional Banking and Finance Series in 1982, we noted the dynamic nature of financial markets beginning in the mid to late 1970s. We expected this trend to continue through the 1980s, as, indeed, it has. Today, the same prospects for dramatic change and the need to monitor and chronicle these changes into the 1990s continues.

We are very pleased with the quality and quantity of output from our continued efforts to publish books written by experts in diverse fields related to our central theme of financial innovation. We expect to continue to publish definitive, authoritative works on specialized subjects for practitioners and theorists, as well as compendiums and handbooks on more general topics, ranging from financial markets and investment policy to consumer, commercial, and investment banking.

It is a continued pleasure for me to work with such a distinguished publisher, and I look forward to a productive association in the years leading up to 2000. Of one thing I am sure: the constant innovations in banking and finance will provide fertile ground for generating ideas and topics for important new works in this series.

EDWARD I. ALTMAN

Max L. Heine Professor of Finance
Stern School of Business
New York University

Contents

PART 3. TRANSACTIONAL ACTIVITIES

PART 4. SPECIALIZED FINANCIAL INSTRUMENTS

PART 5. TAX-EXEMPT FINANCING

PART 6. BROKER ACTIVITIES

PART 7. COMMERCIAL BANKS AND INVESTMENT BANKING

PART 8. INVESTMENT BANKING OUTSIDE THE UNITED STATES

APPENDIX: THE LEADING 75 MANAGERS OF UNDERWRITTEN OFFERINGS

Investment Banking as a Profession: Pathway to Glory or Road to Oblivion?

PETER D. GOODSON

Individuals considering careers in investment banking today face far more complex decisions about the profession than those of us who entered the field in the mid-1960s.

Some decisions compare similarly with those made twenty years ago. Then, in the middle of the Go-Go Years, investment banking was a high-paying, glamorous profession in which hard-working people could go very far very fast. Banking houses vied with each other to attract the top graduates of the best schools. Mergers and acquisitions was a controversial subject eliciting much heated debate among corporate management, academics, and the government. There was enormous uncertainty as to the future of Wall Street. Bankers starting out did not know what shape the industry would take, but were convinced major changes would be coming. Commissions were fixed, NASDAQ had not been invented, and no one had a personal computer.

Everyone who has succeeded on the Street during the past two decades has done so, first, by being adaptive in response to a dramatically changing environment and, second, by being innovative in continually discovering new ways to bring to the table something of value. The same qualities are essential for anyone starting out now.

But despite the similarities, a decision about the profession twenty years ago was much simpler than one today. Most importantly, in deciding to step into the culture of Wall Street, we did not have to wonder whether we were placing our morals at peril. We knew, as well as we knew anything, that the system had integrity. We never had to question our bosses' honesty because it was plain fact that the leaders in the banking industry were individuals of principle and character. The culture of the Street was competitive, aggressive, demanding; but it was ethical.

A universal tenet—self-evident in its correctness—assumed that the profession of banking rested upon the virtue of honesty, and this assumption upheld relationships of trust among investment banks and clients, among partners and peers, and among senior and junior members of firms.

LOOKING BACK: INVESTMENT BANKING PROFESSIONALISM AND CLIENT RELATIONSHIPS

The strength of Wall Street's very business derived from trust and the professional relationships built upon it. Clients did not merely do business with bankers; rather, an investment banking relationship was maintained over many years. Companies were identified with specific banking firms, and individual bankers built careers serving the financing needs of particular clients over years and decades. Commitments formed that were recognized as having value, both for the client companies and their bankers, far beyond the dollar measure of any particular transaction. Through the mid-1960s, the professional worth and contribution of investment bankers were broadly acknowledged to meet the needs of clients.

Banking expertise must be commensurate with the technology utilized in the capital markets. Through the mid-1960s, professional investment banking did indeed fit the technology of the era. Issuers of securities had less access to market information than today, and buyers of securities operated with less information about the companies in which they invested. The expertise of bankers, together with their record of performance, served to bridge these gaps and to provide the support the market needed in order to function.

Viewed with today's clarifying hindsight, the inefficiencies of the market at that time are very evident. The long time frames involved in effecting large trades and in floating issues (often a matter of months) would be intolerable now, and modern pricing practices could not exist if they depended upon the information processing techniques of the 1960s. During the past two decades, market efficiency has increased dramatically as the market has improved enormously in size, liquidity, and diversity—to the betterment of all participants.

However, these beneficial changes carried a price, which generally involved diminished appreciation by clients of relationships with banking professionals. That loss—the deterioration of the perceived value of banking professionalism—reaches to the central worth of banks and bankers. In analysis of that loss may be found the direction of a successful career in banking today.

LOOKING AROUND NOW: TRANSACTIONAL BANKING AND ALIENATED CLIENTS

The changes that occurred in the Street beginning in the early 1970s carried enormous consequences for the financial community and its methods of operating. Most significant were the technological changes permitted near instantaneous transfer of information and, concomitantly, vastly superior processing and analysis of information.

The financial community lives on information. If more information is available, if it can be processed faster, and if more sophisticated analysis is employed, a superior competitive position is attained. The technological advancements of the 1970s in information processing and transmission were optimally suited to the business of the securities market, in which everything can be reduced to a quantified value . . . to bits of data zapped from computer to computer.

As the market became instantaneous and global, the perceptions of clients' banking needs changed. Issuers and investors discovered new opportunities, both in the broadened scope of information available to them and in the greatly truncated time frame required to execute transactions. The many weeks once required for securities offerings shrank to days and hours. As institutions became the dominant investors, a logical consequence was that block trading with negotiated commissions became a core business of Wall Street.

The influence and importance of the computer advanced symbiotically with the development of the global capital market and of the myriad new financing techniques that have emerged in recent years. The sheer ability to access capital markets around the world in a timely manner made it possible to structure and sell whole new spectrums of financial products to a hugely expanded marketplace. These new products—futures, options, swaps, hedges—are, of course, completely dependent on high-technology processing, which is needed to analyze, structure, and sell these products.

In many ways, all these changes were wonderful. The cost of participating in the capital markets dropped for both buyers and sellers. The new importance of trading capabilities and the vastly expanded array of new products (which needed to be created, sold, and traded) opened up fabulous career opportunities for many people whose talents and skills had not previously been in such demand. Changed environments created new opportunities.

The negative aspect of this change, however, was that the standard for measuring the quality of investment banks was often reduced to performance in transactions. The bankers' value-added was seen simply to be executional capability.

Many investment bankers readily acquiesced to this turn. The measure of their own career success became transactions. The focus of their work became product, not client need, and they became product salespeople. This has been particularly true in the merger and acquisition area, where some firms' M&A departments came to comprise large staffs of hyperaggressive people demonstrably devoted to product revenue rather than to the best interests of the clients.

THE LOSS OF PROFESSIONALISM

In a banking system that is essentially transaction-based, clients become alienated from the profession of banking. They inevitably tend to view the value of the bankers' input as being limited by the immediate dollar worth of a given transaction—of the product being purchased today—whether it is a refinancing, a currency swap, or a major acquisition. The value gained in these transactions does not necessarily relate to anything else. The contribution of a banker on a given transaction in such a system is accidental to the value to be gained from a banker on any other transaction.

Carried to its extreme, banking on these terms becomes a commodity business. Capital is the commodity and the only question is who provides capital most cheaply. Bankers become money-hawkers and deal-pushers looking for buyers; and a client "accesses" Wall Street to execute transactions, much the same as retail banking customers access their accounts through ATMs.

Note that with the introduction of competitors such as the immense Japanese firms, Europen banks, and the U.S. commercial banks (and the steady erosion of the Glass–Steagall Act), the system is rapidly moving much closer to a commodity operation. This trend is compounded by the consolidation taking place globally in the banking business.

Consolidation is a driving force because investment banking has become a capital-intensive industry. Massive amounts of capital are necessary both to support the enormous trading systems required today and to participate in modern merchant banking in which banks put their own capital to use on behalf of their client's transactions. Because the capital needed to compete often exceeds the banks' own resources, many investment banks are aligning themselves with large capital bases to ensure their future viability. This is essential to continued existence, but much diversity within the banking community is lost as a result. The eventual, inevitable consequence is a global banking industry dominated by a small number of enormous financial-service companies. The economics of the capital markets will not permit anything else.

This is not to say that there is anything wrong with providing capital as cheaply as possible, or that anything can or should be done to stop the movement in that direction. The issuers and buyers of securities quite properly require the market to make capital available at the most competitive prices.

But if that is the end of the story, it bodes ill for people considering careers in banking because a "premium element" for professionalism is missing from the matrix. There is no place in purely transaction-based banking for the banker's unique value-adding capability. For many of us, the basic professional goal—the mastery of which may direct a career—is then absent. If banking is permitted to continue to be molded overwhelmingly by the technology-driven forces of transaction-based business, it will not offer much in professional fulfillment.

THE CLIENTS' LOSS

The mere fact that some of us who did well under the old order and found great professional satisfaction in that system might like things to be different is not the issue. More significantly, transaction-based investment banking is not good for clients themselves because it deprives them of a distinctive, important added value which can only be derived from professional investment banking.

The essence of investment banking—that aspect of it that brings the highest value to clients and provides the most rewarding career path—does not reside merely in executing transactions but rather in bringing unique perspective to the problems of the clients and providing them with value creation that would otherwise not be available to them.

A critical contribution of bankers is drawn from their position in the marketplace. Bankers access the dynamics of all aspects of the market. Bankers know the sellers of securities; they can evaluate a company, its prospects, and its opportunities in a distinctive context. Bankers also serve and are close to the buyers of securities; they know what products and prices command a premium and where purchasers reside. Optimally bankers are, themselves, the crossroads of the capital markets.

Bankers develop this perspective by working hard over time, capitalizing on the singular vision bankers alone can acquire. There is a cumulative expertise that comes with experience. It leads to wisdom. Without it, bankers are order-takers. With it, bankers are distinctly valuable contributors to corporate managements' strategic planning and program execution.

This value-added element—the unique perspective bankers bring to client opportunities—is the critical element of banking professionalism.

Most corporate managements do a major deal once or twice in a career. Bankers do deals continuously. Corporate managements have, as their primary mission, the maximization of the operations of the companies they are responsible for; their primary mission is not to ride the markets. But bankers ride the markets every day, and the banker's organization is dedicated to maximizing opportunities in a changing world market. The experience of bankers comprises a unique perspective that cannot be attained strictly from the corporate side.

In sum, technology-driven, transaction-based banking has elbowed out much of the professional relationship traditionally considered an important part of banking. But clients need more than just reactions. Banking clients—issuers and buyers— benefit significantly from the addition of the banker's value-added perspective. They need the inputs that are the critical essence of banking professionalism.

The question, therefore, is how to structure the banking industry to ensure the benefits of professional investment banking to clients. A parallel question is how to structure an individual career in investment banking to garner the fullest professional satisfaction.

LOOKING AHEAD: INVESTMENT BANKING PROFESSIONALISM REBORN

New dimensions of professional banking expertise must be developed, for the sake of clients and bankers. In creating and exercising this expertise, bankers must take a vital, proactive part. They must reach into the apparent chaos of today's market and exert themselves to shape their own professional worth. They must identify opportunities in a timely manner. There is no more possibility of a "transom" career in banking.

Creating and supporting such expertise in the global market also requires a new and different type of bank. The bank must house specific industry expertise as well as transactional expertise. It must comprise comprehensive equity and debt desk capability, fully dedicated to the needs of the client. Those of us responsible for the management of banking firms today must accept the responsibility to build environments that instill the banker's perspective in our professionals.

The future will go to those who reestablish banking professionalism as an identifiable quality valued by clients. That is the mandate of the times. Clients need it, and the smart ones know it. The banking industry needs it. Those individuals who stay on top of changing times and deliver to clients the value of a true banking partnership are certain to enjoy careers as fulfilling as they can imagine.

A PROFESSION BUILT ON TRUST

Banking is not now, and never has been, static. It is as dynamic as the changing business world it serves. Specific answers are never the same from one banking era to another, and new solutions to the basic problems of financing must always be invented. But the honesty and trust underlying banking professionalism always remain.

It is a tragedy, but undeniable, that some important bankers have shown themselves to be crooks. They had been classmates, cohorts, peers. Now they are admitted felons. They betrayed the profession. There is nothing any of us can do to erase that.

The challenge now is to rebuild trust in the banking industry, and those who do so will win the competition among the next generation of bankers. The job is not simply one of finance. It is one of defining ethics and of creating and maintaining cultures of honesty and trust.

PATTERN OF SUCCESS

In reviewing the turbulence in banking in the past twenty years, it is tempting to abrogate responsibility for the state of affairs by concluding that events are totally dominated by the changing environment—that the forces shaping the global capital markets dictate the nature of the firms working in those markets and the career activities of bankers themselves. But this is not so.

Looking closely at all that has happened since the Go-Go Years, one can ascertain a certain pattern of success—demonstrated in the careers of persons and firms—that is clearly the consequence of specific, individual decisions as to how to conduct banking business. This discernible pattern doubtless offers the clearest guideline to personal success available, and the most trustworthy.

The pattern of success in banking—the high road of professionalism still to be followed—incorporates several criteria.

1. An understanding of the clients themselves. The most basic element of investment banking professionalism is an accurate perception of client needs. As "The Music Man" says, "You got to know the territory."

2. The technical capability required to deliver the full array of modern banking products. It's said that if your only tool is a hammer, the solution to every problem is a nail. Bankers are no better than the tools at their command, and a sine qua non of banking success is a solid base in executional capability.

3. The ability to anticipate industry trends. A client who is the manager of a telecommunications company needs a banker who understands the telecommunications industry. A client in the retail business will wisely be drawn to do business with a banker who has first-hand knowledge of retailing. And so on through the industries. The banks that are succeeding in today's markets are those that attract and retain in-house staff with specific industry knowledge.

Providing clients with true professional banking counsel implies anticipating of opportunities and then positioning the client to gain maximum value from the changing business environment. Bankers must take their knowledge of the client's industry and their own banking resources and link them with a vision of opportunity that creates true value for the client. When this happens, corporate management realizes that bankers are a unique resource.

4. Dedication to the client. It is a flat truism that integrity is important. The measure of bankers' counsel must be the client's best interest, not the impact on their own income nor the public relations value that doing the deal may add in promoting their reputation. The short-term, self-gratification precepts of the "me" generation have no place in banking. The standard must be what is best for the client, even if that means taking a strong stand against a deal the client may be eager to do.

Some advice: Base your career on solid ethics. The market needs it. Your clients need it. Your career needs it. If you find yourself in a situation where things do not seem to be completely on the level, go to your boss. If the problem happens to be your boss, go to the big boss. If the big boss proves to be the problem as well, quit. You will never regret it.

5. A genuinely collegial culture within the banks themselves and among bankers. Achieving and maintaining banking professionalism necessarily calls for a team approach. The market cannot be mastered by any one person, no matter what the scope of his or her individual talents. The needs of clients are too diverse, complex, and changing to be met adequately on any basis other than a team basis. We are all in this together but, together, we can continue to provide the values of banking professionalism to a world that needs those values more and more. In doing so, we can enjoy careers as full as anything we may imagine.

PART 1 INVESTMENT BANKING TODAY

In the first of the four chapters in Part 1, Sam Hayes, Michael Spence, and David Marks trace the origins of investment banking in the United States. They detail the competitive structure of the industry, an aspect of investment banking that has never been more important than it is today. The past few years have seen sharply increased competition among U.S. investment banking firms, new competition from commercial banks eager to take on investment banking, and growing foreign competition as financial markets have gone "global."

Fred Fisher's chapter moves us to the global perspective. Again focusing on competitive structure, he describes the emergence of the Euromarket, the integration of markets worldwide, and the consequences of competition in a market largely free of regulation. Merchant bankers, commercial bankers, and investment bankers all compete freely in the Euromarket. The patterns of competition, the instruments and markets they have devised, and the services they have invented point the way to the future of investment banking in Europe and the United States.

In Chapter 3, Charlie Ellis writes from the perspective of one who regularly surveys the clientele of investment bankers. His advice on attracting corporate clients in the face of more intense competition stresses what corporate clients want and how their choices are made.

While Charlie Ellis takes the point of view of the investment banker attracting business, Joel Stern and Clifford Smith, in Chapter 4, take the client point of view. Distinguishing between what really matters in financial structuring and what might be called "cosmetic" finance, they provide a means for separating good investment banker advice from what is mediocre or poor. In particular, Chapter 4 presents a wealth of empirical evidence on the market's response to a variety of financial transactions.

1 Investment Banking Competition: An Historical Sketch

SAMUEL L. HAYES III
A. MICHAEL SPENCE
DAVID V.P. MARKS

Investment banking in the United States evolved gradually out of the hodgepodge of financial services first available in the early 1800s. Viewed historically, the process by which these financial institutions developed both their relationships with clients and their methods of doing business reveals much about the industry's enduring dynamics of competition.

The development of investment banking owes much, of course, to local circumstances and influential personalities. Had there been no J.P. Morgan or Jacob Schiff, or had there been no need for railroad financing, the way that General Motors sells new equity would not be precisely what it is today. But it would not be all that different, either. What history makes clear is that the flow of capital through the hands of underwriters tends to seek out its own level.

Since the early 1800s, U.S. investment bankers have managed the growing demand for capital through the use of underwriting syndicates. These syndicates have consistently taken on a pyramidlike shape and have been managed by the handful of firms at the pyramid's apex. Relationships of considerable loyalty and duration have existed between underwriting houses and client firms. In theory, pyramidal syndicate organizations, apex firms, and banker–client loyalty are not inevitable. In practice, they have been so. Something else—something more than the mere need to adapt to changing circumstances—has been at work.

THE EUROPEAN BACKGROUND

The European background of investment banking bears directly on its evolution in the United States. Although the interest of U.S. banks in, for example, the retailing of securities in secondary markets was the product of market conditions in the United States, the transnational careers of individual bankers and joint ventures between European and U.S. houses did help to shape financial services in the United States. More important for our purposes, the early course of developments in Europe offers an especially clear glimpse of the industry's underlying competitive dynamics at work.

The Loan Contractors

By the 1780s, England possessed a reasonably coherent market for public bills and securities. A genuine investor class existed, and subscriptions to public loans were generally open to limited combinations of wealthy private individuals and influential politicians. Within a decade loan contractors appeared who took on subscriptions in order to resell them at a profit. Heated discussions arose at the time as to whether (in Fritz Redlich's words) "the loan contractor was an independent link in a chain or a mere representative of [ultimate] subscribers; or, in other words, whether loan contracting was a business enterprise."[1]

The question was eventually settled: soon after the turn of the nineteenth century, even the wealthiest individual investors began to be crowded out of the original market for new subscriptions by the middlemen—James Morgan, Walter Boyd, the Barings, and Goldsmid and Co. are examples—with comparatively large pools of capital at their disposal. Direct government efforts to keep loan contracting competitive often produced the opposite result. For example, William Pitt's decision in 1784 to solicit public subscriptions to the government debt merely consolidated that debt in professional hands. Competition favored not the emerging investor class with its limited savings but rather the banking firms or partnerships with ample capital resources. These resources provided the large sums required for the initial purchase of securities and for stabilizing the market for their later resale.

To achieve their privileged standing, contractors often cooperated in putting together secret lists or embryonic syndicates for sharing the risks in a subscription bid. Although the use of lists was itself not new, their composition was. No longer limited to ultimate investors, the lists now included first the contractors and sub-contractors and only then private individuals, who had to apply to the contractors for admission. The contractors negotiated the details of the loan, committed those whose names appeared on the list to the pledged amount of their subscriptions, assumed liability for the timely provision of the funds thus pledged, and stabilized the secondary market for loan securities against the manipulations of bearish stock-jobbers.

Early Investment Bankers

English practice during this period developed somewhat apart from that on the Continent. Many of the families that would soon dominate English finance—the

---

[1] Fritz Redlich, *The Molding of American Banking: Men and Ideas*, pt. II, New York: Hafner, 1951, p. 307.

Barings, the Warburgs, the Rothschilds—were of European descent, and though there was some international cooperation, these cross-influences were not extensive.

On the Continent the need for public funds was still largely met by the private resources of well-to-do individuals. But another financing mechanism was also in operation. A group of middlemen—among them the Gebruder Bethmann in Frankfurt, and Hope and Company in Amsterdam—had appeared who

> did not take shares in a subscription outright as did the English loan contractors . . . [but] "negotiated" whole issues on a commission basis . . . [and then] disposed of the securities, with the sale of which they were charged, as fast as possible directly to capitalists, soliciting by letters, circulars, and advertisements.[2]

The wall between these Continental practices and English loan contracting was effectively breached in some of the major public financings after the Congress of Vienna in 1814–1815. In the process, Redlich argues, something legitimately called investment banking was born:

> Like the English loan contractors the early investment bankers took new security issues outright and not on a commission basis, as had done the Continental bankers. But, on the other hand, they dealt with complete issues, as had been customary on the Continent, and unlike earlier eighteenth-century loan contractors they did not compete with institutional or other ultimate investors for mere parts thereof. (To be sure, the English development was already turning in this direction after 1800.) Furthermore, although acquiring the issues outright in English fashion, the early investment banks received a commission following Continental practice. Or to look at the matter from a different angle, the transactions corresponded to what would have been called "private subscriptions" in eighteenth-century England. But they differed from the latter in that only middlemen participated, i.e., bankers who meant to sell to speculators and ultimate investors and who received a commission.[3]

For Redlich, then, the point at which public financing crosses over into investment banking proper occurs when competition for new securities no longer exists "between direct investors and individual speculators, on the one hand, and loan contractors, on the other, the latter being defined as enterprisers who currently subscribe to new security issues in order to profit from resale."[4] Investment banking exists when ultimate investors abandon to professional middlemen the original market for new subscriptions.

The Emergence of Apex Firms

The real significance of this departure of ultimate investors from the original securities market is that a mere handful of the most prominent investment houses came to dominate the flow of long-term capital into public securities. Heated competition

[2] *Ibid.*, p. 318.
[3] *Ibid.*, p. 320.
[4] *Ibid.*, p. 326.

did persist, however, among the smaller firms that desired to be included in the confederations or lists managed by the most influential firms.

What rapidly developed, in Redlich's phrase, was "some kind of oligopoly at the apex of the pyramid . . . supported by chains of middlemen."[5] Competition was not less fierce at the top of the pyramid than at its base. The threat of new entrants and of new alliances among established firms remained quite real. The risks involved in taking on major flotations could suddenly leave even the biggest firms badly exposed. When Walter Boyd, for example, who had dominated English loans during the mid-1790s, became overextended, the other members of his syndicate first reduced the size of his participation and then excluded him altogether. Similarly, the Barings were finally driven from their preeminent position by the Rothschilds. A break in the secondary price of the French *rentes*–probably engineered by the Rothschilds–had caught the Barings sufficiently exposed that they could save themselves only by canceling contracts and thus sacrificing their reputation.

The profits to be made from such flotations were so immense and the mutual benefit of maintaining discipline among syndicate participants in the flow of capital was so clear that the competitive pyramid was an indisputable fact by the 1820s. The early division of firms between the apex and the body of the pyramid was thus a natural outgrowth of competitive dynamics as they then existed. Ultimate investors had not yet developed into a diversified market, although the means for trading securities were already in place. The variety of financial products available to investors was not extensive. Loan participations differed, of course, in maturity, rate of interest, and degree of risk, but the loans themselves were relatively standard. The borrowers, sovereign states or their subordinate units, had—with the exception of wars and other emergencies—a predictable and recurring need for funds. In the early 1800s, even the demand for war loans had a certain regularity.

Although the universe of borrowers was quite small, the threat of their joining to dictate terms to the banking industry was largely offset by the endless political maneuvering among them. Their large financial requirements and the confidential "reasons of state" often underlying those requirements made timely access to capital and assurance of discretion essential. And these could be supplied only by firms able to "manage" the workings of the developing capital markets.

Indeed, the needs of governments virtually forced the emergence of apex firms and the discipline they were able to impose throughout the rest of the financial chain. But they ruled at a price: the erection of protective, though not impassable, barriers around the apex firms. Competition among them did not disappear but shifted from price to considerations of service: broad geographic access to capital, quality of service itself, reputation for reliability, proven ability to deliver as promised, and degree of control over a security's value on the secondary exchanges.

Then, as later, the industry's Achilles' heel was the availability of adequate capital. Because even the apex firms typically did not have the cash to meet their own loan repayments as they came due, they would often have to sell inventoried securities precipitously in the secondary markets. They wold also borrow funds

[5] *Ibid.*, p. 321.

against the securities they kept in inventory, a practice that put them at the mercy of professionally bearish speculators. Only later would the Rothschilds teach the industry more advanced techniques of stabilization by actively orchestrating buying and selling activities on the various European exchanges to keep securities prices up.

U.S. DEVELOPMENTS UP TO WORLD WAR I

Developments in the United States lagged several decades behind those in Europe. Until the Civil war and railroad building of the mid-nineteenth century created ever-increasing requirements for capital, financial services were provided by auctioneers and speculators, merchants like Stephen Girard and John Jacob Astor, brokers of every description, and incorporated commercial banks like Nicholas Biddle's United States Bank of Pennsylvania. By the 1840s, many providers of these services decided to become private bankers dealing in securities transactions. Some, like John E. Thayer and Brother, had originally been foreign exchange brokers; others, like Alex. Brown and Sons, had been merchants and shippers.

Influences from Abroad

The American need for capital attracted representatives of such European houses as the Barings, the Rothschilds, and the Speyers. Alexander Baring, for instance, came over in person to work out the tricky financial arrangements for Jefferson's Louisiana Purchase. August Belmont, who quickly established his own banking operation, was initially an agent of the Rothschilds. Belmont retained close ties with them for many years, which in practice meant privileged access to their financial backing.

Soon thereafter, a number of German-Jewish immigrants with commercial, if not directly financial, family backgrounds—most notably the Seligmans, the Lehmans, Abraham Kahn, Solomon Loeb, and Marcus Goldman—moved from assorted mercantile activities into private banking. Like such Yankee houses as Lee, Higginson and the several Morgan establishments in New York, London, and Philadelphia, the Jewish firms prospered because of their privileged access to European capital. Unlike the Yankee houses, however, they often enjoyed the business advantages of extensive family ties.

There were also numerous joint ventures between European and U.S. firms. The Revolutionary era, of course, saw major efforts of short duration to raise money abroad. In the early nineteenth century, however, funding the public debt sent both government officials and commercial bankers like John Sergeant and Charles Wilkes to London, where they learned a great deal from the Rothschilds and the Barings about loan contracting and securities issues. In fact, until the post-1837 depression, London proved a most reliable source of capital for U.S. needs. Some of these international alliances were temporary—domestic bankers trying to place small issues of local securities abroad. Others, like the association of Prime, Ward, and King in New York with the Barings, lasted even through the bleakness of the 1840s.

By the time Cooke & Co. failed, precipitating the great financial panic of 1873, the industry gave clear promise of its later development. Even though foreign buyers and large domestic institutions still absorbed the lion's share of new flotations, Jay Cooke's imaginative approach to selling government paper during the Civil War showed the value of aggressive sales tactics and a nationwide distribution system. It also identified the small individual investor as a potentially important dimension of the securities market. This attention to mass retailing had a distinctly American flavor. Loan subscriptions open to the public had enjoyed some success in Europe, especially France after 1850, but aggressive retailing found greater acceptance in the United States.

It was Cooke's genius to tap this universe of potential investors by establishing a nationwide, but centrally controlled, network of distribution agents and by supporting them with mass advertising. His appeals to patriotism helped, but earlier patriotic appeals without Cooke's retailing expertise had fallen on deaf ears. Cooke's grasp of the techniques needed to reach middle-class investors and his willingness to support the price of securities in the market defined the mix of sales technique and stabilization characteristic of post-Civil War syndicates.

On balance, then, European influences transmitted a working knowledge of certain financial practices, and European houses controlled much of the later refunding of Civil War loans. They did not, however, have great effect on U.S. investment banking structure or dynamics. Conditions general to underwriting activity and particular to the domestic U.S. market for securities counted for more.

Services and Relationships

By the post-Civil War decade, the market for financial services was changing in important ways. Much in evidence, for example, was so-called active investment banking—banker influence (through membership on corporate boards or finance committees) upon the policies of client companies. In general, investment banking activity expanded by providing technical assistance with new issues and by supplying a wide array of financial advice and supporting services. As these involvements became more varied and extensive, longer-term loyalties between banker and client quite naturally emerged. These relationships, however, were based on more than familiarity.

Bankers' services, general financial advice, and reputation were highly enough prized that the client companies gradually came to encourage long-term alliances with selected investment houses—their "principal bankers." Although neither party was legally bound to maintain the alliance in the course of future flotations, as Vincent Carosso puts it,

> Close, continuous relationships between railroads and the investment houses that financed them, whether formal or informal, were encouraged by both bankers and railroad officials because both benefited from them. The banker's presence on the board facilitated sales of a road's securities; it gave investors confidence that their

interests were being better served; and it appeared to constitute either an endorsement of the issue's "investment quality" or "practically guaranteed" it.[6]

For the bankers, relationships meant assured access to a substantial income, which in turn was necessary to attract and motivate the talented people who serviced the clients. As has been true throughout the history of investment banking, without unusually talented people to keep the banks flexible enough to meet new needs as they appeared, even established houses—like that of the Seligmans—could fall on hard times.

Still, bankers had innumerable ways to make money. There were fees for underwriting managements or participations, fees as registrar or transfer agent for securities, fees for financial consulting, fees for redeployment of a client's deposited funds, fees for overseeing consolidations or reorganizations, and fees for distributing security issues. However large the profits, the premier firms did not monopolize their industry. If anything, as flotations increased in size and retailing grew in importance, the leading houses relied more and more on the collaboration of second- and third-tier distribution firms around the country. As at virtually ever stage of its evolution, investment banking exhibited an obligopolistic industry structure that was roughly pyramidal in shape, with a handful of powerful firms at the apex.

Leading houses like Morgan wanted to cement their own positions, but smaller establishments like N.W. Halsey & Co. found their own lucrative niches, as did nonapex commercial banks outside the Eastern money centers. Local and regional issues often attracted the second- and third-tier firms, many of which also had a relatively open field in distribution operations. The flotations of utility companies did not typically appeal to the major houses, just as a generation or two later the flotations of retailers like Sears and of consumer-oriented light industries would not generate much apex interest. Kuhn Loeb, for example, had little use for industrial, as opposed to railroad, flotations until virtually the end of the nineteenth century.

The firms at the top of the pyramid did not try to compete in every niche of the market. Their strength lay in their ability to put together a group of investors—particularly institutional investors—more effectively than anyone else. As a result, they could absorb the risks of ever larger flotations, remunerate the talented professionals who managed the services on which both profits and client loyalty depended, and move quickly whenever a new competitive opening was spotted.

As the resources of commercial banks, trust companies, and—most particularly—life insurance companies skyrocketed, institutions came to invest heavily in the securities issues managed by apex firms and quite understandably sought closer managerial involvement with them. These overtures were both welcomed and reciprocated. Officers of each of these various institutions typically owned the securities of the others or sat on their boards or finance committees. George W. Perkins, for example, was both a Morgan partner and chairman of the finance committee of New York Life Insurance Co. In 1913, as the Pujo investigations

[6] Vincent P. Carosso, *Investment Banking in America: A History*, Cambridge, MA: Harvard University Press, 1970, p. 32.

revealed, officers of five New York banks (Morgan, First National, National City, Bankers' Trust, and Guaranty Trust) held 118 directorships in 34 banks and trust companies, 30 directorships in 10 insurance companies, 105 directorships in 32 transportation companies, 63 directorships in 24 producing and trading companies, and 25 directorships in 12 public utility companies. Thus this group of men held 341 directorships in 112 companies having aggregate resources of $22 billion. The Morgan partners alone held 72 seats, and George F. Baker, Chairman of New York's First National Bank, personally held 58.[7]

With institutional cooperation assured, the trust companies banks, and insurance companies benefited from the apex firms' reputation and influence as well as from a predictable supply of high-grade paper. For their part, the investment bankers enjoyed a more extensive and reliable supply of both short- and long-term capital. Even so, a single investment banking house could rarely by itself supply the money or absorb the risk involved in a major flotation. As a result, the use of formal syndicates became commonplace in all sorts of new-issues activity.

Conventions of Syndicate Organization

The underwriting syndicates in which investment bankers participated had, according to Carosso, four historically distinct functions: (1) origination, the determination of the kinds, amounts, and terms of the securities to be underwritten; (2) purchase, the actual purchase of securities from issuer or originating house for distribution and resale; (3) banking, the provision by commercial banks of funds to purchasers, when resale was not quickly accomplished, so that they could keep obligations to issuers and originators; and (4) sales and distribution, the placement of securities with dealers or ultimate investors either on a straight commission or a contract basis. In practice, however, the first three functions were the responsibility of the originating house (or houses), usually an apex firm. This manager (or co-manager) function stood clearly separate from the distribution function.

The managing firm had a number of distinct tasks and a wide range of discretion. It established the size and composition of the syndicate, formulated the terms governing origination and sales, determined the size of each member's participation, stabilized the issue's market price during the distribution and selling phases, enforced obligations and liabilities assumed by syndicate members, kept the syndicate's records, and passed out the syndicate's profits—for all of which it received a special manager's fee.

These arrangements represented an extension of earlier practice. Just as linkages grew between banks and their favored clients, so syndicate-based linkages grew among banks themselves. Inclusion in a syndicate-especially as a managing house—yielded the substantial profits and heightened prestige in which competitive success rested. Being asked to join a syndicate managed by others and, even more

---

[7] Sheridan A. Logan, *George F. Baker and His Bank, 1840–1955*, Lüneburg, West Germany: Stinehour, 1981, p. 156.

important, acquiring the power to ask others to join one's own syndicate dominated the attention of all investment banking houses.

The rules by which such offers were extended, though never really formalized, were broadly understood and generally followed. Sufficient financial strength and expertise to meet syndicate obligations were necessary, but they did not guarantee participation. The loyalties developed in a house's past relations with an issuer, if mutually satisfactory, were strongly considered in new flotations, as was the desire of managing firms to assure their own inclusion in future syndicates managed by others. According to one banker, "Participations in syndicates are given for the sake of getting participations in syndicates . . . [and are] taken for the sake of being able to offer participations in syndicates."[8]

These informal understandings, which were most often the product of simple oral agreement among what Jacob Schiff of Kuhn Loeb spoke of as a "circle of friends"[9] did not come without strings attached. A firm that did not meet its syndicate commitments or that sought inclusion only in the most profitable financings or that gained in any of a thousand ways a reputation for not pulling its own weight would quickly find itself left out of future arrangements.

"Every bank or banking house to whom we addressed the syndicate letter offering it participation in the syndicate," testified Morgan's partner Thomas Lamont, "has an absolute right to reject it."[10] Lamont did not, however, report on the generosity of spirit with which the House of Morgan would look upon the exercise of that right. As *The New York Times* asserted, "Firms and individuals . . . cannot discriminate between promising and unpromising syndicates without being excluded altogether in the future.[11] In a financial universe that offered very attractive profits in return for being a responsible "member of the club," the rules may have been informal—a "matter of custom and business honor"[12]—but they were binding nonetheless.

This unspoken code provoked deep suspicion among the industry's critics. The specter of a few powerful houses controlling in secret and in seeming collusion the fate of U.S. business could not help but stir up public suspicion. And these suspicions could not be allayed by simple assurances from leading financiers about their honorable behavior. The perception of a few apex firms sitting atop a pyramid of several hundred lesser ones and ruling them with the aristocratic strictness of an English public school headmaster was likely to create trouble. And, in the wake of the 1920s excesses, it did.

[8] Wallace B. Donham, "Underwriting Syndicates and the Purchase and Sale of Securities through Banking Houses," lecture notes on "Corporate Finance," Harvard Graduate School of Business Administration, 1908.

[9] New York State Legislature, II, Albany: J.B. Lyon, 1906, pp. 1021–1022.

[10] U.S. Senate, Hearings before the Committee on Finance, 72nd Congress, 1st Sess., pt. 1, Sale of Foreign Bonds or Securities in the United States: Hearings . . . , 4 pts., Washington, DC: 1931–32, pt. 1, p. 23.

[11] *The New York Times*, September 24, 1905.

[12] Adricos H. Joline, "The Method and Conduct of the Reorganization of Corporations," two lectures delivered at the Harvard Graduate School of Business Administration, April 4 and 6, 1910, copyright A.H. Joline, 1910, p. 58.

Some historians have argued that this public image implied a degree of competitive regimentation that did not in fact exist. The market for investment banking had become increasingly segmented after the 1870s, however, and the apex firms simply did not regulate competition in every market niche. Only a few of the larger houses (e.g., Lehman Brothers and Goldman Sachs) interested themselves in the affairs of small, family-owned manufacturing or retailing companies. Still fewer bothered with municipal or local utility issues; most left those issues to aggressive regional houses. And as Carosso notes, "alert men [continually] organized new firms to meet local and regional needs and to cater to new investors with new services."[13]

But even in major corporate financings, the established houses differed in the services they provided and in their sources of profit. For instance, they varied considerably in the attention paid to establishing branch offices and to the retailing of securities. Kidder Peabody and Lee, Higginson jumped eagerly into such brokerage activity and used their retailing skills and distribution systems to win participations in syndicates run by confirmed wholesalers like Morgan and Kuhn Loeb.

The major houses no longer had their chosen field to themselves. Substantial roles in new flotations went to the bond departments and security affiliates of commercial banks, as corporate deposits increasingly permitted them to act as institutional investors. Ambitious trust companies with liberal state charters also participated. In fact, access to investment capital anywhere throughout the country and to distribution systems able to tap that capital were sufficient means for new players to enter the industry. From a distance, the industry may have seemed relatively frozen in its disciplined commitment to "good form" and venerable custom; up close it looked more like a beehive of competitive activity—though a beehive in the shape of a pyramid.

RESPONSE TO CONDITIONS AFTER WORLD WAR I

Looking back on these developments half a century later, Judge Harold Medina in the early 1950s in *U.S. v. Morgan*—the antitrust case launched by the government against 17 major investment banking firms—put these changes in industry structure into perspective. It was, Medina contended, preposterous to assume, as the government prosecutors did, that these firms had first "entered into a combination, conspiracy, and agreement to restrain and monopolize the securities business of the United States" in or about the year 1915.[14] The industry had taken on modern form well before that. More important, this form—a pyramid with apex firms, and with the whole linked together by syndicate organizations—had been the basic shape of the industry at each stage of its development.

But neither this shape nor the position of firms within it had become frozen, Medina maintained. It was not a financial straitjacket, but represented the responses of countless individuals and institutions to certain recurring financial needs. It could,

---

[13] Carosso, *Investment Banking*, p. 108.

[14] United States v. Henry S. Morgan et al., 118 F. Supp. 621, 629 (S.D.N.Y. 1953).

of course, be misused, but there was little sense in arbitrarily painting the whole with the broad brush of monopoly.

Medina reasoned that, because the flotation of a security issue was so complex, the process was not a standardized "it" that a few banking houses could monopolize. And because each issue was unique, bankers competed not by offering a commodity-like package of services at the lowest price but instead by trying to "establish or continue a relationship with the issuer," based on past performance, current reputation, and faithful adherence to the industry's informal code of conduct.

As a result, when speaking of competitors, "nothing but confusion will follow unless we first determine what is the 'it' for which the competitors are supposed to be competing." Put simply, Medina saw the industry pyramid as embodying a considerable amount of competitive activity because the "single, entire, unitary transaction" involved in a major underwriting is really the sum of many different banking services.[15]

Nor were these services "the product of accident or secret arrangement among the more powerful firms." They were, as Medina stressed time and time again, "the product of a gradual evolution to meet specific economic problems created by demands for capital, which arose as the result of the increasing industrialization of the country and the growth of a widely dispersed investor class." They were all "part of the development of a single effective method of security underwriting and distribution." In short, they represented over the years "the normal and natural reactions of businessmen with common problems to the course of economic events." Even so, individual firms demonstrated a "conspicuous lack of uniformity" in their manner of participation in the industry—or, in Medina's memorable phrase, a "pattern of no pattern."[16]

Though this conclusion may have been clear to Medina in retrospect, it was not clear to the public in the first third of the twentieth century. Fears of an anticompetitive "money trust" rarely seemed to die down, and in fact were fueled by the gradual discovery not of secret plots or backroom collusion but of professional incompetence, irresponsibility, and out-and-out fraud. Public reaction to the industry's gentlemen's-club mystique had always been ambivalent. But following the great crash of 1929, public confidence in the system evaporated, as events continually gave the lie to the industry's reputation for sober and responsible management.

Along with this loss of reputation, bankers no longer had vast discretion in their stewardship of the nation's private economy. Revelations of stock waterings, bank mismanagement, and slipshod practices on the stock exchanges finally broke the terms of the long-implicit compact between bankers and society. Industry self-regulation was no longer enough. Demands for external regulation could no longer be avoided. A new legal order was needed—or so ran the social consensus—to police the industry's workings. But what that consensus did not foresee was that the arrival of explicit legal obligations would hasten the demise of an older, informal sense of personal and institutional responsibility. By 1930, no man or group of

---

[15] *Ibid.* at 652, 689, 690.
[16] *Ibid.* at 650, 633.

men had the acknowledged standing to do what Morgan had done to stem the Panic of 1907.[17] More to the point, few if any still felt the obligation to do so.

In such a climate, indictments of bankers' lack of probity went hand-in-hand with familiar accusations of excessive concentration and banker control of industry. Although these new charges and the investigations they inspired occupied public attention, they often missed the significance of structural changes. First in New York and then in many other states, for example, life insurance companies were explicitly barred from further participation in underwriting syndicates and, in general, were forced to pull back from their close ties to various banking institutions—except, of course, as ultimate purchasers of securities. As a result, Carosso notes, syndicates became on average much larger than they had previously been, because it took many banking and brokerage firms to absorb the risk and amass the capital of a single insurance company. Syndicates therefore became more open to new entrants, and competition increased among old ones.

Partly in response to these developments, the established modes of syndicate operation began to feel new pressures. Financial houses outside New York started to raise technical questions about the way undistributed securities were divided among syndicate members. Also, as both syndicates and flotations they managed grew larger, their life spans grew shorter and the arrangements among participating firms became more complex and more detailed. Selling syndicates (with either limited or unlimited liability) and selling groups came into wider use, but their members were very much at the mercy of originating houses.[18] The need to distribute a greater volume of securities more quickly than ever before—and at a greater distance from the origination process—diminished these firms' ability to know everything about the goods they sold. At the price of enforced ignorance, the firms found a niche for themselves in the industry. This compromise was by nature unstable, and the strain showed.

There were other noteworthy shifts in the industry's structure. As the speculative tide of the period spilled over into institutional changes, it carried all but the most conservative houses at least part way along. Kidder Peabody, for one, went rather far in this direction and paid for it dearly later on. Few private houses could resist altogether the blandishments of investment trusts or public utility holding companies, just as few incorporated banks could withstand the allure of securities affiliates. In fact, by 1930 commercial and investment banks were handling roughly equal amounts of securities business. Fevered speculation in overpriced paper would, in retrospect, further tarnish the industry's reputation for sober good sense. It did, however, provide the opportunity for new or newly aggressive firms, like Halsey, Stuart and Blyth—many of them located outside the New York orbit—to become major issuing houses.

Fundamental changes were less conspicuous. With the prosperity of the 1920s the national appetite for securities became almost insatiable. Although the volume of stocks finally passed that of bonds in 1929 and the popularity of municipal and

---

[17] Logan, *George F. Baker and His Bank*, p. 142.
[18] Carosso, *Investment Banking*, p. 424.

utility issues grew apace, there was still not enough sound product for the major houses to float and dealers to sell. Nationwide distribution networks appeared to sell what there was. Even a huge increase in the placements of foreign securities could not meet the clamorous demand.

Only for the handful of leading originating firms at the top of the pyramid did the post-1929 world continue to work pretty much as it had a generation before. Although the apex firms would be severely buffeted and some upset, in general they were able to keep, if not their absolute, then their relative places—like corks in the ocean. For the rest, the world had in a sense turned upside down. No longer did supply drive demand. Market demand was now in the saddle and drove everything before it.

GLASS-STEAGALL AND ITS AFTERMATH

In the 1930s a long history of suspicion and questionable behavior finally caught up with the investment banking industry. After years of functioning without stringent external regulation, the industry became, in the course of a decade, one of the most heavily regulated industries in the country. A variety of New Deal enactments— the Revenue Act, the Securities Act, the Securities Exchange Act, and of course the Glass-Steagall Act—wrought great changes. Yet when the dust finally settled the resulting landscape had quite a familiar look about it.

Procedural Revisions

Flotations now had to meet strict new standards of disclosure, and a waiting period separated the registration of an issue from its distribution. With only a few high-grade, low-risk issues to float, underwriting spreads declined and the need for elaborate multisyndicate participations fell off significantly. Originating houses continued to use their own retailing skills and passed the rest of the task along to commission-based selling groups, which had no underwriting responsibilities or liabilities. By and large, as one observer noted, syndicates now consisted of

> a few large underwriting houses who sign the purchase contract with the issuer, dividing the liability in fixed proportions among themselves, and a far larger selling group which does no underwriting, the members receiving a substantial selling commission only for the securities actually sold by them.[19]

Although these developments were mostly evolutionary in nature, they created uncertainty and prompted both issuers and underwriters to protect their flanks. Underwriters insisted on pricing issues at the very last moment and on creating escape clauses for themselves if the market should turn sour, the issuer's standing

---

[19] Jules I. Bogen, "Changed Conditions in the Marketing of New Issues," *Journal of the American Statistical Association*, 33 (March 1938), p. 34.

turn doubtful, or the information in registration statements prove inaccurate. For their part, issuers began to turn to private placements as a way of getting around disclosure requirements, ensuring an immediate commitment for their securities and speeding up the whole flotation process. As always, shifts in institutional procedure followed hard on the heels of environmental change.

Structural Rigidities

But some institutional adjustments touched more than procedures. The Glass–Steagall Act, signed into law in June 1933, erected a barrier between investment and commercial banking. The Act had three objectives: discouragement of speculation, prevention of conflicts of interest, and promotion of bank soundness. Regarding speculation, the Act's proponents argued that if banks were affiliated with brokers, the former would have an incentive to lend money to customers of the latter. These customers might, in turn, invest their borrowings in securities rather than in what were believed to be more productive investments, such as hard assets. The conflicts-of-interest rationale hinged on the fear that commercial banks that had underwritten a firm's securities might then make imprudent loans to the firm to buttress the firm's financial structure while the bank had an equity interest. Perhaps most important was the soundness objective. Proponents of Glass–Steagall feared that banks' soundness could be threatened both by direct losses on securities held by a bank and by adverse effects on the public's confidence should a bank's securities affiliate falter. The Glass–Steagall Act was intended to respond to some of the glaring abuses that had encouraged, some thought, the bank failures and depression of recent years.

As a result of the Act's passage, established private bankers had to choose whether to give up their depository or their underwriting business; commercial banks had to sever relations with securities affiliates and to scale down the activities of overgrown bond departments. Some firms disappeared. Others, including many small regional houses, emerged in a new guise. New firms appeared to occupy vacant niches. Morgan, for example, chose to keep its position in commercial banking, but several partners left to form the investment house of Morgan Stanley. The First Boston Corporation was patched together out of the cast-off securities affiliates of several commercial banks.

Despite this flurry of organizational rearrangement, investment banking houses still provided much the same range of services as they always had. Indeed, the most significant result of the Act was that it froze investment banks out of commercial banking and commercial banks out of investment banking. Thus in effect it precluded entry into investment banking by a group of institutions that had formerly been among the industry's heartiest competitors—the commercial banks. Of course competition persisted, but it did so within an arena better safeguarded against intruders than ever before. And where entry was possible, lagging business conditions and the availability of capital through various New Deal agencies further narrowed industry spreads and made entry unappealing.

Within this protected arena, syndicates continued to function much as they had previously. The major firms on the scene by the late 1930s were, for the most part, composed of people and organizational units that had been parts of other firms before the mid-1930s. Since the complicated work of bringing securities to market still depended on close working relationships between bankers and issuers, new syndicate participations were still conditioned by past relationships. They were also conditioned by the financial competence and proven expertise—especially in distribution and sales—of individual houses. At the same time, however, newer forms of expertise—such as the provision of advice on private placements or on issues put up for competitive bidding—added significantly to the competitive repertoire of some firms.

On balance, therefore, a major effect of Glass-Steagall was to sharply curtail the natural entry of firms. Some established participants—the commercial banks, for example—were forced to leave the industry, much as the life insurance companies had been forced to leave in the wake of the Armstrong investigation a generation before. For the houses already in place and for the houses recently formed out of abandoned or disbanded institutional units, however, restrictions on the ebb and flow of competitors proved a boon.

Persistence of the Pyramid

The sheer staying power of these competitive dynamics—even in the face of the important structural changes wrought by Glass–Steagall—argues strongly that the industry should be viewed along three different, though related, dimensions. The first is the various functions and services it provides. Considered in functional terms, the industry has remained virtually impervious to all outside forces—excepting, of course, the ever present need to adapt to the changing financial requirements of the larger society. The second is the individual firms themselves. Here, too, the dominant impression is of constancy, with the unfolding evolution of the few great houses overshadowing the ceaseless comings and goings of other firms. Finally, there is the industry's institutional structure—the syndicate-based pyramid that has accompanied each stage of its evolution.

Typically, the industry's critics have lumped these three dimensions together, confounding their displeasure with specific houses with the inescapable dynamics of industry operation. When, for example, traditional banking relationships came under suspicion, more and more elaborate tests were designed to ferret out the lingering continuities between past and present firms that Glass–Steagall was to have abolished. Statistical data were used to show the persistence of a pyramidlike arrangement, which was dominated as before by a handful of apex firms. As Carosso observes, "In the four and a half years between January 1, 1934, and June 30, 1938, forty investment banking houses headed 94.2 percent of all managed issues in terms of value and held 82.6 percent in terms of value of all underwriting participations."[20] The real point, though, was not whether the pyramid still existed but whether it was being misused.

[20] Carosso, *Investment Banking*, p. 424.

Even when, after the mid-1930s, rulings by the SEC and ICC required various classes of securities to be put up for public, sealed competitive bidding, the pyramid organization of the bidding syndicates duplicated rather closely in form and in membership that of other underwriting syndicates. In fact, the decline in bankers' gross spreads, for which competitive bidding was more than a little responsible, hurt the small regional dealers it was designed to help by encouraging the larger houses to offset reduced spreads by doing more of their own securities retailing. Still, not all of the major firms leaped quickly into this field—Morgan Stanley, for example, did not—and not all of those which did were equally successful. Halsey, Stuart, according to Carosso, went from managing less than 1 percent of underwriting syndicates in 1940 to managing 29 percent in 1948, but that was quite unusual.[21] Thus, despite the hopes of its advocates, competitive bidding had as its major effect not a disruption of the pyramid but instead the gradual movement of some originating houses into permanent retail operations.

INVESTMENT BANKING AFTER WORLD WAR II

The evolution of investment banking after World War II divides into roughly three phases. The first phase, which carried over into the first half of the 1960s, was characterized by unusual stability in the hierarchical structure. Two factors help explain the stability. First, as we have said, the Glass–Steagall Act, by barring commercial banks from participating in most aspects of underwriting, created barriers to entry that effectively excluded the best-positioned potential competitive entrants. Second, for a considerable period following the end of the war, the volume of underwriting and other corporation finance business was relatively stable—not rapidly growing—so that despite the apparent profitability of these activities the ground was not fertile for upward mobility among lesser firms in the investment banking hierarchy.

The essential sluggishness of capital markets until the mid-1960s, especially when combined with the protective barriers against new entrants raised by Glass–Steagall, did indeed help buffer the industry's structure from major change. Figure 1.1, which tracks the growth in dollar volume of corporate issues since 1935, shows only a modest—and uneven—upward trend before 1965. Much the same is true for the annual volume of shares traded on the New York Stock Exchange, another proxy for activity in the capital markets. Table 1.1, which follows data on share volume since 1930, shows a pronounced upward movement only after the mid-1960s.

For nearly 20 years after World War II, then, not enough new business existed to strain the industry's traditional pyramid structure, reinforced as it had been by the provisions of Glass–Steagall. Intrapyramidal competition at the apex—that is, the slow jockeying for position among established houses—continued, of course, at its normally unhurried pace. But this rate of adjustment had never provided the

[21] *Ibid.*, p. 451.

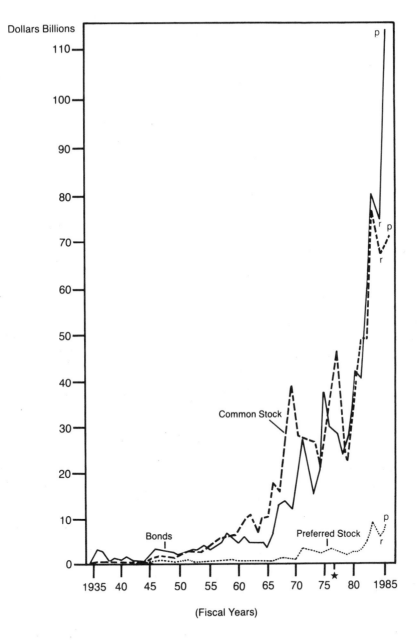

★ In 1977 Fiscal Year End Changed from June to September.
　Data for Transition Quarter July - September 1976 Not Shown on Chart:
　Bonds $5.1 Billion, Preferred Stock $.4 Billion, Common Stock $6.8 Billion
r = Revised
p = Preliminary

Figure 1.1. Dollar volume of corporate securities issued 1935–1985.

**Table 1.1. Selected Annual Share Volume
on the New York Stock Exchange[a]**

	Total Volume (Millions)	
	Shares	Value
1930[b]	1,108.0	$ 61,300
1935	514.0	13,335
1965	1,809.4	73,200
1966	2,204.8	98,565
1967	2,885.7	125,329
1968	3,298.7	144,978
1969	3,093.6	127,675
1970	3,123.5	102,494
1971	4,095.2	145,917
1972	4,328.8	158,617
1973	4,228.0	145,117
1974	3,661.4	96,859
1975	4,839.4	131,705
1976	5,518.7	165,748
1977	5,418.9	155,302
1978	7,370.8	205,590
1979	8,335.5	244,523
1980	11,561.5	382,447
1981	12,049.4	396,070
1982	16,669.3	495,130
1983	21,845.7	775,337
1984	23,308.6	773,426

[a] SEC data 1940–1968. NYSE data in other years.
[b] Estimated.

driving force for substantial alterations in pyramid structure or in the relevant
dynamics of industry competition. When such change had occurred, it had traditionally
been fueled by the distributional skills and upward ambitions of the smaller houses
below the apex. With minimal real growth in the volume of securities to be underwritten
and retailed, therefore, these smaller houses had little on which to base such a move
upward in the pyramid. Table 1.2, which lists for 1950–1980 (at five-year intervals)
the top 20 investment banking houses in terms of the dollar volume of public
offerings managed or comanaged, confirms this postwar state of affairs. Minor
alterations in position do continually occur, but no substantial changes take place
at the pyramid's apex. In fact, as Table 1.2 indicates, six of the top eight firms in
1950 remained among the top eight firms three decades later.

   In this environment the syndicate system—which had by then been refined into
a very effective instrument for allocating risk and for managing distribution in
public underwritings—also functioned as a de facto manager of the hierarchical

Table 1.2. Top 20 Underwriting Firms, 1950–1980[a]

Firm	1950 Rank	1950 Volume	1955 Rank	1955 Volume	1960 Rank	1960 Volume	1965 Rank	1965 Volume	1970 Rank	1970 Volume	1975 Rank	1975 Volume	1980 Rank	1980 Volume
Merrill Lynch	4	339	15	203	5	609	4	1,342	2	6,398	1	14,066	1	21,298
Salomon Brothers	11	145	16	202	18	144	7	924	4	4,589	3	11,884	2	17,213
First Boston	3	556	2	894	1	1,340	1	2,362	1	7,023	2	12,198	3	12,701
Morgan Stanley	2	645	1	1,019	3	970	5	1,101	5	4,094	4	11,226	4	11,668
Goldman, Sachs		—		—	16	180	11	707	8	2,905	5	8,502	5	11,058
Lehman Brothers	7	233	8	441	4	610	2	1,706	3	5,101	7	6,450	6	10,246
Blyth Eastman	6	265	4	748	6	603	3	1,549	6	4,019	6	7,141	7	9,262
Kidder Peabody	5	289	11	301	8	374	8	825	9	2,864	9	5,768	8	9,082
Dean Witter		—	19	101	20	143	12	610	13	1,393	11	4,256	9	6,770
E. F. Hutton		—		—		—		—		—	15	2,596	10	5,420
Lazard Frères		—	18	142	19	143	9	799	14	1,327	18	1,704	11	4,659
Bache		—		—		—		—		—		—	12	4,621
Smith Barney		—	9	321		—	14	508	12	2,155	10	4,333	13	4,051
Warburg		—		—		—		—		—		—	14	3,668
Dillon, Read	12	121	12	271	12	230	18	242	16	1,270	17	2,135	15	3,534
Drexel Burnham	18	41		—		—		—	19	899	16	2,210	16	2,939
Shearson		—		—		—		—		—		—	17	2,451
Bear, Stearns		—		—	17	159		—		—		—	18	2,413

(Table continues on p. 30)

Table 1.2. (*Continued*)

Firm	1950 Rank	1950 Volume	1955 Rank	1955 Volume	1960 Rank	1960 Volume	1965 Rank	1965 Volume	1970 Rank	1970 Volume	1975 Rank	1975 Volume	1980 Rank	1980 Volume
Rothschild, Unterberg	—	—	—	—	—	—	—	—	—	—	—	—	19	2,364
Donaldson, Lufkin	—	—	—	—	—	—	—	—	—	—	—	—	20	1,452
Halsey, Stuart	1	724	3	868	2	1,097	13	591	7	3,077	8	6,201		
Paine Webber					13	205	17	362	15	1,273	12	3,719		
Kuhn, Loeb	14	97	6	472	9	357	10	768	18	1,145	13	3,568		
White, Weld	8	210	7	458	7	578	6	1,050	10	2,629	14	3,552		
Loeb, Rhoades											19	1,503		
A. E. Ames & Co.											20	1,129		
Eastman Dillon			20	94	11	308	16	423	11	2,543				
Stone & Webster	10	170	14	206	10	310	15	439	17	1,246				
duPont Glore Forgan									20	718				
Equitable Securities	17	51					19	185						
Harriman, Ripley	13	102	17	163	14	200	20	176						
Glore, Forgan	15	79	5	493	15	184								
Alex Brown & Sons			10	302										
Union Securities	9	183	13	264										
Wood, Gundy	16	61												
Harris, Hall	19	34												
Blair, Rollins	20	34												

Source: Investment Dealer's Digest.

[a]Full credit was given to all managers of comanaged offerings. In many cases, firms disappear from the top 20 because they merged into other firms. Volume figures are in millions of dollars.

structure of competition itself. A firm's relative position in the industry's pyramid largely determined its access to lucrative future business as well as to substantial current income. Standing was indicated not only by the frequency with which a firm managed or co-managed a major syndicate but also by the frequency of its participations, and the status and prestige following from them. In many ways, then, a firm's overall syndicate standing, which was most graphically expressed in the "tombstone" ads that appeared (and continue to appear) in the financial press, was a symbol of its real power in the industry.

The tombstone ads, like the pyramid they represented, divided syndicate members into several categories or, in the accepted phrase, "brackets." A few apex or special-bracket firms—Morgan Stanley, First Boston, Kuhn Loeb, and Dillon Read—topped the list during much of this period and enjoyed the largest participations. Below this apex group came the "major-bracket" and then the "major-out-of-order" firms, which had been granted major-bracket status only provisionally. Last came several degrees of submajors, each with a relatively small participation but included primarily for their retailing abilities. If a firm's inclusion among the submajors depended on a good track record in distribution, elevation to major-bracket status was far more complex. It rested upon such factors as the professional and, to a less extent, the social standing of the firm's partners, the firm's possession of an adequate capital base, its strength and staying power in distribution, and, perhaps most important, its ability to generate major business, which could be shared with other houses.

To receive the blessing of increased syndicate participations from the leading underwriting firms, other securities firms had in effect to add their support to its extant structure. Some tried more aggressively than others to exploit their competitive strengths and gain improved position. But this was the way syndicates and pyramids had always functioned, ever since their informal beginnings in late-eighteenth-century Europe. These mechanics represented no radically new phenomena. They were but the latest incarnation of a familiar set of institutional arrangements.

Up to the early 1960s, then, competitive dynamics remained pretty much as they had been, at least in outward appearance. Inwardly, however, something important had changed. Pyramid discipline, whose origins lay in the necessary mechanics and client loyalties of large-scale finance, had always received informal support. Among gentlemen, the code of responsible stewardship—though it worked to the advantage of apex firms—was worth supporting in and of itself. It was part of a system that merited willful adherence even from those to whom it offered only a modest share of the available benefits. Just after World War II the code, for the most part, still held. But developments were in the works which would alter that.

The ability of the syndicate system to maintain discipline within the investment banking business came under increasing pressure during the 1960s, a second phase in the evolution of postwar investment banking. A long economic expansion, accompanied by rapidly rising underwriting and secondary market trading volume, created conditions that allowed lesser firms in the pyramid to challenge the prevailing apex firms.

These aspiring firms perceived that although the underwriting portion of Wall Street's total revenue stream was relatively small (approximately 10 percent for NYSE members in 1969, for example) it was also less cyclical, less burdened by heavy overhead, and in general much more profitable than, say, the retail brokerage end of the business. The sustained profitability of both retail and institutional brokerage activities during the 1960s and the rapid rise in underwriting volume (see Figure 1.1), which enhanced the value of distribution capacity to underwriting syndicates, worked to the advantage of several ambitious securities firms, allowing them to push their way into the apex group of syndicate leaders (see Table 1.2). Among the most successful in moving up were Merrill Lynch and Salomon Brothers, both of which achieved their advance, at least in part, by exploiting their leading positions in areas of the distribution business. Salomon Brothers climbed from eighteenth place in the underwriting volume rankings in 1960 to fourth place in 1970. Merrill Lynch climbed only three notches during the same period—from fifth to second place—but its advance was particularly significant, having taken place at such a high level of the pyramid. As a result of their ascent, both Salomon Brothers and Merrill Lynch achieved the status of special-bracket firms, initially in certain—and subsequently all—types of offerings. Meanwhile, as these and several other firms, including Goldman Sachs, ascended the hierarchy, they supplanted other firms whose declining fortunes resulted in demotion to a lower place in the pyramid. Halsey, Stuart, for example, fell from second place in 1960 to seventh place in 1970, and Kuhn Loeb fell from ninth to eighteenth. Both of these firms later disappeared as independent entities through merger.

In the 1970s, the third phase in the history of the postwar securities industry, there were other forces effecting change. Inflationary pressures exacerbated the high-volume "back office" snarls that were afflicting a number of the distribution firms, and a series of liquidations and mergers hit the brokerage sector of the industry. The introduction of negotiated brokerage commission rates in 1975 dramatically altered the economics of the brokerage business and precipitated further mergers and consolidations. In the same period, a new generation of finance professionals took over the reins from a generation more sensitive to institutional loyalties. This intensified the pressures on underwriting compensation for conventional securities offerings and on the securities firms to provide an increasing array of services and transactional capacity, with their attendant human and capital commitments.

Adding to these pressures was an increasing volatility in the financial markets, particularly in the wake of the 1979 shift in Federal Reserve monetary policy. This pushed corporations and their investment banking intermediaries to seek ways to accelerate capital-raising moves so as to minimize their exposure to possibly adverse securities price movements.

The Securities and Exchange Commission was in basic agreement with these streamlining efforts. It had implemented "integrated disclosure" during the late 1970s, a means by which, it believed, corporate issuers could more efficiently and cheaply fulfill their responsibilities for providing public investors with up-to-date information about their companies. These new procedures were believed adequate to supplant the traditional "due diligence" investigations which the Securities Act of 1933 had required as a prelude to any new issuance of securities to the public. The Commission was thus becoming more and more impressed with the "efficiency" of the U.S. securities markets in setting fair prices and absorbing the impact of fluctuations in capital supply and demand with only a minimum of regulatory interference. It was in this context that the Commission proposed that well-known companies be allowed to register blocks of securities without a specific sale date in mind and then to hold them on the "shelf" in anticipation of a later favorable marketing opportunity. This procedure, implemented as Rule 415 under the 1933 Act, was introduced on a trial basis in April 1982 and made permanent at the end of 1983.

In the beginning of 1986 this procedure had established itself as an important dimension of capital raising in the U.S. financial markets. "Shelf" registrations accounted for more than half of the total annual volume of negotiated debt financings; "shelf" financings were a much more modest proportion of the equity financing category, possibly because of the perceived adverse market price consequences of an "overhang" of securities with their future potential for earnings dilution.

While the growth in popularity of shelf financings did further loosen the historic ties binding certain corporations and investment banks, it did not fundamentally alter the traditional, pyramidal competitive structure of the industry. On "shelf" financings, a number of securities firms now competed vigorously for what were essentially competitive bid underwritings. But the recently enhanced volatility of the financial markets placed a special premium on a firm's capability for effecting a speedy placement with institutional investors and, until that was accomplished, its capability and willingness to purchase those securities for its own inventory. As it turned out, essentially the same group of apex securities firms that had occupied dominant positions before "shelf" offerings were introduced sustained their positions after "shelfs" had become an established financing phenomenon, in large part because of their excellent institutional contacts and large capital bases.

And, though the relative positions of several of these leading firms shifted within the apex, the industry's competitive structure actually became even more concentrated than it had been before. Thus the tradition of evolutionary rather than revolutionary competitive developments within investment banking—a hallmark over such a long historical period—was once again reaffirmed.

2 Global Market Integration: An International Perspective

FREDERICK G. FISHER III

Rapid change is increasingly moving international financial markets toward an integrated global market for money. Yet there is a spotty understanding of both the workings of these markets and their major participants. This chapter seeks to provide an introduction to them.

First, the chapter traces several important historical threads that have influenced the configuration of contemporary international financial markets. Building on this historical perspective, the chapter examines recent moves to arbitrage world credit markets and to securitize bank credit, and the influences pushing a number of financial intermediaries toward diversification. Each of these changes, in its own way, has made a significant impact on the move toward global market integration. Finally, the chapter discusses the various choices which industry groups and sectors of this marketplace have to meet the resulting increased competition.

HISTORICAL PERSPECTIVE

International finance is not new. Its origins date back at least to the late Middle Ages when a burgeoning European wool trade and other transnational enterprises provided the economic underpinning for financial intermediation. Efficient resource mobilization, as well as existing threats to established trade routes, encouraged the Crusades.Later, the wealth of Florentine merchants and bankers assisted in financing the Renaissance.[1]

International commercial banking began when Italian banks established operations in the City of London in the late thirteenth century. The road at the heart of the city, "Lombard Street," recalls the origins of banking in the city. Following the expulsion of the Jews under the English King Edward I, Italian funds and financial expertise were required to pay for his wars. Two groups, Bardi and Peruzzi,

---

[1] Anthony Sampson, *The Money Lenders*, Coronet, 1982, p. 29.

volunteered this support and looked to a tax on wool exports as a source of repayment. The intermediation of the Italians continued until the reign of Edward III, when the King decided to rely on the domestic merchant class to provide needed finance. Exercising his right as sovereign, Edward III promptly repudiated the Italian debt, precipitating the collapse of both the Bardi and Peruzzi banks.[2]

In all this there seems to be some forewarning to cross-border lenders of a more recent era. In fact, historically few banks appear to have avoided this pitfall. A chronicler of the Medici Bank, for example, observes that "rather than refuse deposits, the Medicis succumbed to the temptation of seeking an outlet for surplus cash in making dangerous loans to princes."[3]

During the period when European powers colonized the New World, international lending was directed toward development finance. Capital transfers were bilateral in nature, linking individual European countries to their respective colonies and trading outposts. Funds for these development loans were raised essentially from wealthy individuals. The unequal distribution of wealth at the time produced a high domestic savings rate.[4] A relatively stable economic and social environment in Europe also encouraged people to invest. Early intermediaries tapped these resources of surplus capital and organized direct loans for foreign borrowers, typically sovereign states or top-quality private enterprises.

Chief financial centers during this period were London, Paris, and Berlin. New York joined the market, too, but at a later stage. There were also smaller financial centers in Italy, the Netherlands, Switzerland, Belgium, and Sweden.[5]

THE MERCHANT BANKS

Practices of the early European financial intermediaries were formalized in the rise of the nineteenth-century merchant banks, whose experience in originating loans was soon transferred to the issue of securities or bonds. As a parallel development, markets for short-term debt, or money markets, began to emerge. Capital-poor merchant houses took advantage of this to raise funds for short periods to finance holdings of newly issued bonds that temporarily were difficult to sell. As a forerunner of underwriting, this practice proved critical to the development of the market. It provided a mechanism for assuring a borrower that its financial requirements would be met irrespective of current market conditions.

Underwriting also reduced the total cost of raising capital. Previously, new issues of securities had to be priced on extremely generous terms to investors in order to attract full subscription. The practice of underwriting allowed for more precise

---

[2] *Ibid.*, p. 30. See also Michael Prestwich, "Italian Merchants in England," in *The Dawn of Modern Banking*, New Haven, CT: Yale University Press, 1979.

[3] Raymond de Roober, *The Medici Bank*, New York: New York University Press, 1948.

[4] See Y.S. Park, *The Eurobond Market: Function and Structure*, New York: Praeger, 1974, Chapter 1, "History of the Eurobond Market."

[5] See Paul Einzig, *The Eurobond Market*, London: St. Martin's Press, 1969, Chapter 3, "Prewar Markets in Foreign Issues."

pricing on terms that balanced the interests of the borrower with those of the investor. To minimize underwriting risk, merchant houses began to share the contingent liability to purchase a fixed amount of securities at a set price, a process known today as syndicating.

European merchant banks, which since have evolved into international bond houses and other financial intermediaries, benefited as well from their location in capital-rich countries that enjoyed virtually uninterrupted balance-of-trade surpluses. The early institutions thus performed a recycling function, by moving capital investment from the established economies of Europe to finance growth in what were then the developing countries of the world. Among other achievements, the railways of Russia, South America, and China were built largely by virtue of bond financings subscribed for by European investors. The rapid industrial expansion of the United States toward the end of the nineteenth century also owes much to this transnational financing.[6]

SHIFTS IN CAPITAL FLOWS

World War I signaled a quiescent period in the international bond market. With defaults on the Imperial Russian bonds, the already crippled mechanism of transnational capital investment received further blows. A massive industrial boom in the United States, which emerged from the war relatively unscathed, absorbed available capital from other nations at the same time that the country enjoyed high trade surpluses. This inward flow of capital was so overwhelming that it threatened the fragile equilibrium of the world financial system as it then existed. Not surprisingly, it was in the 1920s that currency values were first called into serious question. During this period, the so-called gold clause was introduced into borrowing agreements to ensure the value of the obligation by linking the currency of denomination to the price of gold.

By the end of the 1920s there had been a wave of bond defaults by some Latin American borrowers. The Wall Street Crash of 1929 precipitated the Great Depression, which in turn caused a series of bankruptcies and defaults and brought to a standstill an already faltering international bond market. Investors lost heavily as a result of debt repudiations, and confidence in the market evaporated. Only a few bond issues were floated until after World War II.

Following the Second World War, the international financial market remained in disarray. Transnational capital investment chiefly took the form of official aid, such as the Marshall Plan, and a limited number of foreign bond offerings. Directly after the war, financing activities of major borrowers such as the World Bank, the European Coal and Steel Community, and some governments served to reestablish investor confidence in international securities offerings.[7]

[6] U.S. Joint Economic Committee, "Economic Policies and Practices, Paper No. 3: A Description and Analysis of Certain European Capital Markets," Washington DC: U.S. Government Printing Office, 1964, p. 6.
[7] Park, *The Eurobond Market*, p. 3.

DOLLAR PREEMINENCE

Just as the United States emerged from the war as leader of the free world, so too did the U.S. dollar achieve the status of the principal international currency. As the dollar assumed this role in place of the U.K. pound sterling, the focus of international finance correspondingly shifted from London to New York. It was here that many of the bond issues after the war were syndicated, because New York boasted a vigorous and experienced investment banking community. Operating in the international market, investment banks chose as standard issuing procedures the same techniques and disclosure requirements commonly followed for domestic issues. For issues by Western European borrowers, it was normal practice for a major U.S. investment bank to act as lead manager (organizing the issue), with other New York investment banks playing the roles of either co-managers or underwriters. European financial institutions who were invited to join in the syndicate typically had their participation limited to the international selling group.

In brief, European borrowers were coming to New York to have their issues sold back into their own geographic region, largely through European institutions, thus creating a "turntable" financing structure.[8] This procedure continued through the 1950s and early 1960s. However, during this period the European institutions learned the pricing, underwriting, and syndication techniques of U.S. bond offerings and later modified them to meet the particular circumstances of the European market.

It is quite possible that turntable financings might have persisted, thus further consolidating New York's positions as the international market center, had they not been discouraged by new legislation. During the late 1950s and early 1960s, the United States began to experience persistent balance-of-payments deficits, stemming from a negative trade balance (reflecting the overvaluation of the U.S. dollar) and the increasing export of capital by domestic corporations seeking to establish overseas operations. International payments in those days were settled by transfers of gold, and public concern became aroused as the persistent deficits led to a dwindling of the nation's gold reserves.[9]

The international bond offerings organized in New York contributed to the payment outflows. These bonds were denominated in U.S. dollars, with the funds transferred to Europe by the borrower once the financing was accomplished. In 1960, about $850 million in long-term loans and bond issues by foreigners flowed out from the United States. By 1962, the outflow had increased to $1.2 billion, and in the first half of 1963 alone it reached $1.5 billion.[10] By mid-1963, the U.S. government took remedial action.

On July 18, 1963, President Kennedy addressed Congress about the worsening balance-of-payments problem. Among corrective measures, he proposed a new levy called the Interest Equalization Tax (IET) to be imposed on the purchase price of

[8] See H.C. Donnerstag, *The Eurobond Market*, London: The Financial Times, 1975.

[9] Park, *The Eurobond Market*, p. 7.

[10] See U.S. Joint Economic Committee, "Economic Policies and Practices, Paper No. 3, A Description and Analysis of Certain European Capital Markets," Chapter IV, "Foreign Lending and European Capital Markets." Washington, DC: U.S. Government Printing Office, 1964.

foreign bonds or equities acquired by U.S. citizens. The tax rate varied with the maturity of the bonds, starting at 2.75 percent for bonds of at least three years' life, and increasing in steps up to 15 percent for bonds of more than 28½ years' remaining maturity. Common stock shares also were taxed at the rate of 15 percent.

Although the tax was paid by the investor, the borrower had to compensate for this by increasing the interest return correspondingly. In theory, then, the IET imposed on international bonds put the low interest rates prevailing in the United States on an equal footing with the higher rates in Europe. (This was the derivation of "Equalization" in the name.) At the time, it was estimated that the varying percentages of tax equaled a percent annual increase in borrowing costs over the life of the instrument.

The tax did not solve the U.S. balance-of-payments deficits, but it did bring to a halt important segments of the international bond market based in New York. So effective was the tax that only those foreigners with specific exemptions bothered to use the New York market at all. Canadian issues were free of the tax, as were borrowings by developing nations (such as Mexico and Brazil) and by certain international organizations in which the United States had membership (such as the World Bank). Although it was intended only as a temporary measure, the tax was extended on four occasions, and only finally eliminated in June 1974.

BIRTH OF THE EUROMARKET

There was no exemption from the IET for European borrowers, who effectively were forced back to their own capital markets. However, what seemed at first to be a great U.S. advantage turned out to be something quite different. With the imposition of the IET came the birth of the Eurobond market, supported by indigenous financial institutions that had been well schooled in the capital-raising techniques of the New York market, and that were prepared now to refashion these techniques for even greater efficiency in the European setting. Today, it seems ironic that a tax originally intended to work against the interests of certain foreign borrowers should have provided the creative force behind the largest international capital market that the world has known—the Euromarket.

This new market, with headquarters in London, has now spread around the world, uniting various national and regional markets and creating the world's first truly global market for capital. It comprises all the financial centers of Western Europe and North America, together with centers in Japan, Hong Kong, Singapore, Bahrain, the Bahamas, the Cayman Islands, and Panama. The geographical growth of this market has made the term "Euromarket" of generic relevance only.

It is difficult to overemphasize the importance of the global capital market. Table 2.1 shows that during 1985 alone some $285 billion (U.S. equivalent) of new international financings were recorded in the statistics compiled by Morgan Guaranty Trust Company.[11] The size of this market gives it political as well as economic

---

[11] Morgan Guaranty Trust Company of New York, "World Financial Markets," published monthly.

Table 2.1. Table of International Financings 1981–1985 (In Millions of U.S. Dollar Equivalents)

	1981	1982	1983	1984	1985
I. International bonds					
A. Eurobonds					
U.S. dollar	26,830	43,959	38,428	63,593	97,782
Deutsche mark	1,277	2,588	3,817	4,604	9,491
British pound	501	748	1,947	3,997	5,766
Japanese yen	368	374	212	1,212	6,539
European composite units	309	1,980	2,019	3,032	7,038
Other	2,331	1,996	2,078	3,020	10,114
Subtotal	31,616	51,645	48,501	79,458	136,730
B. Foreign bonds					
U.S. dollar	7,552	5,946	4,545	5,487	4,655
Deutsche mark	1,310	2,952	2,671	2,243	1,741
British pound	746	1,214	811	1,292	958
Swiss franc	8,285	11,432	14,299	12,626	14,954
Japanese yen	2,457	3,418	3,772	4,628	6,379
Other	1,019	1,435	1,730	1,677	2,339
Subtotal	21,369	26,397	27,828	27,953	31,026
Total bonds	52,985	78,042	76,329	107,411	167,756
II. International bank credits					
Eurocurrency credits	N.A.	N.A.	74,222	112,605	110,317
Foreign credits	N.A.	N.A.	7,852	13,317	6,648
Total loans	133,379	85,015	82,074	125,922	116,965
Grand total	186,364	163,057	158,403	233,333	284,721

Source: Morgan Guaranty Trust Company, "World Financial Markets." See also note 11.

relevance. Several nations, and increasingly the United States, are dependent on it to meet their domestic financing needs. Once viewed as a threat to national currency values, the market now is accepted by many as a fact of life—even if an unwelcome one. Indeed, certain countries have changed their laws (as well as their attitudes) in order to improve their competitive position in tapping its funds.

INTEGRATION OF WORLD CREDIT MARKETS

Some years ago, it was fashionable to talk of different national and regional markets for capital. Repeat borrowers planned their financings so that they tapped each such sector in turn. This was done to introduce the borrower's name to the greatest number of markets in the world (thus deepening potential capital resources). This strategy also limited the amount of paper that would be offered in any particular market at a single time, both to preserve the scarcity value of the name and (at least in theory) to influence the issuing terms in favor of the borrower.

For a long time, people referred to an Asian dollar market made up of institutions that provided U.S. dollar financings in the Far East.[12] A similar regional market was supposed to exist in the Arabian Gulf. People found, however, that financings placed in these two investment pockets tended eventually to turn up elsewhere— usually in Europe. This phenomenon was referred to as "flow-back."

There were also various national markets where foreigners were allowed to originate issues called "foreign bonds."[13] One of the largest such markets was the U.S. market for foreign bonds, the "Yankee" bond market. A similarly colorful name attached itself to foreign bonds in Japan—the "Samurai" market. The largest foreign bond market was located in Switzerland, with smaller ones in Germany, Luxembourg, and the Netherlands. All these markets still exist to some extent, but a variety of forces have contributed to the breaking down of national boundaries to capital flows.

ARBITRAGING DISPARITIES

Both borrowers and investors in the contemporary international market have grown in sophistication. Technological advances have reduced transaction costs, and vast improvements in communications allow participants to monitor the world's markets on a minute-by-minute basis. Where once it was standard procedure to plan an issue for a specific market and implement it according to an established timetable, issuing procedures have been simplified and greatly accelerated, permitting borrowers to consider issues in more than one market at a time. It is not unusual for an international borrower to arbitrge yield levels, say, in the Yankee market against those offered by Eurodollar bonds. Investors also have access to the same market information; they are prepared to shift from one sector to another to arbitrage

---

[12] A.K. Bhattacharya, *The Asian Dollar Market: International Offshore Financing*, New York: Praeger, 1977.

[13] Several definitions will be helpful at this point:

"International bonds" are securities sold largely outside the country of residence of the borrower. Such offerings may be divided into two categories: "Eurobonds" and "foreign bonds."

"Eurobonds" are offered to the general public, where permitted by law, through an international syndicate of financial intermediaries, and sold principally, and at times exclusively, in countries other than the country of the currency in which the bonds are denominated.

"Foreign bonds," by contrast, are underwritten by a syndicate of financial intermediaries from one country only. They are distributed in much the same fashion as domestic issues in that country and are denominated in the national currency. Both Eurobonds and foreign bonds usually are available in bearer form, preserving anonymity of beneficial ownership, and interest is payable free and clear of withholding and other taxes at source.

The other major form of international financing is, of course, the "syndicated loan" (or medium-term credit) which typically refers to a loan of two or more years' maturity provided by a group or syndicate of international commercial banks. There are, additionally, a plethora of hybrid instruments such as floating-rate notes and the increasingly popular Euronotes, which operate like commercial paper in the United States.

whatever opportunities present themselves. Their actions have the effect of eliminating differences across markets.

Financing techniques available to both issuers and investors also allow them to compare sectors of the international market that once were wholly separate. An example of this is the use of the foreign exchange market to hedge a bond issue's principal and interest payments in one currency against another specific currency, typically the national currency of the borrower. This process, referred to as "creating" dollars or deutsche marks or Swiss francs or whatever, allows the borrower to straddle two seemingly independent markets.

The action of borrowers and investors playing one market off against another forces a convergence of all markets. The mechanisms of financial engineering have bridged different sectors that once were separated by currency, maturity, and types of interest payments (i.e., fixed versus floating). Market pressures have brought down barriers to capital flows around the world. Although some have survived, most isolationist tendencies of national monetary authorities have been consistently overwhelmed. And with each new breakthrough, the competitive edge of the market becomes sharper and more keen to cut the remaining red tape.

UNFETTERED INNOVATION

The trend toward integration of the world's capital markets has been greatly advanced by the competitive thrust of international financial intermediaries. Unfettered by national regulation, such institutions are free to innovate and experiment with any new financing idea that is proposed. Commercial banks pursue financial innovation in part for the fee income it provides. For the smaller investment and merchant banking units, competition by way of inventiveness or financial engineering has long been the norm. What is novel is that growing innovation has come to challenge other foundations of the market, such as market leadership.

Just as the breakdown of capital barriers generates its own momentum, so too does innovation within the global market. The success of imaginative financial institutions creates imitators who challenge the leader with their own new ideas. There are no patents on ideas, and everyone is free to experiment. Leaders are forced to run faster all the time just to stay in the same place. Innovation is becoming institutionalized as well, as different banking groups create independent think tanks for new product ideas. As spreads and fees are squeezed by competitive pressure, innovation becomes a means of compensating for the declining income realized from older products.

The life cycle of financial products is shortening in a manner consistent with the fungibility of money. Innovative institutions, consequently, are the ones now showing greatest promise. Creative individuals accordingly are sought after in the job market, and their salaries reflect the competitive pressures felt throughout the industry. "Golden hellos" and "golden handcuffs" indicate the magnitude of imbalance between supply and demand for key people, as well as the impact of a powerful bull market over the past four or five years.

In the United Kingdom, rising specialist salary levels in anticipation of fianancial markets' deregulation in October 1986 prompted reinterpretation of the tax treatment of lump-sum transfer fees. With young bond traders earning as much as their prime minister, the whole question may have assumed an unwarranted political dimension. Unfettered, globalized markets act to eliminate discrepancies—even between the salary levels of participants operating on opposite sides of the globe. It should be no surprise then that terms of employment are being equalized between London and New York, particularly as the large U.S. institutions have been aggressive in their purchase of teams of successful employees and even entire investment houses in the City of London.

REGULATION AND GROWING CONGRUENCE

Competitive pressures, shifting capital flows, and the sheer momentum of change have encouraged national authorities to deregulate their domestic markets. The abolition of exchange controls in both Japan and the United Kingdom in 1979–1980 were important steps in this direction.[14] The lifting of the U.S. withholding tax in July 1984 led in turn to the repeal of similar taxes in Germany and France. Hunger for capital has prompted other nations to make such liberalizing moves.

Surplus countries, such as Japan, have been encouraged to open their markets as a means of facilitating the rebalancing of world capital flows. Restrictions on borrowers seeking access to the Euroyen market have, for example, been loosened. It is also now possible for non-Japanese institutions to act as lead managers in Euroyen issues, and the withholding tax on Euroyen bonds offered by Japanese companies has been repealed—thus further encouraging such issues.

Germany, too, fell into line by dropping its earlier prohibition against floating-rate notes (FRNs), swap-related bonds, and zero-coupon issues. The Dutch followed suit early in 1986 by permitting guilder FRNs, certificates of deposit (CDs), and commercial paper. And, as Table 2.2 indicates, both the Italian and French markets were opened (or reopened) during 1985 for Eurobond issues.[15]

Deregulation has opened new sectors and encouraged more institutions to participate in the full product line of the world credit market. Progress is rarely smooth, however. The pace of deregulation and innovation does vary from one sector to another, and change can be frustrated by what appear to be insignificant events or attitudes. One example is in the repeal of the U.S. withholding tax.

Because of tax advantages and the special status of prime U.S. corporate names in the Eurobond market, at one time it was possible to issue such debt in Europe at a rate lower than could be achieved in the domestic market. Clearly, as the two markets merged, such discrepancies would have to disappear. With the lifting of

---

[14] *Bank of England, Quarterly Bulletin*, "Developments in International Banking and Capital Markets," (March 1986), p. 59.
[15] *Ibid.*, p. 60.

Table 2.2. Issuing Activity in Deregulated Markets (In Millions of U.S. Dollar Equivalents)

	1985			
	Q1	Q2	Q3	Q4
I. Euroyen				
Fixed-rate bond issues by nonresidents	1,264	278	2,427	1,782
Bond issues by Japanese borrowers	—	320	94	442
Floating-rate notes	—	—	63	70
Credits for nonresidents	—	—	414	208
II. French francs				
Eurobonds	—	393	442	524
III. Italian lire				
Eurobonds	—	—	—	272
IV. Deutsche marks				
Floating-rate notes	—	1,034	179	1,975
Zero-coupon bonds	—	163	—	72

Source: Bank of England. See also note 15.

the withholding tax, yield levels did equalize, except for yields on U.S. government securities. And here, the problems that arose were all self-inflicted.

While the withholding question was being considered, a debate began between the U.S. Treasury and the Internal Revenue Service. With a huge deficit to finance, the Treasury was eager to raise funds in the relatively cheap Euromarket. Because of this market's preference for anonymity, it was suggested initially that the government Eurosecurities be issued in bearer form (which would not expose the identity of the ultimate investor). The IRS, fearing that U.S. citizens would find this an attractive way to evade domestic income taxes, moved to block the bearer option and insisted that all government bonds be placed with European investors on a registered (or named) basis only.

Furthermore, penalties were proposed for noncompliance. Investor attitudes in Europe naturally stiffened, and for a while it looked as if the government might be forced to cancel its international debut. Finally, an uneasy compromise was forged. "Specially targeted" government bonds could be purchased in the names of European financial institutions without requiring them to reveal the identities of the investors. Institutions provided instead a "negative certification" that the ultimate beneficial owners of the securities were not liable for the payment of U.S. income tax. Subsequent issues of Treasury bonds and notes were judged reasonably successful, but the yields levels achieved were never as attractive as had been hoped originally.

The experience of the U.S. government in the global market illustrates how certain anomalies do persist to compromise the efficiency of the marketplace. The higher-yield levels on Eurotreasuries will be paid for eventually by future generations of U.S. citizens. Frequently, anomalies are created by misunderstandings of the market. In this case, the IRS simply failed to see that there was such an abundance of highest grade or "AAA" dollar paper in the Euromarkets at the time as to provide investment opportunity for all U.S. tax evaders. Floating U.S. government bearer bonds did not provide a major new inducement to avoid paying tax.

Despite setbacks in certain areas, the general trend toward integration of the world's credit markets seems clear. In the United Kingdom, the financial services sector experienced a radical restructuring in October 1986. One major change is the blurring of functional distinctions among brokers, jobbers, and merchant bankers. Some institutions anticipated these changes by constructing financial conglomerates with the capacity to provide a number of services ranging from commercial banking to investment advice and management and securities underwriting.[16] Previously excluded English and foreign institutions now are permitted membership in the London Stock Exchange.

The cumulative effect of the various liberalization steps is improved efficiency in the world's capital markets, providing borrowers freer access to financial resources at a reasonable cost and investors a wider range of investment alternatives featuring attractive returns. Financial intermediaries benefit through a broadening of their role and through executing a greater volume of transactions. Public sector authorities value both the increased availability of capital resources at reasonable cost (to fund deficits or investment programs) and the improved ease of capital movements (to redress current account imbalances). With so many beneficiaries, the international markets have acquired a powerful constituency of interested supporters. This will work to assure continued progress and greater efficiencies.

SECURITIZATION OF BANK CREDIT

The unification of the global market proceeds along more than one dimension. Besides convergence of different market sectors, there is a trend toward the merging of different financial instruments. Instruments once totally unrelated are beginning to blend into each other. As this evolution continues, the market gains still more in efficiency. This development points toward the ultimate objective of interchangeable financial instruments in a unified world capital market.

The difference between debt and equity is becoming less distinct. In recent years, for instance, U.S. commerical banks have been authorized to issue bonds and count them as primary (equity) capital if they were either convertible into or refunded by primary capital securities. The British National Westminister Bank also originated a perpetual FRN (without fixed maturity) that did not require timely payments of interest. If for some reason the bank decided against paying (or could not pay) dividends on its ordinary shares, the FRN interest was simply deferred. There was no default, not even a technical one. In short, very little separated these FRNs from

---

[16] *Ibid.*, p. 59.

the bank's own equity, and indeed the financing was structured so that it could be counted as an addition to the bank's equity-capital base.

The present pace of financial innovation is especially fast in the area of commercial banking operations, largely because that industry sector is going through a period of crisis, with implications fundamental to future world capital flows. A major factor is the illiquidity plaguing many international banks. Overburdened with Third World and Eastern European debt reschedulings, banks are making many new loans for the purpose of providing the borrowers with funds to keep interest payments or incumbent debt current. The hopeless position of certain sovereign state borrowers has led to massive write-offs or to a treatment of the debt as quasi-equity. Indeed, many ingenious approaches to the resolution of Latin American debt appear to involve exchanging it for equity in domestic business enterprises, particularly export operations. As with big waves, crises in commercial banking seem to have come in threes. Following the debt problems of Latin America and Eastern Europe, the once-prosperous Arab world appears to be heading toward a debt crisis itself because of overconsumption of imports and greatly reduced revenues from cheaper oil exports.

Partly as a recognition of these problems, central bank authorities have over the years grown increasingly insistent that banks strengthen their balance sheets. This has prompted new equity fund-raising exercises and the invention of such instruments as the near-equity bonds already referred to.

A major focus of central bank attention, particularly in the United Kingdom, is asset liquidity. This priority has helped to shape the trends in the banking sector. Banks now are looking more seriously at debt instruments or other short-term investments that can be bought or sold quickly. There is, thus, an increasing preference for tradable securities evidencing indebtedness.

At the same time, international investors have not been oblivious to the position of the banks. Following such rescue operations as those launched for Continental Illinois and Johnson Matthey, investors have tended to opt for lower rates of return than commercial banks find acceptable, in exchange for greater security. Thus, certain prime sovereign and corporate borrowers are perceived as better credit risks and can frequently raise debt finance in the form of marketable securities at very low spreads. This tendency has now progressed to the point that such high-quality borrowers can issue their debt at a cost even lower than that at which the banks can attract funds themselves. It is not uncommon to hear of new securities offerings priced at a margin *below* LIBOR—the interest rate that prime international banks themselves pay for deposits in the open market.

THE DECLINE OF SYNDICATED LOANS

The substitution of securities offerings for syndicated bank credits is probably the major product-line trend in today's market.[17] The significance of this shift may be

[17] Bank for International Settlements, "Recent Innovations in International Banking" (April 1986), p. 13.

Table 2.3. International Loans and Securitized Instruments (In Billions of U.S. Dollar Equivalents)

	1981	1982	1983	1984	1985
I. International bonds					
and notes of which	44.0	71.7	72.1	108.1	162.8
floating-rate notes	7.8	12.6	15.3	34.1	55.4
convertible bonds	4.1	2.7	6.8	8.5	7.3
II. Syndicated Euroloans[a]	96.5	100.5	51.8	36.6	21.6
of which:					
managed loans[b]	—	11.2	13.7	6.5	2.4
III. Euronote facilities[c]	1.0	2.3	3.3	18.9	49.4
	141.5	174.5	127.2	163.6	233.8

Source: Bank of England. See also note 18.

Notes:

[a] Excludes U.S. takeover-related standbys.

[b] New money element of rescue packages.

[c] Includes revolving underwriting facilities, multiple component facilities (if they include a note-issuance option) and other Euronote facilities.

illustrated by the contraction in new medium-term syndicated loans, particularly if "managed" or nonspontaneous lending to large, third-world debtors is excluded. Table 2.3 shows that somewhat under $100 billion was raised in the form of syndicated Euroloans in 1981, but this figure dropped to $38 billion in 1983 and to $19 billion in 1985 (after deduction of managed facilities).[18]

These figures actually overstate the strength of the medium-term loan market. Its real contraction has been far greater, as may be demonstrated by excluding from the statistics the loan amounts used simply to refund maturing facilities. Such an adjustment shows that net new lending declined from about $28 billion in 1980 to $4.5 billion in 1983. During 1984 and the first nine months of 1985, the market actually shrank by $1 to $2 billion in each period.[19] Statistics compiled by both the Bank of England and Morgan Guaranty Trust include with loan figures the amount of Euronotes and related facilities that were acquired by commercial banks. If these were deducted as well, the true syndicated loan sector would be seen to have been contracting at the rate of $5 to $10 billion in each of the past two years.[20]

Set against these data are the replacement holdings of marketable securities by commercial banks. To satisfy liquidity objectives, banks may attempt either to trade their existing loans or to alter their asset preference in favor of securitized instruments. A market for loan swapping has developed and flourished, particularly where tax advantages could be more efficiently distributed. One constraint on further development of this business is the valuation risk banks might run if the price level of these

[18] *Ibid.*, p. 130.

[19] *Ibid.*, p. 131.

[20] *Ibid.*, p. 131.

Table 2.4. Bank Holdings of International Bonds and FRNs

	1981	1982	1983	1984	1985
(In Billions of U.S.-Dollar Equivalents)					
Estimated total holding	46.7	59.2	76.7	99.5	157.7
Holdings of banks in the United					
Kingdom (including CDs)	16.8	22.9	32.4	41.7	64.6
of which: FRNs	N.A.	4.2	9.9	16.7	30.8

Source: Bank for International Settlements (note 20). See also note 21.

transactions were taken as the actual worth of similar credits held in portfolio. Indeed, it is normal to swap loan against loan, which reduces cash settlements to marginal compensation for inferior risks.

A tidier approach involves direct investment in marketable securities and increases in such holdings over time to counterbalance less liquid assets. Table 2.4 shows that bank holdings of bonds and FRNs increased from over $46 billion in 1981 to nearly $158 billion in 1985, a threefold rise. When CDs are added into the figures for London-based banks, the increase is nearly fourfold.[21]

THE EURONOTE

Banks also are becoming heavy investors in a hybrid instrument frequently referred to as a Euronote. These instruments are known also by a variety of other colorful names, such as NIFs, RUFs, PUFs, SNIFs, and TRUFs, all denoting the latest variation in terms of this rapidly evolving security. Such financings typically involve the issuing of notes that mature in under a year, say, six months. If the investor no longer wishes to hold a note to maturity, the underwriting syndicate supporting the facility buys it and places it with another willing buyer. These underwritten facilities can extend for years into the future and thus are easily tradable in a highly liquid secondary market. In these two respects they are similar to public bond issues. Euronotes share a number of common characteristics with syndicated loans. Frequently they are categorized with bank credits, because banks are normally the chief purchasers, and the interest-payment mechanism is identical to that of a syndicated loan. During 1985, some $58 billion of Euronote offerings were brought to market, up from $15 billion in the preceding year.[22]

A parallel development has been the explosive growth of Eurocommercial paper. During 1985, just under 100 of these programs were arranged for a potential outstanding volume of approximately $16 billion. This figure does not include another half-dozen programs that were of unspecified size.[23] The competitive advantages of Euronotes and commercial paper over traditional syndicated credits

---

[21] *Ibid.*, p. 136.

[22] Christian Hemain, "International Financing Review," (January 4, 1986) p. 4.

[23] *Ibid.*, p. 5.

appear to be overwhelming. They are cheaper for borrowers, longer in potential maturity, and much more marketable. Commercial banks may be reluctant to be disintermediated by the new hybrid instruments, but in reality they may have no choice.

This growth in Euro commercial paper tends to disintermediate commercial banks in the short-term market just as Euronotes have replaced medium-term syndicated credits. U.S. banks are aware of the impact of commercial paper, but the lesson still has to be learned by the international community. There are signs, too, that bank regulators are altering their views on the operation of deposit-taking institutions. Their concern arises naturally enough from the proliferation of the stand-by commitments which often support the new securitized instruments and the use of other off-balance-sheet commitments not only to boost fee income but also to circumvent capital-ratio guidelines.[24]

The underwriting commitment assumed by a bank when issuing a Euronote has common characteristics with a stand-by letter of credit, and probably it should be figured into risk ratios accordingly. If buyers for Euronotes cannot be found, the banks themselves are committed to lend virtually without condition. Such an event probably would correspond to a dramatic weakening in the underlying credit—not the best time to be a lender. In the face of such difficulties, the supposed marketability of such notes could evaporate, leaving them just as illiquid as the traditional syndicated loans they replaced. Furthermore, the more diffuse nature of the Euronote market erodes the traditional customer relationships built up by banks, thus complicating any rescheduling or negotiations that might be required.

Related concerns involve the blurring of distinctions between commercial and investment banks. Historically, commercial banks have been subject to relatively strict supervision because of their sensitive role as deposit-taking entities. Any major losses in asset values jeoparized the savings of the public. Now that securitized products are replacing loans, the responsibility for asset creation and quality also appears to be shifting more toward the investment banks. Not only are such institutions frequently unregulated in the international market, but their greater propensity for new product innovation also appears to outstrip the established mechanisms for regulation. The Bank for International Settlements itself admits that, given the ability of capital market institutions to innovate rapidly and flexibly, it is now "more difficult than in the past to design policy changes and be confident that those changes will for long achieve desired results, without unwanted side effects."[25] Thus the very success of the new instruments is viewed by the regulators as a challenge to monetary and macroprudential policies.

The advent of short-term Euronote facilities also has an effect on borrowers. Previously, little differentiated a prime credit from one of lesser standing in syndicated loans. Interest margin might give a clue as to credit quality, but in the heyday of medium-term lending the huge volume of petrodollars looking for placement and

---

[24] See, Bank for International Settlements—Committee on Banking Regulations and Supervisory Practices, "The Management of Banks' Off-Balance-Sheet Exposures: A Supervisory Perspective," 1986.

[25] *Ibid.*, p. 2.

the competition among commercial banks had the effect of depressing interest margins across the board until there was little or no differential for relative risk. Now the higher-quality names have dispensed with syndicated loans altogether in favor of the cheap-note-issuing facilities. This leaves the lesser credits alone in the loan market. A tiering of borrowers is becoming more evident, and as loan syndication declines in popularity either the lower-tier borrowers will find it harder to raise financing, or banks concentrating on second-tier borrowers may experience an overall decline in the quality of their portfolios.

THE SWAP AS AN ARBITRAGE VEHICLE

We have seen that technical innovation in the global market tends to blur once clearly drawn boundary lines. The difference between floating-rate interest (typically used in commercial banking transactions) and the fixed rate of interest traditionally payable on a bond has been bridged by the wizardry of the interest-rate swap. Although a highly sophisticated financing technique, it is basically a way of exchanging the different forms of interest between borrowers on a basis more advantageous than if each had raised the preferred funds on its own. An established bank might, for instance, issue a fixed-rate bond and swap these funds for floating-rate borrowings which could be raised by a little-known corporation. At the end of the exercise each institution would have the type of interest payment most suited to its operations—and at a significant savings in yield. Increases in this type of swap activity have spurred rapid growth in the international bond market.

In fact, this financial technique provides a good indication of where the market is heading. Differences between markets provide opportunities to either make or save money or gain some other benefit. Given natural competitive pressures, there will always be an incentive to innovate in those areas where anomalies can be turned to one's advantage. The swap is a means by which financial intermediaries can generate further business and at the same time improve the efficient operation of the marketplace. The success of swap activity has led market innovators to search for other anomalies that might be exploited. Electronic communications are so efficient today that aberrations anywhere in the world can be detected quickly and arbitraged for whatever gain might be made before the differences are reduced. The efforts of national bureaucracies may impede and delay this process, but the pressures of the market are unrelenting as the demands for cheaper capital are irresistible. Thus, while these global market developments may well attract more interest on the part of central bank regulators, the forces supporting the process of integration should not be expected to decrease.

FUTURE PRODUCT INNOVATION AND DIVERSIFICATION

Against this backdrop of the global market and the competitive forces that shape it, international financial intermediaries will find no alternative except to expand geographically (to cover its various sectors) and to diversity product lines (to match services offered by competitors). The drive to innovate requires the continued development of new product ideas. As innovation established itself as an accepted mode of competition, the speed of change within the global market is bound to accelerate. New-issue ideas will become a daily event, and financings will be tailored more finely to a borrower's specific requirements. Rather than offering a range of established alternatives, the financial intermediary of tomorrow will devise a specially customized instrument suited to the detailed requirements of the client. Investors, too, will be treated in a similar fashion. More time will be spent identifying their precise needs with a package tailored to meet those needs. Capital markets, which historically have been largely borrower-driven, will be in the future concentrate more on the specific requirements of investors.

The process of product innovation naturally will lead to a wider range or diversification of product lines. Larger international intermediaries will thus take on the appearance of financial supermarkets. This trend will be reinforced by competitive pressures that will force certain institutions to diversify simply to survive. Full participation in the global market requires a substantial balance sheet to handle the volume of business needed to cover expensive overheads. Such costs include office space in all the financial sectors of the world, administrative backup, computer, and highly elaborate communication devices. Organizations meeting these requirements will of necessity be large.

This very size factor, though, will provide opportunities for others to remain small and flexible as so-called boutique operations. Large organizations typically take longer to react because of multiple layers of decision making. Further, they can only concentrate on markets or deals above a certain size threshold to justify the commitment of their substantial resources. A small, nimble-footed organization can easily live off the opportunities that are too small for the behemoths. This can already be seen in London as small groups operate in discount brokerage, gray-market trading, and the unlisted securities market. Because of their modest capitalization, they are highly vulnerable to changes in the marketplace. But, given the current optimistic outlook, they will probably survive in sufficient numbers to build a sustainable niche for themselves.

TALENT VERSUS CAPITAL

An interesting question is whether the brains of innovation or the brawn of capital will be the key to survival in the unfolding markets of the future. In the mid-1980s, it appears that innovative talent is gaining the upper hand. One look at the identity of the top lead managers of Eurobond issues gives a good indication. During 1985, of the top 10 book-running managers, six were investment banks (four U.S., one Japanese, and one U.S./Swiss). Indeed, four of the top five—or five of the top five, if you count Morgan Guaranty's merchant banking arm—were investment banks.[26] (See Table 2.5.) The large, capital-rich commercial and European universal

---

[26] Hemain, "International Financing Review," p. 30.

Table 2.5. Eurobond Lead Managers League Table[a]

1978	1985
1. Deutsche Bank	1. Credit Suisse First Boston
2. Westdeutsche Landesbank	2. Merrill Lynch
3. Amsterdam-Rotterdam Bank	3. Morgan Guaranty
4. Dresdner Bank	4. Salomon Brothers
5. Credit Suisse First Boston	5. Morgan Stanley
6. Commerzbank	6. Deutsche Bank
7. U.B.S. (Securities) Ltd.	7. Goldman Sachs
8. S.G. Warburg	8. Nomura
9. Banque Nationale de Paris	9. UBS (Securities)
10. Hambros Bank	10. Paribas

[a] Full credit to book runners only.

Source: AGEFI.

banks have been pushed into a secondary role. This represents a major shift from the relative positions of these two groups since the late 1970s.

At that time, the large European banks had pushed themselves to the top of the league table with the muscle power provided by hugh capital backing. People openly talked about muscle power and that is precisely what they meant. Deutsche Bank, to pick a name, could purchase whole bond issues if it felt that secondary trading was unsatisfactory. It dictated to the market the terms it thought appropriate, disciplining smaller financial intermediaries that misbehaved in new-issue syndicates.

Conventional wisdom in those days was that placing power was all-important. Placing power was the ability to sell bonds to end-investors or to make a commitment to hold them in the intermediary's portfolio until they could be sold at an acceptable price. Investment banks with their small capital bases were viewed as "weak hands." The fear was that the investment banks' relatively small capital bases would not permit them to hold sizable positions of bonds and that therefore they would be forced to dump them at the worst possible time with a disastrous impact on price levels. In many instances, such concerns were justified.

Investment banks did, however, persevere, and although the reasons for their success are many, two are paramount: reaction time and innovation. The market's development over the past few years favors the more agile organizations that mobilize individual performance unfettered by the constraints of a top-heavy bureaucracy. The intermediary institution still matters, but the individual is growing in importance, because it is only the individual who can create and innovate. Committees work by consensus, not inspiration.

The capital-rich international banks also have failed to live up to their own past standards of success. The herd mentality and short-term profit objectives that contributed to the past fad of sovereign state cross-border lending have exposed the weaknesses of these institutions. At the very least, the problems of banks' existing loan portfolios will constrain their operating flexibility in the foreseeable future.

One strategic alternative might be for these institutions to consider moving toward the investment banking model, with the prospects of high fee income. Banks attempting this new role, however, must brace themselves for a major modification of their procedures and corporate culture. Decision making must be decentralized and hierarchies flattened if the requisite innovative climate is to be created. Administrative and compensation policies will have to be revised to identify and reward individual contribution. Emphasis must be placed on the quality of executive staff and not merely on containing their numbers. Salary levels should be allowed to rise in order to attract and retain key staff members. Reaction time will need to be cut in operations relating to tradable financial instruments.

A lumbering bureaucratic organization will no doubt face the same fate as the dinosaur. The speed of market innovation requires a different type of organization. The survivors of the coming decades in the global market must be prepared to refashion themselves to suit the new and dynamic challenges ahead.

Some commercial banking operations have already attempted the transformation. A notable example is Bankers Trust, which sold its retail banking network and adjusted its policies to support more of an investment banking perspective. Morgan Guaranty Trust also announced a reorientation toward merchant banking. This move follows the enormous success of that bank's innovative London subsidiary in the international bond market, which made it the third most active institution there during 1985.

There will be room in the market, too, for commercial banks to revert to traditional direct lending, particularly if central banking authorities place constraints on the future expansion of off-balance-sheet facilities. Such business will, however, still place a premium on high-quality staff as the more prosaic skills, such as credit analysis, reacquire the importance they deserve. What will suffer a demise, and deservedly so, is the mechanistic, and now profitless, business of telex banking.

The process of diversification need not take place through internal reorganization alone. Some institutions have recently decided that acquisition is the best way to add new product lines. Nowhere is this strategy more evident than in the City of London where there was a scramble to buy up brokerage firms before the 1986 deregulation. U.S. commercial banks were foremost among the aggressive buyers. Chase Manhattan managed to acquire two firms. The enthusiasm for these linkups led to high purchase prices that will be a challenge to justify in the years ahead. Another challenge, already mentioned, will be the retention and motivation of key staff members, many of whom profited handsomely from the sale of their firms. The great attraction of these mergers to the commercial banks is the acquisition of securities industry skills, particularly if the relevant laws are liberalized in the United States.

The markets of today and the foreseeable future are and will be dominated by financial innovation, which is people and not capital-dependent. A strong balance sheet and good name will always be important, but the challenge facing most established commercial banking institutions is how quickly and successfully they can modify their business orientation to confront new market realities.

For the same reasons that institutions merge or reorganize their operations to adjust to market trends, so too individual employees must learn to master not one but many areas of financial intermediation. A number of investment houses now require people to rotate among different departments to acquire valuable experience in fields that will have a bearing on whatever career path is eventually selected. Some bond houses have gone so far as to merge once totally separate departments. It is frequently felt advisable, for example, to mix syndicate personnel with corporate finance. This not only provides one group of people with a sympathetic understanding of another sector of the business, but it also adds to cross-fertilization of ideas and experience. However this objective is achieved, the end result is highly beneficial to the organization.

Training procedures should reflect the general trends in the marketplace. Thus a broad-based exposure emphasizing the interdependence of different sectors and instruments appears to offer the greatest relevance. Training programs need to follow the interplay of the different functions of financial intermediation. As the markets grow more homogeneous, the real lessons are the common characteristics of once-separate forms of financing. The practitioner of tomorrow will need to be not only a master of many trades but also capable of understanding the interconnections that unite different financing approaches. So important is this lesson that wherever product areas overlap within the fast-moving international capital markets, a generalized training will be indispensable. The current trend toward employee specialization should be reconsidered in this light. Short-term gains may be achieved by focusing attention and energy, but the movement of the markets requires an intellectual approach favoring integration rather than segregation.

CONCLUSION

Banks and international financial intermediaries of tomorrow will have to be prepared to operate with a range of instruments simultaneously in different market sectors. The freedom and growing integration of the international marketplace dictates that its participants adopt a global approach to financing. The speed of innovation driving the converging global markets compels international institutions to analyze their strategic options at their earliest opportunity. Those who operate primarily in a carefully regulated and structured national market have more time to consider their position. But these institutions too will eventually face the winds of global competition. Regulatory factors that have separated competing groups are bound to weaken. The movement of international commercial banks into investment banking product lines, for example, seems inevitable, just as investment banks will move to exploit attractive opportunities within traditional commercial banking territory. Consequently, as markets internationalize, regulatory restrictions imposed by a single country—such as the Glass–Steagall Act in the United States—will become increasingly academic.

In the same way, a number of European-based institutions must eventually seek to diversify and/or merge, if only to strengthen their position against their rapidly evolving U.S. rivals. The creation of the global market will favor institutions prepared to take advantage of its supranational character and to spread their operations on a worldwide basis offering a full range of financial services. There will still be room for boutique operations and their specialized products. But the institutions that will dominate the market in the coming decades will be the ones that do their business as the markets develop—on a global basis.

3 Attracting Corporate Clients

CHARLES D. ELLIS

Investment banking has been—and is virtually certain to continue to be—an increasingly intensively competitive business as the capital markets and the securities industry adapt to many important changes and as each firm strives to earn an increasing share of the lucrative fees paid to the firms that develop and demonstrate exceptional capabilities to conceive and execute innovative and complex transactions.

As background to an examination of the ways in which investment banks compete, a brief review of the most important changes in their competitive environment will be useful.

The changes are several and they are interactive. Change forces include:

1. Emergence of institutional investors as the dominant participants in the captial markets. Two decades ago, professional or institutional investors bought and sold only 25 percent of all securities; today they buy and sell over 75 percent. As a result, they dominate the pricing of securities.

2. Internationalization of the capital markets. U.S. corporations raised more debt-capital in the London Eurobond market than in New York in 1982. U.S. institutions are investing more and more actively in European and Japanese companies' stocks. British and Danish companies are "going public" in the United States rather than in their national markets, and the dominant secondary market for the common stocks of several leading European corporations is in Wall Street.

3. Infusions of technology in telecommunications and data processing that enable investment banks—and their customers—to organize and distribute extraordinarily different amounts and kinds of information than could have been even conceived possible just a decade ago. Today, investment bankers care even more about being in the center of the "information flow" than in the center of "capital flows."

4. Volume is up. Even though the volume of transactions has moderated following last year's extraordinary record level, the volume of business done—measured in number of transactions or in scale of transactions or in fees—is by normal historical standards simply extraordinary.

5. Complexity is greater. The 15-year fixed-rate sinking-fund bond has been displaced by variable-rate negotiable-term issues. The crucial success factor in

mortgage securities is proprietary software with which to calculate the optimal match of security to the mortgages' actuarial experience expectations. Hedging and synthetic securities are now basic ingredients in major underwritings. Compounding this complexity is processing *speed*.

6. Innovation is common. New "products" are being developed at a remarkable and clearly unprecedented pace. In the past half-decade, the industry has developed such novelties as safe-harbor leasing, floating-rate preferreds, zero-coupon bonds, underwritings under Rule 415, interest-rate swaps, debt defeasance, unrated commercial paper, floating-rate notes, and mortgage securities of many different kinds.

7. Product has eclipsed service. The traditional *service* orientation of the generalist investment banker of the 1920s, 1940s, and 1960s is being replaced by the development and packaging of defined *products*. The difference is crucial: services are *client*-centered while products—no matter how astutely matched to the market's demands—are *producer*-centered.

8. Capital market capabilities are replacing institutional intermediating capabilities. The clearest evidence of this change is the disappearance of the great underwriting syndicates of a generation ago and the appearance of Rule 415 shelf underwriting aimed at bursting through short-lived market "windows of opportunity."

9. Commercial banks are becoming increasingly active and effective competitiors, particularly in international investment banking.

None of these changes is nearly so important, however, as is the fundamental change in the *concept of the business* of investment banking.

Gone forever are the stable, long-term, almost "captive" relationships of the kind build up over many, many years by such bankers as J.P. Morgan and Jacob Schiff. These traditional bankers did not compete for business; they would not ever think of propositioning another firm's clients, any more than gentlemen would read one another's mail.

Today, however, every major corporation is considered "fair game" and is actively courted by many different investment banks.

Even more important, that's the way the corporations want it. No longer willing to accept submissively the judgment of a dominant investment banker, chief financial officers and their able staff experts want to comparison-shop the market, seeking the most capable firms for each service, and inviting investment banks to present their particular capabilities—and then competing for business with their best new ideas.

The *typical* large corporation now does one or more specific transactions with four or five different investment banks. And this same corporation will be solicited by an *average* of eight different investment banks. One-third of the nation's large corporations are solicited by more than 10 different investment banking firms. Both the number of firms used and the number of firms soliciting the typical large corporation have increased steadily over the past decade. There is no evidence that would indicate a slowdown in the future.

Despite the use of multiple firms and the encouragement of other firms to solicit business and demonstrate their capabilities, established relationships are still given considerable importance by chief financial officers.

The CFOs' overwhelming policy preference is to conduct most of their business with their traditional investment banks—and also to invite specialists to compete in their particular specialties.

In a recent study, here's how corporate executives divided on the policies they follow in selecting investment banks for specific transactions:

"All business is done with our corporation's traditional investment banking firms."   12%

"Most business is done with our corporation's traditional investment banks, but other firms are encouraged to compete for our business."   71%

"The investment bank to use in each transaction is decided on the capabilities of particular firms in that specialty."   17%

So long as corporate executives are interested in learning the capabilities of firms they have not used or used extensively in the past and so long as investment bankers want to increase their volume of business—and both phenomena are now designed into the structure of the system—the extraordinary competitiveness of the last several years will come to be recognized as normal.

This dual policy is made practicable by the investment banks. These firms so quickly match any new service or product developed by an important competitor that their traditional clients have little or no need to "walk across the Street" to find the skills they need. Their traditional firms will do the new things for them.

This dynamic response to competitors' innovations has two effects: (1) it makes the business seem more competitive, more transactional, and less stable to the investment bankers who must hurry to make changes—or lose out to competitors, and (2) it makes the business seem more stable and less transactional to the corporate executives who get more new services from the same traditional investment banks.

While a capital market of intermediation process is certainly far more transactional than an institutional system, those experienced with such clearly transactional markets as the Eurobond market or the domestic bond market will know that close, effective, useful working relationships with customers are central to competing successfully in a market-driven intermediation.

The difference is that the relationships are much more likely to be controlled and directed by the buyer than by the seller. In such a situation, smart buyers will accelerate the competition, and will drive the market to be increasingly transactional.

The smart seller will meet the requirements of the marketplace on transactional capabilities and deliberately develop strong, mutually beneficial relationships through which transactions will be executed.

As with chickens and eggs, transactional capabilities are required to build and maintain relationships, and good relationships are needed to win an unfair share of the transactions—on favorable terms. So the movement to a capital markets system of intermediation changes, but certainly does not eliminate the importance of good working relationships between investment bankers and their corporate clients.

Explicit separation of the investment banker's two previously integrated functions—business *getting* and business *doing*—into two coordinated but organizationally separated functioning groups removes the size limit that governed in the past, allowing each organization to expand the scale almost without internal limits on size of firm or volume of business done.

The only limit on these "corporate" firms' size is that they cannot be small. Their natural inclination is to get bigger and bigger.

The reason they feel an imperative to expand is that their costs are high and rising. Costs are rising because these firms compete for market share by increasing the breadth and depth of their capabilities—and increasing capabilities increases costs. (Costs in people. Costs in systems. Costs in capital at risk.) So the firms need more volume to keep up their market share—and their profits.

The best of these firms are truly magnificent in their wealth of talent, speed and precision, their innovation and creativity, and their ability to do what has not been done before.

But there may be a dark side that could haunt investment banking. In the near term, investment bankers must *innovate* useful products and give more intensive service to corporations. But in the long run, the imperative to do more and more business with *customers* may not be as fully balanced by the firm's feeling equally

Table 3.1. How Use of Investment Banking Services Varies with Company Size

Service	Total Industrials	001– 100	101– 200	201– 300	301– 400	401– 500
Commercial paper dealer	45%	79%	59%	64%	35%	19%
Financial advice	38%	53%	29%	44%	35%	43%
Advice on acquisitions	40%	52%	53%	47%	40%	32%
Industrial revenue bonds	33%	43%	51%	31%	28%	23%
Advice on divestitures	31%	49%	53%	26%	21%	15%
Public bond offering	16%	29%	22%	17%	13%	8%
Advice on takeover defense	31%	32%	32%	33%	46%	32%
Project financing	21%	35%	28%	23%	15%	9%
Public stock offering	14%	15%	13%	13%	13%	21%
Leasing	19%	35%	26%	9%	22%	13%
Private placement of debt	15%	19%	19%	13%	15%	9%
Stock-for-debt swap	22%	32%	34%	16%	25%	17%
Interest-rate swaps	14%	21%	15%	19%	7%	4%
Real estate financing	12%	21%	15%	11%	10%	8%
Pollution control financing	14%	35%	16%	11%	10%	8%
415 bond offering	8%	20%	13%	10%	3%	0%
Debt defeasance	11%	19%	10%	9%	18%	8%
415 stock offering	5%	3%	9%	6%	6%	8%

Table 3.2. How Solicitations for Services Vary with Company Size

Service	Total Industrials	001–100	101–200	201–300	301–400	401–500
Advice on acquisitions	68%	81%	79%	74%	71%	47%
Interest-rate swaps	62%	75%	81%	70%	68%	42%
Commercial paper dealer	52%	77%	63%	66%	54%	25%
Private placement of debt	46%	52%	50%	59%	47%	36%
Public bond offering	44%	68%	62%	61%	32%	21%
Leasing	41%	60%	47%	46%	43%	25%
Financial advice	37%	44%	34%	44%	40%	34%
Public stock offering	37%	45%	49%	44%	32%	30%
Advice on divestitures	46%	57%	69%	53%	41%	28%
Industrial revenue bonds	38%	53%	49%	41%	43%	21%
Debt defeasance	37%	57%	49%	44%	32%	17%
Real estate financing	23%	48%	31%	24%	19%	13%
Advice on takeover defense	34%	36%	46%	37%	35%	26%
Project financing	23%	37%	37%	29%	22%	9%
Pollution control financing	24%	40%	40%	24%	19%	13%

compelled to take the long-term responsibility to be right that is inherent in a professional relationship with *clients*.

Use of investment banking services varies substantially—both by service and by size of corporation, as shown in Tables 3.1 and 3.2. (In fact, the variety of services has become so great that most competitors do not offer all services.)

Note that the demand data are given only for *industrial* corporations. Relative to industrials, utilities are more frequent users of such services as private placements, pollution control financing, and commercial paper, and, for obvious reasons, less frequent users of merger and acquisition services. In a similar way, transportation companies, particularly airlines, are much more active users of leasing.

Bank holding companies are more frequent users of interest-rate swaps. They also use investment banks as issuing dealers in certificates of deposit and bankers' acceptances, and to issue floating-rate notes.

In brief, investment bankers gain a larger share of a client's business by earning credibility with senior corporate management, by understanding company's needs better than other investment bankers, and by coming up with more new and better ways than other investment bankers can to solve those client needs. (See Table 3.3.)

Evaluating investment banks and the capabilities most important to their corporations, chief financial officers consider three factors *most* important:

1. Understand our company.
2. Earn credibility with our senior management.
3. Make useful recommendations to our company.

Table 3.3. How Importance of Firm Characteristics Varies with Industry Group

Characteristic	Industrials	Utilities	Thrifts	Banks
Understand company	50%	64%	38%	64%
Credibility with senior management	45%	40%	41%	68%
Useful recommendations over past years	38%	36%	24%	34%
Understand industry	23%	48%	34%	55%
Innovative financing techniques	25%	16%	28%	22%
Frequency of contact over many years	23%	24%	28%	23%
Expertise in bond market	15%	20%	14%	9%
Institutional distribution	10%	20%	3%	9%
Special expertise in specific service	20%	20%	17%	25%
Willing to commit capital	15%	20%	14%	13%
Expertise in equity underwriting	7%	8%	3%	11%
Specific recommendation	0%	4%	0%	5%
Expertise in Eurobond market	3%	0%	0%	5%
None	3%	0%	0%	0%
No answer	10%	0%	7%	7%
Uncertain	0%	0%	0%	0%

The *least* important factors are:

1. Expertise in Eurobond market.
2. Expertise in equity underwriting.

CFOs at larger industrial companies attach substantially greater weight to five characteristics:

1. Understand our company.
2. Expertise in bond market.
3. Institutional distribution.
4. Special expertise in a specific service.
5. Useful recommendations.

Chief financial officers at utilities, thrifts, and banks give more weight than do their industrial colleagues to investment bankers' understanding their particular industries.

Bank holding company CFOs give particular emphasis to an investment banker's credibility with the bank's senior management.

Of course, the competition between investment banks is continuous—and intense. They not only compete vigorously for clients, but also compete even more vigorously for a larger share of the transactions done by each client. The competition is very intense because the incremental profitability of each incremental transaction is extraordinarily high and because the fixed and near-fixed costs of being a leading firm are very high.

The reasons specific firms gain importance to their corporate clients are very similar to the characteristics the executives consider most important. Here are the reasons investment banks gain importance:

1. Credibility witht the client corporation's senior management—earned over several years.
2. Understanding the client company's needs for service and its financial goals and policies.
3. Making useful recommendations to the company over a period of several years.
4. Innovating with new financing techniques.
5. Having special expertise in a specific service.
6. Recommending a specific transaction.

During the past decade, investment banking has gone through extraordinary change: from self-controlled oligopoly to intense free-market competition; from relatively small professional firms to sizable corporations; from generalists to specialists; and with major infusions of capital and technology. Of all the changes, the most important may be the increasingly important and powerful role played by the corporate customer.

It will never go back.

4 Evaluating the Advice of Investment Bankers

A. MISACCOUNTING FOR VALUE

JOEL M. STERN

An investment banker is a financial intermediary whose principal client functions are to select the "right" financing instruments and provide advice on corporate finance policy that can be expected to maximize the client's share price.

We can examine both functions to determine whether they are consistent with the principles of modern financial economics. If an investment banker's advice is inconsistent with theory and (more important) with evidence on the functioning of financial markets, managers can expect suboptimal resource allocation and consequently a lower market value for their shares.

Part A of this chapter reviews the conceptual foundations of financial economics that relate to how markets respond to a firm's financial policies and the role of investment bankers in the process of financial policy making. The first section contrasts the fundamental discrepancies between the popular accounting model of the firm and the preferred alternative economic model; specifically, the three popular accounting measures of corporate performance—earnings, earnings per share (EPS), and earnings growth—are compared with the economic model's free cash flow. Value is shown to be critically dependent on cash generation and the associated level of risk. Emphasizing the accounting implications of business and financing decisions can corrupt and render useless a value-maximizing criterion for corporate performance.

Part A goes on to review a large and growing body of evidence on the effect of financing policy on share price. It can help the investment banker respond to management's questions about the probable impact of changes in capital structure on the client's share prices.

PERFORMANCE MEASUREMENT

Measuring corporate performance and, equally important, designing an effective management incentive compensation system, depends on a clear, consistent, and valid statement about what determines a firm's market value.

Stated most simply, a firm's value is equal to the present value of its expected future performance. Present value involves a discounting of the expected future free cash flows at the required rate of return on similarly risky opportunities elsewhere:

$$\text{Value} \; = \; \frac{\text{Expected future corporate returns}}{\text{Required rate of return}} \tag{1}$$

Given the denominator, which is determined exogenously in the market, the relevant question is: What makes up the numerator, the corporate returns? This is important because, given the denominator, maximizing the numerator maximizes value.

Under the accounting model, the return is net profit after the provision for taxes (NPAT). This measure has numerous implications and shortcomings:

1. Bookkeeping entries that have no effect on cash allegedly do affect value. Examples include the provision for deferred income tax and amortization of goodwill, both expenses that involve no cash outlay. By reducing NPAT, such entries supposedly reduce a firm's value.

2. Cash outlays recorded on the income statement allegedly reduce value, while if these items were capitalized on the balance sheet and written off more slowly, the firm's value presumably would be greater, even allowing for greater payment of taxes earlier.

3. Arbitrary decisions that affect cash can suboptimize value creation. Take the FIFO–LIFO choice for inventory valuation. Remaining on FIFO for most firms, given even modest inflation rates, costs out the earliest and least expensive inventory acquired first, minimizing cost of goods sold and, thus, maximizing gross and net profit, but also taxes paid, thereby reducing the firm's present value of cash generated. LIFO, in contrast, does the opposite, maximizing cost of goods sold, minimizing gross and net profit and therefore taxes paid, thus conserving cash. Supporters of the accounting model allege that FIFO, in maximizing net profit, maximizes value despite the unnecessary and voluntary payment of taxes sooner.

4. If Company A commanding a higher price-earnings ratio (PE) acquires, with an exchange of shares, Company B for a PE less than its own to form AB, A's earnings per share (EPS) will increase. That is, AB's EPS will exceed A's. Accounting model advocates applaud the resulting combination as value-creating even absent any synergy. If, on the other hand, B acquires A to form BA, that is, the lower PE company acquires the firm selling the greater PE, B's EPS falls. BA's EPS is less than B's. Thus, according to EPS proponents, BA is bad and AB is good for value-creation. How can this be, as AB and BA are the same firm? Yet the accounting model recommends AB and discourages BA. These same proponents, in order to combine A and B in the form BA, usually will recommend senior securities or cash to finance the acquisition of A to prevent so-called EPS "dilution."

5. A key objective for accounting-model advocates is to maximize the earnings growth rate. Here again we have perverse policy. The rate of growth in profits depends on the rate of return on capital (r) and the rate of new investment (i.e., increase in capital, I, divided by current earnings):

$$\text{Earnings growth rate} = r \cdot \frac{I}{\text{Earnings}} \qquad (2)$$

Consider three cases, X, Y, and Z. X has a return on capital of 0.30, Y 0.15, and Z 0.075 but all have the same 15 percent growth rate. How? X invests 50 percent of its earnings in new capital, Y 100 percent, and Z 200 percent by seeking additional capital from new debt and/or equity:

$$\text{Earnings growth rate} = r \cdot \frac{I}{\text{Earnings}}$$

$$
\begin{array}{lll}
\text{X} & 0.15 = 0.30 & \times\ 0.50 \\
\text{Y} & 0.15 = 0.15 & \times\ 1.00 \\
\text{Z} & 0.15 = 0.075 & \times\ 2.00 \\
\end{array}
$$

Note that the earnings growth rate, as a performance measure, indicates that all three firms are performing equally well. If the required return is the same for all three firms, say 15 percent, however, clearly X is creating the most value, Y is the second best performer, and Z is the worst. Using earnings growth as an indicator, Z performs as well as X and Y by spending its way to success!

6. The accounting model measures only the magnitude of results. It fails to include any indicator of risk.

The economic model of the firm, in contrast, uses only one financial statement, cash receipts and disbursements. And because it includes the time value of money that is also a function of the risk associated with the generation of cash, it acknowledges that cash now is superior to the same amount of cash later. These are its principal characteristics:

1. Bookkeeping entries that have no effect on cash have no effect on value. Thus, deferred tax and amortization of goodwill are ignored. This means that in measuring results these items are not subtracted from sales, and if they have been deducted as expenses on published accounting statements, making sense of these statements requires that such items be added back to earnings to arrive at economic earnings.

2. The faster one can expense items on the income statements for tax purposes, the better it is for the creation of value. This is simply the principle that cash now is better than cash tomorrow, despite the lower reported earnings that inevitably result.

3. As long as LIFO reduces taxes paid, a switch to LIFO adds to value; remaining on FIFO diminishes value.

4. The AB-BA example is best described as the "AB-BA fallacy." Value is not simply the rote multiplication of a PE by a firm's historical EPS. Rather, where there is no synergy, improvements or reductions in EPS arising from share exchanges between firms with different PEs, must involve changes in PE in the opposite direction to the change in EPS, by the same degree, to keep the buyer's share price unchanged.

5. Earnings growth rates do not matter per se. What does matter is the comparison of properly calculated expected rates of return for a given degree of risk.

6. Finally, if r is the properly measured rate of return and c is the cutoff rate of return required for the risk of the project, a substantial body of evidence indicates that:

$$\frac{r}{c} \approx \frac{MV}{RBV \atop (EBV)} \tag{3}$$

where MV is the market value, RBV is the realizable book value in economic book value (EBV), not accounting book value, terms, using current-value accounting to minimize distortions created by inflation and original cost accounting, and where $\approx$ is the indicator of strong correlation. The relationship says that expected rate of return in relation to required returns moves closely with the relationship of market value to properly measured realizable economic book value. Or, if returns exceed expected required returns, a firm will sell at a premium to its realizable economic book value.

Returning to the valuation model, the economic model describes the numerator as expected future free cash flow (FCF), that is, the amount of cash expected to be generated over time that is distributable to both lenders and shareholders. It is NOPAT, net operating profit before finance charges and before bookkeeping entries having no effect on cash but after taxes paid, minus net new investment (I) on the balance sheet. I can be calculated as the increase in total assets minus the increase in non-interest-bearing current liabilities (accounts payable and accrued expenses), the latter being spontaneously generated with current assets. In terms of conventional financial statements, FCF is NOPAT minus I.

Is the most value created when any year's FCF is positive, zero, or negative? When positive, NOPAT exceeds I. When zero, NOPAT equals I, and when negative NOPAT is less than I. The answer depends on r in relation to c. If expected returns exceed the required returns, the more investment the better, and, therefore the more negative FCF, the better it is for value-creation.

This discussion has critical implications for management policies. In point of fact, it means that economic value is created only when r exceeds c. That is, an investment banker's suggestion to a client to make an acquisition is beneficial only if returns measured in economic terms are greater than those required for the risks borne based on the price paid for the deal. The accounting implications of deals are irrelevant. Financing questions are not issues that deal with probable effects on net earnings or EPS, but rather with how the financing will affect taxes paid and risk, and accordingly their effect on c.

EFFECT OF FINANCING ON SHARE PRICES

Until very recently, much of what passed for corporate financing advice from investment bankers not only was dominated by the accounting model—reported earnings, EPS, and earnings growth, and definitely avoid any earnings "hit"—but also was lacking a comprehensive, objective, and testable conceptual basis.

Serious researchers have begun to overcome the popular intuitive responses that casual observers of market behavior often offered, because research has countered the one-dimensional correlation inherent in the intuitive approach with well-thought-out causality that is the basis of the principles of modern financial economics.

The most fascinating such development deals with the impact of new debt and equity on a publicly traded firm's share price. As long as 27 years ago, Professor David Durand of Massachusetts Institute of Technology's Sloan School espoused the view that small increments or even significant amounts of debt in relation to equity have no impact on the riskiness of a firm's shares. Earlier still, the popular view was that favorable financial leverage—using debt or other senior securities bearing a fixed cost less than the return on assets—by boosting EPS would increase a firm's share price. Professor Durand's position at least modified this position, limiting it to modest amounts of debt.

In the early 1960s, valuation and portfolio theory and evidence made two critical advances in modern finance to help practitioners deal with the capital structure question. First, in their seminal papers on valuation, professors Franco Modigliani (MIT) and Merton H. Miller (Chicago) suggested that the only value-creating function debt financing could provide was derived from its tax shield. That is, because interest cost is tax-deductible and dividends are not, thereby reducing a firm's cash-out, the present value of the annual expected tax shield would be impounded into a borrowing firm's share price. Notice that this necessarily means that the favorable financial leverage effect of debt on EPS is totally irrelevant; it has no effect whatsoever on share price. For all degrees of financial leverage, an increase in a firm's debt-to-equity ratio creates financial risk for the shareholders in the form of an increased expected variability in distributable cash that offsets the greater EPS.

Second, portfolio theory demonstrated that in well-functioning markets, risks and rewards are very highly correlated, which means that the market is a fair game: investors get what they pay for. This is the case even for small degrees of risk and small increments of reward.

In the past decade an additional development has led to a startling conclusion. In his presidential address to the American Finance Association in 1976, Merton Miller asserted that debt is unlikely to be cheaper than equity after all, despite the earlier tax-shield position, and therefore the tax shield would not offer additional value to shareholders. Lenders, he argued, gross up the pretax interest cost to borrowers so that the after-tax cost is no lower than it would be if there were no tax deduction and no grossing up.

Furthermore, he maintained that if debt were less expensive than equity, debt-to-equity ratios certainly would be much higher than they actually are especially because important research performed at the University of Chicago has found the bankruptcy risk of debt to be trivial for investors holding well-diversified portfolios.

The view today among serious researchers is that even if debt is less expensive than equity because of the tax shield, it is not a great deal less expensive. The tax shield is significantly half the size that had been believed. Why then should firms use debt? Why do they use debt? One answer could be that managers using debt believe, given their inside information, that their equity is not yet fairly priced. This "informational asymmetry"—that management's knowledge is superior to that of outside analysts—is the popular view of many current researchers. [See the *Midland Corporate Finance Journal* (Spring 1986). Six articles in that issue are discussed below.]

The current stock of knowledge for the right-hand side of the balance sheet has two implications for policy:

1. Debt may be less expensive than equity, but only because lenders are unable to fully gross up the pre-tax interest cost of debt. The benefit of debt is in no way related to the impact of leverage on the popular accounting earnings measures— NPAT, EPS, and earnings growth—because any benefit is offset by the greater risk shareholders bear whenever any senior securities are used to finance the firm.

2. Estimating upper limits for a firm's debt-to-equity ratio requires specific desired levels of risk taking, which cannot be easily derived from ad hoc accounting data. Rather it involves estimates of the expected variability in future cash flow.

Six papers on raising capital are noteworthy (all of them from chapters in the issue of the *Midland Corporate Finance Journal* referenced above.)

1. "Raising Capital: Theory and Evidence," by Clifford W. Smith.
2. "Equity Carve-Outs," by Katherine Schipper and Abbie Smith.
3. "Evaluating Your Investment Banker's Performance in Bond Offerings," by Robert Rogowski and Eric Sorensen.
4. "Evaluating the Costs of a New Equity Issue," by Robert Hansen.

5. "The Certification Role of the Investment Banker in New Issue Pricing," by James Booth and Richard Smith.

6. "The New Competitive Environment of Investment Banking," by Robert Rogowski and Eric Sorensen.

Clifford Smith's paper (which is reproduced below as Part B of this chapter) especially provides key lessons for policy and the utility of the investment banker's function. Smith set himself two objectives: (1) To examine the theory and evidence about how the market responds to security offer announcements; (2) to evaluate the different methods of marketing securities—rights offerings versus underwritings, negotiated versus competitive bid contracts, and traditional versus shelf registrations.

His research confirms that, on average, the market's reaction to all security offerings, including debt and equity, straight and convertible, industrial issues and utilities, is either negative or about zero. What is at least as interesting is that the market's response to issues of common stock is more negative than its response to preferred stock or debt issues. It is also more negative for convertibles than for nonconvertibles, and more negative for industrials than for utilities.

Smith evaluates various explanations to account for these findings. The simple accounting model excuse—dilution of EPS—is dismissed as an illusion. He is skeptical likewise about the "price pressure" argument, a kind of huge supply effect that needs a discounted price to be absorbed, an unlikely explanation given the volume of traded shares that well-organized markets handle with ease.

The best explanation, he maintains, is the "informational asymmetry" hypothesis. This argument states that management not only may possess inside information that it can use to take advantage of outside investors by issuing overvalued securities, but that the mere announcement of an intention to issue equity or equity-related securities sends a negative signal to the market about the firm's intrinsic worth.

The informational asymmetry argument is used to explain why firm-commitment offerings predominate over rights offerings, negotiated over competitive bids, and traditional over the rapidly growing (but still smaller number of) shelf registration. The effect of inside information causes potential investors to demand that the issuing firm hire a reputable certification agent (i.e., underwriter) for new securities. Assurance of quality is deemed to be strongest when a firm-commitment offering is negotiated with a single investment banker rather than auctioned through a competitive bid, and strongest when registered using traditional rather than shelf registration.

The paper by Katherine Schipper and Abbie Smith identifies the only kind of equity offering that elicits a positive response upon announcement, the "equity carve-out." Traditional announcements of new equity cause an average 3 percent decline in share price, while equity carve-outs result in an average 5 percent increase. The popular explanation of this latter phenomenon has been that an equity carve-out allows an analyst to better see, study, and appreciate on a stand-alone basis the values that earlier were hidden deep within a consolidated enterprise. This is a rather weak argument, for there should be sufficient incentive for analysts to uncover opportunities that otherwise might remain undervalued. A more convincing explanation is that it is possible that periodic involuntary disclosure can affect perception of the value of new stand-alone units. And a more intuitively appealing reason is that carve-outs can be expected to improve a unit's operating efficiency, especially if there are changes in management incentive compensation tied to value-creation.

The remaining four papers I have cited are devoted to one of the basic themes of this chapter, the role of the investment banker in raising capital. The articles of greatest interest to senior management are likely to be Robert Rogowski's and Eric Sorensen's "Evaluating Your Investment Banker's Performance in Bond Offerings" and Robert Hansen's "Evaluating the Costs of a New Equity Issue."

Rogowski and Sorensen maintain that issuing costs in bond offerings consists of two components, the "spread" and underpricing of the issue. They show that underpricing for the period 1981–1985 on average was significant: reoffering yields were 8 to 12 basis points too high. The authors provide an objective measure that an issuer can use to evaluate the performance of an investment banker and, perhaps more important, to exact concessions from the underwriter.

Calculating the costs of an equity issue is more complex. Hansen identifies six distinct components, of which the three most impressive are: (1) underpricing, on average one-half of 1 percent of the proceeds; (2) the market's negative response to the announcement, about 3 percent on average; and (3) granting the "Green Shoe" option. Hansen also provides a formal model for estimating a "fair" cost to the issue.

"The New Competitive Environment of Investment Banking" is an historical perspective on the changing investment banking environment since the introduction of shelf registrations in 1982, the rise of the "bought deal" to replace syndication—where an underwriter purchases an entire issue without any preselling activities, increasing competition in the Euromarkets, commercial banks' challenge to the Glass–Steagall Act, and the invasion of the U.S. markets by overseas merchant banks.

The lessons to be taken from these papers and from 30 years of earlier research are these: (1) simple accounting-based decisions on corporate finance policy can be expected to harm shareholders; (2) capital structure decisions should entail a thorough assessment of risk and the informational signaling that could be contained in individual announcements of new debt or equity; (3) the fees of investment bankers appear to be identifiable; and (4) issuers using simple models can be expected to be more aggressive in negotiating the terms of their relationships with an underwriter.

This is only the beginning of what we can expect serious researchers to tell us. Research will aid managers to better understand the structure and functioning of the financial markets and to control the costs of raising capital. The result: maximizing share price.

B. RAISING CAPITAL: THEORY AND EVIDENCE*

CLIFFORD W. SMITH, JR.

Corporations raise capital by selling a variety of different securities. The *Dealers' Digest* (1985) reports that over $350 billion of public securities sales were underwritten between 1980 and 1984. Of that total, 63 percent was straight debt, 24 percent was common stock, 6 percent was convertible debt, 5 percent was preferred stock, and the remaining 2 percent was convertible preferred stock. Besides choosing among these types of securities, corporate management must also choose among different methods of marketing the securities. In issues that accounted for 95 percent of the total dollars raised between 1980 and 1984, the contracts were negotiated between the issuing firm and its underwriter; in only 5 percent of the offers was the underwriter selected through a competitive bid. Shelf registration, a relatively new procedure for registering securities, was employed in issues accounting for 27 percent of the total dollars raised; the remaining 73 percent was raised through offerings using traditional registration procedures.

Despite the critical role that capital markets play in both financial theory and practice, financial economists have only recently begun to explore the alternative contractual arrangements in the capital-raising process and the effect of these choices on a company's cost of issuing securities. This article has two basic aims: (1) to examine the theory and evidence concerning the market's response to security offer announcements by public corporations; and (2) to evaluate the different methods of marketing corporate securities (rights versus underwritten offers, negotiated versus competitive bid contracts, traditional vs. shelf registration, etc.), with attention given to the special case of initial public equity offers.

MARKET REACTIONS TO SECURITY OFFER ANNOUNCEMENTS

A public company seeking external capital must first decide what type of claim to sell. In making that decision, it is important to understand the market's typical reaction to these announcements.

---

* This portion of Chapter 4 is reprinted by permission of the Midland Corporate Finance Journal. It is based on "Investment Banking and the Capital Acquisition Process." *Journal of Financial Economics* (1986). This research was supported by the Managerial Economics Research Center, Graduate School of Management, University of Rochester.

Presented in Table 4.1 is a summary of the findings of recent academic research on the market's response to announcements of public issues (grouped by industrial firms and utilities) of common stock, preferred stock, convertible preferred stock, straight debt and convertible debt. Perhaps surprisingly, the average abnormal returns (i.e., the price movements adjusted for general market price changes) are consistently either negative or not significantly different from zero; in no case is there evidence of a significant positive reaction. Furthermore, the market's response to common stock issues is more strongly negative than its response to preferred stock or debt offerings. It is also more negative to announcements of convertible than nonconvertible securities, and more negative to announcements of offerings by industrials than utilities.

I would first like to examine potential explanations of these findings. Let me start by briefly noting a number of arguments that have been proposed to account for at least parts of this overall pattern of market responses, and then go on to consider each in more detail.

EPS Dilution. The increase in the number of shares outstanding resulting from an equity (or convertible) offering is expected to reduce (fully diluted) reported earnings per share, at least in the near term. New equity is also expected to reduce reported ROE. It has been suggested that such anticipated reductions in accounting measures of performance reduce stock prices.

Price Pressure. The demand curve for securities slopes downward. A new offering increases the supply of that security relative to the demand for it, thus causing its price to fall.

Optimal Capital Structure. A new security issue changes a company's capital structure, thus altering its relationship to its optimal capital structure (as perceived by the market).

Insider Information. Management may possess important information about the company that the market doesn't share. Investors recognize this information disparity and revise their estimate of a company's value in response to management's announced decisions. This effect works through two channels:

1. *Implied Cash Flow Change.* Security offers reveal inside information about operating profitability; that is, the requirement for external funding may reflect a shortfall in recent or expected future cash flows.

2. *Leverage Change.* Increases in corporate leverage are interpreted by the market as reflecting management's confidence about the company's prospects. Conversely, decreases in leverage, such as those brought about by equity offers, reflect management's lack of confidence about future profitability.

Table 4.1. The Stock Market Response to Announcements of Security Offerings

In the columns below are the average two-day abnormal common stock returns and average sample size (in parentheses) from studies of announcements of security offerings. Returns are weighted averages by sample size of the returns reported by the respective studies listed below. (Unless noted otherwise, returns are significantly different from zero.) Most of these studies appear in the forthcoming issue of the University of Rochester's *Journal of Financial Economics* 15 (1986).

| Type of Security Offering | Types of Issuer | |
	Industrial	Utility
Common Stock	−3.14%[a]	−0.75%[b]
	(155)	(403)
Preferred Stock	−0.19%[c],*	+0.08%[d],*
	(28)	(249)
Convertible Preferred Stock	−1.44%[d]	−1.38%[d]
	(53)	(8)
Straight Bonds	−0.26%[e],*	−0.13%[f],*
	(248)	(140)
Convertible Bonds	−2.07%[e]	n.a.[g]
	(73)	

[a] Source: Asquith/Mullins (1986), Kolodny/Suhler (1985), Masulis/Korwar (1986), Mikkelson/Partch (1986), Schipper/Smith (1986)
[b] Source: Asquith/Mullins (1986), Masulis/Korwar (1986), Pettway/Radcliffe (1985)
[c] Source: Linn/Pinegar (1986), Mikkelson/Partch (1986)
[d] Source: Linn/Pinegar (1986)
[e] Source: Dann/Mikkelson (1984), Eckbo (1986), Mikkelson/Partch (1986)
[f] Source: Eckbo (1986)
[g] Not available (virtually none are issued by utilities)
* Interpreted by the authors as not statistically significantly different from zero

Unanticipated Announcements. To the extent an offer is anticipated, its economic impact is already reflected in security prices. Thus, market reactions to less predictable issues should be greater, other things equal, than to more predictable issues.

Ownership Changes. Some security offerings accompany actual or expected changes in the ownership or organization of the company, which in turn can influence market reaction to the announcement.

Before considering each of these possibilities at greater length, let me emphasize that some of the above arguments have more explanatory power than others. But no single explanation accounts, to the exclusion of all others, for the complete pattern of market responses documented by the research.

EPS Dilution

Many analysts argue that announcements of new equity issues depress stock prices because the increase in the number of shares outstanding is expected to result in a reduction, at least in the near term, of reported earnings per share. The expected fall in (near-term) EPS causes stock prices to fall.

Underlying this argument is the assumption that investors respond uncritically to financial statements, mechanically capitalizing EPS figures at standard, industrywide PE multiples. Such a view is, of course, completely at odds with the theory of modern finance. In an efficient market, the value of a company's equity—like the value of a bond or any other investment—should reflect the present value of all of its expected future after-tax *cash flows* (discounted at rates which reflect investors' required returns on securities of comparable risk). This view thus implies that even if near-term EPS is expected to fall as the result of a new equity offering, the issuing company's stock price should not fall as long as the market expects management to earn an adequate rate of return on the new funds. In fact, if the equity sale is perceived by the market as providing management with the means of undertaking an exceptionally profitable capital spending program, then the announcement of an equity offering (combined perhaps with an announcement of the capital expenditure plan) should, if anything, cause a company's price to rise.

There remains a strong temptation, of course, to link the negative stock price effects of new equity announcements to the expected earnings reduction. But to accept this argument is to mistake correlation for causality. We must look to other events to assess whether it is the expected earnings dilution that *causes* the market reaction, or whether there are other, more important factors at work. I believe that studies of stock price reactions to accounting changes have provided convincing testimony to the sophistication of the market, which contradicts the claims of the EPS dilution argument.[1] Such studies provide remarkably consistent evidence that markets see through cosmetic accounting changes, and that market price reactions generally reflect changes in the expected underlying cash flows—that is, in the long-run prospects for the business. In short, there is no plausible theoretical explanation—nor is there credible supporting evidence—that suggests that the reductions in expected EPS accompanying announcements of stock offerings should systematically cause the market to lower companies' stock prices.

Price Pressure

In a somewhat related explanation, some argue that the price reduction associated with the announcement of a new equity or convertible issue is the result of an increase in the supply of a company's equity. This price-pressure argument is based on the premise that the demand schedule for the shares of any given company is downward-sloping, and that new shares can thus be sold only by offering investors a discount from the market price. The greater the proportional amount of new shares, the larger the discount necessary to effect the sale.

Modern portfolio theory, however, attaches little credibility to the price-pressure argument—not, at least, in the case of widely traded securities in well-established secondary markets. The theory says that investors pricing securities are concerned primarily with risk and expected return. Because the risk and return characteristics of any given stock can be duplicated in many ways through various combinations

---

[1] For an excellent review of this research, see Ross Watts, "Does It Pay to Manipulate EPS?" *Chase Financial Quarterly* (Spring 1982), reprinted in *Issues in Corporate Finance*, New York: Stern Stewart, 1983.

of other stocks, there are a great many close substitutes for that stock. Given this abundance of close substitutes, economic theory says that the demand curve for corporate securities should more closely approximate a horizontal line than a sharply downward-sloping one. A horizontal demand curve in turn implies that an issuing company should be able to sell large quantities of new stock without any discount from the current market price (provided the market does not interpret the stock sale itself as releasing negative insider information about the company's prospects relative to its current value).

What does the available research tell us about the price-pressure hypothesis? I will simply mention a few studies bearing on this question.

The first serious study of price pressure was Myron Scholes's doctoral dissertation at the University of Chicago. Scholes examined the effect on share prices of large blocks offered through secondary offerings According to the price-pressure hypothesis, the larger the block of shares to be sold, the larger the price decline would have to be to induce increasing numbers of investors to purchase the shares. By contrast, the intrinsic-value view suggests that the stock price would be unaffected by the size of the block to be sold. It says that at the right price, the market would readily absorb additional shares.

Scholes found that while stock prices do decline upon the distribution of a large block of shares, the price decline appears to be unrelated to the size of the distribution. This finding suggests that the price discount necessary to distribute the block is better interpreted as a result of the adverse information communicated by a large block sale than as a result of selling pressure. This interpretation was reinforced by the additional finding that the largest price declines were recorded when the secondary sale was made by corporate officers in the company itself—that is, by insiders with possibly privileged information about the company's future.[2]

In another study on price pressure, Avner Kalay and Adam Shimrat recently examined bond price reactions to new equity offers. They reason that if price pressure (and not adverse information) causes the negative stock price reaction, there should be no reduction in the value of the company's outstanding bonds upon the announcement of the stock issue—if anything, the new layer of equity should provide added protection for the bonds and cause their prices to rise. The study, however, documented a significant drop in bond prices, suggesting that the market views an equity offering as bad news, reducing the value of the firm as a whole.[3]

Another recent study of price pressure was conducted by Scott Linn and Mike Pinegar. They examined the price reaction of outstanding preferred stock issues to announcements of new preferred stock issues by the same company. They found that the price of an outstanding preferred stock did not fall with the announcement

---

[2] For the published version of Scholes's dissertation, see "Market for Securities: Substitution versus Price Pressure and the Effects of Information on Share Prices," *Journal of Business*, 45 (1972), pp. 169–211.

[3] Avner Kalay and Adam Shimrat, "Firm Value and Seasoned Equity Issue: Price Pressure, Wealth Redistribution, or Negative Information," New York University working paper, 1986.

of an additional new preferred issue, thus providing no support for the operation of price pressure in the market for preferred stock.[4]

In short, there is little empirical evidence in support of price pressure in the market for widely traded stocks. The observed stock price declines, as I shall suggest later, are more plausibly attributed to negative "information" effects.

Optimal Capital Structure

Financial economists generally agree that firms have an optimal capital structure and a number of researchers have suggested that the price reactions documented in Table 4.1 reflect companies' attempts to move toward that optimum. This explanation might be useful if we found broad samples of firms experiencing positive market responses to their new security issues. But because the market reaction to most security offerings appears systematically negative (or at best neutral), it is clear that any attempt by firms to move toward a target capital structure is not the dominating factor in the market's response. If we were to use the market's reaction to new security offerings as the basis for any useful generalization about companies' relationship to their optimal structure, we would be put in the embarrassing position of arguing that new security offerings routinely move companies away from, not toward, such an optimum. Thus, I raise this possibility largely to dismiss it.

Information Disparity between Management and Potential Investors

The documented reductions in firm value associated with security sales—which, after all, are voluntary management decisions—thus present financial economists with a puzzle. One possible explanation is that new security sales are optimal responses by management to changes for the worse in a company's prospects. Alternatively, a company's current market valuation may seem to management to reflect excessive confidence about the future, and it may attempt to exploit such difference in outlook by "timing" its equity offerings. Investors habituated to stock offerings under such conditions will discount, as a matter of course, the stock prices of companies announcing security offerings. In such circumstances, even if a security sale increases the value of the firm by allowing it to fund profitable projects, it could lead potential investors to suspect that management has a dimmer view of the company's future than that reflected in its current market value.

It is now well documented that managers have better information about the firm's prospects than do outside investors.[5] There is also little doubt that outsiders pay attention to insider trading in making their own investment decisions. Given these observations, I believe that the findings in Table 4.1 are driven in large part by

---

[4] See Scott Linn and J. Michael Pinegar, "The Effect of Issuing Preferred Stock on Common Stockholder Wealth," unpublished manuscript, University of Iowa, 1985.

[5] See Jeffrey Jaffe's seminal study of insider trading, "Special Information and Insider Trading." *Journal of Business*, 47 (1974), pp. 410–420.

this potential disparity of information between management and the market, and the incentives it offers management in timing the issue of new securities.

Furthermore, I would argue that, as a result of this potential information disparity, new security offerings affect investors' outlook about a company through two primary channels: (1) the implied change in expected net operating cash flow and (2) the leverage change.

Implied Changes in Net Operating Cash Flow. Investors, of course, are ultimately interested in a company's capacity to generate cash flow. Although a new security offering might imply that the company has discovered new investment opportunities, it might also imply a shortfall in cash caused by poor current or expected future operating performance. As accounting students learn in their first year of business school, "sources"must equal "uses" of funds. Consequently, an announcement of a new security issue must imply one of the following to investors: (1) an expected increase in new investment expenditure, (2) a reduction in some liability (such as debt retirement or share repurchase) and hence a change in capital structure, (3) an increase in future dividends, or (4) a reduction in expected net operating cash flow. If new security sales were generally used only in anticipation of profitable new investment or to move capital structure closer to an optimal target ratio, then we should expect positive stock price reactions to announcements of new offerings. But if unanticipated security issues come to be associated with reductions in future cash flows from operations, then investors would systematically interpret announcements of security sales as bad news.

This argument can be generalized to consider other announcements which do not explicitly link sources and uses of funds. Using the above line of reasoning, we would interpret announcements of stock repurchases, increases in investment expenditures, and higher dividend payments as signaling increases in expected operating cash flow and, thus, as good news for investors. Conversely, security offerings, reductions in investment expenditures, and reductions in dividend payments all would imply reductions in expected operating cash flow.

The academic evidence on market responses to announcements of new securities sales, stock repurchases, dividend changes, and changes in capital spending (summarized in Table 4.2) is broadly consistent with this hypothesis. As shown in the upper panel of Table 4.2, announcements of security repurchases, dividend increases, and increases in capital spending are greeted systematically by increases in stock prices. The market responds negatively, as a rule, to announcements of security sales, dividend reductions, and decreases in new investment (an exception has been the oil industry in recent years, in which case the market's response to increases in capital spending has been negative, and positive to announced cutbacks in investment). On the basis of this evidence, the market appears to make inferences about changes in operating cash flow from announcements that do not explicitly associate sources with uses of funds.

I should point out, however, that although this explanation helps to explain nonpositive price reactions to announcements of all security sales, it provides no

Table 4.2. The Stock Market Response to Announcements of Changes in Financing, Dividend, and Investment Policy

In the columns below are the average two-day common stock abnormal returns and average sample size from studies of changes in financing, dividend, and investment policy grouped by implied changes in corporate cash flows. Returns are weighted averages by sample size of the returns reported by the respective studies. (Unless otherwise noted, returns are significantly different from zero.)

Type of Announcement	Average Sample Size	Two-Day Announcement Period Return
Implied Increase in Corporate Cash Flow		
Common Stock Repurchases:		
Intra-firm tender offer[a]	148	16.2%
Open market repurchase[b]	182	3.6
Targeted small holding[c]	15	1.6
Calls of Non-Convertible Bonds[d]	133	−0.1*
Dividend Increases:		
Dividend initiation[e]	160	3.7
Dividend increase[f]	280	0.9
Specially designated dividend[g]	164	2.1
Investment Increases[h]	510	1.0
Implied Decrease in Corporate Cash Flow		
Security Sales:		
Common stock[i]	262	−1.6
Preferred stock[j]	102	0.1*
Convertible preferred[k]	30	−1.4
Straight debt[l]	221	−0.2*
Convertible debt[l]	80	−2.1
Dividend Decreases[f]	48	−3.6
Investment Decreases[h]	111	−1.1

[a] Source: Dann (1981), Masulis (1980), Vermalen (1981), Rosenfeld (1982)
[b] Source: Dann (1980), Vermalen (1981)
[c] Source: Bradley/Wakeman (1983)
[d] Source: Vu (1986)
[e] Source: Asquith/Mullins (1983)
[f] Source: Charest (1978), Aharony/Swary (1980)
[g] Source: Brickley (1983)
[h] Source: McConnell/Muscarella (1985)
[i] Source: Asquith/Mullins (1986), Masulis/Korwar (1986), Mikkelson/Partch (1986), Schipper/Smith (1986), Pettway/Radcliff (1985)
[j] Source: Linn/Pinegar (1986), Mikkelson/Partch (1986)
[k] Source: Linn/Pinegar (1986)
[l] Source: Dann/Mikkelson (1984), Eckbo (1986), Mikkelson/Partch (1986)
* Interpreted by the authors as not significantly different from zero.

insight into the questions of why investors respond more negatively to equity than debt sales, to convertible than non-convertible issues, and to sales by industrials rather than utilities.

Information Disparity and Leverage Changes. Suppose that a potential purchaser of securities has less information about the prospects of the firm than management. Assume, furthermore, that management is more likely to issue securities when the market price of the firm's traded securities is higher than management's assessment of their value. In such a case, sophisticated investors will revise their estimate of the value of the firm if and when management announces a new security issue. Furthermore, the larger the potential disparity in information between insiders and investors, the greater the revision in expectations and the larger the negative price reaction to the announcement of a new issue.

Because debt and preferred stock are more senior claims on corporate cash flows, the values of these securities are generally less sensitive to changes in a company's prospects than is the value of common stock. Thus, this problem of potential insider information that management faces whenever it issues a new security is most acute in the case of equity offerings. Similarly, the values of convertible debt and convertible preferred stock are also generally more sensitive to changes in firm value than nonconvertible debt and preferred because of their equity component—but less sensitive, of course, than common stock; hence the information disparity should be more problematic for convertible than for straight securities.

The case of utility offerings is somewhat different. In the rate regulation process, managers of utilities generally petition their respective regulatory authorities for permission to proceed with a new security issue. This petitioning process should reduce the price reaction of utilities announcements relative to industrials for three reasons: (1) it could reduce the differential information between manager and outsiders; (2) it could limit managers' discretion as to what security to sell; (3) it could reduce managers' ability to "time" security offerings to take advantage of inside information. Because of this regulatory process, utilities do not face as great a problem in persuading the market to accept its securities at current prices.

Thus, while this information-disparity hypothesis does not predict whether the response to announcements of debt and preferred issues will be negative or positive, it does predict that the reaction to common stock sales will be more negative than the response to preferred or debt, more negative to convertible than nonconvertible issues, and to industrial than utility offerings.[6]

This second, leverage-related channel through which the information-disparity problem operates can be distinguished from the implied cash flow explanation by examining evidence from events that *explicitly* associate sources and uses of funds: namely, exchange offers, conversion-forcing calls of convertible securities, and security sales in which the proceeds are explicitly intended for debt retirement. Research on announcements of these transactions (summarized in Table 4.3) documents the following: (1) the market responds positively to leverage-increasing trans-

---

[6] But if the evidence across classes of securities is consistent with the information-asymmetry hypothesis, some data within security classes is apparently inconsistent. When Eckbo (1986) and Mikkelson Partch (1986) disaggregate their bond data by rating class, neither study finds higher rated, less risky (and thus less sensitive to firm value) bonds to be associated with smaller abnormal returns. Eckbo also finds more negative abnormal returns to mortgage bonds than nonmortgage bonds. B. Esben Eckbo, "Valuation Effects of Corporate Debt Offerings," *Journal of Financial Economics*, 15 (1986), 119–51; and Wayne H. Mikkelson and M. Megan Partch, "Valuation Effects of Security Offerings and the Issuance Process," *Journal of Financial Economics*, 15 (1986), 31–60.

Table 4.3. The Stock Market Response to Announcements of Pure Financial Structure Changes: Exchange Offers, Security Sales with Designated Uses of Funds, and Calls of Convertible Securities

Below is a summary of two-day announcement effects associated with the events listed above. Because each of these transactions explicitly associate sources with uses of funds, they represent virtually pure financial structure changes. (Unless otherwise noted, returns are significantly different from zero.) Full citations for all studies mentioned can be found in the reference section at the end of the article.

Type of Transaction	Security Issued	Security Retired	Average Sample Size	Two-Day Announcement Period Return
Leverage-Increasing Transactions				
Stock Repurchase[a]	Debt	Common	45	21.9%
Exchange Offer[b]	Debt	Common	52	14.0
Exchange Offer[b]	Preferred	Common	9	8.3
Exchange Offer[b]	Debt	Preferred	24	2.2
Exchange Offer[c]	Income Bonds	Preferred	24	2.2
Transactions with No Change in Leverage				
Exchange Offer[d]	Debt	Debt	36	0.6*
Security Sale[e]	Debt	Debt	83	0.2*
Leverage-Reducing Transactions				
Conversion-forcing Call[e]	Common	Convertible	57	−0.4*
Conversion-forcing Call[e]	Common	Preferred	113	−2.1
Security Sale[f]	Convertible Debt	Convertible Bond	15	−2.4
Exchange Offer[b]	Common	Debt	30	−2.6
Exchange Offer[b]	Preferred	Preferred	9	−7.7
Security Sale[f]	Common	Debt	12	−4.2
Exchange Offer[b]	Common	Debt	20	−9.9

[a] Source: Masulis (1980)
[b] Source: Masulis (1983) (Note: These returns include announcement days of both the original offer and, for about 40 percent of the sample, a second announcement of specific terms of the exchange.)
[c] Source: McConnell/Schlarbaum (1981)
[d] Source: Dietrich (1984)
[e] Source: Mikkelson (1981)
[f] Source: Eckbo (1986) and Mikkelson/Partch (1986)
* Not statistically different from zero.

actions and negatively to leverage-decreasing transactions; (2) the larger the change in leverage, the greater the price reaction. Accordingly, debt-for-common offers have larger positive stock price reactions than preferred-for-common offers, and common-for-debt offers have larger negative price reactions than common-for-preferred offers.

In Figure 4.1 the analysis of the two channels is combined to provide additional insight into the information disparity explanation. The events to the upper left of the figure tend to have positive stock price reactions, those in the lower right tend to have negative reactions while those along the diagonal tend to be insignificant. Hence, a common stock offering, which implies both a reduction in future operating cash flow and a reduction in leverage, prompts the largest negative market response of all the security offers. A stock repurchase, by contrast, suggests increases both in operating cash and leverage, and accordingly receives strong endorsement by the market. It seems to provide a credible expression to investors of management's confidence about the company's future performance (at least relative to its current value).

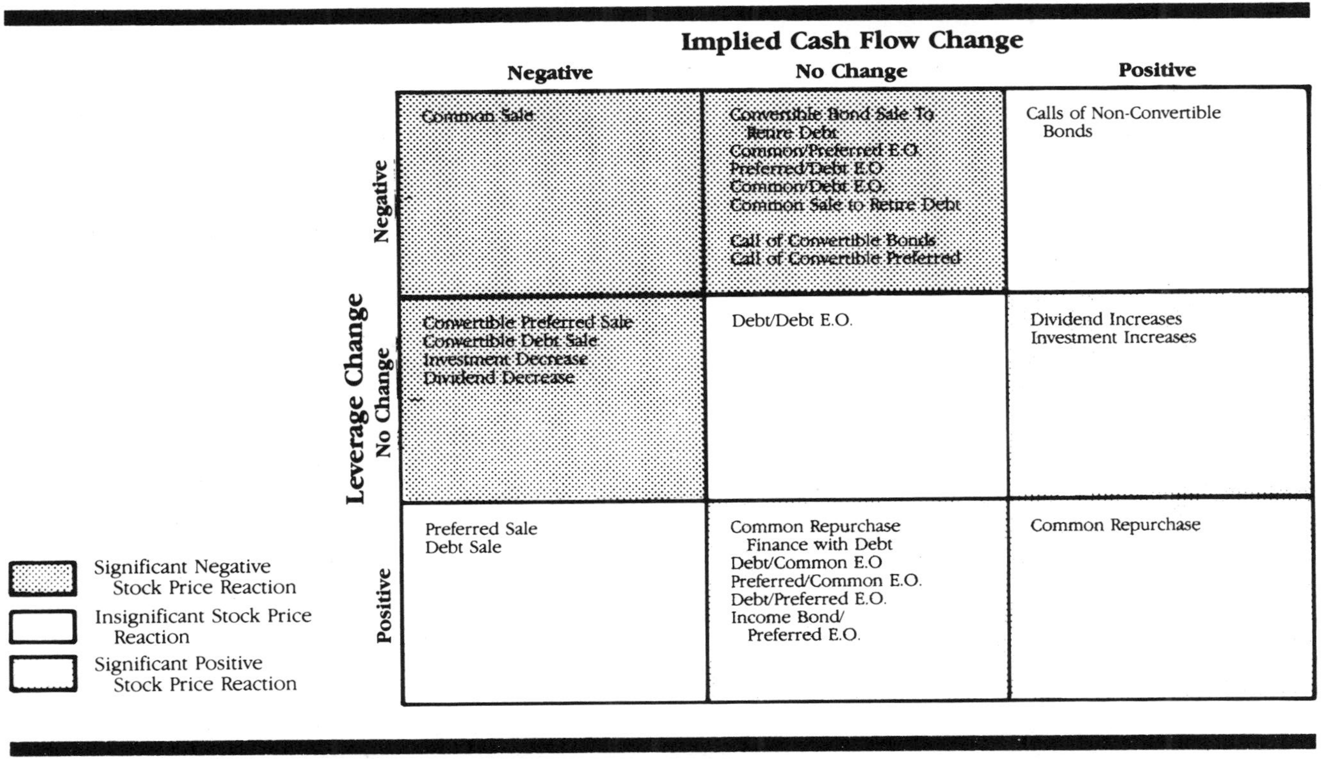

Implied Cash Flow Change

Leverage Change	Negative	No Change	Positive
Negative	Common Sale	Convertible Bond Sale To Retire Debt, Common/Preferred E.O., Preferred/Debt E.O., Common/Debt E.O., Common Sale to Retire Debt, Call of Convertible Bonds, Call of Convertible Preferred	Calls of Non-Convertible Bonds
No Change	Convertible Preferred Sale, Convertible Debt Sale, Investment Decrease, Dividend Decrease	Debt/Debt E.O.	Dividend Increases, Investment Increases
Positive	Preferred Sale, Debt Sale	Common Repurchase Finance with Debt, Debt/Common E.O., Preferred/Common E.O., Debt/Preferred E.O., Income Bond/Preferred E.O.	Common Repurchase

Legend:
- Significant Negative Stock Price Reaction
- Insignificant Stock Price Reaction
- Significant Positive Stock Price Reaction

Figure 4.1. Implied cash flow change

Unanticipated Announcements

Because stock price changes reflect only the unanticipated component of announcements of corporate events, the stock price change at the announcement of a security offering will be larger, all else equal, the more unpredictable is the announcement. For example, debt repayment (either from maturing issues or sinking-fund provisions) requires the firm to issue additional debt to maintain its capital structure. Given a target capital structure and stable cash flows, debt repayment must be matched with a new debt issue; hence the more predictable are principal repayments, the more predictable will be new debt issues. similarly, the predictability of earnings (and thus internally generated equity) will determine the predictability of a new equity issue. Therefore, one should expect a new debt issue to be more predictable than a new equity issue because principal repayments are more predictable than earnings.

Another reason for the greater predictability of public debt offerings is related to the cost structures of public versus private debt. Flotation costs for publicly placed debt appear to have a larger fixed component and more pronounced economies of scale than bank debt. Thus a firm tends to use bank lines of credit until an efficient public issue size is reached; then the firm issues public debt and retires the bank debt. If investors can observe the amount of bank borrowing and the pattern of public debt issues, then more predictable announcements of public bond issues should have smaller price reactions.

Utilities use external capital markets with far greater frequency than industrials, thus making utility issues more predictable. For this reason alone, we would expect utilities' stock prices to exhibit a smaller reaction to announcements of new security sales. In short, the relative predictability of announcements of security offerings helps explain both the observed differences in market reactions to common stock versus debt issues and to the offerings of industrials versus those of utilities.

Changes in Ownership and Control

Some security sales involve potentially important changes in ownership or organizational structure. In such transactions, part of the observed price reaction may reflect important changes in the ownership and control of the firm. For example, equity carve-outs (also known as partial public offerings) are transactions in which firms sell a minority interest in the common stock of a previously wholly owned subsidiary. In contrast to the negative returns from the sale of corporate common stock reported earlier, equity carve-outs are associated with significant *positive* returns of 1.8 percent for the five days around the announcement.

In this case, the problem of the potential information disparity which appears to plague equity offerings seems to be offset by positive signals to investors. What are these signals? As Katherine Schipper and Abbie Smith argue,[7] equity carve-outs may suggest to the market that management feels the consolidated firm is not receiving full credit in its current stock price for the value of one of its subsidiaries.

---

[7] "Equity Carve-outs," *Midland Corporate Finance Journal*, 4 (Spring 1986), p. 23.

If such is the information management communicates by offering separate equity claims on an "undervalued" subsidiary, then carve-outs could provide a means of raising new equity capital that neutralizes the negative signal released by announcements of seasoned equity offerings. Also worth noting, the public sale of a minority interest in a subsidiary carries potentially important control implications. For example, the sale of subsidiary stock allows management of the subsidiary to have a market-based compensation package that more accurately reflects the subsidiary's operating performance. In fact, 94 percent of the carve-outs studied adopted incentive compensation plans based on the subsidiary's stock.[8]

Academic research in general suggests that changes in ownership and organization affect stock prices (see Table 4.4). The evidence summarized in the upper panel suggests that voluntary organizational restructuring on average benefits stockholders. The research findings summarized in the lower panel suggests that announcements of transactions that increase ownership concentration raise share prices while those that reduce concentration lower share prices. For example, in equity offers where a registered secondary offering by the firm's management accompanied the primary equity, the average stock price reaction was -4.5 percent, almost 1.5 percent more negative than the average response to industrial equity offerings. This is the case, incidentally, in which the information problem becomes most acute: not only is the firm issuing new stock, but management is using the offering to further reduce its ownership stake—the reverse of a leveraged buyout.

SUMMING UP THE MARKET'S REACTION TO SECURITIES OFFERINGS

Figure 4.2 offers a pictorial summary of the various hypotheses and how each contributes to our understanding of the research findings on new security issues. Those arguments focusing on the information gap between management and investors appear to have the most explanatory power. The extent to which announcements are unanticipated helps explain differences in the market's response to debt versus equity offerings, and to industrial versus utility issues. And in the special cases when the offer accompanies ownership or organizational changes, there are important additional insights available. The price-pressure hypothesis may have some validity, but for widely traded securities I remain skeptical. The dilutive effects on EPS and ROE of new equity and convertible offerings are nothing more than accounting illusions; *given* that the security is fairly priced at issue, and that management expects to earn its cost of capital on the funds newly raised, there is no real economic dilution of value caused by a new equity offering. Finally, optimal capital structure theories, at this stage of development, seem to offer little insight into the general pattern of price reactions to new security sales.

[8] *Ibid.* See also the academic piece on which that article is based: "A Comparison of Equity Carve-outs and Seasoned Equity Offerings: Share Price Effects and Corporate Restructuring," *Journal of Financial Economics*, 15 (1986), pp. 153–186.

Table 4.4. The Market Response to Announcements of Organizational and Ownership Changes

In the columns below are summaries of the cumulative average abnormal common stock returns and average sample size from studies of announcements of transactions which change corporate control or ownership stucture. Returns are weighted averages by sample size of the returns reported by the respective studies. (Unless otherwise noted, returns are significantly different from zero.)

Type of Announcement	Average Sample Size	Cumulative Abnormal Returns
Organizational Restructuring		
Merger: Target[a]	113	20.0%
Bidder[a]	119	0.7*
Spin-Off[b]	76	3.4
Sell-Off: Seller[c]	279	0.7
Buyer[d]	118	0.7
Equity Carve Out[e]	76	0.7*
Joint Venture[f]	136	0.7
Going Private[g]	81	30.0
Voluntary Liquidation[h]	75	33.4
Life Insurance Company Mutualization[i]	30	56.0
Savings & Loan Association Charter Conversion[j]	78	5.6
Proxy Fight[k]	56	1.1
Ownership Restructuring		
Tender Offer: Target[l]	183	30.0
Bidder[l]	183	0.8*
Large Block Acquisition[m]	165	2.6
Secondary Distribution: Registered[n]	146	−2.9
Non-Registered[n]	321	−0.8
Targeted Share Repurchase[o]	68	−4.8

[a] Source: Dann (1980), Asquith (1983), Eckbo (1983), Jensen/Ruback (1983)
[b] Source: Hite/Owers (1983), Miles/Rosenfeld (1983), Schipper/Smith (1983), Rosenfeld (1984)
[c] Source: Alexander/Benson/Kampmeyer (1984), Rosenfeld (1984), Hite/Owers (1985), Jain (1985), Klein (1985), Vetsuypens (1985)
[d] Source: Rosenfeld (1984), Hite/Owers (1985), Jain (1985), Klein (1985)
[e] Source: Schipper/Smith (1986)
[f] Source: McConnell/Nantell (1985)
[g] Source: DeAngelo/DeAngelo/Rice (1984)
[h] Source: Kim/Schatzberg (1985)
[i] Source: Mayers/Smith (1986)
[j] Source: Masulis (1986)
[k] Source: Dodd/Warner (1983)
[l] Source: Bradley/Desai/Kim (1985), Jensen/Ruback (1983)
[m] Source: Holderness/Sheehan (1985), Mikkelson/Ruback (1985)
[n] Source: Mikkelson/Partch (1985)
[o] Source: Dann/DeAngelo (1983), Bradley/Wakeman (1983)
* Interpreted by the authors as not significantly different from zero.

ALTERNATIVE METHODS OF MARKETING SECURITY OFFERINGS

Once having decided on the terms of a security to sell, management then must choose among a number of methods to market the issue. it can offer the securities on a pro rata basis to its own stock holders through a rights offering, it can hire an underwriter to offer the securities for sale to the public, or it can place the securities privately. If management chooses to use an underwriter, it can negotiate the offer terms with the underwriter, or it can structure the offering internally and then put it out for competitive bid. The underwriting contract can be a firm commitment or a best efforts offering. Finally, the issue can be registered with the Securities

Research Finding

	Returns ≤ 0	Common ≤ Debt or Preferred	Convertibles ≤ Non-Convertibles	Industrials ≤ Utilities
Optimal Capital Structure	No	No	No	No
Implied Cash Flow Change	Yes	No	No	No
Leverage Change	No	Yes ⁺	Yes	Yes
Unanticipated Announcements	No	Yes	No	Yes
Ownership Changes	Yes*	Yes*	Yes*	No
Price Pressure	No	No	No	No

Potential Explanations

+ But only for Debt, not Preferred
* In Special Cases

Figure 4.2. Research finding

and Exchange commission under its traditional registration procedures; or, if the firm qualifies, it can file a shelf registration in which it registers all securities it intends to sell over the next two years.

Let's look at the major alternatives for marketing securities to provide a better understanding of why certain methods predominate.

Rights versus Underwritten Offerings

The two most frequently used methods by which public corporations sell new equity are firm-commitment underwritten offerings and rights offerings. In an underwritten offering, the firm in effect sells the issue to an investment bank, which resells the issue to public investors (or forms a syndicate with other investment banks to do so). The initial phases of negotiation between the issuing company and the investment banker focus on the amount of capital, the type of security, and the terms of the offering. If the firm and its chosen underwriter agree to proceed, the underwriter begins to assess the prospects, puts together an underwriting syndicate, prepares a registration statement, and performs what is known as a "due diligence" investigation into the financial condition of the company.

In a rights offering, each stockholder receives options (or, more precisely, warrants) to buy the newly issued securities. One right is issued for each share held. Rights offerings also must be registered with the SEC.

Despite evidence that the out-of-pocket expenses of an equity issue underwritten by an investment banker are from three to 30 times higher than the costs of a non-underwritten rights offering,[9] over 80 percent of equity offerings employ underwriters.

[9] See my paper, "Alternative Methods for Raising Capital: Rights versus Underwritten Offerings," *Journal of Financial Economics*, 5 (1977), pp. 273–307.

Perhaps the most plausible rationale for using underwriters is that they are effective in monitoring the firm's activities and thus provide implicit guarantees to investors when they sell the securities. This monitoring function would be especially valuable in light of the information disparity between managers and outside stockholders discussed in the first part of this article.

Thus, in addition to providing distribution channels between issuing corporations and investors, the investment banker performs a monitoring function analogous to that which bond-rating agencies perform for bondholders and auditing firms perform for investors and other corporate claimholders. While such activities are expensive, such monitoring of management increases the value of the firm by raising the price investors are willing to pay for the company's securities.

Negotiated versus Competitive Bid Contracts

The evidence also suggests that competitive bid offerings involve lower total flotation costs than negotiated offers.[10] In fact, it has been estimated that companies which use negotiated contracts can expect their total issue costs to be higher, on average, by 1.2 percent of the proceeds. Nevertheless, the primary users of competitive bids are regulated firms which are required to do so. Companies not facing this regulatory constraint (Rule 50 of the Public Utilities Holding Company Act) appear overwhelmingly to choose negotiated offers.

This behavior may be attributed partly to the fact that the variance of issuing costs has been found to be higher for competitive bid than for negotiated offers. Executives whose compensation is tied to accounting earnings might prefer a more stable, if somewhat lower, bottom line resulting from the use of negotiated offerings. Another potentially important problem with competitive bids is the difficulty in restricting the use of information received by investment bankers not awarded the contract. Hence, companies with valuable proprietary information are likely to find the confidentiality afforded by negotiated bids more attractive.

Probably most important, though, is that the monitoring, and thus the guarantee provided investors, is much more effective in the case of negotiated offerings than in competitive bids. With a negotiated offer, the issuing firm has less control over the terms and timing of the offer; hence, investors have fewer worries that the issue will be structured to exploit their information disadvantage.

This leads me to generalize about the kinds of companies which are likely to benefit from using competitive bids. The less the potential disparity between management's and the market's estimation of the value of the company, the greater are the likely savings to a company from using the competitive bidding process. For this reason, regulated utilities (those not already subject to Rule 50) stand to benefit more from the use of competitive bids than unregulated firms. Also, in the case of more senior claims such as debt and preferred stock, the informational asymmetry problem is less pronounced, as I have suggested, because the value of the claim is

[10] See Sanjai Bhagat and Peter Frost, "Issuing Costs to Existing Shareholders in Competitive and Negotiated Underwritten Public Utility Equity Offerings," *Journal of Financial Economics*, 15 (1986), pp. 233–259.

less sensitive to firm value. Thus straight debt, secured debt and nonconvertible preferred stock should all be sold through competitive bids more frequently than common stock, convertible preferred stock, or convertible bonds. And this is apparently the case.[11]

Shelf versus Traditional Registration

Prior to any public security offering, the issue must be registered with the SEC. Using traditional registration procedures, the issuing firm, its investment banker, its auditing firm, and its law firm all typically participate in filing the required registration statements with the SEC (as well as with the appropriate state securities commissions). The offering can only proceed when the registration statement becomes effective.

In March of 1982, however, the SEC authorized Rule 415 on an experimental basis, and it was made permanent in November 1983. It permits companies with more than $150 million of stock held by investors unaffiliated with the company to specify and register the total dollar amount of securities they expect to offer publicly over the next two years. The procedure is called shelf registration because it allows companies to register their securities, "put them on the shelf," and then issue the securities whenever they choose.

After the securities are registered, management can then offer and sell them for up to two years on a continuous basis. Rule 415 also allows the company to modify a debt instrument and sell it without first filing an amendment to the registration statement. Thus shelf registration allows qualifying firms additional flexibility both in structuring debt issues and in timing all security issues.

Because of the additional flexibility afforded management by the shelf procedure, there is greater opportunity for management to exploit its inside information and issue (temporarily) overvalued securities. Thus the information-disparity problem attending new issues should be especially great in cases of shelf registration. Potential investors anticipating this problem will exact an even larger discount in the case of shelf offerings than in offerings registered through traditional procedures. Hence, stock price reactions to announcements of new offerings registered under Rule 415 could be more negative, other things equal, than those under traditional registration procedures.

It is largely for this reason, I would argue, that shelf registration has been used far more frequently with debt than with equity offerings.

A Special Case: Initial Public Offerings

Private firms that choose to go public typically obtain the services of an underwriter with which to negotiate an initial public equity offering (IPO). IPOs are an interesting

---

[11] See James R. Booth and Richard L. Smith, "The Certification Role of the Investment Banker in New Issue Pricing," *Midland Corporate Finance Journal*, 4 (Spring 1986), p. 56. The article is based on their study, "Capital Raising, Underwriting and the Certification Hypothesis," *Journal of Financial Economics*, 15 (1986), pp. 261–281.

special case of security offers. They differ from offerings previously discussed in two important ways: (1) the uncertainty about the market clearing price of the offering is significantly greater than for public corporations with claims currently trading; (2) because the firm has no traded shares, examination of stock price reactions to initial announcements is impossible. The first difference affects the way these securities are marketed; the second limits the ways researchers can study the offerings.

Underpricing

The stock price behavior of IPOs from the time the initial offer price is set until the security first trades the aftermarket demonstrates unmistakably that the average issue is offered at a significant discount from the price expected in the aftermarket. In fact the average underpricing appears to exceed 15 percent. (For a summary of the results of studies of offer prices for initial public equity offerings as well as new issues of seasoned equity and bonds, see Table 4.5.) Once the issue has begun trading in the aftermarket, however, the returns to stockholders appear to be normal.

In an IPO, as suggested, there is a large amount of uncertainty about the market-clearing price. Furthermore, as some observers have argued, this uncertainty creates a special problem if some investors are considerably more knowledgable than others—for example, institutions relative to, say, individuals (especially since the Rules of Fair Practice of the NASD prohibit raising the price if the issue is oversubscribed). Assume, for the sake of simplicity, that we can divide all potential

Table 4.5. The Underpricing of New Security Issues

Presented below is a summary of estimates of the underpricing of new securities at issuance by type of offering. Underpricing is measured by the average percentage change from offer prices to aftermarket price.

Type of Offering	Study	Sample Period	Sample Size	Estimated Underpricing
Initial Public Equity Offering	Ibottson (1974)	1960–1969	120	11.4%
Initial Public Equity Offering	Ibbotson/Jaffe (1975)	1960–1970	2650	16.8
Initial Public Equity Offering	Ritter (1984)	1960–1982	5162	18.8
		1977–1982	1028	26.5
		1980–1981	325	48.4
Initial Public Equity Offering	Ritter (1985)	1977–1982		
Firm Commitment			664	14.8
Best Efforts			364	47.8
Initial Public Equity Offering:	Chalk/Peavy (1985)	1974–1982	440	13.8
Firm Commitment			415	10.6
Best Efforts			82	52.0
Equity Carve-Outs	Schipper/Smith (1986)	1965–1983	36	0.19
Seasoned New Equity Offering	Smith (1977)	1971–1975	328	0.6
Seasoned New Utility Equity Offering:	Bhagat/Frost (1986)	1973–1980	552	−0.30
Negotiated			479	−0.25
Competitive Bid			73	−0.65
Primary Debt Issue	Weinstein (1978)	1962–1974	412	0.05
	Sorensen (1982)	1974–1980	900	0.50
	Smith (1986)	1977–1982	132	1.6

investors into two distinct groups: "informed" and "uninformed." Under these conditions, if the initial offer price were set at its expected market-clearing price, it is not difficult to demonstrate that uninformed investors would earn systematically below-normal returns. If an issue is believed by informed investors to be underpriced, then those investors will submit bids and the issue will be rationed among informed and uninformed investors alike. If the issue is overpriced, however, informed investors are less likely to submit bids and the issue is more likely to be undersubscribed. In this process, uninformed investors systematically receive more of overpriced issues and less of underpriced issues.[12]

Recognizing their disadvantaged position in this bidding process, uninformed investors will respond by bidding for IPOs only if the offer price is systematically below their estimate of the after-market price in order to compensate them for their expected losses on overpriced issues. Such a bidding process would also account for the well-documented observation that underpricing is greater for issues with greater price uncertainty.

The above explanation has been tested using data from IPOs in the following way. Given that there is an equilibrium amount of underpricing (i.e., one which has proved to be acceptable to issuers in order to sell the issue), we can hypothesize that an investment banker that repeatedly prices issues below this equilibrium level will lose the opportunity for further business. If the investment banker repeatedly overprices (or does not underprice by enough), however, he loses investors.

A recent study by Randy Beatty and Jay Ritter estimated an underpricing equilibrium and then examined the average deviation from that level of underpricing by 49 investment bankers who handled four or more initial public offerings during the period 1977–1981. When they compared the subsequent deviation from their estimated normal underpricing was greatest with that of the remaining 25 underwriters, the market share of those 24 firms fell from 46.6 to 24.5 percent during 1981–1982; and five of the 24 actually closed down. For those 25 with the smallest deviation from the estimated underpricing equilibrium, market share goes from 27.2 to 21.0 percent, and only one of the 25 ceases operation. (The remaining 54.5 percent of the business in 1981–1982 was underwritten by firms which did fewer than four IPOs from 1977–1981.)[13]

As Table 4.5 shows, security issues by public corporations are also typically underpriced, but much less so than in the case of IPOs. Seasoned new equity issues have been found to be underpriced by 0.6 percent. There is some disagreement about the degree of underpricing of seasoned bonds, with estimates ranging from 0.05 percent to as high as 1.2 percent of the offer price. Seasoned equity issues by utilities, however, appear to be *overpriced* by 0.3 percent.

---

[12] For a systematic formulation of this "informed-uninformed" investor dichotomy and its effects on IPO pricing, see Kevin Rock, "Why New Issues Are Underpriced." *Journal of Financial Economics*, 15 (1986), pp. 187–212.

[13] See Randolph P. Beatty and Jay R. Ritter, "Investment Banking, Reputation, and the Underpricing of Initial Public Offerings," *Journal of Financial Economics*, 15 (1986), pp. 213–232.

Best-Efforts versus Firm-Commitment Contracts

There are two alternative forms of underwriting contracts that are typically used in IPOs. The first is a firm-commitment underwriting agreement, in which the underwriter agrees to purchase the whole issue from the firm at a specified price for resale to the public. The second is a "best efforts" agreement. In such an arrangement, the underwriter acts only as a marketing agent for the firm. The underwriter does not agree to purchase the issue at a predetermined price, but simply sells as much of the security as it can and takes a predetermined spread. The issuing company gets the net proceeds, but without any guarantee of the final amount from the investment banker. This agreement generally specifies a minimum amount that must be sold within a given period of time; if this amount is not reached, the offering is cancelled. From 1977–1982, 35 percent of all IPOs were sold with best efforts contracts. Those issues, however, raised only 13 percent of the gross proceeds from IPOs over that period, implying that larger IPOs tend to use the firm-commitment method.

The choice between firm commitment and best efforts comes down, once again I think, to resolving the problems created by the information disparity between informed and uninformed investors. The preceding argument for underpricing firm commitments can be contrasted with the incentives in a best efforts contract. Consider that in the case of a best-efforts IPO, if the issue is overpriced and the issue sales fall short of the minimum specified in the underwriting contract, the offer is cancelled and the losses to uninformed investors are reduced. Structuring the contract in this manner reduces the problem faced by uninformed potential security holders, and thus reduces the discount necessary to induce them to bid.

Thus the relative attractiveness of the two types of contracts will be determined, in part, by the amount of uncertainty associated with the price of the issue. The prohibition against raising prices for an oversubscribed issue (imposed by the NASD's Rules of Fair Practice) means that the company has effectively given a free call option to potential stockholders. Thus, relative to a best efforts contract, the expected proceeds to the issuer in a firm commitment IPO are reduced as the amount of uncertainty about after-market prices increases. In a best-efforts contract, the firm provides potential investors not only with an implicit call option (because of the rule against raising the price), but also gives them the option to put the shares back to the firm if the issue is undersubscribed. Because of these implicit options provided investors in best-efforts contracts, the greater the uncertainty about the after-market price of an IPO, the more attractive are best efforts contracts to investors; hence, the more likely are issuers to choose that form over a firm commitment.

To summarize, firm-commitment offerings are more likely the less the uncertainty about the market-clearing security price. Consistent with this hypothesis, one study found that the average standard deviation of the after-market rates of returns for 285 best-efforts offerings was 7.6 percent in contrast to a 4.2 percent standard deviation for 641 firm commitment offerings.[14]

---

[14] See Jay Ritter, "The 'Hot Issue' Market of 1980," *Journal of Business*, 57 (1984), pp. 215–240.

Stabilization Activity and the Green Shoe Option

Underwriters typically attempt to stabilize prices around the offer date of a security. In the case of primary equity offers by listed firms, this stabilization is accomplished by placing a limit order to purchase shares with the specialist on the exchange. I believe this activity represents a bonding mechanism by the investment banker— one that promises investors that if the issue is overpriced, they can sell their shares into the stabilizing bid, thereby cancelling the transaction.

The Green Shoe option (so named because it was originally used in an offering by the Green Shoe Company) is frequently employed in underwritten equity offers. It gives the underwriter the right to buy additional shares from the firm at the offer price. This is equivalent to granting the investment banker a warrant with an exercise price equal to the offer price in the issue. The total quantity of shares exercisable under this option typically ranges between 10 and 20 percent of the offer. Obviously, the option is more valuable if the offer price is below the market value of the shares; thus, the Green Shoe option is another potentially effective bonding mechanism by which the investment banker reassures investors that the issue will not be overpriced. That is, if a new offering prospectus contains a Green Shoe provision, potential investors (especially the less informed) will reduce their forecast of the probability that the issue will be overpriced because the returns to the underwriter from the Green Shoe are lower if the warrant cannot be exercised.

IMPLICATIONS FOR CORPORATE POLICY

Recent research on the stock market response to new security offers consistently documents a significant negative reaction (on the order of 3 to 4 percent on average) to announcements of new equity issues by industrial companies. Convertible issues, both debt and preferred, also typically are greeted by a negative, though smaller, price change (of roughly 1 to 2 percent). By contrast, the market reaction to straight debt and preferred issues appears to be neutral.

The critical question, of course, is—Why does the market systematically lower the stock prices of companies announcing new stock and convertible offers? Such financing decisions, after all, are voluntary choices by management intended, presumably, to increase the long-run value of the firm by providing necessary funding.

After consideration of several possible explanations, I argue that the primary cause of this negative response is the potential for management to exploit its inside information by issuing overvalued equity (or convertibles, which of course have an equity component). Investors recognize their vulnerability in this process and accordingly reduce their estimate of the firm's value. The result, in the average case, is that the new equity is purchased by investors at a discount from the preannouncement price.

This theory and evidence has a number of managerial implications. Perhaps the most important is that management should be sensitive to the way the market is likely to interpret its announcement of a new issue. For example, if the company is contemplating a primary equity offering and an executive asks to include a registered secondary in the offer, the board of directors should recognize that this can be a very expensive perk; in such cases the market price typically falls by almost 5 percent upon the announcement. This is probably the surest means of arousing the market's suspicion that insiders have a different view of the company's future than that reflected in the current stock price.

Perhaps the best way for management to overcome this information problem is to state, as clearly as possible, the intended uses for the funds. For example, if management intends to use the proceeds for plant expansion, management should say so—emphatically. We know that the market responds positively, on average, to announcements of increases in capital spending plans (with the exception of the case of oil companies in recent years, where the reverse has been true).[15] Consequently, short of revealing proprietary information which could compromise the firm's competitive position,[16] management should benefit from the attempt to be as forthright as possible in sharing with the investment community its investment opportunities, corporate objectives, capital structure targets, and so forth.

This strategy is not meant to contradict the obvious: namely, that current stockholders benefit when management issues stock or convertibles when the market price proves to have been high; and that debt or preferred stock is better if the company proves to be undervalued (though, in the absence of significant inside information, I would suggest that this can only be determined with hindsight). The problem, however, is that this kind of managerial opportunism may prove an expensive strategy for a firm that wants to maintain its access to capital markets. If management develops a reputation for exploiting inside information, the price discount the market exacts for accepting subsequent new issues could be even larger.

In the second part of the article, I attempt to show how the use of investment bankers as underwriters also helps to solve this financing problem arising from the possibility of insider information. The fact that management may have an incentive to issue overvalued securities causes a demand for "bonding" the firm's actions— that is, investors will offer more for the securities if they are provided a credible promise that they will not be exploited.

In those cases where the information disparity between management and investors is likely to be greatest, and to have the worst potential consequences for new investors (i.e., for equity holders, and especially in the case of smaller firms in less heavily traded markets), the demand for the bonding or certification provided by the banker is also likely to be the greatest. For this reason I have argued that underwritten issues provide stronger guarantees to investors than rights offers; issues

---

[15] A study by John McConnell and Chris Muscarella ("Corporate Capital Expenditure Decisions and the Market Value of the Firm," *Journal of Financial Economics*, 14 (1985)) found that announcements of increases of corporate capital spending were accompanied by a 1 percent increase, on average, of the announcing company's stock price.

[16] For example, when Texas Gulf Sulphur discovered substantial mineral deposits in Canada, immediate release of that information would have substantially increased the cost of adjacent mineral rights then under negotiation.

with negotiated underwriting contracts are more strongly bonded than competitive bid issues; issues registered using traditional procedures are more strongly bonded than those employing the new shelf registration procedures; and issues containing a Green Shoe option are more strongly bonded than those without. Therefore, for example, an industrial equity issue should more frequently be registered using traditional rather than shelf registration procedures, and sold under a negotiated, firm commitment rather than a competitive bid contract; it is also more likely to include a Green Shoe option. By contrast, a nonconvertible debt issue by a utility is more likely to be sold under a competitive bid contract and registered using the new shelf registration procedures.

The above argument is not to deny that shelf registration procedures have significantly lowered the fixed costs of public issues for some industrial companies. In fact it should be especially cost-effective for large, well-established companies, especially in the case of the public debt offers.

To take greatest advantage of the potential savings from shelf registration, I believe that management must change some of its practices with respect to debt offerings. Instead of using a line of credit at a bank until a large public issue can be made, qualifying companies could use the shelf registration process to place several smaller issues. In order to retain the additional liquidity in secondary markets associated with larger issues, I expect companies to begin offering multiple issues with the same coupon rate, coupon dates, maturity dates, and covenants—instead of designing all new issues to sell at par.

PART 2   RAISING CAPITAL

Raising capital is traditionally what investment banking is all about. The chapters in Part 2 deal with different kinds of capital raising.

In Chapter 5, Jim Freeman and Peter Jachym describe what has historically been the heart of investment banking: syndication. The process has changed dramatically in recent years, with the introduction of Rule 415 permitting "shelf registrations," and the rise of offerings in the Euromarket.

Charlie Wolf's chapter deals with the private, as opposed to the public, offering process. Private placements have for decades been an important part of raising capital. While commercial banks have become active as intermediaries in private placements, investment bankers have a well-established position. The chapter discusses the private placement process and describes a number of examples.

Chapter 7 turns to the special case of the initial public offering—a company's first venture into the public marketplace. Dennis Logue describes the mechanics of an IPO and focuses on forms of compensation to underwriters and the critical pricing decision. The compensation and the pricing are closely related, and the chapter presents an economic analysis, supported by a substantial body of empirical data, to indicate how pricing is and should be done.

Bob Towbin and Peter Williamson deal with another special case: high-tech, growing companies. Chapter 8 describes the financing of these companies from their beginnings to a first public offering, and the role of an investment banker in that financing.

Chapter 9 discusses opportunities for investment bankers in the venture-capital business. Ned Hazen describes the financing process, including raising capital and evaluating prospective investments. He analyzes the economics of the business, and identifies sources of profit to those who invest in and manage venture-capital funds.

In Chapter 10, Paul Kazilionis deals with another specialized area: real estate. Some investment banking firms have established extraordinarily profitable real estate financing departments, and this chapter describes their activities and the basis for success.

5 Syndication

JAMES L. FREEMAN
PETER C. JACHYM

Investment banking syndicates have been used historically to diversify risk among their members. Until recently, most investment banks had small capital accounts relative to the underwriting risk they assumed in public offerings. In the post-Glass-Steagall period, this strain on capital required the creation of syndicates to spread the risks and the rewards of any one transaction. Although risk was the primary concern, the need for distribution strength was nearly as great. Most investment banking firms lacked the distribution capability to sell the offerings they generated until the late 1960s and 1970s. Consequently, the syndicate was devised as a way of spreading the financial risk of a public offering and rewarding the members who could distribute the securities to buyers.

More recently, investment banks have become dominant forces as broker/dealers (e.g., Morgan Stanley) and broker/dealers have become important underwriters (e.g., Merrill Lynch). This phenomenon, among others, has led to a major consolidation within the industry over the last 20 years. A small number of highly capitalized firms now have become financial supermarkets. Some are directed to the institutional or wholesale market; others dominate the individual or retail market; a few try to do both. This change in capital size and distribution ability among the major underwriters has caused significant changes in syndication methods. In the past that was far less true when one size and structure fitted all syndicates regardless of the nature of the underwriting.

Today, the size and the role of the syndicate can vary considerably depending on the type and size of the securities offered. In a small debt transaction, the syndicate tends to be relatively small and the managers will sell most of the securities. In such a transaction, the role of most members of the syndicate may be limited, for the most part, to underwriting the securities. On the other hand, for a large initial public offering of common stock, the company offering securities and its lead investment banker may choose a broad syndicate of up to 120 firms. In this case, the syndicate would be expected to sell much more of the stock and the company would look to some of the firms in the syndicate to provide research coverage and to create liquidity in shares in the secondary market after the offering.

THE TOMBSTONE AD AND PROSPECTUS LIST

The best description of investment banking syndicates and their structure can be found in the second section of the *Wall Street Journal* or Section D of the *New York Times* on virtually any business day. In these newspapers and in other financial publications appear the "tombstone" advertisements for investment banking transactions. An example of a recent tombstone ad appears in Figure 5-1. Notice that the ad states explicitly that it is not "an offer to sell or a solicitation of an offer to buy" the shares. Investment bankers may offer securities only by means of a prospectus filed with the Securities and Exchange Commission. A typical tombstone ad will also include the relevant terms of the offering: the size of the offering in dollars (or other currency) for debt securities, or the number of shares for equity securities, the name of the issuing company, and the interest rate for debt securities or dividend rate for preferred stock.

The remainder of the tombstone ad is what really interests us here. First, the offering of 4 million shares is divided into three parts. Banco Central is a Spanish bank and the underwriters were tapping the U.S., Canadian and European markets. The United States offering consisted of 5 million American Depositary Shares or Receipts (ADRs). What happened was that 2.5 million shares of Banco Central were deposited with a trustee (the Morgan Guaranty Trust Company) which in turn issued 5 million ADRs. So one ADR represents a claim to half a share of Banco Central. The ADR form is useful because holders of ADRs can trade them in the United States far more easily than they could trade the underlying Banco Central shares.

For the U.S. offering, a number of underwriters are listed in the ad. Notice that the names are not strictly in alphabetical order. They are organized by what are called "brackets." In Figure 5-2, the same tombstone ad has been marked to identify the brackets.

The first bracket consists of the *managers*, in this case three firms. The management group can consist of a single firm or of several. The decision as to the composition of the management group rests largely with the company issuing the securities. The company will make this decision based on the type of security to be issued, the overall relationship between the company and a number of investment banks, and the company's perception of the abilities of the banks. One of the managers will be chosen to be the lead or book-running manager. The name of this firm normally appears first, or on the left side of the tombstone ad. The typeface used in the ad will be the typeface unique to that firm. In our example, however, the normal procedure was not followed. First Boston was actually the lead manager, although one would think from an examination of the ad that this position was held by Shearson. Shearson had had a long-standing relationship with Banco Central, and in recognition of this, First Boston agreed to place Shearson's name in the normal position for lead manager. (The typeface, however, is the First Boston typeface.) A detailed description of the functions of the lead manager will be given later in this chapter.

If the tombstone ad were for an offering of debt securities, the next bracket would be the *bulge* or *special* bracket. In a debt offering, capital strength and distribution ability of underwriters are especially important, and the firms that appear in the special bracket are those that historically have been the largest and the most prominent in generating business and placing securities. Usually, special bracket firms are at the top of the "league tables" for capital raised.[*] Currently the special bracket firms are The First Boston Corporation, Goldman Sachs, Morgan Stanley, Merrill Lynch, Salomon Brothers, and Shearson Lehman Brothers. Shearson is the most recent member, as a result of its deal generation in recent years. In the case of equity offerings, such as that of Banco Central, there is generally no special bracket.

Next is the *major* bracket. In our example it begins with Bear, Stearns and ends with Dean Witter Reynolds. The names are in alphabetical order, although they may not seem to be. Alex. Brown uses "Brown" and Dean Witter Reynolds uses "Witter" for purposes of alphabetizing. The reasons for this go back to the origins of the firms and industry traditions. The firms in the major bracket are quite large and have substantial ability to distribute shares. Some may be critical to the success of an offering because of their extensive retail distribution networks. In a debt offering, of course, some of these majors would be up in a special bracket. Sometimes a few strong regional or specialty firms may appear after the alphabetical list of majors. If they underwrite the same amount as the major firms they are included in the major bracket, but since they are not included in the alphabetical list they are called "majors out of order." Later in this chapter we will discuss how, why, and when firms appear out of their normal order.

Next is the *mezzanine* bracket. In our example three firms appear in this bracket, in alphabetical order. The mezzanine bracket often recognizes firms smaller than the majors but ones with which the issuing company or the lead manager has a special relationship.

Finally, the *submajor* or *regional* bracket (both terms are used; the former is more apt if the bracket consists of New York firms) includes the remaining firms, listed alphabetically. These are firms that on the whole are smaller than the mezzanine bracket firms.

Why should investment banks care about where they appear in the tombstone ad for an offering? A partial answer is economic and can be found in the list of underwriters associated with the tombstone ad. Figure 5-3 is reprinted from the prospectus for the offering and shows all the firms participating in the underwriting and the number of shares underwritten by each. Notice that the higher the bracket, the more securities the firm underwrites (and the more it profits). All firms within a particular bracket underwrite equal allocations of securities, with the lead manager sometimes taking more than the other co-managers. (In our example the allocations

---

[*] The league tables are compiled quarterly, showing the performances of leading underwriters ranked every conceivable way. The term originated in the Euromarket and is derived from the soccer league (Boxscore) tables.

July 13, 1987

4,000,000 Shares

(of which 3,250,000 Shares are represented by 6,500,000 American Depositary Shares in the United States and Canada)

Banco Central, S.A.

Price $19 Per American Depositary Share

Price $38 Per Share

These securities are being offered in the United States, Canada and internationally.

United States Offering

5,000,000 American Depositary Shares
Representing
2,500,000 Shares

Shearson Lehman Brothers Inc.

The First Boston Corporation

Prudential-Bache Capital Funding

Bear, Stearns & Co. Inc.	Alex. Brown & Sons Incorporated	Dillon, Read & Co. Inc.	Donaldson, Lufkin & Jenrette Securities Corporation
Drexel Burnham Lambert Incorporated	Goldman, Sachs & Co.	E. F. Hutton & Company Inc.	Kidder, Peabody & Co. Incorporated
Lazard Frères & Co.	Merrill Lynch Capital Markets	Montgomery Securities	Morgan Stanley & Co. Incorporated
PaineWebber Incorporated	Robertson, Colman & Stephens	L. F. Rothschild & Co. Incorporated	Salomon Brothers Inc
Smith Barney, Harris Upham & Co. Incorporated		Wertheim Schroder & Co. Incorporated	Dean Witter Reynolds Inc.

Allen & Company
Incorporated   Oppenheimer & Co., Inc.   Thomson McKinnon Securities Inc.   Advest, Inc.

AIBC Investment Services Corp.   Arnhold and S. Bleichroeder, Inc.   Butcher & Singer Inc.   Cowen & Co.

Craigie Incorporated   Interstate Securities Corporation   Janney Montgomery Scott Inc.   Jefferies & Company, Inc.

Ladenburg, Thalmann & Co. Inc.   Cyrus J. Lawrence   Legg Mason Wood Walker   McKinley Allsopp, Inc.
Incorporated   Incorporated

Morgan Keegan & Company, Inc.   Moseley Securities Corporation   Neuberger & Berman

Raymond James & Associates, Inc.   The Robinson-Humphrey Company, Inc.

Tucker, Anthony & R. L. Day, Inc.   Wheat, First Securities, Inc.

Figure 5.1.

100

(*Note:* In its original form this is a one-page ad.)

101

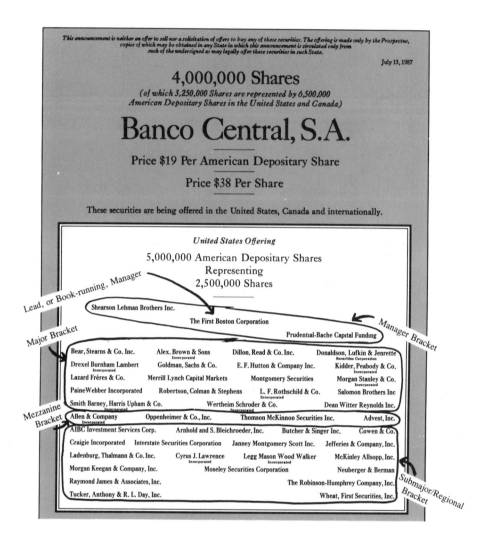

Figure 5.2.

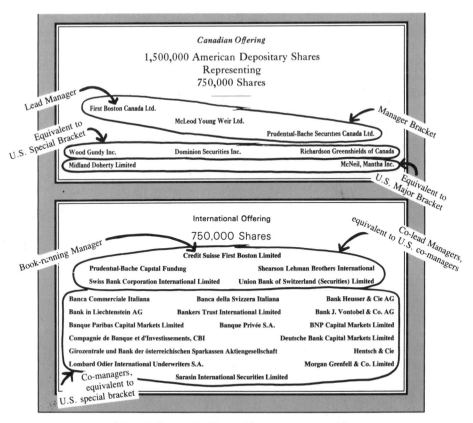

(*Note:* In its original form this is a one-page ad.)

UNDERWRITING

Subject to the terms and conditions set forth in an agreement (the "U.S. Underwriting Agreement"), the Selling Shareholder has agreed to sell to each of the underwriters named in the table below (the "U.S. Underwriters"), and each of the U.S. Underwriters, for whom Shearson Lehman Brothers Inc., The First Boston Corporation and Prudential-Bache Securities Inc. act as representatives (the "U.S. Representatives"), has severally agreed to purchase from the Selling Shareholder the number of ADSs set forth opposite its name below.

Name of U.S. Underwriter	Number of ADSs
Shearson Lehman Brothers Inc.	721,500
The First Boston Corporation	722,000
Prudential-Bache Securities Inc.	721,500
Advest, Inc.	25,000
AIBC Investment Services Corp.	25,000
Allen & Company Incorporated	50,000
Arnhold and S. Bleichroeder, Inc.	25,000
Robert W. Baird & Co. Incorporated	25,000
George K. Baum & Company	25,000
Bear, Stearns & Co. Inc.	90,000
Blunt Ellis & Loewi Incorporated	25,000
Boettcher & Company, Inc.	25,000
J.C. Bradford & Co.	25,000
Alex. Brown & Sons, Incorporated	90,000
Butcher & Singer Inc.	25,000
The Chicago Corporation	25,000
Cowen & Co.	25,000
Craigie Incorporated	25,000
Dain Bosworth Incorporated	25,000
Dillon, Read & Co. Inc.	90,000
Donaldson, Lufkin & Jenrette Securities Corporation	90,000
Drexel Burnham Lambert Incorporated	90,000
A.G. Edwards & Sons, Inc.	50,000
First Southwest Company	25,000
Goldman, Sachs & Co.	90,000
J.J.B. Hilliard, W.L. Lyons, Inc.	25,000
E.F. Hutton & Company Inc.	90,000
Interstate Securities Corporation	25,000
Janney Montgomery Scott Inc.	25,000
Jefferies & Company, Inc.	25,000
Kidder, Peabody & Co. Incorporated	90,000
Ladenburg, Thalmann & Co. Inc.	25,000
Cyrus J. Lawrence Incorporated	25,000
Lazard Frères & Co.	90,000
Legg Mason Wood Walker, Incorporated	25,000
McDonald & Company Securities, Inc.	25,000
McKinley Allsopp, Inc.	25,000
Merrill Lynch, Pierce, Fenner & Smith Incorporated	90,000
Montgomery Securities	90,000
Morgan Keegan & Company, Inc.	25,000
Morgan Stanley & Co. Incorporated	90,000
Moseley Securities Corporation	25,000
Neuberger & Berman	25,000
The Ohio Company	25,000
Oppenheimer & Co., Inc.	50,000
PaineWebber Incorporated	90,000
Piper, Jaffray & Hopwood Incorporated	25,000
Prescott, Ball & Turben, Inc.	25,000
Rauscher Pierce Refsnes, Inc.	25,000

Figure 5.3.

Raymond James & Associates, Inc.	25,000
Robertson, Colman & Stephens	90,000
The Robinson-Humphrey Company, Inc.	25,000
L.F. Rothschild & Co. Incorporated	90,000
Salomon Brothers Inc	90,000
Smith Barney, Harris Upham & Co. Incorporated	90,000
Stephens Inc.	25,000
Sutro & Co. Incorporated	25,000
Thomson McKinnon Securities Inc.	50,000
Tucker, Anthony & R. L. Day, Inc.	25,000
Underwood, Neuhaus & Co., Incorporated	25,000
Wertheim Schroder & Co. Incorporated	90,000
Wheat, First Securities, Inc.	25,000
Dean Witter Reynolds Inc.	90,000
Total	5,000,000

Figure 5.3. (*Continued*)

were 25,000 shares for the submajors; 50,000 in the mezzanine bracket; 90,000 for the majors; 721,500 for two co-managers, and 722,000 for the lead manager.)

In addition, the position of a firm in terms of bracket represents an indication of status, signifying ability and importance of each firm in the generation of deals and the placement of securities. Castes may have died out in India, but not on Wall Street.

Before turning to the Canadian and International portions of the Banco Central offering, we will look at variations on the tombstone ad, shown in Figure 5-4. The tombstone ads in Figures 5-1 and 5-2 appeared in the eastern edition of the *Wall Street Journal*. The ads in three other editions, and in the *New York Times*, were a little different, as shown in Figure 5-4. The manager and major brackets appeared in all ads, but the makeup of the submajor or regional bracket has been varied to give recognition to regional firms in their part of the country.

The Canadian Offering was underwritten by Canadian firms. Three firms are shown in the manager bracket, with First Boston Canada the lead manager. The second bracket is the Canadian equivalent of the U.S. special bracket—especially strong firms. And the third bracket is the Canadian equivalent of the U.S. major bracket.

The International Offering was underwritten by overseas firms. Five firms made up the group of "co-head managers" in European parlance. This group is equivalent to the U.S. manager or co-manager bracket. Credit Suisse First Boston was the book-running manager. (The list of firms for the International Offering is in Credit Suisse First Boston's typeface.) The remainder of the firms (in alphabetical order) constitute "co-managers" in European parlance, equivalent to special bracket firms in the United States.

The First Boston Corporation—Banco Central, S.A.

LOCAL IMPRINTS—Add the following names after Dean Witter Reynolds Inc.

MIDWESTERN WALL STREET JOURNAL

A. G. Edwards & Sons, Inc.	Robert W. Baird & Co. Incorporated	George K. Baum & Company	Blunt Ellis & Loewi Incorporated
J. C. Bradford & Co.	The Chicago Corporation	Dain Bosworth Incorporated	J. J. B. Hilliard, W. L. Lyons, Inc.
McDonald & Company Securities, Inc.	The Ohio Company	Piper, Jaffray & Hopwood Incorporated	Prescott, Ball & Turben, Inc.

WESTERN WALL STREET JOURNAL

Boettcher & Company, Inc.	Dain Bosworth Incorporated	Sutro & Co. Incorporated

SOUTHWESTERN WALL STREET JOURNAL

First Southwest Company	Rauscher Pierce Refsnes, Inc.	Stephens Inc.	Underwood, Neuhaus & Co. Incorporated

NEW YORK TIMES

Allen & Company Incorporated	Oppenheimer & Co., Inc.		Thomson McKinnon Securities Inc.
Advest, Inc.	Arnhold and S. Bleichroeder, Inc.	Cowen & Co.	Jefferies & Company, Inc.
Ladenburg, Thalmann & Co. Inc.	Cyrus J. Lawrence Incorporated	Legg Mason Wood Walker Incorporated	McKinley Allsopp, Inc.
Moseley Securities Corporation	Neuberger & Berman		Tucker, Anthony & R. L. Day, Inc.

Figure 5.4.

WHO ORGANIZES THE SYNDICATE?

If the syndicate is considered so important to the transaction, and the bracketing position is valued, the obvious question is how and why firms are placed in the syndicate. In the preliminary prospectus or "red herring" for an offering, the syndicate list normally does not appear. The list of underwriters must appear in the final prospectus. At the time the red herring is filed with the SEC, the company will have selected its managers for the transaction, and their names appear on the red-herring cover. The lead manager or book-running manager, in consultation with the company, will then invite firms to take part in the transaction in order to form a syndicate of appropriate size and composition. The firms are invited in a telex from the lead manager and are usually given the opportunity to review the prospectus. Investment banks will make the decision whether to participate in a syndicate based on their understanding of the company, what they believe to be their level of potential contribution to the offering, and the adequacy and quality of disclosure in the prospectus. Firms will then accept or reject invitations and respond to the lead manager.

Although the lead manager working with the company is responsible for the composition of the syndicate and inviting specific firms, the bracket in which a particular investment bank appears is largely a matter of historical precedent. However, lead managers have some discretion and often there are minor variations in bracketing. Most of these differences occur below the majors. They reflect special relationships among firms in deference to a regional or specialty firm's new business or distribution capability. The lead manager moves the favored firm up a rung in all syndicates. Aside from these minor variations, firms normally appear in the same bracket for all syndications unless they have a special relationship with the company and the company requests that the firm be moved to another bracket. Occasionally, some specialty firms are moved up to the major bracket when they have particular expertise, such as Conning on insurance deals or Keefe Bruyette on banks.

As we have seen, there is economic significance to which bracket a firm is placed in, because the amount underwritten varies by bracket. Within a bracket, there may be status implications in the firm's location—whether it appears in alphabetical order or "out of order"—but there are no economic differences.

THE FUNCTIONS OF THE SYNDICATE

The three parts of the underwriting fee paid by the issuer to the syndicate correspond in value to the functions of a syndicate. The underwriting fee, called the gross spread, is shown on the cover of the final prospectus and is illustrated in Figure 5-5. The three components of the gross spread are the management fee, the underwriting fee, and the selling concession. The amount of each of these components can vary with a particular transaction. However, typically the management fee will represent 20 percent of the gross spread, the underwriting fee an additional 20 percent; and the selling concession the remaining 60 percent.

The Management Fee

The management fee is retained by the managers for their work in preparing the transaction. This work typically includes carefully examining the company and ensuring that its strengths and weaknesses are properly disclosed in the company's prospectus. This process is referred to as "conducting due diligence." The members of the syndicate depend on the managers' due-diligence process. Consequently, this puts a special burden on the managers, especially the lead manager, to know and disclose all relevant information about the company's operations.

Probably the most important function of the managing underwriters is pricing the issue. This requires a careful understanding of the expectations of the company and an in-depth knowledge of the current market for the security. Certain lead managers get a reputation for being "chicken" and underpricing issues. Eventually, companies shy away from letting them run the book because it costs the companies money. Other managers get a reputation for overpricing issues. This leads syndicate members and institutional investors to become suspicious of any deal that the firm lead-manages.

In addition, in assembling the syndicate, the managing underwriters must try to assure that the strengths and capabilities of the various members will complement

Banco Central, S.A.

5,000,000 American Depositary Shares
Representing
2,500,000 Shares

Each American Depositary Share ("ADS") represents one-half of one Share, stated value 500 pesetas per share (the "Shares"), of Banco Central, S.A. (the "Bank"). The ADSs are evidenced by American Depositary Receipts ("ADRs"), which are listed on the New York Stock Exchange (Symbol: BCM). Only holders of 20 or more Shares are entitled to attend the meetings of shareholders and have one vote for every 20 Shares owned. Holders of fewer than 20 Shares may aggregate their interests and permit one holder to attend and vote at meetings. For a description of the voting, dividend and liquidation rights of holders of Shares and ADSs, see "Description of Share Capital" and "Description of American Depositary Shares". The Shares represented by the ADSs being offered hereby are being sold by Inmobiliaria Central Española, S.A., a wholly-owned subsidiary of the Bank (the "Selling Shareholder"), which acquired the Shares in purchases on Spanish stock exchanges and in off the market transactions. See "Market Information" and "Selling Shareholder". The principal non-United States trading market for the Shares is the Madrid Stock Exchange. The last reported sales price of the ADSs on July 9, 1987 on the New York Stock Exchange was $19 per ADS and the daily quoted price of the Shares on the Madrid Stock Exchange on such date was 5,225 pesetas. See "Market Information". The Shares also are listed on the Barcelona, Bilbao and Valencia Stock Exchanges in Spain and on the Frankfurt, Paris and London Stock Exchanges.

In addition to the 5,000,000 ADSs being offered hereby, 1,500,000 ADSs (representing 750,000 Shares) are being offered concurrently in Canada and 750,000 Shares are being offered concurrently internationally, outside the United States, Canada and the Kingdom of Spain. The Underwriters reserve the right to reallocate the ADSs and Shares among such offerings. See "Underwriting".

THESE SECURITIES HAVE NOT BEEN APPROVED OR DISAPPROVED BY THE SECURITIES AND EXCHANGE COMMISSION NOR HAS THE COMMISSION PASSED UPON THE ACCURACY OR ADEQUACY OF THIS PROSPECTUS. ANY REPRESENTATION TO THE CONTRARY IS A CRIMINAL OFFENSE.

	Price to Public	Underwriting Discounts(1)	Proceeds to Selling Shareholder(2)
Per ADS			
Offered in the U.S.	$19.00	$ .92	$18.08
Offered in Canada	Cdn. $25.14	Cdn. $ 1.2173	Cdn. $23.9227
Per Share			
Offered internationally	Pts. 4,822.0	Pts. 233.0	Pts. 4,589.0
Total(3)(4)	$152,000,000	$7,357,000	$144,643,000

(1) The Bank and the Selling Shareholder have agreed to indemnify the Underwriters against certain liabilities, including liabilities under the Securities Act of 1933. See "Underwriting".

(2) Excludes expenses of the offerings estimated at $1,800,000, payable by the Bank, including $300,000 which the Bank has agreed to pay to the Underwriters as partial reimbursement of their expenses. See "Underwriting".

(3) Canadian dollar amounts are translated at the Bank of Canada noon rate of exchange on July 9, 1987, Cdn. $1.3232 per U.S. $1.00. Spanish peseta amounts are translated at the Noon Buying Rate described herein on July 9, 1987, 126.9 Pts. per U.S. $1.00.

(4) The Selling Shareholder has granted the Underwriters 30-day options to purchase, on the same terms per ADS or per Share set forth above, up to an aggregate of 1,200,000 additional ADSs or 600,000 Shares to cover over-allotments, if any. If such options are exercised in full, the total Price to Public, Underwriting Discounts and Proceeds to Selling Shareholder will be $174,800,000, $8,461,000 and $166,339,000, respectively. See "Underwriting".

The ADSs are being offered by the U.S. Underwriters when, as and if sold by the Selling Shareholder and delivered to and accepted by the U.S. Underwriters and subject to their right to reject orders in whole or in part. It is expected that the ADRs evidencing the ADSs will be ready for delivery on or about July 16, 1987.

Shearson Lehman Brothers Inc.
The First Boston Corporation
Prudential-Bache Capital Funding

The date of this Prospectus is July 10, 1987.

Figure 5.5.

one another and contribute to the success of the issue. The lead manager must educate the syndicate concerning the issuer's strengths and weaknesses. In other words, the firm develops the marketing stance to help the syndicate distribute the issue. It is responsible for the distribution of prospectuses and other related documents to the syndicate members. The lead manager's legal counsel also arranges for qualification of the issue in various states under applicable blue-sky laws. During the marketing of the transaction, the lead manager is responsible for setting up the "road show" with which the company and its management will visit investors in a number of different cities.

Prior to filing with the SEC, the management fee is set between the co-managers according to negotiations with the company. Sometimes the book-running manager (lead manager) will receive a larger percentage of the management fee because of the additional work involved in coordinating the entire issue. The term "running the books" stems from the control the lead manager has in accounting for costs and, most importantly, allocating the securities among underwriters (retention) and controlling the allocation of the institutional pot. More on the importance of being the book-running manager and how the institutional pot works is included under the "Book-Running Manager" section later in the chapter.

The Underwriting Fee

The underwriting fee is the component of the gross spread that is paid to each member of the syndicate in proportion to the percentage of the issue its underwriting participation represents. An underwriter receives the underwriting fee on each share it underwrites without respect to the number of shares it retains (i.e., ultimately sells). This fee compensates the underwriter for assuming the economic liability taken by it as a syndicate member, up to the underwriting firm's percentage of the syndicate. These liabilities stem from losses on unsold securities or from overallotment losses on behalf of the syndicate. Thus, when the underwriting agreement is executed between the company and the lead manager, the underwriters legally own their underwriting participation despite the fact that their alloted "retention" for actual sale may be more or less than this amount. Each underwriter receives its underwriting fee after (net of) its proportionate share of expenses associated with the transaction. These expenses include such items as: advertising; legal and other expenses of the managers, including appropriate direct marketing expenses; correspondence postage, telephone, telex, and facsimile transmissions; road show and information meetings; and any stabilization expenses (discussed in the next section).

If the aggregate underwriting fee exceeds the expenses of the offering, the lead manager sends a check to each underwriter for its proportionate share of the net underwriting fee. If, on the other hand, the expenses of the offering exceed the aggregate underwriting fee, each underwriter receives a bill from the lead manager for its additional liability from the offering. For obvious reasons, the investment banking community looks upon the receipt of a bill from the lead manager with disfavor.

Stabilization

The process of stabilization attempts to ensure an orderly distribution of new securities into the marketplace. If done correctly, once the issue is freed from stabilization the securities will trade *at* the same level or slightly *above* the level of the offering price. In other words, the lead manager stabilizes *at* or slightly *below* the offering price and in doing so buys securities that are being sold in the marketplace.

In order to facilitate the stabilization process and increase the likelihood of an orderly distribution, the lead manager will create a "short position" in the deal. This is done by selling more securities through the syndicate than will be bought from the issuer. The lead manager skillfully sizes the short position based on its assessment of the potential demand for the deal, the size of the offering, the prevailing market conditions, and the quality of the book (the buyers). In an equity deal where stabilization is extremely important to the success of the deal, the short may run from 5 to 20 percent on an initial public offering.

Since it is the syndicate, not the company, that sells the shares short, neither an underwriting fee nor a management fee is paid on them. However, in order for the securities to be distributed, a selling concession must be paid. The costs of this additional selling concession are allocated among the underwriters as one of the expenses paid by the underwriting fee.

If too large a short position is created and excess demand carries the stock up from the original price, the syndicate will lose money by having to cover the short position (i.e., buy shares) at a price higher than the price at which they were sold (the offering price). The cost to the syndicate then would be the selling concession plus the increment over the offering price. If too small a short position is established, the managers either will have to buy shares long on behalf of the syndicate or stop stabilizing. In the former case, the syndicate buys stock that it generally will liquidate at a loss. In the latter case, the syndicate will free the stock to trade too soon, and generally it will trade down. This has the threefold black eye for the book-running manager: making the company look bad, angering customers who bought stock that went down, and incensing the syndicate members who are getting an earful from their customers who are sitting with a loss.

To avoid both of these unattractive alternatives, syndicates often use the "Green Shoe." Under National Association of Securities Dealers (NASD) rules, an over-allotment option exists that permits underwriters to purchase additional securities (up to 15 percent of the number of shares offered) from the issuer or selling shareholders. This option is often referred to as the "Green Shoe" provision (because it originated in an offering for the Green Shoe Company). It is granted for 30 days and may only be used to cover overallotments. Historically, Green-Shoe provisions typically have been used in one of three situations—in an initial public offering where no float exists, in a large issue relative to the previous trading activity in the company's common stock, or in a common stock transaction that had been volatile in a secondary market. Today, such provisions are used in most equity, convertible debenture, and preferred offerings, particularly where the securities to be offered are of an unusual nature and there may be some concern as to the market acceptance of the securities. Consequently, most high-yield debt issues employ the Green Shoe.

The benefit to the issuing company is twofold. First, the underwriter can price the deal more aggressively in a difficult environment, knowing the short is oversized. Second, it can mean more proceeds to the company at that aggressive price.

Selling Concession

As stated earlier, approximately 60 percent of the gross spread goes to the selling concession. The selling concession is the fee paid to the registered representative's (RR) firm for each share sold. The firm then pays out a percentage to the RR according to a constant rate structure (possibly 35 percent for sales to individuals, 20 percent to small institutions, 15 percent to medium-sized institutions, and 10 percent to large institutions). The selling concession is normally larger than the commensurate commission on a similar-sized transaction in the secondary market. In fact, on large institutional orders, it may be many times the equivalent commission. Investors normally do not care about this greater remuneration because they buy the security net of any commission, which some consider a major incentive to participate. Additionally, they can buy in size without disturbing the price. The reason the seller is willing to pay the greater spread is to compensate the underwriters for the out-of-the-ordinary effort by the firms and their RRs in selling the issue, as well as the greater financial risk associated with an underwriting as compared with normal secondary trading.

Selling Group and Reallowance Sales

In many underwritings, the managers set aside securities to be sold by the selling group. The selling group includes nonunderwriters and nonmembers of the syndicate. Firms may choose to be part of the selling group because of political reasons (bracketing problems or conflicts with another corporate client), because the syndicate was small (it has managers and majors only, thus excluding regionals and specialty firms), or because they are firms that do not traditionally underwrite securities.

Members of the selling group buy securities from the syndicate group less the reallowance. The reallowance is a part of the selling concession and varies in spread based on how much the syndicate needs the selling group. It may be approximately 25 percent of the gross spread, but that 25 percent comes out of the selling concession.

Reallowance sales are not restricted to members of the selling group. Often one underwriter has better results selling securities than another. Consequently, that underwriter will buy part of the retention of another underwriter less the reallowance.

THE IMPORTANCE OF BEING THE BOOK-RUNNING OR LEAD MANAGER

Like most things in life, managers are not created equal. The economic rewards of being the lead manager are vastly greater than for being a co-manager in many deals. Earlier it was stated that management fees may be split unequally among the managers to favor the lead manager. Although this is an incentive, it is not the norm, nor is it the real gravy from running the books.

Today, typically more than half of an issue is distributed through a group account set aside by the underwriters to cover demand by institutions—"the institutional pot." Any underwriter can bring in an order to the pot. However, the book-running manager allocates the securities and the portion of the pot to each institutional customer. Not surprisingly, the book-running manager will tend to favor accounts that it trusts and with which it does a volume of business. In turn, the institutional account designates underwriters it wishes to remunerate because of help on the deal, or for research or other services. Not unexpectedly, the book-running manager gets a large chunk of each designation. Since the selling concession is 60 percent of the gross spread, and it is the only part of the gross spread that is not preset but varies with the number of shares sold, the book-running manager, through his control of the pot, has substantial control of the economics of any deal.

COMPETITIVE BID SYNDICATES

Until this point we have discussed only negotiated syndicates. Most syndicates today are negotiated, but historically this has been less true. The statutes creating the SEC and forcing registration rules that are still effective today were enacted in the mid-1930s. These were a reaction to the abuses of the 1920s that accelerated the stock market crash. One of the most flagrant abuses was the creation of utility holding companies. As a reaction, the security financings of most utility companies were required to be by competitive bid. Typically, railroad equipment debentures are also sold competitively.

A competitive bid starts with the company stating the security type, the size, if debt, the maturity date, the date of the bid, as well as the time, place, and other requirements. This fundamental information is posted as a public notice in the *Wall Street Journal*, among other places. Normally a number of syndicates will be created. Some may have a small number of members who are willing to take substantial risk, others may have 8 or 10 majors, all of which will be managers, plus a number of regionals. Typically, the books rotate among managers alphabetically. Although the book runner has a greater say in the pricing, there tends to be a closer relationship between underwriting risk and economic reward in competitive bids. In a tough securities trading environment and where there are a number of groups, sometimes groups will merge to make the bid on a one-time-only basis. In a terrible environment it is possible for a group to be unwilling to make a bid or for the bid to be intentionally low. The credit crunches of 1969–1970, 1973–1974, and 1979–1982 led to the breakdown of competitive bidding as the rule, although it is still widely used by the utility industry.

RULE 415: THE NEW WORLD

In 1982 the Securities and Exchange Commission attempted to streamline the issuance of securities. This experiment was tried for a year and later became law. The main proponents of this rule change were major corporations, which saw it as a more flexible and competitive offering style.

Under Rule 415, major corporations may file shelf registration statements with the Securities and Exchange Commission. Such a statement may or may not name underwriters. It does not really matter because the statement can be amended on nonmaterial factors, as underwriters are considered to be by the SEC. By filing a shelf, the company can be ready to issue within 24 hours using the stated underwriters or other firms if a better proposal is presented. Rule 415 allows corporations to take advantage of attractive price fluctuations, because they can react so quickly. Bonds under Rule 415 tend to be generic offerings and this corporate competitive or semicompetitive issuance form works especially well. The securities are usually investment grade, often of intermediate maturity, and generally with standard indentures and features. Very often the lead manager and perhaps a few co-managers make a proposal to the issuing company. If the company accepts the proposal, it is said the group "bought the deal" or the issue is a "bought deal" and then firms are invited to form a syndicate, with perfect knowledge of size, maturity, and price. Obviously, if the deal is overpriced, the lead manager will have called a party to which no one comes.

Under 415 the bulge-bracket underwriters have become even more dominant. This was not supposed to be the case originally. However, the large underwriting firms are the best risk takers, have the best idea of which customers buy what new issues, and tend to be institutional in customer base in an increasingly institutional market.

DUAL SYNDICATION

The most innovative new product in syndication started in 1984 with a dual syndicated issue for Esselte Business Products. Credit Suisse First Boston ran a syndicate in Europe, while The First Boston Corporation ran a syndicate in the United States. The two lead managers worked closely together to best tap the customer base in both countries. Dual syndication allows a U.S. company to avail itself of the strong syndication ability of the very major European managers in what normally would be a domestic deal. Similarly, it allows a foreign issuer to have access to the largest market for securities in the world—the United States—while also tapping its home market.

This technique has been so successful that a majority of large equity issuers now use the dual syndicate to distribute new stock issues.

SYNDICATE DEPARTMENTS

Every major investment bank and underwriting firm has a syndicate department. The syndicate department does what most people would expect: invites firms into the firm's managed syndicates, accepts invitations from other firm's managed underwritings, sets retention for other firms, tries to get the highest retention for its firm, and so forth.

Because of those duties that require interaction with other firms, the syndicate department has the closest relationship with the Street, not as competitors but as working partners. Consequently, when conflicts arise among firms, it is often the syndicate departments that become the go-betweens. The syndicate department can be said to be the firm's eyes and ears among its competitors.

6 Private Placements

CHARLES R. WOLF

An investment bank's private placement department focuses on the direct placement of corporate securities to lenders. Private placement offers an investment bank its main opportunity for creative financing. Typical deals involve creative features that are absent from financings in the public market.

The private placement market for corporate bonds was created by the Securities Act of 1933, which exempted corporate issues sold to a limited number of professional (and presumably informed) investors from SEC registration. The private placement market has evolved since then to become a major source of funds for companies with lower credit ratings seeking long-term financing. Given that private placements are effectively nonmarketable, terms can be tailored to the particular needs of less financially secure companies. The private placement market also has served as a source of funds in complex financings. Indeed, in recent years, a substantial fraction of high-yield, so-called junk bond, financing has been arranged in the private placement market.

As capital raisers, investment banks have been pivotal in arranging and distributing private financings. This chapter attempts to provide some insights to the private market as it exists today and on the special role investment banks play in this market. The first part of the chapter examines recent trends in public and private financing, then provides a brief overview of the buyers of private placements. Discussed next is the private placement function in investment banking—how it is organized and the services that investment bankers provide in a private placement. The chapter then focuses on recent examples of types of financings done in the private market, and, finally, examines the role of the private placement market in the recent junk bond financing phenomenon.

BORROWING IN THE PUBLIC AND PRIVATE CORPORATE BOND MARKETS

Over the past two decades, financing in the private placement market has accounted for about 30 percent of all corporate borrowing. As Table 6.1 shows, the proportion

Table 6.1. Corporate Bond Financing (Amounts in Thousands)

Year	Public	Private	Total	Percent Private
1966	$ 7,540	$ 7,463	$ 14,904	49.4%
1967	14,444	6,762	21,206	31.9
1968	10,216	6,525	16,741	39.0
1969	12,338	5,128	17,466	29.4
1970	24,365	4,656	29,021	16.0
1971	23,279	6,756	30,035	22.5
1972	16,922	8,706	25,628	34.0
1973	12,899	7,802	20,701	37.7
1974	25,337	6,160	31,497	19.6
1975	31,493	10,173	41,666	24.4
1976	26,089	16,119	42,208	38.2
1977	24,206	18,058	42,264	42.7
1978	20,466	16,977	37,443	45.3
1979	25,814	14,394	40,208	35.8
1980	41,587	11,619	53,206	21.8
1981	38,103	6,989	45,092	15.5
1982	44,278	9,798	54,076	18.1
1983	47,369	21,126	68,495	30.8
1984	73,357	36,326	109,683	33.1
	$520,102	$221,438	$741,540	29.9%

placed privately has varied considerably, though, ranging from a high of 49 percent in 1966 to a low of 16 percent in 1981. Figure 6.1 shows how volatile the volume of public financing was throughout the two decades, compared to the supply of private financing, which was relatively stable through 1976, fluctuating around $6 million per year.

Since the late 1970s, the annual level of financing in the private market has been even more volatile on a percentage basis than the annual level of public financing.

The chief suppliers of funds to the private placement market are life insurance companies. Such lenders with stable cash inflows can make investments in the private placement market that exhibit a stability not found in the public offering market.

The increase in the volatility of private financing since the late 1970s is not easily explained. The change in Federal Reserve policy in 1979, which significantly altered the financing patterns of corporations, and the ensuing increase in both the level and volatility of interest rates were the most likely factors. High interest rates in the early 1980s encouraged life insurance policyholders to borrow on their policies, which substantially reduced insurance company cash flow. Moreover, in recent years insurance companies have become increasingly willing to vary their lending between the public and private market to take advantage of changes in yield differentials. In addition, new lenders have entered the private market as a result

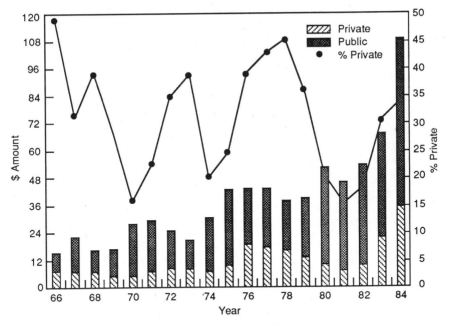

Figure 6.1. Corporate bond financing

of the surge of high-yield financing. A significant fraction of acquisition-related financing, for example, takes place in the private market; this brings a broader range of participants to the market.

LENDERS IN THE PRIVATE PLACEMENT MARKET

A relatively small number of lenders supply funds to the private placement market in accordance with the restriction that private placements be sold to a limited number of lenders. Subsequent interpretations of the 1933 Securities Act have required buyers of private placements to evidence investment intent by holding such issues for a substantial period following their purchase. Regulation D, issued by the Securities and Exchange Commission in 1982, clarified various interpretations of the 1933 Act by specifying that private placements can be shown to an unlimited number of presumably informed investors.

It is unlikely that the private placement market would have attracted a wide spectrum of investors even in the absence of restrictions on distribution. The market is an illiquid one, appealing chiefly to lenders whose cash flows enable them to hold issues indefinitely, if not to maturity, and only a limited number of investors fall within this category.

As we said before, the major institutional investors in the private market have been domestic life insurance companies. Life insurance liabilities are largely contractual in nature, and the cash flows associated with life insurance company liabilities are fairly predictable. To the insurance industry, the higher yields available on the typically lower-quality issues sold in the private market are sufficient compensation for their lack of marketability. Because of their ongoing commitment to the private placement market as a major investment outlet, insurance companies have devoted considerable resources to developing staffs to evaluate such investments. As a result, large life insurance companies typically serve as the lead lenders in most private financings.

At times private and public pension funds have been major buyers of private placements. Because these institutions never invested significant resources in personnel to handle private placements, however, their participation typically has been limited to financially less complex issues. State law also limits state and local funds to higher-quality loans as well. More recently, foreign investors, especially Japanese financial institutions, have become major buyers of private placements. It is estimated that Japanese investors now provide about 15 percent of the funds to the private market.

THE PRIVATE PLACEMENT FUNCTION IN INVESTMENT BANKS

Historically, borrowers in the private market have relied on investment banks to serve as intermediaries in a majority of private financings, and most major investment banks have long been active as agents. Borrowers do deal directly with lenders, however, especially when an ongoing relationship has been formed or in the case of refinancing. In the vast majority of new financings, where the borrower does not have an established relationship with lenders, though, investment banks, and to a lesser extent commercial banks, act as intermediaries to arrange the financings.

Depending on individual histories and evolutions, private placement departments occupy different locations within investment banks. Publicly offered issues are initiated chiefly by corporate finance personnel but underwritten and distributed by the sales and trading departments. In contrast, if they involve a complicated story, private placements can require the private placement groups to perform both corporate finance and distribution functions. As a result, the location of the private finance department within an investment bank depends largely on the expertise developed in the private area.

Investment banks that specialize in complex private financings requiring special selling efforts have tended to locate the private placement department within the corporate finance function. Those specializing in more standard private placements have tended to place the department under sales and trading functions. As a result of the SEC's Rule 415, the so-called shelf rule, corporate finance has evolved into a more transactional business. In investment banks where capital markets groups have been established as liaisons between the corporate finance and distribution functions, the private placement department has sometimes been relocated within this intermediate group. Finally, in some firms the private placement department has been placed in the high-yield group, which handles corporate finance and sales and trading activities involving junk securities.

At Morgan Stanley, for example, the private placement department is part of the high-yield department, while at Salomon Brothers and Goldman Sachs it is part of corporate finance. Fixing the private placement department in corporate finance at Goldman reflects the kinds of private financings traditionally handled by the firm. Historically, Goldman has concentrated on complex financings, those that benefit from the direct input of the private finance people in the distribution process. First Boston has taken an intermediate step, locating the private finance group within the liaison capital markets function. Depending on the complexity of a financing, distribution may be handled by the fixed-income sales force or the private placement department.

A private placement department in an investment bank provides a wide range of services in the distribution of private placements. Many of these involve the close cooperation of the private placement group with other departments within the organization.

Business Development

Business development typically is undertaken by a corporate finance department. It involves identifying a corporation's financing need and selling the investment bank's ability to deliver the desired financing. Frequently, financing opportunities might arise out of "reverse" inquiry from lenders themselves. Reverse inquiry refers to an institutional buyer's request for specific types of investments from an investment bank. With the change in Federal Reserve policy in October 1979 and the subsequent increase in the volatility of interest rates, buyers of both public and private securities have provided increasing input in the structuring of securities to meet specific investment requirements.

The private placement group often participates in business development where the most appropriate financing vehicle is a private placement or where a specific opportunity has been revealed through reverse inquiry. In these instances, private placement and corporate finance groups work together to sell the deal to a potential client.

Structuring the Deal

This is largely the responsibility of the private placement department. Because the issues are effectively nonmarketable, the terms and provisions of a private financing can be tailored to the individual needs and preferences of both the borrower and potential lender.

From its experience as an intermediary, the investment banker knows the type of terms typically associated with a particular financing. It also knows what lenders prefer in the way of terms and which potential buyers of the issue currently have funds to invest. At this stage, the investment banker focuses on such terms as the maturity and amount of the issue, but not the rate. These terms may be set aggressively depending on timing and credit considerations. A borrower with a strong credit rating and the time and options to make smart choices, for example, has far more negotiating flexibility than a company with limited access to the financial markets and a strict financing deadline.

Pricing and Selling the Deal

In pricing the deal, that is, in determining the appropriate coupon for an issue, the private placement department may work with a number of other groups within the firm, depending on the complexity of the financing. The capital markets group, which has first-hand knowledge of competitive rates, is responsible for pricing all new public issues. A firm's institutional salespeople may also provide input, because they are in frequent contact with the potential buyers of an issue. Finally, the private group may obtain price views from the institutional lenders directly, in the event that the financing involves complex terms and provisions. Ultimately, the rate chosen will depend on what lenders are willing to accept. The private group in effect selects a rate that just sells the entire issue.

Depending on the complexity of the terms and provisions of an issue, the private placement department may sell the issue directly to lenders or rely on the firm's institutional sales force. It is more practical to sell complex issues directly, as the private group may be the only one that fully understands and can articulate the deal to lenders. Less complex deals are sold by the institutional sales force. Typically, the firm attempts first to sign up one of the major lenders. Indeed, that lender is pivotal in determining both acceptable terms and an appropriate coupon. Once a major lender, such as Prudential or Metropolitan, signs up for a financing, smaller lenders usually are quick to follow the large lender's "seal of approval."

Negotiating the Terms and Provisions

Once a financing is completed, the private placement group stands as the intermediary between the borrower and lenders in negotiating the terms of the issue. Much of this process has been completed informally in the pricing and sales process, with the final steps fixed at this stage.

Documentation

The final step in the sale of a private placement—and one that can occupy the most time—involves legal documentation of the terms and provisions agreed on by the borrower and lenders. The lending group is responsible for meeting due-diligence requirements for documentation.

THE TYPES OF PRIVATE FINANCINGS ARRANGED BY INVESTMENT BANKS

The types of private financings arranged by an investment bank range from straight debt financings to venture-capital equity deals and leveraged buyouts. This section describes a variety of recent First Boston Corporation financings in the private placement market.

Taft Broadcasting: Straight Debt Financing for an Acquisition. Taft Broadcasting acquired several radio and television broadcasting stations owned by Gulf Broadcast Company in 1985. Taft had to use so much debt to acquire the properties that its credit rating was reduced from A quality to less than investment grade. Because FCC approval of the acquisition was required, the financing provided for the delayed delivery of funds by the lenders conditional on FCC approval. Taft issued $150 million in subordinated debt with a 15-year maturity. The only covenant in the loan agreement was that this issue became *pari passu* with any future debt raised by Taft. Thus, over time, the issue should gradually assume a senior debt status as Taft's currently outstanding senior debt matures.

First Boston arranged the financing in the private placement market because lenders in this market had provided funds to Taft Broadcasting in the past and understood the credit. These lenders were thus in a far better position to assess the quality of the company, its management, and the temporary nature of the financial leverage created by the acquisition than uninformed lenders in the public market. Because of this, First Boston was able to obtain a substantially lower rate in the private market than would have been available on a public offering.

The New York Times Corporation: A Yen Loan Hedged into Dollars in the Foreign Exchange Market. The New York Times Corporation wanted to borrow $25 million for three years. The company hoped to borrow at a rate no more than 50 basis points above the yield on three-year U.S. Treasuries. First Boston arranged for a Japanese bank to lend The New York Times Y5.315 billion, equivalent to $25 million, at a rate of 6.58 percent. The yen loan was then swapped into dollars using the spot market rate in the foreign exchange market. The Times' future interest and principal payments were hedged by a series of forward contracts to buy yen on the appropriate payment dates. Because of the higher interest rates prevailing in the United States, the cost of buying yen in the future becomes increasingly expensive. (Otherwise everyone would sell yen, buy dollars, earn the higher U.S. interest rates, then buy yen back at the same exchange rate in the future.) In combination with the 6.8 percent financing rate, the cost of these forward contracts translated into an overall borrowing rate that was 15 basis points below the rate on three-year Treasuries. First Boston was able to obtain this extremely low rate because it moved quickly to exploit an aberration in the U.S. and Japanese foreign exchange markets during a period of highly volatile interest rates.

Portland General Electric: A Leveraged Lease Financing. Leveraged lease financings are one of the more popular types of financings undertaken in the private placement market. A substantial percentage of all aircraft have been financed in this way. Typically, about 20 to 40 percent of an airplane's cost is represented by an equity investment and 60 to 80 percent by debt financing. The equity investors receive all of the depreciation on and the ultimate residual value of the equipment.

Lenders in turn are protected by the equity cushion, the collateral of the property, and the assignment of the lease. The creditworthiness of the lessee provides the ultimate support to the lenders.

The Portland General Electric financing was a $230 million transaction involving the sale and leaseback of part of one of Portland's coal-fired electric generating facilities to a special-purpose corporation. The lease equity, representing about 20 percent of the financing, was placed with General Electric Credit Corporation (GECC) by First Boston's Leasing Group. GECC's return was comprised of a contractual return (the excess of rent over debt service) and a noncontractual return (tax benefits and residual value at the end of the 29-year lease). The debt portion of the leveraged lease financing was secured by a power purchase contract with San Diego Gas & Electric, a 15 percent interest in the plant, and the lease payment obligation of the special-purpose corporation.

The $186 million debt portion of the transaction was divided into three tranches, in a way similar to a collateralized mortgage obligation. Forty-three million dollars of Series A bonds matured in 1995, $109 million of Series B bonds matured in 1999, and $35 million of Series C bonds matured in 2013. The Series A bondholders received principal and interest payments until the Series A bonds matured. They then received both principal and interest payments until 1999. The Series C bonds were virtually zero-coupon bonds since all principal and interest payments were dedicated to paying the interest and principal of the first two series through 1999. The C tranche began paying principal and interest after the Series B bonds matured in 1999.

By structuring the financing like a collateralized mortgage obligation, First Boston was able to significantly lower the cost of the financing. The loan would otherwise have had a maturity of 28+ years with a 20-year average life. Although the interest rate on the Series C tranche was high, these bonds represented only 18 percent of the issue. The Series A and Series B bonds, with shorter maturities, carried lower rates because the corporate yield curve was upward-sloping. This resulted in a lower overall cost to the borrower than a 28-year single maturity issue. More importantly, perhaps, it is unlikely that $168 million would have been available for a 28-year maturity. First Boston was able to sell the different maturity series to different buyers with specific maturity requirements. Ten insurance companies and one state pension fund participated. The state pension fund was able to participate because the loan carried a single A rating.

United Asset Management: The Use of a Private Placement to Raise Equity. United Asset Management (UAM) is a holding company which acquires institutional investment management firms. These firms continue to operate independently under their own names. UAM provides the acquired firms with investment liquidity and diversification. In return, UAM obtains a reasonably predictable cash flow with almost a 20 percent annual growth rate.

UAM has financed its acquisitions, which total over $8.2 billion under management, through stock and/or cash. The cash is raised through the private placement of equity. The private placement route was chosen because of the short four-year history of the company as well as the comparatively small size of UAM itself. The company does plan public offerings in the future. This will enable the private equity shareholders to register their securities and to sell them at a later date if they wish.

First Boston was the managing agent for UAM's issues, working with two other investment banks. A key role of the agents was to determine the appropriate securities to sell to buyers and to identify the group of buyers who would be most receptive to the financing. After due diligence was completed, the group determined that straight equity would be more attractive to UAM than convertible debentures, the alternative choice. The offering price was based on historic and prospective cash flows. Earnings were not used in the valuation because they were distorted by noncash deductions unique to this transaction. To price the issue, the prospective growth rates in UAM's cash flows were compared to the growth rates of publicly traded mutual fund holding companies. From this, the issue was priced at a multiple of 10 times the latest 12 months' cash flow.

Distribution was conducted by the three agents in the United States and Europe. Approximately 125 offerees were approached. Twenty-six million dollars was raised with 25 buyers eventually participating. The buyers were chiefly money managers, the group most familiar with the asset management industry and UAM's strategy for growth and profitability.

THE ROLE OF PRIVATE PLACEMENTS IN ACQUISITION-ORIENTED FINANCING

Acquisition-oriented high-yield or junk bond financing has come of age in recent years as an integral part of the wave of leveraged buyouts and acquisitions. The private placement market has played an important role in their success. It is estimated, for example, that in 1985 about one-third of the over $20 billion of acquisition-related financing took place in the private placement market. The motives for using the private market in such financings and the ways in which they differ from more traditional private financings are discussed in the following material.

Typically, private placements are used as part of an overall financing package in leveraged buyouts. The dominant motive for using the private market is the speed with which a private placement can be lined up. Speed is usually of paramount importance in such leveraged buyouts and hostile takeovers. A private financing, that is, the commitments to participate in such a financing, can be obtained within a matter of hours or a few days from lenders in the private market. Such commitments provide a signal that an acquiror has the financing available to implement a takeover.

Another motive for using the private market in acquisition-oriented financings is that forecasts of revenues and sales can be provided. In contrast, the SEC does not allow such projections in a public offering. In cases where forecasts of future earnings are important in selling a deal, then, a private placement will normally be used.

A third motive for using the private market is that it enables the deal-makers to reach a large pool of money that would otherwise not be available. The large life insurance companies, for example, prefer to lend in the private placement market provided yields are attractive.

Private financings arranged in conjunction with acquisition-oriented financings differ in one important way from traditional private placements. They typically provide for subsequent SEC registration. Private lenders will accept a more lenient set of terms and provisions on an issue if they have an option to sell their position before maturity. By providing registration rights, then, an acquiror–borrower can avoid the restrictive terms and provisions of a traditional private placement.

In the high-yield market, private placements typically carry yields that are 0.25 to 1.25 percent higher than comparable publicly offered bonds. There appear to be two reasons for this. First, in a leveraged buyout where speed is of the essence, the buyer can extract a premium in exchange for a quick commitment to the deal. Secondly, the yield premium frequently serves as a substitute for an equity kicker which the lenders would otherwise demand for accepting the higher risks of such deals.

The lenders in acquisition-oriented financings are segmented along traditional lines. The buyers of the private bonds are the traditional lenders in the private market—life insurance companies. The buyers of the publicly offered paper are savings and loan associations and dedicated high-yield mutual funds. Fidelity, Putnam, IDS, Keystone, and T. Rowe Price all have high-yield funds with dollar amounts of up to $2.5 billion.

7 Initial Public Offerings

DENNIS E. LOGUE

This chapter deals with the market for initial public offerings (IPOs), which are new issues of unseasoned common stock. It begins with a general discussion of the market, moves to a treatment of underwriter selection and contracts, then focuses upon new-issue pricing, underwriter compensation, and other costs.

THE MARKET

The market for IPOs is perhaps one of the most volatile and erratic of all financial markets. First, the size of the market varies greatly. In 1977, for example, there were only 15 IPOs, raising just $124 million. In 1983, 464 issues of more than $3 million each amounted to $9.5 billion in risk capital. Table 7.1 shows hows volatile the activity in this market is.

Second, the price behavior of new issues of unseasoned stock is just as varied. In some periods, stocks are priced at extraordinarily high multiples of earnings or book value, or, if both of these are negative, sometimes even sales. In other periods, extremely promising companies sell at multiples of earnings or book value that are on a par with those of very mature, often declining firms.

The "hot issue" or "hot market" phenomenon is far more pronounced in the market for IPOs than for other financial assets. That is, activity and price volatility is either very high or very low. There seems to be no "normal" period. This characteristic of the market gives rise to some surprising results.

One would expect that during very slow periods in the IPO market, only the very best companies would come forward to sell stock. Similarly, during the "hot" periods, companies with no earnings or assets and very little promise would flood the market. This pattern would lead one to expect lower corporate failure rates for stocks sold during slow periods than during "hot" periods. In fact, the opposite seems to be the case.

In an interesting yet seemingly overlooked study, Michael Brown [3] showed that "hot" market companies tended to be more successful, at least in terms of survival. Companies going public during quiet periods in the market have experienced

Table 7.1. Initial Public Offerings 1977–1983

	Number of Issues	Amount $Millions
1977	15	$ 124
1978	20	206
1979	48	362
1980	95	1,092
1981[a]	233	2,643
1982[a]	76	999
1983[a]	464	9,451

[a] Data are for issues of $3 million or more only.

Source: Drexel Burnham Lambert, Inc., *Public Offerings of Corporate Securities*, various years.

much higher failure rates. The reason very likely is that strong companies can afford to wait for opportune times to raise capital.

The lesson from this analysis, if there is one, is that both issuers and investors need to be especially careful in selling or buying IPOs. From the issuer's standpoint particularly, it is best to wait for a period of market enthusiasm, rather than to rush to the equity market at the first sign of a need for new equity. Patience generally will yield substantially higher valuations, thereby providing more capital for a given fraction of the company, than would be the case in an unenthusiastic environment.

Although a strong track record is helpful to a company wishing to sell securities to the public for the first time, it is not necessary. Many companies are able to enter this market with very little more than a promise. Full disclosure of performance and open discussion of prospects are crucial, however.

THE OFFERING PROCESS

Securities sold to the public must be registered with the Securities and Exchange Commission (SEC). Registration entails payment of legal and accounting expenses to prepare the Registration Statement. This statement describes the business and how the proceeds of the offering will be used, and includes some background on the principal executives, audited financial statements, and other pertinent data. Many states also have "blue sky laws" that must be satisfied before a corporation can sell securities in those states. These laws, which are designed to protect potential investors, have the principal effect of barring very new, start-up ventures from access to the market in those states. For example, the State of Massachusetts did not permit the sale of stock in Apple Computers to its residents (Brealey and Myers [21], p. 301).

There are two types of registration statements: essentially a short form and a long form. The short form is written under Regulation A (Reg. A) and is intended for issues of $300,000 or less. It is really an offering circular. Issuers who wish to sell more than $300,000 worth of stock must file a complete registration statement; these typically run to 50 or 60 printed pages.

The first part of a registration statement is distributed to investors in the form of a preliminary prospectus or "Red Herring." Using this, underwriters can get a feel for how strong demand for the security will be, although as yet there is no specific price per share mentioned. After the SEC permits use of the preliminary prospectus, the underwriting syndicate meets, sets a price, prints the price in the (official) prospectus, sends it to the SEC for (routine) acceptance, then sells the stock to the public. While it might take two to three months to plan and execute an IPO, only a few days or even hours elapse between SEC acceptance of the preliminary prospectus and sale of the offering.

UNDERWRITING

Issuer's Goals

The issuer's principal concern is in receiving as much as possible for the portion of the company being sold the the public. Underwriters often try to discourage this value maximization. They argue that if an issue is priced so aggressively that its price immediately falls in after-market trading, the investing public will remember and penalize the company by being less responsive to subsequent offerings. In other words, investors will push down the price of the traded stock before the next issue, or underwriters, in order to sell a large new issue, will have to price it below the market price of the traded common stock.

This notion has not been tested empirically, but it is not entirely logical that such a penalty exists or would work this way. The argument assumes a very inelastic demand for the new common stock of seasoned companies, a demand made more inelastic by virtue of the fact that several months (or more likely years) earlier short-term investors in the IPO may have taken a loss.

Another oft-heard reason for underpricing is that it cushions the stock from a market decline that may carry the stock price down. This either causes a disruption in the distribution of the stock or causes a loss to investors in the aftermarket. This may harm the underwriter, but will not affect the issuer if the underwriting contract is the customary firm-commitment contract. In brief the argument, as advanced by underwriters, seems to be quite self-serving.

A more compelling reason why underwriters argue against pricing new issues fully is that the expense of marketing an aggressively priced IPO may exceed the extra money raised by a wide margin. In addition, an after-market price rise reduces the likelihood that any suit will be brought against the underwriter for failure to do a thorough "due-diligence" investigation. (This refers to the underwriter's certification that the material in the prospectus is accurate.) The underwriter's tendency to price low is constrained by the prospect of losing future business. If shares always experience substantial price rises right after the offering, new issuers will not seek out such an underwriter. The nature of competition in the investment banking market places limits on this sort of behavior.

The issuer's second goal is broad distribution. One reason for this is fear of outside interference in the operation of the company. No issuer wants to be vulnerable to a takeover threat soon after going public. The more widespread the distribution of ownership, the more costly it is likely to be for an outsider to accumulate a significant block of stock. The second reason for broad distribution is that it is related to more active trading stock, hence assures greater liquidity and valuation accuracy of the aftermarket.

A third goal of the issuer is an active aftermarket. Frequently, an issuer will deal only with an investment banking firm that can and will make a market in the stock after the public offering.

All these goals are reflected in the issuer's choice of underwriter.

UNDERWRITING CONTRACTS

There are three types of contracts with underwriters that an issuer might enter.

The first is a "firm-commitment" contract, where the underwriter guarantees sale of the issue at a specified price. The underwriter takes the risk here. If an issue fails to sell at the agreed-upon price, the underwriter may lose money because the unsold shares either will be sold at a discount or put in inventory and sold later. From an issuer's perspective, this is the safest way to raise equity capital. It is also the most expensive, because underwriters require compensation for bearing this risk. This is the most common type of offering.

The second form is a "best-efforts" contract. In this case, the underwriter agrees to sell as many of the registered shares at the agreed-upon price as possible. What is not sold is returned to the issuer. If some minimum number is not sold, the deal is canceled, and investors who bought can get their money back. The underwriter bears much less risk in this arrangement; the issuer, however, bears more. The charge for this sort of a contractual arrangement customarily is less than for a firm-commitment contract. Over the period 1977–1982, this method was used in 35 percent of the offerings, accounting for 13 percent of the proceeds of IPOs (Ritter [15]).

The firm-commitment and best-efforts contracts are the most common kinds of underwriting contracts. Most issuers choose one or the other, depending on the value of the "put option" the underwriter offers in a firm commitment relative to the charge for the contract. Generally, smaller IPOs will use best-efforts, while larger IPOs will use or at least try hard to arrange, a firm-commitment contract. The best-efforts contract generally is best when the pricing uncertainty is unusually high. It tends to shift the risk of overpricing to the company rather than to the investment banker. A minimum-sale clause also limits the risk of investors buying overpriced stock. When the minimum is not sold, it means the issue was overpriced, but investors who did buy the stock can get their money back.

The third type of contract is the "all-or-none." It is not used nearly as frequently as either of the other two contracts, but it sometimes appears. In this arrangement, the underwriter either will sell an entire offering or cancel the deal altogether. Risk is borne by both issuer and underwriter. Frequently, if most but not all of an issue is sold, the underwriter will buy the remainder. The charge for this is somewhere between those for the other two types of contracts. The underwriter bears risk in the sense that if all the shares are not sold, that is, if the IPO is very much overpriced, no underwriting commissions are paid. The issuer, of course, gets no money and at the same time must pay accounting, printing, and perhaps some fixed advisory fees to the underwriter.

Syndicates

IPOs are sometimes underwritten by single firms, but it is far more often the case that the IPO is made by a syndicate.

The issue originates with the managing underwriter. This is the firm with which the issuer deals directly. The managing underwriter (or in some cases of very large issues, two or more co-managers) forms an underwriting syndicate. That is, the manager convinces other firms to share the risk of the underwriting. This group constitutes the risk-bearing or underwriting group. It is joined by another group of firms, and together the two groups constitute the selling group. This collection of investment bankers and securities dealers comprise the syndicate.

Of the total underwriting compensation, the manager gets roughly 15 to 20 percent, the underwriting group 10 to 30 percent, and the selling group 50 to 75 percent. A manager who is part of the underwriting group and the selling group collects from all elements of the syndicate.

Decisions on pricing are made by the managing underwriter with the syndicate's approval. Generally, if a syndicate member disagrees with the pricing decision, it will be allowed to drop out of the syndicate. The risk to that member, of course, is being excluded from future, more palatable deals.

Syndicate behavior is dictated by the manager. Syndicate members agree to sell the issue for the same price. That is, so long as the syndicate exists, the stock cannot be sold at any price other than the offering price. This is known as the "fixed price offering system." When a firm commitment moves too slowly, however, the syndicate may dissolve before all the stock is sold. All underwriters then are free to sell securities for whatever price they can get. IPOs that are "overpriced," that is, hard to sell, ultimately may be discounted. The NASD and the SEC prohibit raising the price of an issue that was quite obviously "underpriced" initially; syndicate members cannot mark up the price of an IPO (or any security for that matter) that is in voracious demand by investors. They thus bear downside risk, but have no real upside possibilities in the pricing decision.

During the offering period, the syndicate manager has the approval of the SEC as well as other syndicate members to stabilize the market. This means the manager can buy shares or sell shares short in order to keep the price unchanged throughout the offering period. Although there are no studies of extent and significance of such price stabilization activity, investment bankers report it is an important activity during periods of generally weak demand.

THE PRICING OF ISSUES

Short-Run Price Performance

The evidence is overwhelming that short-run rates of return generated by IPO investment are extraordinarily high. This observation leads to the conclusion that initial prices are set too low. At the same time, it says nothing about how they are set.

Customarily, returns have been estimated as excess returns. That is, the rate of return on a broad-based market portfolio, such as the NYSE Index, the S&P Index, or the NASDAQ Index, is subtracted from the actual rate of return on the stock. The result is the excess return. Some attempts have been made to adjust the excess returns for risk, but such adjustments make little differences in the results: returns on IPOs are, on balance, so much greater than returns on the market that no conceivable risk adjustment would yield a conclusion of no abnormal returns. Table 7.2 shows the broad results of many studies on IPO price performance. All point to exceptional short-run returns. (See also Smith [17] for further evidence.)

There are some regularities in short-term performance. The larger the company and the greater the proportion of the issue that is a secondary offering, the lower returns seem to be. Perhaps underwriters find it easier to price large companies and have strong incentives to price more aggressively when dealing with principals who are selling some of their own shares.

Another regularity has to do with the underwriter. Hayes [4] offers a useful scheme for classifying investment bankers that seems to explain a large portion of new-issue price performance. Logue [8], in a study differentiating underwriters, found that the average excess returns one month after the issue for so-called prestigious underwriters was 20.8 percent. For nonprestigious underwriters it was 52.1 percent.

Table 7.2. Studies on IPOs' Rates of Return to Investors

Study	Time Period	Number of Issues	Excess Returns from Time of Issue	
			One Week	One Month
McDonald–Fisher [10]	1969	142	28.5%	34.6%
Ibbotson [5]	1960–1969	128		11.4
Ibbotson–Jaffe [6]	1960–1970	2650	N.A.	16.8
Logue [8]	1965–1969	250		41.7
Neuberger–Hammond [10]	1965–1969	816	17.1	19.1
Block–Stanley [1]	1974–1978	102	5.9	3.3
Neuberger–La Chapelle [13]	1975–1980	118	27.7	33.6

Table 7.3. Average Excess Return by Underwriter Tier

Time Period for Performance Measurement	Tier I	Tier II	Tier III
Offer—1 week	5.3%	9.6%	43.3%
Offer—1 month	2.5	1.9	58.3
1 week—1 month	−3.2	−3.4	17.4
Sample size	20	32	66

Source: Neuberger and La Chappelle [13], Exhibits 2 and 5.

In a more recent study, Neuberger and La Chapelle [13] divided underwriters into three categories. Tier I firms are special bracket or bulge groups plus major firms. Tier II are the nonprestigious underwriters used in other studies. These include large regional firms. Tier III consists of firms who manage new issues with an initial offer share price of $1.00 or less. Table 7.3 shows these results, which support the notion that there are significant differences among investment bankers.

Literally interpreted, this table suggests that who does the underwriting matters greatly: more prestigious underwriters price more aggressively, hence allow for lower after-market returns. Such a literal interpretation is inappropriate, however. For starters, there are substantial differences in the size and quality of issues that each underwriting tier sells, and features of an offering, such as size and maturity, often make it easier to price some issues closer to their true market value.

There are several competing hypotheses as to why IPOs seem to be so underpriced at offering. One is underwriter risk aversion. The underwriter wants to be sure both of selling the issue and avoiding litigation over inadequate due-diligence investigation. The second hypothesis is cost. It may be less expensive for the issuer to sell stock at what appears to be too low a price than to price it fully and pay the underwriter the necessary fee to market it at that price. While this may account for underpricing of 5 to 10 percent, it certainly cannot account for the magnitude of underpricing that almost all studies observe.

A third hypothesis is underwriter error. The market is just too volatile and uncertain to price securities with any precision. Unfortunately, none of these hypotheses has been thoroughly explored, nor do they seem amenable to testing. (See Smith [17] for an elaboration of some of these.)

Pricing Methods

The art and science of pricing an IPO is fraught with pitfalls. Two approaches can be discussed briefly.

Using Comparable Companies. One method investment bankers use is historical, comparable, or proxy company analysis. They look at recent issues of companies in similar businesses and other recent IPOs of similar size and quality to obtain pricing benchmarks. They examine the pricing of comparable issues and their aftermarket performance, then try to exploit this information in pricing the next new issue they will bring to market.

This approach, alas, is very unscientific, and often can be misleading. Table 7.4 shows some pertinent data from 1983. In this year, the IPO market started strongly, then suddenly faltered. Evaluating comparables issued at a different time, even a day away, could have (and perhaps did) lead to some serious errors.

The table suggests the first two quarters were "hot," while the last two were considerably cooler. Substantial variation quarter-to-quarter reduces the viability of the comparable method. And if anything, day-to-day variation may display even wider disparities than quarter-to-quarter variation, even for companies that seem, at least superficially, to be comparable.

Identifying comparable companies in the high-technology areas is extraordinarily difficult. The products they design, manufacture, or sell are all subtly different, hence so are their markets. One would think identifying comparables is easier in more traditional areas, but that is not the case.

Table 7.5 provides data that might have been gathered in evaluating comparables for the IPO of Knoll International, a furniture manufacturer. It shows a prior furniture company IPO and includes a similarly low-tech company offering made the very same day. It also shows how Knoll was priced and what happened to its price: it dropped but did not trade down to LADD's level. Moreover, all three were priced just about correctly; there was no dramatic up-or-down price movement soon after offering. But the pricing benchmarks, PE and market-to-book ratios differed dramatically among these companies.

On balance, evaluating similar, recent offerings does not provide very good standards regarding earnings multiples, book value multiples, or any other guidelines. The problem is that "comparables" probably are not comparable. Differences in expected earnings growth rates, financial and operating leverage, dividend likelihood,

Table 7.4. IPO Features in 1983

Quarter	Number of Issues of $3 Million or More	Number of Issues that Fell in Price Two Weeks After Offering	Number of Companies Sold with No or Negative Earnings
First	53	9	16
Second	104	17	31
Third	148	68	37
Fourth	159	66	36

Quarter	Average Offering Price/Book Value[a]	Average PE Ratio[a]	Average Two-Week Price Appreciation
First	11.5	37.9	17.2%
Second	19.1	34.3	21.3
Third	9.3	27.7	2.1
Fourth	11.2	19.0	9.8

[a] Based on a sample of issues with positive book values and positive earnings.

Source: Drexel Burnham Lambert, Inc., *Public Offerings of Corporate Securities*, 1983.

Table 7.5. Comparable Data Pricing

Offer Date	Company	Business	Size of Offering ($ M)	Latest 12 Months' EPS	Offering PE	Offering Price Book Value	Returns over Two Weeks
8/4/83	LADD Furniture	Furniture	$36.25	1.31	11.1	6.85	5.2%
8/9/83	Crain Books	Bookstore	$62.50	52	48.1	25.71	−6.0%
8/9/83	Knoll Furniture Internatl.		$56.00	.75	21.3	5.37	−8.6%

and many other factors play a role in making each pricing different enough from other recent transactions to mandate the use of a model that simply does not exist. At the present, there is no publicly available, statistical model that can value all the differences among companies so that benchmark pricing (i.e., using PEs or market-to-book ratios) can be used with any great confidence.

Discounted Cash Flow Analysis

An alternative to the comparable-company method for determining an initial offering price is discounted cash flow (DCF) analysis. For pricing new issues, it works in the following way.

First, project the company's future free cash flow as if the present offering were successful in raising the necessary cash. Carry the projection out several years, or until the time that a company's cash flow growth is likely to approximate the industry growth rate, that is, until the company becomes mature relative to the industry.

Second, project a terminal value for the company. This is the value it is assigned upon its blending into an existing industry grouping. Here again, we are confronted by the question of comparable companies. The only meaningful way to determine a terminal value is to determine a market value at that time. To estimate this, industry average PEs, market-to-book ratios, or industry growth rates are necessary once more. Again, this says our company is like the others.

While this requires a great leap of faith, it is not so great as that required to use comparables directly in the initial pricing decision. The reason is that by the time a company begins to mature relative to its industry, its growth rate approximates that of its industry; and very often its financial and operating leverage does, as well. The company "grows" into comparability. The terminal value can be estimated by taking the company's earnings or its book value and applying long-run industry average PE multiples or market-to-book ratios. Alternatively, the company's free cash flow in the terminal year can be treated as a perpetuity that will grow at the industry growth rate. (As a practical matter, there will not be much difference in the value of this as a perpetuity or as, say, a 10-year annuity, but mathematically the perpetuity is much easier to handle.)

We now have a terminal value, a market value for the company's free cash flows after its super-growth phase has ended, and a set of free cash flows during the supergrowth phase. (Note: because of reinvestment for growth, the free cash flows during the supergrowth phase may be zero, or negative if more common stock issues are expected to be sold.) This series of flows must next be discounted back to the present. The discount rate must reflect the risk of the company, yet it may not be possible to evaluate risk without some longer history. Accordingly, a reasonable "first-cut" may be made using Ibbotson's estimates of returns on stocks of small companies. He estimates historical returns on different types of investment instruments, and updates them annually. Over the period 1926–1982, small stocks had a geometric average annual return of 12.4 percent.[1]

---

[1] Pricing an IPO should take into account compound returns to investors over a comparatively long period. The arithmetic mean return might provide a good estimate of next year's return, but it has no

The geometric average of 12.4 percent is the long-run return for a stock of average risk. The very small companies that are going to the market initially are likely to involve considerably different risk. Without trading data—lacking by definition for IPOs—it may not be too unreasonable to make a first pass at pricing the company supposing it were of average risk. (Some experimentation using different discount rates may be helpful, too.) To do so, apply the chosen discount rate to the free cash flows and the terminal value, then bring these values back to the present. The result is what the company will be worth after the IPO.

Next determine what portion of the company must be sold to the public to generate the requisite amount of cash. The total value of the company can now be arbitrarily divided into shares. Many underwriters like to price new issues in the $10 to $20 range, so this should be a consideration in determining how many shares the company will have outstanding after the offering. The issue price emerges from these calculations.

To illustrate, suppose the company's current worth is estimated at $20 million. The company needs $5 million, including fees it must pay the underwriter, so 25 percent of the company must be sold to the public. Pick a number of shares to divide the $20 million into; assume two million. Each share will be worth $10. So the offering will be 500,000 shares at $10 apiece. If one million shares were chosen as the total number, the IPO price would be $20 a share for 250,000 shares.

The DCF analysis seems quite precise. It may be more scientific than the comparable approach, but there is no assurance its use will prevent the sorts of return experience, the evidence of seemingly systematic underpricing, that has marked this market in the past.

No matter what method is used, there is no substitute for a good feel for the market at precisely the time of offering. This knowledge can help in adjusting the price so that issuers do not get too little for their stock and investors do not attain rewards far in excess of the risk they bear.

COSTS OF AN IPO

Types of Investment Banker Compensation

Underwriters may be compensated for advising, bearing risk, and distributing securities in three distinct ways. The first is the opportunity to buy the securities at a discount from the offering price. The difference between the IPO price to the public and the price paid the company is the underwriter spread. This is distributed among the manager, the underwriters, and the selling group.

---

multiperiod feature. That is, the arithmetic return over a two-year or longer period will be misleading as to actual returns. Suppose a stock rose by 100 percent this period and fell by 50 percent next period. The arithmetic mean return is +25 percent. The acutal return over the two-year period, however, is zero. And this is clear from the geometric mean return: $[(1.00 + 1.00) (1.00 - .50)]^{1/2} - 1 = 0$ percent. Accordingly, the geometric mean return seems to offer a better estimate of the appropriate market discount rate.

The second type of compensation occurs is warrants. Underwriters often request warrants to purchase the common stock from the issuer as a form of remuneration in addition to the underwriting spread. Such warrants are exercisable for several years and at prices equal to or above the initial offering price. With this kind of compensation, the better the stock does, the more valuable the warrants become. This form of compensation could encourage underwriters to underprice securities at the offering because the conversion price is customarily linked to it. The lower the initial price, the more valuable the warrants, everything else equal.

The third form of compensation is cheap stock. Although the National Association of Securities Dealers frowns upon this practice, on rare occasions underwriters are allowed to purchase securities at prices well below the offering price.

Two other arrangements connect issuers to underwriters. While it is difficult to assign monetary values to them, they are nonetheless financially valuable. First, often the manager of an IPO gets a right of first refusal, generally for a predetermined number of years. First-refusal rights give the underwriter who managed the IPO the opportunity to evaluate every subsequent offering. If the manager can match the best alternative arrangement, the new offering of securities is awarded to that manager. Second, managers often get representation on the board of directors of the IPO firm. They then have the opportunity for direct influence on the future course of the company.

Cash Compensation to Underwriters

It is difficult, if not impossible, to estimate with any precision the monetary value of all the noncash compensation received in a particular deal. The cash component of compensation is readily available. For IPOs, underwriting discounts generally range from 5 to 10 percent, although from time to time isolated issues command slightly higher discounts.

Table 7.6 provides some data on underwriting discounts collected for a random sample of IPOs offered during the period 1981–1983. It shows clearly that underwriting discounts vary inversely by size of issue. In addition, Logue and Lindvall [9] also suggest that the security's risk as well as general market conditions influence the size of the spread.

Other Expenses to an Issuer

An IPO includes other expenses to be paid: legal fees, accounting fees, and printing costs. These will tend to vary with the complexity of the firm and its size. Such expenses for an IPO would not differ from expenses for any company selling securities; all are subject to the same expense, so to provide some notion on their magnitude we can examine such expenses for all public stock issues. Table 7.7 contains measures of such expenses broken down by size of offering.

Note that expenses as a percentage of the offering decline with issue size. This reflects a substantial invariant component. Legal fees, for instance, would not increase proportionally with the size of the issue or the size of the company.

Table 7.6. Underwriters' Cash Compensation (Discounts) as a Percentage of Offering Value (1981–1983)

Size of Issue	Number of Companies					
	5.0–5.99% Discount	6.0–6.99% Discount	7.0–7.99% Discount	8.0–8.99% Discount	9.0–9.99% Discount	10% Discount and Above
$3.0–6.99M	0	0	8	24	49	2 (11.5%)
$7.0–13.99M	0	1	41	6	0	0
$14.0–24.99M	0	15	20	0	0	0
$25.0–49.99M	0	23	13	0	0	0
$50M and above	7	15	3	0	0	0

Source: Drexel Burnham Lambert, *Public Offerings of Corporate Securities*, various years.

Table 7.7. Expenses of an Underwritten Offering

Size of Issue ($M)	Expenses as a Percentage of Offering
0.50–0.99	6.8%
1.00–1.99	4.9
2.00–4.99	2.9
5.00–9.99	1.5
10.00–19.99	0.7
20.00–49.99	0.4
50.00–99.99	0.2
100.00–500.00	0.1

Source: Smith [17], Table 1, p. 277.

Accounting fees, however, will very likely rise with the size of the company and the complexity of the businesses. Not reflected in the data is the value of company management time spent on planning, negotiating, and preparing the IPO.

SUMMARY

The IPO market is an exciting one. It is a market rife with uncertainties and very sensitive decisions. The issuer has to make choices regarding the investment banker, and the issuer and the investment banker have to choose the best investment banking contract (firm-commitment, best-efforts, or all-or-none). Pricing is one of the most difficult parts of the transaction. The empirical evidence suggests that underwriters tend to underprice in an effort to move issues quickly, hence economizing on marketing costs and helping investors to economize on information-gathering costs.

The administrative costs as a percentage of principal value of an IPO vary inversely with the size of issue. This is true for investment banking spreads as well as other administrative costs such as legal and accounting fees.

There are a host of other issues surrounding IPOs. Logue [8] and Logue and Lindvall [9] found that IPOs that contained large amounts of secondary offerings—that is, sales by early investors—did not perform as well as those in which all the proceeds went to the company. Our hypothesis is such sales imply to the market a lack of faith in the company by early investors and founders and thus dampen enthusiasm for the IPO. This market dampening should, however, already be reflected in the initial pricing, not the after-market returns. So why does it seem to manifest itself this way?

Other questions revolve around choices of underwriting contracts and compensation schedules. Again, there are plausible hypotheses regarding why things are as they are, but no solid empirical verifications.

What all this points to is that investors and companies approaching the IPO market should do so with caution and skepticism.

REFERENCES

1. Block, S. and M. Stanley, "Financial Characteristics and Price Movement Patterns of Companies Approaching the Unseasoned Securities Market in the Late 1970s," *Financial Management*, 9 (Winter 1980), pp. 30–36.

2. Brealey, R. and S. Myers, *Principles of Corporate Finance*, 2nd ed., New York: McGraw Hill, 1985, Chapter 15.

3. Brown, Michael J., "Post Offering Experience of Companies Going Public," *Journal of Business*, 43 (January 1970), pp. 10–18.

4. Hayes, S.L., "Investment Banking: Power Structure in Flux," *Harvard Business Review*, 49 (1971), pp. 136–152.

5. Ibbotson, R.G., "Price Performance of Common Stock New Issues," *Journal of Financial Economics*, 2 (1975), pp. 235–272.

6. Ibbotson, R.G. and J.F. Jaffe, "Hot Issue Markets," *Journal of Finance*, 30 (1975), pp. 1027–1042.

7. Ibbotson, R.G., R.A. Sinquefield, and L.B. Siegel, "Historical Returns on Investment Instruments," in D.E. Logue, ed. *Handbook of Modern Finance*, New York: Warren, Gorham and Lamont, 1984, Chapter 18.

8. Logue, D.E., "On the Pricing of Unseasoned Equity Issues," *Journal of Financial and Quantitative Analysis*, 9 (1973), pp. 91–104.

9. Logue, D.E. and John R. Lindvall, "The Behavior of Investment Bankers: An Econometric Investigation," *Journal of Finance*, 29 (March 1974), pp. 203–215.

10. McDonald, J.G. and A.K. Fisher, "New Issue Stock Price Behavior," *Journal of Finance*, 27 (1972), pp. 165–177.

11. Mandelker, G. and A. Ravin, "Investment Banking: An Economic Analysis of Optimal Underwriting Contracts," *Journal of Finance*, 32 (1977), pp. 683–694.

12. Neuberger, B.M. and T. Hammond, "A Study of Underwriter's Experience with Unseasoned New Issues," *Journal of Financial and Quantitative Analysis*, 10 (1974), pp. 165–177.

13. Neuberger, B.M. and C.A. La Chapelle, "Unseasoned New Issue Price Performance on Three Tiers: 1975–1980," *Financial Management*, 12 (Autumn 1983), pp. 23–28.

14. Parker, G.G.C., "Investment Banking," in D.E. Logue, ed., *Handbook of Modern Finance*, New York: Warren, Gorham and Lamont, 1984, Chapter 4.

15. Ritter, J.R., "The Choice Between Firm Commitment and Best Effort Contracts," University of Pennsylvania, unpublished manuscript, 1985.

16. Smith, C.R., "Alternative Methods for Raising Capital: Rights versus Underwritten Offerings," *Journal of Financial Economics*, 5 (December 1977), pp. 273–307.

17. Smith, C.R., "Investment Banking and the Capital Acquisition Process," *Journal of Financial Economics*, 14 (Spring 1986), pp. 000–000.

8 Financing High-Technology, Emerging-Growth Companies

A. ROBERT TOWBIN
J. PETER WILLIAMSON

At the risk of some oversimplification, the financing of high-technology, emerging-growth companies can be classified into three stages: the venture-capital stage, the initial public offering of securities (IPO), and later public or private financing. In this chapter we are concerned with the first two of these stages and with the investment banking firms that provide or arrange for the financing.

Three kinds of investment bankers participate in financing high-tech, emerging-growth companies. One kind is represented by Alex. Brown & Sons, Inc.; Hambrecht & Quist; Montgomery Securities; and Robertson, Colman & Stephens. All are relatively small in size, ranking in capital in 1985 forty-fifth, seventy-second, eighty-third, and unranked, respectively, among all U.S. investment banking firms, according to *Institutional Investor*. (Alex. Brown, however, added to its capital in a first public offering in 1986.) Each has a regional (non-New York City) base and relatively limited capability in fixed-income securities and retail distribution. All have specialized in the financing of emerging-growth companies, and some in high-tech, emerging-growth companies.

The second kind of investment banker includes some of the largest, best regarded national firms, a number of which have only in recent years turned to financing high-tech, emerging-growth companies. Morgan Stanley & Co. and Goldman Sachs & Co. are examples, as are Prudential-Bache Securities, Paine Webber, Inc., Salomon Brothers, Inc., and Smith Barney, Harris Upham & Co., Inc. While some of these firms have a relatively short history at this kind of financing, they can bring enormous resources, including capital and skilled people, to it. Other firms with strength in this kind of financing are somewhat smaller. These include Ladenburg, Thalmann & Co., Inc., and Cowen & Co.

Finally, L.F. Rothschild, Unterberg, Towbin by itself constitutes a third kind of firm, both larger (ranking twenty-third by capital in 1985) and more diversified than most of those that comprise the first kind, yet far smaller and less well-known than most of the examples of the second kind (although clearly a national firm).

C.E. Unterberg, Towbin Co. originated as a small over-the-counter trading firm in 1932. After World War II it became the preeminent investment banker for the high-technology companies of the period. Most of these companies in the late 1940s and 1950s were connected with the aircraft industry, and most developed aircraft instrumentation. In 1977, the firm merged with L.F. Rothschild & Co., a fixed-income sales and trading firm. with arbitrage, retail distribution, and money management.

Both L.F. Rothschild, Unterberg, Towbin and Alex. Brown & Sons made first public offerings of stock themselves in 1986, and some statistics from their prospectuses indicate the volume of business they have done. Table 8.1 is based on the prospectus disclosure. The figures give some indication of the volatility of the business. After a boom in 1983, there was a substantial decline in 1984.

Since the beginning of the 1970s there has been a significant change in the financing of new ventures, particularly high-tech ventures. The expertise of the investment banker, up to the point of a first public offering, has become less important than it once was. Venture-capital organizations, possessing all the necessary expertise and sophistication, now offer to handle the financing stages preceding the first public offering and to provide financing advice to the new venture itself. At this early stage, then, the investment banker may be welcomed as an investor rather than a supplier of expertise.

At the same time, a new company, and the venture capitalists that are financing it, are likely to be aware that at some point an investment banker will be required for a first public offering, so it may be useful to involve two or three investment bankers long before the public offering takes place. Not surprisingly, what these conditions have led to is a perception on the part of investment bankers that the way to get first public offering business is to become actively involved with the company long before the first public offering. As a result, we have seen lively competition among investment bankers to become investors and to join boards of

Table 8.1. Corporate Issues Managed or Co-Managed

	L.F. Rothschild, Unterberg, Towbin				Alex. Brown & Sons	
	Number of Issues		Amount (millions)		Number of Issues	Amount (millions)
	Equity	Debt	Equity	Debt	Equity & Debt	Equity & Debt
1981	39	2	987	200		
1982	22	6	628	260		
1983	66	9	2,331	441	71	2,156
1984	12	3	171	127	26	632
1985	24	12	493	659	41	1,288

directors of promising new ventures at an early stage. Naturally, the venture capitalists and the company to be financed are happy to exploit this competition and play one investment banker against another.

One of the developments that has taken place among investment bankers engaged in the financing of new ventures has been the almost universal practice of establishing a venture-capital fund. Private placements by investment bankers at the early stage of a new venture have not disappeared, but they have largely been replaced by two kinds of venture-capital funds: those that are independent of investment bankers and those established by the investment bankers themselves. L.F. Rothschild, Unterberg, Towbin was formed at a time when the firm and its partners did not have a great deal of capital to put into new ventures. Their primary financing activity then was underwriting first public offerings, as well as arranging private placements of securities with clients of the firm. It was not until the firm had grown and accumulated capital that it was able to make significant investments in new ventures on its own. At this stage, to reconcile the servicing of investor customers and the direct participation of the firm in new ventures, a venture-capital fund was organized.

Competition among investment banking firms is to some extent a function of the size and activity of their respective venture-capital funds. Some of these funds have reached hundreds of millions of dollars, which means that some firms have substantial pools of money to draw on as they approach a new venture seeking private financing. Investment bankers with smaller venture-capital funds, particularly if they cannot supply substantial capital from the firm itself to supplement the fund, are at a disadvantage.

WHAT IS DIFFERENT ABOUT FINANCING HIGH-TECH COMPANIES?

To begin with, a high-tech company at the venture-capital or private financing stage, in anticipation of a first public offering, has a very short operating history. The absence of a track record in achieving and maintaining sales growth and profitability makes the company harder to evaluate and clearly more risky than one with an established record. Analysis of the company is qualitatively different from the analysis of an established business.

The products of a high-tech company almost always have a short life cycle. The risk of company failure here is an industry and technology risk. The company must be able to bring a product to market, exploit its franchise long enough to make that product profitable, and then move on to another product. This risk is very different from the general economic risk, influenced by inflation, interest rates, and growth of the economy, that affects the performance of most established companies.

The management of a high-tech company, at the stage when the underwriter first becomes involved, is likely to consist of engineers, scientists, and technicians rather than business people. The first question than is whether the company has the requisite financial and general management expertise necessary for survival and growth. Some engineers and scientists make good managers and good financial planners, and some do not. Even if the management is capable of handling the company's early years, however, a second question concerns its ability to operate once the company has turned from the invention and product development stage to manufacturing. It is not unusual for founders of a company who are able to deal with the management problems in the early years to find themselves unsuited by temperament and by skill to manage a large manufacturing concern where the critical issues become sales, manufacturing cost control, product quality, inventory, and timely delivery. It is not unlikely that the company will have to go through a significant management change while the underwriter is closely involved with it.

Investment bankers, for the most part, have no compunctions about assisting in the early financing and later underwriting for competing high-tech companies. Indeed, this is beneficial to the investor customers of the firm, who can accumulate a diversified portfolio if they subscribe to many of the firm's underwritings, although those underwritings may be concentrated in high-tech companies, or even a segment of the high-tech industry. Some of the high-tech companies themselves, however, object to their underwriter financing a competitor. This is something to be kept in mind when developing business.

THE IDENTIFICATION AND EVALUATION OF POTENTIAL CORPORATE CLIENTS

We have said above that the evaluation of the high-tech company at an early stage in its development calls for analysis that is qualitatively different from the investor or underwriter analysis of well-established companies or of new companies that are not high-tech.

The promise of the new high-tech company almost always lies in a new product or a new process. It will be crucial to the success of the company that the product or process be valuable, and that the company have some franchise on it. This leads to questions of what the company can do to establish and protect the franchise. Perhaps patent protection is available. The technology may be so difficult to master that a competitor will experience a long learning time attempting to duplicate what the company is doing. In assessing potential competition from large companies, it is commonly assumed that if the market potential for the product or process is modest, enough perhaps to ensure great success for the small new company but not large enough to prove interesting to a large company, then at least one need not worry about competition from the large companies. Also, if the product is likely to be of interest to large competitors, it may be possible to form an alliance with one of them, or find some other way to enable these large companies to benefit from the product without becoming direct competitors.

It is quite likely that the founders of the company will have come up with a first-rate product or process, one that does represent a real innovation. What they may not be as good at doing is assessing the demand for the product, and what they may be least adept at is identifying the basis upon which their franchise must rest. The investment banker probably cannot contribute much to technical improvement of the product or process, but must ensure that any weaknesses in the strategic planning of the management are taken care of by its own research and analytic staff or by consultants hired for the purpose.

Particularly since the new high-tech company does not have an established track record, the reputation of the members of management will be critical. Sometimes these people have a record of establishing and managing new companies. Sometimes they have a record of successful achievement at a larger company. But there are times when they have no track record that will serve to inspire confidence. Clearly this increases the risk of the venture.

We can begin now to pinpoint how the investment banker goes about the evaluation process, and what resources are necessary for this process. Established relationships with the venture-capital community network can be very helpful. Through managements of successful small companies, managements with which the investment banker is closely associated for example, through partners in venture-capital firms, through individual investors, one comes to hear of new opportunities, new companies, and reputable founders of new companies. All this background can help identify an opportunity and build confidence in the managers of the company. Evaluation of the prospects of the new high-tech company is helped by the experience of the underwriter's corporate finance partners with other such companies. This is not so much experience with the technical side of these companies as with the management and financing side and with the economic aspects of exploiting a brilliant product or process.

On the technical side, a strong research group within the investment banking firm is important. The research group can be as helpful to the company itself as to the underwriter. Members of this group can supply information on industry trends that may tend to make the new product or process more or less valuable, as well as developments at competitors or potential competitors that may be important. What they add is a perspective and a broad industry knowledge that the management of the new company may not have. After all, the function of the research group at the underwriting firm is to follow a variety of high-tech industries, while the function of the company management is generally to develop a few products or processes.

For the investment banker to establish a relationship with the company well before the stage of a first public offering means becoming an investor through a venture fund or a private placement at an early stage. It may mean joining the company's board of directors at an early stage. This close involvement provides an opportunity to see what is going on at close range, particularly to evaluate the capability of the management. At the same time, an astute management, possibly aided by a venture-capital firm, will be evaluating the investment banker, or the two or three investment bankers that are likely to be potential underwriters of the company's stock.

STAGES OF FINANCING BEFORE A FIRST PUBLIC OFFERING

The age of the high-tech new venture really began following the Second World War. Most such companies at that time were engaged in developing instrumentation for the aircraft industry. Initial financing took the form of private placements of common stock. The founders of a new company, after they had exhausted their own financial resources and those of their families and friends, would approach an investment banker with a reputation for financing new ventures. The investment banker would assess the opportunity. If it looked attractive it would invest the firm's own money and frequently call on a group of wealthy individuals to participate as well in a private placement of stock. The firm would prepare a booklet on the company, present it to potential investors, and collect a fee from the company for its services.

In the 1960s and 1970s a number of venture-capital firms appeared, raising substantial amounts of money and supplying that money to new ventures. The venture-capital firms do not always purchase common stock. They sometimes buy convertible preferred stock or convertible debt instruments, and often take warrants for the purchase of common stock. These venture-capital funds provide direct competition to the investment banker. Some of them have very large amounts of capital available, they have considerable experience and expertise, and they have developed good contacts in the high-tech, emerging-growth company industry. Their competition, however, is limited to the financing preceding a first public offering. They do not act as underwriters (although one venture capital fund, Cable, Howse & Ragen, has formed an investment banking firm to extend its activities to underwriting).

As the independent venture-capital firms assumed a large role in the early financing of new high-tech companies, investment banking firms changed their way of doing business. A firm creates its own in-house venture-capital fund by putting some of its own money into the fund, with the balance of the money coming from investors. The manager of the fund decides whether to invest in a new venture. The chief benefit of this method of financing over the old method of investing firm money, and perhaps including a group of individual investors, is that there is no longer a question of who participates in the best financings and who in the least attractive. Because the financing is done through the venture-capital fund, no investor, including the investment banker itself, has a priority over any other. If the manager of the fund declines to make an investment, or if the need for funds on the part of the new venture is greater than the amount the venture-capital fund can provide, then the investment banking firm itself or a group of its clients may invest independently of the fund.

The financings we have discussed so far involve either a venture-capital fund or an investment banker or both. Some private placements, however, are made by new companies without the aid of either. The company simply acts on its own to place stock with a small group of investors, a group that may include individuals and corporations and also venture-capital funds or investment bankers. But the latter two simply act as investors here, not as intermediaries.

From the point of view of the investment banking firm that is attempting to develop an underwriting relationship, these early financings are important as a first step in establishing that relationship. Early participation by venture-capital funds that are not affiliated with another investment banker does not present a difficulty. But if another investment banker is in early, probably through its own venture-capital fund, but possibly through providing money in a private placement, and especially through obtaining a seat on the board of directors, then it may be difficult for a competitor to displace that firm when the time comes for a first public offering.

A specific example may help to clarify ways in which an investment banking firm can participate in the early financing of a new, high-tech venture. High Technology (the fictitious name of a real company) was established by a number of engineers who got their early financing from a venture-capital fund within a small investment banking firm, as well as from a few wealthy individuals and a few small venture-capital funds not affiliated with investment bankers. The company had developed a powerful and compact data processing product. Its strategy was an interesting one. It had decided not to attempt to sell directly to users of the product, but exclusively to large and well-established manufacturers of computer hardware. Like a number of companies following this strategy, High Tech obtained some equity capital from the companies to which it sold the product. It also offered to these companies warrants to buy substantial amounts of stock.

Raising equity capital from customers and suppliers has become an established practice for new ventures in the high-tech field in the past 10 or so years. Some companies have paid for component parts with stock and warrants; others, like High Tech, have offered warrants as a special inducement to purchasers of their products. There are two reasons why major U.S. corporations that have an interest in technology have begun to invest significantly in small, start-up companies. First, they expect to make a profit on their investments. Second, they effectively expand their research activities by way of these small companies. In many cases, the large company has simply missed a successful line of research and development, and is faced with how to catch up. Generally speaking, a large company probably would prefer not to tie its investment to the purchase of products from the smaller company, but from the point of view of the smaller company such a tie can be extremely valuable.

High Tech reached the point where a further, small private financing was needed. An investment banking firm learned of this imminent financing and saw an opportunity to establish a relationship with High Tech that might lead to future underwritings.

High Tech already had obtained some financing from a venture-capital fund controlled by a small investment banker, which was in fact represented on the board of the company. The obvious competition then was the small firm already in place. At the same time, one of the largest investment banking firms in the country had indicated an interest in participation, clearly with the hope of becoming the company's investment banker when public offerings were called for. This firm had recently begun the underwriting of first public offerings of high-tech companies and had a high-quality team of investment bankers at work developing opportunities in Silicon Valley.

The competition among investment bankers for high-quality high-technology companies in recent years is probably similar to the competition among investment bankers in the early 1900s for the business of the outstanding steel companies and railroads. There are some significant differences, in that the high-tech companies generally require much less capital than did the steel companies and railroads, and almost all of this capital takes the form of equity rather than debt. And the high-tech companies generally are able to command a much higher price per dollar of earnings or expected earnings than were the steel companies and railroads. But from the point of view of an investment banker, the level of competition is similar.

In approaching High Tech, the investment banker stressed four points. The first had to do with the firm's experience. The small firm in place had considerable experience, too, in high-tech financings, but not as long a record of successful offerings. The very large competitor had relatively little experience, although it offered the services of a team of highly qualified people.

Second, the firm had a substantial retail department. It could offer distribution power greater than that of the small competitor, although nothing like that of the very large wire houses, with thousands of registered representatives. In addition, the firm had a substantial research department, with over 20 professionals focused on high-technology. The research was valuable to the underwriter, of course, but could also carry over to High Tech, in supplying information on competitive products and product development, and trends in the industry.

The third point was that the firm had a very strong over-the-counter trading capability. The importance of market making is discussed later in this chapter. Briefly, what the firm had to offer was its ability to maintain a market in High Tech stock after it first went public, as well as the ability to provide good advice with respect to subsequent financings.

Finally, the firm was able to offer the individual commitment of a senior partner. The smaller competitor could make the same offer, but one of the disadvantages from which the large investment banking firm suffered was that while the individuals who would handle an underwriting would be well qualified, they would not be among the senior members of the firm. The firm's commitment to High Tech, through the participation of a senior partner on its board, and by the active leadership role taken by that partner in any financing deliberations and public or private placements, was a powerful argument.

A final, although less important, point had to do with fixed-income capability. To many small and medium-sized new ventures, a public offering, or even a private placement, of debt may seem rather farfetched. Debt is likely to take the form of bank loans. But if the company is successful and grows substantially, then it is quite likely that a time will come for a debt offering. Most of the small underwriting firms that specialize in high-tech new ventures, including the small competitor in this case, do not have a substantial fixed-income capability. The large competitor, of course, had ample resources.

In addition to these points, which can be organized into an effective presentation by an investment banking firm, a crucial element concerns the personal relationship that is or is not established between the company management and the investment banker. In this particular case, the founder and president of the company initially had a good relationship with the investment banker who had provided early financing and who was on his board. But there had been some disagreements, and this, perhaps more than the objective set of strengths and weaknesses of the three competing firms, opened the way for a change. The senior partner of the firm seeking to break in was able to establish a close, amicable relationship with the company's president, which was probably the most important factor in the company's decision. The firm was invited to participate, through its venture-capital fund, in the private placement. (The company arranged the placement on its own, so the firm participated only as an investor.) The large investment banking firm was also included in the private placement, however, so the company was keeping its options open.

A number of experienced chief financial executives of companies approaching a first public offering believe the leadership in that offering should include a major investment banking firm and also one of the firms specializing in high-growth, high-tech offerings. The Microsoft first public offering in March 1986, for example, was co-managed by Goldman Sachs and Alex. Brown. An Apollo offering of convertible debentures (not a first public offering) in February 1986 was co-managed by Morgan Stanley, Salomon Brothers, and Hambrecht & Quist.

THE INITIAL PUBLIC OFFERING

Underwriting the public offering is what investment banking is all about. This is where the investment bankers' reputation, and much of its profits, are made. Public offerings in the United States historically have almost always involved syndication, and a brief discussion of the syndication process is in order, although the need for a syndicate is today much reduced.

Traditionally there have been two reasons to form an underwriting syndicate. One was to spread the underwriting risk. The second was to distribute the securities. A third reason concerns prestige and public relations. The syndicate leader took pride in displaying its leadership role and its continued ability to assemble a respected syndicate. And the syndicate member took pride in being one of the select few.

Today, the first two reasons are much less important. Except in the case of very large offerings, many investment banking firms have the capital to take the entire risk in a public offering. (Drexel Burnham Lambert, Inc. generally operates without a syndicate.) And many firms, particularly those specializing in offerings of high-tech growth companies, have all the distribution power necessary to dispose of the entire offering. There remain, however, some other reasons for forming a syndicate. If the managing firm is not itself well known, it can be important to the offering to have some well-known firms in the syndicate, and to have their names appear in a tombstone ad. The use of a syndicate makes it possible to share expenses of the offering, which may be attractive to the manager. A number of lesser-known firms may seek the advertising value of being listed in a syndicate, even though they are allocated very little stock, and stand to make little or no profit from the offering. The manager, perhaps at the request or insistence of the issuing company, may include some of these firms even though they are not necessary to the success of the offering.

The nature of syndication as well has changed substantially in recent years. The key position is syndicate manager. Offerings are frequently co-managed, and in this case the co-manager who "runs the books" has the key position. In a tombstone ad, the name of the manager, or those of the co-managers, will appear in the first line of underwriters, separated from the remainder of the syndicate. Traditionally, if there were co-managers, the manager whose name was on the left of the first line was the one running the books. Currently there are exceptions to this practice. A co-manager not running the books may be an important enough firm to insist on appearing at the left of the top line. But in this case, the typeface used in the tombstone ad will be the typeface associated with the co-manager who is actually running the books. Simple observation of the typefaces associated with managing underwriters enables the reader to identify which co-manager is running the books. Notice that in the ad for the INGENE offering the firm running the books is L.F. Rothschild, Unterberg, Towbin, while Bear, Stearns appears at the top left. (See Figure 8.1)

Running the books gives control over the distribution of stock. The manager running the books will make a judgment, in consultation with sales staff and corporate finance people, as to how to distribute the offering between institutional and retail sales. The choice, for example, may be half institutional and half retail. Of the institutional portion, part will be put in an "institutional pot." If 30 percent of the offering is allocated to this pot, then 30 percent of each underwriter's share of the offering is automatically contributed to the pot. Actually, the manager sells these shares, using its own sales staff, but the members of the syndicate will receive credit for the sales.

The manager is in a position to allocate institutional sales to the pot, to take them for itself, or to allocate some to syndicate members who have institutional customers and wish to sell directly to them. Clearly, the manager is simultaneously serving its own interests, attempting to maintain good relations with syndicate members whose cooperation will be needed in future offerings if not in the current one, and seeking to achieve an overall satisfactory placement of the shares.

Placement of the shares is important, and a good manager develops a feel for quality placement. Generally the demand is good for shares in a high-technology first public offering. The manager will have assured the demand or it will not make the offering. The ideal buyer is one who takes part of the offering and then comes back for more in the aftermarket. This enables the manager to dispose of any shares acquired in the course of stabilization, and also tends to support the price after the offering has been completed.

There is always the risk of a price decline during the offering or sometime after, perhaps as the result of a general market decline. If stock has been placed well, it has been bought by investors who will continue to hold it despite a decline in price. Stock in "weak hands," on the other hand, may be sold in panic in the event of a price decline, only driving the stock price farther down or putting a heavy burden on the manager's efforts to stabilize the market. So-called DVP accounts, meaning "deliver to a bank against payment," suggest purchases on borrowed money and the likelihood of a quick sale if the market drops.

Compensation arrangements to the members of the syndicate work something like this: out of every dollar of spread (i.e., the difference between the price paid by the public and the amount received by the issuing company) 20 cents will go to the manager or the co-managers. Arrangements for sharing this amount among

This announcement is neither an offer to sell nor a solicitation of an offer to buy these securities.
The offer is made only by the Prospectus.

June 19, 1986

INGENE
International Genetic Engineering, Inc.

2,000,000 Shares

Common Stock

Price $5.00 Per Share

Copies of the Prospectus may be obtained from the undersigned only in States where the undersigned may legally offer these securities in compliance with the securities laws thereof.

BEAR, STEARNS & CO. INC. — L. F. ROTHSCHILD, UNTERBERG, TOWBIN, INC.

DONALDSON, LUFKIN & JENRETTE Securities Corporation — HAMBRECHT & QUIST Incorporated — E. F. HUTTON & COMPANY INC.

MONTGOMERY SECURITIES — PRUDENTIAL-BACHE Securities

ROBERTSON, COLMAN & STEPHENS — SHEARSON LEHMAN BROTHERS INC.

ADVEST, INC. — ALLEN & COMPANY Incorporated — EBERSTADT FLEMING INC.

A. G. EDWARDS & SONS, INC. — LADENBURG, THALMANN & CO. INC. — MOSELEY SECURITIES CORPORATION

ROTHSCHILD INC. — TUCKER, ANTHONY & R. L. DAY, INC.

ABD SECURITIES CORPORATION — ARNHOLD AND S. BLEICHROEDER, INC. — SANFORD C. BERNSTEIN & CO., INC.

J. C. BRADFORD & CO. Incorporated — CAZENOVE INC. — EUROPARTNERS SECURITIES CORPORATION

FIRST ALBANY CORPORATION — FURMAN SELZ MAGER DIETZ & BIRNEY Incorporated — JANNEY MONTGOMERY SCOTT INC.

KLEINWORT BENSON Incorporated — NEUBERGER & BERMAN — OKASAN SECURITIES, LTD.

THE ROBINSON-HUMPHREY COMPANY, INC. — ROONEY, PACE INC. — SOGEN SECURITIES Corporation

STEPHENS INC. — SWISS BANK CORPORATION INTERNATIONAL Securities Inc. — WHEAT, FIRST SECURITIES, INC.

ADAMS, HARKNESS & HILL, INC. — ANDERSON & STRUDWICK Incorporated — BAER & COMPANY Incorporated — COLEMAN & COMPANY

CRAIGIE INCORPORATED — HAAS SECURITIES CORPORATION — HAMERSHLAG, KEMPNER & CO.

INTERSTATE SECURITIES CORPORATION — JOHNSON, LANE, SPACE, SMITH & CO., INC. — McKINLEY ALLSOPP, INC.

RAYMOND, JAMES & ASSOCIATES, INC. — ROSENKRANTZ LYON & ROSS Incorporated — SILBERBERG, ROSENTHAL & CO.

Figure 8.1. INGENE tombstone ad

co-managers vary from one offering to other. Generally expenses are shared in the same ratio as the compensation. Another 30 cents of the one dollar of spread takes the form of an underwriting fee that is shared by all underwriters of the offering. This is their compensation for the risk involved in the underwriting. It is quite likely that this entire fee will be absorbed by expenses.

Finally, 50 cents of the one dollar of spread takes the form of the "selling concession." A member of the syndicate can earn the selling concession in either of two ways. If stock is allocated to that member and the member sells it, then the selling concession is earned. In addition, sales made via the institutional pot are credited to all members of the syndicate, so each member will earn the selling concession on these sales, even though that member did not actually participate in the sales. In the case of retail sales of stock, the member of the syndicate will allocate the selling concession to the individual salesperson in the firm who makes the sale, as a "sales credit." A portion of the sales credit, perhaps as much as 50 percent, will be paid to the salesperson as a commission. In the case of the institutional pot sales for which the member obtains a selling concession, a sales credit may be given to the institutional salespeople of the firm.

The organization of syndicates until quite recent years depended essentially on personal relationships. Members of "the club" were included in syndicates; non-members were not. For an emerging investment banking firm to become a member of syndicates headed by reputable investment banking firms, and for that emerging firm to persuade other reputable firms to join a syndicate it might be heading, has always been extremely difficult. Cultivating personal relationships, demonstrating financial stability and staying power, and building a respectable underwriting business might have to go on for many years, or even decades, before a firm might expect to be received within the established syndicates.

In recent years, such personal contacts have become a little less significant. An underwriting firm that can deliver a sought-after product, like initial public offerings of attractive high-tech issuers, will find it much easier to attract reputable firms to its syndicates, and in turn to be accepted in other syndicates, than was the case even a decade ago. Performance, rather than whom one knows or who one's parents are or were, plays a greater part today. C.E. Unterberg, Towbin, the underwriting predecessor of L.F. Rothschild, Unterberg, Towbin, which began in the late 1950s to build the relationships necessary to gain access to syndicates and to be able to form syndicates, was helped by its proven success record in bringing initial public offerings to market. What was particularly important was that these companies by and large proved to be successful. Many of them were merged into large, successful, and well-known enterprises. Virtually none of them (perhaps two or three out of 400) turned out to be complete failures.

L.F. Rothschild, Unterberg, Towbin made a decision fairly early to do only high-quality underwritings. Part of its concern for quality stemmed from the firm's wish to establish syndicate relations with other investment banking firms, and for this purpose its reputation as a very high-quality investment banker was crucial. The firm went further, and held off entering the venture capital business when it was first building its reputation as an investment banker. There was some feeling that a conflict of interest might be perceived if an investment banker were taking substantial positions in a company as a venture-capital financier, and then bringing the company public. The firm did not take cheap options as partial compensation in an underwriting. It charged spreads on the order of 8½ to 9 percent on very speculative offerings, down to 7 percent on the more ordinary first public issues.

To return to our example, some months after the second private financing High Technology decided to do a first public offering of stock. The market for high-technology stocks was down, so this was not a particularly easy time for a first public offering. Our investment banking firm was invited to underwrite the offering. The senior partner joined the board of directors of the company, and the partner of the smaller investment banking firm left the board at the same time. The smaller firm was included as a joint manager in the public offering, but the large firm was not included.

The public offering process now goes something like this: the deal is put together between company and underwriter, and then about two weeks are spent preparing a prospectus. The company and its lawyers and accountants prepare a first draft that goes to the underwriter. The corporate finance department of the underwriting firm, and its lawyers, then put the finishing touches to the prospectus. The prospectus forms the bulk of the registration statement, which then goes to the Securities and Exchange Commission.

A good deal of care goes into the disclosure in a prospectus for a high-technology first public offering. Only a few years ago, there was a sense that for a substantial company with a record of successful operations it should not be necessary to elaborate on the risk to investors in the stock. Today, underwriters are more careful. The boom in high-tech offerings in 1983 was succeeded by a general decline in prices in 1984. Most of the buyers of these offerings suffered losses, and lawyers were not slow to file lawsuits. As a result, the principal underwriters of high-tech offerings are later facing a number of suits. Whatever the ultimate outcome of the litigation, defense is expensive, and the current practice is to ensure that prospectus disclosure leaves no doubt as to the risk of loss.

It generally takes two weeks to a month before the SEC responds to the filing. The staff of the Commission will send a letter of comments, which usually are not hard to deal with. They may ask for clarification, for further information, and perhaps for rephrasing or restatement of financials. If the company regards the information requested as confidential, generally it is possible for the Commission staff to treat the information as confidential, and not disclose it or insist on its inclusion in the registration statement. Finally, the registration statement becomes effective, and the public offering can begin.

In the case of High Technology, an interesting problem arose with respect to the use of warrants as an inducement to customers. When the registration statement was filed for a convertible bond offering, some years after the first public stock offering, the SEC took the position that the cost of sales had been understated by the value of warrants issued to induce those sales. Furthermore, the SEC insisted that the relevant value of the warrants was not the value when they were first issued, in order to promote sales, but their value at the time of the bond offering. By this point, the stock price had risen and the warrants had a respectable value. In some cases, the warrants were to purchase stock at $6 and the stock was to be offered at $20. Ultimately, the SEC withdrew its demand for a restatement of cost of sales, but did insist that any future issue of warrants to encourage sale of company products would call for addition of the value of the warrants to the cost of sales.

Once the filing has been made with the SEC, but before it is effective—that is, while the Commission is examining it—actual offering of the securities is not allowed, but some preselling activity is permissible. A "red-herring" prospectus (so-called because a legend is printed in red to the effect that a registration statement has been filed but is not yet effective) can be distributed to prospective investors. But a livelier activity takes the form of "road shows."

The staff of the firm generally designs these shows. They put together a series of slides based upon what is in the prospectus (they do not, however, include any financial projections), designed to provide the clarity that is generally not possible in the formal legal language of the prospectus itself. The slides explain the company, its products, its people, and its finances. For about two weeks, while the new offering is in registration, the show is taken from city to city. Sophisticated investors are invited. These will include portfolio managers for mutual funds and insurance companies, people from investment counseling firms, and representatives from firms included in the offering syndicate. The general public is not invited nor are reporters. An investment banker introduces company managers, who present the slides and answer questions. Every guest receives a red-herring prospectus.

The road shows serve to acquaint institutional investors with the company whose stock is to be first publicly offered. At the same time, they educate the sales force of the investment banking firm, and prepare these people to sell the stock to their customers once the registration statement has become effective.

The last step in the process of preparing for the offering is setting the price, which is done just before the registration statement becomes effective. At least two resources of the investment banker are important in pricing: first is experience with first public offerings of high-tech companies, second is a talented trading department. Experience indicates what investors might reasonably expect in the way of future earnings from the issuing company, and what they are likely to be willing to pay. A trading department can have a good sense of the demand for stock of the kind of company that is being underwritten, price trends, and the prices of comparable stocks.

AFTER-MARKET SUPPORT

The ideal initial public offering is sold out quickly, the price in the aftermarket (i.e., the market for the stock following the offering) rises a little above the offering price, and subsequently there is a continued rise in price. The investors who bought in the offering are pleased to see they have made a gain and that there is a market in which they can sell their shares if they wish to; the investment banker has enthusiastic customers ready for its next offering and another success story to relate to the next company to be underwritten; and the issuing company is pleased to see enthusiasm for its stock and a market that will make the next public offering easier.

Achieving this ideal depends to some extent on luck. A rise or decline in the stock prices of high-tech companies in general is beyond the control of underwriter and issuing company. In 1984, for example, a falling market dragged down the prices of almost all high-tech initial public offerings, leaving a trail of unhappy investors. The experienced underwriter can, however, set the initial offering price so as to maximize the likelihood that the price in the aftermarket will rise and can be sustained. And the market-making commitment of the underwriter's trading department, including its ability and willingness to maintain an inventory—to "position" stock of the company—is a critical element in sustaining the stock price and making possible purchases and sales by investors.

Following the initial public offering, it is important that a market be maintained for the company's stock. This market not only meets the needs of investors wanting to buy and sell shares but also it establishes a market price. The manager of an initial public offering of a high-technology company will anticipate making a market in the shares, and generally hopes to handle 20 to 40 percent of all trading. This percentage of the market will require the maintenance of attractive spreads and a willingness to deal in size. The practice has developed recently, however, of listing shares on a stock exchange contemporaneously with a first public offering. Not every company is able to meet the listing requirements of the American or New York stock exchanges, of course, at the time of a first public offering. But some do, and the result is that the exchange specialist becomes the market maker, depriving the offering manager of an opportunity and also relieving it of a responsibility.

DIVERSIFICATION AND SIZE OF FIRM

When it was smaller, L.F. Rothschild, Unterberg, Towbin could afford to think of itself as focused on underwriting high-tech new ventures. As the firm has grown, though, it has not only built facilities to support that underwriting—including a substantial research staff, corporate finance staff, and trading activity—but it finds itself having to expand into more or less unrelated areas as well just to preserve its position as a major investment banking firm. Mutual funds and the sale of insurance, for example, may seem to have little to do with the underwriting of high-tech, new ventures. But they have a great deal to do with the prosperity and indeed survival of an investment banking firm facing competition from other large and well-capitalized firms as well as from a number of financial institutions (banks at present and ultimately perhaps insurance companies). So one of the consequences of success at the high-tech, new-venture underwriting business is the need to venture farther afield.

L.F. Rothschild, Unterberg, Towbin has also been affected by another change in the investment banking business generally. Largely because of elimination of fixed-commission rates, the nature of sales and trading has changed. Sales has become closely linked to trading, and trading has become a combined sales and trading function. Some years ago, the trader was seen as someone gifted at buying low and selling high. This characteristic is still important, but something further is required: the ability to use the enormous amounts of information that are available now on who owns how much of what, who is buying and who is selling, and where demand and supply exist and are likely to arise in the future.

One dilemma of the investment banker who would like to focus on high-tech new offerings is that the business has changed enough over the years so that it is very difficult to do these offerings without substantial resources, particularly in the form of trading and research capabilities. For a firm to maintain these substantial resources, it almost has to use them for other things than high-tech offerings of new ventures. Another dilemma involves underwritings of marginal quality companies. Offerings that an aggressive investment banker might well want to undertake, and that L.F. Rothschild, Unterberg, Towbin might have undertaken in its earlier years, may now be passed up because such an offering might impair the reputation of the firm with other investment banking firms and with the customer base that it has put together. To some extent, perhaps, the firm becomes a victim of its own success. It has worked to create the image of a very high-quality investment banker, and preservation of that image may require turning down business that someone ought to be doing.

There is probably a place for the small and highly focused firm that is content not to do very many public offerings, and to be displaced when the most attractive offerings come up by larger firms with greater resources. Sometimes the smaller firm is not displaced, but can share in managing an underwriting, because it has unique talents. Alex. Brown (relatively small at least until its public offering in early 1986) has developed a recognized expertise in computer software that is understood by high-tech companies. A software company may not choose Alex. Brown as its lead underwriter, perhaps preferring a firm with greater resources, but it might insist that Alex. Brown be a joint underwriter, simply because the first-choice underwriter does not have the expertise Alex. Brown has.

Probably a firm of ten experienced people, with a small trading department and an analyst, could succeed in underwriting high-tech issues. The firm could earn a living but it could never compete with a firm like Goldman Sachs or Morgan Stanley in underwriting a first public offering of an outstanding high-tech company. Much of the firm's success might rest on connections with people in the high-tech business who are likely to leave established companies and start up new companies, then turn to their contacts in the investment banking world for financing help.

The high-tech companies themselves have become very sophisticated in understanding the capabilities of investment banking firms. They are quite capable of identifying the firms whose expertise is particularly appropriate to a particular issuer, and quite capable of selecting a combination of investment bankers whose collective expertise best fits their needs.

9 Venture-Capital Financing

C. EDWARD HAZEN

Venture, or risk, capital has been profitably invested at least since the Phoenicians mounted trading missions around the Mediterranean. In the United States, institutions and wealthy individuals have been funding new business endeavors almost since European settlers set foot on its soil. The commercial history of the nation—from the earliest days of trapping and trading, to the development of an industrial base founded on textiles and steel, to the railroads, to automobiles, and more recently to computers and biotechnology—has been written largely because of the availability of venture capital for new undertakings. In the years since World War II, modern, institutional venture capital as we know it today has grown into a true "industry." Whereas in the 1950s venture-capital investing was dominated by wealthy individuals or families, such as the Whitneys (J.H. Whitney & Co.), the Phipps (Bessemer Ventures), and the Rockefellers (Venrock) investing their own money, in the 1960s there began to emerge private partnerships dedicated to managing venture-capital investment pools for institutions and wealthy individuals. From the late 1960s, as institutions dedicated greater sums to venture capital, investment banking firms began also to manage such funds.

As a result, venture-capital investment has become an integral part of the product portfolio of most, if not all, major investment banking firms. Investment banks' participation in venture capital ranges from direct investment management of institutional venture-capital pools, to investment of firm or partnership capital as principal in venture-capital situations, to provision of traditional corporate finance services, such as initial public underwriting or merger and acquisition advice, to venture-capital-funded companies. Indeed, some firms, notably Alex. Brown & Sons, Hambrecht & Quist, Robertson, Colman & Stephens, and L.F. Rothschild, Unterberg, Towbin are known for specializing in investment banking for venture-capital-backed companies.

THE WHY OF VENTURE CAPITAL

Investment banks have been drawn to the venture-capital area for a number of reasons. The most important reason is high returns on investment in such ventures.

An investment bank which acts as a general partner of an institutional venture-capital investment pool generally has a carried interest of 20 percent of the profits of the pool. This means that the general partner retains $.20 of every $1.00 of gain over the amount originally invested. Thus a $50 million venture-investment portfolio which appreciates to $250 million yields $40 million to the general partner over the life of the portfolio (generally 10 years). Since the general partner normally invests only 1 percent of the investment funds, the compound annual return on investment (55 percent for 10 years in this example) is highly attractive to the investment bank. In most investment bank-sponsored venture-capital pools, the general partner's carried interest is split on some basis (e.g., 50–50) between the sponsoring firm and the individuals employed by the firm to manage the venture investments. Even so, the return to the firm can be considerable. While returns on venture-capital investing vary widely from one group to another and from one period to another, it is a generally held rule of thumb among venture capitalists and institutions which invest in venture capital that a 35 percent compound annual rate of return across the portfolio of a venture capital partnership is considered to be good performance.

A second reason for an investment bank's participation is that a firm often can add to the return on its general partner investment by directly co-investing firm funds in some or all of the venture capital opportunities in which the firm-sponsored investment pool invests.

For example, ML Ventures, a venture-capital fund sponsored by Merrill Lynch, may invest $3 million in X Co., a potentially attractive new-technology start-up. In fact, X Co. needs to raise $6 million, but ML Ventures' managers do not consider it prudent to invest more than 5 percent of their $60 million fund in one investment. Still, it is an exceedingly attractive opportunity. The solution: Merrill Lynch, the parent company, invests an additional $3 million of its corporate funds directly in X Co.

To extend the example, assume that ML Ventures and Merrill Lynch each have an ownership position in X Co., after their respective $3 million investments, of 25 percent and that in five years X Co., having achieved its promise, is sold for $120 million to a larger company. What is Merrill Lynch's return? This return is a function of Merrill Lynch's various roles in this transaction. It has first earned a return on its portion of the general partner's carry, assuming that Merrill Lynch retains 50 percent of the 20 percent carried interest in ML Ventures. Since the general partner contributed 1 percent of the venture-capital fund's total capital, Merrill Lynch has, in effect, contributed $15,000, or 50 percent of 1 percent, of ML Ventures' $3 million investment in X Co. The compound annual return over five years on Merrill Lynch's general partnership portion of the X Co. investment is 182.5 percent, computed as follows:

Investment:	ML Ventures' investment in X Co.	$ 3,000,000
	General partner's share of ML Ventures' investment (1%)	30,000
	Merrill Lynch share (50% of 1%)	15,000

Return: ML Ventures' investment yield (25% share of
                 $120 million net proceeds) $30,000,000
              Less: ML Ventures' investment   (3,000,000)
              Net yield to ML Ventures   27,000,000
              General partner's carried interest (20% of net yield)   5,400,000
              Merrill Lynch share (50% of 20%)   2,700,000
              Merrill Lynch compound ROI   182.5%

Merrill Lynch is also a direct investor in X Co., having invested $3 million of corporate funds, and thus earns a return on this investment as well. By adding the return on this investment to the return on the general partner's carried interest shown in the preceding breakdown, it can be seen that Merrill Lynch earns a blended return on both investment pieces together of 61.2% percent. However, the total dollar return to Merrill Lynch grows from $2.7 million to $32 million, which has a far greater impact on Merrill Lynch's corporate profitability.

Merrill Lynch's investment in X Co. $ 3,000,000
Merrill Lynch's investment yield
     (25% share of $120 million net proceeds)   30,000,000
General partner's share (from above)   2,700,000
Total yield   32,700,000
Compound ROI   61.2%

This example clearly illustrates why investment banking firms have found that such direct co-investments with sponsored venture-capital funds can provide attractive returns.

The third important reason for investment banks' participation in venture-capital investing is corporate finance deal flow. While many firms consider this reason important, certain firms, notably Hambrecht & Quist and Robertson, Colman & Stephens, seem to place an especially high value on it. These firms, through their venture-capital funds, have made hundreds of investments in early-stage companies. These firms, and indeed most investment banking firms who participate in venture-capital investing, believe that if they are investors in a company, either directly or through a firm-sponsored venture-capital fund, they will be able to win that company's investment banking business whenever investment banking services are needed. The fact that most venture-backed companies are, by their very nature, voracious consumers of capital to fund their rapid growth, makes them attractive investment banking clients. The most common investment banking service required by such a company is an underwritten initial public offering, and perhaps later, secondary offerings. Other investment banking services often rendered to venture-capital-backed companies include assistance in raising mezzanine-stage private financing, merger and acquisition advisory work, and other corporate financial advice.

A fourth important reason for an investment bank's venture-capital activity is that such activity creates opportunities for areas of the firm other than corporate finance. For example, a firm's equity-research analysts are afforded a window through venture-capital investments on technology breakthroughs in small companies and can thus assess emerging competitive and market threats to the larger, publicly traded companies on which they report. In fact, the benefit in a relationship between a venture-capital group and an equity-research group often flows the opposite way as well: the equity analysts can help venture capitalists in identifying and evaluating attractive venture investment prospects. In some firms, notably Robertson, Colman & Stephens, the venture-capital group and equity-research group work hand-in-hand in many venture-capital projects.

Another area of investment banking which can benefit from a firm's participation of venture capital is the institutional and retail sales effort, which may sell investment partnership interests in the firm's venture-capital pools and in R&D investment partnerships for venture-backed companies as described in the following section.

To summarize, there are four primary reasons why investment banks have been drawn to participation in venture capital investing. They are:

1. Attractive returns on investment in managing institutional venture-capital investment pools.
2. Opportunities for direct co-investment with such managed pools.
3. Captive generation of corporate finance deal-flow.
4. Generation of revenue opportunities for other areas of the firm.

THE HOW OF VENTURE CAPITAL: SOURCES OF FUNDS

There are seven primary ways in which investment banking firms participate as venture-capital investors:

1. Managing institutionally funded venture-capital limited partnerships.
2. Managing individually funded venture-capital limited partnerships.
3. Managing pooled R&D investment partnerships.
4. Managing single-project R&D investment partnerships.
5. Syndicating private equity financings.
6. Selling public securities in early-stage companies.
7. Investing firm or partnership funds in venture-capital situations.

Institutional Venture-Capital Partnerships

The most common vehicle for investment bankers' participation in venture-capital investing is the institutionally funded venture-capital limited partnership. Examples of these partnerships include Alex. Brown & Sons' ABS Ventures, Dillon Read's Concord Ventures, Donaldson, Lufkin & Jenrette's Sprout funds and Robertson, Colman & Stephens' RCS funds. In such partnerships, the investment banker, acting as general partner, raises funds from wealthy individuals and from institutions—

including insurance companies, pension funds, corporations, foundations, money managers, and bank trust departments—to be placed in a "blind pool" for venture-capital investments. In this vehicle, the limited partners do not know in advance what investments will be made, nor do they have any control over whether to invest in any given opportunity. All investment decisions are made solely by the general partner. Hence, it is called a "blind pool."

Raising funds for a venture-capital fund from institutional limited partners is often the most difficult step in the entire venture-capital investment process. It can take as long as a year to raise the funds for a partnership. In general, the most important factor considered by the institution in deciding to invest in a blind pool is the venture-capital investment track record of the general partners or other investment decision makers in the venture-capital group. Those with a good record have an easier time; those with a mediocre record or no record have a more difficult time. Nonetheless, there is intense competition among venture-capital firms for the institutional funds available for investment in blind pools.

To some extent, investment bank-sponsored venture investment pools have an advantage in competing for these funds because raising money is the business of investment banks. Investment banks have long and multifaceted relationships with major financial institutions and wealthy individuals. The weight of their corporate resources and reputations behind a venture effort often can buttress the impressions of potential investors.

In fact, venture-capital firms which are not otherwise affiliated with an investment bank sometimes use the services of an investment bank to help to raise their capital. In such arrangements, the investment bank normally is able to participate in the venture pool, either as a "special" limited partner or by retaining a portion of the general partner's carried interest. In either case, the investment bank is able to share passively in the venture fund's success without having to invest its own funds.

Normally, the institutions that invest in venture-capital pools make commitments for a 10-year period, but the funds are actually drawn down by the general partner as needed for new investments in stages over the first two to five years of the partnership.

Because initial investments are usually made in the first half of the 10-year partnership term, most general partners normally are managing two or more limited partnerships at once. The first, having been invested in years 1–5, is being managed and harvested in years 6–10, while the second is being invested initially in years 6–10, with harvesting coming in years 11–15.

As noted earlier, the general partner normally retains a 20 percent carried interest in the profits of the partnership. In addition, the limited partners pay a small management fee, usually 1 to 2½ percent of committed capital, to the general partner to cover expenses incurred in making and managing investments.

Individual Venture-Capital Partnerships

Partnerships funded solely by individuals are similar in most respects to institutional funds. The most significant difference is the source of funds. These partnerships attract investment solely from individuals rather than institutions, and generally in much smaller denominations: where the normal minimum limited partner's investment in an institutional fund is $1–$5 million, individual partnership interests have been sold in units as small as $5000. Other differences are more subtle. For example, institutional partnerships, as noted earlier, generally take down committed capital in stages across the early years of the partnership; individual partnerships generally take down 100 percent of committed capital at inception. Another difference is that institutional partnerships are 10-year commitments. Limited partners cannot withdraw capital before the term of the partnership (except in extreme and rare circumstances). Individual funds, which are in effect mutual funds invested in private companies, usually provide limited transferability of, and a market for, partnership interests.

Individually funded partnerships for traditional private equity venture investing are much less common than institutionally funded partnerships. Examples of investment bank-sponsored individual partnerships among major national firms include Merrill Lynch's ML Ventures and among smaller, regional firms, Boettcher (Denver) and Wedbush, Noble & Cooke (Los Angeles).

Pooled R&D Investment Partnerships

Pooled R&D investment partnerships are partnerships formed to make investments in a number of research and development projects. In such R&D partnerships, capital is provided to a number of companies to undertake specific research and development projects leading to the introduction of commercially viable products. For each such project, a research partnership is formed in which the company sponsoring the research is the general partner, and the pooled R&D investment partnership is the limited partner which provides the capital for the research to be carried out by the research partnership on behalf of the sponsoring company. In fact, this is usually just a bookkeeping structure. The sponsoring company generally does all the research using its own employees but they are paid and supported out of the research partnership "pocket."

The research partnership, in which the sponsoring company typically holds a 20 percent stake and the pooled R&D investment partnership an 80 percent share, "owns" the technology or product developed under its aegis.

The return to the limited partners in the pooled R&D investment partnership in such ventures is provided by a combination of tax benefits (primarily R&D tax credits and operating losses) incurred by the research partnership and a royalty stream paid to the research partnership based on sales of the new product which it "owns."

The tax benefits and royalty income pass through the research partnership to the limited partners of the pooled R&D investment partnership. The royalty stream is generally paid until a predetermined aggregate payout is reached. In some cases, the research partnership "sells" its product or technology back to the sponsoring company for a single cash payment or for equity in the sponsoring company. Again, the proceeds flow through to the limited partners of the pooled R&D investment partnership.

Some pooled R&D investment partnerships are formed with a preselected portfolio of R&D projects (usually 5–10). Others are formed as blind pools, with the investments to be made at the discretion, and based on the judgment, of the general partner.

Insofar as the primary investment objective of these partnerships is tax avoidance, the limited partners normally all are wealthy individuals. For this reason, pooled R&D investment partnerships are often associated with investment banks. The brokerage arms of investment banks are in the business of, among other things, creating and selling tax-related investment opportunities to their individual clients for whom tax minimization is an important investment objective.

These pooled R&D investment partnerships are quite attractive to investment banks: they are investment products created by the firm for distribution through its sales force (which is always seeking new products to sell to key accounts); they generally carry an attractive commission for the firm's salespeople; they generally incorporate an attractive carried interest for the investment bank as general partner; through the sale of the research output back to sponsoring companies in exchange for equity, they carry the potential for the high return associated with venture-capital equity investments; and they contribute to investment banking deal flow. Nonetheless, there have been relatively few of those partnerships offered. The principal reason appears to be that the return record of these pools has generally been poor: the investors have gained their tax deductions, but have seen little additional return. More recently, uncertainty about, and changes in, tax laws have contributed to the unpopularity of those pools.

Sponsors of such pools currently include Merrill Lynch, Morgan Stanley, and Prudential Bache.

Single-Project R&D Partnerships

These partnerships are nearly identical to the research partnerships described previously, except that the funds are used for a single, preselected R&D project.

In these partnerships, the investment bank will raise the funds, in the same way and for the same reasons noted previously, but the general partner of the R&D partnership is likely to be only the company receiving the funds rather than an investment bank. The investment bank's primary role is that of agent, rather than principal, but to the extent that the R&D funds are provided to early-stage, private companies the activity may still be viewed as venture-capital investing.

Private Equity Syndications

Investment banking firms often act as agents in the venture-capital area by syndicating private equity financings of a particular company or opportunity. Many small, local, or regional investment banks commonly put together a syndicate of individual investors to invest in an early-stage company. In larger investments banks, the companies tend to be larger and the investors are more likely to be institutions, but the same steps apply. Large investment banks play this role especially in raising mezzanine, or later-stage capital for venture-capital-backed companies in which they may or may not have a venture-capital investment. While such transactions can be very profitable in their own right for an investment bank, this activity is also thought to provide competitive advantage to an investment bank in winning the right to underwrite a later initial public offering and to provide other investment banking services.

Sale of Public Securities

Certain investment banks have developed a lucrative niche in taking public early-stage companies which might otherwise be viewed as logical candidates for venture-capital financing. Such public financings resemble private equity syndications except that the securities involved are registered and tradable in public transactions.

Perhaps the most widely known currently of such investment banks is D.H. Blair in New York. Since 1980, Blair has taken over 100 companies public, many of which had never showed profits at the time of the initial offering, and a few of which had never even recorded revenues. Blair's client list includes such apparently successful companies as TIE Communications, Genetic Systems (sold to Bristol-Myers) and Enzo Biochem.

Investment of Firm Funds

As noted at the beginning of the chapter, many investment banks invest firm or partnership capital in venture-capital situations. Such "merchant banking" transactions range from periodic opportunistic investments in transactions in which the firm is acting also as an agent, to organized, strategic efforts to regularly invest a portion of firm capital in venture-capital situations. This latter model suggests, in effect, a traditional venture-capital pool in which there is but a single limited partner: the investment bank. Almost all investment banks have pursued this sort of venture capital at one time or another; many, in fact, first decided to enter the business of managing venture-capital funds for others by having initially had success in investing their own funds. Firms that continue today to invest actively in this way include Morgan Stanley, Shearson Lehman Brothers, and Stephens Inc.

One variant on this model is a venture-capital partnership, the only limited partners of which are employees of an investment bank. In many respects such a partnership is a vestige of the days before most investment banks went public or became subsidiaries of large, diversified financial companies. When most major investment banks were partnerships, partnership funds were routinely invested outside normal investing banking activities on behalf of the partners. Both E.F. Hutton and Donaldson, Lufkin & Jenrette, for whom such a fund is a modest supplement to their much larger institutional partnerships, currently manage this sort of employee partnership.

THE HOW OF VENTURE CAPITAL: USES OF FUNDS

There are five key steps in venture capital investing:

1. Finding investment opportunities.
2. Evaluating the opportunities.
3. Structuring investments.
4. Managing investments.
5. Selling off investments.

Finding Investment Opportunities

Venture capitalists are able to earn superior returns on investment primarily for two reasons. The first is that their investment cost is much lower relative to expected return than might be the case in, for example, public equities markets. The higher expected return is required to compensate for the higher risk inherent in such investments. By definition, venture-capital investments involve new companies with new products and technologies, managed by teams which have not necessarily worked together for long periods of time. In many cases, the markets in which such companies plan to compete are themselves new. The investments are illiquid. In other words, such investments bear a higher degree of risk than most alternative investment opportunities and thus demand a higher expected return than is afforded by such alternatives.

The second reason venture capitalists are able to earn a superior return is that the market for venture-capital investing is inefficient. Each new company is unlikely to be seen by every investor who might like to invest, given the opportunity. There is an imbalance in favor of the suppliers of funds, the venture capitalists.

In recent years, however, the number of venture capitalists and the amount of venture capital available for investment has expanded dramatically, thereby increasing competition for attractive venture investments. New capital committed to venture-capital funds rose from $300 million in 1979 to $4.5 billion in 1984.

The key for venture capitalists in maintaining high returns has become to find the most attractive investment opportunities before other potential investors do. To do this, most venture capitalists develop and maintain a network of contacts with bankers, lawyers, accountants, executive recruiters, and other professionals who may be aware of fledgling companies. They attend conventions and trade shows sponsored by industries in which they may have investment interest, in search of new companies. They read trade journals, often very obscure ones, following industry trends, personnel moves, and technological breakthroughs. They maintain relationships with academics and research scientists for additional insight into technological issues. In some cases, they directly approach employees of larger companies to encourage them to go out on their own to start new companies. Investment bank-related venture capitalists may also consult with the equity-research analysts in their firms about promising opportunities. The goal of all this activity is to find and invest in new companies before the "market" is able to increase the investment cost, and thereby lower the return.

As more venture-capital partnerships have been formed, and as more venture capitalists scour the country in this fashion, it has become more difficult to "discover" attractive investment opportunities. Similarly, many entrepreneurs have become more sophisticated in raising capital and are more willing to "shop" their company, looking for a better price.

For these reasons, many venture-capital firms join in loose fraternities in which a small group of firms will share investments within the group by informally syndicating venture-capital financings with one another. As a result, many venture-capital investment opportunities are first seen through referral from other venture capitalists.

Investments found through active prospecting and a network of contacts, and through other venture capitalists, account for the vast majority of venture capital investments. The remainder are discovered hiding among the hundreds, if not thousands, of unsolicited proposals received by venture-capital firms each year. Many entrepreneurs prepare a business plan and mail it to every venture capitalist listed in the many published guides to venture-capital funding sources. While many of these opportunities may have some investment merit, few of these investments are funded by institutional venture capitalists.

Evaluating Investment Opportunities

The process by which venture capitalists evaluate investment opportunities is long and thorough. The investigative period may stretch as long as a year, although one to three months is the norm. In the evaluation process, the venture capitalist is attempting to determine the level of risk in the investment and to identify the evident areas of risk. It is commonly said that risk falls into three general categories: management, market, and product.

Management risk generally receives the most attention because, in many ways, this is the most difficult category to evaluate and because venture capitalists have found that management problems are the most common cause of the failure of venture-capital-backed companies. In order to assess management, the venture capitalist does extensive background checks on each key entrepreneur, talking to former employers, employees, and other professional contacts, even to competitors. The venture capitalist also tries, during the evaluation period, to spend as much time as possible with the key managers in a variety of settings. Some venture capitalists like to put entrepreneurs in competitive situations, such as tennis or golf matches, to test their competitive mettle. Some venture capitalists have assessments of entrepreneurs made by psychologists or psychiatrists. The goal is to find out as much as possible about how the managers think, act, and react.

Market risk is evaluated through analysis of the industry and competitive dynamics of the market in which the new company expects to compete. The venture capitalist talks to industry observers, such as consultants and securities analysts, attends trade shows, reviews the trade press, and talks to competitors, vendors, and customers. The goal here is to develop an independent understanding of the market and its forces and to assess whether the company under consideration has planned an appropriate strategy and tactics for successfully penetrating the market.

Product risk is evaluated on a number of bases. First, can the product be made at all? What is the technological risk? Does the product require any technological breakthrough? The second important question is: Can the product be made at its projected cost? If so, are the margins adequate to support the business strategy? If not, can the price be raised, given market constraints? The third major question is: Is the product truly proprietary? Does it have a sustainable advantage over competing or substitutable products? The fourth key question is: Will the market buy the product? Does it have the features and functions demanded by the market? Can it be sold profitably at the price the market will bear?

To attempt to answer all those questions, the venture capitalist talks again to competitors, vendors, industry analysts, and customers or potential customers. A special consultant may be retained to evaluate the technological and cost issues.

At the end of the evaluation process, the venture capitalist expects to feel "comfortable" with the team of entrepreneurs, to have gained an understanding of the market and the product, and to be aware of likely, if not all, areas of risk to the success of the company.

Structuring Investments

Venture capitalists have traditionally invested in new companies in the form of convertible preferred stock or convertible debt with warrants. The object is to achieve the potential return associated with equity investments while at the same time maintaining a senior position on the balance sheet in the event of liquidation (a not uncommon occurrence among venture-capital-backed companies).

Acquiring ownership control per se is not generally a priority for venture-capital investors. In determining ownership percentage, the venture capitalist is more likely to focus on the prefinancing value of the company and the amount of capital required. The ownership share in this case is merely derived as a function of valuation and amount invested. For example, if a company is seeking to raise $2 million and the entrepreneurs and investors agree that the value of the company before new financing is $4 million, then the new investors will own 33 percent of the company. To the extent that control over an instrument is an issue, however (and it usually is), most venture capitalists rely on mechanisms other than outright majority voting interest. They may include, for example, agreements requiring approval of the venture investors for certain corporate actions, or provisions by which the venture capitalists may control the board of directors without owning 51 percent or more of the company.

Managing Investments

There is a wide range in the degree to which venture capitalists "manage" investments. This is especially true among investment bank-sponsored venture-capital funds. At one extreme are firms which are very active investors, serving on the boards of directors of all their portfolio companies, closely advising management, and participating actively in strategic, if not operating, decisions. At the other extreme are entirely passive investors who make the investment but do not serve on boards or participate in any meaningful way in the affairs of their portfolio companies. Various investment bank-sponsored venture firms fall at both extremes and at each point between, but tend also to constitute a disproportionate percentage of the set at the passive end. This is so because for some investment banks it is enough only to be an investor in a company in order to feel securely positioned to win later investment banking business.

Selling Off Investments

Venture-capital investments are liquified generally through one of three means:

1. Public offering.
2. Merger of the company with a third party.
3. Sale of the company to management.

The investors' goal in most venture-backed companies is to take the company public in 3 to 10 years following the initial investment. In capitalizing the company's earnings stream at a multiple of earnings, the venture investor is normally able to enjoy a steep appreciation in the value of the investment. The public market also affords the private investor an opportunity for liquidity. However, venture investors may also hold on to an ownership position after a company has gone public and benefit from further appreciation based on earnings growth or (better yet) the expansion of the multiple. (Of course, an earnings decline, a multiple contraction, or a downturn in the capital market cycle may also be the result.) Taking a company public also allows the venture investor the opportunity to be flexible (within the limits of pertinent securities laws) in determining when to liquify all or part of an investment through sale in the public market.

However, not all venture-backed companies can be taken public. Some may be too small, some may be in industrial sectors which are out of favor with public investors, some may be managed or otherwise controlled by people who do not want to put up with the burdens of being a public company (such as a heavy commitment to investor relations, pressure to achieve quarterly results in accord with investor expectations, SEC reporting requirement, etc.), and some may not be performing well enough to be taken public.

In many such cases, venture-backed companies are sold to or merged with other companies to provide the venture investors liquidity through receipt of cash or a publicly traded security in exchange for their interests in the venture-backed company. While such transactions commonly involve successful venture companies and can provide returns to investors equivalent to those available in the public market, this path is also used to provide liquidity in less successful companies where the venture capitalists hope only to get some of their investment back, or perhaps all, but with no gain.

In the case of either a public offering or a sale, there is a role for an investment bank, and investment banks which have venture-capital affiliates expect to have access to this role through their venture-capital participation in a company going public or being sold. As discussed earlier, this is one of the important motivations for investment banks to enter the venture-capital business.

In fact, from the point of view of an investment bank, a company in which the firm has a venture-capital investment and which can both be taken public and later sold or merged is the paradigm of a good venture-capital investment. The investment bank is able to profit from a series of transactions.

Home Club, a warehouse outlet offering building and home repair products, is a good example of such a company for Donaldson, Lufkin & Jenrette (DLJ). Home Club was founded in August 1983 by a group of entrepreneurs who raised more than $4 million of start-up capital from a syndicate of venture-capital investors, including DLJ's Sprout Group. In late 1984, DLJ acted as placement agent in a $30 million, mezzanine-stage private equity placement with a number of corporations and institutions, for which it earned almost $900,000. In October 1985, DLJ, with Morgan Stanley and Montgomery Securities, underwrote Home Club's initial public offering, and only six weeks later, in December 1985, DLJ represented Home Club in the sale of the company to Zayre's Corp., a diversified retailer.

So, in slightly more than a year, DLJ earned fees for managing Home Club's private equity placement, for co-managing the Company's initial public offering, and for representing Home Club in negotiating its merger with Zayre's. Meanwhile, over a two-year period, from 1983 to 1985, DLJ's Sprout Group (of which DLJ is a limited partner and a subsidiary of DLJ is a general partner) earned a return of 4.3 times their total investment, in this case equal to a compound annual return of approximately 150 percent. As noted previously, this sort of investment result is the apotheosis of an investment bank's participation in venture capital.

Venture-backed companies which are unable to go public, whether because of company conditions or capital market conditions, and cannot be sold to unaffiliated third parties, but which are stable and can survive without infusion of additional capital, are often sold to their managements in leveraged transactions. In such transactions, the venture investors' returns are normally much lower than those present in a public offering or third-party transaction, but if a company cannot be sold or taken public, and its future prospects are at best uninteresting, venture capitalists generally seek liquidity on whatever terms they can.

THE WHO OF VENTURE CAPITAL

There are literally hundreds of venture-capital firms and small business investment companies (SBICs) in the United States, and thousands of individuals who may invest privately as "angels" in early-stage venture-capital-type companies. However, there are a much smaller number of firms for which professional venture investors

Table 9.1. Investment Banks' Venture-Capital Activity

Firm Majors	Venture Capital Since	Committed Capital (Millions)	Source of Funds
Alex. Brown & Sons	1982	$108.0	Institutional
Dillon Read	1982	100.0	Institutional
Donaldson, Lufkin & Jenrette	1969	240.0	Institutional
Drexel Burnham Lambert	1979	40.0	Institutional
First Boston	1981	67.0	Institutional
Hambrecht & Quist	1968	500.0	Institutional
E.F. Hutton	1981	20.0	Firm
Merrill Lynch	1982	130.6	Individual/R&D
Montgomery Securities	1969	99.7	Institutional
Morgan Stanley	1984	130.0	Institutional/R&D
PaineWebber	1970	54.0	Institutional
Prudential Bache	1978	150.0	Firm/R&D
Robertson, Colman & Stephens	1980	136.7	Institutional
L.F. Rothschild	1984	20.0	Firm/Institutional/ Individual
Salomon Brothers	1985	60.0	Institutional
Shearson Lehman Brothers	1984	250.0(2)	AMEX in 17 Partnerships (Firm)
Smith Barney, Harris Upham	1972	120.0	Institutional
Regionals			
Bateman Eichler, Hill Richards	1983	$ 9.7	Individual/R&D
Wm. Blair & Co.	1982	50.7	Institutional
Boettcher & Company	1984	10.7	Individual
Butcher & Singer	1983	10.0	Institutional
Cable, Howse & Ragen	1977	132.0	Institutional
Piper, Jaffray & Hopwood	1986	14.0	Institutional
Rotan Mosle	1983	18.5	Institutional/ Individual
Rothschild Inc.	1984	56.0	Institutional
Seidler Amdec Securities	1970	10.0	Individual
Stephens, Inc.	1933	10.0	Institutional
Wedbush, Noble, Cooke, Inc.	1986	0.0[a]	Firm/Institutional

[a]Firm has contributed $3 million. Wedbush, Noble, Cooke, Inc. is currently looking for institutional sources to reach $20 million.

Source: *Pratt's Guide to Venture Capital Sources*, 11th ed. (Wellesley, Mass: Venture Economics, 1987)

manage institutional or individual pool of funds greater than $10 million. Included in this group are 28 investment banks, listed in Table 9.1 (some of those firms manage smaller amounts, as can be seen in the table).

Surprisingly, given the $1 billion+ in venture capital under management by these investment banks, the firms listed in Table 9.1 employ fewer than 150 people, *in the aggregate*, in full-time venture-capital investing.

These venture capitalists have a range of backgrounds and experiences ranging from newly minted MBAs, to former investment bankers and equity-research analysts, to management consultants, commercial bankers, and operating executives with 25 years of industry experience. Certainly, there is no consistent pattern as to the length or kinds of experience that make a successful venture capitalist.

Those who do succeed seem, however, to have a number of qualities in common, including:

1. A good understanding of people which is necessary to evaluate the management team of prospective investments and to guide those teams in building their companies.
2. Creativity and persistence, which is necessary to uncover attractive investment opportunities and to help in devising solutions to the problems experienced by emerging companies.
3. Analytical rigor, which is necessary in overall assessment of investment opportunity and in devising strategies for companies in which investments have been made.
4. Humility, which is necessary in light of the fact that most venture-capital investments do not turn out anywhere near as well as predicted by the venture capitalist at the time of investment.
5. A little luck (see item 4).

10 Real Estate Finance

PAUL D. KAZILIONIS

The evolution of real estate activities among investment banking firms on Wall Street varies significantly by firm. It is important to understand that real estate service is a relatively recent offering with a scope that is still being defined by the industry. The discussion here focuses on several issues: the varying commitment of investment banks to real estate services; specific products and services provided by real estate departments; and the integration of real estate with more traditional investment banking services.

REAL ESTATE AND INVESTMENT BANKING

Traditionally, investment banks have thrived on a narrow business base—sourcing capital in the form of securities offerings for large, established corporate clients. As capital markets have become more complex, and as the investment banking industry has become increasingly competitive, most firms have broadened their array of financial service offerings. Some examples of expansion of activities include high-yield securities, leveraged buyout, mergers and acquisitions, and various transactions in which investment banks, as principals, invest their own capital.

Extension into real estate services has been a product of diversification as well. This expansion occurred relatively recently and has taken one of two forms: (1) acquisition of an existing commercial and/or residential real estate brokerage franchise; or (2) development of in-house expertise augmented by external hires from the real estate industry. (Two Wall Street firms are exceptions.) These methods have enabled investment banks interested in serving their corporate clients to acquire both geographic real estate market knowledge as well as invaluable experience in arranging real estate sales and financings, resulting in an immediate presence and influence in a relatively diffused industry. In some other cases, units have been established primarily for the tax-shelter benefit of a firm's partners. These units often specialize in real estate development and technical offerings motivated by various tax incentives.

As investment banks establish their commitment to real estate through various methods, so they continue to differ with respect to emphasis. Some of the larger wirehouses target securitized residential real estate, seeking underwriting and trading profits, while advice-oriented firms focus on the private placement of securitized financing of larger commercial properties (i.e., office and industrial buildings, retail projects, and hotels). Most firms offer investment sales, mortgage placement, and valuation advice, a few offer more sophisticated financing alternatives, including securitized offerings, and fewer still are involved in more active roles as asset managers, leasing agents, and/or developers.

That there are many differences among firms helps to highlight an important point—the precise role played by a real estate arm of an investment bank is yet to be clearly defined. Capital commitment (i.e., investment dollars for principal activities as well as direct spending to build a real estate group) varies widely and services offered rarely overlap completely across firms. As competition continues to increase among investment banks and independent real estate services companies, these large distinctions are likely to fade.

PRODUCTS/SERVICES

We try here to represent the real estate investment banking industry as a whole rather than to profile a typical firm within it. The real estate investment bank acts in one of two roles, either as an agent or as a principal. The former is characterized by a no-risk mediatory or advisory position. Acting as a principal on the other hand, the firm places its own capital at risk to generate trading or development profit.

Agency Functions

Traditionally, agency functions have centered on transactions related to the sale or financing of a major single asset or portfolio of domestic or international real estate. As an advisor, the firm serves all real estate players including developers, operators, corporations, institutions, users, and investors. Agency fees are structured primarily upon a percentage basis of the total sale or financing proceeds. There is a wide range of agency products and services that includes, but is not limited to, the following.

Construction Financing. Construction financing provides the funds required to construct various real estate projects. A construction loan is intended to cover only the costs associated with predevelopment planning through initial lease-up, and usually is structured for a term of three to seven years. Construction financing can take several forms, including traditional commercial bank and insurance company lending, commercial paper construction financing, and other public debt issues.

Intermediate/Permanent Financing. Because of the risk premium and the short time period, construction financing is refinanced into longer terms of approximately 7 to 15 years as soon as the underlying property demonstrates sufficient earnings potential. In contrast to construction financing, permanent financing can be achieved through a wide variety of methods, including: first or second mortgages, where a fixed-rate or floating-rate loan is secured by a senior or subordinated lien on the property; lease-backed notes; zero-coupon bonds; collateralized mortgages; rated commercial mortgages; and convertible or participating mortgages, where the investor return is determined by a fixed rate on the loan as well as a portion of after-debt cash flow from the underlying property. This increased flexibility is attributable partially to the decreased risk associated with investing in an operating versus a speculative project that makes more capital sources willing to supply permanent, as opposed to construction, financing. Given the number of potential capital sources and potential financing structures, it is easy to see the value of employing an investment bank to solicit and select the most effective alternative.

Advisory Assignments. Financial advisory services provided to owners of major real estate portfolios and large real estate projects may include partial or complete liquidation of real estate companies or real estate investments, acquisition of major real estate properties or assets, reorganization or restructuring of real estate portfolios, project evaluation, and lease negotiation. An investment banker's expertise in accounting, tax, and securities disciplines is invaluable in this case, especially with respect to publicly traded companies involved in real estate. Besides financial advice, the investment bank can also provide guidance on development and real estate investment (i.e., asset management).

Sale/Brokerage. The firm acts as an agent and intermediary by representing clients in the sale or purchase of office buildings, shopping centers, hotels, office/industrial parks, and multifamily residential properties. Sources of capital for this type of transaction typically come from major international and domestic public and private institutions and corporations, as well as wealthy individual investors. It is the ability to access these sources of capital (i.e., potential purchasers) that may dictate success in a sales assignment.

Development Counseling. Many investment banks provide advice to institutions, corporations, and developers in the conception and construction of major real estate projects. A firm may perform market feasibility studies; select architects, developers, and other consultants; negotiate for zoning and usage rights; and develop and execute a financing plan.

Mergers and Acquisitions/Leveraged Buyouts. Real estate groups often are involved in the acquisition or divestiture of real estate service companies or real estate subsidiaries of large corporations. In these assignments, an investment bank's real estate group may provide an evaluation of management, an analysis of the synergy created by merging two operations, insight on current and future opportunities within the industry, and valuation of a target company and the real estate it owns. Upon concluding a transaction, the investment bank may be required to provide a written opinion for the shareholders or policyholders as to the fairness of the transaction from a financial point of view.

Available Products

Sale Leasebacks. Sale and leaseback of corporate real estate can often represent the optimum structure for monetizing appreciated real estate assets. Such a transaction can provide all the benefits of selling an asset for maximum proceeds without relinquishing control. The major benefits of this type of transaction include raising funds by taking advantage of the appreciated value of real estate assets, access to nontraditional sources of equity, continued asset control through net leasing, a potential future repurchase option, and off-balance-sheet financing. Lease terms typically run 10 to 25 years with renewal options. Rental payments usually are favorable to the seller in the early years with inflation adjustment or predetermined increases in rental structure to compensate the purchaser in future years. The real estate typically includes corporate headquarters buildings, manufacturing facilities, and other single-purpose properties.

Commercial Paper. Commercial paper is a short-term, floating-rate financing vehicle, generally irrevocably and unconditionally guaranteed by a domestic insurance company or foreign bank, that must be reissued approximately every 30 days. Commercial paper generally is associated with companies with high credit ratings, but some lower-quality companies using a third-party guarantor (such as a private real estate developer) can access this growing market. A nonrecourse commercial paper program with credit support can be an effective alternative to conventional sources of construction financing and, in some cases, interim financing for periods of up to 10 years.

The advantages of commercial paper are numerous: the cost of borrowing is relatively low because the dramatic growth in commercial paper programs has created a liquid market for investors looking to avoid exposure to volatile interest rates; the borrower gets access to public markets without SEC registration requirements; short-term notes can be placed both domestically and in Europe, allowing the issuer to take advantage of the most favorable market conditions; a program can be limited or nonrecourse; and there is considerable flexibility in meeting future cash flow needs.

Although commercial paper is floating rate, an interest-rate swap can be utilized in order to obtain a long-term, fixed-rate cost of debt. Using interest-rate caps, floors, and collars, a developer can create its own interest-rate risk environment for the life of the commercial paper program.

Real Estate Investment Trusts (REITs). A REIT is a corporation or business trust that avoids corporate-level taxation by conforming to specific requirements of the Internal Revenue Code. Cash flow from the real estate is paid out as dividends without taxation at the corporate level, thus avoiding the double taxation that many other partnerships encounter. The market for REITs is primarily a retail one, which requires a relatively high initial return on invested equity.

There are three basic types of REITs: an equity REIT (ownership of real property), a mortgage REIT (a portfolio of loans secured by real property), and a hybrid REIT (a combination of equity and mortgage REITs). The advantages of a REIT include direct cash flow to investors, elimination of double taxation, potential accounting gains, and the possibility of continued asset control when the investor acts as advisor to the trust. Disadvantages include not maximizing sale proceeds for asset sales, the possibility of creating an undesirable taxable event, shares generally trading at a discount to the market value of their properties, and meeting strict IRS requirements to retain tax-exempt qualification.

Master Limited Partnerships (MLPs). An MLP is a publicly traded limited partnership vehicle sold primarily in the retail equity market. As a practical rather than legal term, an "MLP" can refer to a large partnership made up of several smaller partnerships or to any partnership in which interests are publicly registered and tradable.

Creation of an MLP is complex and may take several forms. A company (sponsor) may sell assets to an MLP, which raises funds through an initial public offering of units representing limited partnership interests. A sponsor can contribute assets and liabilities or operations or subsidiaries to an MLP, receiving units in exchange for the contribution; the sponsor can then retain a portion of the units and distribute the rest. Or an MLP may be organized by a sponsor who acts as the general partner in several existing nontradable limited partnerships. MLPs began in the oil and gas industry but recently have sprung up in the real estate, transportation, and communications industries. Corporations can use MLPs to sell or spin off assets and, as in the case of REITs, eliminate taxation at the corporate level.

The advantages of MLPs include: flexibility for holding and managing real estate or other portfolio assets; appreciated asset value while maintaining sponsor control as general partner in the partnerships; use as an antitakeover defense mechanism; and potential accounting gains by eliminating double taxation. Disadvantages include not maximizing sale proceeds from asset sales because of high-yield requirements of investors, risking possible taxation as a corporation, and signs that the market may be oversold.

Securitization and Mortgage Products. In order to issue a public note backed by real estate, often it is necessary to provide additional guarantees beyond the value of the underlying property. As part of the issuing process, the investment bank's real estate group will coordinate a rating for the offering through Standard & Poor's. Another possibility is for a real estate group to find a third-party guarantor who will meet timely payment of principal and/or interest to note holders in the event the property does not generate sufficient cash flow.

Other securitized products are available in the form of debt secured by mortgages on real property. Two examples are collateralized mortgage obligations (CMOs) and mortgage-backed securities. In these instances, mortgages are pooled together with the principal and interest payments offered to investors. While these instruments are implicitly backed by real estate, their liquidity and marketability make them more suitably handled by sales and trading professionals.

European Debt Issues. The European market for dollar-denominated commercial paper and medium-term notes recently has expanded dramatically. Often this presents an attractive alternative for U.S. clients, real estate related or otherwise, seeking debt financing. The obvious advantages to European debt issues include the expanded investor market, access to a growing and sizable investor group seeking liquid investments besides time deposits and CDs, competitive borrowing costs, and flexibility with respect to timing, maturity, and issue amount. Real estate backed debt instruments issued in Europe trade on the borrower's name and credit as opposed to the quality of the real estate. This can be an added advantage, especially for a corporate client looking to refinance a lesser-credit real estate project.

Principal Functions

Real Estate Development. Besides engaging in real estate development indirectly as agents, certain investment banks invest in development projects for their own accounts. This activity reached its peak in 1982–1985, fueled by real estate tax benefits created by the Economic Recovery Tax Act of 1981. Many partners of a privately held investment bank sheltered a great deal of their earnings from taxation through real estate developments for the firm's account.

The Tax Reform Act of 1986 greatly alters the tax treatment of real estate investments. Depreciation has been extended from 19 to 31½ years, reducing tax benefits and resultant property values, as well as changing investment criteria from shelter-based to income-based. Additionally, the elimination of preferential capital gains treatment has made property sales less attractive. The totally tax-shelter-motivated syndication market has been all but eliminated with loss of the ability to offset earned income with passive losses from public real estate tax shelters. Repeal of the Investment Tax Credit, application of at-risk limitations, and the switch from amortization to capitalization of construction period interest costs and taxes also reduce the attractiveness of real estate as a tax-motivated investment.

It should not be surprising that these tax law changes, coupled with the relative softness of most real estate markets, have reduced development activities at most investment banks. Other factors, including lower returns on invested capital in real estate projects in comparison with other principal activities in an investment bank, and the continuing problem of the illiquidity of real estate assets, have made real estate development less attractive to investment banks—entities that redeploy their capital daily to take advantage of rapidly changing market conditions.

INTEGRATION WITH TRADITIONAL INVESTMENT BANKING OPERATIONS

Discussion of real estate products and services offered by investment banks would be incomplete without acknowledging that integration with other investment banking services is vital to realizing maximum value from a firm's real estate operations. Consider the following examples.

Mergers and Acquisitions. Real estate professionals within an investment bank often work jointly with mergers and acquisitions specialists in order to best serve a client's needs. The most obvious example of this occurs when there is a need to sell a client's real estate assets as part of an overall divestiture program, a restructuring, or a defensive response to a hostile tender offer. In the case of major corporate acquisitions, the primary transaction typically is followed by a spinning off of redundant or superfluous assets. Real estate often may be a secondary line of business which new management deems as nonessential to operations. Valuation and disposition of this real estate can be offered as an additional investment banking service by the mergers and acquisitions professionals.

Commercial Paper and Interest-Rate Swaps. We previously noted that commercial paper programs can be a cost-effective, short-term financing method for a real estate client. Issuing commercial paper for a real estate project requires a joint effort of two departments. The short-term finance specialists review pricing and market conditions as well as execute the public offering, while the real estate professionals provide detailed information on the underlying real estate and work to arrange a third-party guarantee. A firm's swap group also may be called upon to determine the cost to the borrower of trading floating- for fixed-rate debt. The swap group can offer a variety of interest-rate alternatives including caps and floors.

Private Placement/Syndication/Public Securities Offerings. Whenever a real estate investment is placed with more than one capital source, other resources within an investment bank are called upon. In this type of offering the real estate group will arrange a sale or financing structure to be offered to potential investors through the appropriate domestic or international desk, including syndicate, private placement, and equity sales. Suppose a REIT is assembled by the real estate group. The client is advised as to the properties to be included and the cash flows they will generate. The initial public offering then is handled by an equity sales force with product-specific knowledge provided by the real estate group.

High-Yield Securities. Because real estate investments are often below investment grade, high-yield, (or "junk" bond) financing is sometimes used. Real estate expertise is combined with knowledge of the appropriate high-yield financing vehicle to best meet a client's objectives.

International Coverage. International sources of capital are often targeted as sources for domestic real estate investment. Given the number and dollar magnitude of recent international acquisitions of domestic real estate, an investment bank's ability to reach Far and Middle Eastern and European investors interested in domestic real estate projects is of considerable value.

CONCLUSION

The relatively recent expansion of investment banking services to include real estate expertise is but one element of the universal growth and sophistication of the financial markets. In the ever expanding search for new areas of profitability, the imperfect real estate markets have encouraged most investment banks to establish real estate subsidiaries.

Two opposing characteristics have come to mark real estate in investment banks. First, the emergence of liquid real estate investments has allowed new products to be offered as standard, or mainstream, capital-raising techniques, understood and appreciated by most investor markets. On the other hand, however, real estate remains a complicated investment requiring extensive experience and knowledge. This had led investment banks to create real estate units that offer specialized market expertise as well as access to traditional investment banking resources.

PART 3   TRANSACTIONAL ACTIVITIES

The chapters in Part 2 dealt with the raising of capital for business, activities in the primary market. The chapters in Part 3 turn to the secondary market, where securities are bought and sold among investors.

In Chapter 11 Jim Freeman covers the trading of equity and debt securities in an investment banking firm. This has become an enormously important activity in major investment banking firms. Institutional and retail sales, the role of analysts in support of trading, risk arbitrage, and program trading are significant aspects of equity trading. High-yield bonds, medium-term notes, floating-rate instruments, and mortgage-backed securities are important parts of the fixed-income market. The chapter concludes with a discussion of trading in foreign markets.

Chapter 12 discusses leveraged buyouts, one of the more spectacular investment banking activities in recent years. Some investment bankers have been particularly successful in managing LBOs and the profits have been high. Warren Law discusses the role of investment bankers, the structure of an LBO, and the motivations of the parties involved.

In Chapter 13, Peter Williamson describes mergers and acquisitions, another of the recently glamorous and highly profitable investment banking activities. The chapter deals with the various types of transactions, and focuses on the roles played by different kinds of investment banking firms. Varied resources are called upon for M&A work. The chapter concludes with a review of defensive strategies in attempted takeovers.

Investment management is a prominent feature of some investment banking firms, while others avoid this activity. In Chapter 14, Jeanne Gustafson discusses how investment bankers got into the money management business, how this business relates to other investment banking activities, and how profitable the business can be.

11 Sales and Trading

JAMES L. FREEMAN

Twenty years ago, sales, research, and trading were separate activities within most investment banks. These activities began to be integrated 10 years ago with the aim of enhancing a firm's effectiveness in distributing securities in the primary and secondary markets, (i.e., new issues and the market for outstanding securities). Today sales, trading, and research are fully integrated functions in state-of-the art financings as well as secondary market transactions.

This progression reflects the increasingly sophisticated needs of security issuers as well as the institutionalization of financial assets into large, professionally managed pools of money. Some background may help to understand what has produced these circumstances.

During World War II, in order to raise the vast quantities of capital needed to finance the war, the U.S. government adopted a policy of forced savings. For years, the country and corporate America were nourished by this forced liquidity. In the booming postwar economy, both borrowers and lenders were highly liquid. Corporations had only minimal need for external funds because of the high return on assets they were earning. Those needs were easily met by individuals, who controlled the vast amount of investable funds during the early postwar period.

By the 1960s the mutual fund industry had begun to institutionalize a part of personal wealth, that is, to attract liquid savings and investment in professionally invested pools. By the early 1970s, changes in the pension laws encouraged the buildup of increasingly larger pools of retirement savings managed by financial institutions. ERISA, the Employee Retirement Income Security Act passed in 1974, and new deferred savings plans have increased the size of these professionally managed pools so that the pension system now exceeds $1 trillion and IRAs, individual retirement accounts, exceed $300 billion.

Meanwhile, in the past 25 years, corporate America has had to learn to deal with inflation, credit crunches, recessions, and then disinflation, in short order. The appetite for capital became ravenous. Partly this reflected the lessened ability of corporations to finance their growth internally in an era of extended inflation in the 1970s and early 1980s. The recent unlocking of hidden assets through mergers, leveraged buyouts, restructurings, and divestitures has led to increasing need for debt capital.

Another huge pool of investable funds, the Eurodollar market, was created overseas when the U.S. dollar became the international settlement currency. With its growth accelerated by the rise of the petrodollar empire in the 1970s and exacerbated by U.S. trade deficits, among other factors, the Eurodollar market now represents nearly $2 trillion of "fast money" seeking high returns on financial assets.

Finally, in the 1980s we have seen a once-in-a-generation phenomenon—disinflation. Extended disinflationary trends have always increased the integrity of financial assets. When this happens, financial assets become attractive to investors—individuals, institutional investors, and corporations alike. Thus financial assets have become the commodity of the 1980s, spurring development of increasingly sophisticated investment vehicles in the primary and secondary markets, and the brave new world of synthetic securities was born.

Today investment banking is at a crossroads. On the one hand, there are immense financing needs to solve ever more sophisticated corporate and government problems. On the other hand, managers of enormous institutionalized investment pools with a global perspective have hired the best and the brightest talent to allocate their financial assets to achieve the highest returns consistent with specified levels of risk. Wall Street's challenge is to understand these needs, and to create added value simultaneously for both sides.

This chapter attempts to explain how the investment banking community is bringing together primary issuers and secondary sellers, with buyers in the equity and taxable fixed-income markets. These markets, which have always been linked by investors' economic outlook, are also related through asset-allocation efforts now being used by institutions and pension plan sponsors.

EQUITIES

Traditionally, articles explaining the equity area break it down by function. What does a salesperson, a trader, or a research analyst do? As mentioned earlier, evolution in investment banking has moved toward the integration of those functions in order to create products and execute transactions. This trend makes it efficient to discuss the area by product group rather than by function. Product groups include:

1. Institutional group
   a. U.S. stocks
   b. International stocks
   c. Convertible securities
   d. Over-the-counter stocks
   e. Futures/options/index options

2. Retail group
   a. Sales
   b. Administration
3. Proprietary group
   a. Risk arbitrage
   b. Futures/options/index options
4. Capital markets
   a. Traditional syndicates
   b. Block trades
   c. Multiple syndication
5. Program trading
   a. Arbitrage
   b. Liquidity
   c. Money market

Institutional Group

Institutional equity business now accounts for around 70 percent of the volume of all transactions on the major domestic equity exchanges. Moreover, approximately 50 percent of all volume is now traded in block transactions of 10,000 shares or more. The institutionalization of the market has brought with it ultrarapid transaction response times and a high degree of price volatility. Where institutional investors once made a clear distinction between investment advice and the liquidity function—that is, a willingness to provide capital to execute volume transactions close to the market—now the demands of institutions have merged, requiring the integration of research, sales, and trading to create a successful transaction. The heart and soul of this group, although not the most profitable area on a fully costed basis, is the domestic institutional equity business.

Investment ideas are generated by a research department made up of 35 to 50 industry and strategy analysts (Merrill Lynch is an exception with 100 plus) who carry out in-depth industry, corporate, and value analysis in order to recommend a definitive course of action—buy/hold/sell.

Research analysts, who once were thought of as green-eyeshade intellectuals, have become well-rounded marketers of the products and ideas they create. This transformation was motivated by the elimination on May 1, 1975, of fixed commissions on transactions conducted on the New York Stock Exchange. Before "May Day," research analysts were essentially purveyors of information about companies and industries. Institutional investors paid for this service with the high commissions generated on their trades. After that date, with the erosion of transaction commissions paid by institutions, research analysts worked in conjunction with their firm's sales force and traders to create transaction opportunities.

An analyst spends approximately half of his or her time analyzing, visiting, and preparing information on a given industry and on companies within the group. Another 35 to 40 percent of the analyst's time is spent marketing to institutions. This includes seeing major customers at least once a year and making 100 to 200 telephone calls a month as follow-through. The sellside analyst has an institutional buyside counterpart: an analyst or portfolio manager who covers a group of industries for the money management organization. Their interaction allows the sellside analyst to understand and become part of the investment decision-making function at an institution. If the analyst is respected, the telephone calls and visits—that is, demand for information—flow both ways. Continuity and consistency of service are of primary importance in maintaining a valued relationship between the analyst and his or her counterpart.

Once an analyst generates an idea and delivers it orally or in writing to the firm's sales force and to the institutional analyst counterpart, the sales force interacts with its counterparts. The equity sales force in most institutional brokerage firms consists of two groups. The first group, the research or portfolio salespeople, interacts with the research department, strategists, and portfolio managers of buyside institutions. Salespeople call their counterparts at the institutions assigned to them for the purpose of generating investment/transaction decisions. Simply passing on information, like a "cold, wet fish," is a waste of time. The portfolio salesperson calls with an action recommendation: that a position should be bought, sold, or held—and why. As in the case of the analyst, the object here is to establish two-way feedback between the institution and the salesperson. Every offering of information and recommendation in a salesperson/portfolio manager relationship should bring a response that leads to a decision on an investment course of action or inaction.

The second group in the equity sales force consists of sales traders or coverage traders. This group is assigned institutional customers who have an active order desk or highly transaction-oriented portfolio managers. The coverage trader passes significant information quickly to the institution's trading desk, normally by direct tielines. The major purpose of the functional link between these two areas, however, is to communicate information on the large amount of transactions (called inquiry) in the form of bids, offers, and swaps that are being worked on currently by the firm's sales and trading group. The sales trader does not execute orders but acts as a conduit and aids the institution's transaction decisions in order to get the best execution price. Once again, the sales trader's part of the decision-making function is essential to the success of the system.

The sales trader interacts with the investment bank's position or block traders. That trader executes all orders by pricing the order inflow. In some cases, one inquiry can be matched with another institution's inquiry on the other side. A large percentage of institutional transactions, however, involve principal (i.e., the investment bank's own capital) risk. First, block traders make "upstairs" (i.e., away-from-the-floor) markets in major issues in that trader's area—assigned industries. Second, the buyside and sellside may not match exactly in size—a 100,000-share buyer versus a 125,000-share seller, for example. The 25,000 is often positioned by the trader.

Finally, as a service to major institutions, investment banks execute trades as principals in the transaction. Because this is a service, part of the commission is expected to be lost in trading losses. At the same time, the best houses with the strongest trading desks know how to price and distribute this risk quite well. They rely on an excellent sales trading distribution system, the trader's "feel" for the price that will create buying or selling interest, and the use of futures and options to hedge the risk in the positions.

To complete the circle, the trader, who is an expert in the trading pattern of a stock, maintains a close relationship with the analyst covering the same industry. Here, fundamental information—the timing of potential information flow, such as earnings reports or management presentations—is combined with information as to who has been interested in knowing more about the stock, whether from the buyside or sellside. This is one of the ways analysts spend the remaining 10 to 15 percent of their time. To sum up, there is an integrated effort by the research, sales, and trading groups to interact with investors in the decision-making and execution functions that end up as business on an institutional block desk.

Although this example has been in listed securities, similar functions exist in the international, convertible, over-the-counter, and futures/options areas. The level of sophistication of both investment banks and institutional money managers has upped the ante so that each area requires specialized groups. For most transactions, the system described earlier will work, but for the 50 to 100 institutions most active and sophisticated in a particular area, a special coverage group will have primary responsibility for its area.

The international or the non-U.S. stock department may have its own research group. This may be a subset of the equity-research department that concentrates on providing service to a specialized group of salespeople, traders, portfolio managers, and analysts interested in international equities. International groups face the added demand of 24-hour trading. In most cases, desks with research, sales, and trading groups are set up in Tokyo, London, and New York. This should become an increasingly important function following the opening of the Tokyo market to U.S. houses which happened in late 1985 and the deregulation and unbundling of functions in London during October 1986. "Big Bang," as it has come to be known, is in many ways reminiscent of "May Day" 1975 in the United States. It will provide new opportunities as well as trying times for major U.S. investment banks (as well as the locals).

It is not our intention to give short shrift to the convertible (bonds and preferreds), futures and options, and over-the-counter areas. To avoid repetition, it is necessary only to state that these products function as a group in the same integrated manner as the listed common stock area; each interacts with the institutional decision makers in their specialty.

Retail Group

Dealing with retail customers requires considerable commitment of sales and administration resources. Capital for trading is of less importance, yet a certain level is necessary for regulatory capital purposes as defined by the New York Stock Exchange and the National Association of Securities Dealers (NASD), which maintain self-regulatory arms to enforce rules and regulations.

The integration of functions described in the preceding section is less important in the retail product. Marketing depends almost entirely upon the individual salesperson. Many retail houses repackage their equity research to highlight the pertinent points and to make the product more of a streamlined marketing piece than a detailed analytical document.

Salespeople are the essence of a retail organization. The salesperson tends to operate as a small proprietor within the organization, an entrepreneur using a system. The quality of business that good retail salespeople generate tends to be underestimated. Further, the strong retail salesperson acts as an advisor to his or her customers, anticipating needs and understanding what financial decisions are important. The salesperson is often multimarket-oriented, tending to be equally accomplished in recommending stocks and municipal bonds, for example. In some cases, knowledge of commodities and now financial asset-based commodities is essential. Familiarity with short-term investments as well as the state-of-the-art tax shelters also may be important.

Registered representatives (another name for salespeople) tend to sell the products with which they feel comfortable. Their customer base reflects their talents. Success is a measure not only of selling skills but also of an ability to fulfill the customer's expectation.

Another major element essential to running a successful retail operation is a high-quality administrative infrastructure. Here the integration of data processing, back-office clearing, and order-desk execution is paramount. Excellence in performing these functions is essential to keeping the customer and to making the product profitable.

Profitability in retail sales is an asset accumulation and banking function as much as it is a marketing function. The "box," or the large pool of securities controlled by a member firm through hypothecation in margin accounts, is important. These securities can be borrowed at will to provide arbitrage or hedging strategies. Also, the cash balances that customers maintain are paid interest at a rate that is somewhat less than the firm can earn when it aggregates all cash balances. The spread between the interest rate which is charged to margin accounts and the rate paid on free credit balances is positive because the member firm has a better credit rating than the individual account.

Strength in sales and administration allows the successful retail firm to be profitable, with a substantial amount of its profitability resulting from its role as a banker—a gatherer of financial assets.

Proprietary Group

Trading functions for all products—taxable fixed-income, municipal securities, or equities—can be categorized as institutional or proprietary. The proprietary trading group's function is to make money for the firm. In many firms it is totally separated from the institutional effort, in order to minimize any conflict of interest. The largest equity proprietary product is risk arbitrage, which today covers a multitude of speculative strategies normally (but not exclusively) related to merger, acquisition, and divestiture activities.

Risk arbitrage requires a trading mentality. Decisions are made quickly. An inherent ability to assess potential and risk is essential, but careful attention to detail is important too. Risk-arbitrage groups employ analysts specifically to evaluate the financial integrity, legal regulation, and business rationality of any potential combination. This arena presents some of the most lucrative opportunities for the firm and the risk arbitrageur, as the rewards are huge for those who combine strong intellectual, decision-making, and risk-taking talents. This is the "dollar-a-point" bridge game of Wall Street. it is normal for the daily profit/loss in the area to swing in the millions of dollars, and it is not usually for the P/L to move in the $10-million-or-more range during a week.

Capital Markets

The equity new-issue business, much like the corporate bond area, has moved up the risk ladder. Capital brawn is as much a factor as quality of investment banking service.

Traditional syndicates still exist and are widely used by smaller firms and in initial public offerings. In the former case, the book-running manager does not want to shoulder the underwriting risk. For initial offerings it is necessary to gain broad enough distribution to achieve an optimal trading balance or possibly to obtain listing status, which is dependent on getting enough round-lot shareholders.

With the consolidation of the investment banking industry, a greater dependence on capital has developed. Corporate issuers (like institutional customers) increasingly demand liquidity, and the traditional syndicate does not afford the flexibility to respond "on the wire." Consequently, many capital market transactions are executed single-handed or with a limited group of co-managers. Often the transactions are executed as block trades under a registration statement. They can be printed on an exchange or off-board. The issuer gains more timing flexibility, a higher assurance of execution, and a lower execution or transaction cost. The investment banker assumes far more risk for a lower spread but hopes to make it up in volume. Moreover, the book-running manager and to a lesser extent the co-managers generate nearly all the sales interest in most new-issue transactions so they might as well take the risk and earn the rewards.

The capital markets group represents the ultimate integration of research, sales, and trading. Research analysts often help in understanding and advising the corporate issuer. Respected analysts know all the senior management within their area of expertise. Similarly, once the issue is filed, it is the analyst who best understands the positives and negatives of a company he or she covers. Thus the education of the sales force and institutional customers is dependent on an analyst's understanding of the company, its potential, and its competitive position. The salesperson presents the ideas to his or her account base, as in the case of other research ideas. The sales trader also shows the merchandise to the institutional trading desks, with more depth and background than the run-of-the-mill trading inquiry. Finally, the position traders become involved at the time of pricing as they would with any large block transaction.

In this capital-intensive activity, success depends on the integrated efforts of research, sales, and trading.

Program Trading

Program trading refers to portfolio or multistock transactions, as distinguished from individual stock transactions. Typically, a derivative security, such as futures or index options, is used in conjunction with or as a proxy for the portfolio being traded. This sounds more complex than it is. Traditionally, portfolio managers made decisions to buy or sell a stock. Now they often decide to buy or sell a whole portfolio. If it were not for their ability to lay off a large portion of the risk in the futures market, investment banks would find the risk of such transactions too great to make as principals.

Some of the strategies that typically result in program trades are:

1. *Index Funds or Passive Management.* This is a major portfolio technique that evolved from the need to manage the risks and aggregate performance of vast pools of pension fund money. AT&T realized years ago that the results of individual managers could vary, but the performance of its overall fund tended to track the S&P 500 stock index, less fees and transaction costs. If a fund were so large that it could only track the S&P 500, the best way to improve performance, then, was to lower fees and transactions costs. Recognition of this by pension fund sponsors has led to nearly a quarter of a trillion dollars of equity funds being indexed to one of the benchmark averages, from the Dow Jones 30 to the Wilshire 5000 index.

On any given day an index fund may want to buy or sell a dollar amount of the fund. The investment bank promises the customer a basket normally priced at the last sale at the close of trading, and then covers its risk in the futures or index options market. The securities are bought or sold, normally in waves on the exchange floor. Such massive transaction volume usually calls for more floor talent than a firm has in-house, so many two-dollar (independent) brokers are employed. A large program, say $100 million or more, may take numerous (five or more) waves. After each wave is completed and the transactions are executed, the program trader at the investment bank lifts part of the hedge, so that the firm is as close to neutral exposure as possible.

2. *Selling and Buying Portfolios.* This often happens when one advisor loses a piece of pension business to another advisor. Instead of dribbling the portfolio out and taking market risk, the new advisor shows the portfolio or a profile of the portfolio to a program-trading house. A profile may include the dollar amount, the number of stocks, size of individual positions, the liquidity of individual positions, frequently defined as number of trading days of volume contained in the position, and a beta-coefficient profile of the whole portfolio, but not the names of the

individual securities. A profile instead of actual names prevents the investment bank from trading on this information beforehand, but it significantly increases the risk that a program-trading group must incur in effecting a trade. Based on the profile, the program-trading group presents alternative fee proposals to the customer.

The greater the risk the group takes, the higher the cost. A pure agency transaction, for example, may cost only a few cents per share. A blind bid struck off the last sale price, which concentrates all the risk on the investment bank, may well cost the customer $.25 per share or even more. Active management portfolio transactions of this type are inherently riskier than index portfolio transaction. There is no perfect hedge to offset the portfolio risks. In a program trade involving an index, one knows the exact composition of the portfolio. In contrast, when selling actively managed portfolios, the trader not only does not know what is there, but more often than not may encounter a few little surprises that potentially can be extremely costly.

3. *Money Market Substitute.* It is hard to believe that the world has come to a point where large money market accounts will buy a basket of stocks and sell stock-futures contracts normally one to three months out in order to beat the return on commercial paper or certificates of deposit, but it is true. The account goes long a stream of dividend-paying stocks. By selling the futures contract that is exactly the same as the basket at a given spread, depending on the length left in the futures contract, the account has accomplished a riskless arbitrage that at expiration renders a predetermined return. When the spread is right (the premium is enough), tens of billions of dollars of this type of transaction may be in place.

4. *Asset Allocation Changes.* An account or a plan sponsor (the corporation that owns a pension plan run internally or by advisors) may decide to change the asset mix among cash, stocks, and bonds. These transactions can be very large, over $100 million, and given the size and the mix of products only a very few investment banks are willing or able to execute this sort of program. Over time, however, this capability will become increasingly important, as asset allocation is in the early stages of strategic understanding.

5. *Premium Arbitrage.* Futures and index options tend to trade within a band relative to the underlying index. Often index funds or program-trading departments will trade the premium, selling stocks and buying futures at a large enough discount, or the reverse, to make an arbitrage profit. In addition, futures and index options may trade in bands relative to each other, setting up the potential for attractive intraderivative arbitrages. Unlike the money market arbitrage, which is a "true" or riskless arbitrage, this type of trading activity is not. It is not unusual for the Dow Jones to outperform or underperform the Wilshire 5000 for months or even years. Therefore, the trader may make the right spread decision and still lose.

Program trading encompasses a vast number of strategies, normally using a derivative hedge in the futures or index option markets. The large size of many programs and the hedged position may cause these trades to be disruptive to the market on any given day, because it matters little to the customer or the program-trading group at what price the transactions are executed. The important function is the "basis" spread (measured in basis points between the future/option and the index itself, i.e., premium/discount). Consequently, a large program may cause short-term volatility in the averages but have little effect on the basis spread. Within a short period of time these aberrations normally are corrected.

TAXABLE FIXED-INCOME SECURITIES

"Where there is no money there is no change of any kind, not of scene or of routine."

MOSS HART

No area of the securities industry has adapted to world economic changes with more dynamism than the fixed-income markets. The investment banking industry has won the admiration (and occasionally the scorn) of borrowers for its ability to create new products (and profits) despite or possibly because of the cathartic pains that have engulfed the credit markets during the last 20 years. The breadth of products resulting is so great that a few pages cannot do justice to the many brilliant innovations. The description following is the proverbial Chinese dinner, with a tidbit from the government menu, a sampling of a securitized asset, a taste of capital markets. The reader who is hungry a short time later will want to learn more on his or her own.

It is probably worth a few minutes to explain how taxable fixed-income products have evolved since World War II. The cliché—necessity is the mother of invention—could not be more apt.

A brief backdrop of recent credit history will bring into perspective the need for some of the publicly traded fixed-income products that will be discussed. The preceding section of this chapter noted that World War II was a period of forced savings for U.S. corporations and individuals alike. In the late 1940s industry cautiously changed over to the production of peacetime goods. Arising out of forced abstinence, consumer spending for homes, cars, and appliances was easily financed through savings and liquidity in the banking system. Before long, corporations realized this was no aberration, but rather the beginning of a prolonged boom, leading to a need for sizable, incremental investments in plant and equipment. At the same time, attempting to rebuild its trading partners and remedy poor financial liquidity abroad, the United States set out through the Marshall Plan and its successor programs to provide grants and preferential loans in dollars to nations within its sphere of influence. The dollar became the international currency of record, the reserve backing for other countries' treasuries. Thus began what is now the vast Eurodollar pool.

In the 1950s the balance sheets of U.S. industry generally were good, so financing growth took fairly conventional forms. Capital expenditures were financed by long-term bonds, preferred stock, and, occasionally, common equity. Inventories were financed by bank loans. Residential housing was financed primarily by savings and loan institutions, commercial banks, and savings banks. Other consumer durables were funded by the financing arms of the automobile or retailing industry (General

Motors Acceptance Corp., for example) at the point of purchase or by a local bank. The U.S. Treasury funded most of its needs through tax receipts or the Treasury bill market.

Rates were heavily stratified by the government, which acted somewhat like a benign dictator in the credit markets. Until 1951 government bond rates were pegged by the Federal Reserve Board. Until 1978, rates paid on savings were set by government agencies, and in return the government blessed the safety of savings accounts.

Changes, however, started in the early 1950s when the Federal Reserve unpegged the rates on government bonds. Then in the early 1960s the government began to withdraw from the foreign loan market to finance the Great Society and later the Vietnam conflict. The banking industry stepped into the void to provide liquidity to those nations that were important to the United States' sphere of influence. By 1965, the country's guns-and-butter policies had brought credit shortages and worries of economic overheating. Hoping to slow the runaway demands for goods, services, and money, in 1966 the Federal Reserve heavily restricted credit, especially for housing loans. Thus started the first in a series of postwar credit crunches with the housing market as the primary sacrificial lamb. The benign dictator began to lose control, and the accepted pattern of easy credit at low rates through normal lenders was lost.

The sins of disintermediation set the stage for winners and losers within the financial system. Accelerating embedded inflation led to increasingly cathartic credit crunches in 1966 to 1967, 1969 to 1970, 1980, and 1981 to 1982. It is against this background of spiraling inflation and interest rates that the investment banking industry learned to engineer financial products to cope with and capitalize on the increasingly severe bouts of disintermediation and credit demand that plagued the world.

The publicly traded fixed-income products that we are going to discuss, and the ways in which they are traded, are these:

1. Government securities
   a. Treasury bills
   b. Coupons
   c. Agencies (nonsecuritized issues)
2. Corporate fixed income
   a. Bonds
   b. Preferreds
   c. High yield
   d. Medium-term notes
3. Short-term and floating-rate products
   a. Commercial paper
   b. Certificates of deposit
   c. Bankers' acceptances

   d. Floating-rate notes

   e. Adjustable-rate preferreds

4. Asset-backed products

   a. Mortgage-backed

   b. Automobile-securitized

   c. Credit card and other securitized loans

5. Capital markets

   a. Solicitation and coordination with corporate finance

   b. Competitive bid changes under Rule 415

   c. Bought deals

6. Foreign markets and securities

   a. Eurodollar bonds and notes

   b. Nondollar financing

   c. Opening of the yen market

7. Financial futures and options

   a. Futures

   b. Options

   c. Warrants

8. Proprietary trading

   a. Arbitrage

   b. Yield curve

   c. Intermarket and credit trades

Government Securities

Once upon a time the government market was an arcane, quiet area dominated by such little-known firms as C. J. Devine, Discount Corp., Aubrey Langston, and a number of institutions known for other activities—Morgan Guaranty, Citibank, Salomon Brothers, First Boston. All that changed in the late 1960s and early 1970s. Now interest rates in other capital markets are measured in relation to the government yield curve. As the most active debt market, the government market provides the most accurate indication of supply and demand conditions in the market at any time.

The government market, like all other fixed-income markets, is an over-the-counter market. It is maintained by a large number of dealers who "make markets" in the various issues comprising the government's debt, that is, they act as principals in completing trades in the market. The Federal Reserve has designated the 36 most active dealers as "reporting" dealers who must report their trades to the Fed, which compiles statistics to keep track of the market. The "reporting" dealer designation is important, because the Federal Reserve itself trades with only these dealers when conducting open-market operations and transactions for other accounts. Such trades represent about 10 percent of all activity in the government market, so these dealers are well compensated for their reporting activities. Reporting dealers also are expected to participate in all Treasury sales of new issues, but most dealers in governments would do so anyway.

A small group of government "brokers" are active in making firm bids and offerings or swaps on an anonymous basis between dealers. Dealers make markets as principals (at risk). The brokers act as agents (nonrisk). Finally there is a fourth market—an electronic market where bids and offerings are projected instantaneously by television monitor—sort of an ultimate high-stakes video game.

An investment bank's government group has sales, trading, and research areas. The research product is part of a wide range of fixed-income research a firm will make available, here dealing mainly in quantitative relationships between various sectors of the yield curve under various assumptions of change. In all fixed-income sales one salesperson provides economic, strategic, and trading information to a given customer. Similarly the portfolio manager at the institution usually does the research, portfolio, and trading functions in a particular area. All government dealers make active markets in all "on-the-run" issues (current-coupon issues that are active) and are expected to make bids and offerings in any other issue upon request. The sales force is responsible for transactions with customers, such as bank portfolios, fixed-income investment advisors, other dealers, or government arbitrage firms. Typically, a trader talks to other reporting dealers' trading desks by direct wire. Interdealer trading creates substantial liquidity that aids all participants. Salespeople and traders work closely together to best position their firm to trade profitably in what has become a volatile environment. They are strategically aided by their quantitative research units.

The government market is huge. Some $1.559 trillion of marketable government securities are outstanding. The daily trading volume in the cash market averages over $100 billion and multiples of that trade "notionally" (by value of the contract, not the money put up) in the futures and options markets.

Because the total market is huge, the markets made by the traders are huge; round lots range up to $10 million in bills. Additionally, the spreads are thin, a few 32ds. Profits are made by trading actively with customers, being properly positioned for the intraday swings in the markets, and from the "carry." The carry is the interest-rate differential between the current yield on a government security carried in a dealer's inventory and the overnight borrowing rate to finance it. (The carry is not always positive.)

Corporate Fixed Income

The corporate bond began to come of age in the 1960s when corporations no longer were able to finance most of their capital needs with internally generated funds. Traditionally, bond salespeople and traders on Wall Street dealt in corporate bonds. Today these salespeople have become the generalist sales force for the whole taxable fixed-income area, servicing customers who can buy a wide range of debt instruments in pursuit of maximizing total return. Such customers include insurance companies, investment advisors, bank trust departments, mutual funds, and self-administered state and corporate pension funds, among others.

Strategic input on interest rate moves and the shape of the yield curve must be combined with credit evaluation and "spread" (here meaning spread off the Treasury market) movement analysis, based on the market's credit psychology. Maximizing performance in an environment affected by so many variables takes a wide range of research products that must be integrated to make appropriate portfolio decisions. The measurement of returns under different yield-curve assumptions is essential, as is the spread "trade history" at given rate levels and credit analysis covering a wide universe of comparable companies. When firms put time and effort into building extensive data bases, it is necessary to link them together simultaneously to earn a decent return.

Research for the fixed-income area is more quantitative than is equity research. Even spread differences based on quality are quantified in order to determine value. The fixed-income mentality is more mathematical and defined while equity analysis may seem more philosophical or conceptual.

Sales, research, and trading work closely together to produce customized work for any given account's needs. Those needs are based on a rate and credit environment set by the customer's economic prospects along with the supply-demand relationship in the primary and secondary markets for bonds. In addition, portfolio construction can be based on strategic decisions at the corporate level. This happens when the corporate plan sponsor of the pension fund makes structural changes in its benefit programs to help the corporate parent. Portfoliowide strategies of "defeasing" the future liability of a defined benefit program or "immunizing" a portfolio against future rate changes are strategies a plan sponsor may set (as against his advisor) to benefit corporate goals. These portfoliowide moves are provided by the investment strategy service group of the fixed-income generalist group at investment banks.

An important recent development on the corporate fixed-income front is high-yield bonds—often indelicately referred to as junk bonds. Interest in junk bonds arose out of work originally done at Drexel Burnham Lambert that showed the bond market was too credit-conscious and discounted subinvestment quality paper—BB/Ba and below—well beyond the empirical risk. Recent corporate restructurings through mergers, LBOs, and stock repurchases among others have created a vast quantity of lower-quality paper. Additionally, inherently riskier companies that normally would be financed in the private placement corporate market or by commercial banks now have the opportunity to issue in the public market.

The growth of high-yield paper has brought hefty profits to organizations that have committed major resources to creating a high-yield group of research, sales, trading, and capital markets officers. A successful firm requires a specialized research group whose analytical approach is similar to equity-research analysts, because valuation focuses on projected cash flows arising from different economic scenarios. The sales function also tends to take an equity bent, with salespeople who know "the story" of the issuing company's product lines and outlook.

Although the high-yield area has grown exponentially, only a limited number of issues are liquid—normally the most recent large deals. The liquidity of seasoned issues depends to a great extent on the willingness of the originating investment banker to make markets in such issues. Because the market is large and the liquidity risks are high, spreads in the primary and secondary market are commensurately wide. This gives rise to big profit potential. It is important for the trader not only to know the levels of spreads, but also to know where to go with the paper, that is, who buys a given type of high-yield paper.

High-yield debt is frequently issued with equity warrants as a sweetener. Most often the warrants are separable immediately after the issue is sold, and this is just what happens. High-yield buyers hold the debt and sell the warrants, so warrants are often available cheaply during a distribution. The high-yield trader will trade the debt or the unit, but trading naked warrants excites only the equity department, creating the additional opportunities available in imperfect markets.

In the high-yield area, the origination group also works extremely closely with research, sales, and trading to create a package that has appeal to buyers and is affordable for the issuer. Creatively engineered deals are the norm, not the exception, in the brass-knuckles world of junk securities.

Medium-term notes are a world apart from high-yield bonds. MTNs are a product made possible by Rule 415. They are issued in maturities from 9 months to 15 years. The most usual length is 2 to 7 years. Issuers are normally of investment grade. For the first eight months of 1986, the quality spectrum was as follows:

AAA	13%
AA	29%
A	45%
BBB	13%

MTNs are coupon corporate debt that is sold under a shelf registration statement, making note offerings similar but longer in duration to commercial paper programs. Programs are issued on a continuous basis. These programs are the purest example of Rule 415 flexibility.

MTNs provide investors (buyers) an opportunity to select exactly their maturity and size needs. It is possible to purchase tranches of $2 million or more. Similarly, exact maturity dates within the issuer's maturity ranges are offered investors in order to allow investors to fill exact duration needs or match assets and liabilities.

For the borrower, MTNs represent a method to move quickly and in size. They also offer sellers the ability to issue in maturity ranges that fit the corporation's needs or where the market provides particularly attractive opportunities. But the greatest value is for corporations which have large funding needs that must be filled in a short period of time. Given the continuous issuance, and the size and maturity favorability, MTN programs are a powerful funding system.

Medium-term notes are issued through an investment bank that acts as an agent to the issuing company. The capital markets department tends to be the area within the investment bank that controls MTN programs. Rate levels (maturity and size to be offered on a given day) are normally agreed upon by the company and capital markets with the help of the bond-trading desk.

For the first eight months of 1986, issuers had the following profiles:

Finance Companies	51%
Banks	17%
Industrials	15%
S&L	7%
Other	10%

The future of medium-term notes includes a wide range of potential additional uses. Two areas come to mind with huge potential growth. One is Euro-MTN and Yankee-MTN issuance. This could become the same expansive market that high-quality foreign issuers have used to tap the commercial paper market. Second, under the new tax law it is quite possible that a broad range of municipal issuance may be placed in MTN programs, both taxable and tax-exempt.

Medium-term notes are a capital market product. There is little need to have specialized capital commitment abilities to service the products. The capital market group, the corporate bond desk, and the corporate bond sales force are the natural distribution system for MTNs.

Short-Term and Floating-Rate Products

There are a plethora of short-term securities and some longer-maturity instruments that float, that is, their coupons are regularly reset off short rates. These are sometimes known as money market products.

These short-term instruments are sold to corporations for investment of their cash positions and to mutual funds for liquidity funds, or provided by brokerage houses for in-house accounts. Most large bank trust departments also have similar funds for their in-house managed portfolios.

A separate sales force normally sells these product and calls on a distinct group of portfolio managers who invest large pools of liquid assets as their sole function. Investors have three basic considerations: (1) quality (buyers tend to be highly risk-averse), (2) maturity, and (3) yield. The trading spreads are small. A successful salesperson works at a firm with a broad range of product and hustles to provide the best service possible. This is not an area that requires genius, but rather attention to detail. Good selling skills, patience, and dogged hard work pay off handsomely. Similarly, traders in certificates of deposit, bankers' acceptances, and commercial paper must know their markets, and much of their function is finding "primary product" at the right level. The trader services the issuers in the market area, for they are the sellers of primary product. The trader knows which bank or corporation is a potential issuer for what maturity in what size, matching opportunities against customer–buyer needs.

Commercial paper is issued through one, two, or (rarely) three primary dealers for a corporation. Dealers are investment bankers, although Bankers Trust has led a commercial banking industry foray into the market. Investment bankers distribute the vast majority of dealer paper. A number of issuers also sell directly to institutions ("direct issuers"). These issuers are of high quality, have large appetites, and are constantly in the market. They are typically the finance arms of high-visibility companies; GMAC, Ford Credit, and Sears Credit are the archetypal direct issuers.

The floater market is a newer market, starting with floating-rate notes issued by banks in the middle 1970s. Although maturities may vary anywhere from one to 20 years, the coupons are reset periodically at a designated premium over a well-quoted average such as Treasury bills or the London Interbank Rate (LIBOR). A host of more specialized floating-rate products have developed recently. Many are issued to fill a specific need in a given rate environment. The rage of 1984, for example, was the adjustable-rate preferred (ARPs) that took advantage of the preferred stock intercorporate dividend tax preference (then an 85 percent dividend exclusion). The first issues were priced too cheaply, that is, the reset spreads were set too high. However, each succeeding issue ended up richer and richer (i.e., the coupon was set lower and lower), until every investment bank was finally bagged with an overpriced, unsalable issue.

Asset-Backed Financing

Far and away the bulk of this area is the mortgage-backed securities market. The Federal National Mortgage Association (FNMA or "Fannie Mae") was created in 1938 to provide consistent financing for a housing market that was suffering periodic credit crunches. Fannie Mae today is a government-sponsored corporation that is publicly held. In 1968 the Government National Mortgage Association (Ginnie Mae) was created to help liquify the home mortgage market by securitizing groups of mortgages into pools of $1 million. These pools, which are serviced by the mortgage bankers or savings institution that may have created the mortgages, are guaranteed by Ginnie Mae as to principal and timely payment of interest. The government continued to expand its support of the housing markets through the issuance of pass-throughs of the Federal Home Loan Mortgage Association ("Freddie Mac") which was created in 1970. Freddie Mac packages mortgages similarly to Ginnie Mae, but the underlying credit is that of the agency itself, not the full faith and credit of the U.S. government. In the late 1970s a few commercial and saving banks decided they could generate pass-throughs from their burgeoning mortgage-generation abilities. Some had private third-party guaranties, but others did not. These programs subsequently faded because of credit worries in the early 1980s and the lack of liquid secondary market support.

The mortgage-backed market is extremely complex. There are a huge number of mortgage originators, mostly mortgage bankers, thrift institutions, and commercial banks. The government organizations securitizing mortgages (such as Fannie Mae, Ginnie Mae, and Freddie Mac) are few, secure, and huge. Distribution of the "securitized" pools is through a relatively narrow group with less than a dozen real players, mainly investment banks. Nearly 70 percent of the market is dominated by Salomon Brothers and First Boston.

Mortgage units work in concert as well as with the generalist sales force, since mortgage-backed pass-throughs are often attractive alternatives to corporate bonds. One further element is essential to profitable operations in this arena—a skilled administrative and back-office clearing capability. The two most back-office-intensive activities on Wall Street are equity-program trading and mortgage securities. Mix-ups not only make the business grossly unprofitable, but also considerably alienate the firm's customer base. The importance of the clearance function cannot be overemphasized.

The mortgage-backed unit has its own origination group to create new securitized pools. In order to make active markets in size, new-product generation is essential. Consequently active contact with mortgage bankers, savings institutions, and the government-sponsored agencies, as well as the customer base, is a necessary function linking the mortgage finance group to the trading desk.

Research also plays a part. Pass-throughs are a great idea with great cash flow, security of payment, liquidity; what more could an investor ask for? Compared with government and corporate bonds, however, the timing of repayment is uncertain. This is because the repayment schedule on mortgages contains a large, random, repayment component. Try to understand a security whose maturity, average life, yield, and cash flow all vary depending on the interest-rate environment, right down to the basics such as what is Mortgage Pool A worth versus Pool B! In the beginning, research was inductively theoretical. Later, as obvious deviations from the hypothetical norm appeared, it became deductively based on repayment experience. This process requires huge data-manipulation tasks, including recording and making available the paydown experience on any given Ginnie Mae or Freddie Mac pool.

Recently "collateralized mortgage obligations" (CMOs) have simplified these problems. Typically, a CMO allows the investment banker or a mortgage banker to use pools of mortgages to back a bond that pays interest and principal at regular intervals like a sinking-fund bond. The banker accomplishes this by dividing the pool into tranches of securities that mature at regular intervals in the life of the pool. The holders of the shortest maturity tranche are repaid principal from the re-payment of all mortgages held in the pool until fully paid down. Holders of the second tranche are then repaid principal until it is completely paid down. The originating banker guarantees the CMO holder a coupon and a close approximation to the principal repayment on specified dates. For creating the security the banker receives an underwriting spread, an origination profit, and a service fee.

There are some recent extensions of the asset-backed concept. One is in the automobile finance industry, which is emerging as a new area of gigantic potential. Recently part of automobile industry pricing has been its willingness to subsidize financing rates. The volume of loans has risen, consequently putting capital-footing strains on even the biggest and strongest finance companies. One solution is to securitize car loans and sell them as pass-throughs. Presently a market is also emerging for credit card receivables and appliance receivables among others. (Mobile homes are already included among mortgage pass-throughs).

The asset-backed market has fascinating potential. Success in the business is governed by a firm's ability to combine and control the diverse organizational aspects of the business: penetration of the market by originators, ability to maintain broad sales distribution to move vast quantities of products in any interest-rate environment; and attention to detail in data processing, clearing, and administrative tasks. To complicate the process, trading in mortgage securities is made multidimensional by many derivative securities. There are Ginnie Mae futures contracts, as well as a huge "forward delivery" market in Ginnie Mae and Freddie Mac contracts. These are firm contracts to deliver pools on a given day in the future.

Mortgage-backed securities is a creative and innovative business which requires a large contingent of people with varied skills and a tremendous eye to detail. It has been the single fastest-growing capital-raising market in the last 10 years. Consequently it has been a major career path for many talented young people.

Capital Markets

Capital markets is where the corporate financial department meets the trading floor. Until the last 10 years, investment bankers lived in an insulated world, while sales and trading worked in an arena of screaming and swarming activity. Then came the advent of opportunistic financing. Many of the financing decisions within corporate America, especially short-term debt, moved to lower levels within the corporate ladder. This was the result of specialized personnel working on specialized issues and the ever-increasing financing needs. The capital markets operation brings together the ivory tower of corporate finance and the volatile market where corporations must issue securities. Many of the proactive financing ideas got their beginnings on the trading floor, such as mortgage-backed securities and many money market instruments. Additionally, the capital markets group provides the corporate finance department potential financing proposals as well as working on deal solicitations where a market-oriented person, acquainted with the company, could help describe the full range of financing opportunities.

Obviously this environment intensified greatly under "Rule 415." But before proceeding to 415, it is necessary to describe the traditional syndication process so that the new world of issuance is better appreciated.

When looking at a tombstone ad, one sees a manager or co-managers, often a special bracket followed by the majors, a mezzanine bracket, and then submajors. The managers originate the business and then form and invite a syndicate of other investment banks to help distribute the securities and to share the risk. Placement in the syndicate is in a pecking order based on a firm's ability to generate and distribute new issues. It is for this reason that the syndicate department serves a broader purpose. First it creates the syndicate for an investment bank's own deals. It receives the invitations from other firms and must make a decision to accept or decline the invitation, based on the quality of the corporation to be underwritten, and to some extent, Street politics. Because the syndicate department interacts on a friendly basis with an investment bank's competition, it is the point of general contact with the Street. Part of a syndicate department's purpose, especially for the upper management, is to maintain and act as the liaison with the Street to best position the firm with its competition. When small disagreements between firms crop up, the syndicate department often is the point of contact to work them out.

In-house, the syndicate department works with the capital markets group to set sales strategy. The size of the issues, the size of the "institutional selling pot," the control of "designations" within the pot, the size of the "short position to stabilize" the issue in the aftermarket, the covering of the short position, and finally the termination of the syndicate all are responsibilities of the syndicate department. The syndicate department fights to get securities in deals managed by others. Obviously the syndicate department works with and provides service to the sales force in a very close relationship.

The breadth of the syndication process has changed but not diminished since enactment of Rule 415 of the Securities and Exchange Commission in 1981. Rule 415 allows corporations to register securities to be sold at a future date. The issuer may or may not name underwriters. "Shelf" registration allows a corporation to wait for the most propitious moment for sale.

Traditional broad syndication does not work in the case of shelves. Underwriters make solicited or unsolicited bids to the corporation for the securities. The investment bank buys the deal on the wire (a bought deal), in a manner similar to the high-risk technique originated in the Eurodollar market. This requires the ultimate co-operation between the capital markets group, which interfaces with the issuer, and the trading desk, which must set the levels. There is little difference in risk profile between a 415 bid and a bid for a huge block of securities in the secondary market, although there may be a difference in how the securities will be distributed.

In a bought deal, the investment bank may ask others to join to help share the liability and the position. Sometimes the issuer requests that the investment banker take on some other firms as co-managers. These requests are normally met in order to stay in the good graces of the issuer. There is a certain irony to this practice. The fixed-income syndicate business may be high-risk and marginally profitable, but it also is very prestigious because of the underwriting derby called "league tables." League tables are published quarterly like sports box scores to show the relative ranking of investment banks in all areas of capital raising. Unfortunately, the fixed-income, straight corporate business is more for show than profit.

When Rule 415 started, it was supposed to break the stranglehold of the special bracket on corporate bond deals. It has had just the opposite effect, since the largest special-bracket firms that could afford to take the risk had a risk-taking mentality, and needed to maintain their prestige in order to compete effectively as full-service firms. Realizing that the risks are costs, the major-bracket retail firms decided to spend their advertising money on television and in print rather than go head-to-head with the special-bracket firms on 415 underwritings.

Foreign Markets and Securities

Foreign markets cover a vast arena that will be touched on briefly. It is convenient to divide the area into two sectors: dollar-denominated securities issued abroad and nondollar securities issued worldwide.

More than 90 percent of the dollar-denominated securities issued abroad are in the Eurodollar market. As was mentioned earlier, this country intentionally exported capital for liquidity to Europe in the postwar period. Capital export gave way to trade deficits. In 1971 the Bretton Woods agreement was scrapped, and huge currency fluctuations lent another level of volatility to the Euromarket.

Part of the early appeal of the Eurodollar markets was the interest equalization tax applied to foreign holders of U.S. securities, originally intended as protection for overseas issuers. Eurodollar issues were not subject to tax. Consequently, U.S. corporations would set up offshore subsidiaries, often in the Netherlands Antilles, and then issue in Europe, thereby gaining access to this large pool at lower rates. This charade went on until 1981 when the U.S. government ended the interest equalization tax. Contrary to predictions of the doomsayers, Eurodollar issuance rose dramatically, and, as with Rule 415, it tended to solidify the advantage of the risk-oriented enfranchised players. And the risk level did go up. Bought deals in active issuing periods have become the norm.

What is different about the Euromarket is that many of the underwriters—the London and Continental banks—also are investors. Conflict-of-interest laws are less rigid than in the United states, and underwritten issues can be placed in accounts under management. At one time this may have led to some unwholesome practices, but money management in Europe is becoming as competitive as in the United States. Robbing Peter to pay Paul by burying busted new issues in one's accounts under management is now seen to be bad business.

The Eurodollar market, just as the U.S. market, has many types of issues and maturities. Most floating-rate issues and short-term issues are pegged to the London Interbank Rate. LIBOR has a quoted yield curve out to six months, which is market-driven. Floating-rate notes represents a huge market. European investors tend to have a more conservative bent than their U.S. counterparts. This is reflected in the maturity and quality of Euromarket issues. The size of the floater market and the tendency for fixed-rate financing to be in the 5 to 12 year maturities reflects the short-maturity bias. The quality bias puts a major schism between potential public issuers and those relegated to borrowing from banks. Sovereign credits and agencies of foreign governments are active issuers, but even at this end of the quality curve, buyers are very discriminating. Corporate issuers tend not only to be large and highly rated, but investors have a very strong preference for recognizable names. Moody's, S&P, and Duff & Phelps all have their place, but the touch-and-feel test seems more important to European buyers.

There is a small issuance of dollar-denominated bonds in Japan (nicknamed "Sushi" bonds). This market could grow because of Japan's rise as an international banking and investment banking center.

There is a much larger market for dollar-denominated securities of foreign credits issued in the United States (commonly nicknamed "Yankee bonds"). The Yankee bond market was very active in the 1970s. Its relative size has diminished recently because many of the issuers can now borrow in Europe at competitive rates. The Yankee market also tends to be made up of high-grade visible issuers: sovereign credits, agencies, big corporations. Issues tend to be fixed-rate and longer in maturity than in Europe.

Sales, trading, and issuance of Eurodollar securities are closely related. The underwriters live and die by their abilities in the primary market—new issues. Sales and trading play an important part, but in more of a support function. Because of the unusual pricing practices, sales support is important. So is "placing" power, which is the ability to place securities with other syndicate members, often banks. Because of the fragmented nature of the market, syndication ability typically is required to supplement a strong internal sales effort.

There are two widely used pricing practices in the Euromarket. First is the bought deal. The capital market group, usually organized by country desks, frequently calls many of the active issuers to quote terms available. These quotes can be firmed into bids upon request. The investment banker who buys the securities on these terms rapidly forms a syndicate for placement and sells securities to investors through its internal sales force.

The other type of offering, which is the most widely used, starts with the lead manager and co-managers getting a "mandate" from an issuer to do an issue. When the group enters the market, the issuer is named, the expected size is stated, and the maturity is set. The bonds are then sold firm (as against "circled subject to price") and trade in a gray market before the official pricing takes place, which normally occurs 48 hours later.

As for nondollar-denominated securities, every sovereign country has its own internal government market. Maybe the biggest and most active is the Gilt Market in U.K. government bonds. This market has been heavily regulated to the benefit of an elite few dealers. "Big Bang," in October 1986, brought deregulation to the London Stock Exchange and the Gilt Market and thereby vastly broadened the primary dealer group.

Part of the decision to issue in a foreign market is based on currency risk. Since the end of fixed exchange rates in 1971, the dollar has been weak (some major

Table 11.1. Top 10 Book-Running Managers—All Eurobond Issues—1986

Rank	Manager	Volume ($Million)	Market Share	No. of Issues
1	Credit Suisse First Boston	$ 19,812.4	10.8%	102
2	Nomura Securities	14,803.0	8.1	131
3	Deutsche Bank	12,443.7	6.8	91
4	Morgan Guaranty	9,896.7	5.4	65
5	Morgan Stanley	9,021.5	4.9	74
6	Daiwa Securities	8,963.1	4.9	86
7	Salomon Brothers	8,234.9	4.5	54
8	Banque Paribas	7,002.1	3.8	66
9	Merrill Lynch Capital Markets	5,970.6	3.3	40
10	Nikko Securities (Europe)	5,141.0	2.8	54
	Industry totals	$182,754.5	100.0%	1622

Source: IDD Information Services.

Table 11.2. Top 10 Book-Running Managers—All Eurobond Issues for U.S. Corporations—1986

Rank	Manager	Volume ($Million)	Market Share	No. of Issues
1	Credit Suisse First Boston	$ 4,692.7	12.2%	28
2	Salomon Brothers	3,897.4	10.2	28
3	Nomura Securities	3,857.3	10.1	28
4	Merrill Lynch Capital Markets	3,522.2	9.2	22
5	Morgan Stanley	2,727.0	7.1	17
6	Goldman, Sachs	2,343.3	6.1	11
7	Shearson Lehman Brothers	2,244.9	5.9	16
8	Banque Paribas	1,332.6	3.5	15
9	Morgan Guaranty	1,330.7	3.5	19
10	Daiwa Securities	1,221.6	3.2	11
	Industry totals	$38,364.6	100.0%	311

Source: IDD Information Services.

periods to the contrary). Consequently deals in yen, deutsche marks, or Swiss francs would have been subject to major currency risk. Currency swaps (discussed elsewhere in this book) can mitigate this risk at reasonable cost. Consequently, issuance into stronger currency markets has developed significantly recently. The league tables (Tables 11.1–11.3) show the recent share growth in strong currency-denominated securities.

Earlier we observed that Japan is in the midst of opening up its markets, while extending its interest into foreign financial markets. With its huge savings rate and insufficient securities to feed the consequent demand, Japan's investment banking

Table 11.3. Top 10 Book-Running Managers—All Eurodollar Bond Issues—1986

Rank	Manager	Volume ($Million)	Market Share	No. of Issues
1	Credit Suisse First Boston	$ 17,239.6	15.1%	78
2	Morgan Stanley	8,280.4	7.2	55
3	Morgan Guaranty	8,091.4	7.1	43
4	Salomon Brothers	7,048.8	6.2	38
5	Nomura Securities	6,875.2	6.0	78
6	Merrill Lynch Capital Markets	5,829.5	5.1	38
7	Daiwa Securities	5,199.8	4.5	59
8	Deutsche Bank	4,217.2	3.7	19
9	Shearson Lehman Brothers	4,061.1	3.5	21
10	Banque Paribas	3,824.4	3.3	31
	Industry totals	$114,413.3	100.0%	826

Source: IDD Information Services.

brokerage industry has a big leg up. Most recently, Japanese investors have become voracious purchasers of U.S. government securities and, increasingly, players in the high-stakes Eurodollar bond market. But the Japanese domestic market in yen should continue to provide capital for other Western countries, too. Yen-denominated securities of non-Japanese issuers are nicknamed "Samurai" bonds. Japanese buyers will take long maturities but have a strong preference for quality.

Futures/Options on Futures

The world's largest market is not in oil, or in U.S. government bonds, or in Eurodollars. Guess again; it's the futures and options on futures market for securities of the U.S. government and its agencies. Earlier the concept was broached that bonds and stocks are scarce commodities in the 1980s much as gold, oil, wheat, and so forth were in the 1970s. Any commodity market vastly increases its liquidity, its breadth, and the depth of its participants when it has a futures market in the underlying asset. Like the markets in hard commodities of the 1970s, the futures markets for financial assets now are larger than the cash market. In fact, the "notional" value of government futures contracts outsizes the cash market five to one.

Futures serve many purposes. Most obviously, they give the buyer 20-to-1 leverage, as only 5 percent of the notional value or face of a futures contract has to be maintained by the buyer. The typical reason for buying or selling futures is to hedge positions. A number of houses on Wall Street, as well as the government dealer desks in the spot markets at active banks, maintain inventory positions in securities that add up to tens of billions of dollars. One of the ways to maintain such gross positions is to lay off risk in the futures market. Many hedges are pure, for example, a government long bond versus the government futures contract. Others are proxies such as hedging corporates or agencies with the government bond contract. Typically cash positions are hedged on a ratio basis with the best correlated futures contract, because it is rare to have securities that match exactly as to maturity and quality. Teams of quantitative technicians now populate bond desks with the sole purpose of finding the best derivative hedge for a given position.

Futures vastly aid liquidity in the cash market and in asset allocation decisions. Large structural portfolio moves can be initiated in the futures market and then unwound in the cash market. Typically a pension plan sponsor may want to buy, sell, or "take out insurance" using futures. If a corporate pension plan sponsor wishes to move from 60 percent stocks/40 percent bonds to 50 percent/50 percent in a billion-dollar portfolio, it is possible to make the exposure switch in the futures market in minutes. The specific stocks sold and the specific bonds bought to effect this change can be worked out over the following weeks.

Portfolio insurance is another futures strategy used by a corporate sponsor where the corporation does not want to challenge an investment advisor's risk profile. The plan sponsor can use futures to reduce the risk-reward ratio in order to make sure the comfort level is within range.

Normally an investment bank has a futures department. Sometimes the futures group is independent and services hard commodities, bond, stock, and (most recently) municipal trading departments. In other firms the futures area is part of the product group, that is, equity, bond, and so forth. In either case, futures activity can be segregated into customer and proprietary functions. The customer department has its own sales force, but will depend heavily on the government and generalist sales force to cover most accounts. Trading in futures themselves is not risk-intensive. It is execution driven. All executions must be in the pit on a pure action basis, so the only way to position against a future is by guaranteeing a spread against a cash security.

Research in the futures area tends to be technical. Technical research deals with trading patterns based on price and volume relative to outside and internal (50- to 150-day moving average) patterns.

Proprietary use of futures by investment banks allows the firm to hedge risk, provide liquidity, or seize opportunities for the firm's own account.

Proprietary Trading

Activities in the proprietary fixed-income area are as broad and diverse as the mind can conceive. Strategies fit into two groups: (1) arbitrage and (2) market, yield curve, and quality spread bets.

Arbitrage strategies may be as simple as setting up to take advantage of an aberration between the cash and futures markets, or as arcane as using synthetic securities in a series of linked transactions to hedge one against another. Sometimes the advantage is a dollar spread takeout; sometimes it is to take advantage of a basis spread between similar securities.

Market, yield curve, and quality spread bets are strategies to take advantage of an expected move in rates. The object is to minimize the risk exposure while laying out a strategy to take advantage of anticipated market moves. These are much higher risk strategies.

Proprietary traders defy being typified: some appear to be mad professors, others cardsharks. Much of the work, especially in the arbitrage area, is heavily computer driven. Understanding and conceiving of relationships between securities, then testing and executing a hypothesis, takes tremendous patience and a mind that enjoys dealing with mathematical relationships. Proprietary trading often uses vast amounts of computer power to simulate potential gains and losses. At the same time proprietary traders have an innate understanding of risk and the willingness to act or react quickly.

12 Leveraged Buyouts

WARREN A. LAW

Leveraged buyout (LBOs) have existed for decades, but their use has grown remarkably in recent years. It has been estimated that LBOs grew from about $1 billion in 1979 to more than $35 billion in 1985. By 1986, LBOs, in dollar volume, accounted for almost 25 percent of all U.S. mergers.

Put simply, LBOs involve the heavy use of borrowed money to purchase a company or a division of a company, which is then converted into a privately held concern. A relatively small number of specialist firms made substantial profits in the late 1960s from fees for arranging such transactions and from taking equity participations. As the rewards became evident, the number of players increased, until now most major investment banks and a few large commercial banks arrange and invest in LBOs.

AN EXAMPLE

Although there are several variations on the LBO theme, they have one common characteristic—more leverage in the balance sheet than is "normal." Here, for example, is the change in capital structure resulting from the buyout of Houdaille Industries, Inc., in 1979, one of the first large LBOs.

	Millions of dollars	
	Before	After
Debt	$ 23.8	$305.0
Equity	180.3	51.2
Annual interest expense	1.2	35.3

The Houdaille buyout was masterminded by Kohlberg, Kravis, Roberts, and Co. (KKR), which has been described as the undisputed leader in the LBO field. It illustrates characteristics common to many LBOs:

1. The original impetus was management's awareness of its vulnerability to a takeover after two different purchasers had acquired blocks of the company's stock.

2. Houdaille was extremely liquid, with $41 million in cash and equivalents. After the merger, this was reduced to $8 million.

3. The financing was extremely complex, involving two layers of senior debt, two of subordinated debt, two preferred stock issues, and two classes of common stock. Funding was provided by 23 institutional investors, KKR, and Houdaille management.

4. Officers and key Houdaille employees came out with 11 percent of the voting common stock, financed by options and stock appreciation rights that were exercised at the time of the buyout.

5. KKR received 37 percent of the voting common (for $7 million). It received a $1 million fee for arranging the merger, plus $535,000 per year for management services thereafter.

6. Institutional lenders providing subordinated debt received common stock at no additional cost in consideration for making the loans.

7. Houdaille was a solid but unexciting manufacturer (of industrial products and auto bumpers). Its physical plant was in good shape. Cash flow generated from operations was available to service debt and was not required to finance rapid growth or replace obsolete plant.

8. Substantial tax benefits were available. Accountants estimated the replacement cost of inventories and plant to be $49 million above book value. Writing up the tax bases of assets caused the higher cost of goods sold and depreciation deductions to substantially reduce future income taxes and free up more cash for debt service. (1986 tax changes largely eliminate such benefits now; see the concluding paragraph of this chapter.)

In essence, Houdaille was purchased largely "with its own money," and with the aid of the tax shield resulting from increased interest charges and step-ups in tax bases. Because the tax step-ups would not have been available in the absence of a taxable acquisition of Houdaille, the company literally was worth more to new owners than to old. This partly explains the offer of $40 per share for stock trading at $20¾ on the day before the announcement.

In contrast to the Houdaille LBO, which relied on anticipated cash flows to service the increased debt, recently we have seen the rise of "bust-up" LBOs, which hinge on the subsequent sale of assets rather than internally generated cash to make the deal doable. Soon after the $1.3 billion buyout of Uniroyal in 1986, for example, it was revealed that Drexel Burnham Lambert, a big investor in the deal, already had commitments to sell much of Uniroyal.

ROLE OF THE INVESTMENT BANKER

The investment banker may act only as an agent or deal-maker in an LBO, but increasingly he or she is likely to be a principal with money invested in the deal. In either case, the investment banker will provide most or all of the following functions:

1. *Finding the Buyout.* Often a potential LBO comes to the investment firm, although not always with the intention of being bought out. A client wishing to find a buyer for one of its divisions, for example, may find the banker recommending an LBO. Some bankers search actively for potential buyout candidates, often using a computer to screen for characteristics such as those demonstrated in the Houdaille buyout.

2. *Analyzing and Structuring the Arrangement.* This is a role familiar to investment bankers. It is not intrinsically different from providing analysis and advice to a traditional client planning to raise funds.

3. *Negotiating with Buyers and Sellers.* Again the role is familiar to investment firms that have been active in the merger and acquisition (M&A) area. The investment banker is particularly useful in a corporate divestiture where the buyer may be an executive of the corporation planning to stay with the divested division, who would face obvious difficulties in negotiating with his or her own employer.

4. *Arranging Financing.* Although investment firms may not be essential to carry out the first three functions, without them it is almost impossible to arrange financing as complex as that involved in the Houdaille LBO, which may take months to complete. Resources often unavailable elsewhere include an investment bank's expertise in knowing sources, understanding the markets for various debt and equity instruments, and reconciling the interests of lenders and investors.

When the investment firm also becomes a principal in the LBO, it is following a tradition once common on Wall Street, and still familiar to British merchant banks, French *banques d'affaires*, and a few smaller U.S. investment firms (e.g., Allen and Company and Lazard Frères.) The relatively recent willingness of larger investment firms to become principals is partly a function of the large and well-publicized rewards earned by specialized firms such as KKR in a few early LBOs, and partly a desire on the part of lenders to make sure that someone is overseeing the continuing operations of the highly leveraged firm. The investment bank normally does not take an active role in managing the company, but as possibly the largest stockholder it will have representation on the board of directors and regularly be in touch with the company. Obviously in this case the investment banker's reputation is on the line over a longer period than is customary in a deal-oriented industry.

Finally, the investment banker may act only in the role of an advisor to one party in the deal. In this case, if the company is publicly held, the investment firm may be expected to render a "fairness" opinion, designed partly to protect management against unfavorable stockholder reaction. In the Houdaille LBO, Goldman Sachs filled such a role.

FINANCING

In addition to the usual financing of receivables and inventory, commonly provided by banks or finance companies via lines of credit, financing a buyout requires substantial intermediate- and long-term funds, which are usually provided by banks and insurance companies. In a large LBO, a syndicate of banks or insurance companies will participate, with a lead lender that may have a separate lending division specializing in such transactions.

Commonly there are two or more layers of debt. Senior debt may be secured by assets, although generally cash flow is a more important factor in the lender's decision. (There have been LBOs involving service companies, which typically have relatively few assets.) Subordinated lenders, in view of the risk involved in a highly leveraged deal, usually receive an equity "kicker," in stock or warrants to buy stock. (As noted in the Houdaille case, subordinated lenders received "free" stock.) This level of subordinated debt, which is crucial to most LBO financings, is often referred to as "mezzanine" capital. Indeed, one European firm that has raised overseas money for this type of investment in U.S. LBOs is named Mezzanine Capital Corporation.

Investors at the mezzanine level expect a yield below that in a high-tech venture-capital investment—because the borrower has a track record of past cash flows—but higher than that in conventional private placements. To make it easier for the borrower to service the heavy debt, the interest component of this yield will be relatively low, and may be deferred, with lenders expecting eventual equity appreciation to close the gap.

With several layers of debt and equity, each with different risks and rewards, there are inherent conflicts of interest among those providing the funds. For this reason, LBOs are sometimes structured with "vertical strip financing," with the same investors involved in each level of the capital structure in order to minimize the conflict. In the Houdaille deal, several institutional investors purchased senior notes, senior subordinated notes, and junior subordinated notes, and at least one also purchased preferred stock.

As already noted, equity will be provided by management of the firm being purchased, by the investment firm that organized the deal, and by venture-capital groups. Several mutual funds have been created to provide such equity, and employee stock ownership (ESOPs) sometimes are involved.

MOTIVES OF SELLERS

Possibly the most important explanation for the early growth of LBOs was the stock market's undervaluation of assets from the mid-1970s until the mid-1980s. In 1979, for example, the ratio of stock market value to replacement cost of net assets of nonfinancial corporations was only 0.561. This undervaluation had three results. It was a major cause of the wave of unfriendly takeovers that characterized this period and, as we have seen, fear of such a takeover is one motive for going private via an LBO. Second, firms wishing to divest assets, or owners of closely held firms wishing to sell their companies, did not view a public offering of stock as a feasible or attractive possibility. Finally, with the stock of many public companies selling at less than seven times earnings (the average PE of the Standard & Poor's 500 was 7.4 in 1979), it is quite possible that this price represented a multiple of as little as four times cash flow, in which case an LBO could be arranged so that stockholders could be offered substantial acquisition premiums, still leaving the buyer adequate cash flow to service acquisition debt.

Many LBOs resulted from the deconglomeration movement that began in the 1970s, as many firms divested themselves of divisions acquired in the conglomeration mania of the 1960s after realizing that the division did not fit, was more difficult to manage, or had less profit potential than once believed. (Divestitures in the early 1980s were the source of one-third of all mergers and acquisitions.) Liquidation of these divisions may have been infeasible because of publicity, labor problems, or pension obligations, while sale of the division to its management through an LBO might result in the highest possible valuation, for operating managers are the most informed purchasers, and it is often easier to obtain financing if there is no risk of a change in management. (Moreover, the selling firm may be willing to accept some seller's paper, as it trusts the existing management of the division to be divested.)

A few LBOs have been given impetus by turnaround reorganization of companies in bankruptcy proceedings. Since 1979, the Bankruptcy Code has allowed any party at interest to offer a plan of reorganization if existing shareholders have not submitted their own plan within four months. One attraction is that the reorganized company may retain its tax loss carryforward despite forgiveness of debt by previous creditors.

Numerous LBOs have resulted from the desire of insider stockholders of a public company to go private. This desire may stem from the frustrations of dealing with dissident stockholders, the expense and detail of complying with securities laws, the competitive disadvantage of being forced to reveal sensitive information, or simple desire for profit. In some cases, insiders may be the same people who took the firm public a few years before who since have become disenchanted with the market's valuation of their stock. Because these insiders, who usually dominate the board, may introduce the idea of an LBO, the potential conflict of interest is obvious. Care must be taken to structure the deal in a way that is demonstrably fair to the holders whose stock will be purchased. Here again the fairness opinion of a reputable investment banker is important.

ASSETS VERSUS STOCK

Before 1987 the buyer normally preferred to purchase assets rather than stock. This procedure not only avoided undisclosed liabilities but also preserved the option of stepping up the tax basis of the assets, based upon a fair market appraisal, while the seller was responsible for any recapture of accelerated depreciation or investment tax credits taken on the assets. The Tax Reform Act of 1986, however, has made such write-ups much less attractive (see the concluding paragraph in this chapter).

Sometimes valuable corporate assets can be acquired only through purchase of stock. This is most common when there is a net operating loss carryforward, but it may also be true if the seller has valuable franchises or leaseholds that cannot be assigned.

The seller may prefer to sell stock rather than assets, to avoid contingent liabilities or sales taxes. In this case there is no tax to shareholders until they redeem their shares. When the company being acquired is controlled by a close group of insiders, however, there may be advantages to them in so-called Oppenheimer financing. If the corporation sells all its assets, any capital gain is taxed at the corporate, rather than individual, level, and the corporation becomes a closed-end investment company. If the cash received is invested in tax-exempt securities, all income received is free of tax, even when paid out to shareholders.

In any event, the form of the LBO is a subject for negotiation between seller and buyer.

EMPLOYEE STOCK OWNERSHIP PLANS

Under certain circumstances an LBO may be facilitated by using an employee stock ownership plan (ESOP). In this case, the acquiring company creates an employee stock ownership trust (ESOT), which borrows part of the funds necessary for the LBO and purchases stock in the new corporation, guaranteeing to the lender that it will make annual payments into the ESOT sufficient to repay the debt. This has tax advantages, because payments made to the ESOT (up to 25 percent of total payroll) are deductible by the corporation. Moreover, the 1984 Tax Reform Act allows banks to exclude 50 percent of income earned on loans to finance employee stock purchases. Obviously this device is most useful in a profitable corporation, and where management is willing to have a continuing investment, as shares of stock pledged during the loan become free only when the loan is repaid.

Some critics of this technique have pointed out that workers may thus sacrifice the advantages of a diversified portfolio. They also may feel cheated because management benefits unduly from the LBO (employees have filed at least one protest against an LBO with the Labor Department on these grounds). Moreover, by packaging the LBO as a pension program, management may be held to act in a fiduciary capacity and "solely in the interest" of workers.

GETTING OUT

Usually the entity investor hopes to liquidate his or her investment in five to seven years, after enough of the debt has been retired to make the firm's balance sheet less frightening to a buyer. With luck, favorable market conditions will make a public stock offering possible. If not, the company may be sold privately, and it is not unheard of that the sale will again be an LBO. Obviously the timing of sale and choice of buyer is a potential source of conflict between management of the firm and other outside equity investors.

In a few well-publicized cases, investors have realized extremely large profits in much less time than five years. When RCA cast off Gibson Greeting Cards via an LBO in 1982, the buyers had a public offering the next year that netted the principals more than $100 million. In early 1985, investors in a buyout of Kaiser Steel one year earlier reportedly sold their interest at a 41-to-1 return. Such instances, in fact, have made some sellers reluctant to sell, for as one investment banker put it: "Nobody wants to be the next RCA."

THE FUTURE

By early 1987 the future of LBOs had become uncertain. Changes in tax laws made some less attractive. Commercial banks reportedly were more cautious in financing them, and regulators became more conscious of the quality of loans in bank portfolios, as the chairman of the Federal Reserve Board expressed concern about the volume of LBO loans. Moreover, the number of financial firms looking for potential LBO deals had escalated dramatically, which, coupled with a more buoyant stock market, caused prices being offered to increase substantially. Some veteran players of the LBO game complained that a firm that could have been purchased for seven times earnings a decade earlier commanded a price twice as high by 1985. In such circumstances firms seldom could be bought for less than reproduction cost, and fears of deflation reduced the long-run asset-play aspect of an LBO. On the other hand, acquirers were increasingly able to finance deals by issuing junk bonds, at least partly filling the gap left by banks, and the sharp drop in interest rates since 1982 made it easier to carry debt.

At the same time, LBOs showed signs of becoming an important M&A tool. Some professionals were accused of using an LBO announcement as a stalking horse, with the real intention of "putting the firm into play" by thus declaring it up for sale and establishing a floor price for an ensuing auction. Observers also noted the rise of the tender buyout, a two-step approach in which a company's managers and a deal-maker first tender for its shares and then, once in control, refinance through traditional LBO techniques. Completing the deal in 20 business days (the Williams Act requirement for a tender offer) rather than in several months reduces the chance of losing the deal to a higher bidder. It has been estimated that by 1984 more than half the would-be LBOs of public companies were being lost to other acquirers. In two 1986 cases, SCM and Revlon, the courts ruled against a management team attempting an LBO in favor of a competing bid from a raider.

In a tender buyout it is necessary to squeeze out shareholders who do not tender, because until the acquirer has 100 percent control it can use the firm's cash flow to repay debt only by paying dividends. The greatest difficulty, however, lies in obtaining bridge financing for the tender offer, as margin regulations prevent banks from providing more than half the funds. Moreover, lenders may be worried about the risk that the buyer cannot complete the transaction and that there will be no ready market for the stock securing the loan. One solution has been to involve corporations in financing the tender LBO, as a device for ensuring their acquisition of some assets of the target. For example, Bristol-Myers, in return for helping finance a tender LBO of American Sterilizer, obtained an option to buy the firm's surgical equipment division. Nevertheless, the deal-maker in a tender LBO usually has to risk more of its own capital than in the traditional one, so it is more inclined to look for prospects like those that once epitomized most LBOs—firms with undervalued assets, low stock prices, substantial liquidity, and strong, steady cash flows.

Finally, and perhaps inevitably, the tender LBO is a technique available to any raider willing to make an unfriendly tender. The well-publicized hostile tender by Ted Turner for control of CBS in May 1985 had many of the earmarks of an LBO, except that the original offer was only for 51 percent of CBS stock, and clearly CBS management did not expect to remain in place. Turner planned to divest CBS assets rather than rely on operating cash flow to reduce the heavy debt involved in his offer, a step later taken by CBS management to reduce its vulnerability to similar attacks in the future.

CONCLUSION

As LBOs have become a familiar part of the financial scene, a few observers have expressed unease at their social implications. In the early history of LBOs, there was concern that shareholders might be squeezed out at a time chosen by management, and at an unfair price. There indeed have been a few stockholder attempts to block a proposed LBO on these grounds, but most holders seem willing, even eager, to accept the large premiums over market offered in most LBOs.

Recently criticism has centered on whether the typical LBO produces any true social gain commensurate with the out-of-pocket costs involved, which may exceed $10 million in a large LBO, and whether the resulting highly leveraged balance sheets may not one day trigger difficulties for the U.S. financial system. Some academic adherents of "efficient market" financial theory contend that the fact that buyers offer a premium over the existing market implies that the assets of the firm will be utilized more efficiently after the LBO, while critics argue that the LBO phenomenon is largely tax-induced and that the taxpaying public suffers. Whatever the truth, financial pages continue to be filled with news or rumors of potential LBOs, and KKR, which predicted in 1983 that it could take five years to invest the $1 billion it had raised for this purpose, was able to invest it in two years and promptly set about raising an additional $2 billion.

The Tax Reform Act of 1986 eliminated one of the attractions of LBOs seen in the Houdaille buyout—the ability of the buyer to write up assets for tax purposes. Previously the General Utilities doctrine (named after a 1935 Supreme Court case) allowed purchasers of all a firm's stock to write up certain assets by the difference between their carrying values for tax purposes and fair market values, resulting in increased depreciation charges, lower taxes, and greater cash flow. The 1986 Act eliminated this advantage, and was expected to reduce prices paid in some LBOs. But one investment banker has said: "There is no doubt that we will think up new ways to get deals done." And the 1986 LBO involving Macy's, which was viable only because the financing package included substantial amounts of zero-coupon bonds, lends support to that belief.

BIBLIOGRAPHY

Benjamin, H.E., and M.B. Goldberg, *Leveraged Acquisitions: Private and Public*, New York: Practiscing Law Institute, 1985.

Dannen, Frederic, "LBOs: How Long Can This Go On?" *Institutional Investor*, 20 (November 1986), pp. 151–160.

Diamond, S.C. ed., *Leveraged Buyouts*, Homewood, IL: Dow Jones, Irwin, 1985.

Lee, Steven J., and Robert D. Colman, *Handbook of Mergers, Acquisitions and Buyouts*, Englewood Cliffs, N.J.: Prentice-Hall, 1981.

Lowenstein, Louis, "Management Buyouts," *Columbia Law Review*, 85 (May 1985), pp. 730–784.

Sandler, Linda, "Wall Street Finally Discovers the Leveraged Buyout," *Institutional Investor*, 16 (August 1982), pp. 88–93.

Scharf, Charles A., *Techniques for Buying, Selling and Merging Businesses*, Englewood Cliffs, N.J.: Prentice-Hall, 1964.

Wallner, Nicholas, *How to do a Leveraged Buyout or Acquisition*, San Diego: Buyout Publications, 1982.

13 Mergers and Acquisitions

J. PETER WILLIAMSON

Mergers and acquisitions represent one of several markets in which investment bankers participate. Certain characteristics distinguish this market from the markets for stocks and bonds, the principal markets where investment bankers are active.

Mergers and acquisitions are prompted by a variety of motives and economic conditions. Some corporations are inherently conglomerates; they hold a portfolio of different businesses, adding and selling businesses as the economic outlook changes and purchase and sale opportunities arise. Allied-Signal is one example. Other corporations are intent on becoming larger and/or stronger within a particular industry by a series of acquisitions—James River Corporation, for example. Others are frankly raiders who spot opportunities to make a profit by buying a corporation and selling off its component parts. Sir James Goldsmith is an example. Still others specialize in leveraged buyouts (see Chapter 12), seeking to add value to a corporation by changing the ownership and capital structure. An example is Kohlberg, Kravis, Roberts (KKR).

Charting the future course of M&A activity requires evaluating the probable level of these different kinds of transactions as well as the factors that influence these levels. The regulatory environment has become more permissive in the past several years, paving the way for mergers that might have been challenged in the past as anticompetitive. An example is the Fort Howard Paper acquisition of Lily-Tulip. This favorable condition could change in future years. Falling interest rates have eased the burden of borrowing to finance acquisitions, and the development of high-yield, "junk bond" financing has been important too. Public leveraged buyouts, perhaps the fastest growing segment of the M&A business, are largely the result of innovations in financing instruments and investors' increased tolerance of high leverage.

A host of economic factors are important to the volume of M&A business. Changes in industry structure, technology, and competitive position will shift activity from one industry to another and from one company to another. Some argue that investment bankers themselves generate M&A activity, and there can be no doubt that the personal motivations of individual corporate executives are one important factor.

The M&A market is characterized by a relatively small number of giant transactions (perhaps a dozen in a year, involving over a billion dollars each) and a substantial number (several thousand) of small to medium-sized deals. The expertise of the intermediary is critical in the giant transactions, and even the smaller transactions generally have some unique features requiring special handling.

It is difficult to imagine how one might standardize the trading in the M&A marketplace, as, for example, trading in options contracts was standardized in the 1970s. The market for interest-rate swaps shows signs of developing in the same way, as individually arranged transactions are turning into what some regard as a "commodity" business handled by traders equipped with screens and telephones. It seems unlikely that the M&A market will ever turn into a commodity business, although a number of firms have developed some standard in-house procedures for handling many M&A transactions.

There are some fairly significant barriers to entry into the M&A market, at least on a substantial scale. Ease of entry varies, depending on the role the investment banking firm plays (discussed later in this chapter), but in general it is difficult to establish a large-scale presence.

The overall reputation of the firm is of paramount importance when the firm is to act as an intermediary for major mergers and acquisitions. These transactions may take place once or twice in the career of the chief executive of a major corporation. To that executive, the transaction is enormously important, and he or she is likely to insist on the services of one of the most highly regarded firms in the country. As we shall see, only a very small group of firms have reputations that are likely to meet the most exacting demands.

A second barrier to entry is related to the resources of the investment banking firm. The different roles to be played in the M&A market require rather different resources. A full discussion of the matching of resources to the role chosen by the firm will come later in this chapter. Suffice it now to say that participating as intermediary in a large-scale transaction requires resources that are possessed by relatively few investment banking firms.

There may be some disagreement within the industry on the importance of established relationships in gaining access to the M&A market. The investment banking firms characterized by an emphasis on relationships believe that the success of M&A activities depends considerably on cultivating and maintaining corporate relationships. These relationships in turn depend on the overall reputation of the firm and the variety and quality of investment banking services it offers. Goldman Sachs, for example, was able to build a substantial M&A business among its existing, large clientele. Other firms are characterized as more deal-oriented; they are likely to place less emphasis on the importance of relationships in building and maintaining M&A activity. In these cases the M&A department may have to be more aggressive in seeking business, and its own reputation will be critical.

A further barrier to entry into the M&A market concerns expertise. Expertise can of course be purchased. And the luring away of M&A experts from one firm to another is one of the hallmarks of the business. This is discussed later in the chapter. For the present, what is important is that a substantial expertise must be either developed within the firm or purchased from the outside before a significant amount of M&A business can be done.

Acting as an intermediary in the merger and acquisition business in the United States has not required much capital until recently. Essentially, the investment banking firm provides advisory services. Conditions are changing, however, particularly with respect to leveraged buyouts. A firm that is prepared to guarantee the purchase of debt or equity instruments often has a competitive advantage over a firm that cannot make the guarantee. And leveraged buyouts account for more M&A business each year. Some firms have funds available for investment in LBO securities when these seem attractive. But others may be willing to go much further—to commit capital to carry LBO securities pending resale, and hence to facilitate the firm's agency role. Here is where substantial capital commitments may earn large fees. First Boston is reported to have purchased for its own account 51 percent of the stock of Allied Stores Corp. for nearly $2 billion, to be delivered to Campeau Corp. in the course of its hostile takeover. In Europe there appears to be more use of capital by intermediaries in the merger and acquisition business. There, the principal intermediaries tend to be merchant banks, institutions that perform an investment as well as an advisory function.

THE INTERNATIONAL MERGER AND ACQUISITION BUSINESS

The foreign (as opposed to international) M&A market is very much smaller than the market in the United States. In the United Kingdom, merger volume was estimated at $7 billion in 1985 (compared with $120 to $180 billion in the United States), and all other foreign markets are considerably smaller. The international M&A market, on the other hand, appears to offer interesting possibilities for the future. An appendix to this chapter shows statistics suggesting that the international business amounted to about 10 percent of U.S. business in 1985.

International activity at the present time consists primarily of foreign companies acquiring U.S. companies. This is in part the consequence of prosperity in Europe and Japan, providing foreign companies with cash to spend. It is also due to the decline in the U.S. dollar in 1985 and 1986, and to a long-standing sense that the United States offers more economic and political stability than in any other part of the world. We may be in the midst of a long-term trend in which U.S. companies or parts of U.S. companies are being continuously sold to foreign companies.

In the foreign M&A markets, U.S. investment banking firms suffer from a considerable disadvantage. Foreign banks and merchant banks have well-established relationships with the companies that are likely to be engaged in mergers and acquisitions, and availability of capital effectively to underwrite some transactions may give the merchant banks an advantage. As a result, U.S. firms generally are co-advisors when they are retained in foreign M&A transactions. But hostile takeovers are fairly new overseas, and U.S. firms have more experience defending in hostile cases than do foreign intermediaries. As a result, some U.S. firms have found opportunities to participate in purely foreign deals. In the United Kingdom, for example, 1986 saw a substantial increase in hostile takeovers. Of course, U.K. firms can be expected to develop their own expertise.

While buyers in the international M&A business are generally well connected with foreign firms, U.S. firms are in a much better position to identify and negotiate with targets in the United States. Acquisitions, of course, can lead to divestitures, and there is already evidence that U.S. firms may do a good business selling off U.S. assets for foreign companies. Some international business takes the form of acquisitions of foreign firms by U.S. companies, and here the local advantages of foreign banks and merchant banks have so far kept participation by U.S. investment banks at a low level.

It does appear that to be successful in the international M&A business, it is important to have an office in London and perhaps one in Tokyo. Morgan Stanley through its Tokyo office has established a participation in the M&A business in Japan; it has had an M&A operation in London for a decade. Goldman Sachs established its London merger operation more recently, and First Boston also has established an M&A London operation, through a joint venture with its affiliate Credit Suisse First Boston. Merrill Lynch, Kidder, and Shearson Lehman Brothers have M&A offices in London, and so do Citicorp and Morgan Guaranty.

Staffing a foreign office presents some interesting choices for a firm, as well as difficult career choices for an individual. One approach calls for M&A people to serve a one- to two-year tour of duty in London and then return to New York. This maintains the integrity of the M&A group, but has the disadvantage that at about the time the individual is becoming useful in London, he or she returns to New York. Another approach has M&A people permanently located in London, but spending perhaps two weeks every year or half year in New York. And still another approach mixes permanent London staff with New York people spending three to five years at a time in London.

The U.S. firms generally have preferred to send New York-trained people to London, but some have hired whole M&A staffs from U.K. firms. Bringing in accomplished people who have well-established contacts may be the quickest way to enter the foreign (as opposed to the international) M&A business.

THE VARIOUS ROLES OF AN INVESTMENT BANKING FIRM

In general, the investment banking firm plays an advisory role in the M&A market. In some cases, notably leveraged buyouts, the firm may also put up capital and take a position. But most of the time the investment banking firm is offering advice, perhaps negotiating on behalf of a client, and being compensated through something analogous to a brokerage commission. Fees in mergers and acquisitions generally take the form of a percentage of the value of the transaction. As an introduction to just what the investment banking firm does to earn its fee, it is helpful to distinguish different roles, or levels of activity.

Investment bankers are very sensitive about classification of firms in terms of volume or importance of business. As Table 13.1 suggests, however, it is hard to

Table 13.1. Ranking of Investment Bankers' M&A Transactions Greater than $500 MM Completed and Pending in 1986

Investment Banker	Aggregated Value Offered ($MM)	Number of Deals
Goldman Sachs & Co.	$ 72,106	47
First Boston Corp.	57,097	41
Morgan Stanley & Co. Inc.	55,699	37
Drexel Burnham Lambert Inc.	33,969	25
Lazard Freres & Co.	28,874	10
Salomon Brothers	25,348	22
None Employed	28,108	21
Merrill Lynch Capital Markets	22,757	16
Shearson Lehman Brothers Inc.	17,992	13
Kidder, Peabody & Co. Inc.	17,388	13
Dillon, Read & Co. Inc.	11,183	10
James D. Wolfensohn	7,978	2
PaineWebber Incorporated	5,487	4
Donaldson, Lufkin & Jenrette, Inc.	4,985	4
Bear, Stearns & Co.	4,808	5
Warren E. Buffett	3,557	1
Montgomery Securities	3,230	1
Allen & Co. Inc.	3,000	2
Keefe, Bruyette & Woods Inc.	2,144	3
Mcleod Young Weir Limited	1,553	1
E.F. Hutton & Company Inc.	1,420	1
Goldenberg & Co.	1,420	1
Walter M. Sharp Co.	1,409	1
Stephens Inc.	1,363	1
Prudential-Bache Securities	1,350	1
W. Blair & Co.	1,072	2
Rothschild Inc.	881	1
Bankers Trust Company	775	1
Blackstone Group	749	1
WM Sword & Co.	675	1
Robinson-Humphrey Co. Inc.	600	1
Morgan Lewis Githens & Ahn	600	1
Smith, Barney, Harris Upham & Co.	600	1
Piper, Jaffray & Hopwood	590	1
Morgan Schiff & Co., Inc.	550	1
E.M. Warburg, Pincus & Co. Inc.	520	1
Brian Freeman	515	1
Gibbons, Green, Van Amerongen	500	1
Eastdil Realty, Inc.	500	1
Total	$423,432	299

Source: Morgan Stanley & Co. Firms are given credit for deals in which they are known to have participated.

deny the existence of a top tier of three firms whose scales of operations are roughly comparable and well beyond the activities of other firms. Another six or so firms constitute a less well-defined second tier, and from this point on it is difficult to establish classes apart from the category of some very small firms, the "boutiques" of the M&A business. For the purposes of this chapter, it seems useful to discuss three different levels of activity. At one extreme is the very large-scale operation; at the other is the boutique. And in between is a group of 15 or so firms with merger and acquisition departments that handle a substantial amount of business in some cases.

Only one commercial bank appears in Table 13.1. A number of commercial banks are making a major effect to build M&A activities. At present they are unlikely to be associated with the largest transactions, but still they may do a substantial business in smaller deals. Commercial banks seem to have difficulty attracting and holding strong M&A staffs, but they may do better in time.

Large-Scale Operations

Investment banking firms do not publish specific revenue figures for their merger and acquisition activities. Morgan Stanley in a prospectus issued in 1986 reported gross revenue of $423 million in 1985 from "investment banking." Three hundred million was for "financial advisory activities," of which merger and acquisition activity is one. Within the industry, M&A revenue is estimated at approximately $200 million in 1985 for each of Morgan Stanley, Goldman Sachs, and First Boston. These three firms appear to have the resources necessary to handle the largest merger and acquisition transactions. (Some of the six or so second-tier firms would argue that they are equally equipped.) For these firms, a small M&A transaction is one involving under $100 million, a large one over $500 million.

The firms in this class have substantial merger and acquisition staffs, but statistics on M&A staffs can be misleading. Morgan Stanley has an M&A staff of about 125 professionals worldwide, First Boston has about 120, and Goldman Sachs has under 100. Yet all three firms do roughly the same volume of M&A business. All three can draw on corporate finance staff to handle M&A work, and classification of people as M&A or corporate finance can be somewhat arbitrary. There are probably more corporate finance people spending most of their time on mergers and acquisitions at Goldman than at the other two firms.

But more than formal classification is involved. The M&A business is cyclical, and Goldman may be more conservative than the other two firms in maintaining an M&A staff that will be fully employed at a low point in the cycle, supplementing the staff with corporate finance people at other times.

All the major M&A departments draw heavily on other resources within the firm. Indeed, one way of looking at merger and acquisition activity in firms operating on this scale is to see the M&A work as a way of further capitalizing on an array of resources that by themselves are already profitable. Combining these resources to add another substantial layer of profit is the function of the merger and acquisition department. This is an important point, because merger and acquisition departments have in recent years been enormously profitable. The Morgan Stanley statistics certainly support this conclusion. But it is one thing for a stand-alone department of an investment banking firm consistently to deliver extraordinary profits, and another for that department to tap a variety of resources in the firm, combining and repackaging what these resources have to offer and selling the result at a substantial price. For the firms operating large-scale merger and acquisition departments, the second characterization is probably more apt, although for firms in the middle of the three classes the first may be appropriate.

By and large, the merger and acquisition department draws from other departments of the firm and gives relatively little back. (Some in the M&A business would say that the relationships they develop are valuable to other parts of the firm.) Securities research is one of these parts. Securities research people can generate valuable leads to a merger and acquisition department. Security analysts are in a position to know which companies are in trouble and may welcome advice leading to acquisition or divestiture. They are in a position to know which companies are vulnerable to takeovers, because of undervalued assets. And they are in a position to know which companies are likely to be looking for acquisitions. At the same time, security analysts can answer the questions of merger and acquisition people looking for buyers or sellers to meet the needs of a client.

A strong trading department can be helpful to merger and acquisition activity. Judging the market for new financings to accompany an M&A deal, and particularly estimating the market for a new kind of instrument, requires trading expertise.

More important than a trading department is a risk-arbitrage department. "Risk arbitrage" actually is a contradiction in terms. A true arbitrage consists of the taking of offsetting positions in a security in two markets, or in equivalent securities in one or two markets, to secure a profit without taking a risk. Buying a convertible debenture, for example, for $2000 and simultaneously selling short the shares into which the debenture can be converted for $2001 provides a risk-free profit. In the early days of M&A arbitrage, the transactions were not risk-free, but had some of the characteristics of a true arbitrage. Once it was reasonably certain that corporation X would exchange one of its shares for one share of corporation Y, then buying shares of X at one price and simultaneously selling shares of Y at a slightly higher price achieved a profit that was subject only to the risk that the merger would not be completed. Today, what is called risk arbitrage generally encompasses simple speculation in stocks that are expected to rise during the course of merger negotiations or a takeover contest.

Risk-arbitrage departments are an important part of all major investment banking firms, and a number of risk-arbitrage firms do nothing else. As contested mergers develop, institutional stockholders tend to sell, as risk arbitrageurs buy. In early 1986, it was estimated that 30 percent of the shares of Sperry Corp., the target of Burroughs Corp., were held by arbitrageurs.

Risk-arbitrage people are a constant source of information on market activity. Most large corporations watch the daily volume in their stock and are quickly aware of unusual activity. But to know the causes of the activity they probably need the help of an investment bank and its arbitrage department. Even before it is approached by a corporation, the investment bank may have learned what is going on and be in a position to warn of an impending takeover attempt.

Apart from assisting with new business, risk-arbitrage people can supply current news on offensive and defensive strategies, and can help predict how the market will respond to a package of securities issued in connection with an M&A transaction. To be fair to the trading department, the risk-arbitrage department may be relying on traders' advice in estimating a market response.

As of 1987, with the Securities and Exchange Commission pressing insider trading charges, there was rising concern about the use of inside information in risk arbitrage. Once an investment banking firm undertakes to advise a corporation involved in merger negotiations or a takeover contest, and probably even earlier, at the stage of discussions that could lead to an advisory role the risk-arbitrage department will cease taking any position in the corporation's stock. But these traditional safeguards may not be enough. In 1987 a number of firms were having to reassess the transfer of sensitive information within the firm. In any case, risk-arbitrage departments in investment banking firms generally take positions only in *announced* deals.

The support of a risk-arbitrage group probably is more obviously valuable in cases of contested mergers, where offensive and defensive strategies are important, where market rumors can be significant, and where quick judgments with respect to market response are important. But its value is not limited to hostile cases. In friendly mergers, generally there is a public offering of securities, and advice is needed on how the public will perceive and value the offering.

A corporate finance department obviously is helpful and probably integral to M&A work. Other kinds of M&A activity are discussed later in this chapter, but a significant part of the activity takes the form of financial restructuring, and here the expertise of corporate finance is essential. In fact, it is often difficult to distinguish clearly between corporate finance and M&A in an investment banking firm. In many firms, people move back and forth between M&A work and traditional corporate finance work as the need arises.

An options and warrants department can be helpful to M&A people. The design and valuation of option instruments has become highly specialized, and these instruments may be a significant part of the financing of some M&A transactions.

In recent years a number of corporate pension funds have become overfunded; by terminating its pension plan a corporation may be able to retrieve a substantial amount of cash. The potential for pension plan terminations as a source of cash in a merger has become quite important, and both Goldman Sachs and Morgan Stanley have formed small groups to specialize in pension plan aspects of corporate restructurings.

Finally, most large investment banking firms have what is essentially a relationship department, marketing all the firm's services, maintaining contacts with clients, and generally carrying out many of the activities one might expect to be performed by a relationship officer in a commercial bank. This department supports M&A activities in a number of ways. First, it calls on regular clients of the firm, reminding them of the services that are available and picking up news that may suggest impending merger and acquisition activity, or at least an opportunity for the M&A department to suggest activity. The relationship department also calls on potential clients, once again carrying the firm name and reporting any opportunities it uncovers.

Morgan Stanley has another department—Capital Markets Services—that combines sales and corporate finance activities and that can be helpful in providing advice to an M&A team. Other firms have similar departments.

Innovation is an important aspect of large-scale merger and acquisition activity, if for no other reason than that it enhances the firm's public image. Innovation is likely to show up in the design of financing instruments and packages of financial instruments. It can also appear in strategies for defending against hostile takeovers and in defeating defensive strategies.

The relationship between innovation and a large flow of M&A transactions is important. Innovation can flourish only in the context of a steady flow of deals. And the steady flow is maintained at least in part by constant innovation. Mutual reinforcement of this sort is further evidence of barriers to entry in this business. Some firms feel that innovation is more likely if there are at least a few people in the merger and acquisition department who are not constantly involved in day-to-day participation in deals, but have time to think about the process. Probably only the largest firms can afford this sort of activity.

The role of legal work in M&A activities is crucial. There are perhaps a half-dozen law firms in New York City known for their M&A capability, any one of which will be found representing a party to a major M&A transaction. The two firms probably best known are Skadden, Arps, Slate, Meagher & Flom and Wachtell, Lipton, Rosen & Katz. Most of the innovations in offensive and defensive strategy in hostile takeovers have originated in the lawyer's office.

M&A departments rely heavily on law firms, particularly in contested cases. While some investment bankers probably have favorites among them, there are no ties that link one investment banking firm to a particular law firm.

The merger and acquisition business has been highly cyclical. Traditionally activity varies not only from year to year but also within the year. (Yet since 1980 the dollar volume of business has risen steadily, especially in very large transactions, raising the interesting question whether this business is on the rising part of a long cycle or whether it is simply on a steadily upward trend.) Generally, when a corporation sets out to acquire or be acquired, it wants quick action from its investment banker. And of course in the case of hostile takeovers, the investment banker is expected to be prepared to throw enormous resources into an assignment on a few hours' notice. The dilemma for the investment banking firm is that maintaining the resources to be able to respond quickly is expensive, difficult, and probably risky. But not to have the resources available is to concede important business to a competitor.

Another aspect to cyclicality has to do with specialization. Merger waves tend to reach different industries at different times. Banks, pipelines, oil companies, and food companies all have been the focus of merger activity in recent years. The firm that has a wide variety of industry specialists among securities research and corporate finance staffs has an advantage in being equipped for whatever opportunity comes along. Alternatively, by anticipating the industry that will be next year's focus of activity, a firm can try to develop the appropriate specialization, especially among corporate finance people. Some firms have maintained a particular specialized capability for many years, thereby acquiring a reputation for experience and knowledge of an industry. An example is Goldman Sachs, long known for its expertise in retailing.

Intermediate-Scale Operations

As Tables 13.1 and 13.2 indicate, there are perhaps a half-dozen major investment banking firms participating in a substantial number of large mergers and acquisitions, but falling in volume of business below the top three M&A firms. These half-dozen or so are followed by another half-dozen, some of them major investment banking firms and some of them relatively small firms, doing a respectable merger and acquisition business. And then there are close to two dozen firms, a few large but most small, doing a much smaller business. Note that the tables cover only the major transactions of 1986, so they fall far short of presenting a complete picture of the merger and acquisition business.

The half-dozen or so firms that did a substantial volume in major M&A transactions in 1986 fell below the top three in that year, but all have done substantial M&A work in recent years, and they probably are capable of handling almost any transaction. Lazard specializes in M&A work; for the others this is an important but not a dominant activity.

Within this intermediate class, and especially among the smaller firms, there can be heavy reliance on a small number of professional M&A specialists whose personal reputations are outstanding. The point was made earlier that it is always possible to buy expertise and individual reputations, and hence build a merger and acquisition capability. A few experienced, skillful, and well-known individuals can bring business to the merger and acquisition department of a firm. And in many cases they can manage without the substantial staff support that exists in the top M&A firms.

Building a business on the reputation of one or a few individuals is attractive but risky. M&A work, particularly the handling of an innovative and successful defense in a hostile takeover attempt, can probably lead to more personal publicity than almost any other investment banking activity. And personal glorification in newspapers and magazines can bring in the business. But the firm that wins business by selling the reputation of an individual is very vulnerable to raiding.

Loss of the chief M&A person can lead to another two or three defections. At that point the firm may discover that it simply has no M&A capability. What is actually quite likely is that the firm retains an M&A department that is capable of doing almost all it could do before the defection, but the outside world, which after all was told how important the defector was, perceives the firm to have lost its capability.

Upon the departure of a much-publicized M&A chief, client corporations may maintain retainer relationships until they are approached by another major firm claiming superiority in the absence of the first firm's key person. At that point the

Table 13.2. Ranking of Investment Bankers Participating in the Top 50 M&A Transactions of 1986

Investment Banker	Aggregated Value Offered ($MM)	Number of Deals
Goldman, Sachs & Co.	$ 55,719	22
Morgan Stanley & Co. Inc.	41,302	17
First Boston Corp.	39,433	15
Lazard Freres & Co.	25,785	6
Drexel Burnham Lambert Inc.	24,834	11
None Employed	21,367	10
Merrill Lynch Capital Markets	17,148	7
Salomon Brothers	16,325	8
Shearson Lehman Brothers Inc.	13,255	6
Kidder, Peabody & Co. Inc.	11,957	5
James D. Wolfensohn	7,979	2
Dillon, Read & Co. Inc.	6,917	4
Warren E. Buffett	3,557	1
PaineWebber Incorporated	3,420	1
Montgomery Securities	3,230	1
Allen & Co. Inc.	3,000	2
Donaldson, Lufkin & Jenrette, Inc.	2,970	1
Bear, Stearns & Co.	2,515	2
Mcleod Young Weir Limited	1,553	1
Golenberg & Co.	1,420	1
Walter M. Sharp Co.	1,409	1
Stephens Inc.	1,363	1
Prudential-Bache Securities	1,350	1
Total	$307,808	126

Source: Morgan Stanley & Co. Firms are given credit for deals in which they are known to have participated.

clients may be inclined to move to the new firm. Of course, there is always some risk to even the top firms of loss of people whose reputations are important. But the M&A departments at these firms are strong enough to be able to stand individual losses without serious harm, and, more important, without perceived harm.

Some of the firms in this intermediate scale of operations specialize in the types of business they do. Keefe, Bruyette & Woods, for example, is known for its expertise with banking organizations.

Specialization may indeed be the key to success in the highly competitive M&A business for a firm that does not have the general reputation and large-scale resources of the top firms. Many of those who are experienced in the M&A business believe that a reputation for expertise in a particular industry is one of the most important factors in building business.

Small Firms Specializing in M&A Activity

Among the firms participating in only one of the major transactions of 1985 are some fairly substantial investment banking firms that simply do not have significant merger and acquisition departments, and some very small firms that in fact specialize in mergers and acquisitions. Salim B. Lewis, George Needham, and James D. Wolfensohn operate small, highly specialized firms. George Needham left the corporate finance department at First Boston to establish his firm. James Wolfensohn was with Salomon Brothers before he founded his firm. And Salim Lewis worked for a number of major investment banking firms before establishing his own. Blackstone is a firm founded by Peter G. Peterson and others who left Lehman Brothers. These firms are essentially one-person operations, in the sense that it is the reputation and to a large extent the skill of a single individual upon which the success of the firm rests. They are examples of an interesting industry career following a highly successful stint in mergers and acquisitions at a major investment banking firm. It is possible that one result of the insider trading scandals of 1986 will be increased opportunities for individuals whose experience and judgment are coupled with a reputation for absolute integrity.

RESTRUCTURING

An enormous amount of corporate activity in recent years has involved the redeployment of corporate assets in an effort to refocus a company's lines of business. The conglomerates form in the 1960s and 1970s are prime candidates for such restructuring. The activity probably is dominated by two objectives: improving corporate profitability and enhancing perception of value within the investment community. The first of these objectives is easy to understand; any management should be continually seeking to improve profitability. The second is less obvious. The point is that when the market values a corporation it is valuing a collection of assets, liabilities, and cash flow. It appears that overall valuation can often be improved by restructuring liabilities and making substitutions of assets.

Given the two objectives, there is still the question of what motivates change. Some managements are moved to action simply because of dissatisfaction with profit performance or with the market perception of value. Other managers are alarmed at the possibility of a hostile takeover by someone who believes that profits and value can be increased, in other words, that the company is worth more than its market value. And third, an investment banker may take the initiative in pointing out to management the opportunities for improving profits and value, or, alternatively, the possibility of a hostile takeover.

Restructurings, then, offer a fertile ground for M&A departments. Those that are aggressive and have the expertise can develop a substantial business. Security analysts who can pinpoint companies with problems are helpful, as is a risk-arbitrage department that can identify early indications of takeover interest.

Sometimes what is called for is simply a financial restructuring. The client company, for example, may find its stock selling in the marketplace at a discount from what the management, and the company's M&A advisors, perceive to be its intrinsic value. The problem may have to do with the nature of the business itself, or it may have to do with capital structure. Financial restructuring may take the form of eliminating expensive debt—debt that was issued during a period of high interest rates. Calling debt that is callable, or making a tender offer for debt that is not callable, may be one appropriate change. A repurchase of common stock is another possibility, and a number of repurchases have been undertaken by large, publicly held companies in recent years, both as a useful investment and to increase corporate leverages. Union Carbide's self-tender is an example.

Rearranging the portfolio of business assets, through acquisitions and divestitures, is a richer area for the M&A group than is pure financial restructuring. The challenges are greater, and there is more scope for an investment banking firm to display its skills. Here what comes to the fore is essentially competitive strategy, where the objective is to improve market power and market share, and sometimes to achieve a critical size, as well as to bring about an improved stock market perception of value.

Restructuring work often involves developing or helping to develop a business strategy for a client. And the M&A team may find itself acting initially as management consultants (generally not a very profitable activity compared with the usual M&A work). The M&A group may be favored because it brings a specific expertise to the job, one not necessarily found even in first-rate management consulting firms. The expertise involves the market valuation of the package of assets and liabilities that makes up the corporation. An M&A team may be able to point out that the market appears to perceive a corporation as belonging to one industry when in fact the bulk of its activities lie in another. And if one industry is in relative favor while the other is in disfavor, then the company's value in the marketplace will be enhanced if its activities can be shifted so as to create a market recognition that it is operating in the favored industry.

Divestitures call on the special expertise of an M&A group. Some firms have established a reputation for skill in disposing of particular classes of property. The leveraged buyout has become a popular way of divesting major components of a corporation. The point here is that buyers may be found who are more interested in the financial aspects of a purchase than in acquiring a new business operation. An initial public offering of a parent or a subsidiary is another alternative, where once again the buyer is making a financial investment rather than taking on a business operation.

The role of the merger and acquisition group in these restructurings is a function of the skills and resources it can offer to a manager. First is the market appraisal of a company, and how various asset and liability configurations are likely to be valued in the marketplace. Here the role of security analysts is important, ands the trading and risk-arbitrage people may be helpful. Next is the independent perspective that an M&A team can bring to a management that is preoccupied with its own operations and its own industry. Here it is the experience of the M&A group itself that is probably most important. Third, if divestitures seem to be called for, the M&A group should be able to put a team to work valuing the assets to be disposed of and identifying the most attractive potential buyers as well as the best divestiture process. The support of security analysts may be helpful here, but perhaps even more important is the general business development and relationship activity of the firm that allows it to suggest appropriate potential buyers. Finally, skill that may separate the successful from the less successful M&A group has to do with understanding the corporate culture of the client company.

SUBSIDIARY MERGERS

In a declining industry, a number of companies may discover that there is just not enough business to go around, and that shrinking operations is appropriate. The oil services industry is a good example. One way to reduce expenses without actually withdrawing from the business is for two or three companies to merge their oil services activities into a jointly owned subsidiary. Each company then participates through that subsidiary in the oil service business, but the investment and expense are shared two or three ways.

The pooled operation need not take the legal form of a jointly owned subsidiary corporation. It may be a joint venture. Careful design of the form of organization may enable the participating companies to avoid writing off assets that have declined in value. There may even be opportunity for leveraging the new entity to provide cash to those who have contributed assets.

RECAPITALIZATION

Altering the capital structure of a corporation draws on many talents in M&A and other departments in a firm. The importance of the corporate finance function is obvious. We have mentioned pension plans as a source of cash, and expertise in this area is valuable. A sale and leaseback may be an attractive way to restructure both assets and liabilities, so a real estate department can be helpful.

Stock repurchase plans have become popular in recent years for a number of possible reasons. Stock repurchases may constitute a takeover defense, both by using up corporate cash and concentrating defensive ownership of shares. They may be motivated by the attractiveness of higher leverage, particularly in a period of relatively low interest rates. And they may simply constitute the best available investment for corporate cash.

The expertise of arbitrage and equity trading people will help set the terms for an offer to shareholders. Fixed-income staff can advise on the effect of a share repurchase on debt rating and cost of debt.

Public leveraged buyouts are also examples of recapitalizations designed to increase leverage. This is a fast-growing business, with Drexel a leader largely because of the ability it developed to place debt of highly leveraged companies.

ARRANGING FOR AN ACQUISITION

A not unusual case will present the M&A group with a client company that finds itself confronted by little potential for growth by itself or perhaps within its industry. The task begins with an analysis of the company and the industry, and then a search for an industry that offers a reasonable "fit" for the client company. Sometimes there is no such industry, and any acquisition will have to be in the nature of pure diversification.

The M&A group will identify an industry, then the companies that offer attractive strengthening or diversification possibilities, and then which of those companies probably could be purchased. Finally, a short list of possible acquisitions is presented to the client management.

Next comes the question of tactics in approaching a potential acquisition, and here the judgment of the M&A advisor is critical. The client will have to decide whether it is willing to pursue an unfriendly takeover, or whether the acquisition must be on a friendly, negotiated basis. The M&A group will value the prospect companies and estimate what price the client will have to pay to acquire them. The client decides whether the investment banking firm is to make an approach to the target company, or whether its own chief executive officer or some other person will do the initial negotiating.

Designing the transaction by which a company is to be acquired requires considerable skill and judgment. An important choice, of course, is whether to pay in cash or in securities, or in some combination of cash and securities. The tax position of the seller in a negotiated acquisition can be very important, particularly if the stock of the company to be acquired rests largely in the hands of founders of the company who may have a very large unrealized capital gain on their investment. A tax-free reorganization, involving a swap of stock in the acquiring corporation for stock in the acquired corporation, can offer a very substantial tax benefit to the sellers. A cash payment may call for financing on the part of the acquiring corporation, which has implications for the capital structure of the acquiror. Accounting issues can become important, particularly those that involve the treatment of goodwill.

Often there are questions of protection and compensation for management of the company to be acquired. And it is sometimes possible to create some significant tax benefits for these people.

FORMS OF MERGER

Although the simplest arrangement is probably represented by merger of the target corporation into the acquiring corporation, with shares in the latter distributed to shareholders of the target corporation, a more common scheme is the "triangular merger." The acquiring corporation forms a wholly owned subsidiary; the target corporation is merged into the subsidiary, and the shareholders of the target corporation receive shares in the acquiring corporation (the parent of the subsidiary). The procedure may seem rather roundabout, but it has some clear advantages. As we shall see, a merger is a neat way—probably the only way—to eliminate shareholdings of a minority who refuse to sell. Use of a subsidiary leaves the acquiring company in a position to operate the target as a separate corporation if this is desirable, or to merge it into its parent. And no merger vote by the acquiring company's own shareholders is necessary.

Completion of the merger is likely to require approval by a "super-majority" of shareholders of the target corporation (two-thirds in Delaware and New York). Some states statutes may preclude counting shares held by the acquiring corporation toward this majority. Shareholders who resist the merger generally can be forced to go along, but they may have the right to be paid an appraised value for their shares.

An exchange of shares of the acquiring corporation for shares of the target corporation usually can be arranged as a tax-free reorganization for federal tax purposes, thereby deferring any tax on a gain. A cash purchase, on the other hand, is subject to the usual tax treatment of gains or losses.

The accounting treatment of the merger may be important because it can have a dramatic effect on the balance sheet and reported earnings of the new enterprise. In a "pooling of interests," there is a carryover to the acquiring corporation of the target company's book value of assets and liabilities. At least 90 percent of the target's shares must be acquired, and some other conditions met, to qualify for pooling treatment. Pooling-of-interests accounting will generally lead to higher reported earnings for the new enterprise than will other accounting procedures, because depreciation charges are not increased. "Purchase accounting" applies where 50 percent or more of the target corporation is acquired and pooling is not appropriate. Purchase accounting calls for assets and liabilities of the target to be restated on the acquiring corporation's books at fair market value, with goodwill accounting for any excess of the purchase price over the net fair value. Amortization of goodwill, and probable increased depreciation on the target's assets, will lead to lower reported earnings than would be the case in a pooling of interests. Where 20 to 50 percent of the target is acquired, the "equity method" is used. The acquiring corporation records its investment as an asset, at cost plus a pro rata share of the target corporation's earnings following the acquisition. The share of target income is included in the acquiring corporation's income statement.

TENDER OFFERS

The federal Williams Act sets out a number of procedural steps that must be followed in a tender offer. These become particularly important in the case of a hostile tender, but they apply to all tenders. The Williams Act forms Section 13(d) of the Securities Exchange Act and requires that the acquiror file a public statement when over 5 percent of the target has been purchased. The Securities and Exchange Commission's Form 13D requires a statement of the purposes of the acquisition. A common statement is to the effect that the shares have been acquired "for investment purposes" or as a step to "significant ownership" and that there will be a continuous review of plans and intentions. In a hostile takeover, a blatant declaration of war may deprive the acquiror of the advantages of keeping the target company management in the dark, while any misrepresentation of intentions may provide the target with the basis for a lawsuit.

A tender offer itself must be filed with the SEC, with the target corporation, and with any stock exchange where the target corporation is listed. The filing must include a number of disclosures, including a description of the source of funds to be used for the acquisition and the purpose of the tender offer. The tender offer must remain open for at least 20 business days, and if the tender price is increased, for another 10 days after the date of the increase.

Shareholders of the target corporation who tender their shares in response to the offer have the right to withdraw their shares during the first 15 business days following the offer. Shares tendered but not yet accepted by the acquiring corporation may also be withdrawn (1) during a 10-day period beginning with the announcement of a competing tender offer, and (2) after 60 days from the beginning of the original offer. Where the offer is for less than all the shares of the target corporation, and an excess of shares is tendered, the acquiring corporation may not favor any tenderer, but must prorate the shares accepted. Any increase in price in the course of the tender offer must be paid to all who have tendered shares.

In general, tender offers may be divided into two basic types depending on whether prorating is a factor in the bid. An any-or-all offer states that the acquiror will buy any tendered shares of the target corporation. Typically, the offer is conditional on a minimum number of tendered shares sufficient to ensure control after the offer. In an any-or-all offer, target shareholders know that all their tendered shares will be purchased at the offered premium as long as the minimum conditions are met.

The second type is a partial offer, in which the acquiror sets both a minimum and a maximum. If the offer is oversubscribed, the tendered shares are subject to purchase on a pro rata basis.

A partial offer may be just that, leaving the acquiring corporation with control of the target (or even less than control) but no more. But the partial offer may also be the first of a two-tier offer. The partial offer (the first tier) achieves control of the target, and the second tier takes the form of a merger. In a friendly, negotiated merger, the terms of both the first and second tier will be agreed to by the acquiror and the directors of the target. In a hostile takeover, generally there is no agreement on either tier.

A two-tier tender offer can increase the incentive for target shareholders to tender by offering a high first-tier premium and a relatively low second-tier premium. The greater the difference between the first-tier premium and the second-tier premium, the greater is the opportunity cost to target shareholders of not tendering if the offer succeeds. Under certain conditions, target shareholders perhaps can be induced to tender into a two-tier offer even though its blended premium is less than the uniform premium of an alternative any-or-all offer that is forthcoming.

A report from the Securities and Exchange Commission uses this example. Suppose a target firm with 1000 outstanding shares has a market value of $10 per share before the tender offer, for a total equity value of $10,000. Assume that a bidder is willing to pay $5000 above this market value for control of the target firm. Therefore, the bidder is willing to pay $15 per share in an any-or-all offer. Further assume that there is a strong expectation that in the near future (say, 50 days) another bidder will offer $18 per share through an any-or-all offer.

Despite the expectation of a higher offer in the near future, the first bidder can fashion a two-tier offer to pressure target shareholders into responding while still paying only a $5000 premium. Specifically, the first bidder offers $20 per share for 500 shares on a pro rata basis, and $10 per share for the other 500 shares, to be paid after the first offer is executed. The blended price is $15, which equals the outlay in an any-or-all offer of $15 per share.

Faced with this offer, each target shareholder will reason that: (1) if other shareholders tender, then I should tender to avoid receiving only $10 for all my shares; (2) if other shareholders hold back, then I should tender to receive the first-tier price of $20 per share, with little prorating risk if the offer succeeds. Such reasoning will lead rational shareholders to tender. This result holds even though all shareholders know that concerted, organized refusal to tender would be the best strategy because this course of action would allow all to receive $18 per share in the near future from an alternative bidder. The "prisoner's dilemma" that is created by the two-tier offer causes the shareholders to accept the lower-valued offer with a $15 blended price.

The theory, however, does not seem to be borne out in practice. The SEC studied all control contests involving partial or two-tier offers between 1981 and 1984 for evidence that any-or-all offers are disadvantaged relative to partial or two-tier offers in contests, or that shareholders may be accepting a lower return by approving a partial or two-tier offer. They found virtually no evidence to support the suggestion that two-tier or partial offers can defeat competing any-or-all offers while providing lower prices for target shareholders.

The SEC report concludes:

The data on tendering contradict three important pieces of conventional wisdom. First a surprisingly large fraction of equity holders forgo the opportunity to participate in these lucrative tender offers. Without speculating about underlying motivations for this result, it is notable that, even for the high-response any-or-all offers, there remains untendered on average 14 percent of the outstanding shares.

The second surprising result is that the tendering response is actually less for the supposedly more coercive types of offers. In particular, the response is greatest for any-or-all offers and less for two-tier and partial offers. The tendering response runs directly counter to the coerciveness of the offer, as measured by the difference between tiers.

The third surprising result is that the tendering response for each type of offer is less for nonnegotiated offers than it is for negotiated offers. This contradicts the popular notion that nonnegotiated offers are more coercive than negotiated offers. Apparently, many stockholders heed target management's advice in determining whether to tender or hold.[1]

The SEC study analyzes the outcome of multiple-bidder contests for corporate control between 1981 and 1984 and discusses whether partial or two-tier offers have a tactical advantage over other kinds of offers. Included are all multiple-bidder contests in which shareholders chose between a partial or a two-tier offer involving prorating and an any-or-all tender offer or a merger offer with no prorating. The survey shows that during this period no (nonnegotiated) partial or two-tier tender offer beat an (unenjoined) any-or-all tender offer or merger proposal offering a higher premium.

Of the 18 head-to-head contests between two-tier/partial and any-or-all offers, five were won by two-tier or partial offers. Of these, three (Gulf Oil, HMW Industries, and Interpace) were won with a higher blended premium than that available from the competing any-or-all offer. In a fourth case (Conoco), the higher-valued any-or-all offer was enjoined by the Justice Department. The one case in which a two-tier offer beat a higher-valued any-or-all offer is that of Enstar Corp. in 1984. Here, the success of the two-tier offer was at least partly attributable to certain agreements between the two-tier bidder and the target. The failed any-or-all offer was nonnegotiated and conditional on the rescission of these agreements.

Partial offers have declined in popularity. The development of a market for high-yield debt has made it easier to finance any-or-all cash offers. And that same market has enabled target companies to out-bid a hostile two-tier offer, in the form of a recapitalization.

HOSTILE TAKEOVERS

Generally, at least the more substantial M&A groups within investment banking firms prefer to be associated with defending against a hostile takeover rather than with the aggressor. Drexel Burnham Lambert is perhaps an exception to this rule. All the major M&A groups (perhaps with the exception of Goldman Sachs) occasionally find themselves associated with the aggressor in a hostile case, because the maintenance of long-standing relationships demands that a firm assist a valued

---

[1] *The Economics of Any-or-All, Partial, and Two-Tier Tender Offers*, Securities and Exchange Commission, Office of the Chief Economist, April 19, 1985, p. 21. Other studies from the SEC Office of the Chief Economist include: *The Impact of Targeted Share Repurchases (Greenmail) on Stock Prices*, September 11, 1984; *Institutional Ownership, Tender Offers, and Long-Term Investments*, April 19, 1985; *Shark Repellents and Stock Prices: The Effects of Antitakeover Amendments Since 1980*, July 24, 1985; *Motivations for Hostile Tender Offers and the Market for Political Exchange*, September 25, 1985; *Antitakeover Amendments and Takeover Activity: Testing for Principal-Agent Problems in the Market for Corporate Control*, January 1986; *The Economics of Poison Pills*, March 5, 1986; *Noninvestment Grade Debt as a Source of Tender Offer Financing*, June 20, 1986; *The Effects of Poison Pills on the Wealth of Target Shareholders*, October 23, 1986.

client. But the general rule is always to stand ready to defend a client when that client is attacked, and to be ready to take on clients who need a defense.

Participating on either side of a hostile takeover does call for some special resources. The M&A business is never leisurely, but in the case of a hostile takeover the pace becomes particularly demanding. The firm may get some advance warning of an impending takeover through its risk-arbitrage group or special "watch" groups with responsibility for tracking activity in client stocks. But normally it must be prepared to throw substantial resources into an assignment on a few hours' notice. This means that legal and accounting talent must be available and the M&A analysts must be prepared to respond immediately, regardless of other work the firm and the M&A group may have on hand.

Hostile takeovers have one very positive aspect for investment banking firms— they bring publicity to the firm. At least on the defensive side this can be very helpful, as it will attract clients who feel threatened by a takeover. The value of the publicity will of course depend upon how successful the defense has been. Morgan Stanley, for example, points to its defense of Union Carbide as resulting in approximately a doubling of the price to be paid to the Union carbide shareholders.

The Unocal defense, in early 1985, is an example of a major M&A activity. Dillon Read was Unocal's traditional investment banker, and Goldman Sachs was called in to help shortly after February 14, 1985, when the Mesa Group (Boone Pickens' companies) announced that it had acquired 7.3 percent of Unocal "as an investment."

In March, the Mesa Group increased its Unocal ownership to 13.6 percent, while Goldman Sachs was analyzing Mesa's apparent intention and discussing strategy with Unocal. On April 8, the Mesa Group launched a two-tier offer. A cash tender offer of $54 was made for 64 million shares, enough to bring Mesa ownership to just over 50 percent. The Mesa plan was to acquire the balance of the Unocal shares for a package of unspecified subordinated securities to be worth $54. The cash offer would cost $4 billion, $1 billion provided by banks as margin credit and $3 billion to come from the sale of high-yield bonds placed by Drexel Burnham Lambert.

Goldman Sachs and its lawyers developed a defense that was announced by Unocal on April 17. Unocal offered a $72 principal amount of three newly designed series of Unocal senior debt for all Unocal shares not purchased in the Mesa offer. The offer was conditioned on Mesa purchasing the 64 million shares for which it had tendered, and the offer excluded Unocal shares held by Mesa. As a result of this offer, Mesa could have found itself owning all the outstanding shares of Unocal, financed by $4 billion of junior debt, with Unocal having to issue another $6.3 billion of senior debt. Goldman's risk-arbitrage expertise was critical to the overall defensive strategy; its corporate finance capability was critical in the structure of the new Unocal debt instruments and their indentures; and its fixed-income strength was critical in design and pricing.

The Mesa Group challenged the Unocal offer in the Delaware courts, arguing that Unocal had no right to exclude from the offer shares held by Mesa. The Delaware Chancery Court agreed with Mesa, but on May 17, the Delaware Supreme

Court reversed the Chancery Court, and let the offer stand. In the meantime, Unocal had taken two further steps. It modified the offer to shareholders, relaxing the condition that Mesa purchase the 64 million Unocal shares first. Unocal removed the condition with respect to 50 million shares, but left it in place for 37.2 million shares. This meant that regardless of whether Mesa was successful in obtaining 64 million shares, 50 million shares held by shareholders other than Mesa could be swapped for Unocal senior debt, for a total of $3.6 billion. And in addition, Unocal announced a master limited partnership that would take ownership of about 45 percent of the company's domestic oil and gas reserves.

The Mesa Group had announced on March 28 that it would solicit proxies to adjourn Unocal's April 29 annual meeting. The meeting was postponed by court order to May 13, and at that meeting Mesa failed to win the proxy fight.

On May 20, three days after the decision of the Delaware Supreme Court, a settlement was reached. Mesa was allowed to tender a small portion of its shares for $72 in Unocal senior debt; Mesa agreed to restrictions on sale of its shares of Unocal stock and to restrictions on voting those shares; and Drexel agreed not to finance another offer for Unocal for three years. In May 1986, Mesa sold almost all its 10.9 percent stake in Unocal at $22.50 per share, having acquired the shares for over $40. Some special treatment from Unocal enabled Mesa to break even overall.

In the end, the Unocal defense proved a costly one. As oil prices fell, the company found its heavy debt load increasingly difficult to bear. Interest expense had risen from $37 million to $124 million per quarter. By mid-1986 Unocal appeared ready to sell off assets and reduce debt.

In 1984 and 1985 hostile takeovers seemed to be dominated by "raiders." That is, the takeover offers were primarily not from companies that wished to combine the operations of the target company with their own operations, but from investors who basically were seeking to restructure the target company. Sometimes the objective was even simpler: to extract "greenmail" from the target company (i.e., to persuade the target company to purchase the acquired shares at a price well above what the raider paid for them, in order to end the threat of a takeover). In 1986 the emphasis seemed to have switched somewhat, and although there will continue to be plenty of raids, M&A groups are more likely to find themselves helping a company deal with unsolicited bids aimed at merging their operations into the operations of another corporation.

STRATEGIES IN HOSTILE TAKEOVERS

A hostile takeover generally involves acquisition of at least a controlling number of voting shares for cash. In a friendly, negotiated transaction it may be desirable to arrange a swap of shares in the target company for shares in the acquiror, particularly if there are tax benefits to the target company shareholders. But an exchange of stock, or an offer of securities of the acquiror for shares in the target company, requires the use of a prospectus and is likely to delay the offer to the disadvantage of a hostile acquiror. In any case, in the course of the offering a large proportion of the shares of the target company will have been sold to arbitrageurs who have no interest in shares or other securities of the acquiring corporation.

At the same time, a cash offering imposes a heavy burden on the acquiror, if the transaction is a large one. One answer to the difficulty is the two-tier offer. (Another answer is the increased use of high-risk, high-yield "junk bond" financing.) A cash offer is made for a controlling number of shares, and then a noncash offer is made for the balance. At this second stage, the acquiror has effective control of the target company and need not fear competitive bids or management resistance.

There will always be some shareholders who refuse to sell their shares at any price. Their shareholdings can be acquired in a merger. The Delaware corporation statute, for example, contains a procedure for squeezing out a minority interest by way of a merger between the acquiring corporation and the target company. The holdout shareholders will have to be paid, but they cannot block the merger. So the last stage in a hostile takeover typically is a "squeeze-out" merger.

Generally, the acquiring corporation will buy a small stake in the target on the open market, as a preliminary to a contest. We have already seen that the Williams Act requires the acquiror to file SEC Form 13D after acquiring over 5 percent of the target.

It is likely that during the early open-market acquisition, the market, investment bankers, and eventually the target company will realize what is going on. And even before the filing of a Form 13D, the target may be taking steps to defend itself.

DEFENSES TO HOSTILE TAKEOVER ATTEMPTS

The past few years have been some remarkable developments in the techniques for achieving, and resisting, hostile takeovers. Probably eight or nine of 10 hostile takeover attempts are successful. This is despite the substantial innovation in "shark repellent" devices to assist in defenses against hostile takeovers. For a while legal decisions tended to favor defenders, but in the 1980s (especially 1985 and 1986) there was a series of decisions that significantly reduced the power of the defending companies. Recently there has been a tendency for courts to take a stronger line with respect to the fiduciary obligations of directors of a target corporation. Once it is clear that their corporation is for sale, their obligation is to obtain the best possible price for their shareholders. The Delaware Supreme Court took this position in a case involving Revlon in 1985. And a Michigan federal court took the same position in blocking a management buyout of Fruehauf that the directors had favored over a higher-priced offer from an outside group.

Sometimes the purpose of a company's defense is to defeat an attack and preserve independence. Sometimes it is to delay a takeover until a more congenial merger can be arranged. And sometimes it is to raise the price offered.

Defensive devices may include a series of charter amendments that can be implemented only by a majority vote of shareholders (and sometimes a two-thirds majority is required). Management considering the use of such devices must consider whether the votes will be forthcoming. Institutional investors, for example, have become suspicious of management efforts to discourage tender offers that may bring windfall profits to shareholders, and for many large companies the votes of institutional shareholders are important.

Certain other defensive devices that do not require shareholder approval recently have faced scrutiny by the courts. These include asset lockups, exclusionary tender offers, and various shareholder rights plans.

Charter Amendments

Classified Board. Directors of a corporation are classified, usually into three groups, with the terms of office of one group expiring each year. Directors may be removed from office only "for cause," with removal requiring a super-majority of shareholder votes (often 80 percent of the shares outstanding, which of course implies a greater percentage of the shares actually voted). Vacancies on the board between elections may be filled only by the board.

This device may delay a takeover attempt, particularly a "creeping acquisition," because ownership of even a majority of voting shares, or control of a majority of proxies, allows replacement of only one-third of the directors at a time. Delaying the time when the acquiror actually takes control may facilitate the use of other defensive tactics described in the following paragraphs. A classified board, however, is no defense against a tender for all shares. Institutional investors tend to vote against classified board proposals. In some recent cases (Chase Manhattan and Gillette) a classified board was just barely approved by shareholders.

Super-Majority Provisions. Approval by more than a simple majority of shareholder votes (commonly 80 percent) is required to remove directors, amend the corporate charter, and approve a merger. The super-majority for a merger may be required only for a merger with a shareholder holding a significant stake in the company (perhaps 10 or 20 percent). This device, like the classified board, discourages creeping acquisitions. It may also give veto power over transactions favored by management to a minority coalition of shareholders.

Institutional investors almost always vote against super-majority proposals.

Restrictions on Shareholder Action. The ability of shareholders to vote on a proposal in the absence of a shareholder meeting is restricted. And the rights of shareholders to call a special meeting are restricted.

The result of such restrictions is to force shareholder-initiated action to be deferred to the next regular annual meeting. This delay may help the board to negotiate, and may discourage a creeping acquisition. It is no defense against an offer for all shares of the company.

Institutional investors generally vote against these restrictions.

Fair Price/Anti-Self-Dealing Provision. A super-majority of shareholder votes is required to approve a merger with a shareholder owning a certain percentage (commonly 10 or 20 percent) of the company. The super-majority requirement is waived if the price to the shareholders in the merger is at least as high as any price paid at an earlier stage of the acquisition. The requirement may also be waived by a majority of disinterested directors. A weaker version of this provision calls for a simple majority vote of disinterested shareholders.

The purpose of the provision is to discourage two-tier offers, where the acquiror begins with an attractive offer for shares (the first tier), obtains control, and then can offer less attractive terms (the second tier) to the minority shareholders left.

Institutional investors understand the value of this provision in protecting shareholders when a majority vote of disinterested shareholders is required. But generally they oppose a super-majority requirement.

"Blank Check" Preferred Stock Issue. Shareholders authorize an issue of voting preferred stock and empower the company's directors to set all the terms and to issue the stock without further shareholder action. The directors can use the preferred to place votes in friendly hands, or to complete a defensive acquisition.

Institutional investors are becoming reluctant to approve "blank check" preferreds.

Antigreenmail Provisions. A majority shareholder vote (generally a majority of disinterested shareholders) is required to approve a significant business transaction between the company and a 5 percent shareholder.

This provision discourages raiders whose objective is greenmail—acquiring a threatening amount of shares and selling them at an inflated price to the company. It can, however, limit the board's ability to carry out transactions it believes to be appropriate.

Institutional investors generally favor these provisions.

Devices That Do Not Require Shareholder Approval

Asset Lockups. Confronted by a hostile takeover attempt, the company sells to a third party or gives to the third party an option on valuable assets, sometimes coupled to an undertaking by the company not to seek a higher price from another potential buyer.

Unless the sale is at a fair price, it is likely to be invalidated. The Delaware Chancery Court invalidated a lockup of assets by Revlon in 1985 which was used as a defensive tactic against Pantry Pride, Inc. In reviewing the decision, the Delaware Supreme Court also said that once the directors of a company have decided on its sale their duty becomes one of obtaining the best possible price for the stockholders. And in 1986 the United States Court of Appeals for the Second Circuit invalidated a lockup by SCM, facing a hostile bid from Hanson Trust PLC. In both cases, the directors authorizing the lockup were found to have violated their fiduciary duty to shareholders.

Discriminatory (Exclusionary) Tender Offers. The discriminatory tender device was used when Unocal Corporation fended off a hostile offer by the Mesa Group in 1985. Once Mesa had acquired a substantial block of Unocal stock, Unocal offered all the shareholders *except Mesa* the opportunity to exchange senior debt securities valued at well above the Mesa bid for up to 30 percent of the shares outstanding. The result of the discriminatory offer would have been buyout of a substantial fraction of the shareholdings other than Mesa's at a very generous price, leaving Mesa in control of a company with very heavy debt.

The Delaware Supreme Court upheld the validity of the Unocal offer, partly because of Mesa's reputation as a raider and the likelihood that Mesa's real objective was greenmail.

The threat of a discriminatory tender offer can discourage a raider from accumulating a large position before launching a hostile offer. In May 1986, the Sperry Corporation threatened to use a discriminatory tender against Burroughs Corporation. Burroughs had offered $70 cash for each of 33 million Sperry shares, in what appeared to be the first of a two-tier offer. Rejecting the offer as inadequate, the Sperry board voted that if Burroughs obtained the 33 million shares, Sperry would tender $80 cash for the remaining 29.5 million shares, not to include any shares held by Burroughs. At the time of the $80 tender offer, of course, Burroughs would own over half the Sperry shares. The end result would have been to increase Sperry's debt by $2 billion and reduce its cash by $400 million after Burroughs had borrowed $3 billion to buy it. At the same time, given Sperry's classified board, Burroughs would not be in a position to control the company. The Sperry action generally was interpreted as a mechanism to increase the Burroughs offer to about $75, not to block the acquisition.

Poison Pills (Shareholder Rights Plans). The board of directors of a company declares a dividend in the form of warrants to purchase more shares. The warrants are activated only in the event of a tender offer for the company, or when a person or group acquires a predetermined percentage of the shares (e.g., 20 percent).

The "flip-over" type of poison pill sets the exercise price of the warrant at two to five times the current price of the shares. The warrant then has little or no value initially. Should a hostile acquiror seeking merger attempt to squeeze out the last of the company's shareholders, however, the warrants convert into warrants to buy shares in the new company with a market value twice the exercise price. In the case of Household International, Inc., the company's stock was selling for $30 and the exercise price of the warrants was $100, giving them no initial value. But the flip-over allowed each warrant to entitle the holder to $200 worth of stock in a new company on payment of $100. A potential acquiror would be faced with substantial dilution. The Delaware Supreme Court in 1985 upheld the validity of the Household poison pill in the case of merger. An acquisition not followed by a merger is unaffected, as Sir James Goldsmith found when he bought into Crown Zellerbach in 1985.

The "flip-in" type of warrant is activated by acquisition of a specified percentage of the company by one shareholder or a group, even if no merger is proposed. The warrant in this case entitles the holders to buy shares in the company at half price.

NL Industries, Inc., attempted this defense against Harold Simmons before it was struck down by a New York court applying New Jersey law.

The "back-end" type of warrant entitles the holders to sell their shares to the company for cash or securities at what the board of directors believes to be a fair price. Up to the activation date the warrants generally are redeemable by the company at a nominal amount, so the directors can easily clear them away.

There are other kinds of poison pills. Revlon issued rights entitling shareholders to exchange a Revlon share for $65 face amount of 12 percent one-year notes, if a hostile suitor acquired 20 percent of Revlon shares. The device did not prevent Pantry Pride from acquiring Revlon in a cash tender offer, but Lazard Freres, who represented Revlon, believes the poison pill added $15 a share to the price. The use of the poison pill in this case was upheld by the Delaware Supreme Court.

Poison Put Bonds. Bondholders can be given an option to demand early redemption in cash, or conversion to stock, in the event of a hostile takeover attempt.

W.R. Grace & Co. issued $250 million of Eurobonds convertible into common stock after five years. In the event that a hostile suitor acquires 30 percent of Grace stock, it is stipulated that the bondholders may convert immediately, or demand cash. The put provision makes the bonds attractive to investors, because it enables them to profit from a takeover bid. And it discourages a takeover by raising the effective price.

Defensive Bond Indenture Provisions. Issuing debt with indenture provisions that bar a variety of corporate changes may make a company unattractive to a potential acquiror. Unocal, in its strategy to resist Mesa's takeover attempt in 1985, offered shareholders the chance to exchange stock for senior debt with covenants that limited new borrowing. In the same year Union Carbide issued shareholders new debt with covenants that limit the sale of assets and increases in debt. In May 1986, Viacom International announced an offering of $250 million senior subordinated notes with covenants limiting the ratio of debt to total capital.

An indenture prohibiting the sale of key assets would block one way of raising cash, and a limit on the debt ratio would block another. The effect is to deny an acquiror access to funds it had been counting on to help finance the acquisition.

THE ROLE OF LAWYERS IN M&A TRANSACTIONS

We have said that legal advice is crucially important in M&A work. The leading M&A law firms are in the news almost as frequently as the leading M&A investment bankers. Martin Lipton of Wachtell, Lipton, Rosen & Katz generally can be found advising one of the parties in a major hostile takeover, with Joseph Flom of Skadden, Arps, Slate, Meagher & Flom on the other side. Flom is associated most often with hostile acquirors, and Lipton with defensive strategies. It was Lipton who originated the poison pill defense. In late 1986 the *Wall Street Journal* reported the move of

M&A lawyer Donald G. Drapkin from Skadden, Arps to an investment firm in the manner it usually reserves for defections from important M&A investment bankers.

Most of the significant innovations in the hostile takeover business, both offensive and defensive, have come from lawyers. And lawyers play an essential part in the development of strategy as a transaction unfolds. This has given rise to some resentment from law firms over what have been seen as inequitable compensation arrangements. Generally the investment banker's fee in a major M&A transaction is based on the size of the transaction, often running to many millions of dollars. Lawyers' fees have been much lower, although they have risen in recent years. But a dramatic change came in 1986, when Wachtell, Lipton charged Burroughs Corporation a contingent fee that came to over $7 million, in connection with Burroughs' acquisition of Sperry Corporation. Total legal fees paid by Burroughs in the transaction came to $12 million, while $11 million was paid in fees to Lazard Freres and James D. Wolfensohn. Skadden, Arps apparently also has begun charging contingent fees. In the Burroughs-Sperry case, Skadden, Arps represented Sperry, the loser, and was paid between $3 and $4 million.

For the future, it seems likely that the M&A lawyers will demand the recognition and compensation that investment bankers have been enjoying. But it also seems likely that a trend toward substantial capital commitments by investment bankers may enable some of them to raise their fees beyond present levels.

CAREERS IN MERGERS AND ACQUISITIONS

The merger and acquisition business is notorious for offering a difficult lifestyle. M&A is a service business, and one in which clients normally are in a great hurry. As a rule, a merger or acquisition, and particularly a hostile takeover, is an event of enormous importance to the client company and its management, however ordinary it may seem to the M&A group. It seems unlikely that these characteristics of the business will change. So long working hours, a great deal of travel on very short notice, and frequent sacrifice of weekends and vacations to the needs of clients will continue to be part of M&A work.

Professionals in the M&A business work very hard and are well compensated. They are accustomed to working with a small group of very talented people who also work hard and are well paid. It is difficult to trace the lifetime career of someone in M&A work, because the specialty is still fairly young. The merger boom we see now began in the 1960s, but it was not until the 1970s that investment banking firms organized formal M&A departments. Morgan Stanley was one of the first, establishing its department in 1972. The pioneers are for the most part still fairly young. Some have become partners of their firms, but none has completed an investment banking career.

Someone joining an M&A department in a major firm is likely to spend a year on valuation work—assembling data, interviewing corporate people as part of the "due diligence" part of valuation, and helping prepare selling memoranda. The next stage in a career involves the judgment process—arriving at a valuation and identifying buyers or sellers. The next involves negotiation, and meetings with company people, lawyers, and M&A people from other firms. Joining a takeover defense team is a further possibility at one of the larger firms.

There is some evidence that people do become burned out in this business within 10 to 15 years. And a few of those who have headed major M&A departments have moved on to other activities within investment banking firms. This has been true at Morgan Stanley and Goldman Sachs. Others, of course, leave the M&A business much earlier. What they have learned essentially is a good deal of corporate finance, a good deal about the mechanics of merger and acquisition transactions, a good understanding of a variety of industries, and a familiarity with the relationships among lawyers, accountants, and other specialists in the M&A group. They are also likely to be well connected in the M&A deal network.

A number of those who are very successful in M&A groups go on to establish their own firms, sometimes doing M&A work, sometimes specializing in leveraged buyouts or venture capital. It has been true for some years that the successful individuals in M&A groups probably get more personal publicity than almost any other investment bankers. And this can be very helpful to those setting up on their own.

Those who do well in an M&A group generally are aggressive and creative. For such people, the M&A operation may be the best training ground in an investment banking firm. Mobility from this group is high. Observation seems to indicate that there is almost no downside risk in the M&A group if one can stand the life-style.

APPENDIX

Statistics on merger and acquisition activity are available from a number of sources. Cambridge Corporation (Boston) publishes a yearbook, *Corporate Mergers, Joint Ventures and Corporate Policy*, but does not identify any of the investment bankers participating in transactions. W.T. Grimm & Co. (Chicago) publishes an annual *Mergerstat® Review*, but again does not give information on investment banker activity. Euromoney Publications of London publishes an annual *Euromoney Mergers and Acquisitions Guide* tabulating activity of investment bankers and other intermediaries. *Mergers and Acquisitions* is a bimonthly journal that includes data on intermediaries in merger transactions (and also maintains a proprietary data base).

Tables 13.1 and 13.2, showing M&A activity for 1986, were constructed by Morgan Stanley & Co. from public information. Each firm is given credit for every transaction in which it was known to be an advisor for either the acquiring or the acquired company.

Total M&A activity reported for the preceding year, 1985, in *Mergers and Acquisitions* was: 2773 transactions within the United States, for a dollar value of $120.3 billion; 206 acquisitions of U.S. companies by foreigners, for a dollar value of 417.8 billion; and only 174 acquisitions of foreign companies by U.S. companies, for a dollar value of $1.1 billion.

14 Investment Management in an Investment Banking Firm

JEANNE GUSTAFSON

Investment management is the business of investing other people's money: choosing what types of assets to use (stocks, bonds, real estate) and which securities or properties to buy and when to sell them. Investment accounts can be pooled, representing the assets of a number of clients where each client has a pro rata share of the returns, or managed separately for a single client. Pools include mutual funds managed by brokers for individuals and commingled funds managed by banks and insurance companies for pension funds or other groups. Clients pay a fee for the service, usually based on the size of the assets managed.

The largest investment banking firms are divided on whether to be in the business or not. Salomon Brother does not offer this service: Merrill Lynch does; Donaldson, Lufkin & Jenrette offers it through Alliance Capital Management. (Both DLJ and Alliance are now subsidiaries of the Equitable Life Assurance Society of the United States.)

A number of investment banking firms initially got into the business of investment management by managing the money of their partners, families, and friends. It was a natural extension of this business to offer this service to the public, either to individuals who knew the partners through business or social contacts or to corporations that had dealt with the investment bankers in other relationships. When other investment banking firms decided to go into the investment management business, they could purchase an already existing firm or hire experienced individuals who had established a reputation and clientele in a previous firm.

INVESTMENT BANKERS AS INVESTMENT MANAGERS

There is little synergy between investment banking and investment management,

247

although the market maker can claim an advantage in purchasing new issues. This advantage, however, could be seen as a potential conflict of interest if the investment manager is suspected of placing new issues in an investment account in order to reduce inventory acquired through an underwriting.

An investment management organization within an investment bank operates as a separate entity. The day-to-day management of the business is separate: client servicing usually involves different individuals at the client organization even if they are an investment banking client of the same firm, and investment decisions are quite different from corporate finance decisions. A significant reason for keeping corporate finance and investment management groups separate is to limit potential for insider information and conflicts of interest. It is essential that the investment manager deal with publicly available information and make decisions to buy or sell securities regardless of a company's relationship with the investment bank.

There is more synergy between brokerage and investment management where the availability of first-class research and trading is critical to producing results in both businesses. The investment management divisions of the major investment brokerage firms capitalize on the firm's reputation in the securities industry to enhance their marketing.

It would be unusual, however, for an investment manager to rely solely on the research available from the parent firm. Most often, investment managers collect information from a number of research sources, and many supplement the available research with company visits and manager interviews on their own. There is a tendency to be comfortable with the research analysts the investment manager knows well, so it is possible that an investment manager may feel more confident of the research provided by his or her own firm than by a third party.

These same advantages may present a conflict of interest if the investment manager trades the securities under management in order to generate trading commissions for the brokerage division, rather than improve investment returns. Any manager who "churns" the portfolio for noninvestment reasons should expect to lose the account eventually because of poor investment performance. For these reasons many broker-related investment managers limit the amount of in-house trading on behalf of their investment management clients and use external brokers for the majority of their executions.

An important argument against the broker as investment manager lies in avoiding competition with the best trading customers: investment managers. Rather than risk offending their large institutional clients, brokers may concentrate on maximizing their trading opportunities. This includes developing new investment management techniques to control risk and improve return. These techniques often involve increased trading and the use of options or futures. Several brokers employ special research teams that serve as industry consultants to investment managers, teaching them new techniques and how to use options and futures. These groups do not charge fees but hope rather that their firm will be asked to execute the additional trades and otherwise profit from the enhanced relationships.

MANAGEMENT FEES

The motives for being in the investment management business are several and include profit. Investment management fees vary by the duties of the investment manager, the asset type, size of account, and the firm's reputation. The duties of the manager range from executing trades based on a computer model (such as matching the return of a specified index) to participating in the management of a venture as the general partner on behalf of limited partners, or managing the leases or the building itself in a real estate investment.

Asset types are broadly grouped into equity, fixed-income, and "other." Equity accounts can include common and preferred stocks, stock options, stock index futures, and stock index options. Fixed-income accounts can include bonds, mortgages, convertible securities, financial futures, bond options, and cash equivalents: Treasury bills, certificates of deposit, commercial paper, bankers acceptances, and other short-term arrangements. A variety of more esoteric investments may include collateralized mortgage obligations (CMOs) and other mortgage-backed arrangements too numerous to mention. "Other" usually means real estate, venture capital, and international equity and fixed-income instruments.

The fees for the active management of the simplest fixed-income accounts generally are lower than those for actively managed common stock equity accounts; venture-capital management fees usually are the highest. Fees for passive management such as a stock index or a dedicated bond fund are less than those for active management. Fees range from 5 percent of assets for venture capital and 1 percent for equity accounts to 0.25 percent for cash accounts and 0.10 percent for passive funds. At 1 percent of assets, the fee for a $50 million account is $500,000 per year.

Account size is another factor in charging fees. Managers usually apply a percentage fee that declines for larger accounts. Some managers, however, charge a fixed percentage regardless of account size. Bank trust departments are most likely to follow declining scales. The firm's reputation influences the size of the percentage fee and how much it declines by asset size. More successful firms generally charge higher percentages, raising fees and minimum account size when they want to limit new business.

An example of a declining fee schedule for an equity manager might be 1 percent of the first $50 million, 0.25 percent on the next $50 million and 0.10 percent on the balance. Individual investors generally are charged the highest percentage fees because of their relatively small assets while multibillion dollar state retirement funds enjoy the lowest percentage fees and often negotiate nonstandard charges because of their size.

PERFORMANCE FEES

In November 1985 the Securities and Exchange Commission adopted a rule allowing investment managers to collect performance-related fees. Before this rule change, managers were restricted to basing their fees on asset size, not performance. The new rule applies to accounts of $500,000 or more for investors who have more than $1 million in net assets. Large endowments and foundations quickly adopted new performance-based fees while plans covered by the Employee Retirement Income Security Act of 1974 (ERISA), such as pension, profit sharing, and other employee benefit plans, waited for the Department of Labor to issue an exemption for ERISA plans to use these fee arrangements. In mid-1986, the Department of Labor approved the performance fee schedules of two investment management firms, but did not issue a class exemption. ERISA plans continued to be slow to consider these arrangements.

Performance-based fees allow investors to negotiate a lower standard fee offset by an opportunity to share in the profit, if performance is better than a specific target performance. The performance fee is particularly attractive to performance-conscious institutional funds, because it could reduce fees if performance falls below target.

There are a number of different formulas for performance fees. Some include a minimum or maintenance fee paid regardless of performance, others have no base or floor; that is, managers may receive no fee at all if their performance is significantly below the standard. Generally these fees are based on the manager's current schedule of fees. For example, a manager outperforming the target by 200 basis points will be paid 100 percent of the current fee. A manager only matching the bogey or target, say, the S&P 500, is paid less, for example 60 percent of the base fee. (For a base fee of 0.5 percent, this manager would earn 0.3 percent for matching the S&P 500.) There are a number of variations. Some formulas are set up to penalize the manager more for underperforming than to reward for outperforming; some have just the reverse incentive. Performance fees must be carefully structured to best meet the clients' objectives and to match the manager's style with the appropriate target. It is also important to encourage the manager to take the appropriate amount of risk: not assuming more risk than is desirable and yet actively managing the portfolio.

MEASURING RESULTS

Institutions measure their fund's investment performance monthly and compare it to the results for other funds each quarter. Generally, they compare managers by asset type (equity versus equity, bond versus bond). This horse-race approach subjects investment management firms to wide swings in fortune. Missing a single bond or stock market rally may not the cost the firm many accounts, unless it is a major rally like the August–September rally of 1982 when simultaneous rallies in both markets brought substantial returns to those fortunate enough to participate. Managers who held large uninvested or cash positions at the start of the rallies had difficulty matching the returns of the fully invested managers and the indexes. On the other hand, several equity managers who were fully invested in small company stocks never sold their securities, and their investment declined rapidly in 1983 and

1984 as their stocks dropped steadily in price. Fixed-income managers who held cash through late 1982, then invested in long-term maturities in 1983, compounded their poor relative performance as interest rates climbed again.

Declining markets mean double jeopardy for an investment banking firm offering investment management services: just when its profits are under the most pressure from falling market values, it will be subject to account loss due to poor performance. At the same time, there is generally a lag of several months following poor performance before the investor decides to change money managers, and poor absolute performance does not necessarily mean poor relative performance. Therefore, even if the markets have been negative, a manager's returns can be viewed as satisfactory given certain goals or the performance of other managers.

One measure of relative performance is a manager's percentile ranking in a universe of similar investment managers. Managers boast of "top quartile" performance, meaning they outperformed 75 percent of the others in the universe. Clients should be careful that the time period for the comparison is sufficient to be meaningful and that the universe is appropriate for comparison. For example, comparing equity managers to bond managers is not appropriate because the opportunities available in each asset class can vary widely from year to year.

Performance results are most important to pension clients and relatively less important to multiemployer funds that value the relationship with the investment manager more than performance. Performance is also less critical to individuals where consulting and estate management services enhance the manager-client relationship. Pension funds are highly competitive and compare their results with specialized groups of other pension funds regularly.

MODERN PORTFOLIO THEORY

Another difference in results is related to the amount of risk the manager accepts. A generally accepted principle of portfolio management is that all investors are risk-averse and accept risk only in the expectation of incremental return. The challenge in performance measurement is to define the appropriate measure of risk and to determine whether the manager earned sufficient return to compensate the client for the amount of risk assumed.

The principle of risk aversion is the basis of modern portfolio theory (MPT). Although it has been around for years, there is little agreement about its application. The most accepted use of MPT is in the measurement of equity managers and their "risk-adjusted" returns. Briefly, a manager's volatility is calculated relative to the market's volatility (generally defined as the S&P 500 Stock Index). This relative volatility is multiplied times the "excess" return the market earned over the "riskless" rate (the return on 90-day Treasury bills). This is the amount the manager should have earned over the T-bill return. If the manager did not achieve this risk-adjusted return, the shortfall is attributed to poor stock selection or poor asset allocation decisions. If the manager achieved a higher return, superior discretionary decisions are credited. In this way, two managers who assumed quite different levels of risk can be compared directly, crediting each with the returns attributable to their decisions and not merely market moves.

Along with its application in performance measurement, MPT is fundamental to numerous investment strategies that seek to maximize risk/return. The use of computers is essential for many of these strategies, which compare thousands of combinations in achieving the "optimum" portfolio. Other computer uses include the tracking of a market index where the investment objective is to obtain the same return, or as close as possible, as the market earns, or to match pension liability streams with asset maturity and income dates, or to manage asset allocation to achieve a targeted return.

Computers are also essential for backtesting an investment approach. Backtesting is the simulation of returns that would have been achieved in past years if a certain approach had been applied in each of those years. For example, a manager specifies a certain set of values for each of several stock characteristics (price/earnings ratio, earnings per share growth rate, market capitalization) and the computer selects the stocks in a given universe that meet these requirements. The computer selects new portfolios for each measurement period, subject to turnover or other restrictions. Then the rates of return are calculated for each period.

Investment management firms are often started to implement a new investment approach, in which case the backtesting data become the basis of a marketing strategy to attract clients and explain the firm's decision-making process. The manager rarely adheres absolutely to the model, but uses it as a guide or first test for certain steps in the process.

STARTING AN INVESTMENT MANAGEMENT FIRM

There is a large turnover among investment professionals in most investment management firms. Seasoned investment professionals may break away from a larger organization in order to start their own investment management firms. It is also typical for an investment manager to gain experience at one firm and move to another in order to significantly increase his or her compensation level or equity participation. The departure of a major investment professional from an investment organization is unsettling for the manager's clients. Often an institution can persuade the clients that the firm's philosophy and style will not be altered because of the loss of one or more individuals and that the attention paid to their accounts will be just the same.

If the managers leaving the firm have established a certain style of investment—for example, if they were in charge of running a particular mutual fund—they may be more successful in enticing clients to follow them to their new firm. It is also common for individuals to leave one firm in order to manage money by using a distinctly different investment style—for example, by following an investment computer model that they have developed over the years. Their success in attracting clients is largely dependent on their years of experience and the extent of their reputation in the investment management field.

Generally speaking, large pension funds seek investment management firms with a sufficient asset base under management to demonstrate their capability in managing accounts of the client's size and a sufficient track record to demonstrate the consistency and workability of the firm's investment style. This record may depend on results from the professional's previous firm, but should reflect the style of management and the team of professionals in place in the new firm.

Relative and absolute performance are key criteria which large pension funds use in selecting investment managers. The institution may employ an investment consultant or conduct the search itself. In either case, the manager is often asked to present performance results for several calendar years and for the latest market cycles. This makes it very difficult for a new firm to attract its first account until it has a three- to five-year record managing $100 million or more of assets.

Pension and other institutional investors (profit sharing plans, 401(k) plans and other employee-benefit-related plans) are the most sought-after clients because they are large, continue to grow through contributions, and require relatively little servicing, sometimes only an annual consultation. Total assets of the 1000 largest employee benefit funds exceeded $1 trillion in 1985. The largest 200 funds accounted for over $800 billion of that total.

It is easier for a new firm to attract clients when the firm is started by seasoned professionals who can point to their record or reputation at previous firms, or when the managers have substantial experience in investment-related endeavors, as in a venture-capital firm that plans to invest in companies that have just gone public. The knowledge of such professionals in the emerging venture companies and the market environment should help to evaluate a company's prospects in the next stage of development.

Capital to start an investment management firm is primarily required to renovate office space, lease or buy furniture and office equipment, and pay rent, utilities, and salaries. The largest ongoing expense is salaries. The actual cost of doing business—buying securities and doing research, even leasing computer data bases and software—can be paid for through commissions that are borne by the client, not the manager.

Once the firm is covering its fixed costs, additional revenues flow fairly directly to the bottom line, usually increasing the compensation of the investment professionals. Compensation is very competitive for experienced professionals, and successful portfolio managers/analysts and marketing professionals are very highly compensated ($200,000–500,000 for nonowners).

There are too many variables to specify the amount of assets under management which are required for a firm to break even, but a rough rule of thumb is $100 million for an equity fund. An example may serve to illustrate the potential profitability. Assume an established balanced manager (stocks and bonds), with an average fee of 0.4 percent, managing $500 million ($2 million revenue), with three investment professionals, one marketing person, and four clerical support staff. Rent, utilities, travel and entertainment, and legal and insurance expenses could be as little as

$200,000 per year. (We assume marketing is concentrated at the firm's immediate geographic location, and ignore all the start-up costs of renovating space, acquiring furniture, developing marketing materials, and other first-year costs.)

That leaves $1.8 million for salaries, employee benefits, and bonuses for four professionals and four clerical employees. If the firm's style of management can absorb more assets under management without requiring additional staff, any additional revenues enhance profitability almost dollar for dollar. The only variable costs that increase are client servicing costs: report production and travel to meetings.

Using a fee of 1 percent, which is not uncommon for an aggressive equity manager, the same $500 million of assets under management would generate $5 million of revenues per year. There are many equity-only firms managing several hundred million dollars with two or three investment professionals; given the low fixed costs and the potential size of revenues, these firms can be very profitable.

SOFT DOLLARS

Paying for research and other information by directing commissions to the provider is called "soft-dollar" payment. In spite of negotiated commissions, there is apparently sufficient profit incentive for full-service, nondiscount brokers to offer these "extras."

Pension funds have begun cashing in on the soft-dollar facility by instructing their investment managers to direct transactions to specified dealers, usually discount brokers, to pay for performance measurement, trustees' fees, and other costs of administering the funds. Full-service brokers and some investment managers claim that discount brokers do not always provide the most effective execution and that a fund's performance could suffer if all trades were directed by the plan sponsor rather than by the manager. The Securities and Exchange Commission, however, questions the difference between negotiated and fully discounted commissions, and has recently issued new guidelines on soft-dollar payments by managers. In a May 1986 ruling, the SEC stipulated that payments for research through commission dollars must be limited to those that provide lawful and appropriate assistance to the money manager in the performance of investment decision-making responsibilities. Computer-driven models for decision making, security data bases, and optimization programs may fall within the "lawful and appropriate asistance" category. However, because the SEC is scrutinizing soft-dollar payments, several investment management firms now pay directly for all research and other services, and have established standard commissions for all security transactions for any broker wishing to execute their trades.

THE FUTURE

The future for investment management firms is very promising. Although many corporations have terminated their defined benefit pension plans (to recapture assets in excess of liabilities), the majority of plans continue to exist, and the terminated plans have often been replaced by defined contribution profit sharing plans. Unless new tax laws eliminate 401(k) plans, the growth in employee contributions should continue even as the number of employers offering these plans grows.

There is also considerable wealth accumulating in Individual Retirement Accounts (IRAs). Even though these have been diminished by recent tax changes, the individual is much more aware of investment management issues thanks to bank deregulation, the proliferation of easily accessible investment vehicles, and the very strong market returns of the last few years. As a result, mutual funds are enjoying large cash flows. Innovative marketing and distributing are bringing investment management to the general public through credit cards and bank accounts, further blurring the distinctions among banks, brokers, and other financial institutions. The future will most likely belong to a few full-service financial institutions that, directly or indirectly, own all other forms of financial services, including several investment management specialists.

PART 4   SPECIALIZED FINANCIAL INSTRUMENTS

The chapters in Part 4 deal with four particular kinds of financial instruments. Steve Kirmse discusses commercial paper in Chapter 15. Only in the past two decades has commercial paper become an important corporate financing instrument, and the placing of commercial paper has become the focus of fierce competition between commercial and investment bankers. This competition and the role of intermediaries are described in the chapter.

An even more recent development has been the enormous growth in mortgage-backed securities—what has come to be known as the securitization of the mortgage market. In Chapter 16, Laurie Goodman discusses the reasons for securitization, the instruments themselves, and the markets in which they are traded.

The high-yield debt market is another very recent development, and Ed Altman discusses it in Chapter 17. High-yield or "junk" bonds constitute a distinct class of security, and the market for these bonds has been created by a small number of investment banking firms—one in particular. The growth in leveraged buyouts, discussed in Chapter 12, owes much to the development of a high-yield debt market. Chapter 17 describes the origin of the market, discusses the participation of the principal firms, and reports on the performance of high-yield bonds and the spreads earned by underwriters.

In Chapter 18, Tanya Arnold discusses derivative financial instruments, in particular interest-rate swaps, and the whole process of innovation in financial instruments. Creating new instruments has become an important aspect of competition among investment bankers. And innovation has largely taken the form of new derivative instruments—options, futures contracts, swaps and the like—creating new claims and new obligations tailored to the precise needs of investors and issuing corporations.

15 Commercial Paper

STEPHEN C. KIRMSE

Commercial paper is one of the oldest short-term financing instruments in the United States. Negotiable commercial paper transactions took place in the Colonies as early as 1704. As the country's economy grew, so did the need for short-term financing. In the early 1800s, banks in certain geographical areas sometimes found it difficult to meet demands for loans during peak seasonal borrowing periods. The lack of a nationwide branch system made it difficult for a bank to attract deposits from outside its region and forced merchants to offset the lack of bank loans by selling commercial paper. By the mid-1800s a generally prosperous dealer network existed in New York, buying and selling commercial notes into and out of dealer inventories.

This activity declined in the 1920s, not to emerge in significant volume until the 1960s, when companies again ran into difficulty in meeting all their short-term borrowing requirements from banks. This time the difficulty arose from the Federal Reserve's efforts to regulate money supply by allowing market interest rates to rise. During "tight money" periods, market rates rose above the rates banks were permitted to pay on deposits, and the banks could not fund the demand for loans. In addition, investors became more sensitive to interest earned on short-term funds—until 1980 banks were not allowed to pay interest on deposits shorter than 30 days.

The banks' premier financial and industrial borrowers found they could obtain short-term funds by issuing notes to investors, either directly or via intermediaries, as long as they were willing to pay a market rate (at this time higher than bank CD rates). As lenders became accustomed to holding these notes, they continued to do so even when banks were able to pay competitive rates for 30-day and longer deposits. Furthermore, for the very best credits, investors were prepared to lend at rates close to (and sometimes below) bank deposit rates, which made commercial paper financing more attractive for the borrower than bank loans.

Outstandings grew dramatically, and commercial paper outstripped commercial and industrial loans of commercial banks. (see Table 15.1).

Table 15.1. Commercial Paper versus Commercial and Industrial Loans (in Billions)

	Year-End 1965	Year-End 1975	June 1987
Commercial Paper	$9.3	$48.5	$358.0
Commercial + Industrial Loans	$53.1	$113.7	$275.1

Source: Federal Reserve Bank of New York.

CHARACTERISTICS OF THE U.S. MARKET TODAY

A commercial paper note is a short-term, unsecured, bearer instrument that obligates the borrower (issuer) to pay a fixed amount to the holder at maturity. Notes follow a standard format, which shows little more than the name of the borrower, maturity date, and amount due at maturity. A borrowing backed by a guarantee, letter of credit, or surety bond will refer to the form of support on the note. The minimum denomination is $100,000, although some very large direct issuers will accommodate smaller investors. The typical note size is $1 million or more.

Issuers. Currently there are well over 1300 issuers of commercial paper who are rated by at least one of the two major agencies, Moody's Investors Service, Inc., and Standard & Poor's Corporation. In June 1987, 88 percent of the volume outstanding was issued by financial institutions (bank holding companies and finance companies). Foreign issuers are the fastest-growing segment of the U.S. market, accounting for a 21% share.

Investors. No more than 500 investors account for the largest part of all commercial paper purchases. They include fund managers (money market funds, pension funds, bank trust departments), insurance companies, and corporations. This results in an extremely efficient market because these investors purchase in large individual transactions and make their decisions early in the day. Generally speaking, investors look to commercial paper as a vehicle to invest temporary surplus cash balances. Although yield is important, they place greater emphasis on credit quality.

Intermediaries versus Direct Placement. Commercial paper can be placed in the market either directly by the borrower of through placement agents and dealers. Approximately 54 percent of the total amount of commercial paper outstanding in June 1987 had been sold directly by issuers to investors. Direct issuers tend to be large finance companies and bank holding companies with assets greater than $1 billion. General Motors Acceptance Corporation is the largest direct issuer with outstandings in excess of $35 billion, approximately 10% of the total market. Other direct issuers with sizable programs include Ford Motor Credit Corporation, General Electric Credit Corporation, Merrill Lynch & Company Inc., Sears Roebuck Acceptance Corporation, and Chrysler Financial Corporation. These issuers typically have a large ongoing need to access the commercial paper market, so they find it practical to employ their own commercial paper sales force. While direct issuers represent a substantial part of the total outstanding volume, they constitute less than 10 percent of the total number of commercial paper issuers. The vast majority of issuers use the services of a placement agent or dealer, who acts as an intermediary in locating investors, charging the borrower a fee for this service.

Ratings. The independent rating agencies analyze issuers in a uniform fashion. While some issuers are able to place small amounts in their local markets without being rated, an issuer contemplating a national program should be rated by at least two of the four independent rating agencies: Standard & Poor's Corporation, Moody's Investors Service, Inc., Duff and Phelps, Inc., and Fitch Investors Service, Inc. The highest commercial paper rating is "A1+" for Standard & Poor's and "P1" for Moody's. Borrowers receiving "A1+/P1" or "A1/P1" commercial paper ratings normally correspond to those with "AAA, "AA," or the upper part of the "A" bond rating.

The rating of a commercial paper issue will affect not only its interest rate but also its marketability. Usually there is a difference between the rates paid by an A1+/P1 issuer whose long-term debt is rated AAA, and the rates paid by an A1/P1 issuer whose long-term debt is rated A; similarly the rates charged an A2/P2 issuer are normally higher. Many investors will not purchase paper whose rating falls below A1/P1. The interest-rate spread varies depending on economic conditions. In periods of tight money or of greater concern about credit risk (such as after the Penn Central bankruptcy in 1970), the yield on A2/P2 paper has been as high as 200 basis points above top quality A1/P1 paper. Conversely, in periods of easy money and falling rates, investors attempt to maintain portfolio yields by switching into lower-grade paper, thereby reducing the effect of a higher rating. In such times, spreads have narrowed to as little as 15 to 25 basis points.

Backstop Lines. Most commercial paper issuers are obliged by the rating agencies to have the ability to borrow from a bank or group of banks to pay off commercial paper borrowings as they mature. Banks will provide "backstop" credit facilities for this purpose. Such facilities are designed to provide sufficient funds for the borrower to meet its commercial paper obligations regardless of day-to-day fluctuations in the commercial paper market that could make it difficult to place new paper. Rating agencies thereby judge not only the borrower's credit standing but also the status and origin of the supporting banks and the relative strength of their support.

The amount of bank credit coverage required depends on the overall credit rating of the issuer as well as its cash, marketable securities, and operating cash flow. For example, almost all A1/P1 commercial paper issuers whose long-term debt rating is A/A have a stated policy of 100 percent line coverage, while only 15 percent of A1+/P1 issuers with AAA/Aaa ratings maintain 100 percent line coverage. The type of credit facility arranged to support a commercial paper issue will vary depending on the issuer's general creditworthiness. Most issuers establish lines of credit which are subject to review from time to time, while others arrange committed credit facilities.

MECHANICS

Physical Delivery Market. Investors normally remit funds only upon receipt of a note. This means that at each sale a note must be drawn up and delivered to the investor against payment. Likewise, at maturity notes must be presented by the investor for payment. This function usually is provided by a third-party commercial bank, although some very large issuers draw up, deliver, and pay the notes themselves. Over the years various efforts have been made to promote a paperless "book-entry" delivery system. For the most part, investors have resisted this, although a few large direct issuers currently issue some of their paper on a book-entry basis.

Bearer Instrument. Commercial paper notes generally are not issued in the name of the purchaser. They are bearer promissory notes that are quoted primarily on a *discount basis*, although most issuers are willing to accommodate investors who prefer interest-bearing notes. Settlement is normally *same-day value*, although occasionally paper will be issued for "regular" (one-day) settlement.

SEC Registration. Commercial paper is exempt from Securities and Exchange Commission registration and the extensive financial disclosure requirements associated with it. There are three principal exemptions that may be available for commercial paper. Section 3(a) (3) of the Securities Act of 1933 exempts securities issued to finance current transactions; Section 3(a) (2) exempts securities backed by domestic bank letters of credit, including U.S. branches of foreign banks; and Section 4(2) exempts securities issued in a private placement. Depending on the applicable exemption, there may be restrictions on the maximum maturity or ability to resell.

Placement. Actual placement of paper with investors normally occurs between 9:00 and 11:30 A.M. New York time. Commercial paper rates are heavily influenced by other money market investment rates such as bankers' acceptances, CDs, LIBOR, and the Federal Funds rate.

Direct issuers use their own sales force to approach investors directly, and many make their rates available to investors through Reuters and Telerate.

Placement agents and dealers will advise their borrowing clients of market developments, agree on target amounts, rates, and maturity, and approach investors through their sales forces. Although a few intermediaries maintain a specialist sales staff that sells only commercial paper, most contact investors about a variety of money market instruments. Concentrating on commercial paper permits a salesperson to focus his or her efforts on a particular issuer or instrument, but this may not be the most efficient way of covering investors, because most investors purchase a variety of money market instruments.

Maturity. The average maturity is normally short, 30 days and less, although 60- and 90-day maturities are readily available. While paper is issued out to 180 days, it is very thin at that maturity and subject to wide fluctuation in rate.

Investment Size. Because of the institutional nature of the investor base, the typical investment is in excess of $1 million. In fact, many large funds' managers will not invest less than $5 million per transaction. The minimum note denomination is normally $100,000, although the large direct issuers sometimes are prepared to issue smaller amounts to attract individual investors.

ATTRACTION TO ISSUERS

Cost. Commercial paper offers the well-rated issuer access to some of the least expensive short-term funding available in the domestic market.

Flexibility. The largest investor demand is in the 30-day-and-under maturity range. Because of this the issuer normally is able to issue odd amounts (i.e., not necessarily in multiples of $1 million) and maturities.

Broader Access to Capital Markets. Participating in the commercial paper market introduces an issuer to major institutional investors who are also important purchasers of other instruments such as term debentures, privately placed debt, and equity.

ATTRACTION TO INVESTORS

To the investor, commercial paper provides direct access to highly rated borrowers and an opportunity to choose the exact amount and maturity. In addition, the large size of this market provides assurance that paper can be resold prior to maturity. Mechanically it is very simple to liquidate a commercial paper note before maturity because it is a bearer instrument. An investor wishing to sell a note normally contacts the intermediary from whom the paper was originally purchased and may also contact other investors and intermediaries for a quote. In the case of direct-issuer paper, the investor may contact the issuer to determine if it will prepay the paper (at a discount reflecting current rates). A direct issuer's willingness to prepay depends on its ability to issue new notes to fund the prepayment as well as its relationship with the investor.

Generally speaking, there is very little secondary market activity, because most investors hold paper to maturity. It is estimated that well over 90 percent of all paper sold is held to maturity. This figure is not surprising given the short-term nature of commercial paper. A seller of secondary commercial paper can expect an "on-the-market" bid, particularly if the issuer has a large volume of paper outstanding, because more investors are likely to have approval to purchase paper of that issuer when there is a large supply in the market. For paper that is marketable, the spread quoted by a dealer is likely to be 5 to 10 basis points.

INTERMEDIARIES—PLACEMENT AND DEALERS

A small number of intermediaries handle the lion's share of paper placed through intermediaries. Goldman Sachs Money Markets Inc. and Merrill Lynch Money Market Inc. are the largest, with each accounting for approximately 30 percent of the total volume of paper distributed through intermediaries. Lehman Commercial Paper/Shearson Lehman Brothers, Salomon Brothers, and First Boston Corporation are the next largest with approximate market shares of 10 percent each. PaineWebber, a relatively recent entrant, has been a growing participant. Of the commercial bank placement agents, Bankers Trust Company is the largest, followed by Morgan Guaranty. There are also a number of firms that have only a few clients.

ATTRACTION FOR INTERMEDIARIES

Profits. The average commission charged by intermediaries is one-tenth of 1 percent, computed on a per annum basis (e.g., one-twelfth of one-tenth of 1 percent for placing 30-day paper). The commission level is influenced by a number of factors, including volume of paper placed, relationship with the issuer, and competition. For investment banks, which are allowed to purchase customer paper for their own accounts, there is the further opportunity to take an interest-rate outlook and position paper (i.e., buy it and hold it for a price rise). In most cases, the intermediaries' cost of funding is higher than the return on the underlying commercial paper inventory, particularly for highly rated paper. Because this creates a negative cost of carry, most investment banks try to limit the amount of paper purchased for their own accounts.

Off-Balance-Sheet Treatment. Except for positioning, this business is not included on the balance sheet of the intermediary. As investors and regulators place more attention on capital adequacy and return on assets, this accounting treatment is quite beneficial.

Client Relationship. Maintaining a daily dialogue with borrowers enhances the probability that the intermediary will learn about other business opportunities, such as when the borrower is considering term funding or swapping the dollar proceeds of commercial paper into other currencies. Having the ability to bring borrowers to the commercial paper market can also enhance the credibility of an intermediary structuring a complex financing package. For example, a company making an acquisition may require a large amount of financing within a short time; funds may be obtained best by initially tapping a variety of short-term sources and later obtaining longer-term funding. One of the short-term sources is likely to be the commercial paper market. An intermediary who can bring a client to this market may be in a good position to assist on the longer-term needs.

Organizational Structure. The intermediaries tend to organize themselves around three main areas: origination, pricing/trading, and distribution.

Origination. The origination group is responsible for generating appointments from issuers and in most cases is staffed by corporate finance experts. They identify potential borrowers, present the intermediary's capabilities to the client, and, when new appointments are received, assist in making sure all the necessary documentation is in place prior to the launch of the program. While in some organizations there may be a group of corporate finance officers who specialize only in commercial paper, others cover a variety of corporate finance products. No matter what the organizational structure, the originators must be knowledgeable about a range of products, because commercial paper is just one of many financing options available for the borrower. Also, it is often only one element of a total structure that includes other Treasury management tools, such as:

1. *Interest-Rate Swaps.* Commercial paper borrowing coupled with an interest-rate swap can create attractive fixed-rate financing. This is accomplished by a commercial paper issuer and a counterparty entering into an agreement whereby the issuer receives from the counterparty, at regular intervals, floating-interest-rate payments computed with reference to an agreed-upon benchmark, frequently six-month LIBOR. In return the issuer makes fixed-rate interest payments to the counterparty, also at regular intervals. As interest-rate swap does not provide principal and is merely an exchange of interest payments. By funding itself in the commercial paper market, the counterparty may be able to achieve a floating rate below six-month LIBOR, thereby providing the issuer with a lower effective fixed-rate cost than the actual fixed rate it pays to the countryparty. In many cases, the effective fixed rate paid will be below other fixed-rate alternatives available to the commercial paper issuer.

2. *Financial Futures.* The emergence of the futures market, particularly Eurodeposit futures, has provided the opportunity for commercial paper issuers to hedge their future commercial paper borrowing costs.

3. *Foreign Currency Financing.* Combining commercial paper issuance with foreign exchange hedging or currency swaps will often lead to foreign currency borrowing costs that are lower than local borrowing rates. Fully hedged commercial paper often will be less expensive than the Euromarket for that currency given the relatively low cost base of domestic commercial paper. In addition, it may be less expensive than the local market borrowing cost of that currency unless the local market is insulated by exchange regulations or borrowing costs are controlled artificially.

Strong marketing skills and the ability to analyze a borrower's total needs are key requirements of the originators.

Distribution. The actual placement of paper normally is handled by salespeople who maintain contact with investors. Each salesperson normally has a group of accounts consisting of the large money market investors, and is responsible for knowing the customers' investment criteria and liquidity position. Each morning the salesperson contacts customers by telephone to offer potential investments that in most cases include commercial paper and other money market instruments such as bankers' acceptances and certificates of deposit. At some intermediaries, the same salesperson may handle both short-and long-term investments such as government bonds.

The salesperson knows what instruments the intermediary has to offer via a computer linkup that provides constantly updated information. While traders make the final determination on the terms of each offering, input from the sales force about customer market perception and preferences is critical to a successful placement operation.

Most of a salesperson's day is spent in front of a computer terminal screen and on the telephone. The salesperson must be able to work with numbers quickly to calculate and explain yield-to-maturity and other details to customers, who are looking for both sharp quotes and market commentary. Transactions concluded are not always straightforward. They may involve complicated strategies, such as swapping out of (selling) one instrument into another for a higher yield, extending maturities out the yield curve, or packaging a variety of money market instruments to create the desired portfolio purchase for the customer. At all times, the salesperson must balance the strategies of the trading desk against those of the customer.

Excellent communication skills are critical requirements for a successful salesperson. Many institutions view prior experience on the sales side as a prerequisite to joining the trading/pricing side.

Trading/Pricing. Traders determine the rates to be offered to investors and, in the case of investment banks, the terms under which the intermediary will purchase paper for its own account. The borrower relies on the trader for advice on the amount, timing, rate, and maturity of each issuance. The trader must keep in constant touch with all other sectors of the market that could affect commercial papers, such as Federal Funds, futures, interbank, and bankers' acceptances. The rate set by the trader affects not only the intermediary's ability to place the paper in the market but also the bottom line. In most cases the rate includes commission as well.

Although the trader typically is part of a larger money market trading group, he or she normally specializes only in commercial paper. Because the bulk of all paper is placed within a two- to three-hour period each day, the pressure can be considerable—five basis points on a $10 million 30-day piece of paper can make the difference between profit and loss for the intermediary and perhaps whether the intermediary keeps its appointments as an issuer's agent.

COMMERCIAL BANKS AS INTERMEDIARIES

In recent years a number of commercial banks have become active intermediaries. This followed a logical progression as many of the banks' large creditworthy borrowers moved from short-term bank loans to commercial paper borrowings. The larger banks already had been placing a significant volume of other money market instruments, such as domestic certificates of deposit, bankers' acceptances, and Euro certificates of deposit with investors, so commercial paper was a natural addition. Also, many of the banks already had been providing related services for commercial paper borrowers, such as issuing and paying.

Investment banks have challenged commercial bank entry into this market through a court suit against the Federal Reserve for permitting Bankers Trust Company (the first commercial bank to provide placement services to national issuers) to enter the market. The courts have determined that commercial paper is a security for purposes of the Glass-Steagall act, which means that commercial banks are unable to underwrite or position their clients' commercial paper. Because of this, commercial banks generally refer to themselves as "placement agents" rather then "dealers." In June 1987, the Supreme Court effectively affirmed banks' rights to act as agents in the placement of commercial paper.

Commercial banks have established a position in the commercial paper market within a relatively short period of time. Their entrance coincided with significant growth in commercial paper outstandings. A large number of new borrowers have begun to tap this market, and many of the long-standing issuers have moved from having one intermediary to having several, thereby enhancing a competitive environment for the placement of their paper. Most importantly, the commercial banks have demonstrated broad placement capabilities.

While issuers naturally have varying viewpoints on the desirability of underwriting or positioning, many recognize that positioning paper often represents added cost for the dealer, because in most cases the dealer will fund itself at a higher rate than it receives from the underlying paper. This is likely to be reflected in the commission charged. Converseley, a potential disadvantage arising from the inability of commercial banks to underwrite paper is that a bank may not always be able to provide firm quotes for all maturities because the rates quoted can reflect only investor interest, not a bank's own ability or willingness to position paper. The sophisticated and broad nature of the commercial paper market means that the practical differences to the borrower between underwriting and not underwriting are small. In fact, knowing that their paper is always placed with end-investors, and never owned by an intermediary is comforting to some issuers who are concerned with tracking how their names are perceived by the end-investors. Commercial banks do act as intermediaries in the secondary market, although they may not act as principal. They can and do find buyers for sellers and sellers for buyers.

EURO COMMERCIAL PAPER

Euro commercial paper is evolving as a competitive and reliable source of funding. By June 1987, approximately 350 Euro commercial paper programs had been announced, and outstandings were estimated to be $27 billion.

Euro commercial paper first appeared in the late 1960s when U.S. corporations issued notes directly in the Euromarket to circumvent U.S. capital export controls. The repeal of the interest equalization tax in 1972 eliminated the funding advantage, and Euro commercial paper disappeared soon thereafter. It reemerged in late 1984 as an outgrowth of the Euronote market. Euronote facilities, also called "revolving underwriting facilities" (RUFs), "note issuance facilities" (NIFs), and "multioption financing facilities" (MOFFs), are medium-term standby commitments offering a variety of borrowing options, including the ability to issue short-term notes (Euronotes) to a group of banks forming a tender panel. The one common feature of all these facilities is the commitment by a group of underwriting banks to purchase notes at a preagreed maximum price if all other options fail to attract competitive bids. This underwriting commitment was a critical inducement for early borrowers to tap the Euronote market.

As the investor base expanded, the Euronote option became an important source of funding. In June 1987, there were approximately 400 facilities in place totaling over $60 billion, with over $17 billion actually outstanding.

As market participants became more confident about Euronote placements, they sought to simplify their issuing strategy by eliminating dedicated backstops and improving placement techniques. There was a growing awareness of the shortcoming of the tender panel structure. First, this mechanism may prevent the development of a steady base of investors because each tender panel member is not guaranteed access to paper. Continuity of supply is critical to Euroinvestors once the issuer's name is on their approved investment lists. Disruption in supply considerable limits the investors' interest in a particular issuer. Second, the tender panel procedure can lead to defensive bids from members who consistently fail to obtain paper. Members may underbid other tender panel participants in order to obtain paper, which, while achieving attractive rates for the issuer in the short run, may disrupt the pricing strategy designed for the long-term success of the program. Finally, distribution through tender panels, perhaps involving 20 to 50 banks, can be cumbersome administratively, often requiring five to seven days from requests for bids to availability of funds.

Distribution through dealers was introduced in 1984, in a pattern based in part on the U.S. commercial paper market. This method enables a dealer to commit specialist staff to selling the issuer's name to investors, keeping them informed of its issuing behavior. The dealer is effective in achieving controlled and consistent placement of notes at low yield levels to investors. Because the dealer normally handles a series of issues from different programs, a diverse investor base can be developed for a wide range of credits, maturities, and yields.

Initially, the investor market for Euro commercial paper was dominated by commercial banks and a few central banks. Nonbank investors, however, are growing and now comprise a significant share of the investor market. Commercial banks purchase Euro commercial paper as a form of short-term lending in negotiable form. Euro commercial paper also provides an attractive alternative to sovereign and bank floating-rate notes and interbank lending, and complements dwindling loan demand from corporate clients. Central banks and official institutions find Euronotes of sovereign issuers to be an attractive alternative to Treasury bills and interbank deposits for reserve investment purposes. The nonbank investor group includes corporations, investment managers, and offshore insurance companies.

Euro commercial paper is similar to U.S. commercial paper in that it is placed through dealers. It differs from the U.S. market in three respects: (1) maturities tend to be longer (i.e., 60- 90- and 180-day maturities are standard), (2) rates are generally based off LIBOR/LIBID, and (3) neither ratings nor backstop facilities are technically required. In regard to the last point, a number of issuers have decided to obtain ratings and backstop facilities as it is generally felt ratings will help the notes' marketability with nonbank investors.

Issuers have been attracted by the lower cost and convenience provided through: (1) simple and inexpensive documentation, (2) elimination of expensive and time-inefficient bank syndicates and tender panels, and (3) the fact that ratings are not required in order to issue Euro commercial paper. Also enhancing issuers' interest has been the narrowing spread between U.S. commercial paper rates and LIBOR. Historically LIBOR has been as much as 100 basis points higher than commercial paper rates, but since 1985 the spread has narrowed to 25 basis points, making borrowings based on LIBOR/LIBID more competitive with U.S. commercial paper rates.

Although efficient clearing and settlement procedures have now been developed which allow for the convenience of same-day settlement, Euro commercial paper is most often sold for two-day settlement (i.e., trade Monday for settlement Wednesday). Investors have expressed little interest in the same-day option found in the U.S. market, because it does not allow them to consider other Euro investment alternatives simultaneously; most other Euroinstruments settle with two-day value.

A Euro commercial paper program provides issuers with U.S. commercial paper programs the opportunity to "globalize" paper issuance. Given the time differences between New York and London, an issuer can begin each day issuing in London and then continue issuing in New York. Such a global program provides issuers with arbitrage opportunities and access to a number of different investor groups. As a general rule, borrowing costs in the U.S. market still favor the highly rated U.S. borrowers. The Euro commercial paper market has been of particular interest to U.S. borrowers who either do not access the U.S. market or who are concerned about the quantity of their paper outstanding in the United States. It also is of interest to highly rated non-U.S. issuers, who often can achieve lower rates in the Euromarket because their name recognition may be stronger in Europe, and there is normally a "foreign premium" applied to non-U.S. borrowers in the U.S. market. A number of well-known U.S. names have established Euro commercial paper programs, including General Motors Acceptance Corporation, General Electric Company, IBM Credit Corporation, New York Times, Prudential Funding Corporation, and Time, Inc.

MASTER NOTES

Issuers with large commercial paper programs often utilize master note agreements to obtain a portion of their funding needs. Instead of issuing new notes and negotiating a new discount rate at each maturity, large investors and issuers will come to an agreement to keep a minimum amount fully invested/issued with rates to be determined by a preagreed formula. Master note agreements are arranged primarily with commercial bank trust and investment departments and pension funds. Each agreement normally has a six-month or one-year maturity with borrowings prepayable/callable on demand. Although either party can terminate on demand, in practice some notice is given by each party as a matter of good faith. Master notes are intended as a supplement to commercial paper borrowings and most master note lenders require that the borrower also have outstanding commercial paper borrowings.

Master notes are priced on the basis of a preagreed formula negotiated between the investor and issuer. Some of the frequently used formulas are: (1) 98–103 percent of the Federal Reserve 30-day composite rate for prime industrial commercial paper issuers; and, (2) the higher of the General Motors Acceptance Corporation posted 30- or 180-day rate.

The advantages of a master note program are: for the issuer—(1) certainty of funding; (2) competitive financing cost; (3) administrative ease; and, (4) investor diversification; for the lender—the elimination of the need to roll over individual notes at maturity.

In most cases, master notes are arranged by a third party for an up-front fee. Not surprisingly the most active arrangers of master notes are the large commercial paper dealers and placement agents.

16 Investment Bankers in the Mortgage Markets

LAURIE S. GOODMAN

In the past few years there has been a virtual explosion of securitized mortgage instruments. These mortgage investments range from whole loan sales to collateralized mortgage obligations. They include participation certificates, pass-through securities, mortgage-backed bonds, and mortgage pay-through bonds. Investment bankers serve as conduits in the securitization process. In whole loans or participations, investment banks purchase the loans or loan interest, then resell as is or in securitized form; in mortgage pass-throughs, the investment bankers pool the mortgages and sell the pass-through certificates. Investment bankers also underwrite and distribute mortgage-backed bonds, mortgage pay-through bonds, and CMOs. The importance of this conduit role should not be underestimated—securitization is the basic form in which mortgages can move from originators to ultimate investors.

While investment bankers are important to the mortgage securitization process, mortgages are very important to investment bankers, and becoming more so. For the 1983–1985 period mortgage trading, underwriting, and sales comprised approximately 20 to 30 percent of the profits in the industry. For several individual firms such as Salomon Brothers and First Boston Corporation, the percentage has been substantially higher. As the range of mortgage instruments has grown and mortgages have become an increasingly important financing tool, investment banks who had shown little interest in structured mortgage transactions in the past have begun to build and expand departments for these transactions. There is a realization that this is one area that cannot be neglected.

WHY SECURITIZATION? THE ORIGINATORS' VIEWPOINT

There are three major residential mortgage originators: thrifts (savings and loan associations and mutual savings banks) accounted for a 55 percent share of the market in 1984, followed by mortgage bankers with 21 percent, and commercial banks with 19 percent. Other smaller mortgage originators include life insurance companies and governmental entities. The amount of new mortgage originations and the market share by originator is shown in Table 16.1.

Prior to the early 1970s savings and loan associations and commercial banks held their mortgages in portfolio. Mortgage bankers sold whole loans and loan participations to institutional investors such as life insurance companies.

The first mortgage securitization program was that initiated by the Guaranteed National Mortgage Association (GNMA) in 1970. This program began slowly, then took off by the mid-1970s. It allowed commercial banks and thrifts to remove mortgages from their balance sheets.

As the range of instruments has expanded, so have the reasons for securitization. Currently, securitization of mortgage instruments may occur for any of three reasons:

1. The desire to remove the mortgages from the balance sheet.
2. The wish to use the mortgages as collateral for borrowings.
3. The ability to arbitrage.

The selling of assets has received increased attention in recent years since many banks and thrifts have been under pressure to raise their capital/asset ratios and reduce their interest-rate sensitivity. The retention of the mortgage origination and servicing roles provides fee income at low risk. It should be noted that is generally new mortgages that are sold off; while accounting guidelines provided by the Federal Home Loan Bank Board have made it somewhat easier to sell off existing mortgages at a discount by permitting the loss to be written off over the life of these instruments, the managements of many financial institutions are reluctant to do so.

The use of mortgages as collateral for borrowing is also very important. Thrifts have traditionally borrowed short and lent long. As long the yield curve was stable and short-term rates were lower than long-term rates, this was a profitable strategy. In the current environment, short-term rates have not been stable, and thrifts do not have access to long-term unsecured borrowing. By collateralizing the borrowing, the issuer is able to achieve an AA or AAA rating and fund long-term at 30–60 basis points above long-term Treasury rates. Interestingly enough, this is the same phenomenon that lies behind the rapid growth of the interest-rate swap market since its inception in 1981.

The third reason for securitization is the arbitrage motive. There have been situations in which a transaction can be structured as a CMO and a substantial gain can be achieved. That is, there have been occasions when the cash flows from a group of mortgages are worth more carved up in a different form than as whole loans. This has been the motivation for a number of the CMO transactions issued by investment bankers. These arbitrage opportunities appear much less frequently as the CMO market has continued to develop.

Table 16.1. New Mortgage Origination: Breakdown by Originator (in $Billions; Market Share in Parentheses)

	1970		1975		1980		1981		1982		1983		1984	
Banks	$28.1	(63.4)	$65.8	(76.3)	$98.3	(68.3)	$72.1	(65.4)	$69.4	(63.1)	$151.1	(67.6)	$167.6	(73.4)
Commercial banks	8.1	(18.3)	15.2	(17.6)	28.1	(19.5)	23.2	(21.1)	26.8	(24.4)	48.4	(21.6)	43.5	(19.1)
Thrifts	20.0	(45.1)	50.6	(58.7)	70.2	(48.8)	8.9	(44.4)	42.5	(38.7)	102.8	(46.0)	124.1	(54.3)
Life insurance	2.6	(5.9)	1.4	(1.6)	3.2	(2.2)	1.2	(1.1)	1.0	(0.9)	2.3	(1.0)	2.3	(1.0)
Pension funds	0.1	(0.2)	0.1	(0.1)	0.1	(0.1)	0.2	(0.2)	0.9	(0.8)	0.3	(0.1)	0.3	(0.1)
Government entities (Federal credit agencies, including GNMA)	2.4	(5.4)	3.2	(3.7)	7.3	(5.1)	7.7	(7.0)	6.9	(6.3)	6.0	(2.7)	5.6	(2.5)
State and local governments	0.7	(1.6)	1.3	(1.5)	4.1	(2.8)	2.9	(2.6)	2.2	(2.0)	1.7	(0.8)	1.8	(0.8)
Intermediaries (Mortgage banks)	10.3	(23.3)	14.2	(16.5)	30.8	(21.4)	26.0	(23.6)	29.0	(26.4)	60.3	(27.0)	48.0	(21.0)
Other	0.1	(0.2)	0.2	(0.2)	0.2	(0.1)	0.1	(0.1)	0.6	(0.6)	1.7	(0.7)	2.6	(1.2)
Total	$44.3	(100.0)	$86.2	(100.0)	$144.00	(100.0)	$110.2	(100.0)	$109.9	(100.0)	$223.5	(100.0)	$228.4	(100.0)

Source: U.S. Department of Housing and Urban Development, Survey of Mortgage Lending Activity.

WHY SECURITIZATION? THE INVESTOR'S VIEWPOINT

For an investor, mortgages provide a fairly safe investment at yields considerably higher than Treasury securities. Moreover, securitization allows issuers to alter some of the less desirable features of conventional mortgages.

For most investors, conventional mortgages have three major problems vis-à-vis alternative investments: monthly cash flows, the prepayment option that the lender has granted the buyer, and the credit risk. Each of these will be discussed in turn.

Monthly Cash Flows

Mortgage cash flows are paid monthly and are level over the life of the instrument. That is, the monthly payment is set such that at the end of 30 years (360 payments) the principal would have been repaid in its entirety and the lender would have received the stated interest rate on unpaid balances at all times.

Cash flows from mortgage investments have posed three problems for investors used to dealing in bonds. First, the cash flows are received monthly and must be reinvested monthly. This means that smaller cash flows are received more frequently, and reinvestment requires more planning. Moreover, since bonds are quoted on a semiannual basis and mortgages are quoted on a monthly basis, a yield transformation is necessary to compare the two: thus a 13.0 percent mortgage yield would translate into a 13.36 percent bond equivalent yield. However, when using yield-to-maturity calculations, it has been long recognized that the investor is assumed to reinvest the interest at the yield to maturity. This is questionable for bonds, and even less likely for mortgages. Lastly, the payments contain both principal and interest. These must be accounted for accordingly. For tax purposes, gains and losses on principal, as it is repaid, are treated as ordinary income, rather than as capital gains and losses.

Prepayment Options

In residential mortgages, the borrower has a call option. That is, the borrower can prepay the mortgage at any time. Moreover, if rates go down, the borrower can refinance.

Mortgage call options do not, however, behave like other options. When rates go down, not all borrowers will refinance. For example, there are still 17 percent mortgage pools outstanding. Thus some mortgage options will not be exercised when rationally they should be. When current rates on new mortgages are 13½ percent, some people with 8 percent mortgages will prepay either because they are moving or they do not like having a mortgage. Consequently, other mortgages options that are "out-of-the-money" will, in fact, be exercised.

The options create uncertainty about when the cash flows are to be received; this uncertainty makes it difficult to price mortgage instruments. On a group of 16 percent mortgage pools with 27 years left, assuming a mortgage yield of 12.20

percent, one would be willing to pay 117^{27}/$_{32}$ if prepayments were 8 percent per annum, 112^{21}/$_{32}$ if prepayments were 16 percent per annum, and 109^{18}/$_{32}$ if prepayments were 24 percent per annum.

Credit Risk

While residential mortgages historically have not been very risky, credit risk on mortgage instruments is difficult to evaluate. The credit risk is the risk that an individual mortgage holder will default and the underlying mortgage will not be worth as much as the mortgage.

Securitization allows for two types of credit enhancement—diversification and guarantees. When one owns a single mortgage, credit information is more important than if one owns $\frac{1}{1000}$ of 1000 different mortgages. Moreover, by packaging mortgages, it is relatively inexpensive to obtain guarantees for the package. It would be much more difficult and costly to insure each mortgage separately. When insuring a package, the insurer will not seek financial information on individual loans and appraisals of housing values—instead, he or she will examine the number and size of mortgages in the package, the demographic characteristics, and the loan-to-value ratios.

Table 16.2. Sources of Credit for Mortgage Originations: Net Funds Provided by Investors (in $Billions)

	Thrifts	Commercial Banks	Pension Funds	Life Insurance Companies	Other[a]	Total
Part A: Net Acquisition of Mortgage Loans						
1982	10.0	21.1	1.3	1.0	3.3	16.8
1983	87.5	37.1	1.2	1.9	2.8	130.5
1984	116.5	36.5	.6	1.7	3.4	158.7
Part B: Net Acquisition of Mortgage-Related Securities						
1982	36.1	10.0	11.0	3.4	15.6	76.1
1983	44.1	8.8	15.0	11.3	35.4	114.6
1984	27.6	9.4	9.9	6.1	40.9	93.9
Part C: Total Sources of New Housing Credit[b]						
1982	46.1	31.2	12.3	4.4	19.0	112.9
1983	131.6	45.8	16.3	13.2	38.2	245.1
1984	144.1	45.9	10.5	7.8	44.3	252.6

[a] Other includes mortgage banks, households, corporations, and other insurance companies.
[b] Technically, total sources of new housing credit should equal total originations in Table 16.1. It does not because of statistical problems in the HUD data. (For a detailed description of the problem, see the Appendix to *Secondary Mortgage Markets*, February 1984, published by the Federal Home Loan Mortgage Association.)
Source: Secondary Mortgage Markets, Federal Home Loan Mortgage Association, Summer 1985.

Most forms of securitization alter one or more of the less desirable features of mortgage cash flows: pass-through securities generally provide for credit enhancement; mortgage-backed bonds and pay-through bonds provide for both credit enhancement and semiannual payments; and CMOs provide for credit enhancement and semiannual payments, and they eliminate some of the risk from the prepayment option. Each of these instruments, as well as whole loans and loan participations, will be discussed in the next section.

Table 16.2 shows the market participants who ultimately invest in mortgages and mortgage securities. It is interesting to observe that thrift institutions and commercial banks often sell whole loans that they originated and simultaneously purchase mortgage-related securities. For example, in 1983 thrifts originated $102.8 billion in mortgages (Table 16.1); their net acquisitions of mortgages (originations plus purchases less sales) were $87.5 billion as shown in Table 16.2. However, their net acquisition of mortgage securities (purchase less sales) was $44.1 billion. Thus they supplied $131.6 billion in new housing credit—that is, they supplied more funds for mortgages than the mortgages they originated. The four largest purchasers of mortgage-related securities are thrifts, commercial banks, pension funds, and life insurance companies. This illustrates that originators as well as other money managers like the benefits provided by securitization.

THE INSTRUMENTS

Loan Participations or Whole-Loan Sales

The difference between loan participations and whole-loan sales is one of form rather than substance. In the event of a whole-loan sale, the servicing of the loans can be retained by the originators or transferred to the investors at the time of the sale. If the servicing is passed to the investors there is considerable paperwork involved because the loan files must actually change hands. If the servicing is retained by the originators, the whole-loan sale is sometimes documented as a loan participation.

In a loan participation, the holder of a mortgage portfolio sells a pro rata interest in a pool of loans. This pro rata amount is usually 90 to 100 percent. The seller continues to service the loans and passes through the required payment to the purchasers (this is treated as a sale of assets for the issuer).

Whole-loan or mortgage participations can be sold by the originator directly or through a conduit. The conduits are predominantly private mortgage intermediaries and investment bankers. The conduit may sell the loans as is, or repackage them in other forms (pass-throughs, CMOs, etc.). There are, however, some discovery costs for the conduit and/or the ultimate investors. Each loan participation or whole-loan sale is different since it involves mortgages of different amounts with different geographic and demographic characteristics. The characteristics of the mortgage are of interest, as they indicate credit quality and anticipated prepayment. Moreover, if the buyer of a package of whole loans is planning to pool the loans for FNMA or Freddie Mac, the amount of nonconforming loans is critical. Nonconforming loans are those with less than a stated percentage down payment, those with inadequate documentation, jumbo loans, and so forth.

These loan participations or whole-loan sales preserve the characteristics of the underlying mortgages—the level cash flows, monthly payment, call options, and credit verification problems. There are two additional problems with loan participations or whole-loan sales. First, since the participation is treated as a sale, issuers with underwater portfolios must record a loss. Secondly, if the seller–servicer is a thrift or a bank, there is some uncertainty about the status of the loans in the event of bankruptcy of the financial institution. (That is, rather than a sale of assets the transaction could be viewed as if the seller–servicer has merely used the mortgage as collateral in order to secure a loan from the purchaser.)

Pass-through Securities

Pass-through securities are very much like loan participations in that they keep the cash flow characteristics of the underlying mortgages intact. The major difference between pass-throughs and participations is the legal form and the guarantees.

The most widely known pass-throughs are those issued by the three governmental agencies: GNMA, FNMA, and Freddie Mac. GNMA securities are obligations backed by the full faith and credit of the U.S. government. Both principal and interest payments are guaranteed as to amount and timeliness by GNMA. FNMA and Freddie Mac pass-throughs are guaranteed by the two quasi-governmental agencies. FNMA obligations are guaranteed as to timely payment of principal and interest. Freddie Mac pools are guaranteed as to timely payment of interest and full collection of principal. GNMA securities are backed by FHA and VA mortgages whereas FNMAs and Freddie Macs are backed by conventional one- to-four-family residential mortgages.

Why does it matter whether mortgages are conventional or FHA/VA? FHA/VA mortgages are assumable whereas conventional mortgages generally have due-on-sale clauses. Thus we would expect prepayments on discount pools to be higher for FNMAs and Freddie Macs than for GNMAs. Investors are willing to pay more for the faster prepayments on discount mortgages.

In addition to 30-year conventional mortgages, pass-throughs can be found on 15-year fixed-rate mortgages (sometimes referred to as "midgets"), graduated payment mortgages, growing equity mortgages, mobile home mortgages and, most recently, adjustable-rate mortgages (ARMs). Fifteen-year pass-through certificates have become very popular with homeowners and investors, and tend to trade in very liquid markets.

There are a number of private entities which have issued pass-through certificates: Citicorp, Bank of America, Merrill Lynch, Sears, and Norwest, to name a few. These private entities provide credit enhancement of the securities through insurance policies, guarantees, or letters of credit. A rating for the issues is usually sought after credit enhancement is provided for. Many of these private entities have issued pass-throughs of nontraditional mortgages, including jumbo mortgages, commercial property mortgages, and adjustable-rate mortgages. Some have been privately placed, others publicly offered; in the event of public offerings, the dealer will maintain secondary markets in the securities. As can be seen from Table 16.3, the amount of publicly issued pass-throughs by private entities is very small compared with those of the agencies. Privately placed pass-throughs of private entities are believed to beabout one and one-half times as large as the publicly issued pass-throughs of these entities. Even including these private placements, the private share of the market is very small—approximately 5 percent or so. GNMA is still the largest program, accounting for 43 percent of the total pass-throughs in 1984. Freddie Mac and FNMA accounted for 29 and 22 percent, respectively.

Thrifts may count pass-throughs as interest in underlying mortgages. If savings and loans have more than 82 percent of their portfolio invested in mortgages, they may place up to 40 percent of their taxable income in a special bad debt reserve fund. (The amount is 72 percent of their portfolio for mutual savings banks.) This has favorable tax consequences, as the money is treated as a deduction from total income. If the amount of mortgages drops below the percentage required, the deduction is phased out; at 60 percent of assets it is eliminated entirely. If the institution holds less than 60 percent of its assets in mortgages, additions to the bad debt reserve fund must be based solely on prior experience.

The pass-through structure preserves the basic characteristics of whole-loan and loan participations—the monthly payments and lack of call protection. It does, however, allow for credit enhancement. Morover, it eliminates the legal risk inherent in a participation structure as the loans are legally transferred to the trustees.

For accounting purposes, pass-throughs are treated as a sale by the issuer. This discourages thrifts with underwater debt portfolios from using these, as it requires recording an accounting loss.

Table 16.3. Origination of Pass-through Securities (in $Billions)

Date	Freddie Mac	Fannie Mae	Ginnie Mae	Other Federal Credit Agencies	Private Firms[a]	Total
1970	–	–	.5	NA	–	.5
1975	1.0	–	7.4	NA	–	8.4
1980	4.9	–	20.6	NA	.3	25.8
1981	3.5	.7	14.3	NA	.4	18.9
1982	24.2	14.0	16.0	3.3	1.2	58.9
1983	19.7	13.3	50.5	2.9	2.8	89.2
1984	18.7	13.9	27.8	2.7	1.4	64.5
1984–Q1	2.7	3.8	8.2	.6	.4	15.7
Q2	3.4	1.6	7.0	.6	.3	12.9
Q3	4.3	4.9	6.6	.7	.4	16.9
Q4	8.3	3.6	6.0	.8	.3	19.0

[a]These figures understate private issues since they include primarily publicly placed issues.

Source: Pre-1982: GNMA, FNMA, Freddie Mac; 1982 and after: *Secondary Mortgage Markets*, Federal Home Loan Mortgage Association, Summer 1985.

For tax purposes, pass-through certificates take the form of a grantor trust. That is, there is a fine line in the Internal Revenue Code between a grantor trust and an investment company. In an investment company, interest and profits are taxable. Certificate holders are treated as shareholders. If pass-throughs were considered investment companies, taxes would be due on the mortgage interest as well as on profits on prepayments of low coupon mortgages. In order to avoid these taxes, the grantor trust form is selected. This makes the income taxable only at the individual level, not at the trust level. There are, however, two disadvantages of grantor trusts: (1) assets cannot be managed, and (2) issuing different classes of securities is prohibited. The TIMS (Trusts for Investments in Mortgages) legislation would have overcome these problems by allowing multiple-class pass-throughs. The advantages of this are discussed later in the chapter.

Mortgage-Backed Bonds

Mortgage-backed bonds were first issued in the late 1970s during the thrift liquidity crises; they allowed these institutions to raise funds that would have been very costly to raise in any other manner. These bonds are still issed frequently in the domestic market for intermediate-term financing, and most of the mortgage issues in the Euromarket have been of this type.

Mortgage-backed bonds are debt obligations of the issuers, in which the mortgages are simply used as collateral. These issues are structured so that they eliminate mortgage characteristics entirely. They are, in fact, ordinary bonds with semiannual coupon payments and no prepayment risk. The mortgage backing allows thrifts which otherwise would receive a low rating to receive an AAA rating. In order to achieve this structure, the credit agencies require overcollateralization—120 to 200 percent depending on the circumstances. If interest rates rise, more collateral is often required.

These bonds are very attractive from an investor's point of view. The overcollateralization requirement eliminates the need for any credit investigation. Payments are semiannual, and there are no prepayments. Moreover, mortgages that are underwater can be used to back a bond. While the collateral is valued at market, the mortgage may still be carried on the institution's balance sheet at par.

These mortgage-backed bonds have a number of disadvantages. First, these are considered bonds when held by another thrift, and consequently do not count toward the qualifying mortgages for the purpose of the bad debt deduction. Second, and more importantly, it is an inefficient use of mortgage collateral. The overcollateralization requirement is set to protect the investors against a depression-type scenario, and while the amount is clearly greater than necessary, other uses of the same mortgages are forbidden.

Mortgage Pay-through Bonds

These instruments, while legally bonds, retain the cash flow characteristics of the underlying mortgages. They are, economically, very much like pass-throughs. The issuer of the bonds is usually a single-purpose financing subsidiary. The bond interest is paid semiannually and the debt service is uncertain—essentially the principal repayment, both scheduled and unscheduled, and the interest are passed through.

This is an efficient use of collateral. However, complex calculations are required to convince the rating agencies that the mortgages will produce adequate cash flows to meet the requirements of the bond issue.

The issuer usually obtains financing treatment for accounting purposes. That is, the assets remain on the books at original value while the bond is treated as financing by the issuer. This does not completely eliminate the problem with low-coupon mortgages, as these must find their way into the single-purpose subsidiary.

Collateralized Mortgage Obligations

A collateralized mortgage obligation is simply a multiple-class pay-through bond. The biggest problem with a one-class pay-through bond is that cash flows are uncertain. A CMO tries to eliminate this uncertainly by dividing the buyers into several classes. All but one class receive interest at a stated rate plus repayment of principal. One class usually receives principal repayment and accrues the interest payment. The payments of principal and prepayments are passed through first to the holder of the earliest class of bonds. When these holders are paid off in full, the principal payments are given to the next class. When this class is exhausted, payments pass to the next class, and so forth.

Thus, CMO purchasers are able to select the pattern of cash flow that is the most suited to their needs. The expected duration and maximum maturity of each class is specified. The maximum maturity of each class is based on zero prepayments and will turn out to be shorter. Freddie Mac CMOs specify a maximum maturity less than that based on zero prepayments, but greater than that based on expected prepayments. The agency will guarantee the maturity if prepayments are slower than expected. It should be realized that substantial prepayment risk still remains. If interest rates rise, prepayments will be slower; if they fall, prepayments will be faster. While the duration variability of at least one class of the CMO must be higher than the underlying mortgages, the ability to choose, within a range, the maturity and cash flows on their instrument is valuable.

The calculations involved in issuing a CMO are complex. In particular, the issuer wants to set maturities in order to take maximum advantage of the yield curve. In a very steeply sloped yield curve, the issuer will want a large, short tranche which will have a low yield. A larger class with a very short maturity can be created by having a large zero-coupon class which does not receive coupon payments until after the other classes have been paid off. Thus the coupon payments for this class can go toward repaying the first tranche. The zero-coupon class is an "accrual bond" with an uncertain maturity. Consequently its yield is considerably higher than Treasury strips of the same expected maturity.

A CMO, like its cousin, the mortgage-backed bond, is usually accounted for as debt.[1] That is, collateral is carried at book value and the obligations are considered

---

[1] The Financial Accounting Standard Board has recently issued a technical bulletin which allows CMOs to be treated as a sale under certain very stringent conditions. However, sale treatment is often undesirable for tax purposes in these transactions, particularly in the case of builder bonds.

debt. For tax purposes, the bond interest is deductible while the interest income is taxable. Thus, in a well-structured transaction, the income offsets the deductions, and the tax effects are minimal. When carried by a financial institution, the CMO will affect capital ratios.

A "builder bond" is generally structured as either a CMO or a cash flow bond. Builder bonds provide a method for builders to finance their home mortgages as well as to take advantage of the installment tax credit. This, in turn, makes new construction more salable to homeowners. Builder bonds are analogous to factoring in other industries.

A builder bond is simply a CMO secured by mortgages made by the builder. Once the builder has assembled the mortgages and insured them, he or she will pledge the mortgages as collateral for a bond, usually by transferring them to a wholly owned subsidiary which will issue the bonds. Because the builder has provided the financing, the transaction qualifies for the installment tax credit, which is very favorable since it allows the gains from the sale of the home to be spread out over several years rather than taken immediately.

The volume of publicly issued mortgage-collateralized securities is shown in Table 16.4. This includes mortgage-backed bonds, pay-through bonds, and CMOs. The amount of private mortgage-collateralized securities is again understated because privately placed issues are not included. Even so, it is clear this market is growing very rapidly.

A Future Possibility—Multiple-Class Pass-throughs

As mentioned earlier, in order to avoid taxation of the mortgage interest payments, pass-throughs must be structured as a grantor trust. Such a trust restricts the extent to which cash flow can be managed and allows for only one class of payments. In early 1984 Sears issued a multiple-class pass-through in order to test the IRS rules; the IRS held that the entity was not a grantor trust, but rather an investment company.

Table 16.4. Originations of Mortgage Collateralized Securities (in $Billions)

	Issuer			
Date	Freddie Mac	State and Local Agencies	Private Firms[a]	Total
1982	0	5.0	.7	5.8
1983	1.7	7.0	3.9	12.7
1984	1.8	7.4	9.4	18.6
1984–Q1	.5	1.8	4.1	6.4
Q2	.7	1.8	1.0	3.5
Q3	0	1.7	1.9	3.6
Q4	.6	2.1	2.4	5.1

[a] These figures understate private issues since they include primarily publicly placed issues.

Source: *Secondary Mortgage Markets*, Federal Home Loan Mortgage Association, Summer 1985.

There have been a number of legislative attempts to allow multiple-class grantor trusts. Multiple-class grantor trusts would differ from CMOs in that they would allow mortgages to be taken off the balance sheets of the issuing entity. In the case of thrifts and commercial banks, this can limit the growth of assets and thereby make existing capital go further. We expect to see developments in the area of multiple-class grantor trusts in the late 1980s.

TRADING

Trading of mortgage-backed securities, particularly pass-throughs, is a very important facet of the mortgage services performed by investment bankers. The major government securities dealers stand ready to make markets in the agency pass-throughs as well as in Freddie Mac CMOs. The underwriting firm or firms make markets in the publicly issued bonds or pass-throughs they have underwritten.

Dealers hold inventories of the mortgage securities that they trade. If a customer wants to buy a specific mortgage-backed security, traders stand ready to quote a price that they will sell (offer) it for; if a customer wants to sell a specific mortgage-backed security, traders stand ready to quote a price at which they will buy it. If an offer is accepted and the traders do not own the security they have sold, they must buy it or borrow it so that it can be delivered to the customer; in such cases traders' prices will often be less attractive than those of traders from another firm who own the security. The customer will pick the lowest price. Likewise, if traders do not want to own a security they has been asked to bid on, they will make a bid consistent with an intention to resell it to a third party. Thus their price may well be lower than that of another trader who does want to acquire the securities. The customer will pick the highest bid price.

The bid-ask spreads on commonly traded GNMAs are $\frac{4}{32}$ (as of this writing, that includes GNMA 8s and GNMA 11s through $13\frac{1}{2}$s). Less frequently traded issues have an $\frac{8}{32}$ bid-ask spread. Freddie Mac PCs generally trade with an $\frac{8}{32}$ bid-ask spread.

Trading of mortgage backed securities is very much like trading government bonds, with one major exception—prepayments. The price of a high- or low-coupon mortgage will be very sensitive to the prepayment rate. If interest rates remain constant and prepayments are expected to be higher in the future, the price of a low-coupon security will rise and prepayments on a high-coupon security will fall. Traders keep careful track of how fast mortgages have been prepaying in the recent past. Using this information, plus their expectations about interest rates in the future, they form an estimate of the future prepayment rate. This estimate will be reflected in the price quoted by the traders. Traders will take a long position if they expect the price of a GNMA to rise and a short position if they expect the price of a GNMA to fall.

Traders will also design strategies in order to take advantage of spread relationships between two mortgage securities or between a mortgage security and a Treasury. If, or example, the spread between a current-coupon GNMA and a 10-year Treasury

Table 16.5. Trading of Pass-through Securities (in $Billions)

Date	New Issues	Existing Issues
1982	76.1	230.0
1983	116.6	506.0
1984	100.3	792.0
1984–Q1	26.9	190.0
Q2	20.8	177.0
Q3	23.4	187.0
Q4	29.2	238.0

Source: Freddie Mac estimate published in *Secondary Mortgage Markets*, Summer 1985.

was 125 basis points, and the trader expected it to narrow to 100 basis points, he or she would go long the GNMA and short the 10-year Treasury. If the spread between Freddie Macs with an 8 percent coupon and GNMAs with an 8 percent coupon was 25 basis points, and it was expected to narrow to 10 basis points, the trader would go long the Freddie Mac with an 8 percent coupon and short the GNMA with the same coupon.

All mortgage-backed securities or even all GNMAs with an 8 percent coupon, are not homogenous, since they are based upon a specific pool of mortgages. Some traders look for particular pools which have been prepaying very fast or slow relative to the rest of the group and are expected to continue to do so. For example, if a single pool of GNMA 8s have been prepaying rapidly relative to the average GNMA 8s, and the pool is from a high prepayment state such as California, a trader will inventory that GNMA, possibly paying a bit extra to obtain it.

The volume of pass-throughs traded is shown in Table 16.5. Note the huge expansion in volume since 1982. If it were not for trading operations, securitization would not be as advantageous; it is the ability to trade the instruments in liquid markets that creates a substantial part of the demand for securitization.

TO WHAT EXTENT CAN BANKS PARTICIPATE IN THE STRUCTURED TRANSACTION MARKET?

While Glass–Steagall restrictions, which prohibit the investment banking groups in commercial banks from underwriting securities, have made a significant difference in the ability of commercial banks to compete with investment banks in the mortgage area, there is still a great deal which banks can do. There is a distinction between loans originated within the bank holding company and those originated by third parties. Regulations allow banks to underwrite any type of instrument originated within the bank holding company, as a bank is not considered to be underwriting but rather acting as a distributor of its own paper. With respect to third-party paper,

Table 16.6. Bank Activities

Mortgage Originator	Type of Instrument			
	Pass-through		Mortgage-Backed Bond	
	Private Offering	Public Offering	Private Offering	Public Offering
Internal	Yes	Yes	Yes	Yes
Third party	Yes	Probably	Yes	No

banks are more circumscribed. For private placement, they can underwrite all types of mortgage instruments including mortgage-backed bonds. Legal opinions suggest that banks may do third-party pass-throughs in the form of a public offering, although this has not been done so far. Bank activities are summarized in Table 16.6.

WHAT'S AHEAD?

Securitization of mortgage products has become an integral part of modern capital markets. Investment banks act as a conduit in this market, first by channeling mortgages from originators to ultimate investors and then by maintaining a continuous market by trading these securitized products with fairly narrow bid-ask spreads. The role of investment bankers will continue to expand as more thrifts essentially change their mode of operations to that of mortgage bankers, serving the origination role with no desire to hold the mortgages in portfolio. Moreover, many investment bankers seem interested in purchasing mortgage banking subsidiaries in order to integrate the securitization process vertically. The investment banking divisions of commercial banks already include that integration to some extent.

In addition to vertical integration, we can expect to see further expansion in the range of instruments securitized; commercial property mortgages, jumbo mortgages, and adjustable-rate mortgages are only recent targets for securitization, and represent growth areas. The rating agencies have recently developed a mechanism for rating commercial mortgages, which should spur their securitization. Jumbo mortgages trade like conventional mortgages but cannot be securitized through the government agencies. Adjustable rate mortgages comprise close to half of all new residential lending. In 1982 and 1983, each institution which offered ARMs had its own set of caps—yearly caps on interest rate changes, lifetime caps on interest-rate changes, caps on payment changes, and so forth. A number of standard products—a necessary prerequisite for securitization—began to emerge in 1984. In late 1984 and early 1985 GNMA, FNMA, and Freddie Mac all announced programs based on ARMs.

Securitization of other receivables—automobiles and possibly credit card receivables and computers—also has appeal. The potential of these markets is hard to gauge since the market for automobile receivables is in its infancy, and the markets for credit card and computer receivables are, as of this writing, untested.

17 The High-Yield Debt Market*

EDWARD I. ALTMAN

In recent years the level of new, public, nonconvertible corporate debt issued annually in the United States has risen dramatically, from $22.4 billion in 1978 to over $155 billion in 1986. While the majority of this expansion occurred as a result of falling interest rates in 1984–1986, a significant portion of the growth came from a previously undeveloped subcategory of the marketplace, that of high-yield bonds. (See Table 17.1.)

High-yield or "junk" bonds (also referred to as speculative-grade, low-rated, or noninvestment-grade bonds) are generally defined as publicly traded debt obligations rated as noninvestment grade by at least one of the independent rating agencies. More specifically, they include securities rated below BBB− (Standard & Poor's) or Baa3 (Moody's)—that is, BB or Ba, B, CCC, or Caa, down to D (default)—and certain nonrated securities that may or may not be tracked by the major rating agencies. The nonrated sector generally includes those bonds with promised yields that are within the range of those observed on rated, high-yield debt. For those readers who are unfamiliar with debt ratings, basically the higher the rating the lower the risk of default on either principal or interest payments (AAA being the highest grade and D being in default).

Debt in the high-yield corporate sector carries a very real level of speculative risk, and as a result investors have demanded yield premiums to compensate for that risk. Over the last decade these securities have usually sold with yield spreads (or risk premiums) of between 2.5 and 5.0 percent over comparable long-term government securities. These premiums and the rising interest rates in the late 1970s and early 1980s were major factors in the rapid expansion of the high-yield bond marketplace. Before going further, we should identify the specific parts of the "junk" marketplace that we will be referring to throughout this chapter.

---

* Portions of this chapter are reproduced with permission of Morgan Stanley & Co., Inc. from E. Altman, "The Anatomy of the High Yield Debt Market: 1986 Update," Morgan Stanley, April 1987.

285

Table 17.1. New Nonconvertible Domestic Debt Issues: 1978–1986 ($MM)[a]

Year	Total Par Value New Public Straight Debt Issues		Total Par Value New High Yield Debt Issues		% New Issue Dollars	Variable Rate Debt	
	Amount	No.	Amount	No.	Pct.	Amount	No.
1986[b]	$155,672	1,041	$34,177	234	22.0%	$ 661	8
1985	101,098	1,212	14,670	188	14.5	2,543	12
1984	99,416	721	14,952	124	15.0	3,927	27
1983	46,903	511	7,417	86	15.8	—	—
1982	47,798	513	2,798	48	5.9	40	1
1981	41,651	357	1,648	32	4.0	104	2
1980	37,272	398	1,442	43	3.9	137	4
1979	25,678	277	1,307	45	5.0	—	—
1978	22,416	287	1,493	52	6.7	—	—
Total	$577,904	5,317	$79,904	852	12.0%	$7,412	54

[a] Not including exchange offers, secondary offerings, tax-exempts, convertibles, or government agencies.

[b] In 1985, exchange offers and reorganization issues totaled $3.96 billion; retirements were $1.62 billion and secondary issues were at least $1.1 billion. In 1986, exchange offers and recapitalizations totaled $9.6 billion and retirements were over $8 billion. Private placements coming public totaled $3.4 billion.

Source: Morgan Stanley & Co., Inc. and *Investment Dealers' Digest.*

Securities in both the high-yield and investment-grade sectors can be broken down into several major types of debt (none of which is mutually exclusive), including fixed- and variable-rate issues, convertible securities, zero-coupon bonds and debt with warrants, stock, or other types of "kickers." In addition, debt issues can also be subdivided by the nature of the offering itself, into categories that include fully underwritten primary offerings, "best-efforts" offerings, exchange offerings, and secondary offerings.

In this chapter I concentrate almost solely on high-yield nonconvertible, corporate industrial, finance, and utility securities that are rated by at least one of the rating agencies as below investment grade.

The last decade or so has seen enormous growth in this market in terms of the number of new issues and dollar amounts outstanding. For example, in 1976 there was approximately $8 billion of high-yield nonconvertible debt outstanding, with the average individual issue being $27 million. This amount grew slowly but steadily for the next few years until 1980 when the market jumped to over $15 billion, up from $10.7 billion in 1979. (See Table 17.2.) Since 1982, the high-yield market

Table 17.2. Public Straight Debt Outstanding 1970–1986 ($ Million)

Year	Par Value Public Straight Debt Outstanding Over Year[a]	Low-Rated Debt[b]			
		Straight Public Debt	% of Public St. Debt	Amount Outstanding Per Issuer	Amount Outstanding Per Issue
1986	$505,150	$92,985	18.4	$181	$85
1985	419,600	59,178	14.1	135	55
1984	358,100	41,700	11.6	125	49
1983	319,400	28,223	8.8	93	39
1982	285,600	18,536	6.5	69	33
1981	255,300	17,362	6.8	62	32
1980	265,100	15,125	5.7	59	31
1979	269,900	10,675	4.0	47	30
1978	252,200	9,401	3.7	49	30
1977	237,800	8,479	3.5	46	27
1976	219,200	8,015	3.7	41	27
1975	200,600	7,720	3.8	41	27
1974	167,000	11,101[d]	6.6	59	35
1973	154,800[c]	8,082	5.2	45	29
1972	145,700	7,106	4.9	45	29
1971	132,500	6,643	5.0	45	29
1970	116,200	6,996	6.0	48	32

[a] Average of beginning and ending years' figures (1974–1986).

[b] Source: *Standard & Poor's Bond Guide* and *Moody's Bond Record*, July issues of each year. Defaulted railroads excluded. Also includes nonrated debt equivalent to rated debt for low-rated firms.

[c] Estimates for 1973 and earlier based on linear regression of this column versus the Federal Reserve's Corporate Bonds Outstanding figures *(Federal Reserve Bulletin.)*

[d] Includes $2.7 billion in Con Edison debt.

has exploded and by mid-1987 it totaled almost $130 billion in rated, nonconvertible (or "straight") debt securities, comprising over 18 percent of the public straight debt outstanding, up from just under 6.0 percent in 1982.

WHY THE TERM "JUNK"?

In our society the term "junk" automatically connotes something negative. Hence, we hear the terms "junkyard," "junk food," or just plain "junk" to identify inferior goods, and so it goes for financial securities as well, much to the chagrin of those who participate in this market—issuing companies, underwriters, traders, and investors.

The term "junk" originated in the mid-1970s to describe those corporate securities that had lost their investment-grade status due to a fundamental deterioration in the quality of their operating and financial performance. These so-called "fallen angels" involved both industrial and public utility debt where the default probability was considered sufficiently high so as to drop the bonds from the list of investment-grade securities.

Since the late 1970s, the proportion of high-yield debt made up of fallen angels has diminished through mid-1987 to about 30 percent. The market began to include more newly issued or original issue debt that represented a source of capital for emerging or continuing-growth companies, and those other companies which previously relied solely on private placements (i.e., commercial bank debt placed directly with other institutional investors such as insurance companies). As privately placed debt typically has rigid debt indenture provisions (restricting a firm's financial and operating flexibility to protect a specific lender's interest) many corporate treasurers have been willing to utilize the less restrictive public high-yield market.

Corporate raiders, at the same time, viewed this new-found source of (relatively) restriction-free debt as an effective tool for financing hostile takeovers of firms. A relatively small number of well-publicized takeover battles in 1984 and 1985 has turned the use of junk bonds for acquisitions into an emotionally charged topic of debate.

WHY HAS THIS MARKET GROWN AND WHO IS INVOLVED?

Rising interest rates and rapid expansion of the supply of high-yield corporate debt since the late 1970s led a wide variety of financial institutions to explore the relative attractions of lower-rated debt securities. Investors in investment-grade and even "risk-free" government securities were increasingly disenchanted with low or negative *ex post* returns on their portfolios as interest rates rose and prices declined. Committed to fixed-income investment, especially because equity returns were not much better or worse in some periods, these investors began to "eye" the high-coupon debt securities found in the "junkyard." In addition to the observed superior yields, the high-yield sector offered increased liquidity and diversification potential over what it had just a few short years before.

The entire high-yield, straight debt market at the beginning of 1987 was comprised of over 700 different corporate issuers and had over 1100 debt issues available to choose from. Of course, many of these issues were small, that is, under $25 million in debt outstanding, with an actual floating or tradable supply even lower. Still, the number of rated new issues greater than $200 million in size was 23 in 1985 and 54 in 1986.

The major players in the high-yield debt "game" are (1) issuing companies, (2) investors, (3) underwriting investment bankers, and (4) rating agencies. These are the same participants as are found in the investment-grade segment of the debt market. An increasingly important external constituency has emerged recently, made up of various observer/regulator-type groups, including financial institution regulators, Congressional committees, the media, and a small number of researchers. Investor interest in this emerging field is perhaps best exemplified by the growth in the number of mutual funds in the area, from less than a dozen 10 years ago to 61 as of April 1987. As of December 31, 1986, they had a total net asset value in excess of $25 billion. Interest from the investment banking community has also grown to the extent that competition for new issue underwriting has been active.

Drexel Burnham Lambert, by far the leader and driving force behind the high-yield field, devotes several hundred people to analyzing, underwriting, trading, and writing about high-yield bonds. Only recently have other major investment banks made concerted efforts to jump on the "junk-wagon." High investor interest and lucrative underwriting spreads (fees) will likely cause investment banks to devote additional resources to the area, thereby spurring greater growth and diversification in the near future.

There is no question that 1986 set records for the amount of new high-yield debt issued, the number of issues, the average size of new issues, and the proportion of total new corporate straight debt contributed by high-yield issues. Indeed, the net new high-yield issues totaled $34.177 billion (Table 17.1), which is far more than in 1984 and 1985 combined and brings the total new original high-yield debt issued since 1978 to just under $80 billion. The 1986 total does not include exchange offers and recapitalizations of $9.6 billion and private placements coming public of $3.4 billion.

Of equal interest is the fact that high-yield debt comprised 22 percent of the total corporate straight debt market, easily surpassing the prior year's high (15.8 percent in 1983). The number of issues was 234, a 25 percent increase over 1985. Of the 234 issues, 11 were greater than $500 million in size and 54 (23 percent) were greater than $200 million (Table 17.3) compared with 19 (10 percent) greater than $200 million in 1985. The average issue size was $146 million with the breakdown by Standard & Poor's original issue bond rating given in Table 17.4. Note that about 57 percent of the new issues in 1986 were rated B, comprising 62 percent of the new issue dollars.

I estimate that 50 to 60 percent of the new-issue dollars went for merger and acquisition-related deals, including LBO activity. The reason I am somewhat vague about the exact percentage is that the proceeds from a new issue may not be used entirely for the merger and the purpose is not always clear. Still, over 50 percent is a relatively high proportion and the dollars involved are substantial. We can

Table 17.3. Distribution of 1986 New Issues by Size of Issue

$Million	Number of Issues	Percentage of Total
0.0–24.9	11	4.70%
25.0–49.9	42	17.95
50.0–99.9	52	22.22
100.0– 199.9	75	32.05
200.0– 499.9	43	18.38
⩾ 500.0	11	4.7
	234	100.00%

probably expect that amount to diminish in 1987 if takeovers meet legislative resistance and the stock market continues to rise (as it has in the early months of 1987), making LBOs and other acquisitions more costly.

Exchange debt in 1986 grew dramatically with the total reaching over $9.6 billion on 27 issues (Table 17.5); $5.8 billion of the total was used in LBO activity with $3.8 billion (19 issues) for other purposes. Most of these "other" purposes involved distressed company exchange issues. Some, however, were not successful as in the case of LTV, Crystal Oil, Petro Lewis, and Damson Oil. Still, the default rate would no doubt be higher without these distressed exchange issues.

Table 17.4. Public High-Yield New-Issue Statistics

Year	S&P Rating[b]	Total Amount Issued ($M)	Number of Issues	Average Years to Maturity	Average Issue Amount ($M)
1986[a]	BBB/Ba	$ 765,000	7	10	$109,000
	BB	7,098,000	37	12	192,000
	B	21,260,000	133	11	160,000
	CCC	4,618,000	40	12	115,000
	No Rating	436,000	17	12	26,000
Total:		34,177,000	234	11	146,000
1985	BBB/Ba	1,065,000	11	10	96,818
	BB	2,040,750	23	11	88,728
	B	6,038,033	77	11	78,416
	CCC	1,668,000	14	11	119,143
	No Rating	3,858,641	63	11	61,248
Total:		14,670,424	188	11	78,034
1984	BBB/Ba	1,290,000	5	9	258,000
	BB	4,698,000	23	13	204,260
	B	6,484,500	68	11	95,360
	CCC	1,476,000	9	12	164,000
	No Rating	1,003,469	19	13	52,814
Total:		14,951,969	124	12	120,580

Table 17.4. (*Continued*)

Year	S&P Rating[b]	Total Amount Issued ($M)	Number of Issues	Average Years to Maturity	Average Issue Amount ($M)
1983	BBB/Ba	—	—	—	—
	BB	2,893,738	24	17	120,572
	B	3,713,451	46	14	80,727
	CCC	285,000	5	17	57,000
	No Rating	525,000	11	11	47,727
Total:		7,417,189	86	15	86,246
1982	BBB/Ba	60,000	2	11	30,000
	BB	1,378,000	16	12	86,125
	B	1,122,292	24	14	46,762
	CCC	145,050	2	13	72,525
	No Rating	92,311	4	23	23,078
Total:		2,797,653	48	14	58,284
1981	BBB/Ba	290,000	4	11	72,500
	BB	290,000	6	19	48,333
	B	893,667	15	18	59,578
	CCC	—	—	—	—
	No Rating	174,500	7	11	24,929
Total:		1,648,167	32	16	51,505
1980	BBB/Ba	50,000	1	7	50,000
	BB	418,000	9	18	46,444
	B	878,625	28	19	31,379
	CCC	25,000	1	15	25,000
	No Rating	70,000	4	14	17,500
Total:		1,441,625	43	18	33,526
1979	BBB/Ba	—	—	—	—
	BB	359,000	8	18	44,875
	B	852,600	33	18	25,836
	CCC	91,400	3	15	30,467
	No Rating	40,000	1	15	4,000
Total:		1,307,000	45	18	29,044
1978	BBB/Ba	40,000	1	20	40,000
	BB	407,875	10	19	40,787
	B	1,029,025	39	19	26,385
	CCC	12,000	1	15	12,000
	No Rating	4,000	1	15	4,000
Total:		1,492,900	52	19	28,710
Totals 1978–1986		$79,903,927	852	13	$ 93,784

[a] Aggregate amounts for all public straight debt excluding issues and private placements going public. Also does not include $8.4 billion of convertible debt.

[b] BBB included if Moody's ranked below investment grade.

Source: Morgan Stanley & Co. Incorporated. Does not include convertibles, secondary offerings, exchange, or best efforts offerings.

Table 17.5. High-Yield Exchange Debt Issues, 1978–1986

Year	Number of Issues	Dollar Amount ($MM)	Average Amount ($MM)
1985[a]	27	$9,643	$357
1985	27	$2,725	$101
1984	10	702	70
1983	16	486	30
1982	5	529	106
1981	2	323	162
1980	5	645	129
1979	6	227	38
1978	12	662	55

[a] Includes recapitalization issues and $5.8 billion of LBO-related exchange debt. Non-LBO exchange debt in 1986 was $3.8 billion on 19 issues.

UNDERWRITING ACTIVITY

Much has been made of late about the increased competitive nature of new-issue underwritings in the high-yield debt market and the apparent increased liquidity of issues in secondary markets, as well. Table 17.6 reinforces those observations as it appears that Drexel Burnham Lambert, while still the dominant firm, has seen its market share cut somewhat from 69 percent in 1984 to about 46 percent in 1986. In terms of new-issue size, Drexel's average issue is larger ($191 million) than any other firm's. Merrill Lynch was second in total dollars and number of issues with 11 percent of the market and an average size of $151 million. Morgan Stanley's average size ($188 million) was just below Drexel's and its overall amount put it in a third place tie with Salomon Brothers.

Given the recent, intense competition among underwriters to bring high-yield debt issues to market, it is worth examining the underwriting spreads. From 1978 through 1985 gross underwriting spreads remained constant at about 3 percent with a rather small and constant standard deviation of about 1 percent (see Table 17.7). Spreads in 1984 ranged from under 1 percent for some split-rated (BBB/Ba) issues to 4.75 percent. Fifteen of 120 (12.5 percent) issues studied had gross spreads of 4 percent or greater in 1984 compared with 11 of 70 (16 percent) in 1983. In 1985, the range widened to between 0.45 and 7.5 percent with 33 of the 174-issue sample (19 percent) being done at a cost of 4 percent or higher. This growth in the issues done at 4 percent or more may be a function of new underwriters getting into the market and issuing smaller, higher-risk debt. Separating issues by size—$100 million or more and less than $100 million—revealed, as expected, the average spread on larger issues underwritten between 1978 to 1985 to be somewhat lower (2.7 versus 3.2 percent respectively) than the smaller-sized deals. As the average deal size dropped in 1985, it is reasonable that average spreads would show marginal increases, which they did in most rating categories.

Table 17.6. New-Issue Statistics by Lead Underwriter: 1982–1986 ($ Million)

Underwriter	1986				1985			
	Amount	%	Number	%	Amount	%	Number	%
Drexel Burnham Lambert	15,775	45.86	82	35.04	7,239	49.71	83	44.15
Merrill Lynch	3,782	10.95	25	10.68	666	4.57	9	4.79
Morgan Stanley	2,817	8.16	15	6.28	1,050	7.21	13	6.91
Salomon Brothers	2,814	8.15	16	6.41	1,464	10.06	13	6.91
Shearson Lehman	1,903	5.51	11	4.60	708	4.86	8	4.26
First Boston	1,650	4.78	11	4.60	640	4.39	9	4.79
Goldman Sachs	1,228	3.56	9	3.77	615	4.22	5	2.66
Bear Stearns	1,145	3.32	14	5.86	456	3.13	7	3.72
Kidder Peabody	880	2.55	7	2.93	—	—	—	—
PaineWebber	545	1.58	4	2.93	206	1.41	2	1.06
E. F. Hutton	370	1.07	5	2.09	280	1.92	2	1.06
Prudential-Bache	357	1.03	4	1.67	435	2.99	8	4.26
Donaldson, Lufkin & Jenrette Inc.	338	0.98	7	2.93	—	—	—	—
Others	864	2.50	24	9.62	804	5.52	29	15.43
Total	34,117		234		14,562		188	

(*Table continues on p. 294.*)

Table 17.6. (Continued)

	1984				1983				1982			
	Amount	%	Number	%	Amount	%	Number	%	Amount	%	Number	%
	10,358	69.28	67	54.03	4,346	58.60	46	54.49	1,544	55.18	28	58.33
	530	3.54	4	3.23	427	5.76	5	5.81	699	24.99	7	14.58
	319	2.13	5	4.03	80	1.08	1	1.16	—	—	—	—
	865	5.79	9	7.26	423	5.70	4	4.65	—	—	—	—
	718	4.80	8	6.45	230	3.10	1	1.16	25	0.89	1	2.08
	390	2.61	5	4.03	325	4.38	3	3.49	—	—	—	—
	100	0.67	1	0.81	125	1.69	1	1.16	—	—	—	—
	360	2.41	4	3.23	380	5.12	5	5.81	35	1.25	1	2.08
	—	—	—	—	—	—			—	—	—	—
	65	0.43	1	0.81	235	3.17	3	3.49	225	8.04	1	2.08
	145	0.97	3	2.42	190	2.56	2	2.33	83	2.95	2	4.17
	950	6.35	13	10.48	275	3.71	6	6.98	40	1.43	1	2.08
	—	—	—	—	—	—			—	—	—	—
	152	1.02	4	3.23	381	5.14	9	10.47	147	5.27	7	14.58
	14,952		124		7,417		86		2,798		48	

Table 17.7. Average Underwriting Gross Spreads for High-Yield Issues

S&P Rating	1978	1979	1980	1981	1982	1983	1984	1985	Average
A	.74%	0.83%	0.72%	0.80%	0.80%	0.79%	0.71%	0.62%	0.73%
Number of issues:	122	63	102	72	70	124	106	193	
BBB/Ba	1.88%	—	1.90%	1.25%	1.63%	—	1.59%	1.29%	1.42%
Number of issues:	1	0	1	3	1	0	5	11	
BB	2.62%	2.33%	1.99%	2.38%	1.85%	2.04%	2.16%	2.21%	2.16%
Number of issues:	10	8	9	5	12	23	17	21	
B	3.29%	3.36%	3.27%	2.62%	2.30%	3.04%	2.91%	3.07%	3.04%
Number of issues:	38	33	24	11	21	44	52	71	
CCC	3.75%	4.68%	4.67%	—	3.65%	3.29%	3.21%	3.33%	3.48%
Number of issues:	1	2	1	0	2	3	7	12	
NR	5.5%	6.0%	6.0%	4.5%	3.69%	3.40%	3.32%	3.77%	3.76%
Number of issues:	1	1	2	3	4	11	16	59	
Average high yield:	3.18%	3.29%	3.11%	2.64%	2.35%	2.81%	2.80%	3.11%	
Number of issues:	51	44	37	22	40	81	97	174	

Source: Morgan Stanley & Co., Inc.

Underwriting gross spreads in this market continue to remain substantially above spreads for investment-grade issues. The largest change occurred in the CCC and nonrated issues. Average spreads for those deals fell from the 4 to 6 percent range in 1979 to a low of about 3 percent in 1984. In 1985, they moved upward again to the 3.3 to 3.7 percent levels, respectively. Generally, while spreads have narrowed since 1978, they have held relatively stable in the 1983 to 1985 period (except CCC and nonrated (NR)), even though underwriting competition has heated up. These spreads, averaging three to five times those on A-rated issues, make this market an attractive one to investment bankers.

DEFAULT RATES AND LOSSES

Defaults, defined as either debt issues dropping to a D rating or involved in a formal bankruptcy, whichever comes first, reached record levels in 1986. The $3.156 billion in defaults easily surpassed the next highest year—1985 with under $1 billion (Table 17.8). The actual names and amounts of each 1986 default[1] are given in Table 17.9 with the first nine issuers all involved in the giant LTV bankruptcy in July. I include all defaulting debt in my totals and not just original issue high-yield bonds. Therefore, LTV-related defaulting debt totaled $1.766 billion or 56 percent of the total defaulting straight debt.

The default rate in 1986 was 3.39 percent of the amount outstanding as of June 30, 1986. As Table 17.10 indicates, the 1986 rate was relatively high although not a record, while the amount easily broke the prior calendar year's high. Only in 1977 was the default rate higher than in 1986 and of course the market was much smaller then, consisting virtually of 100 percent fallen angels.

Analyzing the Default Rate

The 1986 default rate is somewhat difficult to analyze. On the one hand, the rate is quite high, especially for a nonrecession year, reflecting an increased overall vulnerability to distress. And the rate would have been higher if exchange issues for distressed firms had not been successful in avoiding some defaults. Defaults were heavily concentrated in steel and energy issues, reflecting the economic realities of the country. One might therefore wonder what will be the default rate in a bad recession year. On the "positive" side, despite the 3.39 percent rate, and a somewhat lower loss rate, the total rate of return on a diversified portfolio of high-yield debt was a respectable 16.1 percent, perhaps even higher according to others' calculations. And the default rate was about 1.50 percent excluding LTV. This is a rate approximating the average annual rate over the 1974–1985 period (1.53 percent). It appears that the combination of a bad recessionary period *and* two or three really

---

[1] The reader is referred to the prior compilation of all defaulting firm names and amounts (1970–1985) in E. Altman and S. Nammacher, *Investing In Junk Bonds: Inside The High Yield Debt Market*, New York: Wiley, 1986, pp. 112–119.

Table 17.8. Public Corporate Debt Defaulting on Interest and/or Principal: 1970–1986 ($MM)[a]

Year of Default	Straight Debt	Convertible Debt	Total Debt in Default
1986	$3,155.16	$ 299.62	$ 3,455,38
1985	992.10	310.02	1,302.12
1984	344.16	279.95	624.11
1983	301.08[b]	111.55	412.63
1982	752.34[c]	243.29	995.63
1981	27.00	52.61	79.61
1980	224.11	31.60	255.71
1979	20.00	10.70	30.70
1978	118.90	73.30	192.20
1977	380.57	74.21	454.78
1976	29.51	83.99	113.50
1975	204.10	115.63	319.73
1974	122.82	165.87	288.69
1973	49.07	150.84	199.91
1972	193.25	79.34	272.59
1971	82.00	42.90	124.90
1970	796.71	135.81	932.52
Total	$7,793.48	$2,261.23	$10.054.71

[a] Also includes those issues whose ratings dropped to D due to missed interest payments, but did not legally default.

[b] Although Baldwin United's debt in 1983 was not rated investment grade just prior to default, we are told that it was not possible to trade these issues after it dropped below triple-B.

[c] Includes $175 million in Johns Manville debt which was rated investment grade prior to default.

large defaults are the necessary ingredients for default rates to rise to the 4–5 percent range in the future. For 1987, a default rate of 4 percent would mean about $5 billion in defaults—a number which "requires" many large defaults.

Of course, one must include LTV in default rate calculations, and the average annual rate over the 1974–1986 period was 1.67 percent with a slightly higher 1.73 percent over the last four years (1983–1986). The default rate on all corporate straight debt—investment- and noninvestment-grade—rose to about 0.20 of 1 percent for the 1970–1986 period and 0.19 of 1 percent for the more recent 1978–1986 period. This reflects the record (except for 1970) rate of 0.636 percent in 1986 (Table 17.11).

Defaults by Industry

The breakdown of defaults by industrial sector over the 1970–1986 period is given in Table 17.12. Comparing this table with the prior compilation through 1985[2],

[2] *Ibid.*, p. 24.

Table 17.9. Defaulting Debt in 1986 ($ Million)

Default Date	Company[a]	Bankruptcy Filing Date	Straight Debt	Convertible Debt	Total Debt
Jul-86	LTV Corp (9)	Jul-86	$ 884.60	$ 0.00	$ 884.60
Jul-86	Jones & Laughlin Ind. (2)	Jul-86	49.10	0.00	49.10
Jul-86	Jones & Laughlin Steel (5)	Jul-86	114.50	0.00	114.50
Jul-86	LTV Intl NV (3)	Jul-86	0.00	43.80	43.80
Jul-86	Lykes Corp.(3)	Jul-86	259.30	0.00	259.30
Jul-86	Republic Steel Corp (3)	Jul-86	259.64	0.00	259.64
Jul-86	Republic Steel O/S (2)	Jul-86	98.50	65.00	163.50
Jul-86	Vought Corporation	Jul-86	17.60	0.00	17.60
Jul-86	Youngstown Sheet & Tubing (3)	Jul-86	82.70	0.00	82.70
Jun-86	American Adventure	—	0.00	10.80	10.80
Jan-86	Argo Petroleum	—	25.00	0.00	25.00
Apr-86	Crystal Oil (5)	—	190.60	0.00	190.60
Jun-86	Damson Oil (4)	—	71.55	0.00	71.55
Jun-86	Digicon Finance NV	Mar-86	0.00	18.00	18.00
Jun-86	Digicon Inc. (2)	Mar-86	35.00	25.70	60.70

Aug-86	Frontier Airlines (2)	Aug-86	5.27	3.82	9.09
Aug-86	Frontier Holdings	Aug-86	0.00	22.50	22.50
Jul-86	ICO Inc (2)	—	60.00	0.00	60.00
Jun-86	Ideal Basic Industries	—	21.10	0.00	21.10
Mar-86	Kenai Corporation (4)	—	49.40	0.00	49.40
Oct-86	La Barge Inc	Nov-86	20.00	0.00	20.00
Jul-86	McLean Ind (2)	Feb-87	243.00	0.00	243.00
Jan-86	Mission Insurance	—	21.10	0.00	0.00
May-86	Na-Churs Plant Food	—	20.00	0.00	20.00
Aug-86	Petro-Lewis (11)	—	278.80	0.00	278.80
Feb-86	Savin Corp (2)	Mar-86	98.70	0.00	98.70
Mar-86	Smith International	—	75.00	0.00	75.00
Jul-86	Texas American Oil	—	25.00	0.00	25.00
Jan-86	Texscan	Mar-86	0.00	40.00	40.00
Mar-86	Towle Manufacturing	Nov-86	0.00	25.00	25.00
Nov-86	Wedtech	—	75.00	40.00	115.00
Dec-86	Western Co NA	—	33.80	0.00	33.80
Apr-86	Zapata	—	41.50	0.00	41.50
Sep-86	Total debt defaulted in 1986		$3,155.76[b]	$299.62[b]	$3,455.38[b]

[a] Number of issues in parentheses.
[b] Without LTV-related debt, straight defaulted debt totaled $1,389.82, convertible defaulted debt totaled $185.82, and total defaulted debt totaled $1,554.54.

299

Table 17.10. Historical Default Rates—Low-Rated, Straight Debt Only ($ Million)

Year	Par Value Outstanding with Utilities	Par Value Defaulted	Default Rate
1986	$92,985	$3,155.76	3.394%
1985	59.078	992.10	1.679
1984	41,700	344.16	0.825
1983	28,233	301.08	1.066
1982	18,536	577.34	3.115
1981	17,362	27.00	0.155
1980	15,126	224.11	1.482
1979	10,675	20.00	0.187
1978	9,401	118.90	1.265
1977	8,479	380.57	4.488
1976	8,015	29.51	0.368
1975	7,720	204.10	2.644
1974	11,101	122.82	1.106
1973	8,082	49.07	0.607
1972	7,106	193.25	2.719
1971	6,643	82.00	1.234
1970	6,996	796.71	11.388

Average default rate—1970 to 1986: 2.216%
Average default rate—1974 to 1986: 1.671%
Average default rate—1978 to 1986: 1.451%
Average default rate—1983 to 1986: 1.727%

note the following important changes. Oil and gas-related defaults went from 18 to 29 with a 12.7 percent increase in amounts. The relative proportion of this sector's contribution to total defaults increased from 15 to over 20 percent. General manufacturing, including steel, showed the greatest increase from 9 percent of the total (1970–1985) to over 29.5 percent, mainly fueled by LTV. Counting LTV as just one default, the number of general manufacturing defaults increased to 23 from 18. [If one includes each of LTV's issuing subsidiaries in the total, 1986 defaults numbered 33 (Table 17.13) and general manufacturing defaults would number 31 over the last 17 years.] Railroad proportions continued to fall from 27 to 16 percent. These statistics show vividly the marked impact of the two sick industries—oil and gas, and steel. The shakeout in these industries is probably not complete.

Defaults by Original Bond Rating

Table 17.14 updates prior compilations of defaults broken down by their rating distributions at various times prior to default.[3] The proportion of "broken" fallen-angel defaulting debt drops from 28.0 percent (based on 125 issues) to 23.6 percent

[3] *Ibid.*, p. 131.

Table 17.11. Historical Default Rates—All Ratings ($Million)

Year	Par Value of Straight and Convertible Public Debt Outstanding[a]	Par Value of All Public Defaults	Default Rate	Par Value of Public Straight Debt Outstanding[a]	Par Value of Straight Debt Defaulted	Default Rate
1986	$542,900(est.)	$3,455.38	.636%	$505,150 (est.)	$3,155.76	.625%
1985	454,900	1,302.02	.286	419,600	992.40	.237
1984	387,750	624.11	.161	358,100	344.16	.096
1983	347,000	412.63	.118	319,400	301.08	.094
1982	317,600	995.63	.313	285,600	725.34	.263
1981	289,900	79.61	.027	255,300	27.00	.011
1980	281,900	255.71	.091	265,100	224.11	.084
1979	281,700	30.70	.011	269,900	20.00	.007
1978	258,600	192.20	.074	252,200	118.90	.047
1977	248,300	454.78	.183	237,800	308.57	.160
1976	229,100	113.50	.049	219,200	29.51	.013
1975	209,900	319.73	.152	200,600	204.10	.102
1974	183,500	288.69	.157	175,200	122.82	.070
1973	162,900	199.91	.123	158,800	49.07	.031
1972	154,400	272.59	.176	150,900	193.25	.128
1971	143,000	124.90	.087	140,500	82.00	.058
1970	125,500	932.52	.743	124,400	796.71	.640

Average default rate—1970 to 1986:   .199%   .157%
Average default rate—1974 to 1986:   .173%   .139%
Average default rate—1978 to 1986:   .190%   .163%

[a] These numbers are averages of beginning and ending year outstanding amounts from 1981–1986. End-of-year totals for prior years. Total corporate, publicly held outstanding debt at the end of 1986 was $591.5 billion. Source (*Prospects for Financial Markets in 1987*, Salomon Brothers, Inc.)

[b] Estimates for 1973 and earlier based on linear regression of this column versus the Federal Reserve's *Corporate Bonds Outstanding* figures (*Federal Reserve Bulletin*).

Table 17.12. Public Defaults by Industry Sector: 1970–1986 ($Million)

	Number of Companies	Straight Debt	Percentage of Total Straight	Convertible Debt	Total in Default	Percentage of Total
Industrial						
Retailers	15	$ 556.74	7.14%	$ 211.87	$ 768.61	7.70%
General manufacturing	23	2,301.49	29.53%	331.64	2,653.73	25.68%
Electronic/computer and communications	22	200.79	2.58%	413.58	614.37	6.15%
Oil & gas	29	1,581.09	20.29%	449.65	2,030.74	20.34%
Real estate— construction, supplies	13	103.93	1.33%	126.55	230.48	2.31%
Miscellaneous industrials	18	570.30	7.32%	177.68	747.98	7.49%
Total industrial:	120	$5,314.34	68.19%	$1,710.97	$ 6,955.91	69.66%
Transportation						
Railroads	9	$1,260.22	16.17%	$ 31.10	$ 1,291.32	12.93%
Airlines/cargo	7	211.81	2.72%	122.81	334.62	3.35%
Sea lines	4	243.00	3.12%	123.10	366.10	3.67%
Trucks/motor carriers	3	48.31	0.62%	9.75	58.06	0.58%
Total transportation:	23	$1,763.34	22.63%	$ 286.76	$ 2,050.10	20.53%
Finance						
Financial services	11	$ 436.09	5.60%	$ 164.04	$ 600.13	6.01%
REITs	12	279.71	3.59%	99.46	379.17	3.80%
Total finance:	23	$ 715.80	9.18%	$ 263.50	$ 979.30	9.81%
Total defaults:	166	$7,793.48	100.00%	$2,261.23	$10.054.71	100.00%

Table 17.13. Number of Companies with Public Debt Defaulting[a]

Year	Non-Railroad Companies	Major Railroads
1986	33[b]	0
1985	18	0
1984	12	0
1983	14	0
1982	17	0
1981	3	0
1980	5	0
1979	3	0
1978	5	0
1977	8	1
1976	7	0
1975	7	1
1974	11	0
1973	9	1
1972	3	1
1971	4	1
1970	9	5
Total	135	10

[a] Includes straight and convertible defaults.
[b] Includes eight subsidiaries of LTV Corporation and two other separately reported subsidiary defaults, otherwise 23 companies.

(based on 182 issues) when we add 1986 statistics. This shows the naturally increasing proportion of original issue high-yield defaults as the market grows and matures. When we shift to one year prior to default, the proportion of investment-grade debt naturally decreases. That proportion is now 6.5 percent, down from 9.1 percent prior to 1986. At the six-month mark, the proportion is now 2.5 versus 2.8 percent in the earlier compilation.

CONCLUSION

The high-yield debt market is now bigger, deeper, more liquid, and more controversial than ever before. Despite the great emotion and relatively high default rate in 1986, the market remains intact and should weather future storms. The first two-month performance in 1987 has been impressive, with total returns exceeding 6 percent compared to about 1.7 percent on the Shearson-Lehman long-term government index. New issue amounts were over $3 billion including just under $850 million in private placements going public. The likely attempts to regulate investments in high-yield debt by state insurance departments and possible legislation on a state and federal level in the insurance field, as well as the takeover arena, would seem to indicate some future rocky periods. In my opinion, however, the market is resilient

Table 17.14. Rating Distribution of Defaulting Issues at Various Points Prior to Default

Original Rating

	AAA	AA	A	BBB	BB	B	CCC	CC	Total
Number	0	3	11	29	26	79	33	1	182
Percentage	0.00%	1.65%	6.04	15.93%	14.29%	43.41%	18.13%	0.55%	100.00%

Rating One Year Prior

	AAA	AA	A	BBB	BB	B	CCC	CC	Total
Number	0	0	2	11	29	81	67	9	199
Percentage	0.00%	0.00%	1.01%	5.53%	14.57%	40.70%	33.67%	4.52%	100.00%

Rating Six Months Prior

	AAA	AA	A	BBB	BB	B	CCC	CC	Total
Number	0	0	2	3	11	77	95	15	203
Percentage	0.00%	0.00%	0.99%	1.48%	5.42%	37.93%	46.80%	7.39%	100.00%

enough to withstand these largely exogenous, and in many cases poorly conceived, shocks. The new tax laws will perhaps reduce debt activity in the coming months as firms sort out the net benefits of debt financing.

BIBLIOGRAPHY

Altman, Edward I., "Testimony on the Impact of High Yield Bonds on Credit Markets" before the House Subcommittee on Banking, Finance and Urban Affairs, Washington, DC, September 19, 1985.

Altman, Edward I. (ed.), *The Handbook of Corporate Finance*, New York: Wiley, 1986.

Altman, Edward I. (ed.), *The Handbook of Financial Markets and Institutions*, New York: Wiley, 1986.

Altman, Edward I. and S.A. Nammacher, "The Default Rate Experience on High Yield Debt," New York: Morgan Stanley, March 1985 and *Financial Analysts Journal*: (July–August 1985).

Altman, Edward I. and S.A. Nammacher, "The Anatomy of the High Yield Debt Market," New York: Morgan Stanley, September 1985, "Update 1985," June 1986, and "Update 1986," April 1987.

Altman, Edward I. and S.A. Nammacher, *Investing in Junk Bonds: The Anatomy of the High Yield Debt Market,* New York: Wiley, 1986.

Atkinson, T.R., "Trends in Corporate Bond Quality," *National Bureau of Economic Research*, 1967.

Blume, M.E., and D.B. Keim, "Risk and Return Characteristics of Lower-Grade Bonds," Working paper, *Rodney White Center for Financial Research*, Philadelphia, PA: Wharton School, 1984, and *Financial Analysts Journal* (July–August 1987).

Bookstaber, R. and David Jacob, "Risk Management for High Yield Portfolios," New York: Morgan Stanley, January 1986.

Bookstaber, R. and David Jacob, "The Composite Hedge. Controlling the Credit Risk of High Yield Bonds," in R. Platt (ed.), *Controlling Interest Rate Risk*, New York: Wiley, 1986.

Drexel Burnham Lambert, *High Yield Newsletter*, Los Angeles, bimonthly, 1982–1986.

Drexel Burnham Lambert. *The Case for High Yield Bonds*, Los Angeles, 1984, 1985.

First Boston, *The High Yield Handbook*, New York, January 1987.

Fitzpatrick, J.D. and J.T. Severiens, "Hickman Revisited: The Case for Junk Bonds," *Journal of Portfolio Management*, 4 (Summer 1978), pp. 53–57.

Hickman, W.B. *Corporate Bond Quality and Investor Experience*, Princeton, NJ: Princeton University Press and the National Bureau of Economic Research, 1958.

High Performance, Morgan Stanley, monthly, 1985–1987.

Hill, J.H. and L.A. Post, "The 1977–78 Lower-Rated Debt Market: Selectivity, High Yields, Opportunity," New York: Smith Barney Harris Upham & Co., December 1978.

Lipper Analytical Services, "Lipper Fixed Income Fund Performance Analysis," monthly.

Moody's Inc., "Rating Changes and Debt Offerings," *Moody's Bond Survey*, January 27, 1986.

Paulus, John D., "Corporate Restructuring, 'Junk' and Leverage: Too Much or Too Little," New York: Morgan Stanley, March 12, 1986.

Platt, Robert, ed., *Controlling Interest Rate Risk*, New York: Wiley, 1986.

Securities and Exchange Commission, "Noninvestment Grade Debt as Source of Tender Offer Financing," Washington, DC: Office of Chief Economist, June 20, 1986.

Soldofsky, R., "Risk and Return for Long Term Securities: 1971–1982," *Journal of Portfolio Management* (Fall 1984), pp. 57–64.

Standard & Poor's "Corporate Debt Default Risk," *Credit Comment*, February 20, 1984.

Standard & Poor's, "Corporate Downgrades Set Record," *Standard & Poor's Credit Week*, January 16, 1986.

18 Innovative Instruments and Transactions

TANYA STYBLO ARNOLD

Innovation on two fronts has played a key role in the investment banking business of the 1980s: (1) new products for issuers and/or investors; and (2) derivative products.

The explosive growth in both sorts of products is a direct result of change in the capital markets. As interest rates continued to be uncertain and volatility increased during the decade, both issuers and investors required new ways to manage greater risk.

Investment bankers had to overcome a number of obstacles militating against innovative ideas in the capital markets. Certain barriers are common to investment banks and issuers–investors; others are clearly internal or external in nature.

For example, all participants in the issuance and investment aspects of investment banking required education in how to evaluate completely new security structures. In addition, most participants needed schooling in newer, sophisticated techniques for evaluating the impact of interest-rate risk in its various forms (market risk, call risk, prepayment risk, reinvestment risk, volatility risk). One internal obstacle is development of product specialists or traders or other "homes" for successful innovation. An external obstacle might be convincing an issuer to be the first in the market to introduce an unproven security structure. Additional obstacles are possible regulatory restrictions and establishment of tax and accounting treatment.

NEW PRODUCTS

Product proliferation in investment banking of the 1980s has centered largely in the area of fixed-income securities. Tax-exempt securities also saw significant innovation in the 1980s, although the volume was lower. Since 1980, notable fixed-income security innovations have been:

Debt Warrants—1980

Typically, bonds are sold with warrants attached to purchase additional bonds at a predetermined date and price.

Original Issue Discount (OID) Securities—1981

Typically, bonds are sold at the time of issue with a low coupon (i.e., at a large discount from par), which offers investors lower reinvestment and call risk than current-coupon securities.

Debt-Equity Swaps

Typically, a corporation offers equity to existing holders of debt. Initially this was a tax-motivated exchange; the tax advantages, however, no longer exist.

Options on Futures—1982

Puts and calls on U.S. Treasury bond futures contracts were listed on the Chicago Board of Trade. Within three years, daily trading volume exceeded that of the cash market for U.S. Treasury bonds.

Zero-Coupon Bonds—1982

Similar to OIDs, although the discount from par at issue is larger due to the lack of coupon (0 percent). Investor acceptance and the need for higher-quality corpus led to stripping and trading of U.S. Treasury securities in 1982.

Interest-Rate Swaps—1982

A contract specifying an exchange of cash flows (typically a fixed-rate versus LIBOR) on a notional principal amount. Market participants frequently view swaps as futures with longer maturities (up to 10 years).

Floating-Rate Preferred Stock—1982

Initially, structures were created using various floating-rate formulas. By 1984, the most popular form used a Dutch Auction to set a rate every 49 days.

Collateralized Mortgage Obligations (CMOs)—1983

Typically, a single pool of mortgages is used to guarantee a multiple-class issue of securities ranging from short to long maturities. By 1986, some CMOs offered floating-rate, short-maturity classes with a capped rate of interest.

Asset-Backed Securities—1985

Typically, a collection of nonmortgage securities are used to guarantee a multiple-class issue of securities. In 1986, the largest deal completed to date in the U.S. capital markets ($4 billion) was of this form.

Capped Floating-Rate Securities and Interest-Rate Caps—1985

Typically, a floating-rate issue pegged to LIBOR is issued with a stated maximum interest rate (the cap). The issuers frequently sell the caps to a third party. By 1986, interest-rate caps had grown into a separate market that was not just linked to capped floaters.

By 1986, the volume of new innovations and variations on previous innovations represented hundreds of billions of dollars. During 1986, new and revived interest was in the areas of risk-controlled arbitrage, foreign currency denominated issues, dual currency bonds, debt/equity warrants, and perpetual floaters.

DERIVATIVE PRODUCTS

Cash market plus risk-management-tool transactions ("derivatives") represent the newest and fastest growing type of innovation. To create a derivative, risk-management tools are used to transform one or more properties of an asset or liability. The portfolio manager begins with at least one investment plus at least one management tool. Similarly, the liability manager begins with at least one borrowing plus at least one risk-management tool. The most common risk-management tools used to create derivatives are:

Futures/forwards
Options/warrants
Interest-rate swaps
Interest-rate caps and floors
Currency forwards
Currency swaps

In derivatives, the risk-management tools available are not able to transform all properties of the asset or liability (e.g., credit or final maturity). Figure 18.1 portrays those properties most often transformed (in part or in whole) by each of the risk-management tools.

A few patterns are clear from the figure:

Futures, forwards, and interest rate swaps all transform the same properties of a security.
Options, warrants, and interest-rate caps or floors all transform the same properties of a security.
Currency forwards and currency swaps both transform the same properties of a security.

For example, a bullish investor may own a 3-year floating-rate security and wish to lock in a fixed rate for the next year. The investor may use interest-rate swaps

Property	Futures/ Forwards	Options/ Warrants	Interest-Rate Swaps	Interest-Rate Caps/ Floors	Currency Forwards	Currency Swaps
COUPON/RATE OF INTEREST						
Transform from fixed to floating (or vice versa)	X		X			
Transform from one floating index to another	X		X			
Set/remove minimum or maximum rate		X		X		
Transform from one currency to another					X	X
PAYMENT OF COUPON:						
Transform to more frequent or less frequent payments	X		X			
PRINCIPAL:						
Transform from one currency to another					X	X
Set/remove option characteristic		X		X		

Figure 18.1. Derivatives

Step 1. Purchase FRCD. Price: 100; Coupon: 3-month LIBOR Q/Q (Quarterly/Quarterly).

Step 2. Enter a 1-year interest-rate swap in which a fixed rate is received, and 3-month LIBOR is paid.

The cash flows for the next year are:

Asset inflow	+ 3-month LIBOR
Swap outflow	− 3-month LIBOR
Swap inflow	+ 7.00% SA
Net Result	+ 7.00% SA

At the end of the year, the swap matures, and the investor's yield returns to a floating rate based on 3-month LIBOR.

Figure 18.2. Floating-rate certificate of deposit plus interest-rate swap

Step 1: Purchase FRCD. Price: 100; Coupon: 3-month LIBOR Q/Q.
Step 2: Buy a strip of 3-month LIBOR (Eurodollar) futures contracts for the last three successive quarters at:

Q_1: 6.75% (current coupon on FRCD)
Q_2: 6.65% (futures contract #1)
Q_3: 6.80% (futures contract #2)
Q_4: 7.00% (futures contract #3)

The investor's return is now locked in for each quarter. For example, if 3-month LIBOR is less than 6.65 percent at the beginning of the second quarter, the combination of the profit from selling the futures contract and the quarterly inflow from the FRCD will equal 6.65 percent.

The investor's average return will be 6.80 percent [this is the average of the four quarterly rates: (6.75 + 6.65 + 6.80 + 7.00)/4 = 6.80%].

At the end of the year, the futures contracts will be sold or will have expired, and the investor's yield returns to a floating rate based on 3-month LIBOR.

Figure 18.3. Floating-rate certificate of deposit plus long futures position

or futures to transform the floating rate of interest to a fixed rate of return. In the swap, a floating rate would be paid and a fixed rate would be received (see Figure 18.2). In futures, a long position in three-month LIBOR (Eurodollar) contracts would be taken (see Figure 18.3). Alternatively, the investor could set a minimum return by buying an interest-rate floor (see Figure 18.4).

The only limit to the number of derivatives is the financial manager's creativity. Many derivatives involve multiple risk-management tools. As an example, consider

Step 1: Purchase FRCD. Price: 100; Coupon: 3-month LIBOR Q/Q.
Step 2: Purchase a one-year interest rate floor on 3-month LIBOR. For a floor of 6 percent, assume the price is 24 points up front, which equates to 6 basis points per quarter.

The investor's cash flows depend on the 3-month LIBOR rate relative to the level of the interest rate floor:

If 3-month LIBOR is less than 6 percent (the strike level of the interest rate floor), the interest rate floor contract will pay the investor the difference between 6 percent and the three-month LIBOR rate received from the FRCD. The investor's return in this case will be 6 percent less the 6 basis points cost of the floor, or 5.94 percent.

If 3-month LIBOR is greater than 6 percent, the floor will not be used, and the investor's return will be the 3-month LIBOR rate received from the FRCD less the 6 basis points cost of the floor.

At the end of the year, the interest rate floor matures, and the investor's yield returns to a floating rate based on 3-month LIBOR.

Figure 18.4. Floating-rate certificate of deposit plus interest-rate floor

an investor who purchases a three-year fixed-rate U.K. government security denominated in sterling and transforms it to a floating-rate U.S. dollar-denominated investment with a minimum rate of return by:

1. Entering into a series of currency forwards in which the sterling to be received (interest and principal) is sold at guaranteed forward rates in exchange for U.S. dollars;

Step 1. On 4/25/86, the investor purchased sterling 7.7 million in the 9½ percent U.K. government securities due 10/25/88 (U.S. $10 million equivalent at a spot rate of 1.30 U.S. dollars to 1 sterling).

Step 2. The investor entered the following currency forward contracts to transform the sterling investment to a U.S. dollar-denominated rate of return:

Date	Asset Inflow (Sterling)	Forward Rate*	U.S. Dollar Equivalent
10/27/86	365,385	1.267	462,942
4/27/87	365,385	1.267	462,942
10/26/87	365,385	1.267	462,942
4/25/88	365,385	1.267	462,942
10/25/88	8,057,693	1.267	10,209,097

* On 4/25/86, the forward rate curve was flat out to two years.

Step 3. The investor entered a $10 million interest-rate swap maturing 10/25/88 paying a fixed rate of 8.82 percent SA ($441,000 per semiannual period) and receiving a floating rate of 6-month LIBOR. This transformed the investor's semiannual flows to a floating rate basis:

Asset inflow	+ $462,942
Swap outflow	− $441,000
Swap inflow	+6-month LIBOR
Net result	+ 6-month LIBOR + $21,942 (44 basis points)

Step 4. The investor purchased a 7 percent interest-rate floor on 6-month LIBOR maturing 10/25/86 for 1¼ points up front, which equates to 46 basis points per annum.

If 6-month LIBOR is less than 7 percent, the interest-rate floor contract will pay the investor the difference between 7 percent and the 6-month LIBOR rate received in the swap. The investor's return in this case will be 7.44 percent (the floor level plus the 44 basis point spread in step 3), less the cost of the floor, or 6.98 percent.

If 6-month LIBOR is greater than 7 percent, the floor will not be used, and the investor's return will be 6-month LIBOR + 44 basis points, less the cost of the floor, or 6-month LIBOR − 2 basis points.

Figure 18.5. Derivative with three risk-management tools

2. Entering into an interest-rate swap in which a fixed rate is paid and a floating rate (six-month LIBOR) is received; and,

3. Purchasing an interest-rate floor on six-month LIBOR.

This derivative involves three risk-management instruments. It is illustrated in Figure 18.5.

THE LIFE OF INNOVATION

The life of innovative instruments and transactions varies. Innovations designed to take advantage of a window in the market typically die (or become dormant) when the window is closed. An example is a foreign currency borrowing transformed to U.S. dollars via a currency swap: many deals are completed when the "all-in" cost of funds is lower than that of a direct U.S. dollar-denominated borrowing. When the cost is higher, that is, when the window is closed, such deals are rarely executed.

Innovations designed to exploit tax or accounting benefits typically die if the benefit is revoked. For example, a change in the tax treatment of original issue discount (OID) securities and zero-coupon securities dramatically reduced the number of taxpaying investors for such securities. The changes eliminated most taxpaying corporate issuers as well.

Innovation designed to take advantage of an expected level of interest-rate risk (whether high or low) has been responsible for the bulk of new products and derivative products launched in the 1980s. It is likely that innovations of this sort will have a permanent role in the capital markets. Traditionally, issuers and investors have had simple expectations of interest rates: over a stated period rates would rise or fall. Today, capital market participants are much more sophisticated. Issuers and investors analyze the behavior of securities in an expanded context of rates as well as the expected pattern of volatility. Such an expanded point of view leads to more dynamic management of assets and liabilities. Using multiple variables representing types of interest-rate risk rather than a single variable representing interest-rate risk has led to an ongoing supply and demand of securities that includes many of the new innovations. These innovations have helped investors to discover new ways to maximize yield. Similarly, issuers have discovered new ways to minimize cost.

There have been billions of dollars realized in successful innovations in only the past few years. Evidence indicates that investment bankers of the late 1980s will continue to find that the ability to innovate and complete new transactions is crucial to their success.

PART 5 TAX-EXEMPT FINANCING

The tax-exempt market is a large and quite distinct part of the fixed-income market. The issuers of tax-exempt debt (states, municipalities, and various other political entities within a state) are very different from issuers of corporate debt instruments. They are organized differently, their objectives are different, and their culture is different. Perhaps for this reason those in investment banking firms who deal with tax-exempt issuers generally belong to a group that is quite distinct from those who deal with corporate clients.

In Chapter 19, Ron Forbes describes the tax-exempt market, its scope (it is very large, growing and somewhat concentrated among a half-dozen or so states), and the distinction between general obligation and revenue bonds. The chapter goes on to discuss the activities of investment bankers in the issue of tax-exempt debt.

In Chapter 20, the same author turns to innovations in tax-exempt financing. Competition among investment bankers has fostered the introduction of tax-exempt commercial paper and variable-rate demand paper, as ways to satisfy special needs of investors and reduce the issuers' costs of borrowing. Options are another innovation, as are zero-coupon instruments and credit-enhancing guarantees.

Chapter 21, also by Ron Forbes and in this case co-author John Petersen, describes the effects on the tax-exempt market of the Tax Reform Act of 1986. The chapter reviews the history of the tax treatment of state and municipal bonds and a series of restrictions imposed by Congress, beginning in the late 1960s, on the tax-exempt privilege. The 1986 legislation imposed significant new limitations, the most important being limits on the volume of private activity debt. At the same time the new Act also affects the attractiveness of tax-exempt interest to investors.

19 The Tax-Exempt Securities Market

RONALD W. FORBES

Interest payments on debt issued by state and local governments are exempt from federal taxation. In 1985, new tax-exempt issues exceeded new issues of taxable corporate bonds by $45 billion, making this market a significant segment of the nation's capital market. Tax-exemption means that interest rates generally are lower than rates on securities not exempt from federal taxation. Traditionally, this has limited the market to commercial banks, property and casualty insurance companies, and individuals facing high marginal tax rates.

Changes in federal tax rates have a significant effect on the demand for tax-exempts and on the level of tax-exempt rates relative to other interest rates. Changes in federal law also cause substantial shifts in the aggregate supply of new tax-exempts. While state and local governments use tax-exempts to finance traditional government-owned capital projects such as roads, water and sewer systems, and schools, federal law also permits governments to issue tax-exempts for certain types of privately owned projects. The changing federal treatment of these private-purpose tax-exempts has fostered substantial volatility in the supply of new issues.

Because of the unique requirements of the tax-exempt market, most investment banking firms have developed specialized departments to provide origination, underwriting, and distribution services to issuers and investors. This chapter describes the workings of the market and the role of investment bankers in new tax-exempt issues.

AN OVERVIEW OF THE TAX-EXEMPT MARKET

There are a number of ways to measure the size of the tax-exempt market. Table 19.1 traces the volume of new issues from 1966 through 1985. New issues climbed from $17.3 billion to $241.3 billion during this period, at an average annual compound rate of growth of 14.8 percent. By convention, new issues are classified as short-term notes or long-term bonds depending on the final maturity of the issue.

Table 19.1. New-Issue Volume in the Tax-Exempt Securities Market, 1966–1985 (Dollar Amounts in Billions)

Year	Bonds	Notes	Total
1985	$218.16	$23.16	$241.32
1984	119.34	31.07	150.41
1983	95.06	38.30	133.36
1982	89.02	44.71	133.73
1981	57.69	37.43	95.12
1980	56.37	27.72	84.09
1979	49.12	21.72	70.84
1978	50.70	21.38	72.08
1977	46.71	24.75	71.46
1976	35.42	21.91	57.33
1975	30.66	28.97	59.63
1974	23.59	29.04	52.63
1973	23.82	24.67	48.49
1972	23.69	25.22	48.91
1971	24.93	26.28	51.21
1970	18.08	17.88	35.96
1969	11.70	11.78	23.48
1968	16.32	8.66	24.98
1967	14.41	8.03	22.44
1966	11.08	6.25	17.33

Source: Original data from Public Securities Association. Totals have been adjusted for small-issue IDBs as reported in Phil Clark, "Private Activity Tax-Exempt Bonds, 1985," U.S. Treasury Department.

Issues with a final maturity of 13 months or less are classified as notes, which are commonly sold in minimum denominations of $5000 with interest payable at maturity.

Table 19.2 traces the stock of tax-exempt debt outstanding. This stock has increased from $105.9 billion in 1966 to $720.4 billion in 1985, an average annual rate of growth of 10.6 percent. The slower rate of growth of the stock relative to the flow of new issues can be explained by the use of short-term notes and serial-bond maturities, which result in a relatively rapid retirement schedule for tax-exempt issues.

Tax-exempt debt outstanding accounted for 9.25 percent of all credit market debt outstanding in 1971. Table 19.2 shows that the proportion of tax-exempts declined from 1971 to 1981 when it reached a low of 7.3 percent. The rapid increase in new issues since then expanded the stock of outstanding tax-exempts to 8.8 percent of the credit market in 1985.

Another perspective on the scope of the tax-exempt market is the size distribution of new issues, summarized for 1985 in Figure 19.1. In 1985, there were more than

Table 19.2. The Stock of Tax-Exempt Debt Outstanding

Year	Tax-Exempt Debt Outstanding ($Billion)	Outstanding Tax-Exempts as Percentage of All Credit Market Debt
1966	$105.9	8.95%
1967	113.7	9.00
1968	123.2	8.98
1969	133.1	8.94
1970	144.4	9.04
1971	161.8	9.25
1972	176.5	9.10
1973	191.2	8.77
1974	207.7	8.63
1975	223.8	8.54
1976	239.5	8.25
1977	262.9	8.00
1978	291.3	7.79
1979	321.6	7.61
1980	351.9	7.58
1981	375.2	7.32
1982	423.9	7.59
1983	481.2	7.73
1984	547.0	7.69
1985	720.4	8.80

Source: Board of Governors of the Federal Reserve System, *Flow of Funds*, 1986.

9800 new bond issues sold and nearly 4400 were less than $5 million in par value. At the other extreme of the market, 492 issues were sold in that year with a par value greater than $100 million, including a $2 billion bond sale by the New Jersey Turnpike Authority.

Most long-term bond issues are sold as serial bonds. Under the serial-bond structure, a portion of the total bond principal is scheduled to mature at regular intervals over the life of the issue. An example of this type of debt structure is provided in Figure 19.2 for a recent bond issue of the Lynn, Massachusetts, Water and Sewer Commission. The $35.35 million bond issue is structured with a total of $20.975 million in serial bonds maturing from 1986 through 2000, and $14.375 million in term bonds maturing in 2005. The term bonds are subject to a mandatory sinking-fund redemption beginning with a required redemption of $2.415 million in 2001. The bonds maturing after 1995 also carry a call option, permitting the Commission to redeem bonds in 1995 and thereafter at an initial call price of 102 percent of par. The sinking-fund and call-option features are standard terms for tax-exempt bonds. Figure 19.2 indicates the bonds are offered in minimum denomina-

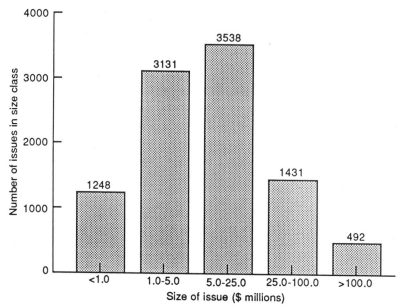

Figure 19.1. Size distribution of new issues of tax-exempt bonds, 1985 (*Source*: Public Securities Association: Dealer's Digest: IDD Information Services/PSA Municipal Database.)

tions of $5000 and the coupon rate, stated as an annual rate, is paid semiannually. More recent bond innovations, discussed in the next Chapter, include variable interest rates (often changing daily), monthly interest payments, and zero-coupon bonds.

Tax-exempt securities are not subject to the regulation and disclosure requirements of the Securities and Exchange Commission; disclosure practices, therefore, vary widely. Large, frequent borrowers may have official statements or prospectuses that range up to 100 or more pages and include full, audited financial statements, while small, infrequent borrowers may provide only brief summaries of relevant credit information. Moreover, issuers of tax-exempt debt are not subject to annual reporting requirements, nor are they required to follow a uniform standard for accounting or financial reporting. Thus updated financial information relevant to changes in credit standing is often difficult to obtain after new debt issues have been sold. The absence of standardized reporting practices, the vast number of issuers, and the many different bond issues sold create high information costs in the tax-exempt market which fosters a geographic market segmentation. Small, local issuers generally are restricted to local markets where investors have first-hand knowledge of the purposes for borrowing and the capacity to repay. Large and frequent borrowers, on the other hand, provide regular detailed reports to facilitate the broad distribution of their securities in national markets.

Government units rarely engage in direct sales of new issues to investors. Most tax-exempts are sold first to underwriting syndicates who then reoffer the securities

In the opinion of Bond Counsel, under existing law interest on the 1985 Series A Bonds will be exempt from federal income taxes and the 1985 Series A Bonds, their transfer and the income therefrom, including any profit made on the sale thereof, will be exempt from taxation within The Commonwealth of Massachusetts; however, the 1985 Series A Bonds and the interest thereon may be included in the measure of Massachusetts estate and inheritance taxes and of certain Massachusetts corporate excise and franchise taxes.

$35,350,000

Lynn Water and Sewer Commission

(A Political Subdivision of The Commonwealth of Massachusetts)

General Revenue Bonds, 1985 Series A

Dated: June 1, 1985   Due: June 1, as shown below

The 1985 Series A Bonds are issuable as fully registered bonds in the denomination of $5,000 or any integral multiple thereof, with interest payable semiannually on each June 1 and December 1, commencing December 1, 1985. Interest on the 1985 Series A Bonds will be payable by check or draft mailed to the registered owner thereof. The principal or redemption price of the 1985 Series A Bonds will be payable at the principal office of the Trustee, State Street Bank and Trust Company, Boston, Massachusetts. The 1985 Series A Bonds will be subject to redemption prior to maturity as set forth herein.

The 1985 Series A Bonds will constitute general obligations of the Commission, which has no taxing power. In addition, the 1985 Series A Bonds will be secured by a lien on and pledge of certain revenues and other moneys of the Commission as described herein. Neither The Commonwealth of Massachusetts nor any political subdivision thereof other than the Commission is obligated to pay the principal of and interest on the 1985 Series A Bonds and neither the faith and credit nor the taxing power of the Commonwealth or any other such political subdivision thereof is pledged to such payment. A municipal bond insurance policy will be issued by

FINANCIAL GUARANTY INSURANCE COMPANY   **FGIC**

to guarantee payment of the principal of and interest on the 1985 Series A Bonds, on stated payment dates, as described herein.

Maturity	Amount	Interest Rate	Price	Maturity	Amount	Interest Rate	Price
1986	$ 865,000	4.90%	100%	1994	$1,405,000	7½%	100%
1987	910,000	5.40	100	1995	1,510,000	7.70	100
1988	960,000	5.80	100	1996	1,625,000	7.90	100
1989	1,015,000	6¼	100	1997	1,755,000	8.10	100
1990	1,075,000	6½	100	1998	1,895,000	8¼	100
1991	1,145,000	6¾	100	1999	2,055,000	8.40	100
1992	1,225,000	7	100	2000	2,225,000	8½	100
1993	1,310,000	7¼	100				

$14,375,000 8¾% Term Bonds due 2005 — Price 100%
(Accrued interest to be added)

The 1985 Series A Bonds are offered when, as and if issued and received by the Underwriters, subject to approval of legality by Palmer & Dodge, Boston, Massachusetts, Bond Counsel, and certain other conditions. Certain legal matters with respect to the Commission will be passed upon by its general counsel, Arthur J. Palleschi, Esquire. Certain legal matters are subject to the approval of Mintz, Levin, Cohn, Ferris, Glovsky and Popeo, P.C., Boston, Massachusetts, Counsel to the Underwriters. It is expected that the 1985 Series A Bonds in definitive form will be available for delivery in New York, New York on or about June 19, 1985.

Merrill Lynch Capital Markets   Morgan Stanley & Co.
Incorporated

May 31, 1985

Figure 19.2. Tax Exempt Offering

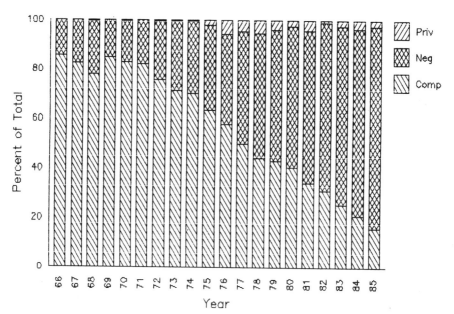

Figure 19.3. New issues of tax-exempt bonds by method of sale (*Source*: Public Securities Association: Dealer's Digest: IDD Information Services/PSA Municipal Database.)

to final investors. As Figure 19.3 shows, negotiated underwritings are now the most common, accounting for more than 80 percent of all new issues (by dollar volume) in 1985. Government units may also solicit bids from competing underwriting syndicates, awarding the securities to the underwriting syndicate with the lowest interest-cost bid. Competitive bidding was used for 16 percent of the new issues in 1985. Private placements typically account for 5 percent or less of new issues sold.

Figure 19.3 indicates that there has been a marked shift in the method of sale used over time. Competitive sales were prominent in the 1960s, accounting for more than 80 percent of new issues. By the 1980s, however, negotiated underwritings came to dominate. The trend toward negotiated financing is related to changes in the purposes for borrowing, changes in the security features on new debt, and market conditions, each to be discussed later in this chapter.

THE REGIONAL DISTRIBUTION OF TAX-EXEMPT NEW-ISSUE VOLUME

Among the more important trends in the tax-exempt bond market has been the changing geographical mix of new debt issues. In 1970–1975, for example, bonds from four northeastern states—Massachusetts, New Jersey, New York, and Pennsylvania—accounted for 33 percent of all new issues sold. Table 19.3 shows that New York government units outpaced all states with $25.7 billion in new obligations representing 18.7 percent of the entire new-issue market. By the first half of the 1980s, however, new-issue volume was distributed more evenly across regions. The shift in the geographic mix of new issues reflects several interrelated forces at work. Tax-exempt financing of government capital facilities is a derived demand that is shaped by underlying demographic factors. The shift in population from "frostbelt" states to "sunbelt" states, for example, has required increased investment in public infrastructure for Southern and Western states. The data in Table 19.3 point out that California, Florida, Louisiana, and Texas have recorded major increases in new debt issuance and in market share, while new tax-exempt obligations from Northern industrial states have declined in market share. The changing regional mix of new issues also reflects the well-known fiscal problems that plagued governmental units in New York, Michigan, and Massachusetts in the mid-1970s. These fiscal problems resulted in lowered credit ratings and led to constraints on market access for governments in these states.

Table 19.3. Leading States in New Tax-Exempt Bond Sales, 1970–1975, 1980–1985

Rank	State	Aggregate Volume ($Billion)	Percentage of Total Volume
		1970–1975	
1	New York	$25.7	18.7%
2	California	9.5	7.0
3	Pennsylvania	8.6	6.3
4	Texas	7.8	5.7
5	Illinois	6.1	4.5
6	New Jersey	5.8	4.3
7	Michigan	5.1	3.7
8	Massachusetts	5.1	3.7
9	Ohio	4.7	3.5
10	Florida	4.3	3.1
		1980–1985	
1	California	$62.5	11.1
2	Texas	53.2	9.5
3	New York	37.3	6.6
4	Florida	36.2	6.5
5	Illinois	25.1	4.5
6	Pennsylvania	24.5	4.4
7	New Jersey	19.1	3.4
8	Louisiana	15.1	2.7
9	Ohio	14.5	2.6
10	Massachusetts	13.7	2.4

Source: Public Securities Association, Dealer's Digest: IDD Information Services/PSA Municipal Database.

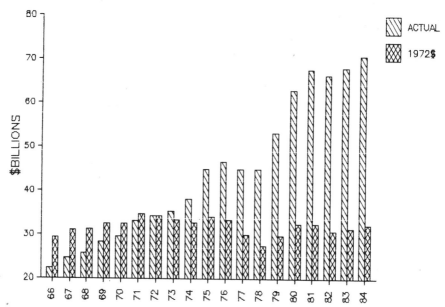

Figure 19.4. State and local government capital outlay 1966–1983 (*Source*: U.S. Department of Commerce, *Government Finances.*)

THE CHANGING PURPOSES FOR BORROWING

Accompanying regional shifts in population has been a significant slowing in overall population growth over the past two decades, a trend mirrored in the tax-exempt bond market. Capital spending by state and local governments has increased in nominal dollar terms from $22.3 billion in 1966 to $70.7 billion in 1984, but most of this increase is due to inflation. Figure 19.4, which compares nominal capital outlays with inflation-adjusted spending, points out that "real" outlays peaked in the early 1970s. Parallel to the trends in population and spending, tax-exempt issues for traditional public works have diminished in market importance. According to Table 19.4, bonds for education declined from 29.5 percent of new issues in 1966–1970 to 7.5 percent in 1980–1985. Highway and transportation bond issues dropped from 11 percent of the new issue market to 1.8 percent, and water and sewer bonds fell from 11 to 4.8 percent over the same period.

THE USE OF PUBLIC CREDIT FOR PRIVATE PURPOSES

In 1975 tax-exempt bonds were virtually synonymous with municipal bonds. Most new capital raised in the tax-exempt market financed government-owned capital facilities. Since then, there has been a steady increase in the use of tax-exempt debt for privately owned projects. These private-purpose bond issues have financed

Table 19.4. Long-Term Tax-Exempt Bond Sales by Use of Proceeds (Percentage)

Use of Proceeds	1966–1970	1971–1975	1976–1980	1981–1985
Education	29.52	18.72	10.38	7.48
Elementary and secondary	21.67	12.54	6.86	3.10
College, university	7.85	6.29	2.63	2.50
Transportation	18.85	11.00	5.91	5.82
Roads, bridges	11.13	6.17	2.81	1.84
Ports, airports	7.72	4.95	2.08	2.58
Utilities	15.08	19.41	18.19	14.30
Water, sewer	10.74	8.57	6.57	4.79
Electric, power	4.34	13.06	7.33	6.54
Social Welfare	7.22	15.89	24.70	26.92
Housing	1.82	6.11	16.79	16.41
Hospitals	3.45	7.25	6.27	7.93
Pollution control	N/A	N/A	4.02	5.58
Small-issue IDB	N/A	N/A	10.36	12.58
Total new capital	99.29	97.29	88.23	71.70
Refundings	.71	2.71	11.77	15.71
Total new bond sales	100.00	100.00	100.00	100.00

Source: Public Securities Association, Dealer's Digest: IDD Information Services/PSA Municipal Database.

capital projects or loans to private colleges and universities (including loans to students attending them); not-for-profit hospitals; commercial bank offices; manufacturing and commercial enterprises; fast food franchises; ski resorts and professional sports stadiums; and single-family home mortgages.

Table 19.5 points out that private-purpose bonds have grown from 22 percent of the new-issue market in 1975 to 60 percent in the mid-1980s. Instrumental in

Table 19.5. New Issues of Tax-Exempt Bonds for New Capital Projects, 1975–1985

Year	Public Purpose ($ Billion)	Private Purpose ($ Billion)	Private as Percentage of Total New Capital
1985	$63.9	$95.5	60%
1984	42.3	64.3	60
1983	30.0	49.3	62
1982	33.6	48.4	59
1981	25.1	30.4	55
1980	21.1	32.2	60
1979	18.7	27.5	60
1978	22.0	17.7	45
1977	22.6	14.6	39
1976	22.4	9.1	29
1975	23.6	6.8	22

Source: Federal Reserve Bulletin (November 1984), p. 796. Figures updated for 1984–1985 from Phil Clark, "Private Activity Tax-Exempt Bonds, 1985," U.S. Treasury Department.

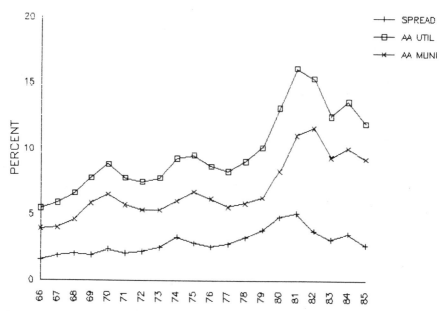

Figure 19.5. Yields on "AA" rated bonds: taxable utility bonds versus tax-exempts (*Source*: Salomon Brothers, *An Analytical Record of Yields and Yield Spreads.*)

the growing use of tax-exempt debt for these purposes has been the potential for significant savings in interest costs. One indicator of the savings is the yield spread between taxable and tax-exempt bonds. Figure 19.5, which traces this spread for AA-rated municipals and taxable utility bonds from 1966 to 1985, shows that the yield spread widened from 155 basis points in 1966 to nearly 500 basis points in 1981. Figure 19.5 also indicates that the yield differential has tended to widen with increases in the level of interest rates, and this has provided additional incentive for borrowers to substitute tax-exempt borrowing for conventional (taxable) loans.

Access to the tax-exempt market in recent years has been controlled by the federal government through legislative changes in Section 103 of the Internal Revenue Code. Congress in 1968 first enumerated a long list of privately owned facilities that were permitted to be financed in the tax-exempt market through state or local governments or their agencies. This list included owner-occupied housing; multifamily rental housing; sports facilities and convention centers; airports and ports; mass commuting facilities; water, sewage, and solid waste disposal facilities; pollution control facilities; and industrial parks. In addition, so-called small-issue industrial development bonds less than $1 million in par value (subsequently expanded to $10 million) were permitted for virtually any depreciable real property.

Since this list of eligible activities was first promulgated in 1968, Section 103 has provided an umbrella for a growing number of nongovernmental borrowers seeking the lower interest rates available in tax-exempt markets. Rapid expansion of this private debt in the 1980s caused Congress to focus on the loss of federal tax revenues from the expanding volume of tax-exempt finance. As a result, recent Congressional actions have attempted to restrict the supply of private-purpose bonds. These limitations have included "caps" or volume restrictions on new issues for specific purposes, and sunset provisions on others that would remove their eligibility for tax-exempt market access after some future date. The tax reform legislation passed in 1986 extends these limitations and places significant restrictions on the future growth of many types of private-purpose borrowing.

CHANGES IN SECURITY FEATURES

Another important change in the tax-exempt market has been the decline in new issues backed by tax-derived revenues of government units. Tax-supported bonds, termed general obligations (GOs), have traditionally been viewed as the most secure of all tax-exempt debts. As stated by Standard & Poor's Corporation:

> An issuer selling a G.O. bond secured by its full faith and credit attaches to that issue its broadest pledge. This security encompasses such things as its ability to levy an unlimited ad valorem property tax or to draw from other unrestricted revenue streams, such as sales or income taxes.
>
> Standard & Poor's Corporation, *Debt Ratings Criteria: Municipal Overview, 1986*

Figure 19.6 provides an example of the full faith and credit pledge for a recent bond issue from Schenectady, New York. The unlimited tax pledge in this instance is based on the provisions of the New York State Constitution.

In the 1960s, most bonds sold were backed by this full faith and credit pledge. Over the last two decades, however, GO bonds have diminished in importance, now accounting for only 25 percent of new issues. Figure 19.7 notes that revenue bonds presently account for 75 percent of new tax-exempt issues. Two broad categories of revenue bond can be defined: those payable solely from the revenues

Security and Source of Payment
    Each Bond when duly issued and paid for will constitute a contract between the City and the holder thereof.
    The Bonds are general obligations of the City and will contain a pledge of its faith and credit of the City for the payment of the principal of and interest thereon. For the payment of such principal and interest the City has power and statutory authorization to levy ad valorem taxes on all taxable real property in the City without limitation as to rate or amount.
    Under the constitution of the State, the City is required to pledge its faith and credit for the payment of the principal of and interest on the Bonds, and the State is specifically precluded from restricting the power of the City to levy taxes on real estate therefor.

Figure 19.6. Summary of security features: $11.122 million bond issue, Schenectady, New York, May 29, 1986 (*Source*: Official statement dated June 15, 1986)

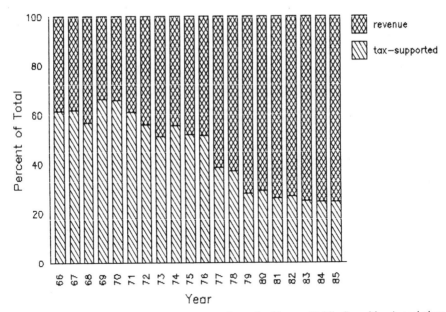

Figure 19.7. Tax-exempt new issues by type of security (*Source*: Public Securities Association: Dealer's Digest: IDD Information Services/PSA Municipal Database.)

of a government-owned enterprise, such as a water or sewer system, and those payable from the income or revenue of private entities or individuals.

Municipal revenue bonds sold by Fort Pierce, Florida to finance capital improvements in the city's municipal utility system are repayable solely from the system's revenues. The debt service has a claim on all revenues after the payment of operating expenses, and the indenture expressly states that the taxing power of the city is not a source for the repayment of these obligations.

Many governments have turned to revenue bond financing for capital projects formerly financed by GO bonds. In some instances, the shift has been necessitated by taxpayer resistance to added tax burdens. The passage in 1978 of Proposition 13, an amendment to the California State Constitution, heralded a wave of taxpayer initiatives in other states that has severely constrained the ability of local governments to pledge general tax support for new obligations. In other instances, revenue bond financing has emerged as governments have organized new public enterprises designed to be self-supporting by user charges.

Most private-purposes bonds are sold through public agencies or authorities that act primarily as financing conduits. These agencies borrow in the tax-exempt market and relend the proceeds to individuals or private enterprises. The principal assets of the public conduits are the portfolios of loans to private borrowers and the cash flow from these loans serves as the security for the bonds. An example of the security features for as conduit financing is summarized in Figure 19.8, which describes the sources of funds pledged for the repayment of a college student loan program of the New England Education Loan Marketing Corporation. As noted, the repayment of student loans financed from the bond proceeds represents the principal source of funds earmarked for the debt service on the bonds.

Revenue bonds generally are perceived by the market as more risky than GO bonds because there is no pledge of taxing power behind them. This perception of added risk has been heightened by the recent default on $2.25 billion in bonds by the Washington Public Power Supply System (WPPSS), a wholesale power system established by the state of Washington. In 1977, WPPSS first issued bonds for the construction of two nuclear-powered generating facilities (Projects 4 and 5). The bonds were secured by power sales contracts with BB participating private and public utilities in the Northwest. In 1982, WPPSS terminated construction of these projects because of large cost overruns and mounting evidence that the power needs of the region were far less than originally estimated. In 1983, the Washington State Supreme Court ruled that the public utilities in the state had no legal authority to repay the outstanding debt of Projects 4 and 5; WPPSS subsequently defaulted on the bonds, the largest tax-exempt bond default in history. In light of the WPPSS default, it is noteworthy that wholesale electric power bonds carry yields that are 93 basis points higher than yields on state GO bonds. Figure 19.9 points out, as well, that revenue bond yields are systematically higher than yields on GO bonds from state and local governments.

General

The Bonds are limited obligations of the Corporation, secured by a pledge of and a security interest in the Financed Loans and notes evidencing the same; all moneys and securities from time to time held by the Trustee under the terms of the Indenture; all Revenues and Recoveries of Principal (as hereafter defined); certain rights of the Corporation under Student Loan Purchase Contracts and the Servicing Agreement (both as hereafter defined); and all of the Corporation's rights under the Commitment Agreement (as described below). All such property pledged and assigned by the Corporation to the Trustee is called the "Trust Assets" for purposes of the Indenture and this Official Statement. All moneys and securities held by the Trustee in the several trust funds under the Indenture, and the trust funds themselves, are referred to herein as the "Funds." The Trust Assets are pledged under the Indenture to the Trustee for the benefit of the Bondowners.

The Bonds shall not be deemed to constitute a debt or liability of the Commonwealth or any political subdivision thereof, or a pledge of the faith and credit of the Commonwealth or any such political subdivision. Neither the faith and credit nor the taxing power of the Commonwealth or of any political subdivision thereof is pledged to the payment of the principal of or the interest on the Bonds. The Bonds are limited obligations of the Corporation, and pursuant to the Indenture, the Corporation shall not be obligated to pay the principal of and interest on the Bonds except from the Trust Assets.

Figure 19.8. Summary of security features, $200 million student loan revenue refunding bonds, 1985 issue A, The New England Education Loan Marketing Corporation (*Source*: Official statement dated August 7, 1985)

The following index is based on yields that about 500 major issuers, mainly of investment grade, would pay on new long-term tax-exempt securities. The securities are presumed to be issued at par; general obligation bonds have a 20-year maturity and revenue bonds a 30-year maturity. The index is prepared by Merrill Lynch, Pierce, Fenner & Smith Inc., based on data supplied by Kenny Information Systems, a unit of J.J. Kenny & Co.

OVERALL INDEX
7.20   −0.11

REVENUE BONDS
Subindex   7.35   −0.09

	11−5−86	Change in Week
AAA-guaranteed	7.14	−0.07
Airport	7.52	−0.02
Electric−retail	7.37	−0.10
Electric−wholesale	7.58	−0.11
Hospital	7.36	−0.03
Housing	7.36	−0.13
Miscellaneous	7.20	−0.08
Pollution control/industrial development	7.42	−0.09
Transportation	7.33	−0.09
Utility	7.27	−0.14

GENERAL OBLIGATIONS
Subindex   6.79   −0.17

Cities	6.87	−0.17
Counties	6.75	−0.19
States	6.65	−0.16
Other districts	6.91	−0.17

The transportation category excludes airports; utility excludes electrics. Other districts include school and special districts.

Figure 19.9. Municipal bond index, Merrill Lynch 500, week ended Wednesday, November 5, 1986 (*Source: The Wall Street Journal*, November 7, 1986)

The proliferation of complex new security features, coupled with the vast number of new issues each year, has focused attention on credit quality. Historically, the tax-exempt market has relied on the credit rating agencies—Moody's and Standard & Poor's Corporation—to serve as information intermediaries, and ratings still serve as important signals to investors. But new forms of credit monitoring have been developed including credit enhancements—letters of credit and bond insurance. These enhancements are supplied by commercial banks and insurance companies with the purpose of reducing information costs for investors and borrowing costs for borrowers. Chapter 20 describes these credit enhancements in detail.

THE DEMAND FOR TAX-EXEMPT SECURITIES

Among other factors such as marketability and the availability of competing tax-sheltered investments, the level of interest rates on tax-exempts relative to rates on comparable taxable investments plays a key role in determining the attractiveness of tax-exempt securities to different investors. Given an investor's marginal tax bracket, the break-even return on tax-exempts can be determined as follows:

$$RTE = RT(1 - t) \; ,$$

where

$$RTE = \text{the tax-exempt rate}$$
$$RT = \text{the interest rate on comparable taxable investments}$$
$$t = \text{the investor's marginal tax rate.}$$

According to this formula, tax-exempt securities are attractive when the yield on them equals or exceeds the after-tax yield on comparable taxable securities.

Conceptually, the aggregate demand for tax-exempts can be portrayed as a supply-of-funds schedule, as in Figure 19.10. Given the yield on taxable investments, each segment of this schedule represents the supply of funds (the demand for tax-exempts) from investors facing a specific marginal income tax rate. This schedule indicates that the supply of funds increases if the tax-exempt rate rises relative to taxable rates; in other words, at higher tax-exempt rates, tax-exempts become more attractive to investors facing lower tax rates. This conceptual framework provides a useful basis for understanding the major trends in demand that have occurred over the past two decades, including the effects of changes in federal tax laws.

The demand for tax-exempts has been concentrated among the three sectors that have faced high marginal income tax rates: commercial banks, property and casualty insurance companies, and high-income individuals. Trends in the holdings of the outstanding stock of tax-exempts by these sectors are displayed in Figure 19.11.

In the late 1960s and early 1970s, bank demand was especially strong and the commercial banking sector owned over 50 percent of outstanding tax-exempts in 1971–1973. Since then, the share of tax-exempts held by banks has declined, and in 1985 they owned only 32 percent of the outstanding stock. Overall, bank demand has been closely tied to bank profitability; tax-exempts have been attractive only when there have been significant profits to be sheltered from the full corporate tax rate.

Until recently, bank demand has also been influenced by banks' ability to engage in a form of "tax arbitrage." Unique among all investor groups, commercial banks

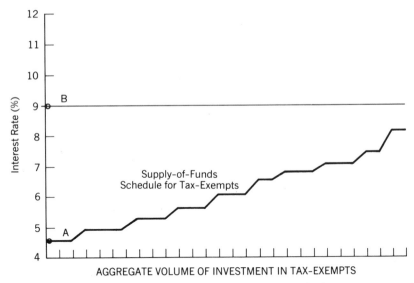

Figure 19.10. The supply of funds from investors (Note: Given the interest rate on taxable investments (Point B, or 9 percent in the schedule, the supply of funds to the tax-exempt market is upward-sloping. Each segment represents the demand for tax-exempt interest by investors in a specific marginal tax bracket, and the segments are ordered (from left to right) from the maximum tax rate to lower rates. In the schedule, Point A represents the demand for tax-exempts from investors in the 50 percent bracket (i.e., break-even tax-exempt rate of 4.5 percent).)

have been allowed to deduct from their taxable income the interest expenses on debt (e.g., time deposits) incurred to purchase tax-exempts. As a result, banks had incentives to borrow and buy tax-exempts as long as the after-tax cost of debt remained below the tax-exempt interest rate. Commercial bank demand also has been conditioned by state regulations, the most important of which have been pledging or collateral requirements for public deposits. Many states require banks to collateralize public deposits with in-state tax-exempts; in states with these requirements, bank demand evidences significant local preferences.

Property and casualty company demand for tax-exempts grew from 1969 through 1980 with their share of the outstanding stock increasing from 11.3 to 22.9 percent. Since 1980, casualty company demand has declined, and by 1985 this segment held only 12 percent of outstanding tax-exempts. Demand from casualty companies, like bank demand, has been primarily a function of industry profitability; the recent declines in demand reflect the significant industrywide losses from insurance underwriting.

When banks and insurance companies do purchase tax-exempts, they have tended to concentrate their portfolios in securities that meet institutional preferences for specific maturities and risk/return characteristics. Bank portfolio composition has emphasized short-term, higher-rated securities, and maturities of 10 years or less traditionally have been referred to as "bank-range" securities. Property and casualty insurance companies, on the other hand, typically have concentrated their holdings in long-term maturities with higher yields and lower ratings; these institutions have been especially important in the markets for long-term revenue bonds.

Given the supply of tax-exempts and the demand for them from banks and insurance companies, any remaining net supply has been absorbed by individuals. With the decline in demand by banks and insurance companies since 1980, holdings of tax-exempts by the household sector have increased from $89.9 billion or 25.5 percent of outstanding tax-exempts to $301.6 billion or 41.9 percent of the stock in 1985.

The need to attract a larger proportion of individual investors has required significant adjustment in the marketing of new tax-exempts. An example of the ability of the tax-exempt market to adapt to changing market conditions can be noted in the growth of unit trusts and mutual funds, both of which are designed to provide portfolio diversification in small denominations.

Unit trusts are investment companies that purchase and hold a fixed portfolio of tax-exempts—in effect, these companies are analogous to closed-end funds with unmanaged portfolios. Investors purchase undivided interests (units) in the trust, and the trust passes through to them the principal and interest on the securities in the portfolio. Estimated unit trust assets at the end of 1985 amounted to $85 billion.

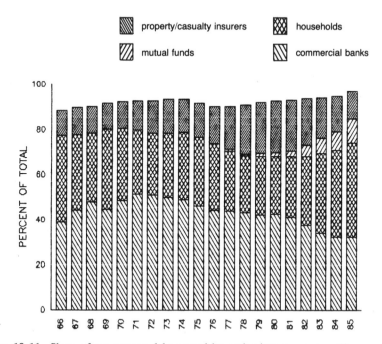

Figure 19.11. Share of tax-exempt debt owned by major investor sectors (*Source*: Board of Governors of the Federal Reserve System, *Flow of Funds*, 1986.)

Open-end, or managed, mutual funds that specialize in tax-exempts held $76 billion in assets at year-end 1985. Managed funds have been developed to offer individuals a broad array of targeted portfolios, including high-risk, high-return portfolios, and short-term, tax-exempt money market funds.

THE BEHAVIOR OF TAX-EXEMPT INTEREST RATES

Figure 19.12 traces the history of yields on 30-year and 1-year maturities of prime-rated tax-exempts over the past two decades. Yields generally increased throughout the late 1960s, then remained on a plateau over most of the 1970s. Beginning in late 1979, yields ratcheted upward, reaching an all-time high of 12.75 percent on 30-year maturities in September 1981. By September 1986, long-term yields had fallen to 6.85 percent and 1-year yields had dropped to 4.25 percent.

The data in Figure 19.12 point to an interesting and unique feature of the tax-exempt market: long-term yields have consistently exceeded short-term rates. The positive slope of the yield curve in the tax-exempt market stands in marked contrast to the behavior of the yield-to-maturity curve in taxable markets. From 1979 through 1981, for example, the average yield differential between 30-year and 1-year U.S. Treasury securities was a negative 116 basis points; for tax-exempts, the average

Figure 19.12. Yields on short-term and long-term tax-exempts, 1966–1983 (*Source*: Salomon Brothers, *An Analytical Record of Yields and Yield Spreads*; data are based on prime municipals, defined as AAA-rated general obligations.)

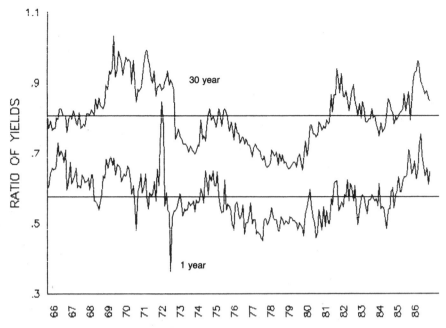

Figure 19.13. The ratio of tax-exempt yields to taxable prime municipals versus U.S. Treasuries (*Source*: Salomon Brothers, *An Analytical Record of Yields and Yield Spreads*; data based on 30-year and 1-year maturity of prime municipals and U.S. Treasuries.)

for the same period was a positive 188 basis points. The persistent upward-sloping yield curve on tax-exempts is generally attributed to the nature of demand in this market. As noted earlier, banks and property/casualty companies have expressed consistent preferences for different ends of the maturity spectrum. Depending on the strength of demand from these institutions, any excess supply of tax-exempts has been marketed to individuals. Most market observers believe that this excess supply systematically increases with maturity. Most also believe that the marginal investors in longer-term tax-exempts have lower incomes and tax rates than investors in short-term securities; therefore, investors in long-term bonds require higher tax-exempt yields to earn returns equivalent to after-tax returns on taxable investments.

Lending support to this view of a segmented market, the data in Figure 19.13 compare the ratios of tax-exempt and taxable yields for different maturities, indicating that the long-term yield ratio has always exceeded the short-term ratio. Moreover, trends in these yield ratios also conform to broad changes in demand by investor sectors. In the long-term market, for example, the downward drift in the yield ratio from 1970 to 1979 parallels the growth of property/casualty insurance company demand. Since 1980, the yield ratio has jumped, which has corresponded to the declining demand from institutions and the increased role of individuals.

Also adding upward pressure on the yield ratios since 1981 has been the significant reduction in marginal tax rates resulting from the Economic Recovery Tax Act of

1981. In the context of the supply-of-funds schedule, the general lowering of tax rates shifted the schedule up; at the new lower tax rates, investors require higher tax-exempt yields to break even with respect to the (higher) after-tax returns on taxable investments.

The pronounced upward trend in the yield ratio on short-term instruments since 1983 also has been influenced by recently enacted limitations on bank interest deductions. The Tax Equity and Fiscal Responsibility Act of 1982 limited bank deductions to 85 percent of the interest expenses of funds used to purchase tax-exempts after 1982. The Deficit Reduction Act of 1984 further limited bank interest deductions to 80 percent for tax-exempts purchased after 1984. The recent tax reform legislation removes all interest deductions (with minor exceptions) for tax-exempts purchased after August 1986. Other aspects of tax reform legislation promise more far-reaching changes in the tax-exempt market which are discussed in the final section of this chapter.

The general upward drift in interest rates over the past two decades has been accompanied by a dramatic increase in the volatility of bond yields. Figure 19.14 records the month-to-month changes in yields on 30-year maturities. Prior to 1979, the monthly changes in yields rarely exceeded 20 basis points. Since 1979, however, monthly yield changes have averaged more than 55 basis points (both positive and negative changes) and moves of 100 basis points have not been uncommon.

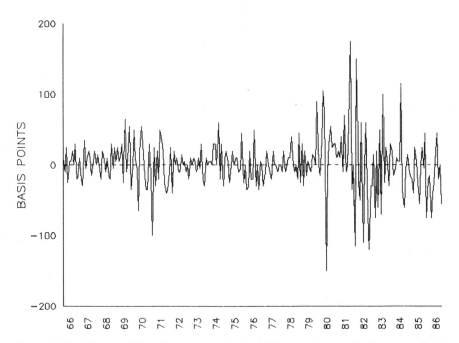

Figure 19.14. The volatility of tax-exempt bond yields: month-to-month changes in basis points (*Source*: Salomon Brothers, *An Analytical Record of Yields and Yield Spreads*; data based on 30-year maturities of prime municipals.)

This volatility has been vexing to issuers, investors, and underwriters, and it has focused attention on the timing of new issues. Although new tax-exempts are exempt from the registration requirements of the Securities and Exchange Commission, the formal steps required to bring a new issue to the market may take up to three months to conclude.

New issues must be legally authorized by the issuing government, which sometimes requires voter approval or public hearings. Moreover, the level of disclosure required in official statements, including audited financial statements, requires time to complete. Some issuers that are frequent borrowers complete these presale activities and then proceeded to accept bids from underwriters "over the wire" when "windows" of market opportunity appear. Most often, these sales have been arranged through existing relationships with underwriters of negotiated debt issues.

THE ROLE OF INVESTMENT BANKERS IN THE NEW-ISSUE PROCESS

Standing between the issuers of tax-exempt securities and the investors who buy them are providers of financial services, including investment banking firms. Most investment banks provide complete packages for the primary market sale of a new debt issue, including origination services, underwriting, and distribution.

Origination (or financial advisory) services refer generally to the range of presale activities necessary to prepare a new issue for the primary market. Underwriting is a risk-bearing service that protects issuers from adverse price changes during the period when new issues are being sold. Distribution services include the activities (and costs) involved in selling and delivering securities to investors. In most investment banking firms, these functions are provided through specialized departments and personnel, coordinated by a central management. Origination services are generally carried out by a public finance banking department; the underwriting division assumes primary responsibility for the initial pricing of a new issue. Distribution falls to the sales and trading division, which also manages the secondary market activities of the firm.

Investment banking firms face competition not only from other investment banks but also from commercial banks and independent financial advisory firms. Although the Glass–Steagall Act of 1933 divided commercial banking from investment banking, the legislation did allow banks to underwrite and trade in U.S. government securities and in tax-supported general obligations of state and local governments. In 1968, the Housing and Urban Development Act permitted banks to underwrite tax-exempt revenue bonds for housing, higher education, and dormitories. In these market segments, commercial banks offer a full line of financial services in competition with investment banks. Commercial banks can also contract as financial advisors with any issuer in the tax-exempt market. Independent financial advisory firms, which do not trade or underwrite tax-exempts, also compete with banks in providing origination services.

Until 1975, commercial banks and investment banks acting as underwriters, brokers, or dealers in tax-exempts were subject only to the general antifraud provisions of the federal securities laws; the comprehensive regulatory system developed for other sectors of the capital market did not apply to tax-exempts. In 1975, however, growing evidence of classic "boiler room" sales tactics and other misrepresentations of securities features spurred Congress to establish the Municipal Securities Rulemaking Board (MSRB). The MSRB is constituted as an independent self-regulatory organization with 15 members, five each from the public, commercial banks, and securities firms. Under the Congressional legislation, the MSRB functions as a rulemaking body; enforcement of its rules is the responsibility of the SEC, the National Association of Securities Dealers, and bank regulatory agencies. To date, the MSRB has enacted rules governing the professional qualifications of personnel in the tax-exempt securities business, transaction-processing activities of firms (e.g., customer account records, confirmations), and syndicate practices, including the role of financial advisors and underwriters.

Financial Advisory Services

Issuers can unbundle the package of services offered by investment banks, and it is not uncommon for them to contract separately for advisory services. Large, frequent borrowers, for example, can perform for themselves many of the functions involved in a primary market sale. Table 19.6 summarizes the advisory services used by issuers, from a recent survey by the Government Finance Research Center. Although most of the services listed by issuers are directly related to a new debt

Table 19.6. Services Provided by Financial Advisors

Services	Number of Governmental Units Using Service	Percentage[a]
Prepares official statement	746	93%
Recommends maturity schedule	708	88
Recommends registration procedures	536	67
Conducts investor relations meeting	363	45
Aids in rating agency presentation	676	84
Verifies bids and aids negotiations	684	85
Analyzes bond sale results	620	77
Analyzes capital budget	98	12
Analyzes debt position	320	40
Analyzes financing options	416	52
Reviews debt management	147	18
Reviews investment strategy	108	13
Prepares annual financial report	110	14
Performs other services	19	2
Total[b]	806	100%

[a] Percentage of respondents using financial advisors who use or have used the service indicated.
[b] Total respondents who use or have used financial advisors.

Source: Government Finance Research Center, *The Price of Advice*, Chicago, IL: Government Finance Officers Association, 1987, p. 29.

Table 19.7. Rankings of Financial Advisors, 1985 (Based on Bonds Sold by Clients)

Rank	Financial Advisor	Total Bond Sales by Clients, 1985 $Billions	Number of Bond Sales by Clients
1	First Southwest Co.[a]	$4.96	191
2	Lazard Freres[b]	3.50	37
3	Prudential-Bache[b]	2.61	38
4	Public Financial Management[a]	1.94	35
5	PaineWebber[b]	1.79	38
6	James J. Lowery	1.56	17
7	Lex Jolley	1.33	5
8	Merrill Lynch Capital Markets[b]	1.31	14
9	Shearson Lehman Brothers[b]	1.31	33
10	Rotan Mosle, Inc.	1.31	56
11	Wertheim & Co., Inc.	1.29	30
12	Smith Barney, Harris Upham[b]	1.17	12
13	Government Finance Associates	1.11	31
14	M.G. Lewis	.99	6
15	Public Resources, Inc.[a]	.92	12
16	Seattle-Northwest Securities	.92	16
17	Dillon Read & Co.[b]	.85	5
18	Evensen Dodge, Inc.[a]	.79	116
19	Rauscher, Pierce[b]	.72	86
20	M. E. Allison	.61	18
21	First National Bank of Chicago[b]	.60	4
22	Interfirst Bank	.58	7
23	Boettcher & Co.[b]	.51	37
24	Caine, Gressel, Midgley, Slater[a]	.50	29
25	Chemical Bank[b]	.47	32

[a] Financial advisory services only.

[b] Firm is also ranked in top 50 senior managers.

Source: Public Securities Association, Dealer's Digest: IDD Information Services/PSA Municipal Database.

sale, the range of services can be grouped into four categories: (1) advice on financial plans and debt policy; (2) technical assistance in structuring new debt; (3) information dissemination; and (4) monitoring. As general financial consultants, advisors may assist issuers in developing capital plans, in analyzing debt and nondebt financing alternatives, and in reviewing debt and investment management policies. As technical consultants, advisors participate in the structuring of new debt issues, in selecting the timing for sales, and in determining the method of sale—competitive bid or negotiation. As information agents, advisors conduct meetings with investors and rating agencies, and they prepare the official statements (or prospectuses) used to discloses relevant information to investors. As monitoring agents, advisors review the proposed terms of sale presented by underwriters.

Table 19.7 shows the top 25 financial advisors for 1985, based on the total volume of bonds issued by their clients in that year. Of these 25 firms, five are specialist firms providing only advisory services. Of the remaining 20 firms, 11 also rank among the top 50 firms in senior managed underwritings, including Merrill Lynch Capital Markets and Smith Barney, which are ranked first and third as senior managers. These rankings suggest that issuers may prefer as financial advisors firms that also have direct experience in the underwriting and distribution of new tax-exempt issues.

Methods of Sale: Competitive Bidding versus Negotiation

As noted earlier, most new issues of tax-exempts are sold through a formal underwriting, either by competitive bid or by negotiation. As the data in Table 19.8 indicate, the method of sale depends to a significant degree on the type of security and the use of proceeds. Ninety-four percent of revenue bonds are sold through negotiation, while tax-supported bonds are divided more evenly between competitive bid and negotiation. Table 19.8 also indicates that debt issues for traditional, government-owned, capital projects are sold more often through competitive bid, while private-purpose bond issues most often are sold by negotiation. More than 50 percent of the tax-supported bonds for elementary and secondary schools, water and sewer projects, and governmental multipurpose bonds are sold competitively, for example, while more than 80 percent of the revenue bonds sold for colleges, housing and hospitals, and industrial development are sold through negotiation.

The preference for negotiated issues is in some instances related to the complex cash flow tests that must be completed at the time of bond sale. These tests are especially important in the case of advance refunding bond issues and mortgage revenue bonds. The proceeds of these issues normally are invested in portfolios of securities—in U.S. Treasury securities for refundings, and in mortgages, for housing bonds. Federal regulations on arbitrage (discussed in Chapter 21) require extensive cash flow tests to prove that the maximum earnings rate on the asset portfolio does not exceed the allowable spread over the present value interest cost of the bond issue. Moreover, rating agencies require detailed cash flow studies to determine that the timing of cash flows from the asset portfolio matches the timing of cash flows for debt service. Investment bankers have developed extensive software to carry out these tests and outside consultants are often employed to verify the results.

The high frequency of competitive bidding on tax-supported bond issues is partly a consequence of state laws that require it. Competitive bidding may also be selected by elected government officials as a method to signal voters that management has been effective in minimizing capital costs. For private-purpose bonds, the choice of sale method may be less important because achieving access to the lower-cost tax-exempt market is itself a signal.

In a competitive sale, the issuer solicits bids through the dissemination of the official notice of sale, which specifies the terms and conditions that underwriters must follow in submitting bids. Among the details supplied in the notice of sale are the time and place for bids, the schedule of bond principal maturities, the basis for awarding the sale, and the coupon constraints or other bid restrictions.

Table 19.8. The Frequency of Competitive and Negotiated Sales by Use of Proceeds and Type of Security, 1985

| | Tax-Supported Bonds | | | Revenue Bonds | | |
| | Total New Issues ($Billions) | Percentage Sold by: | | Total New Issues ($Billions) | Percentage Sold by: | |
		Competitive Bid	Negotiation		Competitive Bid	Negotiation
Total By Use of Proceeds:	$53.50	45.8%	54.2%	$162.81	6.1%	93.9%
Education	5.51	65.2	34.8	11.05	13.0	87.0
Elementary/secondary	4.54	68.9	31.1	.76	31.6	68.4
College/university	.59	35.9	64.1	7.08	15.8	84.2
Transportation	2.48	52.0	48.0	9.48	12.6	87.4
Highway	1.20	49.2	50.8	3.52	1.5	98.5
Ports/airports	.50	18.1	81.9	4.37	14.9	85.1
Utilities	3.73	71.6	28.4	23.41	17.9	82.1
Water/sewer	2.61	72.1	27.9	6.61	25.7	74.3
Electric	.11	36.4	63.6	10.29	15.0	85.0
Social welfare	4.18	59.9	40.1	57.39	4.2	95.8
Housing	1.02	74.5	25.5	35.18	4.0	96.0
Hospital	.25	37.5	62.5	14.85	3.3	96.7
Industrial development	.05	37.0	63.0	13.77	13.5	86.5
Governmental multipurpose	15.42	56.0	44.0	5.40	8.4	91.6
Refunding	19.46	21.7	78.3	38.99	6.1	93.9

Source: Public Securities Association, Dealer's Digest; IDD Information Services/PSA Municipal Database.

The principal of the Initial Bond will come due and mature on June 1 in each year, with installments of principal payable and maturing as follows:

Year	Principal Amount	Year	Principal Amount	Year	Principal Amount
1987	$110,000	1994	$190,000	2001	$325,000
1988	120,000	1995	205,000	2002	355,000
1989	130,000	1996	225,000	2003	380,000
1990	140,000	1997	240,000	2004	410,000
1991	150,000	1998	260,000	2005	450,000
1992	165,000	1999	280,000	2006	485,000
1993	175,000	2000	305,000		

CONDITIONS OF THE SALE

Types of Bids and Interest Rates. The Initial Bond will be sold in one block on an "All of None" basis, and at a price of not less than its par value plus accrued interest to the date of delivery of the Initial Bond. Bidders are invited to name the rate(s) of interest to be borne by each installment of principal of the Initial Bond, provided that each rate bid must be in a multiple of ⅛of 1% or ¹⁄₂₀ of 1% and the net effective interest rate must not exceed 15%. The highest rate bid may not exceed the lowest rate bid by more than 3% in rate. No limitation is imposed upon bidders as to the number of rates or changes which may be used. Each installment of principal (maturity) must bear one and the same rate.

Figure 19.15. Excerpts from notice of sale and bidding instructions on $5,100,000 North Texas Municipal Water District Regional Wastewater System revenue bonds, Series 1986, selling Thursday, May 29, 1986, at 2:00 PM, CDT

For underwriters, determination of the lowest-cost bid can be complex because of the constraints imposed by issuers. For example, the notice of sale for the North Texas Municipal Water District (Figure 19.15) imposes a limitation of 3 percent on the spread between the highest and lowest coupon rates. In markets where the slope of the yield curve exceeds 3 percent, or 300 basis points, this constraint can force underwriters to offer some bonds at a premium and others at a discount. The notice of sale for the New Hanover County bonds, in Figure 19.16 imposes an ascending coupon schedule on the bid, but it limits to six the number of different coupon rates on the serial bonds that mature from 1989 to 2011. Again, this constraint requires underwriters to price bonds at premium or discount.

The multiplicity of bidding restrictions imposed by issuers has led underwriters to develop sophisticated computer software to design optimal coupon strategies. In submitting as competitive bid, underwriters also set coupons and yields such that the expected market value of the bond issue exceeds the amount of proceeds required by the borrower. This difference is the expected underwriting spread. Most bond issues sold competitively are awarded on an all-or-none basis—that is, the winning bidder must purchase the entire bond issue.

In a negotiated sale, issuers select managing underwriters, often as the result of a competition in response to requests for proposals. If more than one firm is selected, a senior manager will be appointed to negotiate simultaneously with the issuer and the other syndicate members. With the issuer, the key terms negotiated include the structure of the debt issue and the gross underwriting spread. Senior managers allocate the gross spread among four categories: (1) management fees (2) expenses (3) underwriting fees, and (4) sales discounts. Management fees compensate the senior manager and the co-managers, if any, for origination and advisory services. Expenses include outlays by the manager on behalf of the issuer, such as fees for legal counsel, bond printing costs, mailing and printing of bond prospectuses, and rating agency fees. Underwriting fees represent compensation for the market risks in a fixed-price underwriting with fees allocated to underwriting members of the syndicate in proportion to each firm's predetermined liability for unsold bonds.

Members of the underwriting group or selling group earn sales commissions— in the trade, the initial takedown—for actual sales to nonsyndicate dealer firms or

Bidders are requested to name the interest rate or rates in multiples of ¼ or ⅒ of 1%, and each bidder must specify in his bid the amount and the maturities of the bonds of each rate. No interest rate named for any given maturity may be lower than any interest rate named for any prior maturity. No bid may name more than six interest rates. All bonds maturing on the same date must bear interest at the same rate. The bonds will be awarded to the bidder offering to purchase the bonds at the lowest interest cost to the District, such cost to be determined by deducting the total amount of any premium bid from the aggregate amount of interest upon all of the bonds from their date until their respective maturities. No bid of less than par and accrued interest will be entertained.

Year of Maturity	Principal Amount	Year of Maturity	Prinicipal Amount
1989	$225,000	2001	$460,000
1990	225,000	2002	495,000
1991	225,000	2003	530,000
1992	240,000	2004	570,000
1993	255,000	2005	615,000
1994	275,000	2006	660,000
1995	300,000	2007	710,000
1996	320,000	2008	765,000
1997	340,000	2009	825,000
1998	370,000	2010	875,000
1999	395,000	2011	900,000
2000	425,000		

Figure 19.16. Excerpts from notice of sale, $11,000,000, New Hanover County Water and Sewer District, North Carolina, sanitary sewer bonds series 1986

to final investors. Syndicate practices generally permit members to pass on a portion of the initial takedown—the dealer concession—to nonsyndicate dealers. Moreover, the concession is sometimes used as a form of "selective underpricing" where institutional investors with large orders can receive discounts from published reoffer prices by purchasing bonds at the concession.

The senior manager also determines (1) the number and mix of firms that will be invited to participate as underwriters or as members of a selling group; (2) the level of underwriting participation; (3) the underwriting fee; and (4) the takedown and concession. These terms are negotiated prior to the signing of the bond purchase contract with the issuer, and the formal contract among syndicate members is the "Agreement among Underwriters." Under Rule G-11 of the Municipal Securities Rulemaking Board (MSRB), the management fee must be disclosed to syndicate members prior to the signing of the bond purchase contract with the issuer.

At the time of sale, the role of the senior manager is similar to that of an auctioneer in a call auction market. The manager announces initial terms (e.g., coupons, prices) for the bond issue and opens the "book" to receive orders for a specified period—the order period. During the order period, the senior manager compiles orders and compares these with the amounts offered; if necessary, the bonds are repriced and offered at a revised auction. An important task of the senior or "book" manager is to preserve order priority. Group orders from institutional investors generally receive the highest priority. These orders are submitted on behalf of the entire syndicate, that is, the sales commissions are allocated among all underwriters according to their participation. Other types of orders that receive priority over member takedown orders include designated orders where an institutional investor designates the commissions to a subset of the underwriters, and group orders at the concession. Under Rule G-11 of the MSRB, these order priorities must be established by the senior manager prior to the first offering of the securities. Moreover, Rule G-11 also requires the senior manager to furnish all members with a postsale report of orders by priority.

Table 19.9 reports the average gross underwriting spread for competitively sold and negotiated water and sewer revenue bonds issued in the first three quarters of 1986. As the table indicates, the average gross spread on negotiated issues ($16.80

Table 19.9. Average Underwriting Spreads Competitive and Negotiated Sales of Water and Sewer Revenue Bonds 1986[a]

	Competitive	Negotiated
Gross underwriting spread	$13.65	$16.80
Management fee	N/A	2.78
Underwriting fee	2.65	.90
Sales discount	10.00	10.31
Expenses	1.00	2.80

[a] Amounts expressed in dollars per $1000 par value of bonds.

Source: Public Securities Association, Dealer's Digest: IDD Information Services/PSA Municipal Database.

per $1000 par value of bonds) is higher than the average on competitive issues ($13.65 per $1000). Most of this difference is explained by the management fee on negotiated issues, which compensates the senior manager and co-managers for origination and advisory services. The origination services required for negotiated financings are also reflected in the higher level of expenses ($2.83 vs. $1.00) relative to competitively sold issues. Partly offsetting the cost of these origination services is the ability of the senior manager to reprice a negotiated financing, which lowers the underwriting risk relative to competitively bid issues. This is reflected in the lower underwriting fee ($.90 vs. $2.65) on negotiated sales.

Rankings of investment banking firms are widely used as indicators of market share and Table 19.10 reports the rankings of the top 10 firms in 1985. The table also reports the rankings of these firms since 1979, determined by assigning the total par value of each issue to the senior manager. These rankings indicate the origination strengths of various firms. In 1985, the top 10 senior managers brought $115.5 billion in new tax-exempt bonds to the market, representing 57 percent of total new-issue volume. Table 19.10 suggests that investment banking has become somewhat more concentrated, because these firms accounted for only 49 percent of all new issues in 1979. The market share of the largest firm, Merrill Lynch Capital Markets, in 1984 amounted to 15.3 percent of the market. By contrast, the leading firm in 1979—Salomon Brothers—managed only 8.65 percent of all new issues.

Overall, membership in the top 10 has been consistent over the past seven years, even though individual firms have moved up or down in rank. Merrill Lynch jumped in rank from seven in 1979 to number one in 1982 and it has retained the top position since then. Goldman Sachs has consistently held down the number two or three ranking, and Smith Barney has consistently remained among the top six firms. Although commercial banks were not among the top 10 firms in 1985, four banks were ranked among the top 20 including Citicorp (11), Bankers Trust (13), Morgan Guaranty Trust (15), and Chase Manhattan (20). The absence of commercial banks from the top tier of senior managers is one consequence of the rapid growth in revenue bonds that banks are not allowed to underwrite. By contrast, commercial banks have retained their traditional role as senior managers in those segments where they are permitted to underwrite. Table 19.11 reports rankings of senior managers for competitively sold tax-supported bonds of local governments. Commercial banks are not only ranked first and second, but they also hold eight of the top 10 spots.

THE IMPACT OF TAX REFORM FOR THE TAX-EXEMPT MARKET AND INVESTMENT BANKING

After two decades of extraordinary change and growth, the tax-exempt market is about to be reshaped in fundamental ways by the Tax Reform Act of 1986. Discussed in detail in Chapter 21, this legislation will alter significantly the demand for tax-exempts by investors and the supply of new issues from borrowers.

Table 19.10. Rankings of Investment Banking Firms by Volume of Senior-Managed Financings[a]

	1985	1984	1983	1982	1981	1980	1978
Rank							
Merrill Lynch Capital Markets	1	1	1	1	2	4	7
Goldman, Sachs	2	3	3	2	3	2	2
Smith Barney, Harris Upham	3	4	5	4	6	6	3
Salomon Brothers	4	2	2	3	1	1	1
First Boston Corp.	5	8	8	7	4	5	4
Kidder Peabody	6	5	6	8	9	9	8
Shearson Lehman Brothers[b]	7	6	#	#	#	#	#
PaineWebber[c]	8	9	7	6	7	7	##
E.F. Hutton	9	7	4	5	5	3	5
Prudential-Bache	10	12	10	14	14	15	10
Amount Managed ($Billions)							
Merrill Lynch Capital Markets	22.98	15.76	10.79	7.34	5.07	2.61	1.81
Goldman, Sachs	20.01	7.57	6.74	6.67	2.61	4.45	2.95
Smith Barney, Harris Upham	13.85	6.39	4.11	5.59	2.21	2.08	2.44
Salomon Brothers	12.35	7.70	7.28	6.48	5.18	4.65	3.74
First Boston Corp.	12.34	3.74	2.88	3.06	2.51	2.47	2.25
Kidder Peabody	10.06	5.94	3.19	2.38	1.35	1.45	1.65
Shearson Lehman Brothers[b]	9.71	5.29	4.37	3.99	1.95	1.33	.57
PaineWebber[c]	8.65	3.25	2.97	3.34	1.93	2.05	2.64
E.F. Hutton	8.00	4.92	4.24	4.35	2.38	2.61	2.05
Prudential-Bache	5.55	2.01	2.22	1.57	.78	.77	1.19
Total	115.5	54.87	48.79	44.77	25.97	24.47	21.29

Market Share (Percentage of Total Dollar Volume)

Merrill Lynch Capital Markets	10.62	15.34	12.48	9.28	10.59	5.38	4.19
Goldman, Sachs	9.25	7.37	7.79	8.43	5.45	9.17	6.82
Smith Barney, Harris Upham	6.40	6.22	4.75	7.06	4.62	4.29	5.64
Salomon Brothers	5.71	7.49	8.42	8.19	10.82	9.58	8.65
First Boston Corp.	5.70	3.64	3.33	3.87	5.24	5.09	5.20
Kidder Peabody	4.65	5.78	3.69	3.01	2.82	2.99	3.82
Shearson Lehman Brothers[b]	4.49	5.15	5.05	5.04	4.07	2.74	1.32
PaineWebber[c]	4.00	3.16	3.43	4.22	4.03	4.22	6.11
E.F. Hutton	3.70	4.79	4.90	5.50	4.97	5.38	4.74
Prudential-Bache	2.57	1.96	2.57	1.98	1.63	1.59	2.75
Total	57.10	60.88	56.41	56.57	54.26	50.41	49.24

[a] Rankings are determined by assigning the par value of each issue to the senior manager.

[b] Amounts, rank, and market share for Shearson and Lehman as separate firms are:

	1983	1982	1981	1980	1979
Rank:					
Shearson	12	13	22	23	N/A
Lehman Brothers	11	9	8	13	19
Amount managed:					
Shearson	2.18	1.75	.54	.45	N/A
Lehman Brothers	2.19	2.24	1.41	.87	.53
Market share:					
Shearson	2.52	2.21	1.13	.93	N/A
Lehman Brothers	2.53	2.83	2.95	1.79	1.22

[c] Amounts, rank, and market share for PaineWebber and Blyth, Eastman as separate firms:

	Rank	Amount	Market Share
Paine Webber	14	.82	1.89
Blyth, Eastman	6	1.82	4.21

Source: Public Securities Association, Dealer's Digest: IDD Information Service/PSA Municipal Database.

Table 19.11. Senior Manager Rankings, Local Government General Obligations Competitive New Issues, 1985

	Amount ($Millions)	Rank	Market Share (Percentage)
Citicorp	1344	1	12.1
Chase	771	2	6.9
Prudential-Bache	756	3	6.8
Merrill Lynch Capital Markets	610	4	5.5
Morgan Guaranty Trust	603	5	5.4
Chemical Bank	580	6	5.2
Northern Trust	443	7	4.1
Continental Illinois	392	8	3.5
Bankers Trust	365	9	3.3
First National Bank of Chicago	342	10	3.1

Source: Public Securities Association, Dealer's Digest: IDD Information Services/PSA Municipal Database.

On the demand site, the Tax Reform Act of 1986 provides for major revisions in marginal tax rates on income. The new tax rate structure, which becomes fully effective in 1988, reduces the present structure of 14 marginal rates to two, and lowers the maximum rate from 50 to 28 percent. The Tax Reform Act also reduces the top corporate rate from 46 to 34 percent. These reductions will shift the supply-of-funds schedule upward as tax-exempt yields adjust to the higher after-tax return available on taxable investments.

The legislation also puts an end to deductibility of bank interest expenses for tax-exempts purchased after 1986 (except for small issues). As noted earlier, previous legislation reduced bank tax arbitrage with the result that short-term tax-exempt rates increased relative to taxable interest rates. The complete removal of bank tax arbitrage opportunities should further increase the ratio of short-term tax-exempt yields to taxable yields, resulting in a less-pronounced upward slope for the tax-exempt yield curve. Moreover, future changes in the slope of the tax-exempt yield curve can be expected to mirror more closely the taxable market, implying that the next cyclical peak in interest rates may generate a negatively sloped tax-exempt yield curve.

At the same time, the Tax Reform Act of 1986 eliminates many other tax-advantaged investments or limits their use, which will indirectly increase the demand for tax-exempts by individuals.

On the supply side, the Tax Reform Act of 1986 introduces significant restrictions on the issuance of private-purpose bonds. Pollution control projects of private firms, sports and convention facilities, parking facilities, and industrial parks will no longer have access to the tax-exempt market. Private colleges and universities and nonprofit organizations other than hospitals are limited to a maximum of $150 million per entity in outstanding tax-exempt debt. Other private-purpose bonds, including single-family and multi-family mortgage bonds, are subject to restrictive volume limitations. Collectively, these bonds are limited by state to $75 per capita or $250 million, whichever is greater, in 1987, and the greater of $50 per capita or $150 million in 1988 and beyond. Based on studies by the Public Securities Association, the application of these limits to the actual volume of bonds sold in 1984 would reduce new issues by $30 billion under the 1988 rules. Other limitations restrict the use of advance refundings by government borrowers and tighten the permissible arbitrage earnings on tax-exempt bond proceeds.

In addition to limiting aggregate volume, the Tax Reform Act of 1986 also places limits on the use of bond proceeds to pay costs of issuance. Applied to all private-purpose bonds, this legislation limits underwriters' spreads, bond counsel fees, financial advisory fees, rating agency fees, printing costs, and other enumerated expenses to 2 percent of bond proceeds. Prior to this legislation, most issuers borrowed a major portion of these costs, which amounted, on average, to approximately 3 percent of bond proceeds. Many issuers and investment bankers perceive this provision of the Tax Reform Act to be a form of price control that may significantly constrain new debt offerings.

Although the Tax Reform Act will reduce the volume of new issues, its impact on investment banking is less certain. Many issuers of tax-exempt debt are developing plans to borrow in taxable markets, including the Eurobond market. For these issuers and their new debts, the origination services offered by investment bankers may be of even greater importance. Investment banking firms that can offer a full range of financing options, including access to international capital markets, will have a competitive advantage with these issuers. As a result, it is likely that the Tax Reform Act will have the indirect effect of increasing the concentration of market share in public finance.

20 Innovations in Tax-Exempt Finance

RONALD W. FORBES

In recent years, borrowers have entered the tax-exempt market with new financing vehicles designed to raise funds for capital projects at lower costs than conventional debt issues. Many of these innovations have been responses to the high levels and increased volatility of interest rates since 1980. In other instances, new methods of borrowing have been designed to circumvent restrictions imposed by statutory or constitutional limits on conventional debt offerings by state and local governments. Much of what is seen as creative in financing can be described more as a "repackaging" of the future cash flows promised to investors. From this perspective, it is useful to review first the "traditional" package of cash flows associated with conventional debt issues and the factors that stimulated the search for alternatives to this traditional package.

As a starting point, Figure 20.1 presents the key features of a recent, but traditional, revenue bond issue for the Atlanta and Fulton County Recreation Authority. This is a conventional "package": the $16 million bond issue is structured with serial-bond principal maturities extending from 1986 to 2007. Figure 20.2 presents the annual cash flows for interest expense and the repayment of bond principal; these annual debt service payments of the Recreation Authority are essentially level over the 22-year term of the bond issue. Viewed as a package, the $16 million bond issue has been recast into a series of "mini-bonds," ranging from a $310,000 issue maturing in 1986 to a $1.5 million issue maturing in 2007. Characterizing this traditional package are the fixed-coupon rate for each principal maturity, the upward-sloping pattern of coupon rate and initial yield to investors, and the semiannual payment of coupons.

From the perspective of an investor, each part of this package generates yet another and quite different "package" of cash flows. The investor purchasing the bonds maturing in 2007, for example, receives 44 semiannual cash payments of $43.50 per $1000 invested and a final payment, of principal, in the year 2007. This particular pattern of cash flows lost favor with many investors during the first half

NEW ISSUE

In the opinion of Bond Counsel, interest on the Series 1985 Bonds is exempt from present federal income taxation and from present income taxation in the State of Georgia under existing laws, regulations, rulings and court decisions.

$16,000,000

CITY OF ATLANTA AND FULTON COUNTY RECREATION AUTHORITY (GEORGIA)

REVENUE BONDS
ZOO SERIES 1985

Dated: December 1, 1985

Due: December 1st, as shown below

The $16,000,000 City of Atlanta and Fulton County Recreation Authority Revenue Bonds, Zoo Series 1985 (the "Series 1985 Bonds") shall be issued in fully registered form in denominations of $5,000 and any integral multiple thereof. Principal shall be paid on the maturity date to the registered owner upon presentation and surrender of each Series 1985 Bond at the principal corporate trust office of First Georgia Bank, Atlanta, Georgia as paying agent (the "Paying Agent"). Interest shall be payable on June 1, 1986 (representing seven months interest), and semiannually thereafter on June 1 and December 1 of each year to the registered owner by check or draft mailed by first class mail to the address of such owner as it appears on the bond register kept by First Georgia Bank, as bond registrar (the "Bond Registrar") at the close of business on the record date.

The Series 1985 Bonds are subject to optional redemption as provided herein.

The Series 1985 Bonds are being issued by the City of Atlanta and Fulton County Recreation Authority (the "Authority") for the purpose of financing the cost of acquiring, constructing and equipping certain renovations, extensions and improvements to the City of Atlanta—Fulton County Zoo (the "Zoo").

The Series 1985 Bonds are secured by a pledge of the Authority's interest in semiannual payments under an Agreement Regarding The Atlanta Zoo, dated as of December 5, 1985, among the Authority, the City of Atlanta (the "City") and Fulton County, Georgia (the "County") (the "Governmental Agreement"), under which the City is obligated to make payments to the Trustee in amounts sufficient to pay the principal and interest on the Series 1985 Bonds and in certain amounts through January 1, 1993 relating to the operation of the Zoo. The obligation of the City to make such payments is absolute and unconditional. The County has contracted to reimburse the City for one-third of such payments made by the City and such reimbursements shall discharge the County's financial obligations under the Governmental Agreement.

The City covenants in the Governmental Agreement that it shall levy such taxes within the limits now or hereafter prescribed by law as may be necessary to make the payments set forth in the Governmental Agreement, provided the City's duty to levy such taxes shall abate to the extent that its resources from other sources are used to make such payments.

The Series 1985 Bonds do not constitute a debt of the City, the County or of the State of Georgia within the meaning of any constitutional or statutory provision, but shall be payable solely from the revenues pledged to the payment thereof, and the Series 1985 Bonds shall not directly, indirectly or contingently obligate the City, County or the State to levy or to pledge any form of taxation whatever therefor or to make any appropriation for their payment. The Authority has no taxing power.

$16,000,000 Serial Bonds

Amount	Year	Interest Rate	Amount	Year	Interest Rate
$310,000	1986	5.75%	$ 650,000	1997	8.00%
330,000	1987	6.25	700,000	1998	8.10
350,000	1988	6.50	770,000	1999	8.20
370,000	1989	6.70	830,000	2000	8.30
400,000	1990	6.90	900,000	2001	8.40
420,000	1991	7.10	980,000	2002	8.50
450,000	1992	7.30	1,060,000	2003	8.60
490,000	1993	7.50	1,160,000	2004	8.65
520,000	1994	7.65	1,270,000	2005	8.70
560,000	1995	7.80	1,380,000	2006	8.70
600,000	1996	7.90	1,500,000	2007	8.70

Price of all Bonds: 100%

(Accrued interest to be added)

The Series 1985 Bonds are offered when, as and if issued by the Authority and received by the Underwriters, subject to prior sale and to the approval of legality by King & Spalding, Atlanta, Georgia and Lawson, Washington & Thornton, Atlanta, Georgia, Bond Counsel, and the approval of certain legal matters for the Underwriters by their Counsel, Arnall Golden & Gregory, Atlanta, Georgia, Rogers, Horton, Forbes & Teamor, Cleveland, Ohio and Harris C. Bostic, Esq., Atlanta, Georgia. It is expected that the Series 1985 Bonds in definitive form will be available for delivery in New York, New York on or about December 31, 1985.

Drexel Burnham Lambert
Incorporated

Bank South, N.A.

Trust Company Bank

December 13, 1985

Figure 20.1. The key features of a recent, but traditional, revenue bond issue for the Atlanta and Fulton County Recreation Authority

352

$16,000,000
CITY OF ATLANTA AND FULTON COUNTY
RECREATION AUTHORITY (GEORGIA)
REVENUE BONDS
ZOO SERIES 1985

Dated: December 1, 1985   Due: December 1st, as shown below

DEBT SERVICE ON THE SERIES 1985 BONDS

The following table sets forth the scheduled estimated debt service on the Series 1985 Bonds.

Debt Service Schedule

December 1,	Principal	Interest	Total Debt Service
1986	$ 310,000	$ 1,296,050	$ 1,606,050
1987	330,000	1,278,225	1,608,225
1988	350,000	1,257,600	1,607,600
1989	370,000	1,234,850	1,604,850
1990	400,000	1,210,060	1,610,060
1991	420,000	1,182,460	1,602,460
1992	450,000	1,152,640	1,602,640
1993	490,000	1,119,790	1,609,790
1994	520,000	1,083,040	1,603,040
1995	560,000	1,043,260	1,603,260
1996	600,000	999,580	1,599,580
1997	650,000	952,180	1,602,180
1998	700,000	900,180	1,600,180
1999	770,000	843,480	1,613,480
2000	830,000	780,340	1,610,340
2001	900,000	711,450	1,611,450
2002	980,000	635,850	1,615,850
2003	1,060,000	552,550	1,612,550
2004	1,160,000	461,390	1,621,390
2005	1,270,000	361,050	1,631,050
2006	1,380,000	250,560	1,630,560
2007	1,500,000	130,500	1,630,500
	$16,000,000	$19,437,085	$35,437,085

Figure 20.2. The annual cash flows for interest expense and the repayment of bond principal

of the 1980s, because of three pervasive uncertainties associated with the then-volatile market conditions:

Uncertainty over future market value

Uncertainty over future wealth

Uncertainty over future investment quality

The uncertainty of market values is a consequence of the greater volatility of interest rates in recent years. As noted in Chapter 19, month-to-month swings of 100 basis points (one percentage point) are no longer uncommon in today's capital markets. Greater volatility means greater uncertainty over market values.

The volatility of interest rates also has increased uncertainty over future wealth for investors with long-term investment horizons. As will be explained later in this chapter, coupon bonds carry a substantial "built-in" reinvestment risk that has become important to many investors. Finally, investors are concerned with the credit quality of their investments. Deteriorating credit quality diminishes the market value of securities while raising concern over the safety of principal.

To borrowers, two persistent characteristics of the tax-exempt market have stimulated new financing techniques. The first, and most nettlesome, has been the high level of long-term interest rates since 1979–1980. Second, and more tractable, the yield-to-maturity schedule has remained very steeply sloped, with short-term rates well below long-term rates. Figure 20.3 traces both factors since 1975. Yields on 30-year maturities of prime municipals jumped from the 5.5 percent range in 1977 to more than 12.5 percent in 1981–1982. Long-term yields have declined since then, but the average level of the 30-year rate in 1985 was still 9 percent. Figure 20.3 indicates that the yield differential between 30-year and 1-year rates has tended to widen in tandem with increases in the long-term rate. In 1982, for example,

Figure 20.3. 30-year bond yield and yield spread, 30-year verses 1-year bonds (Source: Salomon Brothers, *An Analytical Record of Yields and Yield Spreads.*)

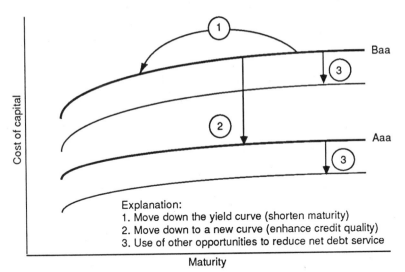

Figure 20.4. Creative financing techniques and the net cost of capital (Explanation: 1. Move down the yield curve (shorten maturity); 2. Move down to a new curve (enhance credit quality); 3. Use of other opportunities to reduce net debt service.)

when long-term rates were at cyclical peaks, the yield differential widened to more than 400 basis points.

As a general guide to the types of innovations that have been developed, "creative financing" techniques can be depicted in the framework of the yield curve as shown in Figure 20.4. A variety of techniques have been designed to shift the cost of borrowing *down* the yield curve, from high-cost, long-term maturities to (initially) lower-cost, short-term maturities. Tax-exempt commercial paper and variable-rate demand bonds are examples. Another technique has been designed to shift the cost of borrowing down to a *lower* yield curve by employing methods of improving the ratings on bonds, such as bond insurance and bank letters of credit. Other innovations attempt to lower the cost of borrowing to governmental units by altering the pattern of cash flows to investors, or by attaching (and exercising) various options to new debt issues. Zero-coupon bonds, put-option bonds, and advance refundings are representative of these innovations.

MOVING BORROWING COSTS DOWNS THE YIELD CURVE: TECP AND VARIABLE-RATE DEMAND BONDS

Historically, governmental units have attempted to capture yield-curve savings by issuing short-term notes with maturities of 3 years or less. Apart from the obvious difference in final maturity, these note sales retained many of the features common to long-term bond sales. Notes typically carried a fixed maturity date and a fixed interest rate. Issues were offered through formal firm-commitment underwritings, quite frequently through competitive bidding. Partly in response to changes in investor demands in the 1980s, other short-term financing instruments have been developed that allow more flexibility than fixed-rate, fixed-term notes. One example is tax-exempt commercial paper (TECP). A transplant from the corporate (taxable) market, TECP is a negotiable, unsecured promissory note with a maturity of 365 days or less.

By contrast with traditional note sales, a TECP program can have a wide variety of maturities outstanding at any point in time. As an example, Table 20.1 lists the maturities for a $7.8 million TECP offering for the Government Development Bank of Puerto Rico in January 1980. At this initial offering, maturities ranged from 29 days to 90 days. As TECP matures, it is commonly "rolled over" or renewed with maturities and rates representative of market conditions at the time. The $3.7 million TECP maturing on February 1, 1980 was reissued on that date with $2.3 million due in 32 days and $1.4 million due in 90 days, on May 1, 1980.

TECP programs effectively permit *the investor*, rather than the borrower, to tailor maturities to his or her investment objectives. This feature has been especially important to select institutional segments, including nonfinancial corporations and mutual funds. Nonfinancial corporations, for example, may accumulate cash or highly liquid financial assets prior to a dividend payment date, and TECP permits tax-free returns with exact maturity dates. Tax-exempt money market mutual funds must hold the bulk of their assets in securities with maturities of 120 days or less. Municipal bond mutual funds require short-term, tax-exempt investments for liquidity to meet redemptions. Bond mutual funds also invest in TECP with maturities scheduled to coincide on the settlement dates for new purchases of long-term bonds. The prevailing practice of immediate (same day) delivery of cash or securities makes TECP a useful tool for tax-free cash management programs.

Issuers of TECP generally do not plan to retire maturing paper; therefore, backup liquidity arrangements are necessary to forestall large, perhaps unexpected, cash demands in the event that maturing paper cannot be refinanced. These liquidity supports (often called "facilities") include bank letters of credit, lines of credit or standby bond purchase agreements, or bond insurance (all to be discussed later). These liquidity facilities do require borrowers to pay fees which add to the "all-in"

Table 20.1. Summary of TECP Maturities, Government Development Bank of Puerto Rico, January 7, 1980 Sale

Amount (000s)	Maturity
$3000	2/1/80
1600	4/2/80
1200	4/2/80
300	3/4/80
1000	2/28/80
700	2/1/80

cost of borrowing, thereby reducing the net savings to borrowers from moving down the yield curve. Offsetting these fees somewhat, dealer fees for marketing TECP range from 1/8 to 3/8 percent of the amount outstanding, or considerably less than the gross underwriting spread charged on a firm-commitment underwriting.

Although its antecedents in the taxable market have functioned well in providing corporate capital for many years, the use of TECP has grown less rapidly. In October 1985, outstanding TECP was estimated at $6.8 billion compared with $281 billion in taxable commercial paper. Additional growth in TECP has been slowed by recent refinancings of outstanding paper with long-term, fixed-rate bonds. Moreover, new issuers of TECP have been deterred by "reissuance risk." Technically, a rollover of maturing TECP constitutes a reissuance—effectively, a new debt issue. The concern over reissuance springs from uncertainties over the tax-exempt status of the debt at the time of rollover—an uncertainty that has been nourished by Congressional tax reform proposals, many of which would ban certain issues and projects permitted under existing laws and regulations.

Variable-rate bonds have been designed to avoid reissuance risks yet retain the interest-rate advantage of short-term instruments. The cardinal characteristics of these instruments are a long-term final maturity date but an interest rate that is "reset" at scheduled intervals. Variable-rate bonds specify daily, weekly, monthly, semiannual, annual, or other periodic interest-rate "reset" intervals.

Original versions of the variable-rate security, often called "floaters," tied the tax-exempt rate to easily available market indices such as the U.S. Treasury bill or bond rate, through a formula. The expectation was that the market value of the debt would remain at or close to par value because the interest payment would reflect current market conditions. The variable-rate security typically contained upper and lower bounds on interest rates ("caps" and "floors") to shield investors and issuers from extreme fluctuations in the market. Figure 20.5 illustrates typical provisions for a formula-based, floating-rate bond. These early versions of variable-

Interest on the Series A Bonds of each issue is payable semi-annually on June 1 and December 1. The interest payable each June 1 and December 1 will be based on a per annum interest rate which is the arithmetic average of all weekly interest indices in effect from the beginning of the interest payment period until five business days before such June 1 or December 1. The interest index determined each week will be the higher of the Short-Term Interest Factor or the Long-Term Interest Factor, determined as set forth below and under "The Bonds". However, each interest index will be subject to a *floor of 6%* and a *ceiling of 14%*.

In general, the *Short-Term Interest Factor is 67%* of the interest rate applicable to thirteen-week United States Treasury ("Treasury") bills and the *Long-Term Interest Factor is 75%* of the interest rate applicable to Treasury securities adjusted to a constant maturity of thirty years.

Figure 20.5. Interest rate indexing provisions on early versions of floating-rate issues (Official Statement, Bucks County Industrial Development Authority, floating-rate environmental improvement revenue bonds, 1980 series A (United States Steel Corporation project).

rate debt encountered problems, however, because the tax-exempt/taxable-yield ratio pegged in the formula (e.g., 67 percent) did not reflect actual market conditions. In 1981–1982, for example, the yield ratio generally exceeded 80 percent; as a result, fixed-formula bonds became unattractive to investors and difficult to sell at the expected par value.

These difficulties prompted the current-day versions of the variable-rate demand bond. These securities are characterized by four distinctive features:

1. A demand feature, that permits investors to redeem their holdings at par at selected intervals.
2. An interest index pegged solely to the tax-exempt market.
3. A remarketing provision which is designed to avoid the need for technical "reissuance" and reduce the probability of drawing down a liquidity facility.
4. A backup source of liquidity or credit enhancement to assure investors of cash on demand.

The demand feature is a form of "put" option, often called a bondholder's tender option, and it is an important component of the variable-rate demand bond. The put option allows an investor the choice of holding an investment or redeeming it at par at specified future intervals. Depending on the frequency of the put-option interval, an investor may convert otherwise long-term maturities into investments with effective maturities as short as one day. In Figure 20.6 the interest-rate "reset" interval is one week. At each interest-rate reset date, the new rate is determined by first calculating an interest index. Pegging the interest index to the tax-exempt market avoids the problems of shifting relationships between tax-exempt and taxable markets. A remarketing agreement backstops the demand feature and provides for a continuous marketing of tendered bonds to new investors.

Figure 20.7 illustrates how a typical remarketing might work. If an investor chooses to exercise the tender option, the bonds are redeemed by that tender agent. Rather than turning to the issuer or a bank liquidity facility for cash, the tender agent first notifies the remarketing agent, who attempts to resell tendered bonds at the new interest rate based on the interest index. The remarketing agent has the flexibility to reset new rates within a prescribed band around the index, in order to reoffer the bonds at par. As new sales occur, the cash is delivered to the tender agent; if all bonds tendered are not remarketed, the remaining cash needs of the tender agent are supplied from the stand-by liquidity facility.

Early versions of variable-rate demand bonds were sold in an "all-or-none" mode; that is, the entire issue was marketed in a single mode, for example, daily, weekly. Many issuers, however, initiated variable-rate bond programs with the intent of refinancing with long-term fixed-rate bonds if and when future long-term rates declined to attractive levels. To avoid the need for a second bond issue (entailing additional underwriting fees), investment bankers and their clients incorporated *conversion* options that permitted borrowers, with advance notice, to convert floating-rate bonds to fixed-rate bonds for the remaining life.

Selected Bond Provisions
Irrevocable Letter of Credit: Citibank, N. A.

Remarketing and Indexing Agent: The First Boston Corporation
Tender Agent: Bankers Trust Company

Adjustable Interest Rate:

Prior to a conversion to a Fixed Interest Rate, interest on the bond will be paid at an Adjustable Interest Rate on the first Business day of each month. The Adjustable Rate Index will be calculated weekly by the Indexing Agent and shall equal the average thirty (30) days or less yield evaluation at par of at least five comparable tax-exempted issues. Interest on the Bonds will be calculated on a 365 or 366 day year and will not exceed 15% per annum.

Bondholders Tender or "Put" Option:

Prior to conversion to a Fixed Interest Rate, each Bondholder shall have the right to demand the purchase of that holder's Bonds on any Business Day which is at least seven days after such demand (the "Purchase Date"), upon presentation of a Bondholder Election Notice to the Tender Agent (or in the case of a Bondholder which is a registered investment company, to the Trustee with a copy to the Tender Agent) at the time of demand.

UNDERWRITERS: The First Boston Corporation
                 Rotan Mosle Inc.

Figure 20.6. Example of variable-rate demand bond provisions: $50,000,000, Texas Health Facilities Development Corporation, adjustable-rate hospital revenue bonds series 1984A, issued May 22, 1984

OVERVIEW OF REMARKETING MECHANICS

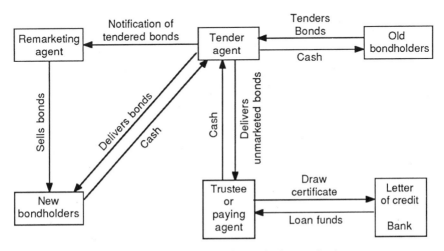

Figure 20.7. Overview of remarketing mechanics

$32,750,000

ILLINOIS HEALTH FACILITIES AUTHORITY
Unit Priced Demand Adjustable
Revenue Bonds
Alexian Brothers Health System, Inc.
(Alexian Brothers Medical Center, Inc. Project)
Series 1985D

Dated: The date of issuance.   Due: January 1 as set forth below

Maturity	Principal Amount		Maturity	Principal Amount
1999	$5,000,000		2012	$5,995,000
2005	5,520,000		2014	5,435,000
2009	5,000,000		2016	5,800,000

Price: 100%

Illinois Health Facilities Authority
Unit Priced Demand Adjustable Revenue Bonds
Alexian Brothers Health System, Inc.
(Alexian Brothers Medical Center, Inc. Project)
Series 1985D

SUMMARY OF INTEREST RATE MODES

	UNIT PRICING MODE	DEMAND MODE	FIXED INTEREST MODE
Interest Payment Date	For Unit Pricing Interest Periods of less than or equal to 180 days: interest paid on the Repurchase Date; for Unit Pricing Interest Periods greater than 180 days: interest paid on each January 1 and July 1 prior to the Repurchase Date and on the Repurchase Date	First Wednesday of each calendar month (whether or not a Business Day); to accrue from the first Wednesday of each month through the Tuesday preceding the first Wednesday of the following month	Each January 1 and July 1
Record Date	If Interest Payment Date is a Repurchase Date: the Business Day next preceding such Repurchase Date; if Interest Payment Date is a January 1 or July 1: the fifteenth day prior to such Interest Payment Date, provided, that if the Unit Pricing Adjustment Date for any Bond falls between the fifteenth day and the Interest Payment Date, the Record Date is the Business Day next preceding such Interest Payment Date	Two Business Days preceding each Interest Payment Date	The fifteenth day of the calendar month preceding each Interest Payment Date
Denominations	For Unit Pricing Interest Periods of less than 365 days: $100,000 and any integral multiple of $1,000 thereafter; for Unit Pricing Interest Periods equal to or greater than 365 days: $5,000 and integral multiples thereof	$100,000 and integral multiples thereof	$5,000 and integral multiples thereof
Tender Option	Mandatory Tender on each Repurchase Date unless the Bondholder notifies the Remarketing Agent by 10:00 A.M. on Repurchase Date of intent to retain ownership	Optional Tender on any Business Day upon 7 days' notice to the Bond Trustee's Agent and the Remarketing Agent and delivery to the Bond Trustee's Agent by 12:30 P.M. on the purchase date	Not Available
Interest Rate/Period Determination	Preliminary determination by 9:30 A.M. and final determination by 12:00 noon on each Unit Pricing Adjustment Date for a period ranging from one day to final maturity (subject to remaining term of Standby Bond Purchase Agreement)	Determined each Tuesday, effective Wednesday (whether or not a Business Day) through the following Tuesday	Determined at the onset of the Fixed Interest Period and effective until maturity
Interest Calculation	For Unit Pricing Interest Periods less than or equal to 365 days: 365/366 day year for actual number of days elapsed; For Unit Pricing Interest Periods greater than 365 days: 360 day year composed of twelve 30-day months	365/366 day year for actual number of days elapsed	360 day year composed of twelve 30-day months

Figure 20.8. An example of an UPDATE (Unit-Priced Demand Adjustable Tax-Exempt Security) which expands the flexibility of debt structuring

360

Further refinements expanded the flexibility of debt structuring to the point where some new issues can be described as "any which way we can" bonds. One example of this flexibility is described in Figure 20.8 UPDATES (Unit Priced Demand Adjustable Tax-Exempt Securities) permit investment bankers to structure all or any part of an issue in one of three modes:

1. The unit price mode, which is similar to TECP. In this mode the remarketing agent establishes an interest-rate scale and investors select the maturity dates they desire, from 1 to 365 days.
2. The variable-rate demand mode, which in Figure 20.8 is a weekly demand mode.
3. The fixed-rate mode which can extend from 1 year to the final maturity date.

Any or all bonds, including fixed-rate bonds at the end of a fixed-rate period, can be converted to other modes upon appropriate notice.

The continuing development of new and more flexible instruments is one sign of a dynamic market response to volatile markets. In 1984, new issues of variable-rate debt amounted to $25 billion; in 1985, volume more than doubled to $56.5 billion. As Table 20.2 shows, virtually all categories of bond finance have at least

Table 20.2. Selected Summary Statistics on New Issues of Variable-Rate Bonds

	1984	1985
Dollar volume (in $billions) of new variable-rate bonds	$27.9	$68.7
Percentage of all new issues	23.0%	30.2%
Volume ($billions) by interest-rate reset interval:		
Annual	$ 3.7	$ 3.9
Semiannual, quarterly, monthly	3.6	4.8
Weekly	13.9	24.4
Daily	2.6	4.3
Flexible	1.8	9.4
Other	.3	.2
Percentage of variable rate debt by purpose:		
Private college/university	2.6%	5.5%
Other education	1.9	4.5
Transportation	8.2	6.7
Utility	15.2	12.7
Housing	7.1	16.9
Hospital	11.6	19.7
Industrial development	36.9	12.4
Pollution control	23.0	7.7
Other	13.0	4.7

Source: Salomon Brothers, *Monthly Report on Tax-Exempts*, May 1987.

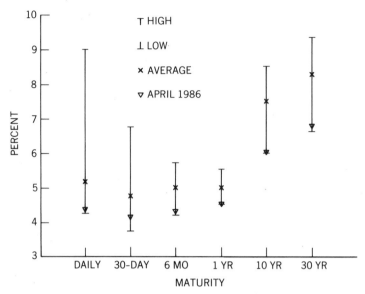

Figure 20.9. The range in yields on tax-exempts by maturity, April 1985–1986 (Source: Salomon Brothers, *Monthly Report on Tax-Exempts*, May 1987.)

experimented with some form of variable-rate debt. Prominent issuers include hospitals ($11 billion), industrial corporations ($6.9 billion), and private colleges and universities ($3.1 billion).

Although variable-rate debt instruments represent a creative approach for moving borrowing costs downs the yield curve, there are added costs and risks to borrowers. Figure 20.9 points out that very short-term instruments—for example, dailies—carried interest rates above yields on 30-day TECP in 1985. The persistence of this yield differential has caused the tax-exempt market to record, for the first time, an inverted yield curve. Reasons advanced for this yield differential focus on the remarketing risk and the determination of investment bankers and borrowers to avoid, even at high cost, the need to draw down liquidity facilities. Figure 20.10 outlines the numerous parties involved in a variable rate demand bond program and it suggests the complex mechanics required to make it work. From a borrower's perspective, this table points up the fact that variable-rate demand bonds involve added costs. Offset against these costs is the fact that demand bonds represent— to the borrower—long-term financing. Once debt is sold, much of the daily management and transaction processing activity is transferred to financing agents that specialize in performing these services.

PACKAGING BONDS WITH OPTIONS

The concept of debt as a package also has been extended to include combinations of traditional debt with other financial instruments such as options. In financial

Agent	Function	Cost of Service
Underwriter	Negotiates original sale of bonds; also may serve as remarketing, tender agent.	Gross spread ranges between $6 and $15 per $1000 par value.
Remarketing agent	Remarkets tendered bonds; generally, senior underwriting manager is appointed.	⅛ to ½ percent of par amount tendered.
Tender agent	Receives and holds tendered bonds until remarketed; usually performed by senior manager.	Included with remarketing fees.
Indexing agent	Prepares and publishes interest-rate index; may be outside service (e.g., J.J. Kenny) or remarketing agent.	Fee ranges from zero when remarketing agent is used to $25,000 per year.
Paying agent	Performs record-keeping functions and records principal and interest payments to bondholders.	$5000 to $10,000 initial fee; $5000 to $15,000 per year depending on number of transactions.
Trustee	Monitors all parties to transactions to ensure compliance with indenture; normally serves as paying agent also.	Same as paying agent.
Commercial bank liquidity agreement	Provides funds for tendered bonds not immediately remarketed.	⅛ to ¾ percent of par amount of bonds outstanding.
Commercial bank, bond insurance company: credit support	Provides credit enhancement for bonds to insure payment of principal and interest to bondholder.	⅜ to 1½ percent of principal (banks) or of principal and interest (insurance).

Figure 20.10. Agents in Variable Rate Demand Bond Transactions

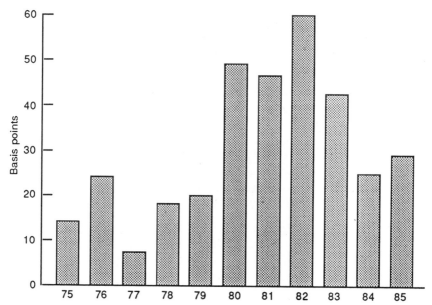

Figure 20.11. Annual average: Absolute value of month-to-month changes in yield, 30-year maturity

markets, options are defined as contractual rights to buy (a call option) or sell (as put option) a particular financial instrument. Normally, option contracts specify the period during which the option may be exercised ("the exercise period") and the price (the "exercise" or "striking" price) at which the instrument may be purchased or sold. Option-pricing theory indicates that the value of options is, in part, a function of the volatility of prices or, for bonds, yields. Figure 20.11 highlights this volatility by tracing the annual average of the absolute value of month-to-month changes in the yield on 30-year maturities of prime municipals. From 1975 to 1979, the average of absolute yield changes ranged from 6.7 basis points (1977) to 22.9 basis points; since 1980, however, the average of absolute yield changes has increased, ranging from 24 basis points in 1984 to 60 basis points in 1982.

It is well known that bonds with fixed coupons must sell at a discount in price during periods when market yields move higher; to a buyer, this discount generates a future capital gain realized at maturity (or, perhaps, on a subsequent sale). Because capital gains are taxable, tax-exempt bonds originally issued at par (100) become partially taxable bonds during periods of rising market rates. An investor factors in this capital gains tax in determining the price for seasoned tax-exempt bonds. In short, tax-exempt bond prices must decline to the point that after-tax yields are in line with current yields on new tax-exempts; the import is that price volatility is even more pronounced than yield changes imply. Long-term maturities exaggerate this effect of volatility, so long-term rates have carried an extra "risk premium" to compensate investors. Borrowers have also recognized investor concerns for price risk by incorporating put options on new bond issues. The previous section described forms of put options, which involved the "sale" of a right to bondholders to put or tender their investments at par on specified future intervals. Depending on the frequency of the put-option interval, investors may convert otherwise long-term bonds to investments with effective maturities as short as one day or one week.

Other put options carry a "deferred put" feature. A deferred put may set the time to first put date 5 to 10 years after the initial bond sale date. Two forms of put have been issued: the one-time put and the continuing put. One-time put bonds may carry a nominal final maturity as long as 30 years, but the put option permits investors to redeem bonds on one specified future date. As an example, a 30-year term bond with a one-time, five-year deferred put date would allow the investor in bonds issued in 1986, for example, to redeem bonds at par in 1991; after that date, the investor not exercising the option would hold bonds with 25 years remaining to maturity.

Continuing put bonds allow investors to redeem bonds at specified intervals, generally annually, from the first put date to the final maturity date. Figure 20.12

$104,750,000

State of New York Mortgage Agency

Residential Mortgage Revenue Bonds, 1981 Series

Dated: November 1, 1981   Due: November 1, as shown below

Under the Trust Agreement, the holders have the right to tender Option Bonds due November 1, 2012 to the Trustee as tender agent for purchase on behalf of the Agency at par on November 1, 1987 and each November 1 thereafter, upon 60 days' prior written notice and tender thereof, provided that as of such purchase date the Bonds are not in default as to payment of principal (including sinking fund payments) or interest. The obligation to purchase tendered Option Bonds is supported by an irrevocable letter of credit of Citibank, N.A. See "Bondholders' Rights to Tender Option Bonds."

Due November 1	Principal Amount	Interest Rate
1982	$ 500,000	9%
1983	925,000	9¼
1984	1,010,000	9½
1985	1,105,000	9¾
1986	1,210,000	10

$100,000,000 Option Bonds 10¼% Due November 1, 2012
Price of All Bonds: 100%
(accrued interest to be added)

Goldman, Sachs & Co.

Salomon Brothers Inc   Bear, Stearns & Co.
The Chase Manhattan Bank, N.A.   Citibank, N.A.
The First Boston Corporation   Smith Barney, Harris Upham & Co.,
                                                                Incorporated

November 6, 1981

Figure 20.12. A summary of the key provisions of a continuing put bond

provides a summary of the key provisions of a continuing put bond. In this example, the term bonds scheduled to mature in 2012 can be redeemed by investors beginning in 1987, six years from the sale date, or on any anniversary date thereafter. The coupon rate on these bonds is fixed for the entire life of the issue at 10⅞ percent.

One key concern in the design of a put bond is the possibility that bonds will actually be tendered, thereby placing a large and uncertain cash demand on borrowers. In the example in Figure 20.12, the liquidity arrangement with Citibank reduces this risk to the borrower, but the particular form of this put option also reduces the probability of a tender. Investors in this bond have three choices on November 1, 1987 and each November thereafter:

1. Hold the bonds for another year or longer;
2. Put the bonds at par; or
3. Sell the bonds to another investor, who may want a one-year investment.

The bonds in Figure 20.12 carried a coupon rate of 10⅞ percent, which is higher than the presently available rate on one-year debt of 4.5 percent. As long as one-year rates in 1987 and thereafter remain below the coupon rate, investors would realize a higher value by selling the bonds in the market, priced as one-year instruments, than they would by tendering the bonds at par. More recent varieties of deferred put-option bonds have married the 5- or 10-year deferred put feature to a subsequent variable-rate conversion option that can be triggered at the first put date. These instruments are often referred to as "fixed/floating-rate" bonds.

CALL OPTIONS AND ADVANCE REFUNDING

Most long-term bond issues include an optional redemption provision that permits issuers to redeem bonds at certain dates prior to the stated final maturity. The optional redemption feature, or call option, can be viewed as a form of contract that is "sold" by the investor to the borrower. The value of this option to the borrower lies in the fact that future interest rates may decline well below the level of coupon rates on outstanding bonds. In that event, the borrower can exercise the call option and redeem outstanding high-coupon debt by issuing new debt at a lower cost. In effect, the call option allows a borrower to buy back outstanding debt at "bargain" prices. As an example, a 20-year "noncallable" bond with a 13½ percent coupon would command a market value of approximately $135.53 per $100 par value if market rates declined to 9½ percent. A typical call option would allow the issuer to redeem these bonds at a price of $102 or $103 per $100 par value.

If a borrower chooses to redeem bonds, the investor will be forced to reinvest the payments at a lower interest rate. Since the timing of the redemption depends on highly uncertain movements in future interest rates, investors must be compensated for this reinvestment risk. Typically, therefore, the borrower compensates the investor by paying higher yields on callable bonds. Rather than a cash payment for the call option at the time the callable bonds are originally sold, borrowers pay, in effect, on an "installment plan." Yields on callable bonds may range from 10 to 50 basis points higher than yields on noncallable bonds, with a higher yield differential at or near cyclical peaks in interest rates.

Most often, bond indentures will prohibit an issuer from redeeming bonds under the call option for a period ranging from 5 to 10 years from the original issue date. This "call deferment period" provides the investor some assurance that the promised coupon payments will be forthcoming for a minimum length of time. Moreover, most call provisions require the issuer to pay a call premium to investors when bonds are redeemed. In the tax-exempt market, these premiums generally range from 2 to 5 percent above par value. These premiums represent taxable income to investors.

Most tax-exempt mortgage revenue bonds used to fund single-family mortgages carry a somewhat exceptional call feature—namely, an "immediate par call option" exercisable at any time. This par call option is used to "pass-through" early prepayments of mortgages by homeowners or to retire bonds in the event that bond proceeds cannot be invested in mortgages at an acceptable interest rate. In some instances, these bonds may have an extremely short life. On April 18, 1986, for example, the Mesquite Housing Finance Corporation called $11.8 million in bonds issued in March 1985; this call represented 60 percent of the original issue.

Borrowers with deferred call options can follow two general strategies for exercising this option when interest rates decline: refundings and advance refundings. At the end of the call deferment period, issuers can carry out a refunding, selling new bonds and using the proceeds to concurrently redeem outstanding bonds. Prior to the first call date, many governmental issuers can undertake advance refundings. Advance refundings also involve the sale of new bonds, but the proceeds are not (indeed, they cannot be) used immediately to redeem outstanding bonds. Instead, the proceeds are invested in U.S. Treasury securities and held in escrow. This escrow fund is used to meet debt service payments and at some future date, usually the first call date, to redeem outstanding bonds. The value of an advance refunding lies in the fact that the borrower need not speculate on lower interest rates at or after the first call date. Instead, advance refundings permit an issuer to capture interest-rate savings from any significant decline in market rates, perhaps as soon as three months after "old" bonds have been sold.

Two common advance refunding techniques are the "standard defeasance" and the "crossover." In the standard defeasance or net cash defeasance, new bonds are sold and the proceeds are used to purchase Treasury securities for the escrow fund. The portfolio of Treasury securities is limited in yield, by existing Treasury regulations, to the yield on the *new* or refunding bonds. The escrow portfolio is structured so that the income and principal will meet *all* debt service on the "old" bonds until the first call date. At that time, the remaining balance in the escrow fund will be used to call the old bonds at the call premium. Figure 20.13, which outlines the cash flows associated with a standard defeasance advance refunding, points out that the effect, for the borrower, is to replace old bonds with new at the time of the refunding bond sale. To the investor, the effect is to transform old bonds, with,

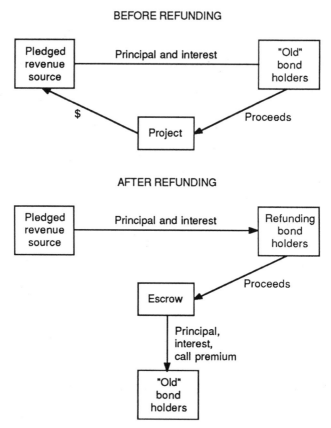

Figure 20.13. An outline of the cash flows associated with a standard defeasance advance refunding

say a 30-year term and a bond rating of A, to shorter-term bonds (e.g., 10 years or less) with a rating of AAA based on the escrow fund. These bonds are commonly referred to as "prefunded" bonds and they represent tax-exempt bonds effectively secured by the U.S. government.

The second major type of advance refunding is the "crossover method"; it differs from the net cash defeasance in that only the bonds that ultimately will be called are refunded in advance. The crossover refunding does not defease the debt service obligations on the "old" bonds prior to the call date. Instead, this refunding method establishes an escrow sufficient to pay only the principal amount of bonds to be redeemed at the call date and the call premium. As with the net cash method, the proceeds of the advance refunding issue are deposited in an escrow fund. However, by contrast, the investment income on the escrow fund is used to pay debt service on the *refunding bonds* until the call date. As Figure 20.14 suggests, the savings to borrowers from a crossover refunding do not have an impact on cash outlays until after the exercise of the call option.

CROSSOVER REFUNDING

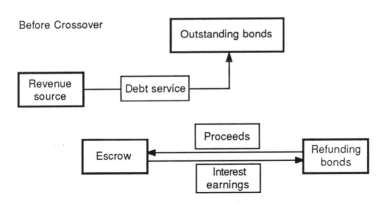

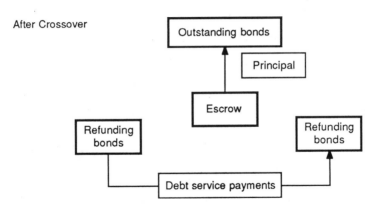

Figure 20.14. Crossover refunding

The volatility of interest rates has increased the value of call options and many issuers have exercised advance refundings. As noted in Chapter 19, the volume of new issues for advance refundings in 1985 exceeded $50 billion.

REINVESTMENT RISK AND ZERO-COUPON BONDS

Investors have, of course, a variety of investment objectives. Some seek current income for consumption spending, while others invest in tax-exempts as a short-term haven for proceeds from the sale of other assets. Still others seek to maximize long-term wealth at some future date. For the investor in this latter category, the traditional long-term, fixed-coupon bond can led to considerable uncertainty over

Table 20.3. Components of Total Future Return: Atlanta and Fulton County 8.70s of 2007 under Assumed Reinvestment Rates (per $1000 Investment)

	Reinvestment Rate		
	8.70%	7.40%	10.00%
Coupon income	$1,914	$1,914	$1,914
Interest-on-interest	$3,597	2,725	4,660
Return of principal	1,000	1,000	1,000
Total return	6,511	5,639	7,575
Realized compound yield	8.70%	8.02%	9.42%

future wealth. The stream of semiannual coupon payments must be reinvested to accumulate, or compound, over the planned investment horizon, but the actual rate earned on reinvesting the interim coupons is not known in advance. Therefore, the total return that will be realized, and the amount of future wealth, are uncertain at the time of an initial investment.

The significance of "interest-earned-on-interest" is demonstrated for the 8.7 percent Atlanta bonds of 2007 in Table 20.3. If all interim coupon payments (of $43.50 per $1000 invested) can be reinvested at the same coupon rate, reinvestment income will total $3597 over the life of the bonds, and the total return will amount to $6511 by 2007. If, however, coupons could be reinvested only a 7.4 percent each period, interest earned on reinvestment would amount to only $2725 and total future returns would fall to $5639. At a higher reinvestment rate, say 10 percent, total future wealth jumps to $7575. As this table indicates, income earned from reinvesting coupons represents the largest portion (50 percent or more) of the total future return on long-term bonds held until·maturity. The dramatic increase in interest-rate volatility in the 1980s has heightened investor awareness of the importance of reinvestment rates, it has increased reinvestment risk, and it has increased the uncertainties over realized compound yields associated with fixed-coupon bonds.

One measure of future wealth that incorporates investors' expectations of future reinvestment rates (or, after the fact, uses actual rates) is "realized compound yield." The realized compound yield (RCY) of an investment is the annualized rate that discounts the total future return at maturity to the initial purchase price. As Table 20.3 shows, RCY is equal to the initial stated yield-to-maturity only when interim coupons are invested at this yield over the life of the bond. One instrument developed by investment bankers to reduce this reinvestment risk is the "zero-coupon" bond (ZCB). There are no interim coupon payments on ZCBs; instead there is a single payment at maturity representing the accumulation of interest compounded from the sale date to maturity.

Figure 20.15 shows one example of the use of ZCBs. It summarizes the debt structure of a recent bond issues for the State of New York Mortgage Agency (SONYMA). Among other features, this issue was structured with serial zero-coupon bonds ("zerials") maturing from April 1, 1997 to October 1, 2002, and

In the opinion of Bond Counsel and Co-Bond Counsel, under existing statutes and court decisions, interest on the Seventh Series Bonds is exempt from Federal income taxes and personal income taxes imposed by the State of New York and its political subdivisions (including The City of New York), and the Seventh Series Bonds are exempt from all taxation directly imposed thereon by or under the authority of said State except for estate or gift taxes or taxes on transfers. See "Tax Exemption."

$200,000,000*
State of New York Mortgage Agency
Mortgage Revenue Bonds, Seventh Series

Dated: December 1, 1985
(Capital Appreciation Bonds and Growth and Income Securities
(GAINS^SM/TM†) dated December 30, 1985)

Due: April 1 and October 1,
as shown below

Interest on the Seventh Series Bonds is payable on each April 1 and October 1, commencing April 1, 1986 except that there will be no periodic payment of interest on the GAINS prior to October 1, 1998 or on the Capital Appreciation Bonds. The Seventh Series Bonds are issuable only in registered form in the denomination of $5,000; in the case of Capital Appreciation Bonds in the denominations set forth below per $5,000 maturity amount; and in the case of GAINS in the denomination set forth below per $5,000 of Accreted Value as of April 1, 1998; or, in each case, any integral multiple thereof. Interest on the Seventh Series Bonds (other than the GAINS prior to October 1, 1998 or Capital Appreciation Bonds) will be paid by check mailed by the Trustee, Marine Midland Bank, N.A., New York, New York, to the registered owners of the Seventh Series Bonds. Principal of the Seventh Series Bonds is payable at the principal corporate trust office of the Trustee.

The Seventh Series Bonds are subject to redemption prior to maturity as set forth herein. The Seventh Series Bonds are special obligations of the Agency payable solely from the revenues, mortgage loans and moneys pledged and assigned under the Mortgage Revenue Bonds General Resolution. The Agency has no taxing power. The Seventh Series Bonds are not a debt of the State of New York or of any municipality and neither the State of New York nor any municipality shall be liable on the Seventh Series Bonds.

Maturity	Amount	Interest Rate	Price	Maturity	Amount	Interest Rate	Price
October 1, 1987	$2,000,000	5¾ %	100%	October 1, 1992	$4,330,000	7 %	100%
April 1, 1988	2,875,000	6.20	100	April 1, 1993	4,485,000	7.20	100
October 1, 1988	3,285,000	6.20	100	October 1, 1993	4,645,000	7.20	100
April 1, 1989	3,440,000	6.40	100	April 1, 1994	4,810,000	7.40	100
October 1, 1989	3,550,000	6.40	100	October 1, 1994	4,990,000	7.40	100
April 1, 1990	3,665,000	6.60	100	April 1, 1995	5,175,000	7.60	100
October 1, 1990	3,790,000	6.60	100	October 1, 1995	5,370,000	7.60	100
April 1, 1991	3,915,000	6.80	100	April 1, 1996	5,575,000	7.70	100
October 1, 1991	4,050,000	6.80	100	October 1, 1996	5,790,000	7.70	100
April 1, 1992	4,185,000	7	100				

$14,555,000 8½% Term Bonds Due October 1, 2004 at 100%
$68,400,000 8⅝% Term Bonds Due April 1, 2011 at 100%
(Accrued interest to be added)

Maturity	Amount	Principal per $5,000 at Maturity	Approximate Yield	Maturity	Amount	Principal per $5,000 at Maturity	Approximate Yield
April 1, 1997	$2,434,932.15	$2,024.05	8.20%	April 1, 2000	$1,014,494.05	$1,485.35	8.70%
October 1, 1997	2,339,053.05	1,944.35	8.20	October 1, 2000	972,182.20	1,423.40	8.70
April 1, 1998	2,194,693.05	1,824.35	8.40	April 1, 2001	918,156.90	1,344.30	8.80
October 1, 1998	1,195,796.40	1,750.80	8.40	October 1, 2001	879,464.95	1,287.65	8.80
April 1, 1999	1,118,788.15	1,638.05	8.60	April 1, 2002	829,366.90	1,214.30	8.90
October 1, 1999	1,072,651.50	1,570.50	8.60	October 1, 2002	794,055.80	1,162.60	8.90

$18,562,228.30 GAINS Due October 1, 2014 Approximate Yield 9.25%
($1,651.15 per $5,000 Accreted Value as of April 1, 1998)

$2,793,637.80 Term Capital Appreciation Bonds Due April 1, 2017 Approximate Yield 9.625%
($264.85 per $5,000 maturity amount)

The Seventh Series Bonds are offered when, as and if issued and received by the Underwriters, subject to prior sale, to withdrawal or modification of the offer without notice, to the approval of legality by Hawkins, Delafield & Wood, New York, New York, Bond Counsel and Wood, Williams & Rafalsky, New York, New York, Co-Bond Counsel to the Agency and to certain other conditions. Certain legal matters will be passed upon for the Underwriters by their counsel, Seward & Kissel, New York, New York. It is expected that the Bonds in definitive form will be available for delivery in New York, New York, on or about December 30, 1985.

Goldman, Sachs & Co.	**Bear, Stearns & Co. Inc.**
Citicorp Investment Bank Citibank, N.A.	**Donaldson, Lufkin & Jenrette** Securities Corporation
Drexel Burnham Lambert Incorporated	**Kidder, Peabody & Co.** Incorporated
Merrill Lynch Capital Markets	**Morgan Stanley & Co.** Incorporated
L.F. Rothschild, Unterberg, Towbin	**Salomon Brothers Inc**
Wertheim & Co., Inc.	

---

* Approximate amount. Actual amount $199,999,501.20.
† GAINS is a service mark and trademark of Goldman, Sachs & Co.

December 11, 1985

Figure 20.15. An example of the use of ZCBs

term ZCBs maturing in 2017. The term bonds carried a present value or price of $264.85 per $5000 maturity amount; given the time to maturity, this translates into a realized compound yield of 9.625 percent. The price of the zerials ranges from $2024.05 per $5000 maturity value to $1162.60, and the RCYs ranged from 8.2 to 8.90 percent. Because ZCBs are sold on the basis of RCY and the avoidance of reinvestment risk, the use of call options is somewhat different from that on coupon-bearing bonds. The term ZCBs in the SONYMA issue, for example, are not callable; they are however, subject to a sinking-fund redemption beginning in 2015. The zerials are callable beginning in 1997, but the call price is based on the accreted (or future) value given by compounding the original price at the stated yield to maturity and the call premium is a relatively high 10 percent of this accreted value.

The SONYMA issue also is structured with $18.56 million in "GAINs" maturing in 2014. These are hybrid securities. They are zero-coupon bonds from the sale date until 1998, when they convert to coupon-bearing bonds. The present value or price of theses GAINs at the initial sales was $1651.15 per $5000 maturity value. In 1998, the GAINs will have accreted to $5000, and from 1998 until 2014, they will carry an annual coupon rate of 9.25 percent. Thus, for an outlay of $1651.15 in December 1985, investors will receive an annual cash flow of coupon income of $462.50 from 1998 to 2014. Effectively, this hybrid security provides a form of tax-free deferred annuity income. The GAINs cannot be called for redemption in the ZCB mode; but they are callable in the coupon mode and they are subject to sinking-fund redemption beginning in 2011.

Figures 20.16, 20.17, 20.18, and 20.19 illustrate how these instruments are integrated into the overall "repackaging" of a debt service schedule. The composite

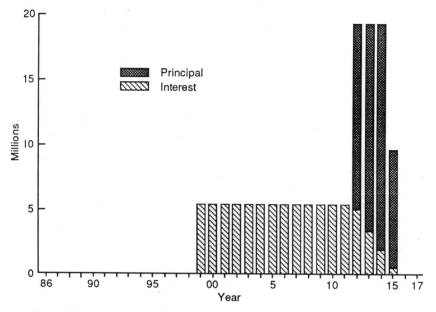

Figure 20.16. New York Mortgage Agency, debt service on "GAINS" bonds

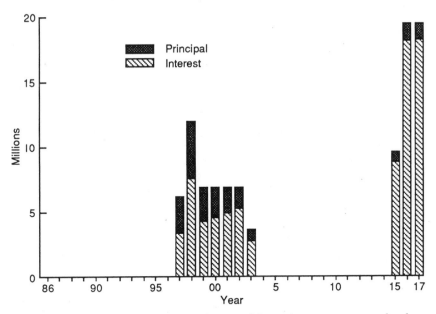

Figure 20.17. New York Mortgage Agency, debt service on zero-coupon bonds

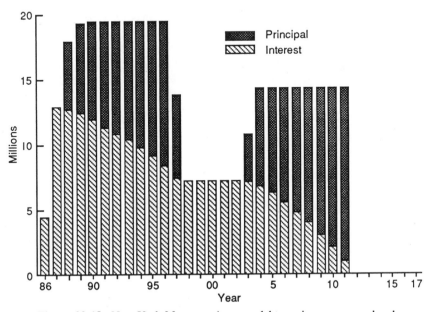

Figure 20.18. New York Mortgage Agency, debt service on coupon bonds

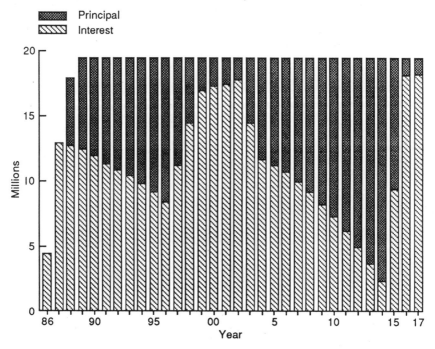

Figure 20.19. New York Mortgage Agency, overall debt service

debt service is structured much as the Atlanta example used at the outset of this chapter (Figures 20.1 and 20.2) to produce level annual cash flows. The ZCBs and GAINs are structured with long-term maturities, where investor concern over reinvestment risk is most significant; these bonds require relatively large future payments of interest. Traditional coupon-bearing bonds are used to "fill-in" the remaining debt service and produce the remaining present value of the $200 million. The use of long-term ZCBs and GAINs provides borrowers with substantial savings in the early years from the coupon payments that would otherwise be required for long-term coupon bonds. These savings are used to structure relatively more serial-coupon bonds in the short-term (and lower-cost) end of the yield curve.

UNCERTAIN CREDIT QUALITY AND CREDIT ENHANCEMENTS

Figure 20.20 shows that yield spreads between prime-grade and medium-grade tax-exempts have increased since 1979, rising as high as 125 basis points in 1982. Fueling investor concern over credit quality has been the trend in bond rating changes. Table 20.4 summarizes rating changes for Moody's Investor Services since 1979 and these data point out that downgradings have been far more frequent than upgradings. In 1983–1984, for example, 938 ratings were lowered while only

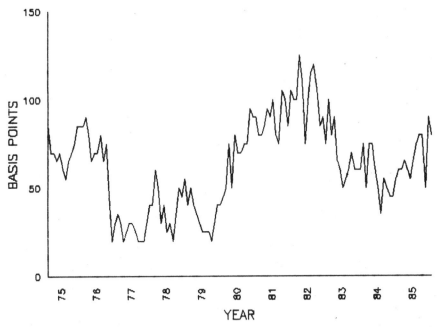

Figure 20.20. Yield spread, medium-grade versus prime-grade 30-year municipals (basis points)

463 were raised. These trends have taken on special significance because of the dramatic changes in the mix of investors in the tax-exempt market. As noted in Chapter 19, demand from traditional institutional investors—banks and property/casualty insurance companies—has declined since 1980 and individuals have been called upon to purchase the new supply of debt. Individual investors, however, are less likely to have the time or expertise to analyze lengthy and complex security provisions. As a result, so-called third-party credit enhancements have become an important feature of the tax-exempt market.

Credit enhancements are contractual commitments by private entities—normally, financial institutions that are not "users" of bond proceeds—to provide funds to meet principal and interest payments on tax-exempt bond issues. According to data

Table 20.4. Trends in Bond Rating Changes by Moody's Investor Services

	Rating Changes						
	1979	1980	1981	1982	1983	1984	1985
Downgradings	220	112	171	263	293	350	295
Upgradings	125	103	91	136	121	101	241

in Table 20.5, the par value of bonds with some form of credit enhancement amounted to $36.5 billion in 1984 and $81.3 billion in 1985. Data compiled by the Public Securities Association indicate that more than 200 private intermediaries are engaged in supplying credit enhancements, including bond insurance companies, other insurance companies, domestic and foreign commercial banks, and thrift institutions. Table 20.6 points out that the principal uses for "enhanced" bonds re advance refundings, multifamily rental housing, hospitals, and single-family mortgage revenue bonds.

Credit enhancements have two purposes: to reduce borrowing costs to issuers and to reduce information costs and risks to investors. Those that supply enhancements (e.g., banks) indicate their willingness, for a fee, to substitute their credit standing and resources for those of the borrower. The "oldest" form of third-party credit support is bond insurance and it has been available for just over a decade. The standard bond insurance contract runs for the life of the insured bonds. In the event an issuer of tax-exempts fails to make principal and/or interest payments in full and on time, the insurer will do so. The payments to investors by the insurer are made according to the original maturity schedule on the bonds; there is no acceleration of the maturity date in the event of a default by the borrower. Insurance premiums may be paid by borrowers or by underwriters. Premiums are scaled to perceived risks and they range from 0.75 to 1.75 percent of the *total* debt service scheduled over the outstanding life of the bonds. Most often, these premiums are payable in full when the bonds are initially sold. Issuers can insure an entire bond issue or only a portion of the issue. In April 1986, four private insurance companies were active in supplying bond insurance: Municipal Bond Insurance Association (MBIA); American Municipal Bond Assurance Corporation (AMBAC); Financial Guaranty Insurance Company (FGIC); and Bond Investors Guaranty Insurance Company (BIGI). All four carry an AAA rating from Standard and Poor's; two—MBIA and FGIC—are rated AAA by Moody's. The savings in interest costs to borrowers that

Table 20.5. Volume of New Tax-Exempt Bonds with Credit Enhancements, 1984–1985

Type of Credit Enhancement	Par Value of Bonds[a] ($ Billions)	
	1984	1985
Private bond insurance	$18.2	43.6
Letters of credit—Total	17.3	34.6
Domestic commercial banks	10.7	12.3
Foreign commercial banks	5.9	20.6
Thrift institutions	.6	1.7
Surety bonds	.5	2.3
State guarantees	.4	.2

[a]Amounts include par value of all bond issues fully or partially insured.

Source: Public Securities Association, Dealer's Digest: IDD Information Services/PSA Municipal Database.

Table 20.6. Issues of Tax-Exempts with Credit Enhancements, 1985

Use of Proceeds	($Millions)	Percentage of Total
Education		
Secondary	2,026.6	2.49
College	2,991.1	3.68
Student loan	1,932.5	2.38
Other education	346.2	.43
Total education	7,296.6	8.98
Transportation		
Surface transportation	366.4	.45
Ports	264.6	.33
Airports	318.8	.39
Other	435.8	.54
Total transportation	1,385.5	1.70
Utility		
Water/sewer	3,889.8	4.78
Electric power, gas	2,775.0	3.41
Other	3,972.4	4.89
Total utility	10,488.9	12.90
Social Welfare		
Multifamily	9,248.5	11.38
Single-family	5,678.7	6.99
Other housing	452.0	.56
Hospitals	8,685.2	10.68
Other	4,675.0	5.75
Total social welfare	28,739.4	35.35
Industrial Development		
Pollution control	3,685.4	4.53
Other	1,719.5	2.12
Total industrial development	452.0	.56
Other New Capital		
Public services	764.1	.94
Recreation	660.8	.81
Miscellaneous, various purposes	6,082.3	7.48
Total: Long-term issues for new capital	60,822.6	74.82
Refunding	20,471.7	25.18
Total: New long-term tax-exempt bonds	$81,294.3	100.00

Source: Public Securities Association, Dealer's Digest: IDD Information Services/PSA Municipal Database.

have their bonds insured depends on the level of interest rates, the relative spreads in rates among bonds of different quality, and the form of insurance. In early April 1986, bonds with 1996 maturities carried yields of 6.75 percent with MBIA insurance, 6.80 percent with FGIC insurance, and 7.00 percent with AMBAC insurance. At the same time, uninsured A-rated bonds carried yields of 7.00 percent and uninsured AAA-rated bonds carried yields of 6.20 percent.

Bank credit supports or facilities can be liquidity supports or letters of credit (LOCs). The liquidity support generally provides only liquidity for the issuer's debt and is subject to numerous qualifications. Most notably, lines cannot be used if the borrower is in default on its obligation. Lines of credit are used most often to support short-term or variable-rate debt with frequent "put" options. Banks generally impose two charges for lines—a commitment fee and a "draw-down" rate. The commitment fee, which may range from ⅛ to ¾ of 1 percent of the principal, can be viewed as an "insurance premium"—it is the cost to the borrower of maintaining access to cash at a future date. The "draw-down" fee is the loan rate charged by the bank when the line actually is used by the borrower. These loan rates can range from 60 percent of the U.S. Treasury bill rate to a premium over the (taxable) prime rate, with higher rates charged as the value of tax-exempt income to banks declines.

The letter of credit provides investors (or the trustee) with a direct claim against the bank in the event that debt service is not fully paid on time by borrowers. The LOC is, therefore, much like bond insurance, and LOC-backed bonds substitute the credit of the bank for that of the borrower. Reflecting the stronger form of commitment, fees and loan rates are generally higher for LOCs, ranging from ⅜of 1 percent to 1½ percent of principal. Generally, the term of the LOC is shorter than the life of the bonds—terms run from 5 to 10 years, with provisions included for future renewals. In the event that a bank notifies an issuer that it will not renew, the bond covenants may stipulate that the bonds will be subject to mandatory redemption prior to the LOC expiration date. Thus, while investors receive some added assurances about the safety of their expected future incomes stream, the duration of this added safety is uncertain.

This discussion also leads to the observation that credit enhancements can be viewed as a form of "put" option to investors, where the exercise of the "put" is contingent on the default by a borrower. The lower yields on bonds with credit enhancements indicate that investors value these options supplied or "written" by well-known financial institutions. But it is also appropriate to underscore the fact that the underlying credit risk of the borrower has not been erased—it has merely been shifted to another party which *may* have special talents or resources that can better analyze or price these risks. Moreover, investors in bonds with credit enhancements have also substituted the underlying risk of the supplier for that of the issuer. In the period from January 1985 to April 1986, more than $2 billion in tax-exempt bonds backed by credit enhancements have received lowered ratings because of changes in credit quality and ratings of various suppliers, including the Bank of America, TICOR Mortgage Insurance Company, and Industrial Indemnity. In part because of theses lowered ratings, the value of the implicit "put option" has also been somewhat reduced.

SUMMARY

This chapter has highlighted some of the many innovative financing techniques that have been employed in the tax-exempt market in recent years. Most of theses innovations have been driven by the yield curve and by the compelling attractions of shifting borrowing costs downs the yield curve (or to lower yield curves), At the same time, some innovations have proved to be short-lived, a result of quickly changing market dynamics that rendered the specific innovative form itself obsolete. Other creative financing tools have emerged in their place and many of them continue to endure. For some of these financing vehicles, the testing time has yet to be faced. The inherent risks of variable-rate financing, for example, may be vastly different if and when the tax-exempt market faces an inverted yield curve in a future period during which interest rates reach a new cyclical peak.

21 The Impact of Tax Reform on the Tax-Exempt Securities Market

JOHN E. PETERSEN
RONALD W. FORBES

After several years of rapid growth, new issues of tax-exempt bonds declined by 31 percent in 1986, to $147 billion. New-issue volume continued to decline in early 1987. Average monthly volume in the first two months—$7.4 billion—dropped 45 percent from average 1986 volume and 61 percent from 1985 volume. The contraction of the tax-exempt, new-issue market has taken place in the face of dramatically lower interest rates. Yields on 30-year maturities of prime (AAA-rated) municipals averaged 8.95 percent in 1985, dropped to 7.25 percent by mid-1986, and stood at 6.3 percent in early March 1987.

The decline of new-issue volume in the tax-exempt market is attributable largely to the Tax Reform Act of 1986, which significantly changed the rules that govern access to the tax-exempt market as well as the nature of demand by investors. The purpose of this chapter is to review the Tax Reform Act and its impact on the tax-exempt market.

BACKGROUND

The Tax Reform Act of 1986 maintains the federal government's role as an active and controversial participant in the tax-exempt market. Traditionally, state and local governments have sought shelter from federal regulation through the doctrine of intergovernmental tax immunity. In its simplest terms, this doctrine holds that states are free from federal taxation, just as the federal government is exempt from state taxation. It was first established in *McCullough v. Maryland* in 1819, when the Supreme Court struck down a state's attempt to tax a federal bank. The principle was extended in later cases, including *Pollock v. Farmer's Loan & Trust* in 1895, where the Court prohibited a federal attempt to tax municipal obligations.

Since these early judicial decisions, however, the doctrine of intergovernmental tax immunity has been more narrowly construed. In *Graves v. New York ex rel. O'Keefe* (1939), the Court upheld a state income tax on a federal employee, stating that a tax on income is not a tax on its source. Other cases (*Massachusetts v. United States* (1978)) have suggested that federal taxation or other revenue measures are not prohibited so long as they do not discriminate against state and local governments or unduly interfere with their essential governmental responsibilities. At present, in the absence of a direct challenge to the federal exemption of municipal bond interest, the status of exemption must remain uncertain.

Legislatively, the first Internal Revenue Code adopted after the passage of the Sixteenth Amendment in 1916 explicitly exempted interest on municipal obligations from federal tax. Since then, however, there have been numerous attempts to define what types of obligations are tax-free. Concern at the federal level has focused on the concept of tax-exempt interest as a *tax expenditure*. The Congressional Budget Act of 1974, for example, defines tax expenditures as "revenue losses attributable to provisions of the federal tax laws which allow a special exclusion, exemption or deduction from gross income," and it requires Congress to measure and report these tax expenditures.

While revenue losses associated with tax-exempt interest have been of long-standing concern, record levels of interest rates, rapidly growing new-issue volume, and an expanding federal deficit have combined to focus attention on the growing magnitude of these losses. Estimates prepared by the Treasury Department indicate that the revenue loss from tax-exempts quadrupled to $16.4 billion between 1976 and 1984.

Not surprisingly, the confluence of tax reform predicated on tax simplification, and the need to raise revenues to offset much lower tax rates, set the stage for major restrictions on the tax-exempt market. The restrictions on tax-exempts in the Tax Reform Act of 1986 follow a course that attempts to carefully avoid direct assaults on the financing of essential (and traditional) government functions. The primary targets are tax-exempts used to finance private activities, thus continuing a long-standing strategy.

In 1968, Congress reacted to the rapid growth in industrial development bond financing (IDBs) by limiting for the first time the powers of states and localities to issue tax-exempt bonds. The 1968 legislation limited IDBs to a maximum issue size of $5 million, although legislation in 1978 raised the maximum issue size to $10 million (or $20 million if projects were done in conjunction with federal Urban Development Action grants). The 1968 legislation also, for the first time, listed private activities that would be permitted access to the tax-exempt market without any volume limits; these included pollution control projects, nonprofit hospital and higher education facilities, student loans, and home mortgage loans among others. As Table 21.1 shows, these private activity financings began to engulf the tax-exempt market during the late 1970s, accounting for more than 50 percent of all new tax-exempts sold since 1979.

Table 21.1. New Issues of Tax-Exempt Bonds by Type of Activity (Percentage of Total New Issues)

	1976	1977	1978	1979	1980	1981	1982	1983	1984	1985
Governmental purpose	67.43	62.90	59.67	41.09	40.44	43.92	41.58	38.80	36.04	46.65
Private activity	32.57	37.10	40.12	56.88	59.74	56.08	58.42	61.20	63.96	53.35
Single-family housing	2.00	2.13	6.92	15.79	19.30	5.08	10.60	11.79	11.06	5.50
Multifamily housing	4.00	6.18	5.09	5.47	4.04	2.00	6.01	5.68	4.75	10.95
Veterans' housing	1.71	1.28	2.44	3.24	2.39	1.63	.59	.75	1.90	1.01
Nonprofit institutions	7.14	9.17	5.91	6.48	6.07	8.53	10.01	12.54	10.11	17.09
Student loan bonds	.29	.21	.61	1.21	.92	2.00	2.12	3.54	1.04	1.83
Pollution control IDBs	6.00	6.40	5.70	5.06	4.60	7.80	6.95	4.82	7.00	3.39
Small-issue IDBs	4.29	5.12	7.33	15.18	17.83	24.14	17.31	15.65	15.82	8.02
Other IDBs	7.14	6.82	6.52	4.45	4.60	4.90	4.83	6.43	12.19	5.55

Source: U.S. Department of Treasury, Office of Tax Analysis, July 15, 1986.

The growth in these issues would have been even greater except for a succession of Congressional actions designed to clamp down on tax-exempts for private activities. The Mortgage Subsidy Bond Act in 1980 restricted tax-exempt mortgage revenue bonds for single-family homes by placing a cap on the volume that could be issued in each state and by restricting the criteria for qualifying mortgages (i.e., borrowers' incomes and properties' prices). The Tax Equity and Fiscal Responsibility Act of 1982 (TEFRA) placed new restrictions on IDBs, including public hearing requirements, and denied accelerated depreciation for IDB-financed projects. TEFRA also placed a sunset on small-issue IDBs—eliminating tax exemption for them after 1986—and required that all new issues be reported to the Treasury Department.

More sweeping were the limitations placed on private activity bonds by the 1984 Deficit Reduction Act. Following the lead of the 1980 Mortgage Subsidy Bond Act, it placed state-by-state volume limits (or caps) on IDBs and student loans and it scheduled a sunset for mortgage revenue bonds at the end of 1986. Another restriction on the issuance and use of IDBs included stringent requirements that any arbitrage earnings be paid to the federal government.

TAX REFORM AND THE SUPPLY OF TAX-EXEMPT SECURITIES

The Tax Reform Act of 1986 (Tax Reform) continued the approach followed since 1980 by tightening the volume limitations on private activity bonds and by expanding the types of issues subject to these limits. It defines a bond as nongovernmental if 10 percent or more of the bond proceeds (or $15 million in the case of electric and gas output facilities) is used in a trade or business by persons or entities other than states and local governments, and if 10 percent or more of the debt service is secured by revenues or property used in such trade or business. This test is more restrictive than prior law, which allowed tax-exempts to be considered as governmental-purpose financings even if up to 25 percent of the proceeds were used for private purposes. In the case of private loan bonds (e.g., home mortgages), bonds are considered private activity bonds if an amount equal to the lesser of $5 million or 5 percent of the proceeds is used to make loans to nongovernmental parties. Under these new definitions, the interest income on bonds meeting the tests for private activity is subject to taxation unless it is provided with a specific exemption.

Tax Reform generally retains tax-exempt status for qualified mortgage revenue bonds, student loan bonds, nonprofit entity (or Section 501(c)(3) organization) bonds, veterans' mortgage bonds and small-issue IDBs for manufacturing and farming. However, mortgage revenue bonds and small-issue IDBs are slated for extinction, with sunset provisions in 1988 and 1989, respectively.

The following other purposes will also continue to qualify for tax-exempt financing: multifamily rental housing; publicly owned airports, docks, and wharves; sewerage and solid waste disposal; water supply facilities (including irrigation); local electric and gas facilities; and mass commuting facilities. Two new purposes added to the list of allowable IDBs are hazardous waste and qualified redevelopment bonds.

In most cases, the types of private activity financings that retain tax-exempt market access become subject to tightened programmatic requirements. Mortgage revenue bonds, for example, are subject to additional restrictions regarding first-time homeowner requirements, purchase prices, and mortgagor incomes. The Act requires that 95 percent of the net proceeds of a qualified mortgage bond (compared with only 90 percent under prior law) be used for first-time homeowners. The purchase price requirement limits home prices to 90 percent or less (down from 110 percent) of the average area purchase price. Family income is limited to 115 percent of the median income except in targeted areas where two-thirds of the bond proceeds allocated to such areas must be provided to families with incomes less than 140 percent of the area median income (prior law had no income limits on targeted area lending).

In addition to stiffening the test for private involvement, Tax Reform places two other major limits on tax-exempt issuance: it repeals tax-exemption for several categories of currently exempt-purpose bonds and it imposes volume caps on most other private uses that retain tax exemption. The list of activities no longer exempt includes IDBs for: pollution control; sports, convention, and trade show facilities; parking facilities; and industrial park and hydroelectric generating facilities. Tax Reform institutes a new unified state volume cap which applies to most IDBs, student loans, and mortgage revenue bonds. Prior law had established two volume limits. Student loan bonds and most IDBs were limited on a state-by-state basis to the greater of $150 per capita or $200 million. A separate cap limited mortgage revenue bonds to the greater of $200 million or 9 percent of the prior three-year average of mortgage originations.

The new cap is the greater of $75 per capita or $250 million in 1987, and $50 per capita or $150 million annually after 1987. Exempt from the unified volume limits are government-owned airports, docks, wharves, and solid waste disposal facilities. Nonprofit entities are also exempt from the unified volume limits, except that nonprofit entities other than hospitals are limited to total tax-exempt debt outstanding of $150 million per borrower. Nonprofit institutions (e.g., private colleges) that already exceed this limit are not required to accelerate the retirement of their debt, but they are foreclosed from future tax-exempt market access.

The data in Table 21.2 provide some perspective on the impact of the new volume caps for new issues. The table shows the maximum permitted volume for each state using current population estimates from the Bureau of the Census. The maximum volume of capped bonds that can be issued in 1987 is $21.3 billion, which is 60 percent less than the actual volume sold in 1984 and 72 percent below the 1985 volume. If 1984 is representative of the potential supply of new issues, the 1987 limits indicate that private activity bonds in many states will be severely restricted under Tax Reform. New-issue activity in 1984 is a useful benchmark because that was the last year in which new-issue activity was not dominated by impending tax law changes. using this benchmark, California will be rationed to $2.0 billion in 1987 compared with $5.4 billion in 1984; Texas will be cut from $3.5 billion to $1.3 billion; and Virginia will lose nearly 80 percent of its 1984

Table 21.2. 1987 Volume Caps for Private Activity Bonds Compared with 1984 and 1985 Issuances[a]

State	1985 Volume ($Million)	1984 Volume ($Million)	1987 Volume Cap ($Million)	Percentage of 1984 Volume Lost Due to 1984 Cap
Alabama	$ 964	$ 649	$ 304	(53.2)
Alaska	780.9	950	250	(73.7)
Arizona	1515.3	950	250	(74.2)
Arkansas	484.4	239	250	—
California	13,655.8	5419.5	2023.6	(62.7)
Colorado	2388.9	665	250	(62.5)
Connecticut	1862	601	250	(58.5)
Delaware	439	474	250	(41.3)
Florida	3903.1	2994	875.6	(70.8)
Georgia	2170.7	1595.4	457.8	(71.4)
Hawaii	354	177	250	—
Idaho	76.5	124	250	—
Illinois	4524.2	2302.3	866.5	(72.4)
Indiana	1854.5	709.2	412.8	(41.8)
Iowa	449	451	250	(44.6)
Kansas	567.8	490	250	(49.0)
Kentucky	1000.1	690	279.6	(59.5)
Louisiana	1292.5	1157	337.6	(71.9)
Maine	462.2	168	250	—
Maryland	1973.7	1309	334.7	(74.5)
Massachusetts	1863.1	1107.4	437.4	(60.6)
Michigan	1645.1	1346.4	685.9	(49.1)
Minnesota	2359.1	1497.6	316.1	(78.9)
Mississippi	1140.5	470.4	250	(46.9)
Missouri	1542.9	904.5	380	(58.0)
Montana	249.3	221.6	250	—
Nebraska	515.9	470	250	(46.9)
Nevada	259.7	336	250	(25.6)
New Hampshire	357.8	182	250	—
New Jersey	1816.9	1786	517.6	(68.1)
New Mexico	482.7	242.3	250	—
New York	3406.9	2574	1332.9	(48.3)
North Carolina	876.1	522	474.8	(9.1)
North Dakota	199.2	244	250	—
Ohio	1537.7	1161.9	806.4	(30.6)
Oklahoma	580.2	547.7	250	(54.4)
Oregon	1543.8	539	250	(53.7)
Pennsylvania	3097.4	2741	891.7	(67.5)
Rhode Island	187.2	518	250	(51.8)
South Carolina	627.6	663	253.4	(61.8)
South Dakota	271.2	291	250	(14.1)
Tennesse	2296.2	1280.1	360.2	(71.9)

Table 21.2. (*Continued*)

State	1985 Volume ($Million)	1984 Volume ($Million)	1987 Volume Cap ($Million)	Percentage of 1984 Volume Lost Due to 1984 Cap
Texas	4001.9	3488	1251.2	(64.2)
Utah	437.3	512	250	(51.2)
Vermont	244.5	124	250	—
Virginia	2123	2103.2	434	(79.4)
Washington	692.9	572	334.7	(41.5)
West Virginia	351.6	281	250	(11.1)
Wisconsin	833.4	528	358.9	(22.1)
Wyoming	115	130	250	—
	$76,630	$52,219.2	$21,281.1	(59.3)

[a] 1985 and 1984 volumes do not include activities that lost tax-exempt status as a result of the 1986 Tax Reform Act, or volume issued in those years for 501(c)(3) organizations.

Source: Public Securities Association, U.S. Treasury Department, and Bureau of the Census.

volume ($2.1 billion vs. $434 million). As these data indicate, Tax Reform will have a substantial and permanent effect in reducing new tax-exempts for private activities. Adding in the 1984 volume of private activity bonds that were repealed by Tax Reform—$18.8 billion—the potential reduction amounts to nearly $50 billion.

EFFECT ON MARKETING AND DEBT MANAGEMENT PRACTICES

To borrowers, the principal attraction of the tax-exempt market is a lower cost of capital. An additional advantage has been available from investing the proceeds of tax-exempt issues in higher-yielding (taxable) securities. This arbitrage practice had been circumscribed to a significant extent by federal laws and regulations prior to Tax Reform, but many governmental-purpose borrowings were permitted to earn arbitrage through three special features of these regulations. Under the so-called temporary period rule, governmental borrowers were permitted to invest new-issue proceeds at unlimited yields for three years, and sometimes five years, after the sale date. Borrowers also were allowed to invest a portion of bond proceeds at unlimited yields in "reasonably required reserve and replacement funds" (limited to 15 percent of the issue) for the life of the bond issue. Finally, the definition of the "yield" on the bond issue permitted borrowers to discount future debt service payments to a present value equal to the net proceeds of the sale after all costs of issuance (e.g., underwriters' spread) had been deducted. This discount rate was often as much as 50 basis points higher than the discount rate that equated the present value of debt service payments to gross bond proceeds (the latter rate is often termed the "true interest cost" or TIC).

Under these rules, issuers and investment bankers developed sophisticated methods for "sizing" new bond issues to take full advantage of legal arbitrage opportunities. Long-lived construction projects often were funded in full and in advance to benefit from investment earnings. Bond proceeds were sometimes used to fund, or capitalize, interest payments for three years; and the practice of borrowing to pay underwriters and others was common.

Figure 21.1 summarizes a typical analysis of the sources and uses of funds in a bond issue that points out the importance of arbitrage: investment income amounts to nearly 10 percent of bond proceeds. One measure of the potential contribution of arbitrage is presented in Figure 21.2—the yield spread between 1-year U.S. Treasuries and 30-year tax-exempts. This yield spread reached a peak of 600 basis points in 1981 at the cyclical peak in interest rates. Recognition of the arbitrage opportunities during the early 1980s also contributed to the rapid growth of variable-rate bond issues, described in Chapter 20. These variable-rate bonds pegged the periodic interest rate to the short-term market, and as Figure 21.2 indicates, the arbitrage yield spread between one-year Treasuries and tax-exempts has often exceeded 500 basis points.

Tax Reform drastically curtails arbitrage profits for all issuers of tax-exempts. The overriding rule is that issuers must rebate any arbitrage profits to the federal

ESTIMATED SOURCES AND USES OF FUNDS

The following table sets forth estimates of the sources and uses of moneys available for the construction of the 1984 Expansion, including the 1984B Bond proceeds.

Sources:	
1984B Bonds	$52,200,000
Investment income (1)	5,081,425
Funds already expended	769,000
Total sources	$58,050,425
Uses:	
Estimated costs of construction of the 1984 Expansion (2)	$36,735,000
Deposit to the Debt Service Reserve Fund (3)	6,044,800
Capitalized interest (30 months)	13,846,250
Costs of issuance (4)	1,424,375
Total uses	$58,050,425

(1) Assumes 8.5 percent investment earnings on the Construction Fund, 10 percent investment earnings on capitalized interest and 11 percent investment earnings on the Debt Service Reserve Fund.
(2) See "System Expansion Plan."
(3) Represents the debt service reserve requirement for the 1984B bonds.
(4) Includes underwriter's discount.

Figure 21.1. Metropolitan Government of Nashville and Davidson County, $52,200,000 energy production facility, floating-rate monthly demand-revenue bonds, December 11, 1984

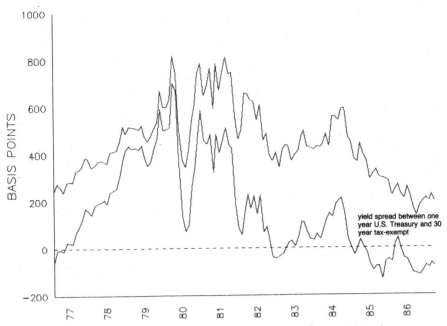

Figure 21.2. Arbitrage Yield Spreads in the Tax-Exempt Market

government. Generally, arbitrage not subject to rebate is permitted only for six months after the sale date and then only if all bond proceeds have been expended for the intended purpose. (Small issuers of less than $5 million are permitted a three-year temporary period.) The discount rate used to determine the bond "yield" has been changed to the TIC, further lowering the permitted yield on investments.

Moreover, the test for arbitrage has been changed from an expectational assurance to an empirical one. Issuers cannot simply aver that they do not intend to earn arbitrage; instead, they must keep records on an issue-by-issue basis of any investment earnings and remit any arbitrage profits to the Treasury every five years. Finally, debt service reserves cannot exceed 10 percent of bond proceeds and investment earnings on these reserves are limited to the TIC on the bond issue.

The new arbitrage rules will increase the sensitivity of new issues to high and rising interest rates during future cycles. Under the former rules, borrowers were insulated from the full impact of cyclical peaks in rates by the high arbitrage profits available. The potential profits available in 1980–1982 are depicted in Figure 21.2. Governmental units also had incentives to borrow at high rates knowing that any future decline in interest rates could produce immediate debt service savings through advance refundings. The technique of advance refunding is described in Chapter 20. Under the former rules, borrowers were encouraged to advance-refund early and often. One indication of the speed with which governments moved to capture these savings is seen in the volume of advance refundings in the nine months after the September 1982 drop in rates: more than $1.5 billion per month, compared with only $270 million monthly for the previous nine months.

Tax Reform also changes the rules regarding advance refundings. In general, new issues sold after January 1986 can be advance-refunded only once. This new restriction will heighten the cyclical sensitivity of new-issue volume and cause issuers to reevaluate the traditional package of optional redemption features. The conventional package—a 10-year deferred call with a premium of 2 or 3 percent—is no longer as valuable now that it can be "exercised in advance" only once. New call-option packages will be developed and more refined analyses will be devoted to optimal refunding strategies.

Private activity bonds are subject to additional restrictions on the marketing of new issues. In particular, no more than 2 percent of the proceeds from tax-exempt securities can be used to finance various costs of issuance. As specified in Tax Reform, items included in the 2 percent limit are:

1. The gross underwriting spread.
2. Legal fees, including issuer's counsel and underwriters' counsel.
4. Fees for financial advisors.
4. Rating agency fees.
5. Trustee and paying agent fees.
6. Fees for accounting services required for the debt issue.
7. Fees for special feasibility or engineering studies necessary for the bond sale.

Some insight into the impact of the 2-percent limit is provided in Table 21.3, which shows the average gross underwriting spread on selected private activity bonds in 1982 and 1986. In 1982, interest rates were near historical highs, and the demand for tax-exempts from banks and insurance companies was weak. Underwriting spreads generally are high under such market conditions, and the table indicates that most private activity bonds carried spreads above 2 percent. By 1986, underwriter spreads had declined, along with interest rates, but small issues continued to carry spreads at or above the new 2-percent limit. The new limits will preclude many borrowers from including the costs of transacting as part of bond proceeds. While issuers may use current revenues to meet these costs, they also can be expected to search for economies in transacting. Pooled borrowings, or bond banks, may be more widely used to achieve lower issuance costs, but other practices—such as direct placements or competitive bidding—will also be explored in this process.

TAX REFORM AND THE DEMAND FOR TAX-EXEMPTS

The effect of Tax Reform on the demand for tax-exempts is difficult to unravel because a variety of tax changes simultaneously affect the relative attractiveness of

Table 21.3. Average Underwriter Spreads on Private Activity Bonds (Percentage of Par Value)

Type of Issue	Less than $5 Million		$5–10 Million		$10–25 Million		$25–50 Million		Over $50 Million	
	1982	1986	1982	1986	1982	1986	1982	1986	1982	1986
Hospitals	3.5%	2.3%	3.4%	2.2%	3.1%	2.1%	2.7%	1.8%	2.6%	1.7%
Small-issue IDB	2.5	2.9	2.4	2.2	2.1	1.6	1.9	1.9	NA	1.1
Airports	2.2	2.4	1.7	1.4	2.1	1.9	2.7	1.3	2.4	2.0
College/university	2.0	1.9	2.6	1.9	2.4	1.6	2.7	1.5	2.0	1.3
Multifamily rental	2.0	2.5	1.9	2.3	2.5	2.6	2.3	1.6	2.5	1.1
Redevelopment	3.3	1.9	2.8	2.3	1.8	2.1	N/A	1.7	N/A	1.9
Single-family MRB	2.4	2.0	2.5	2.0	2.7	1.6	2.8	1.5	2.6	1.5
Average: All issues	2.3	2.0	2.7	1.8	2.5	1.7	2.6	1.6	2.3	1.3

Source: Public Securities Association, Dealer's Digest: IDD Information Services/PSA Municipal Database.

these securities. On balance, the combined impact of these changes suggests that households will continue to be the primary suppliers of funds for long-term bonds, while nonfinancial corporations may supplant banks in the short-term market. For all investors, the new and dramatically lower marginal tax rates on income will increase the required ratio of tax-exempt rates relative to taxable rates.

Household Demand

Tax Reform has pluses and minuses for the household sector. On balance, it will increase the sector's demand for tax-exempts. Demand will increase despite lower marginal tax rates and the imposition of a minimum tax on private activity bonds, because the opportunities for alternative tax-advantaged investments have been decreased. Tax Reform reduces the top marginal tax rate from 50 to 38.5 percent in 1987 and to 28 percent thereafter.

Although it is advertised as a simple system consisting of only two rates, the tax structure for individuals is actually more complicated. The personal exemption is phased out for joint returns over $149,000 and the 15 percent rate is recaptured for joint incomes above $72,000, resulting in an effective marginal tax rate of approximately 33 percent over a wide range of income. At the same time, a number of lost deductions and lost credits—consumer loan interest, dividend exclusions— will increase the percentage of gross income subject to taxation.

The reduction in alternative tax-advantaged investments in Tax Reform may divert a significant supply of household savings to tax-exempts. The Act restricts IRAs and 401(k) deductions, which had amounted in recent years to more than $40 billion. In the long run, the change in capital gains treatment may have the largest impact. Eliminating the special tax treatment of these gains increases the effective rate from 20 to 28 percent, which should shift investment preferences from equities to debt and to tax-exempts. According to federal tax returns through 1983, taxable net long-term capital gains of individuals have amounted to nearly $50 billion. Under Tax Reform, the full amount of these gains is subject to federal taxation.

A complication in estimating household demand comes from the new rules for the individual alternative minimum tax (AMT). AMT liabilities are computed by adding to taxable income certain tax preferences, including interest on private activity bonds issued after August 7, 1986. For most individuals, the AMT liability will not be significant, and any impact on the demand for private activity bonds will be small.

More important in shaping the specifics of individual demand will be state taxes. The reduction in federal tax rates increases the relative importance of state taxes in the total tax bill. Most states do not tax residents on interest for in-state tax-exempts, but they do tax out-of-state tax-exempt income. As a result, regional differences in interest rates are likely to be widened, with high-tax states enjoying a relative advantage in the marketing of new debt. These regional differences are likely to increase the demand for state-specific mutual funds and unit trusts.

Demand for Tax-Exempts by Banks and Insurance Companies

Before reviewing the impact of several special provisions affecting institutional demand, it is useful to discuss the mechanics and implications of the AMT as it is applied to corporations. The tax is greatly strengthened over its predecessor, formulated on the premise that no corporation should enjoy economic income without paying taxes. Although generally similar to the AMT for individuals, the corporate version of the AMT has a further refinement that affects all tax-exempts.

First, the corporation calculates the amount of its taxable income under regular tax rules and determines its tax liability at the 34-percent rate. Then the corporation adds to its regular taxable income (1) the income not included for tax purposes (such as accelerated depreciation), and (2) one-half of its "untaxed reported profits," or excess book income. Untaxed reported profits consist of the amount of income reported by a corporation to the public minus (1) income it reports for tax purposes and (2) its preference income. The AMT rate of 20 percent is then applied to the expanded income base. The corporation pays tax on either the regular or the AMT basis, depending on which method results in the greater tax liability.

Income from municipal securities enters into the corporate AMT calculation in one of two ways: as a preference item or as a component of excess book income. As in the case of the individual AMT, income from private activity bonds issued after August 7, 1986, gives rise to preference income. On the other hand, income from bonds issued before August 8, 1986, and from new bonds issued for governmental purposes or 501(c)(3) organizations is not preference income but does add to excess book income. Because half of the excess income is subject to the AMT rate of 20 percent, the effective rate under Tax Reform is 10 percent.

As in the case of the individual AMT, a relatively large proportion of income will need to come from tax preferences before the tax liability under AMT will exceed that on regular corporate income. Generally, up to 40 percent of total income can be from preference items (including interest on private activity bonds) before the AMT exceeds regular liability, at which point the effective tax rate is 20 percent. However, in the case of governmental and 501(c)(3) obligations, approximately 60 percent is the limit, after which the marginal rate is 10 percent.

Tax Reform also removes an important incentive for commercial bank investment—the deductibility of interest expenses on borrowed funds invested in tax-exempts. This tax deduction is removed for all tax-exempts acquired after August 15, 1986, except that it is retained for purchases of governmental purpose or 501(c)(3) bonds from issuers of less than $10 million in new debt each year. The latter bonds still may be purchased under the previous rule that permits 80 percent of interest expense to be deducted. The combined effects of the loss of deductibility and the exposure to the AMT promise to significantly reduce bank demand.

These provisions also will alter the level of yields required on tax-exempts to attract bank investment. Figure 21.3 provides the formulas necessary to calculate the "break-even" ratio between tax-exempt and taxable rates that results in equivalent after-tax returns. This ratio depends jointly on the percentage of interest costs

Banks not subject to AMT

$$TE = TX - (TX \times MTR) + (CF \times MTR) - (DR \times CF \times MTR)$$

Banks subject to AMT

$$TE = \frac{\begin{array}{c} TX - (TX \times AMT) + (CF \times AMT) - (DR \times CF \times AMT) \\ - (.1 \times CF) - (.1 \times CF \times DR) \end{array}}{.9}$$

Where:

TE = tax-exempt yeild
TX = taxable yield
CF = cost of funds
DR = deductibility ratio
MTR = marginal tax rate on regular income
AMT = tax rate under alternative minimum tax

Figure 21.3. Calculating the "break-even ratio" of tax-exempt yields to taxable yields for commercial banks under tax reform. (*Source:* Cadmus Hicks, "Taxing 'Tax-Exempts': Guidelines for Casualty Companies and Banks," Research Report, John Nuveen & Company, August 25, 1986)

that banks can deduct, the corporate tax rate, and the differential between the cost of funds to banks and the rate earned on fully taxable investments. Under the prior law, with a 46 percent marginal tax rate and the deductibility of 80 percent of interest costs, the break-even ratio of interest rates was 0.63 when the cost of funds equaled the taxable return on assets. Under the new law, with a 34 percent marginal tax rate and the 80 percent deductibility for small issues, the break-even ratio rises to 0.74 for banks not subject to the AMT. For tax-exempts from large issuers, where banks are not allowed to deduct interest costs, the ratio rises to 1.0. When banks are also subject to the AMT, the break-even ratio rises, to 0.91 for small issues and to 1.0 for all other tax-exempts.

The impact of the new tax provisions on bank demand is clear: Banks will find their demand curve for tax-exempts radically shifted and fragmented. Qualified small issuers, where the 80 percent deductibility is retained, should be preferred investments, but even these securities will be unattractive when banks are subject to the alternative minimum tax. What this means in the real world of bank demand remains to be determined, and depends among other factors on the relative supply of small issuer debt. While there is no easily available information on the annual volume by issuer, a reasonable proxy may be found in the distribution of new bonds by size of issue. Issues of less than $10 million in size in 1984 accounted for approximately 60 percent of the number of all issues and 10 percent of the dollar volume. As of early 1987, there are indications that Tax Reform has enlivened the market for "qualified" small issues, with estimates that such issues carry yields 25 basis points lower than yields on otherwise comparable governmental-purpose bonds.

In the mid-1970s, property and casualty insurance companies were major buyers of tax-exempts, but like commercial banks they have been relatively passive in absorbing the heavy volume of new issues since 1980. At year-end 1985, they held $56 billion in tax-exempts, and for the period 1983–1985 displayed virtually no change in their holdings, buying just enough new bonds to replace those that matured.

Traditionally, insurance companies have favored high-yielding, lower-grade revenue bonds with long maturities. But in the 1980s, these institutions accumulated large underwriting losses from insurance and, as a whole, showed negative taxable income. Although profits have recently returned and investment in tax-exempts has quickened, insurance companies have shortened the maturities of new purchases.

Property and casualty companies are subject, as are all corporations, to the alternative minimum corporate tax. They are also subject to a new tax feature that is designed to limit the practice of using tax-exempt interest income to finance insurance loss reserves. Under this new provision, insurance companies are required to reduce their deduction for losses by an amount equal to 15 percent of tax-exempt interest earnings. This amounts to an effective tax of 5.1 percent ($.34 \times .15$) on tax-exempt income and it applies to all tax-exempt securities held by insurance companies.

The consequence of these changes is to raise the break-even ratio of tax-exempt to taxable rates for casualty companies from a minimum of 0.54 under prior law to 0.71 under the new law, due to the reduction in loss reserves. Where a company is subject to the AMT, the break-even ratio rises to 0.775 for governmental purpose bonds and to 0.84 for private-activity bonds.

Other changes in the tax law will increase the tax exposure of property and casualty companies. They will need to include premium income in taxable income sooner and wait longer to deduct some claims, thus eliminating the tax deferral they enjoyed under prior law. With more profits to shelter and fewer options, insurance companies should be good customers for tax-exempts when the ratio of rates exceeds 0.75.

SUMMARY OF TAX EFFECTS: A MEDLEY OF RATES

The Tax Reform Act of 1986 results in new federal tax treatment for state and local obligations that affect both the type of security and the individual or corporate taxpayer. Prior law did not subject interest income from tax-exempt securities to any form of federal taxation: securities either were or were not tax-exempt. (One exception was the inclusion of tax-exempt interest income in determining tax liability for Social Security recipients.) Tax Reform drastically changes and complicates that situation.

Table 21.4 shows the variety of federal income tax exposure, depending on whether a bond is a governmental-purpose or private activity, whether the taxpayer is subject to the AMT, and for property and casualty companies. The rates refer to bonds sold after August 7, 1986, in the case of the minimum tax, except for the excess book income provisions which apply to tax-exempts whenever issued or acquired. The tax rates stated are the maximum marginal rates applicable once the new law becomes fully effective in 1988.

The marginal rates pertaining to interest income from tax-exempt securities, when combined with the top marginal rates applicable under the regular income tax, permit some preliminary estimates of the break-even ratios for various investor groups and types of securities. Generally, corporations subject to the top rate of 34 percent represent the first tier of investor demand (primarily for short-term maturities) when the ratio of tax-exempt to taxable rates exceeds 0.66. This forms the theoretical floor for the ratio of rates (leaving out any potential impact from state or local taxes).

Next come those individuals subject to the highest effective marginal income tax rate of 33 percent, implying a ratio of 0.67. The preponderant demand, however, would seem to appear at the 28-percent marginal bracket, which will apply to most

Table 21.4. Summary of Tax Rates on Income from Municipal Securities under Various Provisions of the Tax Reform Act of 1986

Investor Group and Type of Tax	Class of Municipal Security	
	Governmental[a]	Private Activity[b]
Individual		
Regular income[c]	0%	0%
AMT	0	21
Corporation		
Regular income	0	0
AMT:		
Preference income	0	20
Excess book income[d]	10	10
Property and Casualty Companies		
Regular income	5.1	5.1
AMT:		
Preference income	11.5	20
Excess book income[e]	11.5	20

[a] Governmental and 501 (c) (3).

[b] Not included are those private activity bonds that are fully taxable.

[c] Not including tax on Social Security income prorated to tax-exempt income.

[d] Not including the 0.12 percent Superfund tax on excess book income exceeding $2 million.

[e] Bonds acquired before 8/8/86 are taxed at 10 percent under the excess book income.

households. At this tax rate, the break-even ratio of yields is 0.72. This ratio will also attract property and casualty companies that are not subject to the AMT, but must pay the 5.1 percent tax based on reductions in loss reserves.

As noted earlier, banks, with their dependence on borrowed funds, generally will not find tax-exempts of interest. The major exception is the small-issuer qualified bond, which appears attractive when the ratio of rates is in the low .70s. Individuals and institutions that are subject to the AMT will find tax-exempts viable when the ratio of rates is 79 percent or higher (individuals) or 89 percent (corporations). Yields on private activity bonds must equal those on fully taxable alternatives to be of interest to these investors.

PART 6   BROKER ACTIVITIES

The scope of broker activities varies widely among investment banking firms. Some operate very large retail broker networks, others do no retail business. Most carry on an institutional brokerage business, but the importance of this business shows a wide variation among firms. With the abolition of fixed minimum commissions in 1975, the way was opened for discount brokerage, and the result has been to create new and difficult choices in the face of increased competition. In Chapter 22, Peter Frank discusses the economics of brokerage, including revenue and cost aspects. Chapter 23, by Edward Johnson, deals with what most people (but not the author, for reasons he states clearly) refer to as "discount brokerage."

The clearing function is a much less known but crucial aspect of brokerage, and it is described in Chapter 24, by Van Burger. Clearing has become an important specialty, and Chapter 24 discusses the process, the characteristics of a successful firm, and the economics of the business.

22 The Economics of Brokerage

PETER E. FRANK

Shaping and negotiating investment banking deals and services is only the beginning of a process that brings investors and borrowers together. This investment process generally utilizes the two major groups of investment instruments—equities and debt. Created as a means to raise capital, equities and debt are often purchased and sold countless times through the various securities markets. The sections that follow will provide an overview of:

What these primary investment instruments are

The broker–dealer participants in the markets and their basic function

Some key issues facing broker–dealers today

INVESTMENT INSTRUMENTS

Various types of entities that desire to raise capital, such as corporations and governments, often do so by issuing securities. These securities, or financial instruments, give rights to their purchasers and represent property and value. They are usually:

Equity instruments (stocks), which represent ownership interest (equity) in the issuing entity and entitle the owner to a portion of the company's profits; or,

Debt instruments (bonds), which represent a promise on the part of the issuing entity to repay, at a specified time, a sum of money and an amount of interest for use of the money.

Other instruments of a more speculative nature are stock options and futures, which differ from stocks and bonds in that they are not backed by an issuing corporation (and have no fundamental underlying value). More specifically:

Options are contracts to purchase or sell shares of a particular stock. The contract specifies the security, the purchase or sale price, the life of the option, and the number of shares.

Futures are commitments to receive or deliver a specified quantity and quality of a commodity by a specified future date.

These investment vehicles are the major types of instruments traded today. Increased competition and changing markets have resulted in frequent announcement of new instruments, such as securities representing pools of home mortgages or automobile loans, index options, options on futures, and many more. The creation of new instruments seems likely to continue.

THE BROKER–DEALER

The intermediaries or agents who act for customers (and for themselves) are broker–dealers, frequently called securities firms or brokerage firms. Traditionally, many investors in securities have traded through brokerage firms, whose role is to provide services supporting the exchange and distribution of securities and to give investment management and advice.

A broker–dealer may act as:

A broker, that is, an agent who buys and sells securities on behalf of a client

A dealer, that is, a principal, buying and selling on his or her own behalf with the intention of making a profit

A broker–dealer, performing both functions

Broker–dealers can provide many services, including underwriting, purchase and sale of stocks, bonds, and other investments, development and dissemination of research and market information, and margin services. Depending on the type and extent of services offered, a securities firm can be considered as:

A national full-line firm, providing an entire range of investment services for both retail and institutional customers and having many offices nationwide. Merrill Lynch, PaineWebber, and E.F. Hutton are considered to be national, full-line firms.

An investment banking firm, such as Goldman Sachs and First Boston, primarily providing institutional customers with investment banking services—underwriting, mergers and acquisitions, and distributing, buying, and selling securities for clients and their own accounts.

A regional firm, such as Blunt Ellis & Loewi, Wheat First Securities, and Alex. Brown & Sons, offering a full line of products to customers within a particular geographic area.

A discounter, such as Charles Schwab and Quick & Reilly, offering retail customers lower commissions than other types of firms. These firms do not offer investment advice to their customers, but accept and process orders to buy or sell. Because they do not act as salespeople or marketers, do not require some of the support functions that full-line firms do, and do not pay a percentage of their commissions to salespeople, discounters can offer lower commissions than other firms.

Broker–dealers usually have a headquarters office as well as branches. The number of branch offices a firm has depends on the type of firm, the number and type of customers served, and the nature of services provided. Headquarters generally is responsible for providing supporting services to the branch network and also for administrative activities, operations (the clearing and settlement functions), research, and most investment banking activities.

Sales are the main business of branch offices. Activities there may be geared to either retail or institutional sales or both. Because branch offices are concerned primarily with generation of income through sales, they are considered profit centers. The operations function and other support functions of the firm are non-income-producing and are thus considered cost centers.

BUSINESS FUNCTIONS

Underwriting

Clients who wish to raise capital through the issuance of securities are usually corporations and governments that need the guidance and services provided by an investment banker. The underwriter is an intermediary between the issuer and prospective investors. Underwriting can take the form of either competitive bidding or operating on a negotiated basis.

Under competitive bidding, the issuer accepts bids for the securities offered. This method usually is followed for governments, public utility corporations, and railroads. Negotiated underwriting means that the price of the issue is set by the investment banker and the issuer. In this case, the investment banker may purchase the entire issue of the securities being sold and in turn sell it to the public, or the investment banker may act as agent and market the securities on a best-efforts or all-or-none basis.

In the first instance, when an agreement is made to purchase the entire issue, the underwriter may form a network of underwriters, known as a purchasing syndicate, to share responsibility for the purchase and subsequent distribution. Securities dealers who are clients of the purchasing syndicate form a selling syndicate, which buys the securities from the purchasing syndicate to resell to the public.

When acting as an agent for the issuer, the investment banker does not purchase the entire issue, but only helps to market the securities. The best-efforts and all-or-none methods represent two types of agent agreements.

As part of a best-efforts, or takedown, method, the investment banker contracts to sell as much of the issue as possible through its selling syndicate. Compensation is on a commission-per-share basis. An all-or-none contract requires an underwriter to purchase and distribute a specified amount of a security, but stipulates that the entire issue must sell within a stipulated amount of time or the purchase offer will be withdrawn.

A major goal of the issuer selling securities is to place the issue in the market at the highest price per share (in the case of equities), or the lowest interest rate (in the case of debt instruments), and to obtain the funds generated from the sale. Obviously an important element of underwriting is the price at which an issue is marketed. To determine the price, the underwriter considers many variables, including size and quality of the issue, characteristics of the issuer, current market conditions, and competition of other issues. Evaluating this kind of information is one of the research functions of the investment bank.

Whichever negotiated method is used, the underwriter's major source of profit is the difference between the price paid to the issuer for the securities and the price of the securities then sold to the market. Ideally, the issuer should just sell out. If it is undersold, the offering price was probably too high; if it oversold, the offering price was probably too low. Sometimes the new issue must be allocated to prospective investors if there is intense demand. At other times, salespeople are offered additional incentives to sell the issue.

Research

Firms employ professional researchers to assist underwriters in developing and marketing products and in making recommendations to clients regarding available products on the market. Research evaluations include:

Industry analysis, using a composite of the fundamental business and financial characteristics of companies within a specific industry group. An industry analysis could include comparison of a company's performance to industry averages as well as comparison of performance across different industry groups.

Company analysis, examining a particular organization, its financial condition and prospects, and its securities from an investment perspective, and generally including an investment recommendation (e.g., buy, sell, or hold).

Technical analysis, focusing on the performance of securities in the various markets.

Portfolio analysis, concerned primarily with matching a client's investment objectives with a suitable investment program.

Marketing and Sales

The primary objectives of the marketing function of a broker–dealer are development and promotion of new and existing investment products and services. Marketing often is organized along product lines, such as marketing for fixed-income instruments, for equities, for options, and the like. Besides presenting products though the various forms of advertising media, the marketing department also focuses on promoting products to the sales force of the broker–dealer, who in turn present the products to their customers.

Each broker–dealer has its own sales force. If the firm does business with both retail and institutional customers, there is usually a different sales force for each type of customer, and often for each of the various products being offered.

The people who interact directly with the investing public and who are thus responsible for the sales function, as well as for providing investment advice to customers, are known as "account executives" or "registered representatives" (RRs). RRs are employees of a member firm and must pass specified tests and meet certain requirements to be formally registered. An RR is required to act only in the best interest of the investor and is therefore responsible for understanding the customer's financial condition and learning the customer's investment objectives. RRs may act according to specific customer instructions for each transaction, or may manage a discretionary account that permits the execution of transactions for a customer's account as the RR sees fit.

Commissions are charged to the customer for executing a securities trade. The registered representative receives part of the commission, referred to as a payout, as his or her compensation. Payout formulas are complex, varying by product, by total production for that RR in one or more previous periods, by customer, and by many other factors. Often large bonuses have been paid to high producers to induce them to change firms. Payout percentages commonly approach 40 percent of the commission and often are larger. RRs frequently are paid extra amounts for selling particular securities their firm would like them to sell, for example, from an underwriting in which the firm is participating. Discount firms pay their salespeople salaries rather than a percentage of their sales volume, on the premise that they are order-takers rather than sales initiators.

Execution

Securities are traded either on exchanges or in the over-the-counter markets. Securities traded on exchanges receive most of the coverage in the press and include most of the equity issues of major corporations. The number of securities traded over the counter significantly exceeds the number traded on exchanges and includes many equities, all government and government agency issues, and most of the new products.

The major exchanges operate generally on a specialist system with the specialist charged with maintaining an orderly market. The specialist's responsibility is to match buy and sell orders and to buy or sell for his or her own account, if necessary, to assure an orderly market. The specialist's role is changing steadily as automatic execution systems replace or supplement some of the specialist's former roles.

Over-the-counter securities are traded in a network of dealer firms. These dealers earn profits by trading, that is, by selling securities for more than their purchase price. There can be many dealers making a market in a particular security as opposed to only one specialist per security for an exchange-traded security. Banks are major participants in trading many of the more active issues, particularly U.S. government securities. Trading has seen explosive growth in recent years, fueled by factors described later in this section.

Operations

The operations department of a brokerage firm processes trades and other associated transactions, maintains customer accounts, updates firm records and accounts, and handles cash and securities receipts and deliveries. Operations, also known as the back office, includes the order, purchase and sale, margin, cashier, dividend, proxy, and stock record functions.

Order. An RR receiving or initiating instructions to execute a securities trade sends the order to the order department, where transactions are sorted and routed to the appropriate market for execution.

Market orders, those specifying execution at the current market price, are executed immediately, while limit orders are held until the specified price or other condition is satisfied. Once an order is executed, the department sends information relating to the transaction (such as price) to the RR for his or her records and on to the purchase and sales function for further processing.

Purchase and Sales. The purchase and sales (P&S) department enters the trade on the books of the firm. P&S responsibilities include informing customers of the amounts that will be paid or received for a securities transaction and by what date, and verifying the details of all executed trades with contrabrokers and clearing corporations. In this role, the department will prepare customer confirmations, including computing commissions, taxes, fees, price of the securities, and net or gross amount involved. P&S advises the cashier's department of the details necessary to eventually settle the trade.

Cashier. This department is responsible for coordinating the actual receipt and delivery of cash and securities associated with the settlement of a trade. A purchase, for example, would involve the cashier receiving the securities from the selling broker and arranging payment to that broker for those securities. The cashier is responsible also for receiving payment from the customer. Upon receipt of a security, it is the responsibility of the cashier to prepare and forward the securities for transfer of title to street registration or to the name of a specified customer.

The cashier's department also handles the custody of securities owned by the firm and its customers. This includes providing adequate safeguards for the housing and movement of the securities, ensuring segregation of those securities owned by the firm from those owned by customers, and processing securities for tender offers, subscriptions, and redemptions.

Margin. Customers of a broker–dealer may arrange to operate on a cash basis, a margin basis, or both. A cash basis agreement stipulates that a customer will pay in full by settlement date for any purchase transaction and that the customer will deliver any securities sold by settlement date. A margin account allows the customer to pay part of the purchase price and to borrow the balance, with interest, from the brokerage firm.

The margin department is responsible for monitoring and updating each customer's account. Upon receipt of information about an executed trade, the margin department checks the status of the customer's account to ensure that credit extended is in compliance with limitations set both by the firm and by regulators. For customers purchasing securities on a cash basis, the margin department ensures that cash payments are rendered in full and on a timely basis.

The margin department also is responsible for reviewing each margin account daily to ensure that changing market prices have not caused a customer's equity to fall below prescribed limits. If a customer's account has an outstanding balance beyond firm or regulatory limits, the margin department will initiate a "margin call," requesting the customer to make payment sufficient to bring its account balance to an acceptable level.

Additional Operations Functions. Additional operations functions of a broker–dealer include:

The dividend department, which received dividend payments for all securities held by the firm and distributes these payments to the appropriate customers.

The proxy department, which receives corporate financial reports and stockholder meeting notices applicable to securities held by the firm and forwards this information to the appropriate customers. The proxy department also votes on corporate management issues on behalf of customers who have authorized the firm to do so.

The stock record department, which maintains the firm's records of all securities held, their location, and which customers own the securities.

Electronic Data Processing

Broker–dealers vary in the degree of sophistication of data processing at their firms. One firm, for example, may route trades through the order department and other operations departments as physical tickets, while another firm may have automated the entire process. Volume is often the determining factor in the degree of automation in place at a firm.

The high cost of data processing coupled with rapid technological change has caused firms to examine their method of systems support, and several different approaches are found today, including the use of service bureaus, in-house data processing facilities, and combinations of both.

In-house data processing departments are responsible for all aspects of systems support, including new systems development, maintenance programming, and day-to-day computer operations. Most service bureaus are structured to provide a wide range of services and varying degrees of automation support to external users. Under such an arrangement, a brokerage firm uses the hardware, software, and, to some degree, the employees of the service bureau, and usually pays for the services on a usage (fee-per-transaction) basis. This kind of arrangement makes sense for a firm that does not want to incur the fixed costs associated with maintaining a major data processing operation. A service bureau arrangement is especially beneficial for smaller firms, where per-trade data processing costs for in-house processing would be unacceptably expensive because a relatively large fixed cost would be spread over only a small number of trades.

Data processing generally supports operations activities, accounting, and other administrative functions. Increasingly, data processing support is being provided to RRs, the research department, and to trading and investment banking departments.

Additionally, communications-related information services are in wide use. These include quotation terminals, news services, pricing services, analytical services, and the like—all designed to provide up-to-the-second information about rapidly changing markets. The rapid pace of the securities business, its high volume, and its increasing sophistication has resulted in broker–dealers being among the heaviest users of data processing today.

ISSUES FACING THE SECURITIES INDUSTRY

Many external factors, such as regulatory change, volatile economic conditions, and rapid technological advances, have a tremendous influence on the state of the securities industry. May 1, 1975, when the era of fixed commissions ended and negotiated rates began, signaled the beginning of major changes in the industry. Market volume has increased dramatically since then, and market averages and activity have been dynamic. Mergers and acquisitions continue to be frequent news in the brokerage community, and new products are introduced almost daily. And, perhaps most important, new players are entering the industry. There are many implications to the changes that face broker–dealers today.

Regulatory Change

One of the most significant issues facing the securities industry is the blurring of the lines between the brokerage and banking industries. Historically these industries were clearly divided by the mandates of the Banking Act of 1933 (the Glass-Steagall Act), which separated commercial banking and investment banking (except for trust services offered by commercial banks). Banks, however, are testing the limitations of this law and offering competition to the brokerage industry by issuing commercial paper, by underwriting municipal revenue bonds, by offering discount brokerage services, and by sponsoring money market and other mutual funds. Citicorp and Security Pacific are among the banks at the forefront of this effort.

Other regulatory changes, such as the Tax Equity and Fiscal Responsibility Act (TEFRA) and Rule 415, have affected the securities industry as well. TEFRA requires providers of financial services to verify investors' Social Security numbers and to report dividend, interest, and redemption payments (and in some cases withhold a designated amount of such payments). Major technological change and expense have been necessary to comply with the reporting and withholding requirements.

Rule 415, also known as shelf registration, has changed the process that an underwriter follows in bringing a security issue to market. Prior to Rule 415, an issue date for new securities had to be specified to the Securities and Exchange Commission by the underwriter. Rule 415 now allows an issue to be registered with the SEC and held until the underwriter (and the issuer) chooses to release the securities to the market, preferably when market conditions are most advantageous. The effect of this has been to increase the influence of the issuer over the underwriter (and thereby increase fee competition), in that multiple offerings can be covered by one underwriting.

Fee versus Transaction Income

Volatile markets and rapidly changing economic conditions have caused many broker–dealers to reexamine the source of their income and to take action to stabilize it. Income to a brokerage firm is generated by fee-based services, interest, or commissions. Commissions, or transaction-based income, depend upon the volume and size of trades—the larger the trade, the larger the commission, and the greater the number of trades, the more commissions earned. Commissions therefore are directly tied to market activity and market conditions. During down markets, when fewer and smaller trades occur, brokerage firms have experienced dramatic drops in commission income. Conversely, rising markets have caused significant increases in the commission income of securities firms.

Rapidly changing economic conditions, such as those witnessed in the 1980s, are reflected by turbulent and, for the most part, unpredictable securities markets. Many brokerage firms are consequently expanding their range of services beyond traditional brokerage products and thereby tying income to something more predictable than market conditions. Firms are focusing increasingly on providing fee-based services, such as investment banking, money management, and investment advisory services, trying to strike a better balance between transaction-based and fee-based income to more comfortably weather a down market. Additionally, and especially significant, price competition has steadily eroded the profits of commission business. Growth of the institutional sector of the business, with its fierce price pressure, has diminished the profitability of commission business. Discounters, too, have played a part, with their significantly lower charges for retail customers. Many securities firms are finding that their commission business is at break-even at best, so they are focusing on developing other more profitable sources of income.

Competition

Banks, independent investment advisors, and other nontraditional providers of investment services, such as insurance companies and retailers, are entering the securities business. Many brokerage firms are responding to this competition by offering new and varied products, by becoming more price competitive, and by structuring themselves to be able—as a single, large entity—to provide a full range of financial services. This concept of one-stop shopping has encouraged the combination of many large financial and nonfinancial organizations, resulting in the creation of conglomerates that position themselves to offer a full range of brokerage, insurance, or banking products and services. Some examples of such mergers or acquisitions are: Prudential Insurance Company and the securities firm of Bache Halsey Stuart Shields; Kemper Insurance Company and five regional broker–dealers; and Sears, Roebuck and Dean Witter Reynolds.

The formation of such large conglomerates has coincided with a decline in the number of independent regional securities firms, generally by merger or acquisition. The large financial conglomerates are more highly capitalized and are therefore better able to undertake financings for corporations without forming syndicates, which in effect edges out regional and smaller firms that once participated in these syndicates. In general, larger firms can achieve better economies of scale than smaller firms, due to the fact that fixed costs (such as administration, systems, and communications costs) can be spread over a larger base of business. It is more expensive for smaller firms to maintain the overhead necessary to support the wide range of products and services now being offered by the larger firms.

Despite this, however, many regional firms are doing quite well, because of their strong presence in their local marketplace, underwriting of local securities issues, efficient and effective management, and lack of bureaucratic overhead. Reports of the demise of these smaller firms appear to have been exaggerated.

Three major factors have contributed to these competitive changes: a dramatic increase in the pool of investment dollars, interest rate volatility, and government financing of the growing federal deficit. The pool of investment dollars has been growing because of tremendous increases over the past few years in the size of pension funds, whether from corporate pension programs or from individual pension-related pools of capital, such as IRA, Keogh, and 401(k) programs. These dollars must be invested in various securities, and the resulting flow of funds to investment markets has encouraged many new organizations to offer investment services and many existing securities industry players to offer new products and services. Also, foreign capital has been steadily flowing to U.S. markets over the past few years, adding to the already growing capital pool.

Interest-rate volatility has been partly responsible for growth in the trading of fixed-income investment products. When interest rates were relatively stable, fixed-income products generally were purchased and held to maturity, and trading seldom occurred, either for investment or speculative purposes. Volatile interest rates, coupled with the increasing flow of investable funds, resulted in many opportunities for capital gain as well as opportunities for commission or fee income to securities firms offering execution and other services.

Ongoing increases in the federal deficit have resulted in a major increase in the available pool of investment instruments, particularly U.S. government instruments. As a result, government bond trading has become a major part of the trading activities of securities organizations and investors. It appears likely to remain a major investment activity as long as the federal government continues to increase and maintain its deficit.

Cost Control

More complex products and services offered by the securities industry, and increasing trade volume, have increased securities firms' costs. Many variable costs, notably for personnel, have been replaced with fixed costs for computer systems, communications networks, and the like. This changing cost structure, as well as increases in costs to significantly higher dollar levels, has resulted in a growing cost-consciousness at securities firms and a concomitant emphasis on cost control and efficiency.

Peat Marwick has conducted a "securities industry multiclient performance study" for a number of years. It compares various cost and productivity factors across securities firms. The study is conducted by gathering data from each participating firm according to comprehensive and precise definitions, assuring that cross-firm data is consistent, and producing a matrix of comparative data. Over 400 data elements are produced to enable each firm to compare its performance to that of its industry peers. Among the major conclusions are that securities firms have an increasing awareness of and interest in the costs they are incurring, and are constantly focusing on methods of reducing these costs while maintaining service and productivity levels. In other words, shrinking gross margins brought about by increasing competition have altered the way securities firms operate.

Average trade count breakdowns for all participating firms in Peat Marwick's 1985 study are 68 percent retail, 11 percent institutional, and 21 percent firm. Share breakdowns are, of course, far more heavily weighted toward institutional and firm trading because of higher shares per trade for these activities than for retail. Firm trading includes those transactions that a brokerage firm executes for its own account as well as positioning block trades for institutions. For participating firms which emphasize institutional activity and investment banking, the average trade percentages were 42 percent retail, 17 percent institutional, and 41 percent firm trading. Participating discounter trade counts are, by contrast, almost 100 percent retail.

Participating firms in Peat Marwick's 1985 study achieved a per-trade revenue of approximately $155 from commissions on agency business and trading gains on principal business. Considering that over a third of this income (on average) is paid to the account executive, the remainder must cover all operations, data processing, and other support functions, as well as generate a profit for the organization. Considering also that the $155 per-trade average commission includes quite a few firms generating less than $100 per trade, it is easy to see how significant cost-consciousness has become. Operations costs, including costs of execution, range between $15 and $30 for firms participating in the study. Considering how little operations costs vary with trade size, one can understand the pressure to serve upscale customers and their larger trades—revenue per trade is higher, and the RR payout is higher, but other direct costs are relatively constant.

Execution costs also exhibit some interesting effects. Floor execution on the New York Stock Exchange costs the average firm $12.87 if it uses its own floor brokers. If the firms use a $2 broker (an independent broker on the floor of the Exchange) or specialist, the cost rises to $24.32. Designated Order Turnaround or DOT, the automatic execution system, makes the cost far less. In 1985, participating firms in Peat Marwick's study executed 26 percent of their NYSE trades themselves, used $2 brokers and specialists for 36 percent, and used DOT (now Super DOT) for 38 percent. DOT eligibility has been increasing steadily, so changes in these percentages are likely to continue. OTC trades, of course, have different cost components.

Data processing costs for securities firms show significant economies of scale. Firms processing fewer than 2000 trades per day spent $8.67 per trade in total data processing costs, while firms processing over 10,000 trades per day spent $4.84. The operations-related cost components are $5.08 and $2.51, respectively. Essentially, the break-even point between processing in-house and using an external service bureau is 1500–2500 trades per day, depending on business mix, software availability, and other factors. Beyond this point, in-house processing can become quite cost-effective.

Despite the economics, however, some smaller firms operate their own computing facilities while some large firms use service bureaus. Many brokerage firms, operating with what can be called a trading mentality, simply prefer the variable cost of a service bureau to the higher fixed costs of in-house processing. Other firms go one step farther and contract with another brokerage firm to take over all or part of their operations function. These firms are then known as correspondents.

Securities firms have increasingly focused on increasing net interest income and on improving account executive productivity in their transaction-based business. In many cases, one can view retail brokerage, with its high distribution costs, high processing costs, and competitive pricing, as a break-even business (although, as noted before, many regional firms operate quite profitably in this business). Profits are generated by capital markets products and other fee-based services, which are then distributed through the branch network, and from interest income generated in part by customer debits and other financing services.

Institutional brokerage, which is increasing steadily and generating multithousand-share trades, is subject to fierce price competition, while the retail business, generating far smaller trades, generates far larger per-share commissions but is subject to price competition from the discounters. Therefore, the dilemma for securities firms in selling a commodity product (100 shares of IBM stock is the same no matter what brokerage firm is used) is how to differentiate the firm's products and services while remaining price competitive; how to increase service while cutting costs and reducing prices.

23 A New Product for the Securities Industry: Call It Anything But Discount Brokerage*

EDWARD C. JOHNSON III

What's in a name? Sometimes everything, and all the wrong things. From that perspective, "discount brokerage" is only half-bad as a name for the fastest-growing segment of the securities industry. Brokerage it is, discount it is not. But that is only one of the myths about the product that has come to be known as discount brokerage since a 1975 SEC decision to deregulate all fixed commissions on securities.

Let's set the record straight on just what discount brokerage is and where it came from. To do that means looking at three major phenomena that converged in the mid- to late-1970s: a changing legislative and regulatory climate, advances in computer technology, and the emergence of a new breed of financial consumers. Each served as both cause and prerequisite for the dramatic success of what, for lack of imagination, has come to be known as discount brokerage. Any one condition without the other two would have dramatically altered the course of financial history.

SEVEN YEARS TO MAY DAY, AND THEN SOME

On May 1, 1975, the Securities and Exchange Commission issued its historic order to end rate fixing on the major exchanges. But history had been in the making for at least seven years. The "May Day" decision was the exclamation point to a lengthy yet resolute declarative statement from diverse sectors of the financial community.

---

* This chapter is based on remarks of the author before the Securities Industry Association, January 19, 1984. Research associate: Margaret A. Malaspina, Fidelity Investments.

It was another year or more after the SEC order before the effects of the decision were translated into savings for the consumer. And several more years elapsed before discount brokerage really began to take shape as a serious competitor in the industry.

Deregulation, then, had extended over nearly a decade. The first public proposal for an end to fixed commissions came in 1969, from none other than the president of the New York Stock Exchange. It was a move immediately supported by such Wall Street powerhouses as Merrill Lynch and Salomon Brothers. They and other large brokerage houses were concerned at the loss of institutional business to the over-the-counter markets, where commissions were negotiated as part of the stock price.

Institutions had in effect been the beneficiaries of de facto price deregulation for some time. Large Wall Street firms witnessed the trickle of institutional business swell to constitute over half of the entire securities market in two brief decades. When they spoke out against the fixed-price commission structure, it was with the wisdom of those who knew better than to buck the tide of the marketplace.

But in 1969, when the first cuts in rates on the major exchanges were introduced on trades of 1000 shares, there was little indication that deregulation would extend to the smallest retail customer. Indeed, the next several waves of change were also directed at the institutional business. In 1971 commissions on orders in excess of $500,000 were opened to negotiation. And yet another year later that threshold was lowered to $300,000.

The mood of the marketplace was clear. The purveyors of the spirit of free enterprise were now called upon to live also by its letter. In 1974 the SEC agreed to a trial period of negotiated commissions. By May 1, 1975, the order to end all fixed-rate brokerage commissions came more as an acknowledgment than an edict of radical change. A year later, when the SEC required floor brokers to negotiate their commissions as well, the fixed-price system was dead forever.

TECHNOLOGY: THE GREAT ENABLER

Technology was on the side of discount brokers. Computerized data and communication systems had reached a new level of sophistication in the late 1970s. With the most up-to-date computer equipment, the costs of trading, order processing, and back-office record keeping could be reduced by as much as 20 percent.

An additional 30 to 40 percent savings could be achieved by using passive sales techniques, thanks to the telephone and data systems that made it possible to deal in high volume. Salaried order-takers could handle 100 calls a day—or 20 to 30 executions—as opposed to commissioned salespeople whose volume was about one-third of that number.

A new product was taking shape. The SEC provided the legal structure for discount brokerage, but technology was its great enabler. The systems made the product possible; now all it needed was a market. The third factor shaping the development of discount brokerage was the consumer.

THE INDEPENDENT INVESTOR

Not since the 1920s had the country seen such drama in the financial community as it did in the 1970s. The stock market was a roller coaster—up in the first couple of years, then down as the decade approached its midway mark, then back up again in 1975, and down as the decade began to wane. The sharp increase in consumer prices, coupled with an even steeper climb in retail and mortgage credit rates, sent even the average household looking for new ways of protecting itself against the ravages of double-digit inflation.

Out of this environment came the first money market mutual funds and a host of other fixed-income products. They appealed to an investor group with a distinct psychographic profile: confident in making investment decisions independent of an advisor, and responsive to direct marketing techniques.

The money fund's first customers were investors, but near the end of the decade the savers entered the market. For them, the money fund offered a panacea: attractive yields that promised to stay apace of inflation, liquidity, and relative safety. It was not insured and usually was not available through a local institution with a name and address as familiar and reassuring as the local bank. Yet, to the surprise of many, there was an enormous public willing to clip a coupon, write a check for thousands of dollars, and send it to a post office box half-way across the country.

Here was another distinct characteristic of a financial consumer who behaved differently from his or her counterpart of a previous generation. Any lingering fear that the depository institution would become insolvent had been displaced by the immediate realization that inflation was gnawing away at basic capital. Both groups—investors and savers—were independent and informed. There was growing evidence that convenience drove their transaction choices and rates determined their selection of product. Financial institutions reached out from everywhere to tap this emerging market. Fidelity Investments was one of them.

THE METAMORPHOSIS OF A MUTUAL FUND COMPANY

In 1975—the year of the SEC deregulation order—Fidelity Investments was primarily a regional investment company with nearly a dozen mutual funds that were distributed primarily through a network of broker–dealers. On the brink of celebrating 30 years in the money management business, Fidelity launched itself into a new era.

The company's network of broker–dealer sales was dissolved, and Fidelity Distributors was created to market Fidelity funds through a new distribution channel: direct-response advertising. Over the course of the next few years, several equity funds were transformed into no-load funds to enhance their appeal. New fixed-income funds were added to the product line. And they were no-load. Fidelity Daily Income Trust, the company's first money market fund, grew steadily at first, then exponentially.

Assets under management soared. The source of new accounts was this new breed of financial consumer—self-motivated, informed, asserting the initiative to *buy* rather than waiting to be *sold*. Fidelity had opened a door on a new segment of the market that seemed to be eager to take charge of its own financial future.

Were there other products that appealed to this market? For several reasons, the next logical match appeared to be with discount brokerage. At least two stories about how Fidelity entered that business are worth telling.

Fidelity Brokerage Services, Inc.

The chairman of a certain brokerage firm that also had a very small mutual fund business was walking down the street with me one day. "I came up to Boston to buy myself a mutual fund company," he announced with a self-assurance that is not uncommon to chairpersons of brokerage companies. He mentioned the name of the company and added, "I think we might get it."

There was a casualness to his attitude, as if to say, "Well, you know, we've got this little mutual fund business. Why don't we quadruple the size? We'll just go out and buy a mutual fund management company!"

It struck me that if a securities company could enter the mutual fund business so simply, maybe Fidelity could emulate its competition and do the same. The knowledge gap between the two businesses was not so great, and the odds for success seemed pretty good. The chance meeting with my colleague stirred an interest, and I decided to sound it out.

Bob Gould, the first president of Fidelity Brokerage, managed the development of Fidelity Brokerage Services, Inc., and his is another story: "Fidelity had developed a successful direct marketing system in the mid-1970s with the introduction of money market mutual funds, fixed-income funds, and no-load equity funds. The company's capability in advertising, marketing, and servicing was well established, and it made sense that our expertise would be applicable to products other than mutual funds."

"Discount brokerage was an ideal candidate for three reasons: it called for many of the same direct-marketing techniques we were using with existing products; it appealed to the same independent investor who evaluated and chose his or her own financial products; it depended on the advanced computer technology that drove the systems of our existing products. In reality, the forces that drove the industry itself were the very same forces operating within Fidelity."

Around the middle of 1977, we surveyed our existing shareholders and found that brokerage was the single most desirable financial product Fidelity could add to its growing family of funds. Several subsequent surveys confirmed that a high percentage of Fidelity shareholders were already customers of full-service brokers, discount brokers, or both.

We also looked at redemptions, especially of our money funds, and found that a large number of checks were being written to brokers. It only made sense to create a product that would keep that money at Fidelity and broaden the shareholders' options. By September 1978, when the brokerage business was incorporated, a Fidelity shareholder could select from a range of equity, fixed-income, and money market products that, with brokerage added to the list, was unmatched in the industry.

CALL IT ANYTHING *BUT* "DISCOUNT" BROKERAGE

The term "discount" brokerage came out of a retail movement in the 1960s, when discounting was quite the rage. Strictly speaking, "discounting" means doing something for less money than someone else charges for doing the same thing. As a pricing strategy it has rarely been successful; and those who call themselves successful "discounters" usually are not discounters at all.

Freddie Laker was a discounter. He judged that he could offer the same product that his large competitors offered, but at a lower price. He might have designed an airplane that could move twice as many people as his competition, yet keep them just as comfortable. He might have figured out a new reservation system whereby the right number of people always ended up at the airport. In either case, he would have been able to radically alter his costs and offer an improved product at a lower price.

But he did not do that; he slugged it out with his competitors on price alone, and they all came out bloodied. That is discounting. And that was not the business Fidelity had in mind when it founded Fidelity Brokerage Services. The message was clear, and not accidental when the company was named. We do not call it Fidelity Discount Brokerage. Fidelity does not discount anything, because the company does not believe in giving away what it need not give away.

Fidelity saw an opportunity, brought together by three socioeconomic factors: We looked at the consumer market and saw the emerging profile of a competent, independent investor and a younger, more aggressive saver. These people were capable of making decisions without the assistance of an intermediary or salesperson, and they demonstrated the willingness to invest large amounts of money in response to advertisement.

Secondly, we saw technology capable of revolutionizing the securities transaction. And each technological advance of the seven years since we entered the brokerage business has brought new capabilities and further lowered the cost of the transaction.

Thirdly, we saw an opportunity to expand our distribution channels. Our business had started with a single distribution channel: the brokerage community. We moved to direct marketing through mass advertising and telephone sales with money market and no-load equity mutual funds. That avenue was also compatible with our brokerage product. In the past few years, Fidelity has expanded its network with regional investor centers in 28 cities around the country. And we were the first in the market to introduce brokerage through banks, expanding our alliances with the banking community to create a massive wholesale distribution channel.

What we did not do, though, was adopt a discounter's mentality and pursue a strategy based on price alone. Some of the early entrants into the field did precisely that and failed, or failed to grow at any appreciable rate.

If you look at the cost components of full-service brokerage, you find that some 30 to 40 percent of the total cost is the broker's commission. Without the sales representative to tell the customer, "You've got to have it!" Fidelity conveys its message in product literature, in the media, and over the telephone, telling the customer: "There it is. Take it or leave it!"

Fidelity's brokerage product is fully priced to reflect its costs. Efficient, direct sales techniques are key to arriving at a price substantially lower than that of a full-service brokerage product. So is state-of-the-art systems technology. Rapidly advancing computer technology combined with a high volume of transactions can account for another 10 to 20 percent cost savings for the so-called discounter.

A third factor, and one that is central to distinguishing a full-service product from its lower-priced cousin, is eliminating the research component. Some who have charted the history and development of this business want to minimize the significance of the research component. And it may well be that the advice a lot of full-service brokers give is bad. But it is hard to dispute that, from the customer's point of view, *advice* is precisely what distinguishes the two types of brokerage products. And that advice, or the lack of it, coupled with service and systems, determines the price at which the product can be offered.

Today's brokerage customer has a real choice between two distinct products. One has a high service component, a personal relationship with a broker and advice on what purchases to make; the other simply consists of the transaction. But, make no mistake! They are different products, and they are priced to reflect their differences. There is a substantial difference between furnishing a room or an office through a professional decorator and marching yourself down to the showroom to place the order for your own selection. A desk is a desk is a desk, but when the decorator looks at your living space and makes the recommendation that you buy Desk A, you pay for it. The company that sells Desk A off the showroom floor, or takes your order for it over the phone, is not discounting anything: Different products, different costs, different prices.

WHAT'S IN A NAME?

What is in a name? Names have a way of shaping our images and attitudes and even our understanding. There are distinctions between the two extremes of brokerage products, so a name can either clarify the differences or confuse the customer. The industry is still evolving, so it is safe to say that today's products will be tomorrow's history, and there is probably some variant of Gresham's Law that suggests that nomenclature will always lag behind enlightenment.

In the past few years, more full-service brokers have been moving toward lower prices, certainly more negotiated prices, and discount brokers have begun to offer information on a fee basis. What made news as a revolution in brokerage products is really an evolution that began much longer than 10 years ago. All the phenomena that I have described—deregulation, changing technology, savvy consumers— have led to an unbundling of services that is far from over. It has spurred a healthy competition in the securities industry and led to a profitable expansion of all financial products.

Ten years ago there was hardly a prognosticator who would have forecast that discount brokerage would ever account for 20 percent of the retail brokerage business. Today there are some who believe that we have seen only the tip of the proverbial iceberg. And most observers will agree that discount brokerage, by this or any other name, will continue to play a major role in reshaping the financial services industry.

24 Perspectives on Clearing

VAN V. BURGER, JR.

The clearance business chugs along in the mechanical room of the securities industry as a billion-dollar-a-year subspecialty. Providing operational and financial services that broker–dealers would otherwise have to supply themselves, the clearing firm makes its customers viable competitors against frequently larger and better-capitalized financial concerns.

In line with this function, the range of services a clearing broker provides may be much broader than the term "clearance," with its connotation of financial settlement, suggests. Core services offered by clearing firms, or correspondents as they are also known, include order execution, clearance, and communications and account-maintenance services. Clearance firms also may provide investment products, such as participations in underwritings or tax shelters, and investment services such as research. Discount purchasing plans, back-office accounting packages, software development, or marketing assistance may all be part of the mix.

The list can mushroom—by geographic location, security type, and service feature—into a complex menu. Equities are traded at multiple stock exchange locations around the country as well as in the over-the-counter market. Similarly, options trade on various floors as do futures contracts. Fixed-income securities trade primarily in an upstairs-dealer market, but corporate bonds also have a floor-trading component. Every broker–dealer with a customer order has to work out a logistical system for getting that order to the appropriate marketplace and employ or designate an agent to execute it upon arrival.

MECHANICS OF ORDER EXECUTION AND SETTLEMENT

To understand the role of the clearing firm it is important to understand the mechanics of order execution and settlement. Because equities, options, bonds, and futures contracts all have differing execution and clearance mechanisms, it simplifies the discussion to describe the process in terms of a trade in a stock listed on the New York Stock Exchange.

Equities normally settle on a five-business-day cycle. Perhaps the easiest way to review the process is to do so in terms of the four relevant time periods: trade date, the trade date–settlement date interval, settlement date, and postsettlement.

Trade Date. Orders are transmitted to the floor and executed either through an electronic execution system or by floor brokers trading in the crowd with the specialist or other brokers. As orders are executed both sides take note of price, quantity, and the identity of the other party to each trade. The execution is reported to the customer and details of the trade are recorded for overnight processing.

On the evening of the trade date, transactions are submitted to the National Securities Clearing Corporation (NSCC) or to one of the regional clearing corporations for comparison. Meanwhile the broker prepares a written confirmation of the trade to be mailed to the customer.

Trade Date–Settlement Date Interval. The day after the trade date NSCC advises brokers of any uncompared trades which arise when buyer and seller submit different input as to price, quantity, or contrabroker. The process of resolving these differences results in modifications to the initial input to NSCC and possibly revised confirmations to the customer.

Settlement Date. On settlement date most compared trades will settle through participants' accounts at the central depository (Depository Trust Company) on a continuous, net-settlement basis. This means that all the buys and sells in a particular security net down to a quantity of shares to be charged or credited to a participant's account. At the same time the net value of all the day's activity also hits the account. Meanwhile customers are expected to pay brokers for their purchases and deliver securities pursuant to their sales.

Postsettlement. After settlement date brokers will either hold stock for customers or transfer it into the name of the customer and mail it to them. If the stock is held, the broker incurs such tasks as collecting dividends for the customer, supplying proxy material and other corporate information, and submitting stock for reorganization or tender. The broker also has an obligation to mail periodic statements of account.

This is an oversimplified view of the process into which the clearing broker may insert himself or herself at one of various junctures. Figure 24.1 presents the process and the position of the clearing firm in schematic form.

The clearance aspect of the trade has two components: settling with brokers and settling with customers. The so-called street side refers to settlement between the broker effecting the buy and the broker effecting the sale. Typically settlement operates on a continuous net basis within an industrywide clearing mechanism. Clearing firms that represent brokers only with respect to street-side activity are said to clear on an "omnibus" basis. Firms operating on a "fully disclosed" basis offer both street-side functions and customer settlement. Under a fully disclosed arrangement, the clearing broker carries the customer's account, produces confirma-

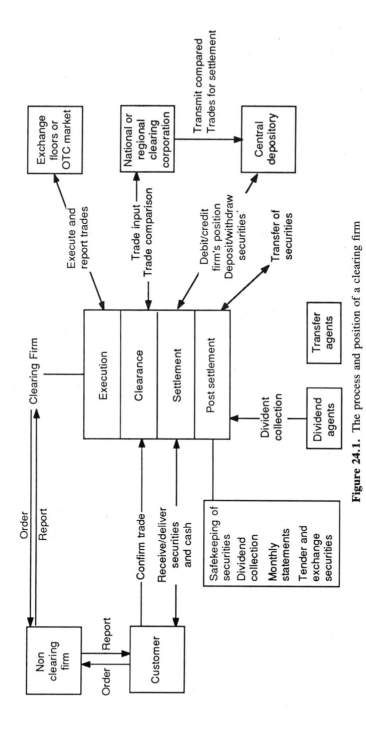

Figure 24.1. The process and position of a clearing firm

tions and statements, and provides margin financing, dividend collection, and maintenance of cash and securities.

Every transaction includes these component tasks of execution and settlement. The resolution of those tasks is, in effect, a make-or-buy decision for the broker with the order in hand.

WHY USE A CLEARING FIRM?

The clearing firm provides the alternative to integrated in-house capability. Typically, the determinants of a firm's decision to use a clearing firm include:

Scale of Operation. To some extent, the function of a clearing broker is to relieve broker–dealers of fixed costs represented by such components as exchange memberships, data processing and communications facilities, clerical staff, and the cost of capital. The primary appeal of clearing arrangements for many broker–dealers is the variable-cost aspect of the relationship. Normally clearing deals provide for X dollars per trade, X percent of the gross commission, or some other variable formulation. The lurches in levels of activity for which the brokerage industry is notorious make variable-cost structures very attractive for many firms.

The self-clearing decision can be represented graphically, to find the number of trades necessary to support the fixed costs associated with clearing (see Figure 24.2). Intersection A indicates the point at which a firm might rationally self-clear. In the real world of competitive factors, however, the intangible benefits of a clearing relationship, management skills, and a host of other variables may come into play.

Location. As suggested earlier, the fact that there are several exchange locations prescribes some use of outside vendors for all but the largest firms. At one time the industry infrastructure was so concentrated in New York that to clear listed securities meant either maintaining an office in New York or using a correspondent.

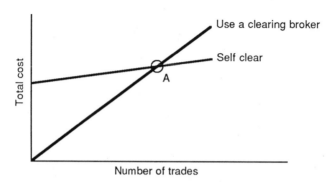

Figure 24.2. Graph of a self-clearing decision

For non-New York firms, the time, expense, and inconvenience of maintaining a New York presence were persuasive deterrents. The systems interfaces between clearing organizations and the availability of local depositories now make it possible for firms to self-clear from most locations. At the same time, access to qualified personnel and other geographically determined factors continue to make location a key consideration in a firm's clearing decision.

Capital. Industry capital requirements mandate higher thresholds for firms that carry customer accounts than for firms that clear fully disclosed through one another. The activity a firm generates gives rise to ongoing capital requirements computed under complex regulatory formulas. A single large trade that failed to clear on a timely basis could trigger a violation in the case of a firm with moderate capital. Many firms simply do not have the capital to self-clear, while others view the capital deployed in clearing as a poor alternative use of funds. Additionally, large clearing firms have access to higher levels of customer account insurance than are available to smaller firms. The clearing broker can provide the ultimate customer the security of its own balance sheet as well as the extra tranche of account insurance.

Technological Resources. The Resources to stay on top of the technology of the business are flatly beyond the capability of most firms. At the same time, these firms require access to this technology if they are to service customers and recruit salespeople. Clearing firms offer this access either through their own facilities or through integration with other outside vendors.

Management Orientation. This factor includes such considerations as image and allocation of time. Do customers react favorably to the fact that their business is cleared by a large, financially secure entity, or does this third-party involvement diminish the role of the introducing broker in their eyes? Do they care? Every firm takes a different fix on its customers' attitudes. A firm with operations-oriented management may be more apt to self-clear than a firm with sales-oriented management, simply because its managers enjoy involving themselves in the process.

Recognizing the factors that shape a firm's decision to uses a clearing broker, clearance firms attempt to position themselves strategically around those same determinants: What can a clearing firm offer in light of industry trends and competitive considerations to exploit operating leverage, geographic location, capital, technical resources, and commitment to the operations aspects of the business? The answers inform pricing strategy, market segmentation, new product introduction, and so on.

FACTORS THAT DIFFERENTIATE CLEARING FIRMS

To understand differences among clearing firms requires a senses of the objectives of competing clearing firms, the various types of customers, and the business cycle that governs the industry.

Compensation

Clearing firms get paid in several ways. First, they receive payment for the various services they perform: execution and clearance, as well as ancillary services they may provide, such as communications, bookkeeping, software development, or research.

Second, they perform various banking functions that generate interest income. Customers borrow to finance securities transactions, collateralizing the loan with securities and paying interest on the loan. The firm funds the loans with its own capital or in one of several other ways. It has customer credit balances that it may use to lend to other customers. It has access to bank borrowing. It also has the use of securities pledged by customers against margin debits. These become a source of cash in two ways. If a customer sells stock short or fails to make timely delivery on a long sale, the firm may use pledged securities to make delivery to the buyer. In that instance, the firm takes in funds that it does not pay out until the customer delivers the stock. Alternatively, the firm may lend pledged securities to another broker against cash, typically splitting the interest opportunity on some basis with the borrowing broker.

In addition to clearing charges and interest income, a clearing firm may have opportunities to leverage the orders it receives from customers. For instance, it may be able to find the other side for an order, creating a second commission on the trade. Another type of opportunity is to act as principal in odd lots, over-the-counter stocks, fixed-income items, or other issues that characteristically trade in a principal market. The firm has the opportunity to use its customer's order to recapture the dealer spread that otherwise would go to another dealer performing that function.

In effect, the clearing firm receives direct payments from customers for clearing and execution services and it also receives indirect payments in the form of interest and trading opportunities. The competitive characteristics of the business require that a firm be both a low-cost competitor with respect to clearance and also a skillful exploiter of indirect opportunities for profit.

Participants in Clearance

Clearing firms competing for customers include a diverse range of participants. A core group of major firms commits substantial resources to across-the-board facilities. Other large retail organizations are smaller and more intermittent players; during volume lulls idle capacity induces them to seek out clearance customers. When volume picks up, they forswear clearance activity in favor of other higher-margin opportunities. Specialists and market-making firms offer clearing services to other professional trading entities. Floor brokers on all exchanges compete for the execution component of the service. Service bureaus are competitors with respect to communication and information-processing aspects. Discount brokers are natural competitors for clearing customers. The clearing business, after all, is simply discount brokerage on a wholesale level.

Perhaps most important in determining the shape of the competitive playing field are the stock exchanges themselves. The exchanges and the NASD have spearheaded changes with respect to execution and clearance that have had the effect of narrowing the range and specializing the commercially relevant services that clearing brokers can provide.

For example, electronic execution facilities have changed the role of clearing brokers in executing small orders. The percentage of trades executed electronically without floor-broker involvement continues to rise. The trades manually handled by brokers are increasingly larger, more complex deals that fall outside the limits of the electronic system. These facts obviously bear on the manner in which firms package and price their services and on the type of business they seek out. Similarly, on the clearing side, the evolution of continuous net settlement and the interfaces between the clearing corporations of the exchanges and between the depositories have reduced the relevance of "omnibus" clearing. Such changes have led many firms to convert more resources to fully disclosed clearing and to target somewhat different markets.

Business Cycles

At the same time, clearing firms deal with the exigencies of a business cycle characteristic of high fixed-cost industries. This one is exacerbated by violent and unpredictable swings in volume. Predictably enough, when volume drops more firms pursue low-margin clearing business as a means of contributing to their fixed costs. The ensuing overcapacity puts pressure on prices. The history of the business suggests that the long-term survivors rarely and reluctantly give up market share. The game is to outlast the competition. The competition process often results in irrational pricing, which leads to failures and consolidations. Well-positioned survivors hope to catch the wave when volume returns. In the clearing business, volume usually redeems all folly.

Obviously the problems of technological change, price competition, and a sometimes hostile cycle are not unique to the clearing business. These environmental factors, however, tend to make it crucial either to be a low-cost competitor or to develop a specialized niche.

Customers/Marketing Opportunities

In view of these imperatives, a clearing firm must match the opportunities presented by the various market segments with its own capabilities. Different types of customers give rise to different types of revenue opportunities. By the same token, different types of resources are required to exploit those opportunities. The market or clearing customers may be segmented as follows:

Retail brokers
Institutional brokers
Professional trading firms (floor specialists, option market makers, arbitrageurs)
Foreign brokers
Financial institutions, for example, banks, S&Ls, insurance companies

An oversimplified outline of market opportunities might look like that in Table 24.1.

While it is obvious that a retail firm may be a candidate for a variety of services, it is not likely to have many orders of a size that might be used to generate offsetting trades. This implies that a clearing firm needs a different set of resources to deal with a retail firm than with an institutional firm that might generate that type of order. Similarly, the settlement of an institutional trade has different interest implications from those of a retail trade. Professional traders require instantaneous execution, which normally precludes any opportunity to look for the other side. Yet the short sales and leverage characteristics of this type of customer create opportunities to generate an interest spread. Foreign brokers resemble domestic institutional brokers. Financial institutions or banks, on the other hand, resemble retail firms, except that they jealously guard all interest opportunity.

A firm tailors its own capabilities to the revenue opportunities it pursues. For example, it is futile to pursue professional traders without a first-class execution capability, strong stock loan and money management skills, and tight credit controls. Quality service to retail firms requires a different blend of skills, those targeted at customer service and satisfaction of the needs of individual salespeople. While opportunities imputed to different market segments will change over time, this pairing of opportunity with the resource required to exploit it bears heavily on a clearing firm's profitability.

The dynamic nature of the securities business means that new opportunities sprout up continually. New products proliferate, each requiring a delivery mechanism that clearing firms are well positioned to construct. Growth of derivative products—options, futures, index contracts—creates new execution and clearing opportunities that can be further enhanced by the arbitrage that emerges among those products. Growing internationalization of the investment process gives rise to new service opportunities with foreign firms. Entry of financial institutions into brokerage pre-

Table 24.1. Clearance Market Opportunities

	Fees for Execution	Opportunity to Generate Offsetting Trades	Opportunity to Trade as Principal	Clearance Fees	Interest Opportunities	Ancillary Services
Retail brokers	X		X	X	X	X
Institutional brokers	X	X	X	X		
Professional traders	X			X	X	
Foreign brokers	X	X	X	X		
Financial institutions	X		X	X		X

cincts lengthens the list of prospective clients. The securitization of new types of assets and liabilities implies an increase in the volume securities that need to be cleared. Every amalgamation of large firms triggers the formation of new businesses by clusters of salespeople or other producers who do not like the deal; each such offshoot is a prospective clearance account. Self-clearing firms seeking to remain independent but also to recast their capital structure often convert to fully disclosed clearing arrangements.

The diversity and energy of the securities business ensure a flow of new prospects, new markets, and new technologies. Those are the growth factors affecting the clearing business together with the historic trend of increasing stock market volume. Rising market activity and increasing numbers of market participants mean that clearing firms will continue to occupy a unique niche in the securities industry: a bridge between market professionals and the customers and markets they serve.

PART 7 COMMERCIAL BANKS AND INVESTMENT BANKING

Since the 1930s, the Glass–Steagall Act has separated commercial from investment banking in the United States. In Europe and in England, on the other hand, the two activities can be combined in a single firm. Canada, having enforced a separation for several decades, is slowly relaxing it.

Many U.S. commercial banks have carried on successful investment banking operations overseas and are doing their best to enter the field in the United States. They have pushed the limits of the Glass–Steagall Act, often finding ways to justify activities that until recently were thought to be the preserve of investment bankers.

Tony Saunders and Ingo Walter, in Chapter 25, discuss from a public policy viewpoint the need for separating commercial from investment banking, and conclude that removal of the separation is desirable.

In Chapter 26, Sam Hayes discusses the extent to which commercial banks have moved into investment banking, and the reasons for the move.

David Dougherty, in Chapter 27, discusses the particular case of Bankers Trust. The chapter deals with the investment banking activities Bankers has chosen, and the competitive advantages it has in those activities. In Chapter 28, Howard Platzman does the same for Chase Manhattan, discussing Chase's reasons for entering investment banking and the resources it is able to employ.

25 Bank "Uniqueness" and the Securities Activities of Commercial Banks

ANTHONY SAUNDERS
INGO WALTER

In recent years bank holding companies have redoubled efforts to secure congressional authorization to engage in originating, underwriting, and dealing in domestic corporate securities through separately capitalized affiliates. Commercial banking subsidiaries of these same holding companies have underwritten general obligation municipal bonds for many years, as well as engaged in discount brokerage and various advisory functions. At the same time, their foreign affiliates have been active in Eurobond underwriting and dealing. While in this country banks themselves have long engaged in arranging private placements of corporate debt, their underwriting of domestic corporate securities has been expressly prohibited since the enactment of the Banking Act of 1933, the Glass–Steagall Act.

One of the central issues in the ongoing debate over allowing bank holding company affiliates to underwrite domestic corporate securities is the degree to which commercial bank subsidiaries provide a unique set of services to society, as well as the extent to which these services might be endangered if bank holding company affiliates were permitted to engage in a corporate securities business. If banks indeed do provide unique and socially valuable services, and if dealing in corporate securities by bank holding company affiliates involves risks that could threaten the integrity of those services, a case could be made to support the existing legislative prohibition. On the other hand, if corporate securities business is no more risky than the other activities bank holding companies engage in now, and if positive advantages can be shown to exist, there may be reason to modify the Glass–Steagall prohibition. This is especially true if there are procompetitive (or market) benefits to be gained from allowing banks to engage in corporate securities activities.

This chapter addresses these issues from an economic perspective, including the question of bank uniqueness in the context of views expressed by representatives of the Federal Reserve System (the Fed), as well as in the economics literature. We analyze the potential economic benefits and costs of allowing bank entry into the securities business, concentrating on three basic issues: (1) effect on bank safety and soundness; (2) potential for conflicts of interest; and (3) gains from increased competition in the securities industry.

THE UNIQUE OR SPECIAL FUNCTIONS OF BANKS

Summaries of views of the Federal Reserve System regarding the special or unique functions of banks can be found in Corrigan [1] and Volcker [14]. Corrigan identifies three characteristics that distinguish banks from other kinds of financial and non-financial institutions:

1. Banks offer transaction accounts.
2. Banks are the backup source of liquidity for all other economic institutions.
3. Banks are the transmission belt for monetary policy.

Corrigan argues that the single characteristic of banks that distinguishes them from other classes of institution is that they issue transaction accounts, that is, accounts that in law, in regulation, or in practice are payable on demand at par and are readily transferable to third parties.

Economists generally agree with the view that offering transaction accounts is the unique function of a bank, and that any institution or firm undertaking this function should be defined as a bank. Thus, if a savings and loan or mutual savings bank offers transaction accounts, it also should be viewed and regulated as if it were a bank.

With respect to the second criterion—banks as suppliers of backup liquidity to other institutions—a number of financial institutions, such as life insurance companies, provide long-term loan commitments to borrowers, and nonfinancial firms provide credit lines through trade credit to customers. It could be argued that banks can provide credit at a lower price than other institutions, because legislated interest ceilings on deposits have in the past placed an artificial limit on the average cost of bank funds. However, it is not clear that such ceilings have reduced the true cost of funds when both explicit and implicit interest payments, such as undercharging for check clearing and other services, are included, as Startz [13] has shown. Indeed, in a competitive financial system the explicit and implicit costs of funds to different classes of institution (banks, nonbank financial institutions, and corporations) tend to be equalized after adjusting for risk, maturity, and convenience. Finally, even if interest ceilings indeed do lower the cost of bank funds, they also serve to increase the extent of financial disintermediation, which reduces the ability of banks to act as the backup suppliers of credit or liquidity in the economy.[1] Disintermediation,

---

[1] An example from the 1970s is the effect that Regulation Q ceilings on time deposits had in spurring the growth of money market mutual funds.

in turn, has accelerated the demise of Regulation Q ceilings and their potential role in reducing the cost of bank funds in the United States.

The logic behind the third criterion—banks as the transmission belt for monetary policy—is that the government issues only a small proportion of the total money supply, namely currency or notes and coin (so-called outside money), which can be exchanged at par for commercial bank deposits (so-called inside money).[2] It is usually argued that the growth of the quantity of inside money has to be constrained; otherwise, banks acting under competitive pressures will tend to expand the supply of inside money to accommodate private-sector demand. If this process were to proceed unchecked, it would result in price-level indeterminacy and, ultimately, hyperinflation, which in turn has important adverse effects on real economic activity—usually in the form of a decline in real output and employment. It also eventually eliminates the value of the government's seigniorage from currency issuance, and thus has important fiscal implications as well.[3]

One mechanism by which the growth of inside money typically is constrained involves imposing non-interest-bearing reserve requirements on banks in the form of vault cash or deposits at the central bank. Because such requirements create a clearly defined need for reserves, and as long as the supply of reserves can be controlled by the Fed through open-market operations, the quantity of inside money—therefore the money supply itself—ultimately can be controlled by the monetary authorities. However, there is absolutely no basis in theory for monetary policy to be carried out in this fashion.

Both Fama [2] and Patinkin [7], among others, have noted that the only necessary conditions for price-level determination in an economy are that the monetary authorities control one price and one quantity—that is, the price of a currency unit and the quantity of currency outstanding. Generally, the public will have a real demand for currency because of its utility or convenience in transactions. Further, as inside and outside money are instantaneously convertible through the banking system, banks will always find it prudent to hold some quantity of outside money as a reserve asset.[4]

Given a stable demand for currency, by changing its supply (e.g., through open-market operations) the Fed can affect the relative price of currency in relation to the price of real goods (the price level) and achieve approximate price-level stability. Therefore, assuming that the main objective of monetary policy is to maintain price-level stability, there is no sound theoretical reason for banks to be singled out for special attention, via reserve requirements, as the transmission belt for monetary policy.[5]

---

[2] Virtually a perfect substitute for bank money.

[3] This notion has given rise to an extensive literature on the optimal rate of inflation (tax) the government should allow.

[4] Because banks will hold less cash in the absence of non-interest-bearing required reserves, reserve requirements create an involuntary reserve system that is similar to taxation.

[5] There might, however, be good empirical reasons, especially if the demand for reserves is more stable than the demand for currency.

This leaves the first characteristic—that banks offer transaction accounts—as the unique function of the banking system. The role of banks in supplying transaction account services that permit an efficient transfer of purchasing power is logically independent of the role of currency as the numeraire in the economy—a unit of account that can be exchanged or converted at par with bank deposits. This independence is not clearly evident in Corrigan's description. Yet even in a hypothetical nonmonetary economic system, where currency does not exist and some other good acts as the numeraire (or unit of account), banks still would play the role of transaction agents. As Fama [2] clearly shows, the only major difference in this case is that debits and credits would be calculated in units of the *new* numeraire. The ability of banks to maintain their (transactions) agency role still would depend on the efficiency with which they carry out the transfer function between economic agents, and the confidence these agents have in the integrity of banks in accomplishing this task. Precisely the same is true for a monetary economy, where currency is the numeraire good that is readily convertible at par into bank deposits.

Clearly, in either a monetary or nonmonetary economy, doubts or crises of confidence on the part of asset holders with respect to the integrity or safety of the transaction account mechanism would represent important social costs. There are real losses of economic welfare as less efficient means of wealth-transfer, such as barter, take hold. Examples of this phenomenon exist in the monetary histories of many countries around the world (e.g., Germany in the 1920s). Indeed, the social costs that accrue whenever there is a major crisis in confidence regarding the payments system constitute a major rationale underlying the provision of deposit insurance to the banking system.

Consequently, it is the efficiency and safety of the transactions account (or wealth-transfer) mechanism that appears to be of foremost concern to regulators in considering the advisability of bank holding companies expanding into corporate securities or other activities. Any loss of confidence in the integrity of the banking system would adversely affect the convertibility of transaction accounts (deposits) into currency, leading to instability and decline in the demand for deposits, and reductions in nominal and real GNP, as people seek to substitute currency and other assets for bank deposits in their portfolios.

Thus, given that disruptions in the transactions mechanism provided by banks do result in real economic costs to society, it is legitimate to consider the nature of activities banks should be allowed to engage in if we are to preserve confidence in, and the integrity of, the transactions mechanism. Specifically, can the corporate securities business be included in those activities?

The Fed's view, as outlined by Corrigan, is that banks must meet two essential criteria in engaging in outside activities: that these other activities (1) should not entail excessive risk of loss, and (2) should not impair the impartiality of credit decisions. The risk-of-loss criterion involves basic questions relating both to the impact of securities activities on bank safety and soundness (or risk) and on bank profitability (or conduct and performance). The second criterion essentially is concerned with potential and actual conflicts of interest that may arise if banks engage in securities activities.

THE COSTS AND BENEFITS OF ALLOWING BANKS TO ENGAGE IN CORPORATE SECURITIES ACTIVITIES

As discussed in the previous section, the crucial question whether commercial banks should be allowed to undertake corporate securities activities revolves around possible effects on their safety and soundness. Indeed, the prohibition on commercial banks underwriting and dealing in corporate securities in 1933 was one part of an effort by Congress to restore order to a severely strained financial system during a period unprecedented in its economic turbulence. Given the unquestioned abuses in U.S. capital markets that led to the financial panic of 1929, it is understandable that lawmakers faced great pressures to try a variety of remedies in their search for appropriate solutions to restore stability. Of paramount importance was the institution of federal deposit insurance and carefully crafted securities market regulation. By themselves, these measures contributed critical elements of stability that were badly needed.

The Glass–Steagall legislation, however, appears, in hindsight, something of an oddity. Flannery [3] and Kelly [6] have proposed that the activities of commercial banks in securities underwriting and dealing had little to do with the financial abuses that took place during the 1920s, or with large-scale bank failures, as proponents of Glass–Steagall suggested at the time. If this view is correct, it follows that the separation of commercial from investment banking may have imposed significant economic costs on the U.S. economy during the past half-century. While obviously it is impossible to say with any certainty how the U.S. financial system would have evolved in the absence of Glass–Steagall, the evidence suggests that vigorous competition, market efficiency, and the overall contribution of the financial services industry to capital formation and sustained economic growth might well have been enhanced in its absence.

Repeal of Glass–Steagall: Potential Sources of Gain

If the net economic costs of the Glass–Steagall prohibitions to the U.S. economic and financial system are to be evaluated, we must consider the competitive structure, conduct, and performance of the commercial and investment banking industries, as well as economies of scale and economies of scope in the financial services industry.

Pugel and White [8] have suggested that competition in several segments of the U.S. investment banking industry is not as vigorous as it might be. Their opinion is that the increased number of participants, if commercial banks entered the securities markets, certainly would tend to enhance the degree of competition in corporate finance with lower fees, better service, broader access, improved secondary markets, and greater innovation. Conversely, it seems probable that the entry of affiliates of investment banks into commercial banking likewise would enhance competition and dynamism in that industry, as in a sense has already been demonstrated by Merrill Lynch's introduction of cash management accounts (CMAs) in 1970s. Thus far, the commercial banks have favored interpenetration of markets and open competition, while the traditional investment banks have fiercely resisted deregulation [11], which suggests that the excess returns attributable to restricted competition may fall mainly on the investment banking side.

If deregulation in investment banking is indeed defensible in economic terms, it must be justified in large part by substantive changes in competitive performance in the provision of corporate financial services. There is already substantial competition between investment banks and commercial banks in a wide variety of such services, as well as in the international capital market. In areas where there have been no artificial barriers to competition, the degree of efficiency and innovation that characterizes the various competing financial services firms has been very high indeed, with commensurate benefits accruing directly to the users of those services and more broadly to the economic and financial system as a whole.

It is only a domestic underwriting and dealing in corporate securities that entry has continued to be artificially restricted under the Glass–Steagall legislation. Economists generally work under the assumption that any such limitation of competitive opportunity will involve a reallocation among potential competitors of the gains from the economic activities involved in favor of those who benefit from protection, as well as a reduction in the efficiency with which resources are allocated—the *static* dead-weight losses associated with protected markets. There also are adverse *dynamic* consequences (such as accelerated financial innovation) that make themselves felt over a period of time; these ultimately may be substantially more important. Measuring the static and dynamic efficiency and redistributional effects of protection involves estimating what a number of key variables would look like in the absence of existing constraints on competition.

As there is no way to run the world twice, this must be done either by examining these variables before and after distortions have been imposed or removed, or by means of cross-sectional comparison between distorted and undistorted markets. Both approaches involve serious empirical problems of research design, comparability, data availability, and interpretation of results. The conclusion of Pugel and White [8], that more competition in securities underwriting and dealing is better than less, comes as no great surprise either from the standpoint of efficiency or equity, and seems well justified in terms of the inferential evidence they present on concentration and competitive structure, size and stability of underwriting fees, quality of service provided to small issuers, and systematic underpricing of new issues. Comparison with the market for general obligation bonds of state and local governments appears to reinforce this evidence, as noted by Silber [12]. So, despite the fact that no credible data are available on the actual returns to factors of production used in underwriting and dealing in corporate securities, the inferential evidence suggests that protection involves costs, and that deregulation would generate material benefits to the users of corporate financial services and to the economy at large.

Repeal of Glass–Steagall: Potential Costs

If there are potential benefits associated with the deregulation of corporate financial services in the United States, there also are potential costs (see [1], [14]). These have both economic and political dimensions, which focus on (1) possible implications for the stability of the banking system, and (2) conflicts of interest within financial institutions undertaking commercial as well as investment banking activities.

The first question concerns the riskiness of corporate securities activities that might be undertaken by commercial bank affiliates. That these activities involve risks is clear. If there were no risks, such activities would produce far smaller gains, both to the direct participants and to society. Risk can be managed through astute evaluation, diversification, and exposure limits, as well as by using the growing array of hedging vehicles (such as options and futures). But beyond this there is the empirical question of how risky corporate securities activities in fact have been in the United States.

Risk can produce either gains or losses for securities underwriters. It may be traced to specific developments affecting a given security issue, or to general developments in financial markets that occur during the underwriting process or (in the case of dealing) thereafter. Specifically of interest here are the potential downside risks associated with securities underwriting and dealing (especially the probability of a big loss taken by an individual firm on an individual issue) and their bearing on the safety and soundness of financial institutions, and the nature of the risk–return trade-offs in the market for corporate securities.

It is impossible to obtain direct data on securities underwriting profits and losses, but one can presume that such activities have been profitable over the years—a presumption that is reinforced by the vigor with which the investment banking community argues its case for continued protection from increased competition. One can also glean some additional evidence from the movement of stock or bond prices during the underwriting process to ascertain possible gains or losses to securities firms during the period in which the securities could have been held.

Giddy [4], for example, finds that the potential gains from underwriting U.S. equity issues during 1976–1982 did indeed far outweigh the potential losses. Moreover, even ignoring gains entirely and focusing on the loss side, under certain worst-case assumptions, Giddy found nothing to indicate that equity underwriting losses in any sense impaired the viability of the securities firms involved during this period. Corporate debt underwriting, which is generally held to be less risky than equity underwriting, appears to have exhibited an even more limited loss profile under worst case assumptions during the same period of time, although the absence of adequate price data prevented empirical verification comparable to that in the analysis of equities.

If a bank holding company is allowed to add a range of financial services activities—whose returns are imperfectly correlated with those of traditional banking activities—it may be able to enhance its earnings stability. This suggests that safety and stability in a modern and competitive financial services environment, one that has significant efficiency and growth benefits for the economy as a whole, may depend more on careful balance or diversification of activities engaged in by firms in the industry than it does on traditional notions of narrow activity limitations and controls.

In examining the question of how corporate securities underwriting and dealing accords with the general imperative of banking safety and soundness, Saunders [9] has concluded that greater activity diversification may indeed contribute to greater institutional stability. He includes evidence in support of the view that the structure of economic incentives and disincentives driving the management of bank holding companies that combine commercial and nonbanking activities tends to ensure effective insulation of nonbanking activities from commercial banking—even in the absence of the legal constraints. Given the latter, Saunders found it improbable that even major underwriting or trading losses on the part of the securities affiliate of a bank holding company would seriously impair the capital adequacy of the bank itself.

Indeed, the 1984 Continental Ilinois difficulties, clearly attributable to asset-related problems within the traditional definition of commercial banking, may have been exacerbated by legal and regulatory impediments that effectively constrained management's search for profits to a relatively narrow set of activities, thus limiting the ability to diversify. On the liability side as well, the bank's funding alternatives were limited by state and federal branching restrictions that prevented the development of a broad and stable retail deposit base. Quite apart from management errors of judgment and control, had Continental Ilinois enjoyed access to a substantially broader range of assets and liabilities, as well as been able to offer related financial services, its stability might well have been enhanced.

There is a potential for conflicts of interest between commercial and investment banking activities undertaken in the same holding company, as there has long been between each of these industries and their fiduciary activities. There are three potential dimensions to such conflicts: (1) between fiduciary activities and commercial banking (2) between fiduciary activities and investment banking, and (3) between investment banking and commercial banking.

The first two have not presented a major problem in the United States. Trust and investment business traditionally has been handled by a variety of financial services firms, including commercial and investment banks, that are engaged in many other lines of activity as well. Although there are indeed serious potential conflicts of interest related to efficiency and equity aspects of information access and dissemination, these have been contained quite effectively by a combination of institutional, behavioral, legal, and competitive constraints. Chinese Walls exist, legal sanctions threaten, but ultimately competition and the discipline of the market limit the factual importance of conflicts of interest involving fiduciary activities. For large trusts, there are simply too many actual and potential competitors in the investment management business, and it is too easy to gauge comparative portfolio performance, for management to deviate very far from serving the basic interests of their fiduciary clients. Moreover, even for smaller trusts, the potential for conflict will continue to erode as information flows, and the associated technologies, continue to improve.

If potential fiduciary conflicts can be handled effectively under the existing institutional framework, the addition of securities affiliates of bank holding companies should involve few incremental problems. Merrill Lynch and Shearson Leman Brothers engage in both fiduciary and investment banking activities, while Bankers Trust and Morgan Guaranty engage in both fiduciary and commercial banking activities. So the remaining question is whether there are serious potential conflicts of interest between investment and commercial banking activities undertaken by separately capitalized affiliates of the same institution. One can point to the fact that commercial banks in the United States already engage in a broad range of investment banking business with the notable exception of corporate securities activities—and even in corporate securities business outside the United States—without encountering significant conflicts of interest.

Kelly [5] has traced the historical roots of the conflict-of-interest issue and has examined the institutional and legal safeguards that now exist to contain their exploitation. He concludes that these safeguards are more than adequate to cope with the deregulation of investment banking. Saunders [10] has assessed the economic and behavioral dimensions in terms of the structure of incentives and disincentives that underlie the exploitation of conflicts of interest. In his view, such exploitation is fundamentally inimical to the economic interests of the firm and its shareholders—which is the maximization of the value of the enterprise as a going concern, and in particular the maintenance of its reputation. The competitive nature of the markets for financial services provides sanctions against deviations from this standard that are both timely and effective. Moreover, institutional factors that drive the behavior of managers—such as the structure of bonus schemes, the use of profit centers, and the market for corporate control—tend to ensure that behavior at variance with fundamental corporate interests is not tolerated for long.

In an environment where performance information is readily available, consistent and profitable exploitation of conflicts of interest is thus impeded both by market competition that aligns managerial behavior with the fundamental interests of the firm and its shareholder and by legal and institutional constraints that help to align the behavior of the firm with the fundamental interests of society.

CONCLUSION

This chapter has argued that the net benefits from removing the remaining barriers between investment and commercial banking revolve around three major issues: (1) the competitive impact (2) the impact on potential conflicts of interest, and (3) bank safety and soundness. Findings of recent research on these issues strongly suggest that the private and social benefits from allowing commercial banks to underwrite and deal in domestic corporate securities would more than outweigh any costs. Consequently, eliminating the Glass–Steagall barriers would be central in any overall plan of deregulating the financial-services industry.

REFERENCES

1. Corrigan, Gerald E. "Are Banks Special?" Federal Reserve Bank of Minneapolis Annual Report, 1982.
2. Fama, Eugene. "Banking in the Theory of Finance," *Journal of Monetary Economics*, pp. 39–57.

3. Flannery, Mark J. "An Economic Evaluation of Bank Securities Activities Before 1933," in Ingo Walter, ed., *Deregulating Wall Street*, New York: Wiley, 1985.

4. Giddy, Ian H. "Is Equity Underwriting Risky for Commercial Banks?" in Ingo Walter, ed., *Deregulating Wall Street*, New York: Wiley, 1985.

5. Kelly, Edward J. III. "Conflicts of Interest: A Legal View," in Ingo Walter, ed., *Deregulating Wall Street*, New York: Wiley, 1985.

6. Kelly, Edward J. III. "Legislative History of the Glass–Steagall Act," in Ingo Walter, ed., *Deregulating Wall Street*, New York: Wiley, 1985.

7. Patinkin, Don. "Financial Intermediaries and the Logical Structure of Monetary Theory," *American Economic Review*, pp. 95–116.

8. Pugel, Thomas, and Lawrence J. White. "An Analysis of the Competitive Effects of Allowing Commercial Bank Affiliates to Underwrite Corporate Securities," in Ingo Walter, ed., *Deregulating Wall Street*, New York: Wiley, 1985.

9. Saunders, Anthony. "Bank Safety and Soundness and the Risks of Corporate Securities Activities," in Ingo Walter, ed., *Deregulating Wall Street*, New York: Wiley, 1985.

10. Saunders, Anthony. "Conflicts of Interest: An Economic View," in Ingo Walter, ed., *Deregulating Wall Street*, New York: Wiley, 1985.

11. Shad, John S. et al. "Round Table Discussion," Washington, DC; Securities and Exchange Commission, 1984.

12. Silber, William L. *Municipal Revenue Bond Costs and Bank Underwriting: A Survey of the Evidence*. New York: Salomon Brothers Center for the Study of Financial Institutions, Graduate School of Business Administration, New York University, Monograph Series in Finance and Economics, 1979.

13. Startz, Richard. "Implicit Interest and Demand Deposits," *Journal of Monetary Economics*, 5, pp. 515–534.

14. Volcker, Paul A. Statement Before the Committee on Banking, Housing and Urban Affairs, United States Senate, September 13, 1983.

26 Investment Banking: Commercial Banks' Inroads*

SAMUEL L. HAYES III

The evolving competition between securities firms and commercial banks has come into increasingly sharp focus in recent years. This chapter examines some of the historical antecedents and contemporary market forces at work in both the retail and wholesale sectors of the securities business which bear on its interface with commercial banks. This examination leads to some suggestions about possible direction and speed of future competitive change in these market sectors.

HISTORICAL EVOLUTION

Since 1933, the traditional role of U.S. commercial banks has been reasonably clear; the niches occupied by various groups of securities firms during this period have been less well understood. Some observers see the securities business as a relatively homogeneous activity; others see it as a disparate series of independent, easy-entry "lines of commerce." Neither of these stereotypes mirrors reality. Instead, competitive factors have divided the business more practically into "retail" investor services and "wholesale" services to corporate, municipal, and institutional customers.

Securities firms and deposit-taking commercial banks have undergone separate mutations in response to broader developments in financial services, but the historic routes and influences that have brought them to their current positions have much in common. The post-World War II U.S. commercial and investment banking structure grew out of legislation and regulatory interpretation in the 1930s. The Banking Act of 1933, the socalled Glass-Steagall Act, threw up a Chinese Wall

* This chapter first appeared as an article in The Federal Reserve Bank of Atlanta's *Economic Review* (May 1984), pp. 50–60 and is reprinted here with permission of the Bank.

between deposit-taking and securities-dealing firms and thus created an industry structure that is mirrored only in Japan, among industrialized countries.

This structural dichotomy survived for several postwar decades without major challenge, perhaps in part because the United States was enjoying an unprecedented era of secular growth accompanied by relatively high savings, nominal inflation, and low interest rates. Each group of financial intermediaries was comfortable, protected, and able to prosper within its assigned niche in the industry structure.

The McFadden Act and the Douglas Amendment protected and nurtured local and regional banks and curbed the money center banks' market shares in domestic lending and deposit-seeking. But these large banks diversified and grew by following corporate customers into the largely unregulated international arena. Likewise, insurance companies were major beneficiaries of the postwar institutionalization of savings, and thrifts prospered by fueling the growth in home ownership with fixed-rate, long-term mortgages.

On the other side of Glass-Stegall's Chinese Wall, an ever-expanding base of individual stock ownership and overall market trading volume promoted growth and consolidation within the retail securities sector. Increasing corporate and municipal underwriting volume also yielded attractive profits to the wholesale investment banking sector. Growth in institutional investor demand, which first came into focus in the early 1960s, created yet another dimension for postwar securities industry growth. Over time, that dimension has come to be associated and identified more closely with the wholesale investment banking function.

Meanwhile, beginning in the 1960s, changes in the domestic and world economy conspired to upset the equilbrium in this financial services structure. Several important factors that particularly affected competition between commercial and investment banks were the rise of the Euromarkets, the increasing sophistication of both institutional investors and corporations, and the acceleration of inflation and interest rates in the 1970s, with a consequent realignment of securities values and investor preferences.

Originally minimized in the mid-1960s as a minor and temporary phenomenon, the Euromarkets' evolution into a large and permanent "supranational" market has created an arena outside the jurisdiction of Glass-Steagall where participation is open to diverse financial institutions willing and able to assume the attendant risks. This market, abetted by the advances in—and application of—electronics technology, has spearheaded the rapid evolution toward a global market in money. Linkage of the various national capital markets with the Euromarkets and accompanying aggressive arbitrage on rates and terms have established money as a truly fungible commodity, whose movement across national and currency frontiers is increasingly difficult to control.[1] It has thus become more and more compelling for U.S. financial-service organizations to accommodate this global market.

In the United States, the inexorable institutionalization of savings had, by the beginning of the 1980s, raised the institutional sector share of the New York Stock

---

[1] See, for instance, Theodore Leavitt, "The Globilization of Markets," *Harvard Business Review* 61 (May–June 1983), pp. 92–102.

Exchange equity wealth to 35.4 percent (from 17.2 percent in 1960) and its 1982 share of equity market trading to 83.8 percent (from 24.3 percent in 1960).[2] Money market funds have grown from nothing in the early 1970s to more than $175 billion at the end of 1983. This institutionalization has loosened the commercial banks' link to the individual saver and focused much of the securities industry's attention on the large portfolio manager.

Corporations also developed and expanded their internal financial engineering capabilities over this period. The growth of the commercial paper market to a mid-1983 annual rate of $123.7 billion (vs. $4 billion in 1960)[3] reflects large companies' willingness to substitute these less expensive but potentially more volatile short-term funds for traditional commercial bank lines of credit. This development also has diminished an important, moderate-risk revenue stream for the commercial banks and forced them into other, often more risky funds deployments as well as more costly retail lending avenues. After the oil shocks of 1974 and 1979, this redeployment was evidenced by the much greater volumes of foreign, cross-border loans.

Of the forces that increased the pressure on the financial services industry status quo during the 1970s, accelerating inflation and rising interest rates were among the most pervasive. For many years, savings patterns had been fairly stable. Most individual savings were channeled to commercial banks, thrifts, and insurance companies in exchange for a modest interest return.

Although earlier flare-ups in interest rates had failed to disrupt this deposit pattern seriously, inflation and interest rate jumps after the first oil price hike in 1973 appear to have precipitated a structural change in retail savings.

On one side of the Glass-Steagall wall, mandated rate differentials were causing commercial banks and other deposit-gathering institutions to lose deposits to money market funds and other intermediaries capable of adjusting more rapidly to changes in prevailing interest rates. Institutions such as thrifts, holding fixed-rate instruments with greatly diminished value, suffered from badly mismatched maturity funding sources on the liability side of their balance sheets. As retail deposits deserted them for substantially better returns elsewhere, their options were to turn to the higher-cost wholesale markets for replacement funds or else sell their assets at substantial losses from their original value. Unlike the commercial banks, they had few alternativestrategies for survival until passage of the Garn Act in 1982.

On the securities side of the Glass-Steagall wall, higher inflation and interest rates also created serious dislocations. The consequent downward revaluation in the market prices of securities created disaffection among retail and institutional investors and disrupted the markets for new issues of securities as well as for secondary market trading. Concurrently, inflation substantially increased securities firms' operating costs, especially since their overhead is heavily weighted with the

---

[2] *New York Stock Exchange Fact Book–1969*, p. 48. *New York Stock Exchange Fact Book–1983*, p. 8.

[3] *Federal Reserve Bulletin* (January 1961), p. 192. Federal Reserve Statistical Release, December 30, 1983.

"people" costs and electronics support systems deemed in necessary to stay competitive.[4]

Break with the Status Quo. These developments have impelled various financial service institutions to seek out new—and hopefully more promising—business niches. On the deposit-accepting side, various legislative and regulatory changes initiated at the behest of industry lobbyists have facilitated this development. Deregulation of the interest payments permitted on deposits (Regulation Q), for instance, has helped spur intensive competition for retail deposits. While these deposits are more expensive than they were prior to the deregulatory measures, they are seen as a stabilizing counterbalance to the banks' and thrifts' mismatched asset maturity structures.

To help attract those deposits and to spread the overhead of the infrastructure and marketing costs, banks and like institutions have sought both to broaden their retail product offerings and to explore alternatives for delivering them, including radically different electronic distribution systems. There also has been a more concerted search, particularly by commercial banks, for additional products and services to strengthen relationships with traditional corporate customers.

In building new ties to both the retail saver and the corporate customer, commercial banks and a variety of other nonbank institutions have moved to break through the Glass-Steagall wall to get into new areas of the securities business. They have noted the growth in securities trading volume and the industry's greatly enhanced revenue stream.

Securities firms focusing on individual investors, however, have not themselves been comfortable with their own situation. They recognize that a large part of their profit derives from their role as banker for their customers and that their own historic "deposit base" (free credit balances), like that of the traditional deposit-taking institutions, has come under attack from the money market funds and other higher-yielding instruments. They have responded in part by creating their own in-house savings vehicles to hold those deposits and by creating an even wider variety of products and services both to retain customers and to spread their overhead across a wider base.

A consequence of that deposit-protecting and product diversification strategy has been for securities firms to emulate competing financial intermediaries on the deposit-taking side of the Glass-Steagall wall. They have initiated moves to break through that wall into the territory of the commercial banks, thrifts and insurance companies by offering de facto checking and savings accounts, consumer loans, home mortgages, and various insurance products.

These retail brokerage firms also have sought to combat accelerating overhead and squeezed margins by attempting to integrate backward into the "manufacture" of their financial products. They have created special "think tank" groups to devise new marketable instruments such as unit trust, tax-advantaged investments, and

---

[4] Seen for instance, *Staff Report on the Securities Industry in 1979*, published by the SEC.

various "stripped" securities. It also has propelled them into a more active competition for leadership in new corporate underwritings, thus obtaining securities that are typically attractive products for their retail (and institutional) clientele and whose management and underwriting fees add incremental revenue to the selling commissions they traditionally have received.

Both retail securities firms and commercial banks have noted that wholesale investment firms were not hurt seriously by any of the major international or national money market developments in which their institutional and corporate customers were active during the 1970s and early 1980s.[5] To be sure, the banks often were prodded into making massive incremental investments of people and money to accommodate structural changes in their institutional and corporate markets. But they found ways to cushion their revenues even when the volume of underwritings declined cyclically.[6] The activities and employment within these firms increased dramatically during the 1970s,[7] and profitability held up much better than was true for the retail brokerage firms.[8] Notably, one of the wholesalers' diversifying moves was into the lucrative high-net-worth sector of the retail brokerage business— primarily because it was a profitable exploitation of their in-place research and trading activities rather than as a way of ensuring distribution for their underwritings.

These competitive "migratory" moves are noteworthy. Some of them appear to be in defiance of the spirit, if not the letter, of the 1933 Act. Challenges to the long-held interpretation of the limits on business activity imposed by the Act surfaced only as a result of economic and competitive forces in a more fragile and volatile environment. Industry competitors began to discover that, like the Wizard of Oz, the Glass-Steagall wall was much more formidable in appearance than in reality. Once tested by restive competitors with inventive legal counsel in an environment generally sympathetic to deregulation, gaps opened up that allowed competitors to cross through the wall in both directions.

It is still too early to predict with confidence the durability or success of many of these competitive moves. Nonetheless, we can learn something about their dynamics by looking at specific market segments. To do that, let us search for likely longer-term competitive patterns in two segments of the securities business.

RETAIL DISCOUNT BROKERAGE

An industrial organization view of the retail securities sector would depict a number of traditional, full-service brokers in the center, with individual savers on the one hand and the various capital users on the other. Primary and secondary transactions

---

[5] *Ibid.*

[6] Samuel L. Hayes III, A. Michael Spence, and David VanPraag Marks, *Competition in the Investment Banking Industry*, Cambridge: Harvard University Press, 1983, p. 44.

[7] Samuel L. Hayes III, "The Transformation of Investment Banking," *Harvard Business Review* 57, (January–February 1979), pp. 153–170.

[8] Superscript author provide footnote.

in traditional stocks and bonds have declined in importance as new products, many of them devised by the firms themselves, have grown in variety and volume.

A number of new firms have entered this business in recent years, including wholesale securities firms seeking to skim the cream through appeals to wealthy customers and discount brokers aiming at the price-sensitive, independent investor. Discount brokers emerged after securities commission rates were deregulated on May 1, 1975. In the immediate aftermath, rates on institution-sized transactions fell by almost 50 percent, whereas rates on trades under 200 shares actually rose by almost 10 percent.[9] During the first couple of years of the negotiated commission era, the retail discounters made little progress, perhaps in part because of inertia on the part of individual investors. The discounters' market share began to grow materially after 1977, however, and by the beginning of 1984 fully 14 percent of the retail trades on the New York Stock Exchange were handled by discount brokers.[10]

Commercial banks and thrifts moved into discount brokerage beginning in 1982.[11] Many leading money center banks have acquired or affiliated with established discount brokerage operations.[12] Other banks have set up their own operations but clear the trades through a conventional securities firm.[13] In some instances, commercial banks and thrifts have even invited brokerage firms to set up booths on their banking floors, much as Dean Witter is doing within the retail stores of parent Sears, Roebuck.

The number of commercial banks and thrifts offering brokerage services has grown from virtually none in 1981 to an estimated 1500 at the end of 1983.[14] One market observer has predicted that, with the growing participation of the commercial banks, discounters' share of the retail securities market could grow much larger within the next several years.[15]

With the effective neutralization of the Glass-Steagall legal barrier that had prevented banks from offering brokerage services, the question remains whether economies of scale or other barriers will inhibit the commercial banks, thrifts, and others from maintaining a sustained presence in the retail brokerage business. In an earlier study, Irwin Friend and Marshall Blume suggested that economies of scale are relatively modest in the brokerage business.[16] Certainly these new bank entrants, whose overhead costs are largely covered by other service activities, appear

[9] *Staff Report on the Securities Industry in 1979*, published by the SEC, p. 47.

[10] William B. Hummer, "Bankers March on Discount Brokerage 101, *Bankers Monthly Magazine* (January 15, 1984), p. 27.

[11] Chemical Bank made an earlier abortive attempt to enter the brokerage business in the 1970s.

[12] For instance, in January 1983 Bank of America acquired Charles Schwab & Company and Chase Manhattan acquired Rose & Company.

[13] Pershing & Company, a division of Donaldson, Lufkin & Jenrette, provides trading and clearing services to banks as do a number of other securities firms. (See Chapter 24.)

[14] Hummer, *supra* note 10, at 26. Other estimates range considerably higher than this number.

[15] Hummer, *supra* note 10, at 26.

[16] Irwin Fried and Marshall Blume, "Competitive Commissions on the New York Stock Exchange," *The Journal of Finance* 28, (September 1973), p. 795.

to enjoy a current price advantage over full-service brokerage firms. That could change as the full-service brokers cut costs and spread their remaining overhead across an ever-broadening array of products and services. It could also be altered if commercial bank entrants move from discount transactions into a more full-service configuration. While trade reports indicate several banks have abandoned brokerage operations because of disappointing profits, the primary motivation for a number of others may be different. If this activity generates incremental retail deposits and other attractive retail "cross-selling" opportunities, it may become a permanent fixture in the banks' product line regardless of its profitability.

WHOLESALE SERVICES

In contrast to the fluidity of the retail sector, the wholesale securities sector, catering as it does to corporate, municipal, and institutional clienteles, is resisting intrusion more effectively. That appears to be the case from the viewpoint of either an aspiring retail securities firm trying to integrate backward into product "manufacuture," or a nontraditional intermediary attempting to penetrate the wholesale business.

Competitive patterns in the wholesale sector appear to differ materially from those in the retail sector. A variety of investment banking intermediaries are competing for the business of increasingly sophisticated capital-raising corporate clients on the one hand, and a group of "savers" heavily dominated by sophisticated institutions investors on the other hand. The growing competences of the traditional corporate clients and the heavily reinforced staffs of the wholesale securities firms[17] have accelerated the pace of "new product" and service innovation. Increasingly, the character of innovation has drawn on the secondary market intelligence generated by the wholesalers' trading floors. A number of firms have even moved part of their corporate finance groups down to those trading floors to provide better what their corporate clients identify (and pay for) as "value-added" services.

Some wholesalers entered the institutional markets seriously in the early 1970s as a defensive move to service their corporate clients better. Others that already had substantial positions in trading used this as a lever to obtain new corporate business. The institutional investors, for their part, have escalated the quid pro quo for their business, so that to be an investment banking participant in the institutional services (and therefore the corporate) sector requires a large commitment of capital and human resources. For some wholesalers the serious commitment to trading was originally a means to an end, but in some instances that activity has become so large that it rivals the firms' corporate finance activities.[18]

Retail securities firms' efforts to integrate backward into this wholesale sector have been modestly successful at best. The top eight wholesale firms' grip on various parts of the business has, if anything, grown stronger in recent years. This is true in the underwriting of corporate securities, whether one looks at a volume

[17] Hayes, *supra* note 7.
[18] *New York Stock Exchange Fact Book–1983*.

of corporate securities managed[19] or revenues from corporate underwriting activities (see Table 26-1). The same also holds true for municipal finance,[20] for perceived trading competence among institutional clients,[21] and for the lucrative merger and acquisition counseling business.[22]

Several new or potential entrants to the securities market have emerged. They include foreign banks, with their merchant banking skills developed and refined in traditionally integrated commercial and investment banking home market settings and in the Euromarkets.[23] They also include a variety of businesses that recently have purchased securities firms with some representation in the wholesale market. Among these are insurance companies (like Prudential), merchandising companies (like Sears), and financial services companies (like American Express). In addition, more and more money center and regional commercial banks have shown interest in parts of the wholesale market which they believe are not closed to them by the Glass-Steagall Act.[24]

These potential entrants believe they have the regulatory license to compete in a wide range of activities. For the commercial banks, some of the more important include Euromarket foreign exchange hedging, underwriting, lending, and trading; U.S. government bond underwriting and trading; interest-rate futures; general obligation, municipal underwriting, and trading; mortgage-backed securities trading; real estate financing; taxable and nontaxable private placements; mergers and acquisitions; venture capital and leveraged buyouts; financial counseling; leasing and portfolio management.

Viewed from a national market perspective, the commercial banking group enjoys major positions in Eurofinancing,[25] leasing,[26] portfolio management.[27] Until now, they have been excluded from underwriting corporate securities[28] and severely re-

---

[19] A.L. Adams, "Salomon's Number One," *Investment Dealers' Digest* 50, (January 17, 1984), p. 8.

[20] *Municipal Securities Market–1983*, New York: Public Securities Association, 1984.

[21] See results of Greenwich Research surveys as reported in various issues of the *Wall Street Letter*.

[22] "1983 Mergers and Acquisitions Tombstone Talley," *Corporate Financing Week*, (January 30, 1984), pp. XXX.

[23] Dwight B. Crane and Samuel L. Hayes III. "The New Competition in World Banking." *Harvard Business Review* (July–August 1982) pp. 88–94.

[24] Almost all of the money center banks have at least a corporate finance group. *The United States Commercial Bank Corporate Finance Directory–1983*, compiled by officials at Northwestern National Bank of Minneapolis, lists corporate finance groups for nine New York City banks, 13 regional money center banks, and eight other regional banks.

[25] "The International Sweepstakes." *Institutional Investor* (September 1983), p. 213.

[26] The American Association of Equipment Lessors reports that, using either equipment cost of $32 billion or total receivables outstanding of $62 billion, commercial banks presently hold approximately 28 percent of the outstandings, compared to 34 percent for independent leasing companies and 13 percent for captive finance companies.

[27] Federal Deposit Insurance Corporation, "Trust Assets of Insured Commercial Banks–1977, Washington, D.C.."

[28] Bankers Trust, however, has recently engineered a "private placement" of Rule 415 "shelf" registration securities and is being challenged in the courts by the Securities Industry Association for undertaking a de facto corporate underwriting.

Table 26.1. Dollar Revenue Concentration: Combined Negotiated and Competitive Securities (All $ Figures in Millions)

	1970	1971	1972	1973	1974	1975	1976	1977	1980	1981	1982
Debt											
Top 4%	32	30	32	36	47	42	42	42	41	39	45
Top 8%	53	50	56	62	68	66	64	67	63	60	64
Top 15%	80	77	79	89	89	88	88	92	86	84	87
Total Universe $	139	141	92	48	140	198	194	153	748	920	1,704
Equity											
Top 4%	44	31	29	30	49	41	39	46	44	41	43
Top 8%	67	51	51	53	72	65	62	67	68	65	67
Top 15%	97	75	77	80	93	89	89	92	88	87	90
Total Universe $	109	268	263	134	86	211	181	159	346	350	289
Debt & Equity											
Top 4%	33	27	27	33	44	39	36	41	42	41	45
Top 8%	55	47	47	53	63	61	58	64	62	60	65
Top 15%	80	73	76	79	87	87	84	91	88	84	88
Total Universe $	253	408	355	182	227	409	375	312	1,053	1,220	1,948

Source: Securities and Exchange Commission Data (1970–1977) released to author/Securities Industry Association (1980–1982) as provided by NYSE adjusted for "universe" of top 25 firms. Data for 1978 and 1979 were not available from the NYSE.

stricted by Glass-Steagall's prohibition on revenue bond financing, which in recent years has constituted approximately three-quarters of municipal underwriting volume.[29]

In the areas of taxable private placements and mergers and acquisition counseling, no legal barriers prevent overt commercial bank competition with securities firms, and yet the results have been disappointing from banks' perspective. Their penetration in private placements has been quite modest, although growing,[30] and their share of mergers and acquisitions assistance at the national level thus far has been nominal.[31] In venture capital, neither commercial banks nor the cadre of leading securities firms have had much impact thus far, although commercial banks have been increasingly active in leveraged buyouts and both groups profess a major interest in venture capital for the future.[32]

Commercial banks have had a similar record at the regional level. Several regional banks have established "investment banking" or "corporate finance" departments,[33] usually well-separated from commercial lending activities. They offer a variety of services, including private placements, mergers and acquisitions, financial consulting, venture capital, leveraged buyouts, valuations and appraisals, various types of asset-based financing, and international financing accommodations. Full-time personnel and revenues tend to be modest; these departments typically have had limited success in mobilizing the sponsoring banks' resources and momentum on behalf of these investment banking activities.

In sum, despite efforts to penetrate the wholesale securities markets, the commercial banks' overall record thus far has been unimpressive. In view of their professed interest in wholesale corporate finance, what are the prospects for the future?

Aside from the regulatory constraints discussed earlier, future progress for many commercial banks may hinge in part on their ability to sell corporate customers on the banks' professional capabilities in providing investment banking services.

It also will hinge on banks' ability to convince themselves that they have those capabilities. Two important aspects of the wholesale investment banking business seem clear: (1) activities within this sector tend to be interdependent, and (2) the successful players in this market have made an important accommodation to the "culture" of investment banking, with its attendant risk and reward structure and high level of personal commitment.

The Interdependent Parts. Many of the key activities in wholesale investment banking are not isolated "lines of commerce" in the classic economic sense but

---

[29] *Municipal Securities Markets–1983*, New York: Public Securities Association, 1984.

[30] See, for instance, *Corporate Financing Week* 14, 5 (February 7, 1983). In reporting on the top 15 leading intermediaries in private placements it notes that "Bank of America, the only bank on the 1981 list, didn't make it in 1982. No banks made it in the 1982 rankings but Bankers Trust came the closest, finishing 16th."

[31] 1983 Mergers and Acquisitions Tombstone Tally, *Corporate Financing Week* (January 30, 1984), a publication of Institutional Investor.

[32] See, for instance, M. Blumstein, "Morgan Stanley Fights for No. 1," the *New York Times* (April 1, 1984).

[33] United States Commercial Bank Corporate Finance Directory–1983.

rather "joint-product" activities that are, to one degree or another, actually interdependent. A leadership position in the annual underwriting "league tables," for instance, is treated by investment bankers as tangible evidence of their market presence and overall corporate finance skill, and is used as a selling tool to convince current and potential corporate clients of their acumen in such areas as financial counseling, private placements and, very lucratively, mergers and acquisitions.

Corporate underwriting leadership increasingly depends on quick and deep access to institutional investors, an access that can be assured only by a continuous presence in the secondary markets. That ongoing market activity, in turn, depends not only on the commitment of people and capital; it also depends on "product" that provides the excuse for securities salespeople to maintain daily contact with institutional portfolio traders and elicit a steady flow of transactions.

Wall Street's response to the introduction of Rule 415 "shelf" registrations demonstrates that investment bankers understand this interlocking system and act accordingly. When the Securities and Exchange Commission first began shelf registrations on a trial basis in March 1982, it expressed hope that the introduction of de facto competitive bidding on these offerings would not only yield savings to corporate issuers but also would boost competition by opening the market to a broader array of competing underwriters.[34]

While corporate issuers have realized significant savings,[35] the leading wholesale firms' responses have further concentrated, not broadened, the group of competing intermediaries.

These traditional underwriting leaders, as noted, have continued to consider high standings in the annual underwriting "league tables" important in soliciting business in other areas. In addition, because they are continually under pressure to generate adequate volumes of marketable products to feed their institutional trading and distribution networks, the shelf registrations, representing well-known credits, are often attractive acquisitions

Perhaps most important, the traditional underwriting leaders have continued to hold onto their ties with certain corporate clients. They act as though the loss of a client's shelf offering to another investment bank could pose a threat to that relationship, with its prospects for other profitable pieces of business.

Thus, in most instances, these traditional leading wholesale investment banking firms have stepped in and aggressively (and often successfully) bid for their clients' 415 offerings. Having won the bid, these underwriting firms often have omitted or sharply curtailed the size of the distribution syndicates, thus further concentrating the new issue business. Investment banks' behavior in connection with shelf registrations helps clarify the interlocking nature of the corporate (wholesale) services business as well as the competitive response that leading securities firms could be expected to make to a new group attempting to enter this market.

[34] See, for instance, hearings before the Securities and Exchange Commission on Rule 415, January 28–July 2, 1982.
[35] See, for instance, M.W. Marr and G.R. Thompson, "Shelf Registration and the Utility Industry," Virginia Polytechnic Institute and State University, Blacksburg, Virginia (June 30, 1983).

Commercial banks, which in theory could be serious competitors in the corporate market, are blocked from a more effective challenge, in part because they lack access to some key components in the interlocking portfolio of products and services. They are legally barred not only from corporate underwriting and trading but also from the big volume industrial revenue bond business. This, in turn, has denied them access to other key components of the product and service "system." The commercial banks cannot aspire to the visibility and stature of a leadership position in corporate underwriting. They cannot benefit from the interaction with corporations that would follow from day-to-day trading in their securities. Absence from the corporate and revenue bond trading markets also can hamper them in providing the latest pricing intelligence to these corporations when new financing strategies are being formulated.

It is not surprising, therefore, that the investment banks have been tenaciously fighting any change in the prohibition on revenue bond underwriting by commercial banks. It probably is not fear of inroads into the profitable revenue bond market that galvanizes investment banks, but rather the spectre of commercial banks gaining greater momentum in secondary market trading and then arguing with credibility for authority to apply that acumen to the U.S. corporate securities markets.

The Bankers' Mindset. While some commercial bankers believe that the only thing standing between them and the wholesale investment banking business is Glass-Steagall, it is much less certain that commercial banks as a group could penetrate this market rapidly if these regulatory barriers fell. Even putting aside the massive counterattack that leading investment banks could be expected to launch, the traditional mindset of commercial banks' management could inhibit successful penetration of investment banking.

While the investment banks talk confidently of their ability to continue fielding the most competent resources in each of their business sectors, they may well fear the trading power that commercial banks might muster. From an initial strategy of "buying" leadership in high volume corporate underwritings such as shelf registrations, and by aggressive trading and principal positioning in the "commodity" end of the secondary markets with the help of their huge capitalizations, commercial banks (and certain other nontraditional entrants) subsequently could move into greater value-added products. Like Salomon Brothers, they might parlay that trading initiative into a credible, broad-based corporate finance competence that could wrest important fee-based corporate business from the current wholesale investment banking leaders.

Field interviews suggest that commercial banks have found it difficult to link the competence and skills of their investment banking groups with their much larger core of lending officers. Some lending officers' reluctance to become familiar with investment banking product and service possibilities and to promote them to corporate customers may indicate a mindset that resists change and fears encroachment by investment banking specialists onto their traditional business "turf."

Envy and resentment at the elite status usually accorded a bank's investment banking personnel also may play a part in some lending officers' unenthusiastic response. These "corporate finance" professionals often are relatively young, deal in what is seen as a more glamorous mix of problems, and have access to the corporate customer group's highest management levels. Lending officers, by contrast, often interact with staff further down the organizational hierarchy. The investment banking staff members usually are paid substantially more than other bank officers, given comparable age, time in grade, and experience. The managements of some lending money center banks believe they already have crossed the psychological barrier to sharply higher compensation levels for their corporate finance and securities trading professionals.[36] Yet at most banks there has been insufficient experience to predict how well mainstream personnel will react to compensation levels of a half million dollars or more for fast-track corporate finance professionals still in their 30s!

Similarly, commercial bank and other nontraditional entrants into investment banking must be prepared to absorb the vicissitudes of the securities block positioning and trading business. As mentioned earlier, a substantial presence in the institutional trading area has become a sine qua non among serious competitors for corporate service business. Inventory levels have risen dramatically in recent years[37] in the face of increasingly volatile securities markets. While hedging strategies have sought to dampen capital risks considerably, players must be prepared to absorb large, unexpected swings in securities inventory values.

On the positive side, commercial banks can point to gains in trading skills and the assimilation of a supportive culture through participation in several arenas, including the domestic market for U.S. government securities, the Euromarkets, the ongoing management of the banks' liability structure, and the emerging secondary markets for commercial, industrial, and foreign loans.

More than a dozen U.S. money center banks[38] are recognized dealers in government securities. These markets are so large and liquid that they often serve as the benchmark from which securities in other markets are priced, either directly or indirectly. Thus banks actively participating in these markets have been able to hone their trading skills and related management systems in anticipation of later access to the corporate securities markets.

Euromarkets have offered commercial banks another arena in which to gain securities market experience, and some of the large U.S. multinational banks have become important participants there. While underwriting syndicates have been active in that market since the 1960s, secondary markets in Eurosecurities are a relatively recent phenomenon. Nevertheless, several U.S. money center banks have already captured significant positions in these markets. Some U.S. commercial banks have developed impressive worldwide financial networks with which to exploit the evolving global market for money.

---

[36] G. Hector, "Bankers Trust Takes on Wall Street," *Fortune* 109 (January 9, 1984) pp. 105–107.

[37] See *Staff Report on the Securities Industry in 1979*, other years, Securities and Exchange Commission.

[38] The "recognized dealers" include: Bank of America, Bankers Trust Chase Manhattan, Chemical, Citicorp, Continental Illinois, Crocker National, First Interstate, First Chicago, Harris Trust, Morgan Guaranty, Northern Trust, Manufacturers Hanover, and Bank of Boston.

As commercial banks and other deposit-taking institutions have moved from primary dependency on savings and demand deposits toward greater reliance on the "wholesale" money markets, they have been propelled into an active trading mode. The constant money-raising efforts of banks' treasury operations and the increasing use of forward hedges and other sophisticated risk-management techniques to accommodate the gap between asset and liability maturities have fostered skills that find ready application in investment banking.

Similarly, on the asset side of their balance sheets, many commercial banks are moving toward a "transaction" as opposed to a "yield" management philosophy, in which each asset is priced as though it were a candidate for resale. As regulatory pressures have mounted on commercial banks to improve their capital bases relative to loans outstanding, one goal has been to increase the velocity of asset turnover through the temporary or permanent sale of their domestic loans[39] to correspondent banks and institutional or foreign investors willing to take a slightly smaller spread. Thus the selling bank is able to reduce its asset base, improve its loan-to-deposit ratio, and enhance the return on those assets. It also can foster a transaction orientation among lending officers that supports the development of a trading culture.

CONCLUSION

Changing economic and demographic patterns have broken the long-standing status quo that prevailed in the post-World War II financial services industry. Each part of that industry has reacted differently to these changes, reflecting competitive dynamics specific to a particular niche. This pattern is mirrored in the intrusion of commercial banks into the securities business. Entry into discount brokerage has been quite rapid because there appear to be few barriers. Penetration of the wholesale investment banking business has been slower and more difficult. Regulatory barriers limit banks' ability to offer the trading and underwriting services necessary if an institution is to compete successfully in the wholesale securities business. The securities industry has recognized this and has moved in both the markets and the courts to limit banks' entry. Even removing regulatory barriers would not assure banks of rapid success, however. Despite the experience and success some banks have gained in permitted securities activities, they must learn to manage differences between commercial and investment banking cultures in order to penetrate the wholesale securities market.

---

[39] There have also been reports of the creation of an informal secondary market for LDC loans, particularly in the case of Mexico. See Gary Hector, "The Banks' Latest Game: Loan Swapping," *Fortune* (December 12, 1983), p. 111.

27 Investment Banking at Bankers Trust Company

DAVID E. DOUGHERTY

In 1978, Bankers Trust Company began charting a new course for itself with the decision to sell its consumer banking operation and concentrate on its greatest strength—wholesale banking. Bankers Trust sought to become a preeminent financial institution worldwide by devoting its considerable resources and energies to four core businesses: commercial banking, corporate finance, money and securities markets activities, and fiduciary services.

The progression of that concept led to Bankers Trust's adoption in 1983 of a merchant banking strategy that has further expanded the frontiers of both commercial and investment banking. Today, Bankers Trust is a leading merchant bank offering a full line of corporate finance services competitive with the major Wall Street firms. By closely integrating the efforts of corporate finance, commercial banking, and money and securities markets professionals, the organization has become a powerful force in wholesale financial services.

Merchant banking at Bankers Trust has several key characteristics. First, it brings together the on-balance-sheet lending capabilities, a broad base of relationships, and wide range of noncredit services unique to a commercial bank with the entrepreneurial spirit and intermediary capabilities of an investment bank. Second, merchant banking means leadership in fulfilling both the origination and distribution functions. Third, it overlays a transaction orientation on the bank's well-established relationship orientation, enhancing the bank's responsiveness to client needs and market opportunities.

The client base to which the bank targets its efforts includes commercial and industrial companies, governments, other financial institutions, and select individuals.

The bank's responsiveness is a function of its culture and the people it has attracted. Through its efforts to flatten out its hierarchy, Bankers Trust has been able to create what it calls a "partnership of professionals" who thrive in an atmosphere encouraging independence and initiative.

In less than a decade, Bankers Trust has evolved from a fledgling to a major force in wholesale finance. Today the bank is recognized as a leader and pioneer in many segments of the business. The bank's corporate finance activities range from the capital markets—including interest-rate and currency swaps, Eurobonds, private placements, and interest-rate caps—to lease financing, mergers and acquisitions, tax-exempt financing, and leveraged buyouts.

COMPETITIVE ADVANTAGES

Since in a very real sense Bankers Trust is both more than an investment bank and more than a commercial bank, it can offer a mix of products and services others cannot. As a result, the bank can fulfill a broad range of client needs. Bankers Trust offers a unique blend of capital, distribution power, and creativity.

In the leveraged buyout area, for example, Bankers Trust can not only provide or arrange all the financing for companies desiring a leveraged buyout, corporate expansion, or divestiture, but is also available to structure and negotiate the transaction. Through these efforts, the bank has built a very high degree of confidence among both clients and potential investors. During the 1980s Bankers Trust has played a meaningful role in nearly every substantial leveraged buyout, including the buyouts of Beatrice Companies and Safeway Stores.

In leveraged lease financing, the bank has displayed well-rounded skills and a strong commitment to the deals it structures. This was demonstrated when Bankers Trust played several important roles in a leveraged leasing transaction for the U.S. Navy. The bank managed the largest lease equity syndication ever done in a single transaction—a $1.3 billion lease of eight vessels to the Military Sealift Command. In addition, the bank invested in part of the transaction for its own account.

Putting together the investor syndicate required special care; the efforts of two departments of the bank were critical to this phase. The successful meshing of the bank's transaction and relationship orientations resulted in both Philip Morris and United Parcel Service joining the investor syndicate.

Bankers Trust has established close relationships with both lessees and lessors, thereby keeping it close to the market. Where large, tax-oriented transactions are concerned, the bank's lease financing professionals possess unexcelled market knowledge, with expertise extending to ships, aircraft, and special facilities, among them co-generation and geothermal plants. The scope of its experience has earned Bankers Trust respect as advisors to all parties involved in leveraged leases. The bank is able not only to react to changing markets but also to create markets when opportunities arise. The bank has consistently developed and executed innovative leasing structures for clients.

Just as the teamwork between the bank's corporate finance specialists and relationship managers is important, so too is their relationship with the sales, trading, and funding function. As one of the market leaders in total volume, trading over $20 billion of securities daily, the bank's sales and trading professionals are able to provide up-to-the-minute market information to their colleagues in other departments. Bankers Trust's commitment to the financial markets is a major one. The bank is one of the top five government securities and foreign exchange dealers, and has earned a reputation for innovation in liability management as well as for its capabilities as a municipal securities dealer.

INNOVATION AND LEADERSHIP

Bankers Trust is an innovator in the financial services industry, a critical quality in an environment where change has become the norm. Once, the "products" of investment banking were simple and few: bonds, preferred stock, common stock, commercial paper, convertibles. Today, they include a variety of hybrid instruments, pooled and stripped securities, futures, options, and currency- and coupon-swap contracts.

It is important to realize, however, that such product proliferation works only if it ties into an origination and distribution network that welcomes it. Most opportunities for innovation arise out of a nonstandard inquiry from either the origination or the distribution side, both of which need to be highly alert to such opportunities.

Bankers Trust has long been an innovator in the tax-exempt financing arena. Its public finance professionals pioneered the tax-exampt variable-rate demand note in June 1981. Since then, the market has grown to an estimated $116 billion, with these highly liquid instruments purchased by tax-exempt money market funds, corporations, and bank trust departments.

Bankers Trust was also the first institution to introduce its own rate service for pricing variable-rate demand notes—TENR™. With the bank already a leader in the short-term, tax-exempt market, the TENR rate service was accepted readily by both issuers and investors. Bankers Trust again broke new ground when it combined a tax-exempt bond refunding with an interest-rate swap, resulting in a significantly lower interest rate for the client.

Since 1982, Bankers Trust has served as managing underwriter or placement agent on over 560 variable-rate transactions totaling $8.8 billion, and on over 130 fixed-rate transactions totaling $9.7 billion. The group's professionals assist borrowers, including municipalities, governmental authorities, and corporations, in all phases of designing and marketing tax-exempt programs.

Another market in which Bankers Trust has been in the forefront is interest-rate and currency swaps. Once thought to be a passing arbitrage product, the swap has proved to be a valuable financial instrument to corporate treasurers, bank liability managers, and government finance officers. As a result, the swaps market has grown dramatically—from approximately $3 billion in 1982 to an estimated $600 billion in 1987. The growth of the market has been due, in large measure, to the imagination and ingenuity displayed by its participants in designing swap structures. Superior distribution capabilities and global presence have also been essential ingredients for success.

Bankers Trust is a world leader in the highly competitive interest-rate and currency-swaps markets, and was ranked number one in overall performance by customers in a *Euromoney* survey published in 1987. The bank's creativity was displayed when the European Economic Community wanted to raise $350 million in floating-rate dollars. Traditionally, the EEC had awarded its business to a select group of European banks. It had also raised its floating-rate dollars in the floating-rate note market. Bankers Trust proposed the largest swap-related bond ever—a fixed-rate bond issue and simultaneous swap into floating-rate funds—whereby the EEC could achieve significant savings of over 50 basis points annually.

Ultimately, several elements tipped the scales in Bankers Trust's favor. Critical was a global capital markets capability, with specialists based in New York, London, Tokyo, Zurich, Hong Kong, Sydney, and Toronto to meet client needs 24 hours a day. Several other attributes also were important to the EEC: the ability to attract a first-class syndicate, the resources to stand behind large bond issues, top-flight distribution capabilites, and a strong track record in the secondary market. The transaction was successfully completed through the close cooperation of two departments of the bank.

Bankers Trust is also one of the top three participants worldwide in the rapidly expanding interest-rate protection market. The bank was one of the first to develop the interest-rate cap, which has grown into a market exceeding $50 billion in size.

GLOBAL REACH

Today the integration of the international capital markets is proceeding rapidly. This movement is being promoted by several factors, including sophisticated voice and data technologies and deregulation. Legislation, particularly that dealing with tax policy, has also been of major importance in removing barriers to integration.

In their performance overseas we can see clearly the success achieved by banks in the broad scope of market activities. Free from the restrictions imposed by the Glass-Steagall Act, U.S. banks, operating through merchant banking subsidiaries, routinely underwrite and deal in corporate securities abroad. The track record of U.S. banks in this area has been excellent.

The international bond markets have grown in volume and prominence in recent years. In 1982, a watershed year, the Eurodollar bond market leapfrogged ahead of the U.S domestic corporate bond market in terms of new issue volume for the first time. There was another change in 1983: the volume of new international bank lending was far smaller than the volume of international bond issues for the first time. The international bond market has thus become an important alternative financing source to bank credit. U.S. banks have occupied top positions in these markets and have built solid reputations.

Even as the environment in which the international markets operate changes, the elements critical to competing internationally remain essentially the same: a substantial capital base underlying strong underwriting and distribution skills.

Bankers Trust has long been an active participant in the international capitals of finance. Through Bankers Trust International Limited (BTI), its merchant bank in London, the bank has increasingly made its presence felt in the Eurobond market.

Specialists at BTI in capital markets, lease financing, mergers and acquisitions, and project finance have played an important role in advancing these businesses world-wide.

For example, Bankers Trust has brought to bear its international resources to meet the ongoing financing needs of Unilever, one of the world's largest consumer products companies. Specialists in syndications, corporate finance, and the money and securities markets, among other areas of the bank, have worked with the relationship managers responsible for Unilever and its subsidiaries on a wide variety of transactions. Transactions for Unilever in a single year included structuring an innovative $1 billion Euronote issuance program, lead or co-lead managing Euro-bond issues to raise fixed-rate funds, and executing a sizable currency swap.

Recent years have also brought the globalization of the mergers and acquisitions market. A strong desire on the part of corporations for geographic diversification, along with their search for new markets and technologies, has fueled this trend. As a result, cross-border mergers and acquisitions have grown in importance.

In 1986, Bankers Trust served as financial advisor for 48 transactions worldwide with a total value of $4.7 billion, ranking us among the most active M&A advisors. Fully half of these transactions involved a foreign buyer or seller. The bank has more than 60 professionals located in domestic and foreign offices, including New York, Los Angeles, London, Tokyo, Paris, Frankfurt, and Sydney. By integrating the efforts of the banks' M&A professionals with the activities of corporate relation-ship managers around the globe, Bankers Trust offers potential buyers and sellers access to senior executives of a vast number of large and medium-sized companies worldwide.

The quest to enhance their worldwide engineering capabilities has led U.S. automakers to seek to acquire small European design and engineering firms. This was the attraction of Britain's Group Lotus PLC—a company known for its high-performance cars and advanced technology—to General Motors Corporation. Bankers Trust acted as financial advisor to British Car Auction Group PLC and JCB Investments Ltd. in the sale of their stake in Lotus to GM. Mindful of Lotus's prestige image, GM, which acquired a controlling interest in the company as a result of the transaction, intends that it continue operating independently as an engineering and research consultant.

When Lagoven S.A., the largest affiliate of Petroleos de Venezuela, decided to look for international joint-venture opportunities, it turned to Bankers Trust for assistance. The bank canvassed the U.S. market for companies that would represent a strategic fit for this client, which is the largest producer of crude oil in South America. After reviewing the merits of potential partners and assessing their economic value, Bankers Trust provided general financial advice in two separate transactions involving large U.S. refining and marketing companies: the purchase of a 50 percent equity interest in Citgo Petroleum and the purchase of a 50 percent interest in the Gulf Coast assets of Champlin Petroleum. These transactions, whose total value approached $500 million, represent the first acquisition of U.S. refinery and mar-keting operations by a foreign state-owned oil producer.

CONCLUSION

Bankers Trust is a dynamic institution in a dynamic industry. It is poised for significant future growth, firmly backed by two resources critical to advancement—capital resources and human resources.

In all that has been discussed, the human element is pivotal. The aggressive, imaginative, highly knowledgeable merchant banker, able to translate the concept of excellence through common purpose into action, is the key to the continued success of Bankers Trust.

28 Investment Banking at Chase Manhattan

HOWARD PLATZMAN

You cannot read anything about the world capital markets these days that does not contain the word "innovation." This chapter will be no exception.

With the rise of the commercial paper market in the 1970s, U.S. money center banks have been faced with a clear choice: innovate or die. This may sound overly dramatic, but the fact is that commercial banking has undergone a sea change in the 1980s. As large corporate customers have increasingly bypassed traditional lenders to tap financial markets directly, innovation has become a necessity.

CHALLENGE

Five years ago, investment banking activities at Chase were concentrated in Euromarket loan syndications. It was apparent, however, that narrowing spreads on commercial loans would have to be compensated for by increased fee-based income. To hold on to old relationships, and generate new ones, we would have to redefine our role as financial intermediaries.

No longer could we think of Chase merely as a conduit through which depositor savings are passed on to corporate borrowers. We had to become more active and more creative, searching out new pools of capital and linking investors in one corner of the globe with capital-hungry firms in another. In short, we had to become investment bankers.

Commercial lending would continue to be an important part of commercial banking, but other methods of corporate finance would have to be employed to meet the changing needs of companies operating in a global marketplace.

This task was complicated by the Federal Reserve Board's decision in 1979 to switch tactics in combating the double-digit inflation of that era; henceforth, it would abandon its focus on exchange rates and try instead to regulate the money supply. While this policy was a great success in subduing inflation, it brought new headaches in the form of wildly fluctuating exchange and interest rates.

As a result, Chase faced a double challenge: (1) devise alternative means of corporate financing, and (2) arrange such financing in a way that minimizes exchange and interest-rate risk.

OPPORTUNITY

It used to be that investment banking was primarily a relationship-oriented business. Corporate finance officers looked to their investment bankers to provide a total package of securities services, and they tended to remain loyal to their banks.

While traditional relationships remain an obstacle to commercial banks with investment banking aspirations, the financial environment is much more competitive today than it was just a few years ago. One reason for the changed environment is that CFOs are more sophisticated than ever before. As a consequence, corporations are more apt to parcel out their business to a number of investment banking providers, including commercial banks.

Another significant factor has been SEC Rule 415—"shelf registration"—which permits a corporation to get the commission's preapproval for a securities issue before choosing an underwriter. Under this rule, the filing is publicly announced, and then would-be underwriters engage in competitive bidding for the right to handle the issue. The resulting erosion of long-standing corporation–investment bank relationships has created an opening for commercial banks to carve out a share of the investment banking business.

Thus Chase had the motive (declining margins), the opportunity, and the means (an international network, a large capital base, and a growing staff of investment banking experts) to develop and market a broad spectrum of corporate finance products.

SUCCESSES

The same capital markets expertise that has enabled Chase to generate $1.4 billion in external funds for its own use between 1981 and 1985 serves to bolster the capital resources of our corporate clients. Despite the Glass-Steagall ban on domestic underwriting, Chase has managed to establish itself as a major force in the international capital markets.

This has been accomplished by the creative adaptation of existing corporate finance techniques and the market-responsive development of new financial instruments, and by high-volume private placement activity and high-visibility Euromarket underwriting.

In 1982, Chase Manhattan Capital Markets Corporation (CMCMC), a wholly owned subsidiary, was formed to integrate a growing array of investment banking products. Since then, over 200 professionals have been added to the investment banking staff, boosting Chase's worldwide total to over 700.

The result: fee-related income in 1985 was up over $100 million compared with 1984, and fee income in the first quarter of 1986 was up 88 percent over the first quarter of 1985.

STRATEGIES

Chase's investment banking strategy is to pursue broadly based growth by capitalizing on the bank's particular strengths. These include: (1) its global presence; (2) its specialized knowledge of various industries; (3) its technological capabilities; and (4) its size and large capital base.

Global Presence

Managing risk is a continuous game requiring timely information on interest rates, currency values, and political developments. The Chase network of offices in over 100 countries offers a natural competitive advantage.

Through this network, Chase is able to tap distant pools of capital and provide relatively low-cost financing to its corporate clients. By contrast, a single-line competitor has to make a special effort, and incur extra expense, to maintain the same level of contact with foreign investors and multinational corporations.

One way Chase leverages its global network is by linking two separate national capital markets via a currency swap. Recently, a major aircraft builder announced a routine shelf registration of a bond issue. Chase proposed instead that the bond be denominated in Swiss francs and then swapped into dollars at better terms than a straight issue. The transaction saved the issuer 35 basis points.

This is a fairly simple, "plain vanilla" deal, but financings can be breathtakingly complex. Another transaction might include a leveraged lease with the equity sourced in one country, the debt in another country, and two currency swaps to denominate the rental payments in the currency of a third country, all on behalf of a lessee residing in a fourth country.

This international network has also boosted merger and acquisitions (M&A) activities. Recently, a long-time Chase commercial banking customer announced its intention to sell about $1 billion of assets. We were able to identify an Australian subsidiary as a suitable candidate for divestiture. Chase had just joined with a major Australian insurance company to open a bank in the country, and we were mandated the sales agent in large part because of the local expertise Chase AMP Bank could offer.

Specialized Knowledge

Chase's corporate sector is organized on an industry basis with about 20 technical directors, and so is better able to evaluate the overall feasibility of proposed ventures than an investment banking firm relying principally on stock analysts.

Technical specialists in mining, energy, electronics, chemical engineering, and other fields provide crucial assistance to the investment banking unit, especially in project finance and M&A. For example, CMCMC, working closely with technical directors in primary metals, recently helped a large energy firm divest certain mining properties. Financial advisory and other activities also benefit from such expertise.

Technology

Until recently, a corporation looking to hedge against short-term interest-rate risk typically turned to the interest-rate futures market. With the development of Chase Electronic Swaps System (CHESS) in 1985, interest-rate swaps became a more attractive alternative.

Before CHESS, arranging a swap was strictly a manual operation. A client would come to us seeking a swap partner and we would telephone around to locate a suitable counterparty. Now, CHESS gives corporate treasurers the ability to: (1) scan a listing of available swap opportunities; (2) simulate the costs of alternative transactions; (3) project their results under varying interest-rate scenarios; and (4) custom-tailor swaps to fit the liability profiles of their companies.

Another breakthrough product, originated for the French domestic credit and commercial paper markets, is PACT (the French acronym for "short-term advance issuance facility"). PACT is a combination computer program and telex facility that permits a borrower–issuer to solicit bids from competing banks, thus saving administrative and relationship costs for both parties to the transaction.

Size

Chase is among the lowest-cost swaps producers in the world because its "book" is one of the largest in the world. This frequently translates into greater flexibility and lower prices. Some investment banking firms have tried to duplicate this approach, but they have thus far failed to overcome the reality that their transaction base is confined to futures markets, their reach is less global, and their technology is less sophisticated than ours.

Size is also important to one of Chase's long-term goals, the repeal of Glass-Steagall's restrictions on domestic securities underwriting. Experts estimate that the credit needs of the U.S. economy could reach $17 trillion by the turn of the century. The huge capital stocks of commercial banks will have to supplement the financial resources of traditional investment banking companies if the financial markets are to meet those needs.

ACTIVITIES

Have commercial banks made serious inroads into the business of traditional investment banking firms? How strong is Chase in the world capital markets?

In general, commercial banks have large market shares in swaps and international leasing—Chase is strong in both these areas—and lesser shares in M&A and corporate securities underwriting.

What follows is a brief product-by-product survey of investment banking services Chase offers as of this writing, with Chase innovations highlighted. One caution, however: by the time you read this, the dizzying pace of market change will have turned these remarks into history.

Swaps

Because of the power of CHESS and the size of its book, Chase has become one of the top five interest-rate swap providers in the world. Because of long experience in foreign exchange trading, Chase is among the top 10 currency-swap arrangers. In 1985, Chase arranged over $10 billion of these transactions, and the swaps business has doubled in each of the previous three years.

Leasing

Chase has done $3 billion in lease deals in the last three years, financing everything from single machines to whole factories. It is the world leader in yen-denominated leases, which have been structured for lessees in South America, Asia, Europe, and the United States.

Recently, Chase arranged the sale/leaseback of a large New Jersey bank's corporate headquarters, effectively transforming a fixed asset into over $30 million of new liquidity for less than the cost of a commercial mortgage.

Chase's lease capabilities have been bolstered by the development of Chase Lease Evaluation and Accounting System (CLEASE), which allows a corporation to project tax benefits based on a model of the tax laws and general financial conditions of the countries in which it operates. This software has become the most widely used analytical tool to structure leases.

Euro Commercial Paper (ECP)

Chase is among the top five dealers in Euro commercial paper, currently the fastest growing product in the world capital markets. Large multinational corporations are increasingly opting for ECP—Eurodollar-denominated promissory notes—over revolving credits offered by commercial banks. Over a recent six-month period, Chase handled 16 issues for major U.S. and foreign corporations and had secondary market involvement in 85 other issues.

Technology has played an important part in Chase's ECP activity. Commercial Paper Manager is an on-line computer system allowing issuer, agent, and dealer to communicate electronically. It facilitates the management of CP issues by simplifying the construction of maturity ladders, highlighting overlaps, and providing up-to-the-minute data on the amount and weighted cost of paper issued. Another computer product, Same-day Securities Settlement, routes funds to issuers and investors as quickly as possible via a direct link with a major European clearinghouse.

New Instruments

Chase has pioneered many new financing tools to meet the capital needs of its clients.

Note Issuance Facilities

NIFs allow corporations to raise funds at a rate close to the London Interbank Offered Rate (LIBOR), the benchmark rate for interbank lending in the Euromarket. NIFs are similar to ECP in that they are short-term notes, but they are a contingent liability of the bank while ECP is issued directly by a customer and sold by the bank on a "best-efforts" basis. Although ECP issues have replaced NIFs for many large corporations, NIFs remain a major source of funding for middle-market companies lacking direct access to the world capital markets. Chase has taken a management role in over $18 billion of NIFs.

Callable Floating-Rate CDs

Originally designed to aid Japanese banks seeking medium-term floating rate Eurodollar deposits, these are now a standard instrument in the Euromarket.

Dual Currency Financings

These match issuers seeking liabilities in one currency with investors seeking assets in another. Chase's first such financing involved a Swiss franc bond offered publicly by a U.S. company in Swiss markets but payable at maturity in U.S. dollars. More complicated multicurrency financings, over a broad range of loan and securities products, have since been devised to further increase flexibility and reduce costs.

Adjustable-Rate Preferred Stock

This stock, which Chase developed in 1982 to facilitate its own capital growth, has become a major source of new funds for foreign and domestic corporations.

Mergers and Acquisitions (M&A)

Chase has been assisting corporations in acquisitions and divestitures for over 25 years, specializing in the electronics, financial services, and energy businesses. Activity in this area has increased substantially of late—with M&A fees doubling in each of the past three years—as Chase has broadened its expertise to include additional industries. For example, CMCMC recently lured a major Swiss-based pharmaceutical firm from its traditional investment bank and arranged the purchase of a U.S. maker of contact lenses. In another deal, Chase arranged the sale of a

U.S. textile firm to a West German corporation. Chase is also heavily engaged in structuring leveraged buyouts and leveraged acquisitions.

Project Finance

Chase is among the few institutions with the resources and the depth and breadth of knowledge required to finance the construction of large projects, such as mines, oil fields, and pipelines. Minimizing the risks inherent in project finance requires command of a wide range of technical and financial information. While industry specialists assess the technical viability of a project, legal, accounting, tax, and regulatory factors are addressed by other Chase professionals. The resulting financing package often involves dozens of parties and multiple contractual agreements.

Private Placements

Private placement of corporate securities particularly benefits middle-market companies that lack ready access to the public debt market. For example, CMCMC recently arranged a 12-year placement backing real estate acquisitions by a U.S. fast food chain. The deal provided financing at a lower cost than a straight commercial loan, and, unlike a typical loan, did not restrict the chain's future debt or dividend payments.

Chase is also strong in the private placement of tax-exempt securities. Because commercial banks are forbidden by law to underwrite municipal revenue bonds, these issues must be handled as private placements. Recently, CMCMC acted as lead placement agent for $220 million in housing bonds issued by a Puerto Rican public corporation. Over the last few years, Chase has placed more than $1 billion of such securities.

Loan Syndications

Despite the proliferation of new financial instruments, loan syndications remain a popular form of corporate financing. With the increasing internationalization of capital markets, syndications can now be custom-designed to include multiple lenders and multiple currencies. Chase is among the top lead managers in Euromarket syndications.

Securities Underwriting

Although prohibited from underwriting in the United States, commercial banks are permitted to underwrite stocks and bonds abroad. Even so, they generally lag investment banking houses in Euromarket underwriting, even in underwriting for U.S. companies. Recently, Chase has started to reverse this trend by acting as lead manager for the 100 million Swiss franc Eurobond issue of a major U.S. auto rental company. In addition, purchase of the London firm of Simon & Coates will give Chase entry into underwriting for the British middle market.

Asset Sales

Where in the past Chase booked loans and held them to maturity, in 1985 the bank sold $28 billion in loans and acceptances in order to free capital for new financing. More and more, the Global Bank originates loans and then places them with financial institutions throughout the world. Mortgages, auto loans, student loans, and credit card receivables are other candidates for this treatment.

Loans sold to investment banking houses are often repackaged and sold as securities in a process known as "securitization." While commercial banks often earn fee income by continuing to service the loans they sell, only investment banks may underwrite these issues. Bank profitability, as well as system safety, would be enhanced if banks could diversify their sources of profit to include underwriting profits from asset-backed securities.

Financial Advisory Services

Chase advises clients on everything from capital structure to liability management to tax planning. Such services may entail new financing or other sorts of transactions, such as asset sales or debt-for-equity swaps. Recently, Chase advised the British government on its plans to build the "Chunnel," a tunnel across the English Channel.

Securities Trading

Today's corporations must manage their assets and liabilities more actively than in the past. Hence the buying and selling of securities has become steadily more important, both for our customers and for ourselves. Chase is a market maker in over 1000 securities issues and has a secondary market trading volume of over $4.5 billion a month.

At Chase, trading operations are grouped in a separate part of the Global Bank, but traders work closely with CMCMC on many investment banking transactions. Because they deal for their own account around the clock, Chase traders are able to translate their knowledge of where the market is—and where it is likely to go—into financing priced as low as possible and risks hedged as well as possible.

Trading rooms in 20 countries, together with a distribution network covering 75 countries, are a major advantage. The recent acquisition of Laurie, Milbank & Co. will further expand Chase's trading capabilities to include "gilts," British government securities.

GOALS

The paramount goal is to further unify Chase's commercial and investment banking functions. Because the distinction between loans and other forms of corporate finance has grown increasingly blurred, it is necessary to have a coherent, integrated, wholesale banking strategy. To this end, investment banking, securities trading, cash management, and traditional relationship-management activities—on behalf of corporate, institutional, and government clients—have been grouped under one umbrella, the Global Bank.

Another goal is to double the number of overseas locations out of which Chase's investment banking products are delivered, from 25 to 50. Just as Chase grew into a multinational lender in order to serve U.S. clients who became multinationals in the 1960s and 1970s, so in the 1980s and 1990s Chase's capital markets prowess will have to be extended to more and more locations around the world.

Last but not least, we need to press on with the technological innovation that has been the source of much of Chase's success. Although investors and issuers may be far apart physically, continuing technological advances will bring them closer and closer electronically. In today's competitive environment, it is not enough to have the right answer; one must get there with it first.

STYLES

While all agree that the future belongs to the fast, doubts are still expressed about the ability of bankers to be responsive enough to meet clients' needs. The evidence of the last few years should convince doubters that the time-honored image of bankers as stuffy and slow-moving is a hoary cliche. The changing nature of the relationship between Chase and its corporate customers has fostered a more service-oriented culture at the bank. The new-breed Chase banker has had to adopt a deals-oriented, willing-to-work-around-the-clock-if-necessary style of doing business.

This has been accomplished by bringing in experienced investment bankers from Wall Street and by reorienting Chase bankers to the realities of the current financial marketplace. The traditional credit training program designed to produce loan officers is giving way to a Global Bank Training Curriculum designed to produce corporate finance professionals.

Management style is also in the process of changing. The heightened need for teamwork and coordinated action has begun to alter the traditional hierarchical bias of commercial bank management.

PROSPECTS

Over the next decade, we foresee Chase taking its place as one of a dozen or so "universal" or full-service megabanks. For a company to enter this pantheon, it will have to attract the top graduates of the leading business schools. In fact, this is already happening at Chase.

More and more, newly minted investment bankers are choosing to forgo the prestige of working for an old-line firm, where they typically start their careers, and sometimes get mired, in less-than-challenging sales positions. Instead, they are opting for the excitement of helping to build a new business, with all the opportunity for creativity and mobility that that entails.

PART 8 INVESTMENT BANKING OUTSIDE THE UNITED STATES

The global nature of the financial markets was described in Chapter 2, international securities trading was discussed in Chapter 11, and frequent references appear in other chapters to activity beyond the United States.

The Japanese market is a particularly important one, and in Chapter 29 Toshiaki Kamijo discusses it. The chapter deals with the investment banking industry and the activities of securities firms, and the primary and secondary markets in Japan.

The United Kingdom is important because London is the center of the Euromarket. In Chapter 30, Tad Rybczynski discusses the organization and functioning of the London market as it has been shaped by the deregulatory "big bang" of October 1986.

Canada, like the United States, has experienced a separation of commercial from investment banking that is breaking down at the insistence of the commercial bankers. In addition, Canada is relaxing a tradition of protecting its securities industry from foreign competition. Calvin Potter, in Chapter 31, describes the competitive structure of the investment dealer business in Canada, as deregulation is in process.

Chapter 32, by David Shaw, provides a discussion of the Canadian securities firm. While many of the characteristics of firms in Canada are similar to those of U.S. firms, there are differences. The chapter describes the unique context in which Canadian firms find themselves and the markets in which they operate.

29 Securities Markets and Investment Banking in Japan

TOSHIAKI KAMIJO

BASIC REGULATIONS

The Securities and Exchange Law, which governs conduct of the Japanese securities markets, was enacted in 1948 while Japan was under the control of the United States. It was influenced heavily by such U.S. laws as the Securities Act of 1933, the Securities Exchange Act of 1934, and the Banking Act of 1933. Although a few revisions have been made since enactment, the law retains its basic framework, so the structure of the Japanese securities markets resembles that of the United States in many ways.

The purpose of the Securities and Exchange Law is "to ensure fair issuing, buying and selling and other forms of transactions of securities and smooth circulation of securities in order to contribute to proper operation of the economy and protection of investors."

For this purpose, the law first requires a registration statement system, which assures disclosure of the financial condition of the company issuing securities so as to provide investors with the accurate and explicit information necessary for an investment decision. It next establishes a system of regulations for tender offers intended to protect investors and preserve an orderly securities market. It also regulates organization of securities companies, securities dealers' associations, stock exchanges, securities finance companies, and other principal institutions carrying out the functions of the securities market.

All parties to securities transactions are enjoined from fraud and misconduct. Securities exchange trading laws prohibit the manipulation of stock prices, provide a price stabilization system, and restrict short selling and other such market practices. The regulation also forbids any actions by company officers and other insiders to profit from trading in their own company's shares on the basis of inside information.

Article 65, one of the most important provisions in the law, requires separation of the banking and securities businesses. Intended to protect depositors and avoid the ill effects of financial oligopoly, the provision has contributed to a drastic change in the structure of Japan's capital market, elevating securities companies to the level of other financial institutions.

That the U.S. securities market model has functioned well in Japan owes much to the Americanization of Japan's economic structure and to the life-style of the Japanese people.

SECURITIES COMPANIES

Issuing and trading of securities is done exclusively by securities companies, except in the case of government bonds, municipal bonds, and government-guaranteed bonds (where the government guarantees the reimbursement of the principal and payment of interest).

Securities companies issue and trade securities with the approval of the Minister of Finance, as specified in Article 2 of the Securities and Exchange Law. When the law was enacted, Japanese securities companies followed the same registration system as U.S. companies. This provision was replaced with a licensing system when the law was revised in 1965 following an economic recession in the first half of that decade. The licenses are of four types:

1. *Dealing Business.* Trading in securities by securities companies on their own account.
2. *Brokerage Business.* Trading in securities on orders from customers.
3. *Underwriting Business.* Underwriting new securities or making a public offering of outstanding securities.
4. *Selling Business.* Engaging in a retail distribution of securities offered publicly.

Companies may hold more than one type of license. As of the end of December 1983, of the total 239 securities companies (excluding foreign companies, which will be described later), 67 held all four types of licenses, while 151 held three types of licenses, one company held two types of licenses, and 20 held one type of license.

Before granting a license, the Minister of Finance screens the applicants according to the following criteria: (1) soundness of financial resources; (2) training and background of personnel; and (3) ability to engage in the securities business from the viewpoint of the business environment in the region in which the applicant wants to do business.

The minimum level of capitalization for a company is set by law depending on the type of license, content of business, location of offices, and whether it belongs to a securities exchange. In November 1980 the Ministry of Finance (MOF) published desirable capitalization levels as well (see Table 29.1).

Table 29.1. Minimum Capital Stock Required for Securities Companies

Classification	Legal Minimum	MOF Guideline
Exchange regular member company:		
Regular member of Tokyo or Osaka SE	¥100 mil.	¥200 mil.
Regular member of Nagoya SE	¥ 50 mil.	¥100 mil.
Regular member of any other SE	¥ 30 mil.	¥ 60 mil.
Nonmember company:		
Located in 23 wards of Tokyo or in Osaka City	¥ 30 mil.	¥ 40 mil.
Others	¥ 20 mil.	¥ 40 mil.
Company dealing solely with securities company:		
Located in Tokyo or Osaka	¥ 4 mil.	
Others	¥ 1 mil.	
Underwriting securities company:		
Managing underwriter also engaged in other securities business	¥ 3 bil.	
Managing underwriter specializing in underwriting	¥ 1 bil.	
Nonmanaging underwriter	¥200 mil.	¥300 mil.

Securities companies with capitalization of ¥3 billion or more that act as managing underwriter and also are engaged in other securities businesses are called "integrated" securities companies. At the end of 1983, there were 15 such companies, which play an important role in the securities exchanges.

A foreign securities company wishing to operate in Japan has three ways to enter the market: (1) establish a branch office, (2) establish a Japanese subsidiary, or (3) acquire an existing Japanese company. Actually, only the branch office method has been used for entry into the Japanese market.

Entry by foreign companies is governed by the Law on Foreign Securities Firms enacted in September 1971. Foreign securities companies receive a license from the Minister of Finance for each office they establish in Japan. The types of licenses and screening standards are roughly the same as those for domestic securities companies. Because foreign securities companies are headquartered abroad, however, they must deposit a set amount of guarantee money before they start operation in order to protect domestic investors.

As of the end of June 1984, the following nine companies (through 10 branches) were doing business in Japan:

Merrill Lynch International Bank, Inc.

Vickers da Costa, Ltd.

Bache Securities (Japan), Ltd.

Smith Barney, Harris Upham International, Inc.

Jardine Fleming (Securities), Ltd.

Salomon Brothers Asia, Ltd.

Kidder Peabody & Co., Inc.
Goldman Sachs International Corp.
Morgan Stanley International, Ltd.

Merrill Lynch has offices in Tokyo and Osaka, while the others have offices only in Tokyo.

MARKET

The size of the securities issuing market varies depending on the economy and on financial market conditions, but generally it has shown an expansionary trend. Table 29.2 shows securities issues in 1983 by type of issuer and by method of issuing. Of the total issue amount of ¥50,354 billion, 41 percent or ¥20,407 billion, was in government bonds. Total public bonds including local government bonds and government-related agency bonds (government-guaranteed bonds and special bonds)

Table 29.2. Size of Securities Issues by Type of Issuer and by Method of Issue in 1983

	Publicly Offered	Privately Placed	Total (¥ Billion)
Public bonds			
Government bonds	11,994	8,413	20,407
Long-term, interest-bearing	6,800	8,069	14,869
Medium-term, interest-bearing	4,702	343	5,045
Discount bonds	492	—	492
Local government bonds	699	1,906	2,604
Government-guaranteed bonds	2,619	—	2,619
Special bonds	105	3,176	3,281
Subtotal	15,416	13,494	28,910
Private corporate bonds			
Ordinary bonds	648	34	682
Convertible bonds	827	—	827
Bonds with warrants	10	—	10
Subtotal	1,485	34	1,519
Yen-denominated foreign bonds	720	179	899
Bank debentures			
Interest-bearing	6,320	59	6,377
Discount	10,993	961	11,954
Subtotal	17,313	1,019	18,332
Total bonds and debentures	34,934	14,726	49,660
Shares	577	118	695
Total	35,511	14,844	50,355

Source: The Bond Underwriters Association and others.

accounted for ¥28,910 billion, or 17.4 percent of the total. Securities issued by private-sector companies included ¥695 billion in shares, ¥682 billion in ordinary corporate bonds, ¥827 billion in convertible bonds, and ¥10 billion in bonds with warrants, amounting to ¥2,214 billion or 4.4 percent. In 1983 the issue of convertible bonds reached an all-time high, exceeding the issue of shares due to increased investor interest resulting from high share prices. Other securities issued include yen-denominated foreign bonds issued by overseas agencies (¥899 billion, 1.8 percent) and bank debentures issued by designated financial institutions (¥18,332 billion, 36.4 percent). Bank debentures are somewhat different from other securities, as they are issued by six specified financial institutions in place of taking long-term deposits.

Private placements are relatively small, except in the case of long-term, interest-bearing government bonds and local government bonds. Private placement in Japan refers to direct issues to trust banks and life insurance companies and subscription by the Trust Fund Bureau (in the case of long-term, interest-bearing government bonds) and direct subscription by local banks (for local government bonds).

Corporate shares are issued in one of three ways: (1) distribution of new shares at par value to existing shareholders; (2) public offering at near-market price; and (3) allocation of shares to specified third parties. The last method is included in private placement in Table 29.2. Through the first half of the 1970s, the popular method of new share issues was by distribution to existing shareholders. Since then public offering at near-market prices has become more popular. In 1983, public offerings, at ¥44 billion, were more than triple the amount of distribution to existing shareholders, which stood at ¥133 billion.

Public offering of securities, with the exception of share issues to existing share-holders and direct offering of bank debentures, is made by indirect issue through underwriting companies. Specified financial institutions, such as securities companies and city banks, form bond subscription syndicates for the issue of government bonds, local government bonds, and government-guaranteed bonds. In the case of other securities, securities companies underwrite them exclusively.

Although the issuing terms of securities fluctuate according to market conditions, at a given moment there is a clear interest-rate structure by issuer and maturity. Ordinary corporate bonds are rated in four categories (AA, A, BB, B) determined mostly by the level of the corporation's net assets. The rating of a company is rarely revised downward, and Japan has not yet followed the U.S. practice of changing the rating of a corporation according to its profits. However, eligibility standards for bond issues, such as net asset multiples, the equity ratio, interest-coverage ratios, and dividend ratio, are enforced strictly. Consequently, ordinary corporate bonds are highly safe investments, and default occurs only in extremely rare cases.

With respect to the secondary securities market, there are securities exchanges in eight major cities of Japan, including Tokyo, Osaka, and Nagoya. Under the Securities and Exchange Law, securities exchanges may be organized only by securities companies on a membership basis. The establishment of securities exchanges requires licensing by the Minister of Finance. The membership of securities exchanges is limited to securities companies and foreign securities companies. The number of members on each exchange is stated in its constitution. The Tokyo Stock Exchange, for example, includes 83 regular members who conduct sales and purchase operations in securities in the exchange, both for public investors and on their own account, and 12 *Saitori* members who act as intermediaries for securities transactions among regular members in the market of the exchange.

The Tokyo Stock Exchange, the largest of the eight securities exchanges, is an offshoot of the Tokyo Stock Exchange Co., Ltd., which was founded in 1878. It was reopened after World War II, at the same location, in 1949. At present, it is the largest securities exchange in the world after New York, in terms of total market value and the number of shares traded (see Table 29.3). In Tokyo, Osaka, and Nagoya, listed companies are divided into two sections depending on their scale and the liquidity of shares. Newly listed companies first are listed in the second section; they are switched to the first section when their capitalization, number of shareholders, and trading volume reach standards set by the securities exchange.

As the end of 1983, 1441 companies were listed on the Tokyo Stock Exchange, 1003 in the first section and 438 in the second section. In addition to the sections, there is a foreign section, which was established in December 1973. Ten U.S. companies, including Dow Chemical Co., IBM, General Motors, Sears, Roebuck & Co., and Dutch Robeco N.V., are listed here, but trading is not so active.

The stock exchanges require their members to concentrate trading of listed shares on the exchanges to assure fair price formation, and the principle of competitive bidding is practiced on the exchanges. Trading on the exchanges is based on the principle of spot trading. Future trading, the mainstay in the pre-World War II Japanese stock markets, is prohibited. However, in order to add speculativeness and to facilitate trading, securities companies are allowed to extend credit to investors, so margin transactions are common.

Stock transactions fall into three groups depending on the interval between the date of contract and the date of settlement: (1) "cash" (settlement is made on the day of contract in principle); (2) "regular way" (settlement is made on the third business day after the contract); and (3) "when issued" (settlement is made on a day designated by the securities exchange after the issuance of shares). More than 99 percent of stock transactions are executed in the "regular way," and orders are carried out as in a "regular way" transaction unless otherwise specified.

At the end of 1983, 659 bonds were listed on the Tokyo Stock Exchange. Except in the case of transactions in a specified range of par value amount by type of bonds, bond traders are not required to concentrate their trading on the exchange. As most bonds are not listed, most bond trading is carried out on the over-the-counter market.

Financial institutions such as banks and insurance companies hold a large proportion of stocks and bonds issued. The ratio of shares held by individual shareholders has declined progressively through the post-World War II years, resulting in a conspicuous institutionalization of the Japanese securities market.

The ratio of individual investors in the holding of all listed shares declined from about 60 percent in the 1950s to approximately 46 percent in 1960, 40 percent in

Table 29.3. Stock Trading on Tokyo Stock Exchange

	Volume (Millions of Shares)		Turnover Ratio (%) (Based on Volume)	Value (¥ Billion)		Turnover Ratio (%) (Based on Value)
Number of Trading Days	Total	Daily Average		Total	Daily Average	
1979 286	98,246	344	50.2	34,911	122.1	51.5
1980 285	102,245	359	50.2	36,490	128.0	49.9
1981 285	107,549	377	50.0	49,365	173.2	58.4
1982 285	78,474	275	34.6	36,572	128.3	38.5
1983 286	104,309	365	44.3	54,845	191.8	48.8

Source: Tokyo Stock Exchange.

1970, and 30 percent in 1980. At the end of March 1984 the proportion stood at 26.8 percent. At the same time, the ratio of financial institutions (excluding investment trusts and securities financing companies) was 38 percent. Of this figure, banks and trust companies alone account for 17.9 percent. Business corporations also have a large share of 25.9 percent. This implies that in Japan groups of companies including banks exist.

However, in 1983, 59.5 percent of all shares traded through "integrated" securities companies were bought or sold by individuals, indicating that individual investors play a predominant role in the secondary market. This is followed by trading by nonresidents, who accounted for 15.9 percent of trading in 1983. The ratio of trading by nonresidents has increased in the early 1980s. Because the spread between their sales and purchases has fluctuated widely, nonresident traders have become a factor with a big impact on share prices.

BUSINESS ACTIVITIES OF SECURITIES COMPANIES

In Japan the investment banking business (underwriting business) is carried out only by securities companies except in the case of public bonds. There is no securities company that engages exclusively in the investment banking business.

The composition of securities firms' income by type of business shows that in the accounting year ended September 1983, 12.5 percent was derived from dealer business, 51.8 percent from broker business, 14.6 percent from underwriting business (including selling), and 21.1 percent from others (see Table 29.4). Note that income from broker business accounts for approximately half the total. Although the composition of income varies from year to year, as the table indicates, the ratio of underwriter business has increased since the 1970s.

The increase in the ratio of underwriter business can be attributed to the expansion of the scale of securities issues, offerings of new share issues at near-market price through underwriters, and proliferation of capital-raising methods that have a higher underwriting fee, such as convertible bonds and corporate bonds with warrants. This business has established itself as an important source of income for securities companies.

Table 29.4. Composition of Securities Companies' Income (%)[a]

	1961–1965	1966–1970	1971–1975	1976–1980	1981–1983
Dealer business	12.3	9.1	10.1	11.2	11.1
Broker business	44.4	52.1	50.1	50.2	49.5
Underwriter business	11.0	12.8	17.1	20.2	16.8
Others	32.5	32.5	26.0	22.6	18.4

[a] Accounting year ends in September.

Source: Ministry of Finance.

Table 29.5. Percentage of Market Share by Groups of Securities Companies (September 1983)

	Big Four	Other "Integrated" Securities Companies	Others
Underwriting			
Shares	80.6	16.1	3.3
Others	70.6	23.6	5.8
Selling			
Shares	63.9	17.2	18.9
Bonds	48.0	26.9	28.1
Beneficiary certificates	73.8	18.9	7.3
Share trading			
Brokerage	28.7	24.3	27.0
Own-account	27.7	19.9	32.4
Total	48.4	23.1	28.5

Source: Ministry of Finance.

Various business activities by groups of securities companies show that, in each field of activity, "integrated" securities companies play important roles, with the "Big Four"—Nomura, Daiwa, Nikko, and Yamaichi—dominating the market (see Table 29.5).

For a long time, financial institutions such as banks have been allowed to subscribe to government bonds, but they have been restricted in their resale businesses. They were also prohibited from engaging in dealing. But between 1983 and 1984, these restrictions were lifted for designated financial institutions that since have been able to resell and trade in government bonds on a roughly equal ground with securities companies. Data so far show that securities companies still have a predominant share in these activities.

Overseas activities of securities companies have made steady progress as the Japanese economy and capital market have become internationalized. As of March 1984, Japanese securities companies had 84 offices in 22 cities in 16 countries, including liaison offices, local subsidiaries with 50 percent or more capital participation, and their branches. For a long time since the opening of overseas offices in the early 1950s, the main activity in these overseas offices was brokerage business for overseas investors to acquire Japanese securities, mainly stocks. Beginning in the 1970s, however, these companies began to serve domestic investors wanting to invest in overseas securities. More recently, they have an impressive record in underwriting the securities issued by both Japanese and local businesses. In Europe and Southeast Asia, they are also engaged in the banking business. Subsidiaries of Japanese banks are engaged in securities businesses in addition to banking business in regions where there is no principle of separation between investment banking and commercial banking.

PORTFOLIO MANAGEMENT

Portfolio management for investors has two aspects. One involves investment trusts and the other investment advice.

Investment trusts are regulated by the Securities Investment Trust Law of 1951. As the law allows only contractual-type investment trusts in Japan, there are no company-type investment trusts as they exist in the United States. Investment trusts in Japan are usually classified as "open" and "unit," depending on whether new principal can be added. In addition, they are divided into share investment trusts and bond investment trusts, depending on whether the assets can be managed in equity. Actually, there is a wide variety of investment trusts depending on the object of investment and the trust period.

The outstanding amount of assets of investment trusts at the end of 1983 stood at ¥14,088 billion, with the breakdown shown in Table 29.6. Among them, medium-term government securities funds, similar to money market mutual funds in the United States, have been popular since their founding in 1980, now accounting for approximately 30 percent of total assets.

Contractual-type Japanese investment trusts require a manager who gives instructions regarding the operation of the trust property, a trustee who administers the trust property in accordance with instructions received from the manager, and of course beneficiaries who benefit from profits from the trust property. The Securities Investment Trust Law stipulates that a manager must be licensed by the Minister of Finance. Qualifications for license require the manager to be a limited company with capitalization of ¥50 million or more and to meet standards in terms of personnel and the capacity to make securities investments.

For approximately 10 years after the reestablishment of investment trusts in 1951, they were managed by securities companies. However, in the mid-1960s, the investment management business split off from the securities companies into separate management companies. With some consolidations occurring since then, there are 11 such companies at present, each historically closely related to a parent securities company. Common practice is for a securities company or a group of companies to sell beneficiary certificates of investment trusts managed by the related investment trust management company.

Table 29.6. Investment Trust Assets (at the End of December 1983, ¥ Billion)

Share investment trust	6,151
Open-type	748
Unit-type	5,404
Bond investment trust	3,710
Medium-term government securities trust	4,227
Total	134,088

Source: The Investment Trust Association.

Trustees must be trust companies or banks engaged in trust businesses. As of the end of 1983, there were six trust companies and one city bank engaged in investment trust business. One manager usually uses three to five trustees.

Investment advisory service is a relatively new business in Japan, and there is no regulation of it. It is estimated that there are hundreds of so-called investment advisors, including companies and individuals. They can be classified into investment advisory departments of trust companies, investment advisory companies related to securities companies, subscription advisors, and individual investment counselors.

Investment advisory services have expanded sharply in recent years because of active international diversification of investment by large overseas individual investors, pension trusts, or oil money, as well as active asset management by domestic financial institutions and business corporations. At the same time, several financial institutions have become deeply interested in the management of domestic pension funds, which are managed exclusively by trust companies and life insurance companies. Among them are foreign banks that have been authorized to engage in Japanese trust business since 1985. Some major securities companies have expressed hopes to ally themselves with these foreign banks to bolster their investment advisory services.

Given the continued expansion of the investment advisory business, the Ministry of Finance plans to establish an investment advisory law requiring those engaged mostly in providing advice and information on investment for pay to register with the Ministry.

FUTURE DIRECTION

The Japanese capital market has been in a period of major transition. In response to the May 1984 report by the U.S.–Japan Yen–Dollar Committee, founded against the backdrop of increasing U.S.–Japan economic friction, the Ministry of Finance has decided to (1) deregulate deposit interest rates on large deposits (to be implemented in two to three years), (2) deregulate the Euroyen market (already implemented), and (3) promote the entry of foreign financial institutions into Japan. However, such liberalization of the capital market cannot be attributed to foreign pressure alone. Japanese investors' increased sensitivity to interest rates, progress in technology, and an expansion of international capital transactions have also played a part. The tempo of liberalization will probably be faster than seen so far.

The deregulation of the Euroyen market has already pulled down the underwriting fees on Euroyen bonds. This may change the structure of underwriting fees for yen-denominated foreign bonds as well as domestic corporate bonds.

Against the backdrop of its massive current account surplus, Japan is expected to play an increasing role as a capital-exporting nation. So far, Japan has responded to overseas investors' expectations as a market with shares of rapidly growing

will meet the diverse needs of those who require funds on a global scale. Toward this end, it will be necessary to increase flexibility in bond issuing terms, to establish a bond-rating system, and to promote listing of foreign companies on Japanese exchanges.

It is certain that Japanese capital markets will continue growing rapidly and will offer abundant business opportunities, especially in the investment banking business.

30 Securities Markets and Investment Banking in the United Kingdom

TAD M. RYBCZYNSKI

Securities markets and investment banking have been an important and integral part of the British financial system for a long time. Their place, role, and functions have been changing as the British economy and its position in the world have been changing. While the pace of change was relatively slow and gradual in the hundred years or so before the early 1970s—during which the basic structure remained virtually the same—the speed and strength of change in the last 10 years or so have been gathering momentum very rapidly. They are still continuing to do so.

It is no exaggeration to say that these two sectors are now in the process of fundamental structural transformation that has not yet run its full course. Some of the emerging features of the new structure have yet to assume their full form. They will be complemented by others that at present either are only beginning to appear or will make themselves felt only when the present period of transformation is complete.

The picture presented here outlines the basic elements of the emerging structure against the background of the previous arrangements and changes now taking place both in the United Kingdom and in other major countries.

SECURITIES MARKETS

Basic Changes in Scope and Nature

For over a century until the 1970s, British securities markets were characterized by the dominance of the London Stock Exchange and its almost exclusive concentration on a limited type of securities denominated in sterling. Although provincial stock exchanges until the early 1960s carried on business independently, they were relatively unimportant as primary and secondary markets. Virtually all securities listed and traded in these markets were sterling securities. They consisted almost entirely of debentures, preference and ordinary shares, and government securities. Business in securities denominated in other currencies was negligible.

Also, since the closing years of the last century, those undertaking business did so in a single capacity, acting either as principal or agent. All broking business was undertaken by agents and restricted to brokers, and principals acting as wholesalers (jobbers) did business only with brokers. Finally, although they were subject to company law, the securities markets were self-policing. Conducting business was regulated entirely by the London Stock Exchange, which was in effect a self-regulatory organization with the self-created power of enforcing its own rules.

This position has been changing rapidly since the early 1970s. Three basic features of change, still under way and marked by the so-called Big Bang, which occurred in October 1986 when fixed commissions came to an end, are: (1) a large increase in the type and number of securities and the currencies they are denominated in, as well as markets where they are traded; (2) the abandonment of fixed commissions, the removal of the limit of 29.9 percent on stakes held by nonmembers in Stock Exchange member firms, and the abolition of single capacity for those participants wishing to act in a dual capacity; and (3) a shift in the regulatory framework from self-regulatory to statutory-backed, but within a self-policing environment.

Type of Securities and Markets

In place of a few types of sterling-denominated securities traded predominantly on the London Stock Exchange, there are now a large number of different sterling- and nonsterling-denominated securities issued in and traded in four markets (to be reduced in the future to three markets). The securities issued and traded comprise not only ordinary shares (equity), preference shares, debentures, and loans, but also a variety of new instruments such as convertibles, warrants, zero-coupon bonds, dual-currency bonds, and traditional and traded options. These and other securities are denominated in sterling and other major currencies, as well as in synthetic currencies such as ECUs (European Currency Units), SDRs (Special Drawing Rights), and others. In addition, there are a number of futures contracts covering interest rates, currencies, and stock exchange indices.

The organized and regulated markets include, at present, the London Stock Exchange with its new title "The International Stock Exchange of the United Kingdom and the Republic of Ireland." Its four different segments have expanded since January 1987 to five segments, and include: the fully listed securities other than Eurobonds; the misleadingly labeled "Unlisted Securities Market" where requirements are less exacting; the recently created segment under the title "The Third Market," where disclosure requirements were even less exacting, and which covers securities similar to those now issued on and traded in the Over-the-Counter (OTC) Market; and, finally, dealers in foreign securities. In addition, the London Stock Exchange has a large number of Eurobonds with full listing coexisting with the Eurobond markets covering other Eurodollar bonds not listed on the London Stock Exchange.

The London Stock Exchange also provides facilities for trading in options and futures.

The London Stock Exchange is a primary and secondary market for British government stock, other fixed-interest, sterling-denominated securities issued by public sector bodies in the United Kingdom as well as by foreign governments and official and corporate bodies, and fixed-interest equity and debt securities denominated in sterling and issued by British companies. It is also a secondary market for nonsterling securities issued originally outside the United Kingdom.

The disclosure requirements to obtain full listing are very exacting. They include a five-year profit record, frequent reporting, and compliance with a number of other detailed rules, including making available 25 percent of shares when first listed. The listing requirements for the Unlisted Securities Market covering smaller companies are less exacting for both disclosure and frequency of reporting. These requirements are even less demanding for listing in the Third Market which came into being in January 1987 and is likely to cover the bulk, possibly all, of the securities now issued on and traded in the Over-the-Counter Market.

Eurobonds, that is, securities issued in currencies of a country other than that in which they are originally sold, with full London Stock Exchange listing, are predominantly issued outside London but apply later for quotation. Until recently this was mainly for convenience and prestige, but now that fixed commissions have been abolished there is a lively secondary market. Dealership in foreign securities covers a number of market makers and dealer–brokers in nonsterling securities whose number is growing.

The still separate and independent market that will probably lose its identity and become a part of the Third Market of the London Stock Exchange is the Over-the-Counter Market. It is a small market for small companies with limited liquidity. As mentioned, its disclosure requirements are significantly less exacting than for companies with full listing or with the status of unlisted securities.

The third independent market at present is the unregulated market for Eurobonds, covering both bonds and convertibles without listing on the London Stock Exchange that are originally issued and listed in other countries, mostly in Luxembourg. It is expected that some time in 1987 this market will become a fully regulated market with its own rules and machinery for the monitoring of such rules and their enforcement.

Finally, there is at present a fourth separate but regulated exchange—London International Financial Future Exchange (LIFFE)—which provides facilities for trading in futures in interest rates, currencies, and Stock Exchange Indices (see Table 30.1.)

The Four New Securities Markets

In December 1986, the London Stock Exchange, which is at the center of the U.K. securities markets, listed 5538 securities, other than Eurobonds, whose market value was £1.3 trillion. Also there were 368 unlisted securities valued at £2.8 billion and 1206 Eurobonds fully listed with a market value of £123.9 billion.

Table 30.1. Securities Markets in the United Kingdom[a]

	March 1979		December 1986	
	Number of Securities	Market Value (£ Billions)	Number of Securities	Market Value (£ Billions)
The International Stock Exchange of the United Kingdom and the Republic of Ireland				
Securities with full listing				
Public sector—United Kingdom and Republic of Ireland	1061	60.9	436	144.0
Public sector—overseas	191	0.5	181	3.1
United Kingdom and Irish registered companies	5690	83.3	4105	344.5
Overseas registered companies[b]	474	177.9	579	831.5
Total	7686	322.6	5301	1323.1
Eurobonds	356	5.6	1206	123.9
	1980			
Unlisted Securities Market[c]	28	negl.	368	5.0
Third Market	—	—	9[d]	(h)
Dealerships in Foreign Securities[e]	na	na	170[f]	na
Over-the-Counter (OTC)[g]	na	na	150	na
Eurobond Market[h] excluding Eurobonds listed on the London Stock Exchange	na	na	na	400/500
London International Financial Future Exchange	na	na	na	na

[a] As in December 1986.
[b] Predominantly companies with capital denominated in currencies other than sterling and originally issued and traded mostly outside the United Kingdom.
[c] Disclosure requirements less exacting than for companies with full listing.
[d] End of February 1987.
[e] Market value at the end of February 1987 about £67 million.
[f] In addition to market-making firms there are a number of broker–dealers and agency brokers covering a large number of foreign securities.
[g] Disclosure requirements less exacting than those applicable to securities with quotation on Unlisted Securities Market; likely to become the "Third Market" of the London Stock Exchange which came into being in January 1987.
[h] Likely to become a regulated market with a status of "Recognised Investment Exchange" in the near future.

Source: Committee to Review the Financial Institutions in the Stock Exchange, the London International Financial Futures Exchange.

The securities with full listing, other than Eurobonds, comprised, first, 436 obligations issued by the British government, the government of the Republic of Ireland, and various public bodies in the United Kingdom; their market value was £144.0 billion. Besides these securities there were 181 obligations of Commonwealth and foreign governments and foreign public bodies with a market value of £3.1 billion. Third, there were 4105 securities issued by companies registered in the United Kingdom and denominated in sterling; their value was £344.5 billion. Finally, there were 816 securities of overseas-registered currencies, denominated almost entirely in currencies other than sterling, whose market value was £831.5 billion.

For some four years or so until 1984 both the number and value of British and Irish government and other public sector securities had been falling, rising interest rates more than offsetting an increase in nominal value associated with the new issue of debt and its consolidation. The value of these securities, though not their number, has been increasing since then as interest rates have dropped, and as those issued by foreign governments and official bodies in London (the so-called Bulldog securities) have increased, following a trend toward the integration of the world financial markets.

This has also been true of securities of British-registered companies, whose number has also been falling for quite a long time because of mergers and amalgamations, but whose market value has been increasing sharply since early 1985. At the same time, both the number and the value of securities issued by overseas-registered companies denominated in currencies other than sterling have been rising sharply—this trend also reflecting the globalization of the world's capital markets, the advantage of having a listing in London, and rising stock market prices in other financial centers, as well as a fall in the external value of sterling.

Eurobond market securities with full listing also have increased rapidly in value and number. The growth in this market reflects the attractions such securities offer, especially the bearer feature, and the fact that they pay interest without deduction of tax.

The Unlisted Securities Market, created only in 1980, has made spectacular progress in the past six years. Companies in this category numbered 368 in December 1986 and had a market value of £2.8 billion. A significant number of companies originally floated in this market have "graduated" to become fully listed companies. Among the companies listed in this group in December 1986 were 14 U.S. companies. With a few other companies they formed the second largest sector, having been attracted by relatively low flotation costs and less demanding requirements than in the United States as regards the release of shares.

The Third Market started operating in February 1987. At the end of February nine companies received listing and their market value was £67 million.

The Eurobond secondary market, covering Eurobonds other than those with full listing in the London Stock Exchange, is a very large, and until recently unregulated, market whose market value at the end of 1986 was estimated at around $650 billion. This has been the most rapidly growing market in the Western World. The business in this market is carried on by members of the Association of International Bond Dealers (AIBD), created under the Swiss legal code, and also the recently set up

British self-regulatory organization, the International Securities Regulatory Organisation, which merged in December 1986 with the London Stock Exchange to form the Securities Association. Following implementation of the new Financial Services Act in 1986, the Eurobond market in London will become a regulated market subject to its own rules and regulations.

There also exists a lively secondary market for securities denominated in currencies besides sterling, other than Eurobonds not listed in London, described as "dealerships in foreign securities." There are some 40 market makers in this segment trading in 170 foreign equities, and a number of dealer–brokers have an interest in this sector. The volume of business transacted by this segment has been increasing rapidly in the recent past and is continuing to do so now.

It should be mentioned here that the London Stock Exchange also runs a market in traditional and traded options and futures in sterling short-term bonds (1991) and long-term bonds (2007), as well as in sterling-dollar and sterling-DM exchange rates and the Stock Exchange Index (FTSE 100 Index). Complementing these markets is the London International Financial Futures Exchange (LIFFE) which offers facilities for trading in sterling and dollar-interest and exchange-rate futures, London Stock Exchange Futures (FTSE 100), as well as traded options in sterling and dollar interest rates, sterling-dollar and DM-dollar exchange rates, and the London Stock Exchange Index (FTSE 100). The latter type of business overlaps that undertaken by the London Stock Exchange. This regulated market, set up in 1982, has been expanding rapidly both with regards to type of contract and volume of business.

Activity

The increase in the scope of the U.K. securities market has been associated with a rise in activity, or turnover (see Table 30.2). Unfortunately, information available covers only the London Stock Exchange and the Unlisted Securities Market, although other evidence, such as number of participants, suggests that activity in other markets, above all the Eurobond market, has been rising quite markedly.

Both the turnover and the average value per trade in listed securities rose significantly in the 11 years ending in 1986. Turnover in fixed-interest securities between 1970 and 1980 rose by a multiple of 13.3, and that in equities by 20.6. As the advance in the number of transactions was small, the value per transaction during this period moved up by a multiple of 13.7 for fixed-interest securities and by 10.8 for equities—both figures comfortably exceeding the rate of inflation.

In the Unlisted Securities Market sector of the London Stock Exchange the turnover increased in the five years ending 1986 nearly tenfold and the number of transactions by nearly 6.5 times, the value per transaction advancing by 50 percent. The Third Market, which started operating in the last week of January 1987, registered in the five weeks ending in February 150 bargains per day.

The most rapidly expanding market has been the Eurobond market—the bulk of such transactions being done in London. There are no official or privately collected statistics covering this market. Some indication of the growth in activity,

Table 30.2. The London Stock Exchange

	Turnover—Listed Securities					
	Value (£Billion)		Bargains—Thousands		Value per Bargain (£'000s)	
	Fixed-Interest	Ordinary Shares	Fixed-Interest	Ordinary Shares	Fixed-Interest	Ordinary Shares
1970	30.0	8.8	1214.1	4097.9	24.7	2.2
1975	76.5	17.5	1261.9	4768.5	60.6	3.7
1980	165.5	30.8	1477.3	4230.7	112.0	7.3
1985	284.9	105.6	1141.7	5567.8	249.6	19.0
1986[a]	389.1	181.2	1148.2	7638.4	338.9	23.7

	Turnover—Unlisted Securities Market		
	Value (£Billion)	Bargains (000's)	Average Value per Bargain
1981	0.282	64.0	£4.406
1984	1.469	287.2	5.115
1985	1.705	335.5	5.081
1986[a]	2.757	414.6	6.651

[a]Not strictly comparable with preceding years in that figures until October 27, 1986, covered "nonmember" trade in a single capacity and excluded business in overseas securities transacted in a dual capacity by international dealers. Since the Big Bang this trade is included.

Source: Stock Exchange Quarterly.

however, is given by the rise in clearings of the two houses, CEDEL and Euroclear, covering business in Eurobonds and other securities. Their clearings advanced from $16 billion in 1974 to $1500 billion in 1984—or by nearly 100-fold in 10 years. By 1986 they amounted to $3500 billion—a figure 2.3 times higher than two years earlier.

Almost as fast an expansion in business has been registered by the London International Financial Futures Exchange (LIFFE). As compared with some 4400 contracts per day in 1982, when the futures business was started, the number of futures contracts in 1986 amounted to nearly 32,000 per day. In addition, some 2400 options were traded daily in 1986 and such estimates as can be made suggest that the value of all transactions in 1986 was around £3 billion.

Ownership of Securities

While a marked rise in turnover in the Unlisted Securities Market is attributable to a higher degree of participation of domestically based investors, there is no doubt that an increase in business in listed securities markets, above all in the British government securities market, comes from a significant expansion in involvement by non-U.K.-based investors. Some indication of these investors' interest in U.K. private sector securities is shown by a rise in their holding of U.K. such securities from £4.5 billion in December 1979 to £96 billion in December 1983 and their holding of British government securities (excluding those held by central banks) in the same period from £2.9 billion to £5.9 billion. (See Table 30.3.)

Such estimates as can be made suggest that following globalization of financial markets and the policy of international diversification this trend has been gaining strength in the last three years, and that foreign holdings of British securities were significantly higher in 1986—in both absolute and relative terms—than in 1983.

Associated with increasing participation in the U.K. securities markets of non-U.K.-based investors has been a change in the relative importance of different types of U.K. securities. The outstanding feature here has been a rise in trading by the institutional investor, excluding depository institutions, and a decline in the involvement of individual investors. Institutional investors held 19 percent of U.K. ordinary shares in 1957, 58 percent in 1981, and 61 percent by 1984. If other depository and allied financial institutions are included, their holdings of U.K. ordinary shares rose from 21 percent in 1957 to 58 percent in 1981 and 61 percent in 1984.

The same trend has been observed for holdings of British government securities. Total holdings of depository and allied financial institutions, as well as of institutional investors, advanced from 44 percent in 1957 to 73 percent in 1981 and 76 percent in December 1984.

Table 30.3. Ownership of Listed U.K. Securities (Percentages)

	December				
	1957	1967	1977	1981	1984
All Institutional Investors[a]					
U.K. company ordinary shares	19	31	44	58	61
U.K. company preference shares	36	59	69	na	na
U.K. company loan capital	75	77	45	na	na
British government securities	17	27	41	52[b]	51[c]
Other Financial Institutions[d]					
U.K. company ordinary shares	2	2	3	na	na
U.K. company preference shares	nil	nil	nil	na	na
U.K. company loan capital	neg	neg	4	na	na
British government securities	27	29	22	21[e]	25[f]

[a]Insurance companies, pension funds, investment trust companies, and unit trusts but excluding financial institutions shown in "Other Financial Institutions."
[b]March 1981; institutional investors include only insurance companies and pension funds.
[c]March 1983; insurance companies and pension funds only.
[d]Banks, discount markets, building societies, savings banks, investment account financial houses, and special financial institutions.
[e]March 1981.
[f]March 1983.

While the policy of privatization pursued by the Conservative government (selling of publicly owned corporations to the public), as well as growing support by employers for employee share participation and the new tax reliefs for individual ownership of equity, have increased and are increasing the *number* of personal shareholders, the proportion of marketable securities held by individuals has continued to decline, resulting in the growing dominance of institutional investors.

To a large extent this development reflects the rapid growth of funded pension funds and of collective savings through unit trusts (referred to as mutual funds in the United States), which has been accompanied by a reduction in the holdings of individuals. This trend can be expected to continue, inasmuch as funded pension funds are still spreading and have not yet reached maturity, and collective savings through mutual funds is less expensive and provides better opportunities of diversification of individual portfolios to meet different demands for income and capital gains.

Regulatory Framework

Accompanying and influencing the changes in the scope and size of the U.K. securities markets have been fundamental changes in the regulatory framework within which they operate. The almost entirely voluntary, self-imposed and self-policing machinery has been replaced now by a new comprehensive system described as "self-regulatory but within a statutory framework." The new system, embodied in the Financial Services Act 1986, comes fully into effect in 1987. Its starting point is the requirement that any firm or individual wishing to engage in the investment business must first obtain the approval of and register with the new supervisory body, the Securities and Investment Board (SIB), or one of the five self-regulatory organizations (SROs) that have already come or will come into being.

The SIB is made up of practitioners and independent members appointed by the Department of Trade and Industry in consultation with the Bank of England. The Department of Trade and Industry (DTI) has delegated to it extensive powers to regulate the business of investment. Rules covering all aspects of financial services must be complied with by every investment firm.

The SIB will authorize, first, various SROs, which will have the power to certify business to carry on investment activity, to implement the rules, and to impose capital adequacy ratios. Second, the SIB will authorize a number of "Recognised Investment Exchanges" (RIEs), which will be responsible for the rules governing trading in securities, listing of securities, membership, and technical matters such as clearing. It should be stressed here that there is no general requirement that trading in securities should take place on a recognized stock exchange. If it does not take place on a recognized stock exchange, however, the reporting and disclosure requirements that must be observed will be very exacting and costly, making it unlikely that such business will be done outside recognized investment exchanges. Finally, members of some professions (e.g., the legal profession) also undertake certain types of investment transactions. To offer such services various professional bodies, such as the Law Society, will have to obtain the SIB's authorization to cover members' activities in the investment area.

The power of the SIB and the SROs is shared with the Bank of England when it covers business in government securities and also certain fixed-interest stocks. The Bank of England approves firms wishing to become market makers, interbroker dealers, and money brokers in such securities, monitors their performance, and imposes capital-adequacy ratios. However, the London Stock Exchange is responsible for the general conduct of their business.

As Table 30.4 shows, at present it is anticipated that there will be three recognized investment exchange and five self-regulatory organizations. The recognized investment exchanges will comprise the London Stock Exchange with its three main segments (securities with full listing, the unlisted market, and the Third Market), the London Eurobond Exchange (yet to be created), and the London International Financial Futures Exchange.

The five self-regulatory organizations will be the Securities Association (TSA), representing the amalgam of the Stock Exchange and the International Securities Regulatory Organisation (ISRO), the Investment Managers Regulatory Organisation (IMRO), the Life Assurance and Unit Trust Regulatory Organisation (LAUTRO), the Financial Intermediaries, Managers, and Brokers Regulatory Association (FIM-BRA), and the Association of Futures Brokers and Dealers (AFBD).

The Securities Association includes 234 firms that had been members of the (old) London Stock Exchange, and 186 members who were members of ISRO, 50 of whom had also been members of the Stock Exchange. The new total of 370

Table 30.4. Regulatory Framework of the U.K. Securities Industry

Department of Trade and Industry (DTI)
Securities and Investment Board (SIB):

  A. Recognized Professional Bodies

  B. Self-Regulatory Organizations (SRO):
    The Securities Association (TSA) (market makers, broker–dealers, agency brokers)

    The Investment Management Regulatory Organisation (IMRO) (investment managers, merchant bankers)

    The Life Assurance and Unit Trust Regulatory Organisation (LAUTRO) (life assurance and unit trusts company salespeople)

    The Financial Intermediaries Managers and Brokers Regulatory Association (FIMBRA) (fund managers and financial advisors)

    The Association of Futures Brokers and Dealers (AFBO) (commodity brokers)

  C. Recognized Investment Exchanges (RIE):
    The International Stock Exchange of The United Kingdom and the Republic

    The Eurobond International Exchange (to be created in 1987)

    The London International Financial Futures Exchange (LIFFE)

firms is likely to increase both as a result of the creation of the Third Market and the admission of new members. They will be able to do business on the new London Stock Exchange and the new London Eurobond market, being created in 1987.

The Structure of the Industry

Four important developments in the last year or so have changed and are changing the basic structure of the securities industry: the abolition of the single capacity, the permission for firms that are members of the London Stock Exchange to be owned by other financial institutions, the abolition of fixed commissions, and the introduction of the new regulatory framework. In addition, there has been a basic change in the mode of operation of the London Stock Exchange, which until recently was based on transactions made on the trading floor but has now changed to electronic, off-the-floor trading based on display of up-to-date information about prices.

The abolition of the single capacity has led to the restructuring of the business undertaken by members of the London Stock Exchange, now forming a part of the Securities Association. In December 1986 there were 27 firms with the status of market makers in British government stocks and 60 in equities of British companies, divided into four subgroups according to their tradability. They are the so-called alpha stocks (about 90 internationally trading companies), beta stocks (440 large British companies trading predominantly domestically), 1100 gamma stocks of smaller companies, and 250 covering the remainder, classified as delta. At the end of December 1986 there were some 175 broker–dealers, including agency brokers, who covered mainly British government and other fixed-interest securities, and some 210 who were concerned principally with equity and allied obligations, a substantial number of which also did business in fixed-interest securities.

Besides market makers and broker–dealers, there are eight interdealer brokers to facilitate trading among members in government securities and other securities, as distinct from business with nonmembers, and seven money brokers lending stock to market makers (see Table 30.5) for business in gilts, six of whom undertake the same function for other sterling securities.

The removal of the 29.9 percent limit on stakes held by outsiders in London Stock Exchange firms, established in the 1970s, has led to over 60 such firms, out of a former total of 218 (17 jobbers and 201 brokers), becoming by December 1986 a part of large British and foreign banks and other financial organizations. The latter include 14 U.K. clearing and merchant banks, 13 other U.K. financial institutions, seven U.S. commercial and investment banks, and another 12 foreign financial firms. In addition, other financial institutions, including British and foreign banks and other depository institutions, have established or are establishing market-making or dealing-brokering subsidiaries. They include one London clearing bank, Japanese securities houses, and Continental banks and other foreign financial institutions. As a result, nearly one-third of the old London Stock Exchange firms that existed before the merger with ISRO are now foreign-owned firms. If allowance is made for new admissions, especially of overseas investment banks, about one-half of member firms are now foreign-owned.

Table 30.5. Structure of the London Stock Exchange—December 1986[a]

	British Government Securities	British Equities with Full Listing				Unlisted Securities Market	Third Market[b]	Foreign Securities
		Alpha	Beta	Gamma	Delta			
Number of securities	124[c]	90	440	1100	250	357	na	170
Number of market makers[d]	27	35		25		na	6–8	40
Number of broker–dealers and agency brokers[e]	148[f]			174		na	na	na
Interdealer brokers	6			6		na	na	na
Money brokers	9			8		na	na	na

[a] The figures must be treated with extreme caution in that new members are added and the number of securities is changing.
[b] Third Market started to operate in January 1987 and is likely to comprise most of the securities and firms now part of the OTC market.
[c] Plus corporations and county stocks and public bonds and so forth of Great Britain and Northern Ireland numbering 215.
[d] Also act as broker–dealers and cover equities.
[e] Excluding market makers who also act as broker–dealers.
[f] Excluding 186 members of ISRO now amalgamated with London Stock Exchange.

The operation of the London Stock Exchange is now based on the electronic system described as the Stock Exchange Automated Quotation (SEAQ)—modeled on NASDAQ used in the United States. This system provides instantaneous screen display of prices, and facilities for telephone dealing and central clearing.

At present, the structure of the new regulated London Eurobond Market, which is coming into being in 1987, is not clear. Its participants will be members of the ISRO, now forming part of the Securities Organisation.

The London International Financial Futures Exchange now has 190 members. They include 66 U.K. banks and 74 overseas banks, besides other British and foreign institutions. A large number of members are also members of the Board of Trade and Mercantile Exchange of Chicago, the Philadelphia Stock Exchange, and similar organizations in Japan, Australia, and other countries.

INVESTMENT BANKING

Investment banking in the United Kingdom includes two types of activities: (1) underwriting, and (2) involvement in corporate mergers, amalgamations, and financial reconstructions. Until about 10 years ago these activities had been entirely in the hands of the merchant banks, other issuing houses, and stockbrokers, but did not extend to large banks and other deposit-accepting institutions. The concentration of investment banking among the former was the result of self-imposed restraints on the part of large deposit banks reinforced by an informal understanding with the Bank of England (acting as the de facto supervisory authority) and was tantamount to the separation of investment banking from deposit banking.

This separation of investment banking and deposit banking between these two groups of institutions has by now disappeared completely. All large British and overseas deposit banks and other financial institutions have already entered this area either by acquisition of the existing merchant bank issuing houses or by entering the field from scratch; and they have been followed by foreign banks and other financial institutions. This development has been reinforced by the changes in the securities markets and the resulting trend toward financial conglomeration, described as "universal banking."

Underwriting, or the sale of new securities on the primary markets in the United Kingdom, includes: (1) sterling securities issued by the British government; (2) securities denominated in sterling and issued by U.K. registered companies in U.K. markets; (3) sterling securities issued by foreign public bodies and corporations in London; and (4) securities denominated in other currencies and sold in the first instance in London.

Sterling securities issued by the British government listed on the London Stock Exchange are at present sold by the Bank of England, acting as its sole fiscal agent either by a tap method (i.e., sold to the buyers) or by tender. However, the Bank of England is about to experiment with the auction method of selling. Auctions will be used alongside the present tap arrangements and there is no intention at present to switch completely to an auction system. Other sterling-denominated securities issued on the primary markets in London can be sold in the first instance on the Stock Exchange, the Unlisted Securities Market, the Third Market, or the OTC market.

New issues of securities with full listing on the London Stock Exchange can be made by way of introduction, public issue, offer for sale, and placing. Introduction consists of obtaining a listing for shares and stock outstanding, and does not involve the issue of new shares to the public. Public issue involves an offer by a company of a fixed number of shares or other securities to the public (using an intermediary) at a stated price (a fixed price or by way of a tender). The issue is made on the basis of a prospectus containing all the information required by the London Stock Exchange and an application form. Offer for sale consists in a company selling a block of shares at an agreed-upon price to an intermediary who resells them to the public. Placing involves a sale by a company of securities to an intermediary that places such securities with its clients. While until recently new issues by companies with full listing had to be offered to existing shareholders, this requirement has now been relaxed leading to the gradual spread of the "bought deal," when an investment house purchases newly issued shares and resells them later, taking the risk that the price obtained may be lower than the price paid.

Issues of new sterling shares on the Unlisted Securities Market can be made using the same methods as those for securities with full listing.

Primary markets in nonsterling securities cover the Eurobond market (at present an OTC market). In this market new issues are normally made by way of syndicated placing.

Financial intermediaries operating in the sterling primary markets (i.e., those who act as underwriters) include issuing houses and stockbrokers. The bulk of issues on the London Stock Exchange are handled by members of the Issuing Houses Association (which includes banks and nonbanks) and seven important merchant banks, although an increasing number are now also handled by other investment banks. Stockbrokers are concerned with every issue and ensure that the Stock Exchange requirements are observed. They handle issues on the Stock Exchange and the bulk of the issues on the Unlisted Securities Market and the Third Market.

In the case of a public issue on the primary market the issuing house or stockbroker acts as an underwriter, subunderwriting it with investment institutions. With offers for sale or placing on the Stock Exchange, an issuing house or stockbroker acts as principal, buying the securities and reselling them to the public. This is also true of placing on the Unlisted Securities Market and of course of issues on the OTC and the Third Market.

The primary issues on the Eurobond markets are handled by a group of banks and other institutions, led by one or two of them, and other institutions underwriting the issue, or buying it outright and reselling or placing it.

The volume of net issues on the London Stock Exchange as well as on the Unlisted Securities Market has increased sharply in the last five years, especially since 1985 (see Table 30.6). The value of net issues on the stock exchange in 1983 and 1984 amounted to £7.5 billion as compared with £2.5 billion in 1980 and 1981. In 1986 the net amount raised increased to £9 billion. The increase is attributable

Table 30.6. Net Issues on the London Stock Exchange (£Billion)

	U.K. Fund-Raisers	Foreign Fund-Raisers	Total
1980	0.8	neg.	0.8
1981	1.7	0.3	2.0
1982	1.0	0.6	1.6
1983	2.7	0.6	3.3
1984	1.5	0.9	2.3
1985	4.5	0.7	5.2
1986	8.5	0.6	9.0

Source: Financial Statistics.

both to a rise in domestic issues, including privatization issues (i.e., flotation on the stock exchange of shares of companies previously owned entirely by the government), and issues by foreign bodies, which since 1979 have not been subject to any exchange controls.

Net issues on the Unlisted Securities Market have increased sharply since its inception, with the rise due almost entirely to issues by U.K. entities, although there have also been some by overseas companies. (See Table 30.7.)

The largest and the most rapidly expanding issues of new securities have been those of Eurobonds (see Table 30.8). They now cover convertibles and, in the last year or so, also equities. In 1986 gross issues of Eurobonds, including convertibles but excluding equities, amounted to nearly $187.0 billion. This figure is nearly four times higher than in 1983 when such issues amounted to $50 billion and exceeded 1975 issues by a factor of 50.

Mergers and Amalgamations and Reconstructions

Three other activities falling within the ambit of investment banking in the United Kingdom are mergers and amalgamations, management buyouts, and financial reconstructions. Mergers and amalgamations have expanded rapidly in the past decade (see Table 30.9). In 1986 the value of such transactions in the United Kingdom

Table 30.7. Net Issues on the Unlisted Securities Market (£Million)

	U.K. Companies	Overseas Companies	Total[a]
1980	8	—	8
1981	41	13	54
1982	85	—	86
1983	154	9	164
1984	155	2	157
1985	175	6	181
1986	271	27	298

[a] Totals differ due to rounding.

Source: Financial Statistics.

Table 30.8. New Issues of Eurobonds (Gross—$Billion)

1973	4.1
1975	8.7
1977	18.6
1979	17.9
1981	26.5
1982	46.4
1983	50.1
1984	81.7
1985	135.4
1986	187.0

Source: OECD Financial Statistics.

was £13.5 billion compared with £7.1 billion in 1985 and £5.5 billion in 1984. These figures comfortably exceed the two earlier peak years of 1968 and 1972, when total value of takeovers (at 1985 prices) was £13.3 billion and £11.4 billion respectively.

Mergers require financial advice to both parties, provided as a rule by merchant banks, issuing houses, foreign investment banks, and stockbrokers. Such intermediaries also act as agents on behalf of the parties concerned both in friendly and aggressive takeovers. The behavior of the parties is regulated by a code issued by the Panel on Takeovers, a self-regulatory body set up in 1968. The Panel retains its status following the Financial Services Act of 1986, although prospective decisions (not historic judgments) can be affected by court rulings.

At present the Panel requirements are that any buyer who obtains 5 percent of ordinary shares of a company should disclose this fact as well as provide details of any additional purchases he makes. Furthermore once his or her purchases reach 30 percent the buyer is obliged to extend his or her offer, at the highest price previously paid, to all other holders of equity.

Mergers and amalgamations are also subject to legislation dealing with competition. When proposals for mergers are announced they are scrutinized by the Office of Fair Trading (OFT), a part of the Department of Trade and Industry. If an investigation concludes that a merger may have adverse effects on competition or is against public interest, the Director of the OFT recommends to the Secretary of State that it should

Table 30.9. Mergers and Amalgamations

Year	Number of Companies Acquired	Value £Billion
1981	452	1.1
1982	463	2.2
1983	447	2.3
1984	568	5.5
1985	474	7.1
1986	695	13.5

Source: Financial Statistics.

be referred to the Monopolies and Mergers Commission (a statutory but independent body) for detailed examination. If the Secretary of State accepts such a recommendation—which he or she is free to reject—the Monopolies Commission is required to submit to the Secretary of State within six months—unless this period is extended—a report with recommendations that a merger should proceed, or should not be allowed to proceed, or that the companies investigated should be required to implement special measures. The Secretary of State is again free to accept or reject such recommendations totally or in part.

However, following a number of large and bitterly fought takeovers in 1986 associated with some irregularities, there has been a lively public debate regarding the procedures and rules of the Panel and its position and policies. Some changes in procedures allowed to be employed were announced early in January 1987. Furthermore, the authorities have stated clearly and unequivocally that if the changes introduced and to be introduced fail to be observed by participants, the self-regulatory character of the Panel will be replaced by a statutory framework.

Management buyouts, not included in Table 30.9, have been growing very rapidly in the last few years and will form a sizable and important segment of investment banking business, involving changes in the capital structure and in ownership. This requires expert advice and the machinery for the implementation of such changes. Both of these are provided by members of the investment banking community who devise new schemes, organize new capital structure finance, and implement the new schemes.

Financial reconstructions cover changes in capital structure necessitated by financial pressures, bankruptcy, and liquidation, and tend to involve merchant banks and investment banks as well as a receiver.

CONCLUSION

The U.K. securities markets and investment banking are still subject to profound structural change. The change involves a move away from a domestically oriented market to an internationally oriented one characterised by: (1) despecialization; (2) participation, on the one level, of international financial institutions, and on the other of those concerned with small and medium-sized companies; (3) a new, all-embracing regulatory framework relying on self-regulating bodies but with statutory backing.

The change also involves, first, the breakdown of the traditional informal divisions between deposit banking and investment banking, which results in a trend toward financial conglomeration or "universal banking"; and secondly, a new approach toward mergers and amalgamations comprising the creation of new rules for those involved in such transactions and their supervision.

The current evolution is an aspect of internationalization of the securities industry. It reflects the transformation of the financial industry toward a market-oriented and securitized system made possible by an official policy designed to strengthen and reinforce the position of London as one of the pivotal international financial centers.

31 The Competitive Setting of Investment Dealing in Canada

CALVIN POTTER

Canada has nothing one could call the equivalent of the Securities and Exchange Commission in the United States, that is, a national securities commission. But there is federal (national) regulation of chartered banks, of federally incorporated trust and mortgage loan companies, and of federally incorporated insurance companies. Moreover, each of the more populous provinces has a provincial securities commission that oversees the practices of stock exchanges and securities dealers within that province. Of these, the Ontario Securities Commission (OSC) is the largest and most influential, and many of its policy decisions are formulated in a national context, for Toronto is the financial center of Canada. Provinces also regulate financial firms, such as credit unions, trust and mortgage loan companies, and insurance companies that are provincially incorporated.

The federal and provincial governments have been increasingly concerned in recent years to achieve a better balance in the regulation of the financial services industry. Heretofore there have been two thrusts to that regulation: the maintenance of functional segregation, referred to as the "four pillars" of the industry—banks, trust and mortgage loan companies, insurance companies, and securities firms—and the encouragement of their functioning with "maximum efficiency." Two public-policy issues bedevil that search for balance—the threat of foreign dominance, and the protection of public investors and depositors. Judicious choice in this matter of balance is further marred by the efforts of industry groups to use federal or provincial regulatory power to cushion the necessity of the industry's competitive response to market and technological developments.

As the title of this chapter implies, we are not going to concern ourselves with the broad question of the organization of the financial services system. But that system is a backdrop for the narrower question of the extent of involvement of financial institutions in the securities markets. This whole setting currently is undergoing rapid change. Investment dealers are both sources in part of the change and respondents to it. To further complicate a forecast of what will be the result, there is a veil of doubt shrouding the question of what approach to the regulation of financial markets will have the support of federal and provincial regulators.

The traditional approach to regulation in the financial services industry is that institutions are confined more or less strictly to defined types of intermediation. This minimizes the difficulty for regulators to protect the public interest in regard to intermediaries' conflicts of interest and the adequacy of their capital. Given this regulatory model, the consumers' choice is somewhat constrained, for competition is limited to the types of intermediation, and, within each type, to the firms within the category.

An alternative regulatory model is one that distinguishes between the institutions and their market functions and regulates the functions. In its purest version, the institutions are completely deregulated. They are allowed to offer whatever range of financial services best suits their particular firm's form and strengths, although the functional sections are still regulated to protect the investment public from fraud and inadequate capital.

Given the possibility of adoption of the latter model—which vastly enlarges consumers' choice—the risk in a forecast of change is apparent. Under a policy of thorough deregulation, the market structure and forms of firms that would survive would be those delivering products and services demanded by consumers at lowest prices while covering costs. Complete deregulation, however, seems very unlikely to win the necessary community consensus because of two issues mentioned above—foreign dominance and the political strength of supporters of the tradition of the "four-pillars" approach.

The issue of regulation versus full competition and the associated social policies of protectionism, nationalism, and deregulation are now under consideration by the federal government and by a provincial task force in Ontario. Without attempting to anticipate their choices, in what follows we will put the issues they face in perspective by focusing upon the structure and function of the securities markets in Canada and upon the philosophies that have motivated the securities regulators. (In the Postscript to this chapter some recent developments are discussed.)

THE THREAT OF FOREIGN DOMINANCE

When, in 1969, one of the old, well-established investment dealers in Canada, Royal Securities, was acquired by Merrill Lynch of the United States through a wholly owned Canadian subsidiary, the merger initiated a public discussion about the ownership and control of market intermediaries in the Canadian capital market. The issue is still reverberating in regulatory halls.

Securities firms that were controlled by nonresidents were not something new in 1969. At that time there were 15 such firms as members of the Investment Dealers Association of Canada.[1] Their presence in the industry was considered a healthy

[1] *Report of the Committee to Study the Requirements and Sources of Capital and the Implications on Non-Resident Capital for the Canadian Securities Industry* (generally known as the *Moore Report*), Toronto: Ontario Government, 1970, p. 158.

injection of competition. But the Merrill Lynch Canada (MLC) intrusion added a new dimension to the scene. It posed a threat not of increased competition within the industry, but of its takeover. Further, because the parent firm, Merrill Lynch, had made a public distribution of its shares, its Canadian subsidiary was in effect a proxy for a publicly held American firm operating in a Canadian market where its competitors were restricted in their form of organization to ownership by industry personnel. Both circumstances were unprecedented. The self-regulating organizations (SROs),[2] which had imposed the capital limitations on their members, had a responsibility to respond on their behalf. The first step was to form an industry committee—the Moore Committee.

The focus of the Moore Committee's deliberations was on the amount and source of capital of securities firms, and their effects upon the risk taking and decision making of such firms. That focus was consistent with the original stimulus for the inquiry, namely, the Merrill Lynch–Royal Securities merger and its implications. At that time the American parent company alone had $271.3 million in its equity capital account, which greatly exceeded the $182.7 million of all 167 Canadian-owned firms in the Canadian industry.[3] Were Canadian-owned firms undercapitalized, and was that state because of the restrictions on the sources of capital?

The Moore Committee concluded that existing industry sources could adequately provide equity capital to meet business requirements in the near to medium term. The status for the long run was more doubtful. Restriction of equity sources to industry personnel would generate a replacement problem when senior personnel retire and their junior personnel replacements have to buy their stock. In the long run, furthermore, some firms would require additional equity capital to expand into capital-intensive areas such as market making and "bought deals."

The committee recommended that the matter of capital sources be reviewed in the future with a view to relaxing existing ownership restrictions "to the extent consistent with the public interest."[4] This latter was defined as entailing:

1. Competition among firms.
2. Good-faith dealings.
3. The avoidance of outside influence.
4. The avoidance of securities firms developing trading markets for their own stock.
5. A policy of maintaining Canadian control of the pillar sectors of the financial markets.

With hindsight, the last two of the foregoing requirements can be interpreted as the opening wedge of protectionism in the securities industry. Requirement 4 could preclude entry into the Canadian industry of U.S. firms whose shares are publicly

---

[2] Comprised of: Montreal Exchange, Toronto Stock Exchange, Alberta Stock Exchange, the Vancouver Stock Exchange, and the Investment Dealers of Canada.

[3] *Moore Report*, p. 159.

[4] *Ibid.*, pp. 6–7.

held. Requirement 5, on the other hand, extended the pillar concept of partitions in the financial markets—that is, separate regulations for different sectors serviced by distinctive financial intermediaries such as banks, trust and mortgage loan companies, and insurance companies—to include as a separate pillar market intermediaries such as investment dealers and stockbrokers. Barriers to free entry into the securities industry would thereby be raised under the guise of maintaining the integrity of the services in the industry (i.e., the avoidance of conflicts of interest and of self-serving schemes) and of protecting Canadian control of the securities industry— this latter at a time of rising nationalism.

Response in Ontario

The agency responsible for overseeing securities markets in the province of Ontario, the OSC, concurred with the Moore Committee's recommendations. The Ontario Securities Act was amended by the government of Ontario to include restrictions on nonresident ownership (NRO) of registered firms; and the SROs amended their rules to follow suit. Effectively, nonresident ownership of a securities firm was restricted to 25 percent of total capital, with no one individual nonresident holding in excess of 10 percent. Existing registered NRO firms that did not meet the conditions were "grandfathered," but constraints were placed on their capital growth relative to that of the industry. The OSC each year would determine the "permissible" capital of each such NRO and then dictate the method by which such a firm's "actual" capital could be increased to reach the "permissible" limit.

The protectionist initiative inevitably affected the economics of the securities industry in Ontario. Limiting the access of NROs to the Ontario securities market would restrict potential increases in market liquidity. NROs could, for example, through affiliated and parent firms, expand the marketplace to other countries, bringing in more investors to purchase Canadian securities, and, conversely, bringing in more securities for Canadian investors to purchase. They thereby would increase both trades and traders. In the process they would give a fillip to Canadian issuers by improving domestic opportunities for a lower cost of financing and a broadened distribution of their securities.

The economics of the industry were also affected by the capital limitations of the SROs. Their insistence on the capital being owned by industry personnel raised the industry's cost of equity capital. The reason for the practice was so that the personal wealth of the members of management would necessarily bear fully the financial effects of their choices as managers. But such insistence precludes the separation of risk taking from decision making. When these functions are undivided, the risk premium on the managers' financial capital is indistinguishable from the risk premium on their career capital. The latter is normally higher than the market premium for risk in financial markets. By prohibiting the specialization of risk taking through the separation of ownership from control, the SROs in effect prevented their members from lowering their cost of capital. It was not an approach all provincial jurisdictions found attractive.

Response in the Province of Quebec

Given the liquidity and cost implications of restricting the amount and sources of capital, the recommendations of the Moore Committee did not fit the particular needs of the province of Quebec, the second most populous province. It set up a committee of its own, the Bouchard Committee, to study the securities industry in the province. The conclusions were very different from those of the *Moore Report*.

The interests of Quebec were different from those of Ontario in two respects. First, the majority of the securities firms licensed to do business in Quebec were not fully based there. Of the 133 firms licensed to deal with the public by the Quebec Securities Commission (QSC), 29 percent had Ontario head offices. Further, a survey by the Bouchard Committee found that of the 15 major firms in the industry (having in excess of $2.5 million capital), only three were based in Quebec.[5] Insofar as the benefit of protectionism was to shield Canadian firms from new competition and insulate them from the need to grow in size and efficiency, the major beneficiary would be Ontario. The burden, on the other hand, of reduced liquidity and increased costs would be borne wherever there were securities markets in Canada.

The second respect in which interest diverged related to industrial structure. The economy of Quebec is much less diversified than that of its neighbor to the west. Small business and entrepreneurship are more vital to economic health than they are in Ontario. Protectionism in the securities industry, as a policy, did nothing to reduce the inefficiency of the capital market in servicing the capital needs of small and developing businesses in Quebec.

Why the Canadian capital market has persistently been inefficient in servicing small and medium-sized businesses is a topic for debate. There are several plausible reasons. The securities industry is very concentrated—the top 5 to 10 firms monopolize the underwriting business. Those underwriting relationships have been formed over long periods of the issuer's and the underwriter's history, and frequently involved reputation transfer (market signaling) from the latter. In such an environment, small and new businesses may find it difficult to compete. When they do, moreover, they may find the cost of going public prohibitive.

All these arguments have equally plausible rebuttals. Traditional underwriting relationships, for example, are no longer sacrosanct; the true deterrent of access to capital may be the small business sector's reputation of poor management; and the Royal Commission on Corporate Concentration illustrated that underwriting costs are not prohibitive.[6]

The Bouchard Committee concluded that economic development in Quebec would be better served by more large securities firms with significant operating control in Quebec. It sought to induce economic change in two respects: (1) industrial structure and (2) the national distribution of securities firms. In respect to the first, the Committee reasoned that if there were more securities firms in the industry, and if

---

[5] *Study on the Securities Industry in Québec*, 1, Final Report (referred to as the *Bouchard Report*), Quebec City: Quebec Department of Financial Institutions, Companies, and Corporations, 1972.
[6] Ottawa: Canadian Government, 1978, pp. 263–264.

those firms had more capital, they would be inclined to increase the size of the underwriting market by taking more risk. In other words, because they wanted more business they would turn more to underwriting small businesses, and because they had additional capital they would be willing to assume the increased risk of underwriting small business.

Concerning the second aim, that is, shifting the national distribution of securities firms, the committee recommended less stringent limitations on sources of capital and on entry into the industry. In regard to nonresident investment in the securities industry, the committee recommended that up to 49 percent of the voting equity be permitted to be held by nonresidents, with a maximum of 10 percent to be held by any one nonresident. It further recommended that ownership by parties outside the securities industry be permitted, as long as a miminum of 25 percent of the equity was held by the firm's insiders resident in Quebec.

The government of Quebec acted on the *Bouchard Report*. The Quebec Securities Commission (QSC) was given broad discretionary powers to determine on a case-by-case basis the fitness of registrants. The registration decision was to be based on the benefits to be derived by Quebec. The power delegated to the QSC gave it wide discretion in granting registration to NROs. In the exercise of such discretion the Bouchard Committee suggested five factors to guide the QSC:

1. The ability to distribute Quebec securities.
2. The capacity to increase the volume of transactions in Quebec's capital markets.
3. The contribution of special expertise.
4. The need to establish and maintain an equilibrium at any given time in order to avoid undue outside influence.
5. Maintenance of sound competition in the industry.

In implementing the *Bouchard Report*, the government of Quebec diverged from the Canadian norm in the regulation of its segment of the financial services industry. It has diluted the four-pillars concept and widened considerably the fields in which financial intermediaries can operate. In return, the latter have had to accept controls exercised by a newly appointed inspector of provincial financial institutions. Quebec also has moved further than the other provinces toward deregulation of access to the securities industry. It has used the capital base of securities firms not as a base for protectionism of the industry, but rather as a stimulus for market competition through allowing capital from any source (nonresidents, financial institutions, or nonfinancial ones), as long as there is some provision for control by the management resident in Quebec.

THE FOUR PILLARS

The Canadian Constitution [Section 91(15)] assigns "Banking, Incorporation of Banks, and the issue of Paper Money" exclusively to the federal government. The

Bank Act, under which banks are incorporated (chartered), is revised every 10 years by the federal government. There is an Inspector General of Banks who, with a staff, is responsible for overseeing the operations of chartered banks. Rules and regulations are designed to protect bank depositors and borrowers—for whom the banks transform the economic characteristics of the claims they deal in (i.e., create utility in terms of risk, maturity, or denomination, through the process of their administrative intermediation). But they also allow for control of the money supply by the central bank authorities—that is, by the management of the Bank of Canada.

Accordingly, traditionally there has been a sharp distinction between those financial intermediaries such as banks that transform financial claims such as deposits, commercial loans, and money market items in a way similar to the technical transformation performed by real commodity producers—that is, for example, make financial claims more or less liquid before passing them on—and other financial intermediaries such as trust companies and insurance companies. These latter, while similar in terms of transforming the economic characteristics of claims, are more marginal in their impact as liquidity producers, because the credit instruments they deal in are largely bonds, stocks, and mortgage loans.

In addition to their contrasts as liquidity producers, each type of financial intermediary has its area of specialization, its core function. Trust and loan companies, for example, accept deposits, issue investment certificates, and engage in term lending. They specialize in fiduciary responsibilities in regard to estates and agency. They can be incorporated by either level of government, federal or provincial, and within each such jurisdiction there is a Registrar of Loan and Trust Companies responsible for the regulation of loan and trust companies. Similarly, insurance companies have a specialization that constitutes a core function. They design group, term, and whole life insurance programs, with low interest earned on savings features. These programs are largely sold through career agents, and the policy proceeds are invested in mortgages, corporate bonds, and equity shares. Insurance companies can be incorporated by either level of government, and within each such jurisdiction there is a Superintendent of Insurance responsible for the regulation of insurance companies.

In contrast to financial intermediaries, market intermediaries such as investment dealer–brokers have a more limited function in terms of the transformation of the financial claims in which they deal. Normally they do not change the claim's risk, maturity, or denomination. Rather they provide administrative intermediation in the form of placement of securities, execution of trades, analysis of information, and counseling of clients.

The cleavage between banks and other financial intermediaries was strengthened by the then-current theories of monetary economics. In that discipline, the quantity of money and its velocity were the conceptual link between monetary policy and financial institutions, on the one hand, and the real economy, on the other. Of course, the deposits of chartered banks were the base of the economy's money supply about which economists were concerned, and the commercial short-term lending of such banks involved the process of deposit creation, with its associated impact on the quantity of money.

In the 1960s, theoretical developments in monetary economics blurred the previously sharp distinction between money and other assets, and between chartered banks and other financial intermediaries. The focus now became a whole spectrum of assets instead of the previous preoccupation with "money" and its velocity. And the link between public policy and financial institutions, on the one hand, and the real economy, on the other, became the structure of interest rates, asset yields, and the availability of credit.

Concurrently, a new view was emerging in regulatory matters. Protection of the lender and borrower from abuse because of economic concentration in financial institutions was no longer so imperative. What was more needed, it was believed, was concern about efficiency and flexibility in the financial system, and this might best be promoted by common participation by the various financial and market intermediaries in the financial system.

It was about this time—the late 1960s and early 1970s—that the SROs in the securities industry embraced the concept of four pillars in the financial system. We noted earlier that the *Moore Report* accepted the notion of pillars that partition the financial markets. As the SROs began in the 1970s to relax their rules governing ownership of securities firms, there was an increasing possibility of firms expanding their capital base and diversifying into other than securities market activities. In 1976 the SROs set up the Fell Committee to recommend guidelines for such diversification. Its report not only concurred in the *Moore Report*'s assumption that pillars subdividing the capital market (the separation of function) were in the public interest, but it also called for the maintenance of the four-pillars concept. It recommended that securities firms be permitted to engage in diversification activities excluding activities of financial intermediaries (except for mutual funds and for incidental investment of up to 10 percent in a financial institution).

In 1978 the *Barron Report* proposed that restrictions on outside ownership of securities firms be relaxed by the SROs.[7] It suggested that up to 40 percent of a firm's capital could come from any one source. But the sources had to be other than financial institutions.

The corollary of the SROs' choice, of course, is strong opposition to the expansion of financial intermediaries into the securities dealers' core area. This opposition was very evident at two subsequent hearings of the Ontario regulatory authority, the OSC, in 1981 and 1983. The first hearing was on whether minimum brokerage commission rates should continue to be established by the Toronto Stock Exchange (TSE). The brief of the TSE[8] opposed unfixing on the grounds, among others, that such unfixing would increase the already excessive market power of the largest financial intermediaries[9] and thereby enable them to set the brokerage rate for those

---

[7] *Report of the Joint Industry Committee on the Subject of Sources of Capital for and Ownership of the Canadian Securities Industry*, Toronto: Investment Dealers Association of Canada, 1978. (*Barron Report.*)

[8] *Unfixing of Commission Rates*, September 15, 1981.

[9] The participation of the 15 largest such institutions in the secondary market between 1976 and 1980 was 23.8 percent.

firms that concentrate on institutional business. The second hearing was on a proposal by a chartered bank to offer integrated access to discount brokerage as a service to its banking customers. The joint brief of the SROs[10] was vehement in its opposition to financial intermediaries expanding into the core market of securities firms. Such integration of the four pillars, it contended, was against public policy.[11]

The OSC in its decision did not concur with the SROs objection to integrated access to discount brokerage. But it did accept the assumption at the base of the SROs' argument that the four-pillars concept was public policy and, indeed, noted that no one at the hearing had questioned that assumption.[12] However, it ruled that provision by financial intermediaries of discount access would not result in integration of the core functions of the four pillars.

What the OSC was recognizing in its ruling was the evolving nature of the pillars concept of the market. Regulatory relaxation had allowed supplementary or ancillary services to be offered by each type of financial and market intermediary. Thus each type was increasingly enabled to compete to a degree in the core areas of the other types. The partitions between once-distinctive functions have in fact become permeable. As encroachments on the core areas have multiplied, the regulatory approach of assuming four quite distinct pillars in the capital market has become virtually obsolete.

The capital market as it operates today encompasses the common participation of financial and market intermediaries in the financial system. As heretofore, each type of intermediary has its main function that is performed by its group—its core function. For example, chartered banks do commercial short-term lending and engage in deposit creation; insurance companies package group, term, and life programs; trust companies engage in fiduciary activities; investment dealers do underwriting; and brokers engage in securities trade executions. In addition, banks do some underwriting, and some serve as conduits for discount brokerage; trust companies do some commercial lending; insurance companies have devised insurance programs with flexible premiums that enable them to compete with investment companies, and they have also begun to solicit personal deposits; and investment dealers assist in the discharge of the fiduciary function in the trusteed operation of registered retirement savings plans, and they are also engaged in deposit taking. This intersectorial competition has blunted the previously sharp distinctions among the different types of institutions in the capital market—the four pillars. Technological change and partial deregulation, by stimulating service and price competition within and between sectorial markets—have become a continuous source of change and adaptation in the capital market, and have significantly effaced earlier distinctions among intermediaries.

---

[10] *Submission . . . Discount Brokerage and the Role of Financial Institutions*, June 10, 1983.
[11] *Ibid.*, p. 7.
[12] *Report on the Implications for the Canadian Capital Markets of the Provision by Financial Institutions of Access to Discount Brokerage Services*, Toronto: OSC, 1983.

TECHNOLOGICAL CHANGE

In Canada there are five stock exchanges, that is, locations for matching trades in listed stocks: the Montreal Exchange, the Toronto Stock Exchange (TSE), the Winnipeg Stock Exchange, the Alberta Stock Exchange, and the Vancouver Stock Exchange. Each has a specialty. The TSE, the dominant exchange, specializes in higher-quality stocks, the Vancouver Stock Exchange in highly speculative stocks. The Montreal Exchange is somewhere in-between. The Winnipeg and Alberta stock exchanges primarily list stocks of regional interest.

Many stocks are interlisted. Because of these stocks there is competition between the exchanges for market share. Normally, such competition fragments the demand for and the supply of securities, thereby reducing liquidity.[13]

In the early 1970s, provincial regulatory power was used to influence market share. The QSC, for example, issued a policy statement requiring that brokers in Quebec execute trades first on what was then the Montreal Stock Exchange, when possible. This requirement led to retaliation by the TSE in the form of arbitrage rules. A state of destructive competition persisted for several years until the regulation was relaxed.

The exchanges now compete on the more constructive basis of exploiting the opportunities created by the electronic revolution. It is no longer necessary, for example, to have one centralized auction market to concentrate trading and thereby improve liquidity. Because of computer advances, it is now possible for the best trade to be found instantly on a computer terminal, by programs that access all exchanges and markets, rerouting the order until the best available match is located and the trade executed. Given that capability, the competitive focus is on the best price, and exchanges recently have been competing by improvement of execution and liquidity through computer links with other international exchanges and through the use of specialists on the floor of the exchange.

PARTIAL DEREGULATION

Minimum Fixed Commission Rates

In 1966 the government of Ontario broadened the mandate of the OSC to include oversight of the operations of stock exchanges in Ontario. This responsibility entailed a review of the TSE's minimum commission rate structure for stockbrokers. The OSC quickly announced it would exercise its new mandate with respect to commission rates by holding public hearings on proposed rate changes. Its proclaimed criterion for judging proposals was the same as that then used by the SEC in the United

---

[13] D. Shaw and R. Archibald, *The Management of Change in the Canadian Securities Industry*, Study Eight, "The Canadian Securities Market: A Framework and a Plan," London, Ontario: University of Western Ontario, 1977.

States, namely, the resonableness of the proposed rate structure. Despite repeated attempts, however, the OSC could not develop a model and measures that would test the reasonableness and fairness of stock brokerage pricing.

Developing experience of the SEC in the United States was similar, and in 1975 it decreed the unfixing of brokerage commission rates and the reliance thereafter on competitive prices negotiated by the client and broker. Canada, however, did not follow immediately in the footsteps of the United States. The OSC decided it did not have sufficient empirical evidence to determine whether the public would be better off under a competitive system of brokerage commission rates. Believing that fixed commission rates subsidized the small retail investor and penalized financial institutions, and that competitive rates might limit securities firms to marginal levels of profitability, the OSC gave several temporary approvals of fixed commission rate schedules while studies were being done on the subject. The final hearing on the issue was in 1981.

The TSE, arguing on behalf of its members, asked at the 1981 hearing for retention of the fixed minimum brokerage rates. The distribution of the stance of its members, however, revealed a split opinion. Fifty-seven of the members had voted for fixed rates and 21 for competitive rates. The latter, interestingly, included all the big, probably efficient, firms. The smaller, presumably less-efficient firms, were in favor of the protection provided by regulation.

The OSC, armed with the six years of U.S. experience in the use of competitive rates, decided the best test as to the fairness of a price was that it had been set by competition. The TSE commission rates were therefore unfixed as of April 1, 1983. The QSC had already decided to unfix commission rates on the Montreal Exchange on the same date. The Vancouver Stock Exchange still has a fixed commission rate schedule (but it provides for negotiation of rates for trades in interlisted stocks).

Scale and Sources of Equity Capital

We mentioned earlier that the regulations of Quebec and Ontario were not fully aligned as to scale and source of equity capital of securities firms; Ontario had imposed tighter restrictions on ownership by nonresidents. In addition, of course, there were also the membership rules of the SROs in the securities industry, which also imposed restrictions on ownership and sources of capital. By the early 1980s some of the contradictions between these regulations were becoming evident. The SROs were arguing for market efficiency through separation of function and investor confidence; for the latter the prerequisite was industry integrity, to be achieved by restricting risk taking and decision making in the main to industry personnel (i.e., by excluding significant participation by those outside the industry). The OSC was promoting market efficiency through price competition, subject to the public-interest constraints of Canadian ownership and the four-pillars concept. The QSC, on the other hand, was seeking structural change in the securities industry by exposing it to regional competition and by encouraging fuller participation.

IN ONTARIO, A DECADE OF SEEKING CONSENSUS

In Ontario over the past decade there have been a number of attempts to achieve a consensus or modus vivendi among the major players in the securities market. In 1972 the OSC endorsed the idea of securities firms having access to new sources of capital (excluding nonresident sources).[14] This recommendation was upheld by a commissioned study of the securities market by a pair of academic specialists (who also thought foreign firms should only be stopped from selling Canadian securities to Canadians).[15] These recommendations elicited no immediate response from the SROs.

In 1978 a joint industry committee was formed by the SROs to study the dilemma of the securities firms. On the one hand, they needed additional capital to promote growth and enhance performance. On the other hand, the introduction of outside capital involved the separation of control from ownership and thereby threatened the professionalism and independent decision making of a firm's officers and employees—the SROs believed.

The committee's report[16] recommended further relaxation of the rules governing outside ownership. It proposed that 40 percent of the total capital could come from external sources, with a 25 percent restriction on voting equity and a 20 percent restriction on any one single holder. Restrictions on nonresident ownership were maintained at 25 percent of the total, and at 10 percent for any single holder. Ownership by financial institutions was excluded. The report was not acted upon directly. But the government of Ontario requested the OSC to review the activities in Ontario of NROs not currently registered in the province.

Nonregistered NROs and the Exempt Market

We have noted that in Ontario in the early 1970s regulations had been adopted prohibiting dealers who are more than 25 percent nonresident-owned from becoming registered as market intermediaries. That prohibition created a category of "suitcase dealer"—an NRO market intermediary unregistered in Ontario—who nevertheless was free to carry on business in Ontario as follows:

To trade *with any person* in "exempt securities" such as debt instruments of governments and certain institutions, and commercial paper issued by Canadian corporations.

To trade *in any security* with certain governments and with "exempt purchasers" (banks, trust companies, loan corporations, insurance companies, and pension funds).

---

[14] *Report of the Securities Industry Ownership Committee of the Ontario Securities Commission*, Toronto: OSC, 1972.

[15] Shaw and Archibald, *Study Eight*, pp. viii–xiv.

[16] *The Barron Report*, 1978.

To engage *with any person* in private placement trades *of any securities* so long as the acquisition cost to the purchaser is in excess of $97,000.

These exemptions were designed to ensure that unregistered NROs were involved only in transactions or securities that generally were of high quality, well known, and understood. Thus they were restricted to that segment of the securities market that was informationally most efficient. Since they were at liberty to operate within that segment as in a free market, their presence was formidable competition for registered dealers.

Solution Is Elusive

In 1979 the OSC as requested reported on its review of NROs in the marketplace. It indicated it had attempted, in vain, to achieve a consensus among the representatives of the major U.S. investment banks and the domestic industry regarding NROs. It recommended a thorough review of matters relating to NRO restrictions within three years.

In 1981 another joint securities industry committee was formed to review sources of capital. It had access to a significant U.S. experience with securities firms that had gone public and had listed their stock on exchanges. And it was confronted with the intention of several Canadian securities firms to proceed with a public distribution of their shares.

The committee's report[17] was issued in the same year. It concluded that the potential problems associated with an external source of capital, such as a public issue of shares by a securities firm, could be dealt with by reliance on the information principle of full disclosure and by other regulatory or agency techniques. But to ensure that in the ensuing separation of ownership from control the decision-making function remained with industry personnel, it recommended that 60 percent of the board of directors must be industry personnel, with the balance to be approved by the SROs. Ownership by individuals outside the industry would be restricted to 10 percent of the voting, participating equity. Existing restrictions on nonresident ownership would be maintained, and financial institutions would be allowed up to 10 percent participation, but could not be represented on the board of directors.

The OSC subsequently published a policy statement (Policy 4.1) that, in general terms, adopted the SROs' recommendations.

By 1984 stress was apparent in the regulatory framework. Disparities between the nonexempt and the exempt markets were becoming measurable. For dealers wishing to trade in the nonexempt segment of the market, entry into the industry was controlled by regulation, as were also the amount of capital of registered NROs and the sources of capital of all registrants. In the exempt segment of the market, on the other hand, there was competition between financial intermediaries and market intermediaries, regardless of residence and unencumbered by restrictions.

---

[17] *Report of the Joint Industry Committee on Public Ownership in the Canadian Securities Industry*, Toronto: Investment Dealers Association of Canada, 1981. (*David Moore Report.*)

This exempt segment, moreover, included the sophisticated element of the investment public—the banks, loan and trust companies, insurance companies, and recognized "exempt purchasers"—those, in other words, aware of the benefits of price competition and conscious of the substitutability of financial products.

The members of the SROs have felt themselves to be handicapped in the past few years in dealing with the sophisticated element of the exempt market. The restrictions on their capital base have apparently limited their ability to provide certain services for the clients such as "bought deals" and interest-rate or currency swaps. Moreover, the restrictions on nonresident ownership preclude joint-venture partnerships of Canadian and nonresident firms that would enable Canadian firms to avail themselves of foreign expertise and entrepreneurial skill, thereby improving the choices they can offer their Canadian clients. Hence the feeling (documentary data have not been gathered) that nonregistrants dominate the exempt market. And hence, also, the perceived grievance of the Joint Securities Industry Committee that nonregistrants have a competitive advantage over regulated firms due both to their avoidance of regulatory costs and to the entry and ownership restrictions imposed by registration requirements.

Some credence has been given to the SROs' grievance by recent developments in the market. A major investment dealer–broker has requested approval for the establishment of an unregistered affiliate whose activities, partially financed by a nonresident institution, would be limited to the exempt market.[18]

The stress in the system is a symptom. The regulatory framework administered by the OSC is no longer as relevant to the needs of participants in the securities market or to the objectives of the commission as is desirable. The commission responded to the malaise promptly. On May 2, 1984, it issued a press release announcing a policy review of the "competitive position of the securities industry in domestic and international financial markets." Public hearings were held in November and December of that year. Written submissions also were received from Canadian investment dealers, nonresident dealers, financial institutions, and other interested parties. On February 18, 1985, the OSC issued its report to the Ontario government, entitled: "A Regulatory Framework for Entry into and Ownership of the Ontario Securities Industry."

RECOMMENDED CHANGES IN THE REGULATORY FRAMEWORK IN ONTARIO

Premise of the Framework

Concern about investor protection is fundamental in securities regulation. Given that concern, the basic objective is to maximize market efficiency and to encourage business responsiveness to consumer preferences. To achieve this objective within a regulatory framework, the Ontario Securities Commission has premised reliance

---

[18] It was turned down by the TSE, and an appeal is now pending at the OSC.

on a "free-market approach." The forces of competition are to be allowed to determine who may act as a market intermediary, subject only to an overriding concern of public policy. The commission identified two such concerns:

Canadian domination of the domestic capital market.

The segregation of the Canadian financial system according to function, that is, the four-pillars principle.

Market efficiency, in other words, is the general objective, but it is subordinated to some degree by two overriding concerns. The risk of excessive domination of the domestic securities industry by nonresident ownership or of control by domestic financial institutions is one. The other is the continued segregation of the Canadian financial system according to function. The recommendations of the report regarding changes in the regulatory framework of the securities market reflect both the foregoing objective and the overriding concerns.

Nonresident Control

In contrast to the existing provision, which limits holdings by nonresidents of any class of securities of a registrant to less than 10 percent individually and 25 percent in the aggregate, the report recommended that nonresidents, individually or in the aggregate, may own securities of a registered dealer granting up to 30 percent of the votes, or the equity participation, of a firm. Where nonresident owners hold more than 10 percent of any class of participating securities, the report recommended a requirement that a "significant industry investor" (industry investor is defined to mean an officer, employee, or partner of the registrant; a group of them exercising their voting rights through a holding company or voting trust would be a "significant industry investor") must own securities carrying more than 50 percent of the votes and more than 50 percent of the equity participation.

Financial Institution Ownership

In contrast to existing provisions of the bylaws of the Toronto Stock Exchange,[19] which limit the investment by a financial institution to less than 10 percent of any class of securities of a member firm, the report recommended that financial institutions be treated in the same manner as NROs. That is, financial institutions may own up to 30 percent of the participating securities of a registered dealer, with the same proviso that if in the aggregate financial institutions own more than 10 percent of the participating securities, the dealer firm must have a "significant industry investor."

---

[19] In the absence either of legislation or of regulations on the matter, investments by financial institutions in registered dealers that are member firms are governed by the bylaws.

Other External Investors

The report recommended that the OSC exercise control over the participation of other external investors in the financing of securities firms. But the constraint here would not be as tight as in the case of financial institutions and nonresident owners. An external investor who is a single resident could own up to 30 percent of the participating securities of a registered dealer, and such investors in the aggregate could own up to 49.9 percent. As in the instance of the NROs and the financial institutions, however, when "other" resident investors own more than 10 percent of the participating securities, there is a requirement for a "significant industry investor," and the OSC would have to give its approval of the arrangement to ensure that the securities held by the "significant industry investor" are voted as a block. The registered dealer also would have to obtain the approval of the OSC for any investor in its participating securities who would own in excess of 10 percent.

Foreign Dealers

The existing provisions limit nonresident owners in the aggregate to 25 percent of any class of securities of a domestic registrant. The report recommended that the ceiling be raised for the existing prohibition, and that a special category be established for those who do not fulfill it. Thus it would create a new category of dealer registration—foreign dealers—for securities firms in which nonresidents own more than 30 percent of the participating securities. The NROs which were "grandfathered" at the time nonresidents ownership was originally restricted would be classified in this category, as would those offshore firms that want to enter the Ontario securities market directly. For a Canadian subsidiary to be registered as a foreign dealer, its parent must carry on a securities business in its home jurisdiction and be essentially a securities firm.

Firms seeking registration in the foreign dealer category would be subject to limitations on their capital and on their entry into the industry. The report recommended that the foreign dealer class be subject to a ceiling on its aggregate capital base. The limit would be approximately 30 percent of the capital employed in the industry, which in the estimate of the OSC is approximately $700 million for the domestic registrants. Thus, if the foreign dealers issued the maximum capital allowed them, the total capital in the industry would be one billion, of which $300 million would be foreign dealers.

The report also recommended a limitation on the capital of the individual foreign dealer. At the time registration is granted, the OSC would set the capital limit of each (with the exception of the grandfathered NROs), and that capital is not to exceed 1.5 percent of the capital of the industry. Thus the maximum capital base the OSC would set for a firm would be $15 million (with the exception noted earlier).

The granting of registration as a foreign dealer would be discretionary. The OSC indicated it would take into account such things as the services the applicant would bring to the Canadian marketplace and the need for those services, the diversity in the country of origin, the historical presence of the applicant in Ontario, and the way the applicant proposed to neutralize any advantages accruing to it in underwriting securities of a Canadian company that is affiliated to a nonresident company for which the applicant's parent acted as underwriter.

The "Exempt Market"

Registration exemptions heretofore have allowed an unregistered market intermediary to trade in any security with "exempt purchasers" (banks, trust companies, loan corporations, insurance companies, and pension funds) and with any person as long as the acquisition cost was in excess of $97,000. The report recommended the removal of registration exemptions for those dealers who rely on exemptions to carry on an underwriting or full-service brokerage business in connection with corporate securities. Effectively, no person or company not registered as a dealer or a foreign dealer could trade in corporate securities (other than financial institution debt securities) as part of an underwriting or full-service brokerage business. With the implementation of this recommendation, the alleged competitive advantage to a dealer or a foreign dealer of establishing an unregistered affiliate whose activities are limited to the "exempt market" would be considerably reduced (such an allegation was the prime mover in initiating the demand for a report).

Financial Institution Registrations

Consistent with the OSC's ruling in 1983 that provision by financial intermediaries of discount access would not integrate any of the core functions of the four pillars, the report recommended that the OSC retain the power to grant registration to applicants who do not fulfill the ownership restrictions, if such application is in respect of an activity that is not one of the protected functions (i.e., underwriting or full-service brokerage) or that does not materially impair the ability of the securities industry to carry on the protected functions.

DEVELOPMENTS IN QUEBEC

In the province of Quebec, the regulatory authority, the QSC, had been empowered to approve ownership structures of securities firms on a case-by-case basis, depending on the benefits to be derived by Quebec. The QSC announced it would approve the external ownership of a securities firm by a financial institution in excess of 10 percent of the voting securities, as long as the senior management of the firm was distinctly separate from that of the financial institution and 40 percent of the directors of the securities firm were employees of that firm. Further, the QSC would not prohibit a financial institution from seeking registration as a dealer, nor would it prohibit a dealer from diversifying into other areas of activities, including those of financial institutions. Moreover, in 1981 the QSC repealed its existing NRO restrictions.

The only ownership restriction now applicable is that no person may have more than a 10 percent equity position in a registrant without first obtaining the approval of the QSC.

DEVELOPMENTS IN THE FEDERAL AREA

In 1985 the Finance Committee of the House of Commons began hearings on the federal government's proposal to overhaul regulations for financial institutions. The proposal would establish a system under which closely held financial holding companies could own a variety of financial institutions, such as banks, trust and loan companies, and insurance companies. This freedom of entry is in contrast, for example, to the present restriction in the Bank Act, specifying that no one is allowed to own more than 10 percent of the shares of a major bank. The proposal also provides strict controls on self-dealings by the owners of the holding companies. Each financial services subsidiary would have to be kept separate, with a so-called Chinese Wall built between the operations of each subsidiary to prevent conflicts of interest.

POSTSCRIPT

By the end of 1986 a political consensus regarding the conditions of entry and ownership in the Canadian financial services system had emerged. Meetings between the government of Ontario and the federal government had resulted in agreement concerning the basic premises of regulatory policy, and protection of the public interest from abuse rising out of economic concentration in financial institutions.

Regulatory Policy

The government of Ontario abandoned the two fundamental limits to which it had subjected the "free market approach" of the OSC, namely:

Canadian domination of the domestic capital market.

Segregation of the Canadian financial system according to function, known as the four-pillars principle.

It announced that it intended to introduce amending legislation that would allow foreign interests to hold up to 100 percent of the voting shares of a domestic securities firm—heretofore they had been restricted to 25 percent. Accompanying that retreat from its policy on nonresident ownership, the Ontario government also appears quietly to have dropped the OSC's proposal of limits on foreign dealers' capital and market share.

The other party to the governmental consensus, the federal government, also abandoned the four-pillars principle. It agreed to amend the Bank Act and the Trust Companies Act to allow 100 percent ownership of securities firms by banks and trusts—something hitherto not allowed. By the middle of 1987, a bank, trust company, securities firm, or insurance company in Canada was able to own firms in other segments of the financial services industry, either by the creation of subsidiaries or through holding companies.

Even without explicit declaration, the segregated compartments in the capital market have been dismantled. At one branch of any bank, trust company, securities firm, or insurance company, a consumer will be able to deposit and withdraw money, obtain loans and mortgages, buy stocks and bonds, and receive advice on financial planning and portfolio management. The one financial service remaining separate is insurance, which will continue to be sold by independent brokers and insurance company salespeople. Further, because banks are under federal jurisdiction, and securities activities are regulated by provincial authorities, banks underwriting equities issues will use separate subsidiaries to allow a clear separation of activities.

Protection of the Public Interest

The second aspect of the governmental consensus—the protection of the public interest from abuse because of financial concentration— also involved government retreat from an earlier policy. The federal government had intended to grant unrestricted freedom for closely held holding companies to fully own a variety of financial institutions. The new policy, effective retroactively to December 1986, is aimed at restricting both the growth of ownership of financial institutions by companies outside the financial sector and the expansion by acquisition or merger of firms already within the financial sector. To discourage the self-dealing associated with closely held ownership, the new rules limit nonfinancial parent companies of financial institutions to a maximum of 65 percent of the voting shares. In other words, there must be at least a 35-percent minority shareholding, with the attendant full-disclosure information policies such a shareholding entails. These new rules, however, do not supersede the present rule for domestically owned chartered banks that places a 10 percent ceiling on any individual or group ownership of such shares. (When wholly foreign-owned Schedule B banks reach $750 million in capital, they will have to comply with the domestic bank ownership restrictions.)

To discourage financial concentration, the new rules will forbid anyone with a significant interest in a financial institution from forming a new trust, loan, or insurance company. Nor can financial institutions now buy a significant position in a trust or insurance company with a capital base of more than $50 million.

In summary, the governmental consensus has made the sweep of deregulation (and reregulation) in the financial services system far more thorough than thought likely at the outset. Its scope reflects Canada's response to the recent emergence of global financial services available on the international scene. The changes made in market structure and regulatory policy allow chartered banks to own 100 percent of the voting shares of a securities firm, ensuring that the securities industry will have the financial clout to compete against the giant investment houses of the United States, Japan, and Britain. Canadian investment houses can thereby remain competitive in the new international market.

32 Securities Firms in Canada

DAVID C. SHAW

Securities firms in Canada (often referred to as investment dealers or brokers) undertake most of the investment banking function in the Canadian capital market as well as acting as investment bankers for Canadian and foreign customers in the United States and Euromarkets.[1] The purpose of this chapter is to describe these firms in the context of the regulatory environment and the investment banking activity; their customers, competition, and organization; and areas of opportunity. The discussion is presented in five parts: first, a description of Canada's regulatory environment in domestic capital markets; second, a description of securities firms and markets; third, a review of the underwriting functions; fourth, a discussion of the competitive environment; and finally, a detailed look at a specific firm, Wood Gundy Inc.

THE REGULATORY ENVIRONMENT

The structure of the Canadian capital market has been based on separation of functions, described as a "four-pillars" system. Foreign firms have had restricted access to these functions. The four core functions (pillars) are (1) commercial lending and deposit taking (performed by the chartered banks); (2) fiduciary activities and trusts (performed by trust companies); (3) insurance of life and property (by insurance companies); and (4) underwriting new issues of securities (by securities firms).

The statutes and regulations of the respective federal and provincial governments have controlled and regulated the various core activities, maintained the separation of functions, and established the level of foreign ownership permitted for the firms operating in the system.

In 1986, major legislative proposals were introduced both at the federal and provincial levels that will significantly change the structure of the market. The four-

---

[1] In Canada, the term "bank" is restricted to companies incorporated under the Bank Act, so the firms involved with bringing new issues to the markets are referred to as "dealers" or "underwriters" rather than investment bankers.

pillars structure based on separation of functions will be substantially dismantled, and the restricted access of foreign firms into the domestic securities industry virtually eliminated. These changes are intended to occur in 1987 and 1988, and are discussed in the preceding chapter.

The Ontario provincial government announced the first major change in the structure of domestic capital markets when it significantly revised its ownership rules for securities firms. Under the new Ontario rules, Canadian financial institutions may enter the securities business beginning July 1, 1987, and foreign firms can carry on a full securities business in the Canadian market beginning July 1, 1988.

The federal government has proposed complementary legislation allowing chartered banks to own securities firms, and allowing trust and life insurance companies to operate securities firms through subsidiary companies.

Banks, Trust, and Life Insurance Companies

The federal Bank Act prescribes the activities and the ownership of the chartered banks. It is reviewed by the federal government every 10 years. Because banking is designated as a function under federal jurisdiction, all banks are chartered and regulated at the federal level. The Bank Act currently prevents banks from undertaking trust activities and limits the extent to which they can transact in securities. The new proposals however, are expected to result in bank involvment in securities, trust, and insurance services.

Trust companies and life insurance companies may be incorporated under either federal or provincial statutes. While there are differences in the governing statutes, the separation of functions has been maintained so far. Deregulation will almost certainly mean that these firms will expand their services.

Securities Industry

Regulation of the securities industry in Canada is the responsibility of the provinces, although pressures have developed at times to establish a federal regulatory body similar to the Securities and Exchange Commission (SEC) in the United States. The dominant position of Toronto, the capital of Ontario, as the financial center of Canada has imbued the Ontario Securities Commission (OSC) with broad powers for regulating the securities industry through the provisions of the Ontario Securities Act. The other provinces have securities acts similar to the Ontario Act.

The major provisions of the Ontario Act include:

1. Disclosure requirements for corporate issuers.
2. Registration requirements of securities firms trading securities.
3. Acknowledgment of the Toronto Stock Exchange (TSE) and the Investment Dealers Association (IDA) as self-regulating bodies under the overall supervision of the OSC.

In broad terms, a public issue of securities in Ontario requires a prospectus to be filed with and approved by the OSC. The securities firms involved in the distribution must be registered with the OSC. These rules cover the general case but there may be specific exemptions with respect to the prospectus and registration requirements.

SECURITIES FIRMS AND SECURITIES MARKETS

Securities firms are responsible for a large proportion of the total market intermediation function in Canada. Market intermediaries accomplish the exchange of securities for cash and vice versa in capital market transactions. A market intermediary may carry out this function by acting in some markets as an agent for one or more of the parties in the transaction, and in other markets as a principal buying the securities for its own account and then selling from inventory. Transactions in existing outstanding securities are referred to as secondary market trades. Transactions in new issues of securities are referred to as primary market trades.

The underwriting function involves one or more market intermediaries acquiring an entire issue of corporate or government securities and selling these securities to investors. Usually an underwritten issue is a primary market transaction, that is, a new issue of securities, but an underwriting may be used to sell a block of outstanding securities. An underwriting usually involves the securities firms acting as principals. A securities firm sometimes will take an issue on a "best-efforts" basis, that is, without assuming liability for the amount of the offering but agreeing to make an effort to sell the securities for the issuer.

Securities firms conduct primary and secondary transactions as market intermediaries for customers from around the world in established markets in Canada for treasury bills, bankers' acceptances and commercial paper, bonds and debentures, preferred and common equities, and options and futures contracts. They trade in the various markets comprising the international capital markets as well. Securities firms also conduct transactions as well in other types of securities contracts, such as mortgage loans, and they arrange private placements of securities for clients. Some firms carry out transactions as intermediaries in commodities and foreign currencies.

The money and commercial paper market includes trades in short-term instruments, usually those with a year or less to maturity, issued by the federal or provincial governments, financial institutions and corporations. These markets operate largely through a network of securities dealers with the active participation of traders in financial institutions. Corporate and government issuers borrow and repay their outstanding notes in this market on a continuous basis. Market players are sophisticated, and transactions involve large dollar amounts.

Longer-term outstanding debt issues are traded in the bond market. Bond traders in securities firms and in banks buy and sell bonds and debentures primarily as principals. A new issue of long-term debt by a corporate borrower involves an underwriting of securities, a process described later in this section.

Orders for trades in outstanding preferred and common equities that are listed on one of the stock exchanges in Canada are routed by the receiving securities firms to the floor of an exchange. The Toronto Stock Exchange (TSE) is the largest exchange, handling about 75 percent of the total dollar volume. The Montreal Exchange (ME), the Vancouver Stock Exchange (VSE), and the Alberta Stock Exchange (ASE) are also active markets. There is an over-the-counter market for unlisted equities where particular securities firms, usually including the original underwriter, trade these issues as dealers. Futures and options are traded in markets operated by the Toronto and Montreal exchanges.

In addition to their market intermediation functions, securities firms may undertake such related activities as advising on and arranging mergers and acquisitions. A few firms undertake a certain amount of financial advisory and consulting activity for corporations involved in rate-of-return hearings, or for shareholders or creditors wishing to pursue an action relating to the value of their shares or claims, possibly during a corporate takeover. Securities firms also engage in professional money management, commodities trading, real estate brokering, and other similar activities.

Types of Firms

Securities firms in Canada can be broadly classified according to the nature and coverage of their customers and their operations. A major firm would be a player in virtually every category and subcategory in the following classifications, while a smaller firm may deal in a narrower range of securities for a regional set of retail customers.

1. *Types of Target Customer*

Institutional
Retail

2. *Type of Securities Traded*

Money market (T bills, commercial paper, and bankers' acceptances)
Bonds and debentures
Equities
Options and future contracts

3. *Role with Respect to New Issues*

Underwriter as a manager or co-manager
Banking group member
Selling group member

4. *Specialty Services Offered*

Research
Trading large blocks
Mergers and acquisitions
Portfolio management

5. *Geographical Coverage*

Regional
National
International

Number of Firms

As of December 31, 1986, about 100 firms were members of the TSE, ME, VSE, ASE, or the Investment Dealers Association (IDA). Together they employed approximately 23,000 people. The IDA is an organization of securities firms recognized by the Ontario Securities Commission as a self-regulatory organization. Many firms have memberships in the IDA and in several stock exchanges, indicating their involvement with both the primary and secondary markets for investment-grade securities (IDA) and the secondary markets for listed equities (TSE, ME, VSE, ASE). These firms collectively held total capital employed of about $1500 million at the end of 1986. An additional five or six firms are registered with the OSC; they are primarily involved in promoting mining and junior industrial issues. These firms are not members of the TSE or the IDA. It is not known how many securities firms operate in Canada without requiring registration and thus trade exclusively in what is known as the "exempt market."[2]

Twelve securities firms in Canada are classified as national integrated firms. In other words, they trade in several markets and have offices located across Canada. The list includes two foreign-owned operations—Merrill Lynch Canada Ltd. and Bache Securities Ltd., both of which operated in Canada before imposition of restrictions on nonresident ownership and were permitted to continue (although with limits on their capital employed). These 12 companies generate over 50 percent of total revenues of all member firms of the IDA and TSE, have over 65 percent of the total capital invested, and undertake much of the domestic underwriting of new issues. Most of these firms cover all markets and have regional offices and a retail sales force. In addition, each has its own research group and a separate institutional sales team. But within the group of 12 there are significant variations in method of operating.

---

[2] The exempt market is described later in this chapter.

A second group of firms is organized to deliver a specialized package of services to a narrowly defined set of customers, usually professional money managers in financial institutions or in corporations managing pension funds. The "products" offered by these "boutique" securities firms are typically research analysis and advice with respect to equities, and trading expertise especially for block trades.

The third major group includes those firms that have regional coverage and serve a specific set of investors with a narrow range of services.

Extent of Activity

The securities industry raised $24 billion in Canada in new issues in the first 10 months of 1986, excluding Canada Savings Bonds and money market investments. Of this amount, 46 percent went to the three levels of government (federal, provincial, and municipal) and 54 percent to the private sector.

Secondary market trading on the stock exchanges in 1986 amounted to approximately $80 billion. Bond trading for the period January to October 1986 reached $243 billion. Trading in money market issues by securities firms amounted to $713 billion in the same 10-month period.

THE UNDERWRITING ACTIVITY

Syndication and Bought Deals

A securities firm underwrites new issues through either syndication or as a "bought deal." Typically in a syndication the lead underwriter advises the corporate client about the type of securities to issue and the timing and terms, prepares the prospectus and expedites its acceptance by regulatory authorities, and prices the issue and guarantees the proceeds. For government clients, the underwriter advises on yield and timing of an issue. When there are co-underwriters, the lead underwriter manages the process, but collectively all co-underwriters price the issue and guarantee the funds.

For a syndicated deal the underwriters sell the issue to a banking group or syndicate of securities firms simultaneously with their purchase of the issue from the corporate or government issuer. The banking syndicate, which includes the underwriters, acquires the issue and assumes liability according to a negotiated percentage for each member. The banking group is responsible for selling the issue and may enlist additional firms for that purpose (including certain financial institutions), but the liability remains with the banking group. A key advantage of the banking group syndicate is the sharing of risk. The actual payment to the issuing corporation or government follows the issue date by about two to three weeks.

Membership and percentage shares in established banking syndicates are highly sought after by many securities firms because they provide new securities for their sales force to distribute. Usually, syndicates are constituted for established issuers, and traditionally they remain intact over several issues. Increased competition in

Each year *The Financial Post*, a weekly business newspaper, presents a ranking of the underwriters of Canadian issues according to various classifications of issues and methods of ranking techniques. The overall results for 1985 were published in the May 3, 1986, issue (p. 16) and are presented here.

These rankings of the underwriters allocate a portion of the amount raised for Canadian corporations, provincial governments, Crown corporations, and municipalities in domestic and international capital markets to the underwriters. Rankings use bonus credit to lead underwriter.

Ranking for 1985	Firm	Amount Raised ($ Millions)	Number of Issues
1	Wood Gundy Inc.	$5,205	275
2	Dominion Securities Limited	4,578	195
3	McLeod Young Weir Ltd.	3,387	144
4	Burns Fry Limited	2,263	72
5	Merrill Lynch Canada Inc.	1,581	116

Figure 32.1. Major underwriters in Canada.

recent years for managing underwriting positions and for improved percentage positions in syndicates, however, has changed many long-standing relationships. Changes in position within syndicates are based on past evidence of distribution capability or lack of it, or because the issuer requests the change.

New syndicates are formed for first-time issuers or when the lead underwriter changes for an established issuer. Syndicate members are chosen for their financial capacity, ability to sell securities, regional coverage, and relationships with both the issuer and the underwriter.

For a "bought deal," which has become an increasingly popular form of underwriting in the past few years, a single underwriter or small group of underwriters buys the issue outright from the issuer at agreed-upon terms, often subject to the filing of required documentation such as a short-form prospectus within a specified time period. The underwriters then sell the issue, usually to institutional money managers, or to individual investors if the issue qualifies for sale to the public.

The "bought deal" requires commitment of greater resources and assumption of more risk by the underwriters. Bought deals generally are available only to corporations with stronger credit ratings and a broad market following. The keys to successful underwriting using bought deals are availability of capital, either in the firm or through an affiliate, and knowledge of the current investment requirements of the major money managers so that the underwriter knows likely buyers for the issue. A few firms with superior block-trading skills in secondary markets have developed as major participants in the underwriting business by their use of the bought deal. Figure 32.1 gives a brief discussion of the major firms involved in the new issues market in Canada and a rank order listing for 1985.

Underwriting fees for bought deals have been lower than those for syndicated offerings. The extent of underpricing on the issue, that is, the relationship of the actual price offered to the issuer to the market value, typically has not been included in calculating the cost to the issuer. Many participants in the new-issues market believe that syndication enables the banking group members to achieve broader retail distribution of the securities over a longer time period and thus obtain a better market price for the issuer than is available through a bought deal.

Underwriters also are involved extensively in private placements of securities. Although this does not usually involve taking a liability position, it requires the skill of developing the financial and other information for the issuing firm and negotiating a price and covenant package with sophisticated institutional investors.

THE COMPETITIVE ENVIRONMENT

In the primary markets, securities firms as underwriters are suppliers of funds to Canadian corporations and governments through their market intermediation activities in domestic and foreign capital markets. In broad terms, these firms compete with other suppliers of funds for all maturities. These competitors, with their particular types of specialty financing, are:

1. Chartered banks in Canada, domestic and foreign-owned, for operating and term loans.
2. Insurance companies, trust companies, pension funds, and other financial intermediaries in Canada for a private placement of securities usually of a longer term.
3. The foreign subsidiaries or affiliates of Canadian banks and other financial institutions operating in foreign capital markets, especially the Euromarket, as market intermediaries and underwriting public issues of securities, debt, or equity.
4. Foreign banks for financing in the Euromarket.
5. Securities firms in other countries, especially in the United States and the United Kingdom, that undertake securities issues in foreign capital markets.

In recent years Canadian corporations and governments have raised substantial sums of money from public offerings of securities in foreign capital markets, using Canadian or foreign securities firms as underwriters, foreign investment banking subsidiaries of Canadian banks such as Orion Royal Bank and CIBC Limited (Canadian Imperial Bank of Commerce), or foreign banks such as Deutsche Bank, all of which underwrite and distribute securities in the Euromarket and in other markets. The interest rates, terms, and conditions in foreign capital markets relative to those available in domestic markets together with the currency exchange rates and ease of trading in currency markets pose the major competitive conditions for securities firms underwriting issues in the domestic market.

There is competition between domestic securities firms and banks for the short-term (under one year) debt financing needs of corporations. The banks offer operating loans, while securities firms provide funds through the commercial paper market, including bankers' acceptances to corporations. For longer-term debt financing, Canadian banks, life insurance companies, and pension funds offer term loans, while securities firms provide funds through public offerings of debt issues. The critical factors on which the various participants compete are overall yield costs, innovative financing techniques, the ability to distribute securities, the relationship with the issuer, and the covenants required. Securities firms believe that they have a competitive edge over financial institutions in terms of their ability to develop new financing ideas, largely because of the entrepreneurial nature of their staff, as well as an edge in marketing securities because of their ability to marshal the organization to achieve a goal.

Institutional money managers in Canada receive proposals from securities firms in Canada, the United States, the United Kingdom, and Japan for Canadian and foreign securities issued and traded in Canadian or foreign capital markets, and from Canadian banks for "exempt" transactions. Exempt transactions are those that do not require the market intermediary to be registered with the OSC, or the issuer to file a prospectus. Trades in all government securities are exempt transactions, and certain institutional investors are exempt purchasers. For orders over $97,000 in a single security, the transaction is exempt; that is, the seller is not required to register with the OSC to conduct the transaction. This segment of the market is referred to as the "exempt market."

While foreign securities firms do not compete with domestic firms on the full range of securities traded in the Canadian markets in 1987, they actively compete for exempt transactions with Canadian and foreign institutional portfolio managers. Examples of such transactions include trades in stocks interlisted on foreign exchanges, trades in debt and equity issues originally undertaken in foreign markets, new debt and equity issues of large Canadian corporations that may be placed in foreign markets, and primary and secondary distributions of private placements in Canada. These trades all became exempt from OSC registration requirements in 1987. Of course the new proposals will enable foreign firms to compete for all business after June 1988.

Individual investors maintain accounts with domestic securities firms and conduct trades in Canadian and foreign securities with these firms. One bank, Toronto-Dominion, has offered a discount order execution access service for its retail and institutional customers, which enables the bank to compete directly with securities firms for customer transactions. Formerly required to place the orders it received through a broker for execution of the trade, the bank was able to handle the transaction through its own operations late in 1987. A few individuals have accounts with foreign securities firms and conduct transactions in Canadian and foreign securities largely by telephone instructions to those firms. Of course, the major competitors for the individual investors' funds are the domestic financial institutions, banks, trust companies, and insurance companies, which have attracted large sums to deposit accounts, retirement savings accounts, and annuity plans.

Competition for retail and institutional customers has several manifestations. Firms compete to offer the best price for the securities involved. In addition, competitors offer a variety of services to their customers as well as executing trades. Securities research and investment ideas are major areas for competition. The quality of the people in the firm developing and presenting the firm's proposals is thought to be a key competitive factor for sophisticated customers. Firms compete for access to customers through the geographical coverage of their office network.

WOOD GUNDY INC.

This section describes a particular firm in order to put the broad descriptions of the various industry activities into an operating perspective. Wood Gundy operates in all facets of the securities markets in Canada, in segments of the capital markets in the United States, in the Euromarket, and to a limited extent in other foreign markets. Wood Gundy ranks as one of the largest firms in the Canadian securities industry in terms of annual revenue earned, capital employed, trading volume of bonds and equities, commissions earned, activity in the money market, new issues underwritten in the domestic market, and involvement in international markets. The company was founded in 1905, and in 1985 it had about 1800 employees, offices throughout Canada, in New York, London, Tokyo, Hong Kong, and Paris, and a joint-venture affiliate in Shanghai.

Services Offered

Wood Gundy is organized to offer three major classes of services or products and a number of minor services and products to its various customers. The three major areas in which the firm offers products and services are new issues, involving the underwriting of corporate and government securities, fixed-income securities, includ-ing trading and sales of these securities, and equities involving trading, sales, and research.

New Issues. Wood Gundy was the lead manager or co-manager of underwriting syndicates in 1986, raising approximately $45 billion in over 440 issues for corporate and government issuers. This does not count participation in the money and commer-cial paper markets and in government of Canada issues. Approximately 60 percent of the funds raised were for Canadian clients. These issues were undertaken in the capital markets in Canada and the United States, and in the Euromarket operating out of London, England. The securities were denominated mainly in Canadian and U.S. dollars, with a few Euroissues in pounds sterling, deutsche marks, and other currencies. The securities issued included bonds, debentures, notes, and preferred and common shares.

Wood Gundy underwrites using both the syndication and bought deal methods. For syndicates organized by Wood Gundy as managing underwriter, Wood Gundy's participation in the banking group would seldom be less than 20 percent and could be considerably higher.

Wood Gundy employs over 100 professional staff members in the new-issues group in four countries to undertake the underwriting and financial advising activity. Within Canada, the new-issues group is organized into the corporate finance, government finance, transaction finance (swaps), real estate, and syndication groups. The largest group is in Toronto, while internationally the firm has staff to handle new issues in London, New York, and Tokyo.

Fixed-Income Securities. The fixed-income division of Wood Gundy includes the bond, money and commercial paper market, and foreign exchange trading functions. The firm operates a fixed-income research group that monitors the credit capabilities of corporate customers. The economics group in Wood Gundy, which is extensively involved in modeling and forecasting interest-rate movements, is part of the fixed-income group as well. The firm operates fixed-income trading desks in Toronto, Montreal, and Vancouver in Canada as well as in New York and London. Corporate and government issuers look to the lead underwriter of their issues to maintain secondary markets and to assist in repurchasing securities when required to satisfy contractual obligations such as the sinking fund.

Wood Gundy is one of 10 securities firms that is entitled to rediscount instruments issued or guaranteed by the government of Canada with the Bank of Canada. This privilege was granted to a few securities firms by the central bank in order to stimulate the development of the official money market in short-term government securities, and to enable the Bank of Canada to exercise more effective control over interest rates and ultimately influence overall economic activity. In addition, Wood Gundy operates as an agent for many financial institutions and corporations in issuing various types of instruments in the commercial paper and mid-term market.

In Canada, Wood Gundy's money market and foreign exchange operations had transaction volume of over $150 billion in 1986. The Wood Gundy bond traders and salespeople in Canada had transaction volume of $34 billion in 1986. The clients are mainly professional money managers working for either financial institutions or corporations.

In New York, the firm has bond traders and sales personnel who specialize in Canadian issues payable in U.S. dollars, and in U.S. government bonds.

In the United Kingdom, the firm has bond traders making markets principally in Euro-Canadian dollar issues and issues by Canadian corporations and governments in U.S. dollars and other currencies. Participation as manager or co-manager in the underwriting of over $30 billion of Euroissues in 1986 shows the significance of the secondary market trading activity in such issues.

Equities. Wood Gundy is a member of the Toronto, Montreal, Vancouver, and Alberta stock exchanges. In the United States, the firm belongs to the New York, American, Midwest, and Philadelphia stock exchanges, as well as to NASDAQ.

For institutional customers, Wood Gundy offers expertise in block trades (over $100,000 in a single stock) both handled through the facilities of the exchange and crossed within the firm. The ability to find the other side ɔf a block order, either with a customer or by positioning the stock in inventory, is a key factor in establishing the firm's position as an equity block trader.

In the United States and the United Kingdom, the equities trading activities largely involve Canadian equities for institutional customers. The firm employs institutional equity sales and trading personnel in Canada in Toronto, Montreal, and Vancouver, and internationally in New York, London, Paris, Hong Kong, and Tokyo.

Research. The firm provides research services mainly to institutional clients, but also to retail customers. The range of service extends from broad industry forecasts to fundamental analysis of specific companies and projection of performance, to charting of market movements. The output of the 20 analysts in Canada includes seminars and workshops with clients, publication and dissemination of information and news relevant to clients, and research reports on industries and companies and on special situations.

In addition to the Canadian activity, the firm has analysts in New York covering a select group of industries and special situations in the United States.

Customers Served

Institutions. The bond traders and bond sales group attempt to maintain continuous contact with bond portfolio managers of pension funds, pooled funds and traders in the major financial institutions, and with managers of separately managed pension funds in corporations. The securities firm representatives try to determine each portfolio manager's strategy and then provide the appropriate products with related services at the best prices.

For equities, the situation is more complex, because the institutional representative must present the firm's research output as well as maintain the same kind of monitoring of strategy and positioning of product as the bond representative. The position is further complicated by the fact that there are more competitors, domestic and foreign, for the equity business. Wood Gundy often takes a position as principal in order to accomplish large equity transactions.

Institutional investors in the United States, the Caribbean countries, the United Kingdom, Europe, Hong Kong, and Japan are contacted regularly by resident Wood Gundy institutional representatives offering a broad range of securities but focusing mainly on those issued by Canadian corporations or governments.

Retail. The firm's retail customers reside in Canada and are served through 40 regional offices. The firm has a retail sales force of about 360 representatives. These representatives market the firm's complete product line, including new issues, stocks, bonds, mutual funds, commodities, futures and options, and Canada Savings Bonds to the retail customers.

The firm undertakes an extensive training program for all new retail salespeople beyond the general training requirements imposed by the various regulatory agencies.

Management and Ownership

Until 1987, Wood Gundy Inc. was owned entirely by its employees, of whom about 600 are shareholders. In June, 1987, the firm announced that the First National Bank of Chicago would pay about $271 million to acquire a 35 percent ownership. The remaining 65 percent would continue to be owned by employees. In late 1987, however, the Bank decided not to complete the planned purchase.

The firm has a board of directors constituted of about 80 members, all employees, with an executive committee of the board charged with primary responsibility for managing the business.

Wood Gundy has two senior executives, the chairman and chief executive officer, and the president and chief operating officer. In addition, the firm has three vice-chairmen, one of whom is based in London and who is responsible for all international, other than U.S., operations.

The firm is organized in a matrix format, major functions on one dimension of the matrix and geographical location on the other. Senior functional managers are in charge of such business areas as new issues, fixed income, and equities. Regional managers are in charge of sales of all products in geographical areas. Sales and expense budgets provide the basis for control. Income determination is carried out for each unit in the matrix.

Most employees follow a career path within a particular activity in the firm. The personality and skill requirements vary substantially across the range of functions, thus limiting somewhat the transferability of personnel across departments. Exceptions to this general rule are found within the new-issues group where members are encouraged to move into a trading or sales function for time. Research members sometimes move to corporate finance or institutional sales.

Opportunities for Growth

In Canada, Wood Gundy is a major player in the domestic market and takes Canadian issuers to world markets. The company sees opportunity to increase its role in arranging foreign financing for domestic firms. Wood Gundy participates to a limited extent in the domestic market in the United States and operates in the international market segment in the United States. Both these areas provide an opportunity for growth for the firm. In addition, the firm intends to bring foreign securities to Canadian institutional investors. The key to accomplishing these objectives of taking Canadian issuers to international markets and bringing international securities to Canadian investors is to develop extensive networks through offices in foreign financial centers with skilled people to recognize these opportunities.

APPENDIX: THE LEADING 75 MANAGERS OF UNDERWRITTEN OFFERINGS, JANUARY 1986–MAY 1987

Underwritten Offerings 1/1/86–5/18/87

	Rank	Dollar Amount (000)	Percentage of Total	Number of Issues Managed	Number of Offices Domestic	Number of Offices Foreign	Number of Employees
Salomon Brothers Inc. One New York Plaza New York, NY 10004 212-747-7000	1	69,000	17.1	582	7	4	4,300
The First Boston Corporation Park Avenue Plaza New York, NY 10055 212-909-2000	2	59,392	14.7	516	12	8	2,600
Merrill, Lynch, Pierce, Fenner & Smith Incorporated World Financial Center 250 Vesey St. New York, NY 10281 212-449-3627	3	46,606	11.5	453	475	50	32,500
Morgan Stanley & Co. Incorporated 1251 Avenue of the Americas New York, NY 10020 212-703-4000	4	43,496	10.8	398	4	5	4,000
Goldman Sachs & Co. 85 Broad Street New York, NY 10004 212-902-1000	5	42,999	10.6	382	12	4	4,700

6	Drexel Burnham Lambert Incorporated 60 Broad Street New York, NY 10004 212-480-6000	40,514	10.0	358	45	14	7,700
7	Shearson Lehman Brothers Inc. American Express Tower World Financial Center New York, NY 10285 212-298-2000	25,391	6.3	374	321	19	21,600
8	Kidder, Peabody & Co. Incorporated 10 Hanover Square New York, NY 10005 212-510-3000	16,033	4.0	252	62	6	6,100
9	Bear, Stearns & Co. Inc. 55 Water Street New York, NY 10041 212-952-5000	7,258	1.8	118	7	5	4,800
10	Prudential-Bache Securities Inc. One Seaport Plaza 199 Water street New York, NY 10292 212-214-5050	6,208	1.5	111	280	48	13,700
11	Smith Barney, Harris Upham and Co. Incorporated 1345 Avenue of the Americas New York, NY 10105 212-698-6000	6,036	1.5	94	98	6	5,700

Underwritten Offerings 1/1/86–5/18/87

	Rank	Dollar Amount (000)	Percentage of Total	Number of Issues Managed	Number of Offices		Number of Employees
					Domestic	Foreign	
PaineWebber Incorporated 1285 Avenue of the Americas New York, NY 10019 212-713-2000	12	5,942	1.5	143	277	8	11,400
Dillon, Read & Co. Inc. 535 Madison Avenue New York, NY 10022 212-906-7000	13	4,239	1.0	52	3	1	500
Dean Witter Reynolds Inc. 130 Liberty Street New York, NY 10006 212-524-2222	14	3,390	0.8	64	375	10	16,200
E. F. Hutton & Company Inc. One Battery Park Plaza New York, NY 10004 212-742-5000	15	3,264	0.8	65	385	19	16,500
Lazard Freres & Co. 1 Rockefeller Plaza New York, NY 10020 212-489-6600	16	2,705	0.7	22	1		500
Alex. Brown & Sons Incorporated 135 E. Baltimore Street Baltimore, MD 21202 301-727-1700	17	2,180	0.5	66	18	1	

	Firm						
18	Donaldson, Lufkin & Jenrette Securities Corporation 140 Broadway New York, NY 10005 212-504-3000	2,068	0.5	46	10	4	2,900
19	L. F. Rothschild, Inc. 55 Water Street New York, NY 10041 212-412-1000	1,968	0.5	53	5	5	1,700
20	Wheat, First Securities, Inc. 707 East Main Street Richmond, VA 23211 804-649-2311	1,900	0.5	35	55		1,100
21	Allen & Company Incorporated 711 Fifth Avenue New York, NY 10022 212-832-8000	1,304	0.3	12	2		200
22	Thomson McKinnon Securities Inc. One New York Plaza New York, NY 10004 212-482-7000	887	0.2	34	170	9	4,900
23	Oppenheimer & Co., Inc. One New York Plaza New York, NY 10004 212-825-4000	822	0.2	17	8	1	2,000
24	Wertheim Schroder & Co. Incorporated 200 Park Avenue New York, NY 10166 212-578-0200	784	0.2	11	4	3	600

Underwritten Offerings 1/1/86–5/18/87

	Rank	Dollar Amount (000)	Percentage of Total	Number of Issues Managed	Number of Offices		Number of Employees
					Domestic	Foreign	
Union Bank of Switzerland	25	643	0.2	5			
Robinson-Humphrey Company, Inc. 3333 Peachtree Road, N.E. Atlanta, GA 30326 404-266-6000	26	517	0.1	28	33		1,000
Citicorp	27	485	0.1	9			
Edward D. Jones & Co. 201 Progress Parkway St. Louis, MO 63043 314-851-2000	28	439	0.1	38	914		3,100
Keefe, Bruyette & Woods, Inc. Two World Trade Center New York, NY 10048 212-349-4321	29	368	0.1	14	3	1	100
Hambrecht & Quist Incorporated 235 Montgomery Street San Francisco, CA 94104 415-576-3300	30	345	0.1	12	5	1	200
Daiwa Securities America Inc. One Liberty Plaza Libery Street New York, NY 10006 212-732-6600	31	321	0.1	2	3		100
William Blair & Company 135 South LaSalle Street Chicago, IL 60603 312-236-1600	32	313	0.1	14	3	1	400

33	Security Pacific National Bank	302	0.1	2		
34	Morgan, Keegan & Company, Inc. Fifty Front Street Memphis, TN 38103 901-524-4100	300	0.1	6	15	500
35	Montgomery Securities 600 Montgomery Street San Francisco, CA 94111 415-627-2000	298	0.1	9	1	300
36	Nomura Securities International, Inc. 180 Maiden Lane New York, NY 10038 212-208-9300	250	0.1	1	4	200
37	Robertson, Colman & Stephens One Embarcadero Center San Francisco, CA 94111 415-781-9700	231	0.1	9	3	100
38	Tucker, Anthony & R. L. Day, Inc. 120 Broadway New York, NY 10271 212-618-7400	230	0.1	12	34	1,200
39	D. H. Blair & Co., Inc. 44 Wall Street New York, NY 10005 212-968-2000	227	0.1	41	1	200
40	Advest, Inc. Six Central Row Hartford, CT 06103 203-525-1421	216	0.1	20	85	1,700

Underwritten Offerings 1/1/86–5/18/87

	Rank	Dollar Amount (000)	Percentage of Total	Number of Issues Managed	Number of Offices Domestic	Number of Offices Foreign	Number of Employees
J. W. Korth & Company, Inc. 29905 Middlebelt Road Farmington Hills, MI 48018 313-855-4500	41	201		6	2		30
Furman, Selz, Mager, Dietz & Birney Incorporated 230 Park Avenue New York, NY 10169 212-309-8200	42	184		10	1	1	200
Dain Bosworth Incorporated 100 Dain Tower Minneapolis, MN 55402 612-371-2711	43	179		13	40		1,200
Rauscher Pierce Refsnes, Inc. 2500 North Tower Plaza of the Americas Building Dallas, TX 75201 214-978-0111	44	167		11	32		900
Ladenburg, Thalmann & Co. Inc. 540 Madison Avenue New York, NY 10022 212-940-0100	45	164		17	4	1	200
Moseley Securities Corporation 60 State Street Boston, MA 02109 617-367-2400	46	161		18	28	4	1,000

Firm	No.				
J. C. Bradford & Co. Incorporated 170 Fourth Avenue North Nashville, TN 37219 615-748-9000	47	143	10	49	900
Ryan, Beck & Co. 80 Main Street West Orange, NJ 07052 201-325-3000	48	140	19	3	200
Piper, Jaffray & Hopwood Incorporated 222 S. 9th Street Minneapolis, MN 55440 612-342-6000	49	129	10	53	1,500
McDonald & Company Securities, Inc. 2100 The Society Building Cleveland, OH 44114 216-443-2300	50	117	9	22	500
Prescott, Ball & Turben, Inc. 1331 Euclid Avenue Cleveland, OH 44115 216-574-7300	51	103	8	47	1,100
Interstate Securities Corporation 2700 NCNB Plaza 101 South Tryon Street Charlotte, NC 28280 704-379-9000	52	95	9	62	900
Legg Mason Wood Walker Incorporated 7 East Redwood Street Baltimore, MD 21202 301-539-3400	53	94	5	38	1,000

Underwritten Offerings 1/1/86–5/18/87

	Rank	Dollar Amount (000)	Percentage of Total	Number of Issues Managed	Number of Offices		Number of Employees
					Domestic	Foreign	
Wedbush Securities, Inc. 615 South Flower Street Los Angeles, CA 90017 213-620-1750	54	90		5	21		600
Butcher & Singer, Inc. 211 South Broad Street Philadelphia, PA 19107 215-985-5000	55	85		9	31		600
Boettcher & Company, Inc. 828 Seventeenth Street Denver, CO 80202 303-628-8000	56	83		8	24		900
The Ziegler Company, Inc. 215 North Main Street West Bend, WI 53095 414-334-5521	57	79		13	32		350
A. G. Edwards & Sons, Inc. One North Jefferson St. Louis, MO 63103 314-289-3000	58	75		6	270		5,000
Blunt Ellis & Loewi Incorporated 225 East Mason Street Milwaukee, WI 53202 414-347-3400	59	71		9	71		1,000

#	Firm					
60	Morgan, Olmstead, Kennedy & Gardner, Incorporated 606 South Olive Street Los Angeles, CA 90014 213-625-1611	68	5	9		300
61	Rooney, Pace Inc. 11 Broadway New York, NY 10004 212-908-7700	66	13	6		300
62	Howard, Weil, Labouisse, Friedrichs Incorporated 1100 Poydras Street New Orleans, LA 70163 504-582-2500	65	6	26		500
63	Sutro & Co. Incorporated 201 California Street San Francisco, CA 94111 415-445-8500	65	5	12		600
64	Johnson, Lane, Space, Smith & Co., Inc. 101 East Bay Street Savannah, GA 31402 912-236-7101	61	4	17		400
65	McKinley Allsopp Inc. 780 Third Avenue New York, NY 10017 212-593-1350	57	9	3	2	60
66	Eppler, Guerin & Turner, Inc. 2001 Bryan Tower Dallas, TX 75201 214-880-9000	55	4	31		500

Underwritten Offerings 1/1/86–5/18/87

	Rank	Dollar Amount (000)	Percentage of Total	Number of Issues Managed	Number of Offices		Number of Employees
					Domestic	Foreign	
First Jersey Securities	67	52		4			
Evans & Co., Incorporated 300 Park Avenue New York, NY 10022 212-753-6200	68	49		9	4		200
Laidlaw Adams & Peck Inc. 40 Rector Street New York, NY 10006 212-306-6100	69	48		7	9	2	400
First Albany Corporation 41 State Street Albany, NY 12201 518-447-8500	70	46		5	24		400

The Stuart-James Company, Inc. 4601 DTC Boulevard Denver, CO 80237 303-796-8488	71	43	10			200
Whale Securities Corp. 650 Fifth Avenue New York, NY 10019 212-397-2250	72	42	9	2		
Muller and Company, Inc. 111 Broadway New York, NY 10006 212-766-1700	73	42		10		
Steinberg & Lyman 1250 Broadway New York, NY 10001 212-714-1470	74	40		9		90
Raymond James & Associates, Inc. 1400 66th Street North St. Petersburg, FL 33733 813-381-3800	75	39		5	33	900

Index